Borderlines

Borderlines

THE SHIFTINGS OF GENDER
IN BRITISH ROMANTICISM

Susan J. Wolfson

Stanford University Press
Stanford, California

Stanford University Press
Stanford, California

© 2006 by the Board of Trustees of the Leland Stanford Junior University.
All rights reserved.

No part of this book may be reproduced or transmitted in any form or by any means, electronic or mechanical, including photocopying and recording, or in any information storage or retrieval system without the prior written permission of Stanford University Press.

Printed in the United States of America on acid-free, archival-quality paper

Library of Congress Cataloging-in-Publication Data
Wolfson, Susan J., 1948–
Borderlines : the shiftings of gender in British romanticism / Susan J. Wolfson.
    p. cm.
Includes bibliographical references and index.
ISBN-13: 978-0-8047-5297-8 (cloth: alk. paper)
ISBN-13: 978-0-8047-6105-5 (pbk: alk. paper)
    1. English literature—19th century—History and criticism. 2. Romanticism—Great Britain. 3. Sex role in literature. I. Title.

PR468.R65W65 2006
820.9'353—dc22

2006004633

for Ron, again

It was scarcely possible to imagine two individual natures more strikingly contrasted—the one so intensely feminine, so susceptible and imaginative, so devoted to the tender and the beautiful; the other endowed with masculine energies, with a spirit that seemed born for ascendency, with strong powers of reasoning, fathomless profundity of thought.

—HARRIETT HUGHES, ON FELICIA HEMANS AND MARIA JANE JEWSBURY (1839)

Lord Byron is a pampered and aristocratic writer, but he is not effeminate, or we should not have his works with only the printer's name to them! I cannot help thinking that the fault of Mr. Keats's poems was a deficiency in masculine energy of style. He had beauty, tenderness, delicacy, in an uncommon degree, but there was want of strength and substance.

—WILLIAM HAZLITT, ON EFFEMINACY OF CHARACTER (1822)

Contents

Acknowledgments		xi
Preface		xv
List of Illustrations		xxi
Chapter One	On the Borderlines of Gendered Language	1

TWO WOMEN

Chapter Two	Felicia Hemans and the Stages of "The Feminine"	39
Chapter Three	The Generations of "Masculine" Woman	78
Chapter Four	Woman's Life and "Masculine" Energy: The History of Maria Jane Jewsbury	92

TWO MEN

Chapter Five	Lord Byron, *Sardanapalus*, and "Effeminate Character"	135
Chapter Six	Gender as Cross-Dressing in *Don Juan*: Men & Women / Male & Female / Masculine & Feminine	164
Chapter Seven	Keats and Gender Acts: "Had I Man's Fair Form"	205
Chapter Eight	Gendering Keats: "The Character Undecided, the Way of Life Uncertain"	243

BODY AND SOUL

Chapter Nine	Sex in Souls?	287

Texts	*317*
Abbreviations	*318*
Notes	*320*
Works Cited	*381*
Index	*419*

Acknowledgments

I am happy to acknowledge several courtesies that have assisted the production of this book. I owe Princeton University Library a wealth of gratitude for the resources therein, and more specific thanks for generous permission to use, gratis, a reproduction of Lady Mary Wortley Montagu from a book in their collection. Paul Douglass kindly supplied an image of Lady Caroline Lamb. With the assistance of Jeff Cowton, John Bugg supplied transcripts of materials in the Dove Cottage Archives, which the Wordsworth Trust, Dove Cottage, Cambria, England, has given permission to reproduce. Ian Burley was splendidly generous in providing technical help in securing, and gratis permission to use, an image of M. J. Jewsbury from the Tamworth Library in Staffordshire. Other galleries kindly allowed reproductions and supplied the necessary materials. A fellowship from the John Simon Guggenheim Foundation provided the gifts of time, support, and encouragement at a crucial early stage in my work.

As my own critical contexts make clear, I am indebted to the pioneers of gender criticism, and our ongoing conversation. Any book so long in development as this, owes much to these currents of discussion, as well as specific accumulated debts for attention, advice, and support. Peter Manning, Anne Mellor, Claudia Johnson, Jerry McGann, Stephen Behrendt, Starry Schor, Paula Feldman, Mary Poovey, Margaret Homans, Elaine Showalter, Karen Swann, Frances Ferguson, Sonia Hofkosh, William Keach, Alan Richardson, Marilyn Butler, Jim Chandler, Garrett Stewart, and Tilottama Rajan have been my vital interlocutors, in various ways inspiring, chastening, and improving my work. Anne Mellor read several chapters in various stages of development with astute commentary from the conceptual to the local; Claudia Johnson reviewed several chapters and was a reliable interlocutor on much else; Jim Engel, Terry Kelley, and Andy Elfenbein honed my thinking about gender and soul; Paula Feldman and Nan Sweet have been my constant colleagues in all things Hemans; and in all things Byron, Jerry McGann—even when (especially when) we've disagreed.

Dennis Low was an enlightening resource on Jewsbury. With informed and generous attention, Doucet Fischer answered every question I had, and then some, about Byron's manuscripts and publication history. Henry Abelove gave timely attention and support to my chapters on Byron, as did Paul Kelleher. Jack Cragwall was dependably sharp, conversant on Byron, and much else. Jeff Nunokawa was a generous reader of it all, crucially supportive, and a valuable friend and colleague—as much fun to teach with as to talk with. Eric Halpern gave a thoughtful and supportive review to the project across several stages of development, and has remained generously interested in, and winningly disinterested about, its publication. Michael Wood has been a valued professional mentor. Billy Galperin and Peter Manning have read more of my work in more of its stages than they probably care to or may even be able to remember, but they won't escape what has now become a lifelong habit of grateful thanks, not just for the attention but for what I always learn from their reliable rigors. Billy, with whom I've talked and laughed about everything, read the entire book with a care both for its foundational interests and their particular engagements. Peter, my friend for decades and coeditor for more than a few projects, has been a consistently valuable intellectual and collegial presence, even when he's not had pages thrust at him.

Princeton University has given me more than a decade of encouragement for my work, both as a teacher and as a writer, and has provided a wealth of material support, in the form of sabbaticals, research funds and assistants (Andrew Krull, Roger Schwartz, Jack Cragwall and John Bugg), a fabulous office and an extraordinary library, and assistance with all matters of production, not just in resources and expenses, but also in the generously helpful staff of the Department of English. In the profession at large, I have been fortunate in being able to test my interests in preliminary, or earlier publications; as I have developed the book, these essays have been heavily rewritten and revised, refitted and updated. Some of my work first took shape in articles and essays in *ELH, ERR,* and various edited collections. I am grateful to these publications for giving me a venue and readers, reactions and correspondence, and I especially thank my editors: Stephen Behrendt, Jerome Christensen, Harriet Linkin, Ronald Paulson, Grant Scott, Hermione de Almeida, Theresa Kelley, Paula Feldman, Carol Wilson, Joel Haefner, and Duncan Wu. Invitations to present some of the work in these pages at UCLA, UC Santa Barbara, the Clarke Library, Northwestern University, University of Southern California, the Wordsworth Summer Conference, the North American Society for the Study of Romanticism, the Romantics Division of the Modern Language Association, University of West Virginia, the British Women Writers Association, and Stanford University have given me valuable opportunities to share my interests and to benefit from sharp, attentive conversation.

The frequency and assurance of such conversations are among the many reasons I'm so grateful to my colleagues and students at Princeton University.

And at every stage, from conception, to conversation, to revision after revision, Ron Levao has provided more sharp and sustained care for this book than anyone has a right to accept across a lifetime, even as an extraordinary blessing. Whatever may register of value in these pages reflects the gift of his critical intelligence, generous attention, and editorial patience. It's a conspicuously insufficient return to say that I'm dedicating this book to him, but I do, with a lifetime of love.

Susan J. Wolfson
Princeton, New Jersey, 2006

Preface

I came to borderlines by directions and indirections. I began to write about issues of gender in Romantic imagination in the 1980s, a decade during which feminist critics and new historicists were reviewing the field, especially the explanatory paradigms. Mapping the biases that had plotted critical discussions and received histories, this critique was soon to shape up a report of two romanticisms, one dominant, another suppressed. There was male/masculinist high Romanticism, formerly the whole story, with no gender marking in the spirit of the age (however contentious). And there was She-Romanticism that, while not necessarily in line with 1980s feminism, was legibly oppositional to high Romanticism in all kinds of ways (genres, values, tropes)—so oppositional that if *feminist* seemed too anachronistic a descriptive, *Romantic* now seemed an unsatisfactory cover term for the literary work in the age. (*Romantic-era* has become our taxonomic compromise, conceding the received history but relativizing its claims.)

It was in no small part because the "Romanticism" refined and institutionalized at the end of the nineteenth century was a men's club, and stayed that way for a long time, that its politics and poetics of gender became a critical subject. A long time indeed. Even as new work and new editions of women writers broke out in the 1970s, the capacious 4th issue of the MLA's *English Romantic Poets: A Review of Research and Criticism* (1985; with no sequel) was content to limit its survey to the twentieth century's "Big Six": Blake, W. Wordsworth, Coleridge, Byron, P. B. Shelley, and Keats. A canon-revolution was marked by the addition of Blake to the second edition, 1957, and no one thought, despite the popularity and influence of the other Shelley's *Frankenstein*, that she deserved admission. The gender gap remained largely unremedied in bicentenary events and the publications soon to follow. Two critically sophisticated commemoratives of 1990 were categorically titled—*The Romantics and Us: Essays on Literature and Culture* (ed. Gene Ruoff) and *Romantic Revolutions: Criticism and*

Theory (ed. Kenneth Johnston &c)—and mostly male focused. And when *The Norton Anthology of English Literature* unveiled its 6th edition in 1993, women still mattered very little in "The Romantic Period": their writing occupied no more than 50 of 890 pages, and it wasn't until the 7th edition (2000) that the ratio swelled, this mostly by the newly hosted *Frankenstein* (following *Longman Anthology* on this initiative).

Yet if *Frankenstein* seems an easy pass, by force of its Promethean fable and the legible connections to canonical male Romanticism, even this hospitality was quite recent. As late as 1989, Harriet Linkin's national survey of 313 representative English departments discovered that this novel was included in only about half the Romantics courses, and it was the most frequently taught work by a woman (554). Jane Austen was there, but not as a "Romantic": she was typically slotted (in critical literature, too) as late eighteenth-century or proto-Victorian. When women's writing entered the story of Romanticism, it was usually to say more about male writers (Dorothy Wordsworth's journals, on William's agons and inspirations) or to amplify themes in the male canon (Harold Bloom's 1965 Afterword to *Frankenstein*). Most female figures, in literary representation and in critical analysis, were arrayed in the lines of men's writing.

One of the reasons I joined the *Longman Anthology* editorial board in the mid-1990s was to offer (with my coeditor Peter Manning) a new array, one that cherished the writers and works that drew us both into Romanticism (those Big Six, and then some, including *Frankenstein*) but with new perspectives: historical and cultural contexts, and female company. It had been only a generation earlier, in the late 1970s, that feminist critics (grateful to a few mid-century pioneers) had begun to review the old ground in earnest, with attention to female authorship and lost writers, with new perspectives on better known ones (Wollstonecraft, Shelley, Austen), and with a theoretical interest in gender. This first-wave (among the most prominent: Margaret Homans, Anne Mellor, Marlon Ross) was attracted to schematic binaries: a "masculine" tradition that was a manifold of egotism, sexism, and power politics, defined and exerted against a more diffuse and permeable "feminine" subjectivity, not inclined to self-assertion or object-appropriation. With reference to such theorists as Carol Gilligan and Nancy Chodorow, and to French feminists Hélène Cixous, Luce Irigaray, and Julia Kristeva, women's writing was said to be inhibited by a masculine tradition and male literary culture (call it patriarchy)—or, if not, then to be venturing a maternally animated *écriture féminine* constituting, in Kristeva's famous Romantic-toned trope, "a revolution in poetic language."

These initiatives got us all talking, but the first proposals, tuned to broad, categorical descriptions and oppositions, seemed to me to elide not only the instabilities and divisions in male representations, but also the assertive critical force of women's writing. Theoretical, often value-laden principles, practices, and traditions (*masculine; feminine*) tended to be hailed in advance of, sometimes in circumvention of, the complex particulars of texts, and the agency these complexities might have in writing the historical and political text of the age. Could textual specifics contest theoretical generalization? What of the potential of literary imaginations to re-imagine, to resist the prevailing paradigms, to open a space in which history is not only disclosed, but made?

Having begun my work in Romanticism with an investigation of interrogative rhetoric—more specifically, the instabilities of male-authored poetry (drawing on formalist criticism and deconstructionist theory)—by the mid-1980s I was turning to the gendered forms of these instabilities, reviewing Byron and Keats. Recognizing that the liberal political spirit of the age—that famous break with received systems of social existence—was contradicted by an *ancien régime* of gender, I was noticing that local plays of writing were rather less systematic. My initial adventures (one on cross-dressing as gender critique in *Don Juan,* one on gender phantasmagoria in the reception of Keats) investigated events of writing that showed men on edge, uncertain of their purchase on "masculine" power, unsure of the borders between masculine and feminine—especially in one strong "spirit of the age": the composition of the aesthetic self by feeling, subjectivity, receptivity. While these events could play into syntax and poetic form (problems I explored in two previous books), I wanted to account for the gender formations driving what Wordsworth's Preface to *Lyrical Ballads* calls the "peculiar language" of literary imagination (*LB&c* 754).

As I was rereading Byron and Keats, two professional women were coming to interest me, one contemporary with Byron and Keats, and one flourishing a bit later. I was curious about this "Mrs. Hemans" whose success as a "literary lady" irritated Byron into nastiness and provoked Wordsworth into impatience; and I was intrigued by "Miss Jewsbury," whose style and wit seemed to fascinate everyone who knew her, including Wordsworth, including even the women of his household who were irked by Mrs. Hemans. Alongside these curiosities, my affection for teaching *Frankenstein* had me reading more of Mary Wollstonecraft. Like Hemans and Jewsbury, she was totally absent from my graduate studies in the 1970s, but I experimentally included her in my first syllabi. They are all in this book.

One map of instability that did emerge in the 1980s, chiefly along deconstructive rather than historicist routes, was Toril Moi's scheme of margin and center, a kind of cartographic rethinking of Kristeva's trope of "femininity as marginality": "If patriarchy sees women as occupying a marginal position within the symbolic order," Moi put it with this nod to Kristeva, then one might transvalue the margin, theorizing it less as depotentiated exile than as a factitious, over-determined frontier: "the *limit* or borderline of that order." On this map, Moi suggested, the feminine works doubly, both to shield "the symbolic order from the imaginary chaos" and, subversively, to mirror what a masculine center exiles and represses but still can't help imagining in alienated feminine form (167). Hence, within male Romantic imaginations, the phantasmic array of patently symbolic female characters, usually with designs on, pressures on, the myth of male self-sufficiency: witches, goddesses (or lovers and goddesses who are witches; *les belles dames sans merci*), dream apparitions, Psyche and epipsyche, emanations and phantoms of delight, spiritual sisters and nurturing mothers, dutiful and rebellious daughters, and forms of "Nature," from nurse to stern deity.

Yet, for all these disparate values, the "feminine" is still the reflex of masculine centricity. What if the notion of border is reconfigured from an outward limit of a concentric structure into a borderline, a differential across which both women and men face each other and continually negotiate, and across which occur more than a few strange shifts and transactions? While less mythically fraught than Moi's map of center and frontier, these borderlines of mutual negotiation are no less revealing of the way men and women lived, wrote, thought, and felt. On these medial lines, senses (and sensations) of gender shape and are shaped by sign systems that prove to be arbitrary, fluid, susceptible of transformation. Hence *Borderlines: The Shiftings of Gender*. Reviewing the map of Romanticism that polarizes those masculinist and feminist (or proto-feminist) orders and practices, *Borderlines* shifts the language of gender essence (culturally organized and supported as it is) into mobile, less determinate syntax, tuned to such figures as the stylized "feminine" poetess, the aberrant "masculine" woman, the male poet deemed "feminine," the campy "effeminate," hapless or strategic cross-dressers of both sexes, and the variously sexed life of the soul itself. On the borderlines, essence figures more as a point of origin, or cultural identity, from which gender, too, is a departure—or even, in extreme instances, a "mistake" (this is Wollstonecraft's bold claim).

Why be *Romantic* about this? While men and women are always reflecting about being men and women, I am certain that the Romantic era, electrified by the French Revolution, with its powerful polemics of the rights and wrongs of *Man*, charged up the discussion to a turning point, or at least a curve of acceleration. With explicit political calculation, Wollstonecraft titled her initiative *A Vindication of the Rights of Woman*. And because writing itself—pamphlets and books, poems and novels—was so involved in the wrongs of woman, its methods and textures are everywhere on her critical agenda. Wollstonecraft was prescient, and is durably potent in treating gender-language as historically contingent. In her address, *Woman* is an ideological and political subject that may be *feminine* or *masculine*. Catharine Macaulay's *Letters on Education* paved the way, but her genre is still eighteenth-century Enlightenment/rationalist. Invoking the revolution-charged word *Rights,* Wollstonecraft channels the political momentum of the 1790s. And if she strategically kept the polemic attached to domestic benefits, contending for a rationally managed home as the first site of good government, she knew she was working a trope: the home that was like a republic implied a republic that could take its cue from by such home-schooled principles.

There is no precise periodizing of the questions that focus *Borderlines*, and that's because the issues are still with us, and continue to recoil in our readings of Romanticism—as my attention to reception, then, later, and now, shall make clear. Wollstonecraft launched nothing less than a methodology, an oppositional gender criticism of literature and culture to be conducted by a close reading of textual structure, right down to words, syntax, grammar, and fleeting allusion, and never forgetting the big stakes. Sharing her commitment to proving (testing, uncovering) large points in local sites, and reading local events into wider registers, I've written *Borderlines* to argue, in effect, that gender theory is most fully realized in such actions.

Illustrations

2.1 *Felicia Hemans.* Edward Scriven's engraving (1839) from William E. West's portrait (1827). In *The Works of Mrs. Hemans.* Edinburgh: William Blackwood and Sons, 1839. Collection of Susan J. Wolfson.

2.2 *Felicia Hemans.* Edward Smith's engraving from a miniature painted by Edward Robertson (1831). In Henry F. Chorley, *Memorials of Mrs. Hemans* (1836). Collection of Susan J. Wolfson.

4.1 *Mrs. Fletcher, Late M. J. Jewsbury,* by G. Freeman, engraved by J. Cochran (1832). Courtesy of Tamworth Library, Sheffield.

6.1 *Lady Caroline Lamb in Page's Costume,* by Thomas Phillips (1814). Copyright Devonshire Collection, Chatsworth. From an image kindly provided by Paul Douglass, reproduced by permission of the Chatsworth Settlement Trustees.

6.2 *The Finding of Don Juan by Haidée,* by Ford Madox Brown (1873). Permission of Birmingham Museums and Art Gallery.

6.3 *Byron in Albanian Dress,* by Thomas Phillips (1813). Permission of the National Portrait Gallery, London.

6.4 Lady Mary Wortley Montagu in Turkish habit, from *The Letters and Works of Lady Mary Wortley Montagu,* edited by her great-grandson, Lord Wharncliffe. London: George Bell and Sons, 1887. Courtesy of Princeton University Library.

8.1 Sketch of John Keats by Charles Brown (1819). Permission of the National Portrait Gallery, London.

8.2 Sketch of John Keats attributed to Mary Newton. Reproduced from Donald Parson, *Portraits of Keats* (Cleveland: World Publishing, 1954), said there (p. 172) to be in the possession of Colonel Claude N. Furneaux. Efforts to trace copyright were unsuccessful; advice welcome.

8.3 Miniature of John Keats by Joseph Severn (1818). Permission of the National Portrait Gallery, London.

8.4 Posthumous portrait of John Keats by William Hilton. Permission of the National Portrait Gallery, London.

8.5 Chalk sketch of John Keats by Charles Wass (1819–20), after a lost original by William Hilton. Permission of the National Portrait Gallery, London.

8.6 Life mask of John Keats taken by Benjamin Robert Haydon (1816). Permission of the National Portrait Gallery, London.

8.7 William Wordsworth, sketched by Benjamin Robert Haydon (1818). Permission of the National Portrait Gallery, London.

For a subsidy to assist in the publication of these illustrations, Susan Wolfson and Stanford University Press thank the Princeton University Committee on Research in the Humanities and Social Sciences.

Borderlines

CHAPTER ONE

On the Borderlines of Gendered Language

At supper my host told me bluntly that I was a woman of observation, for I asked him *men's questions*.
—MARY WOLLSTONECRAFT, 1795

He has, however degenerated sadly, [. . .] to see a person of his age and *sex* so devoted to gossip and scandal, is rather discouraging to those who are interested in his welfare.
—LORD BYRON TO LADY BLESSINGTON ON LORD HOLLAND'S SON, 1823

He appears to know every thing that is going on in England; takes a great interest in the London gossip.
—LADY BLESSINGTON ON BYRON, A WEEK LATER, 1823[1]

The Question of Gender

Literary aesthetics, goes one prevailing critical narrative, insinuate cultural logic, shaping "historical contradiction into ideologically resolvable form" and betraying this overdriven work in gaps and fissures, ruptures and incoherence—all of which it is the call of "ideological critique" (says Terry Eagleton) to expose and interrogate.[2] Some of the most influential accounts of Romantic-period writing, especially on questions of gender, have taken this cue to invoke a determinative socio-historical context, one seen to dictate, or at least underwrite, literary practice. But is literary work necessarily so compliant, so cooperative? While no one would deny the information and force of context, there is a loss in discounting literary agency in the world, and a loss, moreover, in neglecting literature itself as a context in which the ways of the world are refracted by oppositional pressure, critical thinking. Playing across multiple sites, exercising diverse and often competing impulses, writing sensitive to its formation as writing and interpretation has a way not only of resisting the pull of absorption, but also of applying and plying its own structuring power, of testing and contesting the forms and information of habitual understanding.[3]

Back in 1980, when he was advocating a "poetics of culture," Stephen Greenblatt held to a chiasmus, urging an investigation of "the social presence to the world of the literary text and the social presence of the world in the literary," with a sense that social presence was the subject in neglect. It is worth remembering, however, that he was as concerned with the reduction of the literary text to "the expression of social rules and instructions" as he was with the limiting of reference to the author. And not idly: twenty-five years on, post-formal (or anti-formal) polemic has not only suspected the literary text of being "absorbed entirely into an ideological superstructure," but often insists on the inevitability.[4] We can see this view in the most influential gender criticism of the Romantic era, where literary aesthetics are read as complicit with, naively or blindly contained by, these superstructures—in any event, not likely to appear as registers of complex imaginations engaged with complex cultural dynamics.

The issue of ideological superstructure and literary structuring comes into sharp focus with gender, because gender has a long-standing credit as uncontingent explanation: the very word (with its kin *genesis, generate, general*) bears an aura of grounding in "nature" prior to any culture. The language flows into the Romantic decades with this potent validity. So when, in the 1790s, Catharine Macaulay and Mary Wollstonecraft dislodged this ground by proposing the "nature" of gender as a cultural text ("the prevailing opinion of a sexual character," in Wollstonecraft's phrase), it was more than a smart idea. It was a radical challenge—not only to the definition of a sexual character but to any cultural system habituated as inevitable. Educing the invisible, they situated gender as a subject for explanation: a structure of images, values, attitudes and dispositions that could be read and disputed, queried as well as encountered, wondered about rather than simply worn. It is not too much to say that they initiated gender criticism. They did so by putting the language of gender into interrogative syntax (*if. . .*), casting the laws of gender into a field of unsettled negotiation, debate, conflict, and contradiction.

The professional gender criticism that emerged two centuries on took a pattern from this intervention. As with the eighteenth-century gender critics *avant la lettre*, its unidentified system was received opinion: in the case of Romantic studies, the gender of Romanticism itself—its writers, its thematic interests, its literary manners. Indexing definitions drawn from the writing of men, these critics identified a "masculine" bias and a subjected "feminine," both in the literature and in a literary history that suppressed women's writing. Romanticism was then remapped to relativize received tradition: there was the "masculine" canon and the "feminine" of (excluded) women's writing; the first a nexus of values and practices summed (variously) as egotistical, colonizing, appropriative, imperialistic, anti-domestic, sublime; the other, a matrix summed (variously) as selfless, object-oriented, empathetic, sympathetic, communal, domestic.[5] This critique was polemically important; but its poles could feel too sheer, too schematic, slighting not only the aberrations, contradictions, or double-exposures across the divide, but also the instabilities and complexities of particular encounters. Under-reported were slips at the limits of definition, events where the language and logic of gender difference prove uncertain, changeable, contestable, vexing prescriptive grammar into a critical syntax—not just in the Romantic era, but across the social and critical reception of its texts.

Gender and Revolution

It is no wonder that gender criticism often follows and is energized by wider cultural ruptures, and it is no coincidence that Wollstonecraft became a gender critic in the wake of the French Revolution, an international flashpoint for already volatile questions about language in social and political process.[6] While the revolution did not initiate gender questions, it gave hot urgency to the debates; and gender, by force of seeming uncontingent, acquired iconic status. That a crisis (or at least a critical condition) in gender understandings was brewing before this historical rupture was clear enough to John "Estimate" Brown, who broadcast to England this lurid mid-century alarm about sexes and signifiers in perilous decadence:

> The Sexes have now little other apparent distinction, beyond that of Person and Dress: Their peculiar and characteristic manners are confounded and lost: The one Sex having advanced into *boldness*, as the other have sunk into *Effeminacy*. (*Estimate* 51)

A superstructure of displays could not redeem a base corrupted, in Brown's estimate, by a zero-sum economy of advances and deteriorations. The threat of revolution accelerated the crisis. No less than its excitements, its tremors radiated across the Romantic decades, troubling a self-conscious modernism with specters of unknown consequences, and shading new notions of gender, even in otherwise progressive imaginations, with affections for old distinctions.

While the French Revolution was not about gender, gender language magnetized the reaction to it by force of its "natural" grammar. As Wollstonecraft realized, to dislodge this ground was to dislodge its allies: political system and gender system could be reviewed as a constitutive language of "prescription," "prejudice," and "prevailing opinion"—each *pre*-fix identifying an existing but not inevitable situation.[7] At the century's inception, Mary Astell, an educated woman of wealth and independence who moved in upper-class circles, nailed the law of gender. "If by the Natural Superiority of their Sex," men "mean that every Man is by Nature superior to every Woman," she sighed in sarcasm in a new Preface to her *Reflections upon Marriage* (1706), "the greatest Queen ought not to command, but to obey, her Footman: because no Municipal Laws can supersede or change the Law of Nature" (3). While she wasn't disputing the system of monarchy, her *if* is the sort of syntax Wollstonecraft would reiterate into oppositional gender critique. In the question of gender, grammar gets weighted in accumulations of experience that might be otherwise imagined. If a Law of Nature could be ironized by Municipal Law, might "Nature" be a convenient fiction? Wollstonecraft did better, arguing in *A Vindication of the Rights of Woman* (1792) that the law of gender was ready for a "REVOLUTION," a word she set in capitals in her closing call (341; cf. 158). The gender-icons of the French Revolution forced the question. The Republican icons—*La Raison, La Liberté, Marianne*[8]—were poster-femmes that coexisted with women's exclusion from the "rights of man." *Liberté, Égalité, Fraternité* was a fraternity after all.

For liberal women, it was galling that such forward thinkers as Rousseau could be so retrograde on gender. While his *Contrat social, ou Principles du droit politique* (1762) championed a new humanism in the legal equality of men, *Émile ou de l'Education* (also 1762), no less influential in England than *Le Contrat*, upheld the *ancien régime* of gender.[9] Book V, *Sophy, or Woman* (on the cultivation of Émile's ideal mate), not only denied woman the "rights of man" but did so by law of *la raison* itself: "women do wrong to complain of the inequality of man-made laws; this inequality is not of man's making, or at any rate it not the result of mere prejudice, but of reason" (Foxley 323–24). Finding such assertions nothing if not paradoxical, Wollstonecraft subjects Rousseau's "observations" to that syntax of *if,* of question, and satiric critique. Reviewing his claim that woman is "formed to obey a being so imperfect as man, often full of vices, and always full of faults," and so "ought to learn betimes even to suffer injustice [. . .] without complaint," she identifies no logic of reason, just a tyranny of "blind obedience."[10] Then there was the question of agency in *formed,* with Milton's fingerprints. When Milton "tells us that women are formed for sweet attractive grace," she snarks (referring to *Paradise Lost* 4.297–98), it is to insinuate an "insult" about the degraded nature of their grace, continuous with housebreaking into "gentle domestic brutes" (*VRW* 126–27). The specious appeal to nature is exposed by Rousseau himself when he indicates that girls require training "to prepare them for this subjection." Wollstonecraft summons his text into her *Vindication* for critical inspection:

> Girls [. . .] should be early subjected to restraint. This misfortune, if it really be one, is inseparable from their sex. [. . .] They must be subject, all their lives, to the most constant and severe restraint, which is that of decorum: it is, therefore, necessary to accustom them early to such confinement [. . .] and to the suppression of their caprices, that they may the more readily submit to the will of others. (*Emilius*; *VRW* 203)

Stripped of sentiment, Rousseau's obedience-school looks like oppression, and Wollstonecraft provides the critique: to say that "a state of dependence being natural to the sex, they perceive themselves formed for obedience," is "begging the question" (204). The lexicon of "natural" is an array of cultural coercions: *formed for, made for, made to, subjected to.* In another slip that shows "the effect of habit" being invoked "as an undoubted indication of nature" (202), she shows Rousseau admitting that the life of "woman" is not just taught, but also "reduced, by our absurd institutions, to a perpetual conflict with herself." His best rationalization for this unnatural conflict is the old story: it is only "just that this sex should partake of the sufferings which arise from those evils it hath caused us" (*Emilius*; *VRW* 203–4). Like Burke on aristocracy, Rousseau adduces "laws of nature" for partial privilege (*VRW* 162n). Yet nothing is more "grossly unnatural," Wollstonecraft replies, than "the character of Sophia," a freak of culture not only in "the superstructure, but the foundation of her character" (133).

The Rousseauvian view of gender is primed for animadversion no less by its contradictory logic of male priority (super-reasoning and super-vicious) than by its paradoxes on natural female character. A woman, Wollstonecraft proposes, is not born but made, with girls "treated like women, almost from their very birth" (*VRW* 203), "made women of when they are mere children" (246). Wordsworth would argue that the child is spiritual father of the man; Wollstonecraft sees the social genesis of woman in the girl. As her friend Mary Hays writes in 1798, the script is "the composition of Man's woman" (*Appeal* 48). Wollstonecraft's critical de-composition is to make women better readers of the Rousseauvian primer:

> the education of women should be always relative to the men. To please, to be useful to us, to make us love and esteem them, to educate us when young,

and take care of us when grown up, to advise, to console us, to render our lives easy and agreeable: these are the duties of women at all times. (*Emilius; VRW* 200–201)

Of this male-clubbed *they* and *us*, matched by the infinitive projection of female duties as essential and universal, Wollstonecraft dryly remarks, "The *rights* of humanity have been thus confined to the male line from Adam downwards. Rousseau would carry his male aristocracy still further" (210). Identifying "the sexual distinction which men have so warmly insisted upon" as conceptually "arbitrary" and politically a "tyranny" (342), Wollstonecraft closed her *Vindication* with a conspicuous purchase on current political concerns.

That gender is a political text may seem second nature to us now, but the idea was nothing short of electrifying for Wollstonecraft's generation. To refuse sex-determinism and put a female claim on a "manly spirit of independence" (*VRM* 46) was a bracing defamiliarization. Bracing, because gender habits were embraced even by male revolutionaries. Some *citoyennes*, inspired by the new constitution of government, were urging a reform of female education, only to meet a reactionary zeal that was nothing new. An early martyr was Olympe de Gouges, who used feminine nouns in her *Déclaration des Droits de la Femme et de la Citoyenne* (1791) to tweak the exclusionary masculine pronouns of the *Déclaration* adopted by the National Assembly in 1789 (this document would preface the Constitution of 1791, restricting citizenship to men over 25). The reaction of *Révolution de Paris*, a street publication, was a stern sounding of the old order:

> Civil and political liberty is, it is enough to say, unuseful to women and in consequence should be kept from them. Destined to pass their whole life confined in a paternal garret or a marital mansion, born for a perpetual dependence from the first instance of their existence until their passing, they are endowed with only private virtues. A woman is not well off, is not in her place, except in her family or in her household. Of all that goes on outside of her home, she ought to know nothing but what her parents or her husband judge appropriate to inform her of.[11]

The verbs are thoroughly Rousseauvian: *Destinées à, nées pour.* The Society of Revolutionary Republican Women, refusing confinement to "chez elle," kept up the pressure, and provoked everyone—working-class women, bourgeois men, the police, and the Revolutionary council—not just with polemics, but also with the symbolic declarations of their pantaloons and the (male) revolutionary headgear, the tricolor cockade.[12] The cockiness of the last fashion, especially the bid to mandate it as public dress for all *citoyennes,* was quickly registered. These "evildoers," warned the police,

> inspire in women the desire to share the political rights of men. When they have the cockade, they say, they will demand civic cards, want to vote in our assemblies, share administrative positions. (Levy &c 200)

First a hat, then the state.

After a run of heated confrontations, in October 1793 the National Convention abolished women's clubs: women were neither to "exercise political rights and take an active part in affairs of government" nor to "deliberate together in political associations or popular societies." The logic was an *ancien régime* of gender: with the public sphere fanning them to "over-excitation," "heat," and "passion" ("the kinds of disruption and disorder that hysteria can produce"), women were deemed unfit for "affairs of government," and moreover truant from home and family, "the more important cares to which nature calls." Wollstonecraft was in France when de Gouges was guillotined in November. "She wanted to be a statesman," *Feuille du salut public* admonished, "and it seems the law has punished this conspiratress for having forgotten the virtues befitting her sex." Pierre-Gaspard Chaumette of the Paris Commune piled on the gender slanders, warning activist women to "remember that virago, *cette femme-homme,* the impudent Olympe de Gouges," whose "forgetfulness of the virtues of her sex led her to the scaffold." When, within weeks, the Commune was confronted by a deputation of women, it brandished the example of "the impudent Olympe de Gouges [. . .] who abandoned the cares of her household to get mixed up in the republic, and whose head fell beneath the avenging knife of the laws."[13] On this disciplinary arc, the prequel was Charlotte Corday, the assassin of Marat in July. Fuming at "cette femme," *Répertoire du Tribunal Révolutionaire* fanned out a blazon of monstrosity and transgression:

> a virago [. . .] without grace, sloppy, like most female philosophers and wits. [. . .] twenty-five years old [. . .] in our customs, almost an old maid, especially with her masculine bearing and boylike stature. [. . .] Her head was stuffed with books of all sorts. [. . .] this woman has thrown herself absolutely outside of her sex; when nature recalled her to it, she felt only disgust and ennui; sentimental love and its tender emotions never touch the heart of a woman who has pretension to knowledge, to wit, to free-thinking, to national politics, who has a mania for philosophy and who burns to make herself noticed. Decent and amiable men do not like women of this sort.[14]

The insistence on "la nature" is equivalent to its male determination: "absolument hors de son sexe," Corday repels "les hommes bien pensants et aimables."

This is not French law only; its terms played across the channel in British syntaxes.

To name what is unnatural and monstrous is, by reflex, to relay what wise and decent men revere. The primer of this romance for British readers was Burke's *Reflections on the Revolution in France* (1790). "I love a manly, moral, regulated liberty as well as any gentleman," he protests in his opening pages (19), in a mystique of class and gender that comes to full boil in a tour de force on the arrest of Marie Antoinette:

> It is now sixteen or seventeen years since I saw the queen of France, then the dauphiness, at Versailles; and surely never lighted on this orb, which she hardly seemed to touch, a more delightful vision. I saw her just above the horizon, decorating and cheering the elevated sphere she just began to move in,—glittering like the morning-star, full of life, and splendor, and joy. Oh! what a revolution! and what an heart must I have, to contemplate without emotion that elevation and that fall! Little did I dream [. . .] that I should have lived to see such disasters fallen upon her in a nation of gallant men, in a nation of men of honour and of cavaliers. I thought ten thousand swords must have leaped from their scabbards to avenge even a look that threatened her with insult.—But the age of chivalry is gone. [. . .] Never, never more, shall we behold that generous loyalty to rank and sex, that proud submission, that dignified obedience, that subordination of the heart, which kept alive, even in servitude itself, the spirit of an exalted freedom [. . . .] the nurse of manly sentiment and heroic enterprize is gone! (*Reflections* 89)

The heroic paradoxes—proud submission, dignified obedience, free servitude—take the pattern of Christian faith for national identity. An exclamation-pointed "revolution" of English manly heart and spirit trumps the French revolution against "rank and sex." The degradation of gender in this "disaster" (the etymology is keyed to the "star" dauphiness) has rewritten the genre of history: "All homage paid to the sex in general," Burke laments of the new "scheme of things," is to be "regarded as romance and folly" (90).

So radically invested was this mythologizing that its tropes played (in sentiment and parody) for decades. In the immediate wake, Joseph Priestley leapt to ridicule this "idolatry of a fellow creature" (Letter 3, *Letters* 30) and impeach the idolater's manly credit:

> If, Sir, you profess this "generous loyalty, this proud submission, this dignified obedience, and this subordination of the heart," both to *rank and sex,* how concentrated and exalted must be the sentiment, where rank and sex are united! What an *exalted freedom* would you have felt, had you had the

happiness of being a subject of the Empress of Russia; your sovereign, being then *woman?* Fighting under her auspices, you would, no doubt, have been the most puissant of knights errant, and her redoubted champion, against the whole Turkish empire, the sovereign of which is only a *man*. (31)

Priestley subverts Burke's gender-system with travesty, casting chivalric homage as farcical subjection to a queen already cartooned in English letters as the embodied excess of political power and sexual appetite. In 1794 Wollstonecraft looked back on the *ancien régime* as Burkism gone wild. During this "general depravation of manners" (she writes at the head of the second chapter of *View of the Origin and Progress of the French Revolution*):

the young and beautiful *dauphine* arrived; and was received with a kind of idolatrous adoration, only to be seen in France; for the inhabitants of the metropolis, literally speaking, could think and talk of nothing else; and in their eagerness to pay homage, or gratify affectionate curiosity, an immense number were killed. (*W* 6: 29)

Priestley parodied Burke's gender-heroics; Wollstonecraft trains cultural criticism on the public genre. The problem with Burke's glittering morning-star was not just the elevated sphere of celebrity theater; it was the magnetic adulation that corrupts the rational sphere of public life. Conflating Burke's star-struck idolatry with its immediate material sequel (a horrible fire in Place Louis XV, where the theater-crowd had gathered), Wollstonecraft allegorizes the historical catastrophe to come.[15]

Burke, too, knows that culture is theater, but wields gender travesty to conservative ends. The "mixed system of opinion and sentiment" in the revered order (*Reflections* 89) gets its antitype in the gender chaos of the new National Assembly:

They act amidst the tumultuous cries of a mixed mob of ferocious men, and of women lost to shame, who, according to their insolent fancies, direct, control, applaud, explode them; and sometimes mix and take their seats amongst them; domineering over them with a strange mixture of servile petulance and proud presumptuous authority. (81–82)

From this "inverted order" of gender (82) explodes the ghastliest she-issue of the Fall of France: it was amid "horrid yells, and shrilling screams, and frantic dances and infamous contumelies, and all the unutterable abominations of the furies of hell, in the abused shape of the vilest of women" that the royal family was hustled from Versailles to Paris (85). (Nowhere in sight is the material plight Wollstonecraft records: the desperation of these market women from high prices and scarce bread).[16] In a post-Terror public letter of 1796, Burke re-conjures the vile female shape as the enemy not just of patriarchal order but of paternal certainty:

> The revolution harpies of France, sprung from night and hell, or from that chaotic anarchy, which generates equivocally 'all monstrous, all prodigal things,' cuckoo-like, adulterously lay their eggs, and brood over, and hatch them in the nest of every neighboring state. (*Letter to a Noble Lord*; *W* 4: 294)

Though Burke lost a shot in misremembering Milton's more monstrous adjective (not *prodigal* but *prodigious*), he ably whips the hellbound Miltonic inventory into a specter of political reform as promiscuous female infection.[17] "Adulterously" is both a trope of scandal and a prediction of actual female sexual license as another issue of liberty, another curse on male social order:

> These obscene harpies, who deck themselves, in I know not what divine attributes, but who in reality are foul and ravenous birds of prey (both mothers and daughters) flutter over our heads, and souse down upon our tables, and leave nothing unrent, unrifled, unravaged, or unpolluted with the slime of their filthy offal. (*W* 4: 294–95)

With this cue to Virgil, Burke guesses that had this Roman "lived to see the revolutionists and constitutionalists of France, he would have had more horrid and disgusting features of his harpies to describe" (295n). Virgil Redivivus stage-manages the famous opening pages of his widely read *Letters on a Regicide Peace* (also 1796):

> out of the tomb of the murdered monarchy in France, has arisen a vast, tremendous, unformed spectre, in a far more terrific guise than any which ever yet have overpowered the imagination, and subdued the fortitude of man. Going straight forward to its end, unappalled by peril, unchecked by remorse, despising all common maxims and all common means, that hideous phantom overpowered those who could not believe it was possible she could at all exist. (Letter 1; *W* 4: 334–35)

A phantasm of the gothic sublime, the Revolution mob of femmes fatales devastates male fortitude and imagination, masculine political order and civilization. "No man, in a public or private concern, can divine by what rule or principle her judgments are to be directed" (4: 390).

Mindful that men at war may team up on gender, Wollstonecraft opens *A Vindication of the Rights of Men* (1790) with a gendering of class politics. A chief tactical turn is to give old gender-signs new assignments. This Vindicator will use "manly definition" to "contend for the *rights of men*" (2). If a "representative system of government" is one that "presents itself on the open theatre of the world in a fair and manly manner" and "not by fraud and mystery" (204), Burke earns judgment as "unmanly" in angling for a pension (20) and in his mystifications of sentiment, fantasy, and hysteria. His "feminine" rhetoric even solicits female impersonation: "Ladies, Sir, may repeat your sprightly sallies, and retail in theatrical attitudes many of your sentimental exclamations" (5). No man speaking to men, this ladies' man is a study in "sensibility," that female-coded "*manie* of the day"(5).[18] Detaching gender from determination by sex, Wollstonecraft challenges Burke to be more of a man: quit "the flowers of rhetoric" (6), leave off "unmanly servility, most inimical to true dignity of character" (50), abjure devotion to an aristocracy "emasculated by hereditary effeminacy" (97), and meet her standard of "reason" and "manly plainness" (84). Parodying his sigh for "ancient chivalry" (89), she assumes the role of male gallant, solicitous of his feminine delicacy: "it would be something like cowardice to fight with a man who had never exercised the weapons with which his opponent chose to combat" (9). It is the Revolution, she will say at the start of *French Revolution,* that evinces "the enlightened sentiments of masculine and improved philosophy" (v). Noting the conventional gender terms, some 1990s critics detect a "potentially conservative ambivalence."[19] Yet in the 1790s, to substitute rational capacity for "natural" character was to register a revolution, one pivoted not just on politics per se but on the politics of language.

One index of the excitement is Mary Hays's gleeful sequel to Wollstonecraft's parody of male-romanced chivalry: "It is little wonderful that the magnanimous advocate of freedom, and the opponent of Burke, should throw down the gauntlet, challenge her arrogant oppressors, and, hurried away by a noble enthusiasm, deny the existence of a sexual character."[20] Reviewers of the first *Vindication* certainly felt the gender charge. On Wollstonecraft's home court, *Analytical Review* hooted, "how deeply must it wound the feelings of a *chivalrous* knight, who owes the fealty of 'proud submission and dignified obedience' to the fair sex, to perceive that two of the boldest of his adversaries are women!" (8: 416; its next article was on Macaulay's *Observations on Burke*). If the "language may be thought by some too bold and pointed for a female pen," *English Review* was willing to grant the license: "when women undertake to write on masculine subjects, and reason as Miss Wollstonecraft does, we wish their language to be free from all female *prettinesses,* and to express with energy and perspicuity, the ideas they mean to convey" (17: 61). Set to review a transvestite farce, *Gentleman's Magazine* still managed to advertise the initiative:

> The *rights of men* asserted by a fair lady! The age of chivalry cannot be over, or the sexes have changed their ground. [. . .] Mrs. Wolstencraft enters the

lists armed *cap-à-pie,*—as the ladies some years ago took the field at Warley Common. We should be sorry to raise a horse-laugh against a fair lady; but we were always taught to suppose that the *rights of women* were the proper theme of the female sex. (61/1, 151)

Little did they know. If they meant this travesty to point their critique, their notion of "the proper theme" for women unwittingly intuited Wollstonecraft's next *Vindication,* without guessing its attack on the distinctions of which *Gentleman's Magazine* was so sure.

Rights of Woman opens with a dedicatory letter to the French education minister Talleyrand, detailing the gender retrogrades in the revolutionary Constitution (she did not know that the unnamed author of her immediate provocation, his report on national education, had been Mme de Staël.)[21] Mobilizing that syntax of *if,* Wollstonecraft measures the reforms of the revolution against reforms still wanting:

> If the abstract rights of man will bear discussion and explanation, those of woman, by a parity of reasoning, will not shrink from the same test: though a different opinion prevails in this country, built on the very arguments which you use to justify the oppression of woman—prescription. [. . .] tyrants of every denomination [. . .] are all eager to crush reason; yet always assert that they usurp its throne only to be useful. Do you not act a similar part, when you *force* all women, by denying them civil and political rights, to remain immured in their families groping in the dark? for surely, Sir, you will not assert, that a duty can be binding which is not founded on reason? [. . .] if women are to be excluded, without having a voice, from a participation of the natural rights of mankind, prove first, to ward off the charge of injustice and inconsistency, that they want reason—else this flaw in your NEW CONSTITUTION will ever shew that man must, in some shape, act like a tyrant. (103–4)

By naming "the natural rights of mankind," Wollstonecraft tacitly alludes to the contradictory *ancien régime* "laws of nature" for womankind. "The *divine right* of husbands, like the divine right of kings, may, it is to be hoped, in this enlightened age, be contested" (153). The larger question was legible enough to Mary Ann Stodart, writing nervously a half a century on about Wollstonecraft and her prophet Mary Astell, both "strenuous advocates of the mental equality of the sexes": "It is difficult to maintain this theory," she murmurs, "without aiming a presumptuous blow at that wisdom which assigned to man to rule, to woman to obey" (14). Though she wants no part of the politics, delete *presumptuous* and the sentence could have been Wollstonecraft's.

As her rounds with Rousseau show, Wollstonecraft's gender critique proceeds as literary criticism. Also on her syllabus are *Paradise Lost* (implicitly, Scripture), Pope's moral essay on *The Characters of Women,* and the conduct tracts of Dr. Gregory and Rev. Fordyce. Reading gender as a cultural text is the logical extension. The praise of "feminine, according to the masculine acceptation of the word," she reads on a bias, uncovering a "farce" of "specious names" such as *innocent, delicate,* and *beautiful* that convey the "intoxicating" homage which "men condescendingly use to soften our slavish dependence." A language lesson shows the dark side of shining chivalry: "women are systematically degraded by receiving the trivial attentions, which men think it manly to pay to the sex, when, in fact, they are insultingly supporting their own superiority."[22] This much even Hannah More could endorse. Sobered by "common sense" (*Strictures* 5), she was no more eager than Wollstonecraft to "bring back the frantic reign of chivalry, nor to reinstate women in that fantastic empire in which they sat enthroned in the hearts, or, rather, in the imaginations of men" (12). Wollstonecraft satirizes such male imaginations by applying "feminine"-coded terms. In their dubious rational powers, kings, aristocrats, rich men, soldiers, sensualists, gallants, and society wits are she-casts. So, too, weak "reasoners" such as Burke and Milton: of Milton's contradictions in *Paradise Lost* on sexual hierarchy, she remarks, "into similar inconsistencies are great men often led by their senses." Chesterfield is "unmanly"; Rousseau is "unintelligible," full of "nonsense" and "errors in reasoning" arising from "sensibility"; Fordyce is prone to "sentimental rant" and plain "fooleries." In this measure of reason, gender is in free play: rational women may have "masculine" intellect (gainsaying the stigma of "masculine"); foolish boys and servile, or sense-driven men may earn description as "unmanly" and "effeminate."[23] Far from betraying a complicity with adjectival gender-norms, these reversals shape a defamiliarizing satire that draws its force precisely from reference to a still forceful normative hierarchy.[24]

That the rights of women lost out in France was small solace to British conservatives, who quickly registered the force of the idea. A spur for Burke, provoked by new rights in France for bastards and the "license to divorce," was the story "that women had been too long under the tyranny of parents and of husbands"; he warned of the political, social and moral "consequences of taking one half of the species wholly out of the guardianship and protection of the other" (*Regicide Peace* 4: 394). Christoph Meiners saw the fall coming before the Revolution. To let women into the public sphere is to make inversion inevitable: "The men became effeminate, and the women masculine" (3: 418). His best hope amid the Revolution itself was for a new era of Republican security, when women could give up their culottes and liberty caps and withdraw from public life. Dismayed by *Rights of Woman,* he was relieved that Wollstonecraft had at least not pressed for civil and political equality. If this came to pass, chaos would come again: "the men would be transformed into women, or [. . .] the women would be totally diverted from those objects for which nature designed them" (4: 328).[25] With a whiff of Rousseau, he advised, "It is nature herself and not the cruelty of men that has denied them a participation in those rights, offices and pursuits from which they have been excluded in all ages among the nations of Europe" (328). In this story, men are no tyrants, just obedient to the inalienable law of "nature herself," an authority usefully feminine and providentially antifeminist. It helped, too, that there were anti-Jacobin women such as Laetitia Hawkins to write the romance of sequestration: "the whole world might be at war, and yet not the rumor of it reach the ear of an Englishwoman—empires might be lost, and states overthrown, and still she might pursue the peaceful occupations of her home; and her natural lord might change his governor at pleasure, and she feel neither change nor hardship" (*L* 2: 194).

Yet among the women so immured, Hawkins was not alone in some curious latencies. Worrying about the erosion of "respect formerly paid to authority," she cautioned, "she who has early imbibed an aversion towards the kingly character, will easily be persuaded to consider her husband as an unauthorized tyrant [. . .] fancying she has reason on her side" (1: 105–6). The analogy, if not the argument, is Wollstonecraft-wired. So, too, in the next generation when M. A. Stodart toes the line at the outset of *Female Writers* (1842):

> We say nothing, far be it from us, against attention to domestic duties. Home is and ever must be the true sphere for woman and her domestic duties her first duties. Nothing can alter the position assigned to her in Scripture. (9)

Yet for all these strictures, Stodart's peeps of grievance are edged with Wollstonecraft's satires. Her remarks about Boileau (speaking for the old order) might have been Wollstonecraft's on Burke: "Boileau was an unmarried man; how could he for one moment be imagined, to comprehend the mind of women?" His "satire on women is a satire on himself: his quiver is exhausted, and many of the arrows are pointless" (3), she says, not innocent of the sexual jibe. Her protest that women "have been too often delineated by those whose interest it was to keep them in subjection" (25) and the complaint against the system of education that teaches them "that one half of the human species was created for the comfort, the enjoyment, the amusement [. . .] of the other half" (30) seem virtually channeled from *Rights of Woman*. A (singularly long) footnote to the last point not only cites the same lines in *Paradise Lost* on Eve that irritated Wollstonecraft (4.440–43; 634–38), it also involves her rhetoric of "free animadversions" on the "slavish principle" that is "rather too evident in the picture which Milton gives of our first parents. As a republican, his ideas of domestic liberty were not very great, and the inferiority of Eve is most sedulously and sternly maintained" (30–31).

Women Writing

Like Wollstonecraft, these women did not murmur in the peace of the home, but wrote in address to the public sphere. This is the complication negotiated by any woman author, and it was a hot zone if her writing advanced the new philosophies of rights and liberties. The temperate zone hosted the home genres: conduct, sentiment, children, cookery. Even Wollstonecraft began her career on this footing (a book on female conduct and education, a female reader, and a novel of sentiment) and in a mode of modesty (said Godwin's *Memoir*) in "vehement aversion to the being regarded, by her ordinary acquaintance, in the character of an author" (68). Hannah More managed the character of author under the cover of old-school principles: she monitored conduct and arraigned truants, especially female "literary vanity" in disdain of "the duties of ordinary life" and the "sober cares which ought to occupy their sex." Such truancy evinced "an unnatural separation between talents and usefulness" (*Strictures* 218). The advice was self-monitoring, too.

A publishing woman always risked censure, which quickly materialized if her talents were spent against the prevailing opinion of a sexual character—the offense for which "Wollstonecraft," after the scandals blabbed by Godwin, became not just a handy but a magnetic signifier. The female authorial "I" was held to dress-code femininity. In an unsigned essay for *The Liberal* in 1823 that glanced at Wollstonecraft, the author (her daughter, Mary Shelley) stayed mindful of both generic and gender rules: "Half the beauty of Lady Mary Montagu's Letters consists in the *I* that adorns them; and this *I,* this sensitive, imaginative, native, suffering, enthusiastic pronoun, spreads an expressive charm over Mary Wollstonecraft's Letters from Norway" ("Giovanni Villani" 331–32). This *I* creates aura and atmosphere, not polemics. In Wollstonecraft's day, its imprint was a precarious adventure. "In a young writer, and especially a female one," cautioned *General Magazine and Impartial Review* in the wake of the French Revolution, "the little saucy pronoun *I* seldom makes its appearance with a good grace."[26] Conservatives slapped back with two instruments, not always in coordination: conduct-lore on modesty and propriety, and vigilance on the new insurgency. A favorite tactic, as Wollstonecraft recognized, was the stigma of monstrosity, deeming a woman "unsexed by acquiring strength of body and mind" (*VRW* 314). This wasn't just the cry of "libertines" who like a "soft bewitching beauty" (314). It also blazed in the anti-Jacobin tracts that equated female advocacy of liberty with sexual license, civil riot, and national treachery.

An acid alliance of these discourses etches Richard Polwhele's tirade *The Unsex'd Females* (1798). On a polarized anti-Jacobin map, the unsex'd deformation of "Gallic freaks" (20) gets reviewed, then countermanded by "the sex" (177) in proper character. Polwhele opens with calculated sonnet-stanza on the perversion, its climax unveiling a manifold of anti-patriarchal, unnatural, and outlaw rebellion:

> Survey with me, what ne'er our fathers saw,
> A female band despising NATURE's law,
> As "proud defiance" flashes from their arms,
> And vengeance smothers all their softer charms. (11–14)

The title keyword is soon brought on stage: "unsex'd woman vaunts the imperious mien" (16). The conjured ghost is Shakespeare's ambitious regicide, Lady Macbeth, who cries to her spirits, "unsex me here"; she would transform her body "from the crown to the toe" and pervert her "woman's breasts" with an exchange of milk for gall (1.5.41–49). Polwhele previews the sorority of mythic and modern avatars in a footnote just prior (6): "Amazonian band—the female Quixotes of the new philosophy," not just denatured by the sacrifice of a breast to military expediency, but militantly organized polemicists.

Polwhele's foil is no easily dismissed old-school Sophyism (a monstrosity not only to the new philosophy but also to enlightenment rationality). He is, moreover, egalitarian in the republic of letters. In a sentiment that Wollstonecraft might share, he is glad that the "tribunal of criticism" no longer cuts "a female author" any slack "in consideration of her sex," by exercising that "species of gallantry" that would praise "imbecillity." Credit to "literary women" must be secured "with the same rigid impartiality as it seems right to exercise towards the men." While such judgment is rather more partial than it lets on (e.g., "the alarming eccentricities of Miss Wollstonecraft"), what passes muster are the women he met through his mother, women noted for "works of learning or genius" (16–17n). MONTAGUE, CARTER, CHAPONE, SEWARD, PIOZZI, BURNEY, RADCLIFFE—so Polwhele blazons the names through the persona of their disciple More, whom he sets as the center of his reform in female manners: "round their MORE the sisters" (the unsex'd band) gather, with "repentant murmurs" and "blushes" (188–206). To boost More's authority, Polwhele appends a footnote of extracts from the "Introduction" to her *Essays for Young Ladies* on the necessity of observing and preserving the "natural [. . .] distinction" of "sexual character" (36–37n).²⁷ More repays the compliment the next year (1798) by summoning Polwhele's master-tropes at the outset of her *Strictures on Female Education,* where, in the latest political emergency (Napoleonic ambition), she calls on her countrywomen for "patriotism at once firm and feminine," but with no mistake of purpose: "I am not sounding an alarm to female warriors, or exciting to debate female politicians: I hardly know which of the two is the most disgusting and unnatural character" (4). Feminine fortitude is one thing, female transgression quite another.

Polwhele's double-duty of praise and censure is visited on a veteran who might have rushed the More-sorority on the credit of irritating Wollstonecraft with poems in praise of female delicacy. But instead, Anna Barbauld is chastised for forsaking "her songs of Love, her Lyrics" and catching the strain of Wollstonecraft (91–92): "Mrs. B. has late published several political tracts" (17n). And in the genre shift she, too, is "unsex'd." When she published *Eighteen Hundred and Eleven,* a 334-line heroic-couplet tract indicting Britain's imperialism, the Tory *Quarterly* charged into the field of correction with a sex-pointed weapon. Like Polwhele, it was not dead set against a she-pen (it would warm to "Mrs. Hemans"), and certainly no fonder of he-penned opposition (Shelley). The offense is the oxymoron "lady-author," a figure not just on the border of social grammar, but transgressing social practice, by entering the public sphere with command, resolution, and instrumentality:

> We had hoped, indeed, that the empire might have been saved without the intervention of a lady-author. [. . .] Not such, however, is her opinion; an irresistible impulse of public duty—a confident sense of commanding talents—have induced her to dash down her shagreen spectacles and her knitting needles, and to sally forth [. . .] in the magnanimous resolution of saving a sinking state, by the instrumentality of a pamphlet. [. . .] her former works have been of some utility; her "Lessons for Children," her "Hymns in Prose," [. . .] but we must take the liberty of warning her to desist from satire [. . .] writing any more pamphlets in verse. (*Quarterly* 7: 309, 313)

Forgetting the maternal for the military, the knitting needles for the needling pen, the lady-author is not only beaten back with brutal farce and a sarcasm so ungentlemanly that even John Murray, the *Quarterly*'s publisher, was "ashamed," but she is also faintly threatened with official prosecution.²⁸

If this seems like overkill, survey with me Henry Chorley's care, years on (in 1836), to exorcise any stimulus as he introduces a memoir of the very model of feminine decorum, "Mrs. Hemans." He means to champion "the popularity and prevalence of female authorship" as "the spirit of the age," and to put to shame "the contemptuous party-words formerly wielded in attack and defense" (*CMH* 1: 6–7). Yet he halts before the radical claim "that genius is of no sex" and, to reassure the male sex, he satirizes those

> intemperate enthusiasts, who plead their *right* to take up the lion's skin and club, and, assuming the stern and peculiar cares of manhood, would (unwarned by the disastrous example of England's wisest king in the neat-herd's cot) condemn the poor lord of the creation to the small cares of housewifery. (*CMH* 1: 7)

Transvestitism is a durable trope of transgression, as old as Greek myth and Deuteronomy, as new as modern political rioting. Chorley's she-warriors evoke *Gentleman's* farcical butch Wollstonecraft, while his King Alfred allies with More's picture in *Essays for Young Ladies* (1777) of gender-scandalizing Hercules, "who wore a club and a lion's skin in the cause of virtue" but, besotted with passion, let a queen impose "the most effeminate employments" on him (*On Dissipation* 272–73).

Still fresh at the time of Chorley's *Memoir* was Mrs. Sandford's *Woman, In Her Social and Domestic Character* (1831), where she begs the "indulgence of the reader" for woman in the contradictory character of author: her book, she pleads, is "strictly appropriate for a female pen" and safely in the female sphere, "written exclusively for her own sex" (vii). Her credential is to cast Wollstonecraft as the cause of the "folly" of all those "literary ladies" who "plea for assumption":

> The disciple of Wollstonecraft threw off her hat, and called for a boot-jack; and imagined that by affecting the manners of the other sex, she should best assert her equality with them. The female pedant appears in a disordered dress, and with inky fingers; and fancies that the further she is removed from feminine grace, the nearer she approaches to manly vigour. ("The Value of Letters to Woman," *Woman* 25–26)

In this travesty of presumption (cast-off hat, boot-jack, inky fingers), this unsexed female is a disgrace, ridiculous in thinking she can claim equality, or aspire to manly style, in mere theatrical affectations of manners and dress.

Is she Blue? *Blue-stocking* is a transvestite term, derived from men's wear at the eighteenth-century salons.[29] In 1786 More could celebrate this culture in a poem she proudly titled *The Bas Bleu*. But by Sandford's decade, the color was stigma and farce:

> The *bas bleu* is eager for notoriety, and avails herself of her acquirements only to secure it. She does all she can to sustain her claims; she accumulates around

her the materials of learning, and her very boudoir breathes an academic air. Its decorations are sufficient to proclaim her character; its shelves are filled with books of every tongue; its tables are strewed with the apparatus of science; the casket of jewels is displaced for the cabinet of stone; and the hammer and the alembic occupy the stand allotted for the work-box [. . . . all] indulged from the mere wish of being eccentric, and of attracting more than ordinary notice. (*Woman* 118–19)

The decor of displacements—suspect foreign chatter instead of proper she-books, a box of stones instead of the jewel-box, scientific apparatus and tools instead of table china and sewing box—does more than index the travesty; it casts female learning as just one more boudoir farce.

It was not gender deformation that woman-of-letters Maria Jewsbury read in all this; it was social deformation. In a testy (unsigned) review of *Woman* for the *Athenæum*, she contended that "Women rarely make good Mentors to women," because all their "moralities" are corrupted by "a paralyzing fear of man" (282): "all that they decry, and all that they inculcate is subservient," and so (*pace* Sandford) "they hardly ever advise the sex *in print*, without injuring the great and holy cause of female improvement." Jewsbury's mentors in print were the last generation of cultural revolution: "Some forty years ago, a few female spirits, in their eagerness to extend the rights of cultivation, made shipwreck of many things, without which, cultivation is a curse." A historical and moral view of the decades since showed a sad decline and fall: "That reign of audacity among female moralists was succeeded by the reign of timidity; and the present little volume, by Mrs. John Sandford, offers no views brighter, bolder, or more enlarged." Jewsbury herself was not immune. Her home court, the *Athenæum*, for all of its hospitality to smart women (she and Elizabeth Barrett were regular contributors), recoiled at blue signs.[30] When the reviewer of her tale of female genius (*History of an Enthusiast*) challenged the canard "that splendid talents in woman are not compatible with her happiness" to insist "we believe differently," it was not to encourage happy ambition, but to reiterate old strictures:

> Woman is not less happy, and surely not less beloved, because heaven has blessed her with genius; it is only when, scorning the softer affections of her own sex, she aspires to the less amiable and more ambitious feelings of man, that genius becomes the thorn "to prick and sting her,"—it is only then (at least this is our reading of the word) that she becomes a *blue*, and not because she has superlative genius. (1 May 1830, p. 259)

Aspiration to "the less amiable and more ambitious feelings of man" meant professional vocation rather than marriage-marketing—on the same page as the "luxury and damnèd incest" that the ghost of Gerturde's murdered husband hopes will put a thorn of pain into her conscience (*Hamlet* 1.5.83–89). The telltale sign for both sins is *blue*.

In other quarters *blue* purging took on the look of racial or ethnic cleansing. In 1823, the *British Critic* hosted an essay on Hemans celebrating the "womanly nature throughout all her thoughts and her aspirations" (52), but its opening paragraph makes it clear that this was an occasion to go after bigger game:

> We heartily abjure Blue Stockings. We make no compromise with any variation of the colour, from sky-blue to Prussian blue, blue stockings are an outrage upon the eternal fitness of things. [. . .] Our forefathers never heard of such a thing as a Blue Stocking, except upon their sons' legs; the writers of Natural History make no mention of the name. [. . .] Shakspeare, who painted all sorts and degrees of persons and things, who compounded or created thousands, which, perhaps, never existed, except in his own prolific mind, even he, in the wildest excursion of his fancy never dreamed of such an extraordinary combination as a Blue Stocking! No! it is a creature of modern growth, and capable of existing only in such times as the present. (ns 20, 50)

The campy extravagance of this declaration of the wrongs of woman does not disguise the import. Updating the *citoyenne*'s pantaloons and cockade, the transvestite Blue Stocking is an outlaw to patriarchy, history, nature, and even the stretch of literary imagination. At the *British*, harrying the Blue not only advertised "the sound principles, and manly character, of our Review"; it was also a cultural manifesto: "we hereby give notice to all whom it may concern, that it is our intention henceforth, to visit enormities of this description, with the severity they so justly deserve" (51).

Such men's clubbing even liberal *Examiner*-readers could endorse, compacting across otherwise testy class or political differences. Keats muttered of longing "to upset the drawling of the blue stocking literary world." Hazlitt declared his "utter aversion to *blue-stockings*." Byron liked Teresa Guiccioli for "conceal[ing] what she knows," and "know[ing] I am not fond of blues." He also liked Francis Jeffrey's aphorism: "If she has blue stockings, she contrives that her petticoat shall hide them."[31] Even that feminine ideal in Murray's *Quarterly Review* and Jeffrey's *Edinburgh Review,* Mrs. Hemans, didn't contrive sufficiently for Byron. He mocked her to Murray (who published them both) as "your feminine He-Man" or "Mrs. Hewoman's" (*BLJ* 7: 182–83, 158), making a sexual (or unsexed) freak of her professional success. "Mrs. Shemans" was another pet sarcasm, recalled Isaac D'Israeli (Cline 141). Byron clearly preferred women in their place, not his. "I do not despise Mrs. Heman—but if [she] knit blue stockings instead of wearing them it would be better," he snipped to Murray (7: 182).

No wonder women took cover. With rueful satire, Lady Mary Wortley Montagu, who was convinced that "Women are ridiculous, not because they have Learning but because they have it not," advised her daughter to train her own daughter in the "absolutely necessary" art of "conceal[ing] whatever Learning she attains, with as much solicitude as she would hide Crookedness or Lameness"—a deformity that guarantees social misery: "The Parade of it can only serve to draw on her the envy, and consequently the most inveterate Hatred, of all he and she Fools, which will certainly be at least three parts in four of all her Acquaintance" (28 Jan. 1753; *L* 3: 22–23). Almost a century later, in 1845, Byron's friend Lady Blessington wrote a parable for *Heath's Book of Beauty* titled *Le Bas Bleu*. Warned about romancing a learned miss, young Lord Avondale replies with a blue dream: "My own taste for literature [. . .] renders an intellectual wife indispensable to my happiness" (240). But the fantasy is betrayed to a blue cartoon, the wife proving merely pedantic, deeply antisocial, deeply unconjugal. It takes her near death in the birth of a feeble boy (who survives just hours) to reduce her to a proper wife: "weakened by so much suffering, she became docile as a child in [Lord Avondale's] hands. It was now for the first time that Lady Avondale learned to know the value of affection, and as this knowledge dawned on her mind, a sense of her own unworthiness came with it" (247). But if the Bas Bleu learns what true knowledge is, it is not clear what Lady Blessington's true colors may be. Is this a form of the concealment Lady Montagu advised?

It is when actual social practices blur the borders that separate spheres tend to get the sharpest definition, and genre was one of the check-points. George Gilfillan, though he actually liked Hemans's poems, made no bones in *Tait's* about refusing her "the name of poet—a word often abused, often misapplied in mere compliment or courtesy." "A *maker* she is not," he declared (hitting the Greek etymology), then complimented her with mere courtesy:

> Mrs. Hemans's poems are strictly effusions. And not a little of their charm springs from their unstudied and extempore character [. . .] in fine keeping with the sex of the writer. You are saved the ludicrous image of double-dyed Blue, in papers and morning wrapper, sweating at some stupendous treatise or tragedy from morn to noon, and from noon to dewy eve. (*Tait's Edinburgh* ns 14: 360–61)[32]

A Blue attempt at he-genres is both a travesty (her papers and wrapper are curlers and robe, not book-makings) and a mock-heroic caution, mapped on the fall of Satanically confederate architect Mulciber from Heaven ("from Morn/To Noon he fell, from Noon to dewy Eve"; *PL* 1.742–43). Hemans's "keeping" is the aura of "unstudied" nature: "the transition is so natural and graceful, from the duties or delights of the day to the employments of her desk, that there is as little pedantry in writing a poem as in writing a letter, and the authoress appears only the lady in *flower*." Inspired by her "proper sphere and mission," her poetry is "an extension and refinement" of "female influence" (361), showing its grace by knowing its place.

The lady in is both poet and poem: Hemans's signature genre, and stricture, is the effortless effusion. Wordsworth and Coleridge could class and title some poems thus, but only in a regard of the genre as incidental, merely occasional.[33] Hemans sighed of a career of "mere desultory effusions" that had wasted her for the "noble and more complete work" that might crown fame as "a British poetess" (*HM* 300). And Gilfillan would prevent that murmur with the logic of gender. An "absence of original genius, or of profound penetration, or of wide experience" in "our lady authors" (he says generically) disqualifies them for the male sphere of letters: they are not "entitled to speak with equal authority on those higher and deeper questions, where not instinct nor heart, but severe and tried intellect is qualified" (359). Women of severe and tried intellect couldn't qualify either, but were cited for trespass, for penetrating the self-actualizing, vocation-proving male genres. Reading Barbauld's *Eighteen Hundred and Eleven* fresh off the press, Henry Crabb Robinson was certain it would "expose her to the charge of presumption in assuming the character of a philosophic poet or that of a prophetic 'Elegist'" (1: 64). Hemans was just as certain in 1824 of "a prejudice [. . .] against a female dramatist, which it would be hardly possible to surmount" (*CMH* 1: 102). She might have consulted More's introduction to *Essays for Young Ladies* for the long-standing advice that "the lofty epic, the pointed satire, and the more daring and successful flights of the tragic muse, seem reserved for the bold adventurers of the other sex" (6: 263).

But if so, what to do about the author of *Plays on the Passions* (Scott, Wordsworth, and Byron, among her fans)? The fraternity of *Noctes Ambrosianæ*, meeting in the March 1829 *Blackwood's Edinburgh Magazine* (*No. XLI*, v. 25), decided to make half a man of Joanna Baillie, even changing her name:

NORTH. James, who is the best female poet of the age?
SHEPHERD. Female what?
TICKLER. Poet.
SHEPHERD. Mrs John Biley. In her plays on the passions, she has a' the vigour o' a man, and a' the delicacy o' a woman. (380)

This fabrication of the woman as a man's mate is retrofitted into the Shepherd's frame of the feminine: "I'm fon o' a' gude female writers. They're al' bonnie—

and every passage they write carries, as it ought to do, their feminitye alang wi' it." The "best creetishism on her warks," finally, is whether "she would mak baith a useful and agreeable wife" (380).

Such rehabilitation is a common event in otherwise progressive ventures. In 1848 political liberal Frederic Rowton issued *The Female Poets of Great Britain,* a project intended to display the excellence of "Female Intellect" and celebrate "the poetical productions of the British Female mind." On the side of progress, he attributes any deficiencies, Wollstonecraft-wise, to "our system of educating females," and he bluntly disdains the diminutive "Poet*ess*" (his italics) for "Female Poet." But if this gesture seems of a piece with the *Monthly Review*'s insistence, after reading of *Rights of Woman,* on calling Wollstonecraft "the *author* of this treatise—whom we will not offend by styling authoress" (ns. 8 [1792]: 199), other reports in the Introductory Chapter of Rowton's anthology could not be more regressive:

> Man is bold, enterprising and strong: woman cautious, prudent and steadfast. Man is self-relying and self-possessed; woman timid, clinging and dependent. Man is suspicious and secret; woman confiding. Man is fearless; woman apprehensive. Man arrives at truth by long and tedious study; woman by intuition. He thinks; she feels. He reasons; she sympathises. He has courage; she patience. He soon despairs; she always hopes. The strong passions are his; heart is hers. [. . .] Female Intellect seem[s] to be rather negative than positive: [. . .] fitted more for passive endurance than for aggressive exertion. (xxiv–xxv)

Back to basics. That Rowton's anatomy of the sexes sounds merely descriptive disguises its prescriptive force, its fitting out and shaping critical understanding.

The durable paradox of such lessoning is the unsettling stimulus. "Women we have often eagerly placed *near* the throne of literature: if they seize it, forgetful of our fondness, we can hurl them from it," cautioned *Critical Review* when it addressed *Rights of Woman* (ns. 2 [1792] 132). The *ancien régime* lost the French throne, but English censors would sit tight, with the power in reserve of Milton's God. Yet the disciplinary zeal cannot help but expose the question. Polwhele's exercise releases this counter-effect, too. For all his calculation and typographical accent, his scandal-sheet manages to register the insurgent (Wollstonecraft) view of "NATURE's law" as a legislation (what fathers like to see). The footnote he appends to the phrase also has this undertow, first positing an axiom and then, in the rush of discipline, saying too much about the investment: "Nature is the grand basis of all laws human and divine: and the woman, who has no regard to nature, either in the decoration of her person, or the culture of her mind," is likely to "despise government" of all kind (6). This is another one of those contrarian sentences, one that with slight tonal adjustment, could appear in *Rights of Woman*.

Even More's sturdy apartheid registered pressure. When, for example, she lists those genres that "seem reserved for the bold adventurers of the other sex" (*W* 6: 263), *seem* hosts a possible debate, even along Wollstonecraft lines: if "the steeps of Parnassus few [women], comparatively, have attempted to scale with success," the failure is a not nature but education, "when it is considered, that many languages, and many sciences, must contribute to the perfection of poetical composition" (263). Although More is determined to conclude with a brief for the genre-gender law, she can't shake off the force latent in *seem*:

> On the whole, (even if fame be the object of pursuit,) is it not better to succeed as women, than to fail as men? to shine, by walking honourably in the road which nature, custom, and education seem to have marked out, rather than to counteract them all, by moving awkwardly in a path diametrically opposite? to be good originals, rather than bad imitators?—in a word, to be excellent women, rather than indifferent men? (266)

It wouldn't take much to press the rhetorical questions into an argument of questions begged: of the production of men and women by custom, education, and cultural marking out. So, too, Polwhele lets slip a contradiction, on no less a subject that Wollstonecraft. That late footnote in *The Unsex'd Females* honoring and elaborately quoting More on gender orthodoxy begins with a faltering syntax: "Miss Hannah More may justly be esteemed, as a character, in all points, diametrically opposite to Miss Wollstonecraft; excepting, indeed, her genius and literary attainments." That excepting *her* joins the two, and Polwhele makes good on the suggestion by conceding, in the next sentence, "the great natural endowments of Miss W." (35–36). On the political scene, Wollstonecraft symbolizes threats that command censure as unnatural, but in textual encounters, the positive impression warrants a credit to nature after all.

Polwhele's naturally endowed Wollstonecraft wasn't the only contradiction. Recollecting the text and texts of another "highly gifted" woman, DeQuincey, writing from the fraternity at *London Magazine,* confronted a matrix of personal genealogy, cultural anxiety, and theoretical equivocation:

> My mother I may mention with honour [. . . .] For though unpretending to the name and honours of a *literary* woman, I shall presume to call her (what many literary women are not) an *intellectual* woman: and I believe that if ever her letters should be collected and published, they would be thought generally to exhibit as much strong and masculine sense, delivered in as pure "mother English," racy and fresh with idiomatic graces, as any in our language—hardly

excepting those of M. W. Montague. (*Confessions of an English Opium-Eater* [1821], 311; Lindop, ed. 31)

This may seem to add up to the old story: female intellect honored as long as it doesn't pretend to honors. Yet the ground is not so settled. The literary character of this unliterary woman's letters—racy, fresh, *intellectual*—crosses into a "masculine character." And this is no transgression; it is generative of "our language." The "idiomatic graces" are hardly those Milton wrote for "our general mother" ("form'd" for "softness . . . and sweet attractive Grace"; *PL* 4.297–98; 492). How apt that editor Grevel Lindop couldn't trace the source site of this writing in "mother English."[34]

Around the time of the *Quarterly*'s run at Barbauld, de Staël's brainy self-possession was prodding Byron to wonder, in the privacy of his journal, if "she ought to have been a man" (*BLJ* 3: 227). And he was far more vexed by Baillie's capacities than the *Noctes* men were. *Blackwood's* decorously aired the question in 1824, and hit the nerve of male anxiety, when it speculated on the grief Baillie's plays must pose "to the pretensions of the stronger sex [. . .] the distinguished fraternity of bards" (16: 162). It was only with another fantasized regendering that Byron could admire her skill with a genre he was sure had to be a masculine endowment. Musing on Voltaire's remark that "the composition of a tragedy requires <u>testicles</u>," Byron sighed to Murray, "If this be true Lord knows what Joanna Baillie does—I suppose she borrows them" (5: 203). For Hazlitt the caution of Lady Macbeth is more than a borrowing—it is a transformation. In *Characters of Shakespear's Plays* (a virtual conduct manual for men of letters) he quotes her great "unsex me here" aria (20), fascinated by the horror of this "great bad woman, whom we hate, but whom we fear more than we hate" (and he was a good hater). Her terror is her gender-bending, that "masculine firmness" immune to "weak and womanly regrets" in "ascendancy over her husband's faultering virtue" (18–19). Hazlitt liked a manly devil, in manly form.[35]

The Shiftings of Gender

Anna Jameson thought the "preservation of the feminine character" in Shakespeare's wicked women rendered them more terrible than any of "those monstrous caricatures" (13), but this may have been an oblique recognition that the unsexed female was dressing for success in a man's world. In the 1820s, Jewsbury donned the opaque signature "M.J.J."—or disdained any signature. Such operations reflect her hunch about female fiction per se: "when a woman writes fiction" she "fancies herself veiled," and thus released to "enunciate[ ] important truths; the fear of man somewhat departs from her mind, and she becomes (by comparison) free, natural, and unconventional" (*Athenæum* 236: 282). The last string of adjectives liberates "natural" on behalf of the aspiring literary woman. In this same decade, other women writers, especially of unfeminine imaginations, veiled themselves in male names, matching the she-pseudonyms that some literary men (so Goldsmith suspected) used to expand the range of their writing and its commercial opportunities.[36] Making gender into literary performance at once ironizes the system and frees its play from conventional determinations.

An intuition of this potential beset even More in the midst of laboring (in her "Introduction" to *Essays for Young Ladies*) to shore up the "*peculiarly feminine*":

> each sex has its respective, appropriated qualifications, which would cease to be meritorious, the instant they ceased to be appropriated. Nature, propriety, and custom have prescribed certain bounds to each; bounds which the prudent and the candid will never attempt to break down; and indeed it would be highly impolitic to annihilate distinctions from which each acquires excellence, and to attempt innovations. (6: 261–62)

The wavering around *propriety* and the weirdly adjectival *appropriated* (both rooted in *proper*) ripple doubts about whether sexual qualifications are innate or assigned, inborn or (anticipating Wollstonecraft) a sign-system, its agency mystified with a passive participle. Across the chain of "Nature, propriety, and custom" falls a shadow of doubt, too: in its original sense, *propriety* designated *nature*, then evolved to mean *custom*, a term that puts "prescribed certain bounds" into a social text. What, moreover, does More signify with *bounds*: certainties? tendencies? boundaries? obligations? impositions? And if distinctions—admittedly susceptible of innovation, breakdown, or annihilation—are to be maintained, More does this with an appeal not to nature but to the implied antonym of *impolitic*: politic(s). It is telling that when More revisited these sentences "soon after the publication of a work intitled 'The Rights of Woman,'" she tightened them up, taking care to articulate a political errancy and a correction by appeal to divine assignment:

> among the innovations of this innovating period, the imposing term of *rights* has been produced to sanctify the claim of our female pretenders, with a view not only to rekindle in the minds of women a presumptuous vanity, dishonourable to their sex, but produced with a view to excite in their hearts an impious discontent with the post which God has assigned them in this world.
> But *they* little understand the true interest of woman who would lift her

from the important duties of her allotted station, to fill, with fantastic dignity, a loftier but less appropriate niche. [. . .] Each sex has its proper excellences, which would be lost were they melted down into the common character by the fusion of the new philosophy. (*Strictures* 230–31)

Placing text against text—God's assignment against the new philosophy—More now confidently explicates transgression, error, and proper understanding.

Yet when education is not the didactic project but the subject itself, More may wax newly philosophical. In one of those 1771 *Essays*, "Thoughts on the Cultivation of the Heart and Temper in the Education of Daughters," even as she is busily defining a "natural cast of character, and the moral distinction of the sexes," the thought of cultivation imports a trouble to the mind: is it culture working with nature, or enforcement against nature?

> That bold, independent, enterprising spirit, which is so much admired in boys, should not, when it happens to discover itself in the other sex, be encouraged, but suppressed. Girls should be taught to give up their opinions betimes, and not pertinaciously to carry on a dispute, even if they should know themselves in the right. [. . .] It is of the greatest importance to their future happiness, that they should acquire submissive temper, and a forbearing spirit: for it is a lesson which the world will not fail to make them frequently practise, when they come abroad into it. (*Essays* 326)

In these sentences More doesn't just put "natural cast" into question (a girl's spirit may be bold, independent, enterprising); she names the cultural editing in a patter of *should*s: what must be suppressed and acquired, taught and practiced. The performative training for life in the world even has an uncanny reflux on the master trope of "natural cast" as a retrojected first scripting.

As a childless, single, socially active, commercially potent, busily publishing professional woman, More's own life in the world must have forced the question. The "education of women is so defective," she proposes in her *Strictures*, "the alleged inferiority of their minds may be accounted for on that ground more justly than by ascribing it to their natural make" (236). Notwithstanding her horror of Wollstonecraft's politics, she was in accord on education:

> till the female sex are more carefully instructed, this question will always remain as undecided as to the *degree* of difference between the masculine and feminine understanding, as the question between the understandings of blacks and whites; for until men and women, as well as Africans and Europeans, are put more nearly on a par in the cultivation of their minds, the shades of distinction, whatever they be, between their native abilities can never be fairly

> ascertained. [. . .] in Christ Jesus, as there is neither "rich nor poor," "bond nor free," so there is neither "male nor female." (*Strictures* 36–37)[37]

It is striking see More using Galatians (3: 28) to trace sexual difference into a virtual political consciousness (she was an abolitionist), even more striking to see the justifications formerly sought in nature and divine assignment now reorganized: native and natural cannot be known without reference to culture; and the highest existence is taken on faith to be ungendered, exactly that undifferentiated common character that she had just despised as "innovation." As Wollstonecraft theorized, the sexed body is subject to social discipline and political legislation. But if the body can be disguised, or non-corporeal powers, such as soul or mind, become the shape of representation, terms of gender become mobile or even negligible descriptives.

If the practiced polemics of More can erode the boundaries, literary imagination was positively volatile. Feminine idols such as "Mrs. Hemans" struggled with contradictions, female writers such as Jewsbury were passing as men or satirizing male culture, and male writers (especially poets) were becoming ever more familiar with "feminine" feeling and fashion.[38] With a century's retrospect, Virginia Woolf saw even Byron's "manly virtues" fractured: she loved the satires and the letters, but sighed in bewilderment at the raft of poetry that Moore's memoir "quotes with almost speechless admiration": "Why did they think this Album stuff the finest fire of poetry? It reads hardly better than L.E.L." (*Diary*, Aug. 1918; 2–3)—reads, that is, as she-poetry, which Byron penned with a passion in his first ventures. Romanticism is nothing if not a various, ever shifting force field of gender attractions and performances: swooning heroes and capable heroines; men of feeling and women of intellect; women called masculine or manly, men deemed feminine or effeminate; cross-dressers of both sexes. No wonder that when the war with Napoleon was over and England relaxed its military manufacture of the male character, cultural arbiters started to worry about what the poets were effecting.

The reviews of the day monitored sensuous Keats and fantastic Shelley for the contagion of unmanliness. Byron's sly remark that his sometime she-garbed hero Don Juan, once "in England," assumed "a manlier vigour" (11.15) tweaked at a national concern. Byron in his swagger, whether existential grand opera or oppositional satire, made him everybody's favorite man. In 1824, Sir Egerton Brydges beat the drum for his manly genius, in implied antithesis to anything feminine. He "never uses false attractions; he never, in the attempt to please [. . .] resorts to sickly, artificial, or fantastic inventions; he is always manly, direct, and unaffected" (105); his poems "are too manly and vigorous to be ever fantastic; they are never once degraded by any of the petty artifices of poetry" (268); his "most tender and most exquisite feelings" show "something so manly,"

> of so vigorous and healthy a hue, so consistent with a noble daring, so prepared for perils, so strung for action, so adventurous, rather than subject to that shrinking imbecility of action which is the disease that too commonly besets genius, that he seems our protector rather than a sensitive being (as poets generally are) demanding our protection! (285–86)

The next year found Coleridge, who had worried of being "much effeminated" by a love of "sweet Music" (*L* 2: 247), lobbying in *Aids to Reflection, in the Formation of Manly Character* for "the term, Virtue" to be restored "to its original import" in the etymology of *vir*: "viz. Manhood or Manliness to express the quality of Fortitude; Strength of Character in relation to the resistance opposed by Nature and the irrational Passions to the Dictates of Reason; Energy of will in preserving the Line of Rectitude tense and firm against the warping and treacheries of Temptation" (126). Like Bridges's Byron, Coleridge's "Manly Character" makes a stand against feminine-coded antithesis: irrationality, Nature, Passions, Temptation.

What was the fate of literature in the formation and profession of manly character? By the 1840s Stodart felt able to tag the entire business of literary writing as female. Any man ambitious of money and influence, she proposed in *Female Writers*, would disdain life as "a bookseller's drudge," work with no real "social consideration from the exercise of his talent." These days, "men of powerful minds, who might have embraced literature as a profession and risen to the highest ranks in it, enter into some other career; they are to be found in the senate, amid the turmoil of political life; at the bar; and, in fact, in all the learned professions." In the vacated field of literature, only "women, with dwarfish men, step forward" (11–12). Across the 1820s, the decade of the professional "poetess" ("Mrs. Hemans" and "L.E.L."), the male "poet" was already begging for differential credit.

So it was with an audit of the laws of gender that premier critic Jeffrey (cited by Byron on blue-stockings) decided to open his essay on Hemans for the *Edinburgh Review* October 1829 with a lecture on "Female Poetry" and its "essentially and intensely feminine" character (50: 33–34). Yet in his actual measure of the poetic stars of the day, gender essentials start to evaporate into an "essence of poetry" that is no inevitability of sex. It is, in general, the

> fine perception and vivid expression of that subtle and mysterious analogy which exists between the physical and the moral world—which makes outward things and qualities the natural types and emblems of inward gifts and

emotions, and leads us to ascribe life and sentiment to every thing that interests us in the aspects of external nature. (50: 35)

"Eminently a mistress of this poetical secret," Hemans joins male "poets of the highest order" such as Milton and Shakespeare, "the predominant emotion of their minds overflowing spontaneously on all the objects which present themselves to their fancy" (36–37). In this gender-liberal mode, Jeffrey traces (without saying so) the Wordsworthian signature of male poetic power.[39] He does regard Hemans as essentially "feminine": her "taste and elegance," her "tenderness and loftiness of feeling," her "ethereal purity of sentiment [. . .] could only emanate from the soul of a woman" (he says in his last paragraph). But the settlement is unstable: he has just observed that the two most popular male poets of the day, Campbell and Rogers, are loved more "for the fine taste and consummate elegance of their writings" than for "fiery passion, and disdainful vehemence." More she than he. In the poetic culture of the 1820s, the distinctions Jeffrey drew at the top of his essay as a law of nature fail to pattern his survey of the "nature of modern literary fame" (47).

In 1831 Mrs. Sandford listed as first among the "branches of knowledge which are strictly feminine" the "*belles lettres* of every age and country," meaning to recommend nurture "to embellish and refine" the female mind with no loss of propriety (*Woman* 30). Yet the French feminine gender of *les belles lettres* and its designation for "female acquirement" had a way of opening Jeffrey's can of worms: were male poets belles? *Cambridge University Magazine* admired Shelley's "womanly tenderness of heart" (87), and *London Weekly Review* saw a "woman of feeling" behind the "man in intellectual vigour" (107–8). To Gilfillan, the sexual difference of Shelley and Hemans was trumped by a common refinement: "exquisite nervous organization [. . .] so strikingly alike" (*Tait's* n.s. 14: 362). G. H. Lewes ably twinned Shelley to his heroine Beatrice Cenci: the poet exemplified "Gentleness" and "an enduring patience" along with "the obduracy and strength of a martyr; an angel-martyr" (*Westminster* 307); the heroine was "angelic," a "fine and gentle nature, too good for this world," a figure of "patience" with "a firm shield of gentleness" (338).

For other Victorians, such Romantic-engendered similes and similarities spelled trouble. Versed in Romanticism, Tennyson's quatrain *On One Who Affected an Effeminate Manner* lectures about keeping signifiers uncorrupted. "Nature" has a "male and female plan" that can't be confused with manners: "man-woman is not woman-man."[40] If no breach of borders is dreamt of in this philosophy, actual social practice was provoking the disciplinary sermonette. "It may be difficult to trace the precise line of demarcation where the masculine character ends and where the female begins," Revd. Hubbard Winslow conceded in 1838; but he knew transgression when he saw it and, like Meiners and Estimate Brown, called out the dire alarm:

> The man who partakes of the character appropriate to female [. . .] is *effeminate*; [. . .] the woman who partakes of the character appropriate to males [. . .] is *masculine*. These terms, we all know, are intended to designate something out of place, something undesirable and unlovely. We tolerate here and there an anomaly of this kind; but we wish to see such cases "few and far between." We should wisely consider the end of all things not far distant should they become universal. (*Woman As She Should Be* 12)

The asymmetry of *masculine* and *effeminate,* substituting for *masculine / feminine,* is a little fable in itself. *Effeminate* is no real semantic binary, but an adjectival back-formation from a verb about influence: *effeminare,* "to make into a woman," or tropically, "to make feminine."

Writing for *Fraser's* ten years after Winslow, Charles Kingsley found no clearer symptom of "effeminate" culture than the swooning for Shelley: "The private tipping of eau-de-cologne, say the London physicians, has increased mightily of late; and so has the reading of Shelley" (48: 570). Culpable for "all the unrest and unhealth of sensitive young men" of the day, Shelley indexes the pathology of an age as eager to pardon "the lewdness of the gentle and sensitive vegetarian" as to excoriate that "sturdy peer," Byron, "proud of his bullneck and his boxing, who kept bears and bull-dogs, drilled Greek ruffians at Missolonghi, and 'had no objection to a pot of beer.'" Byron "was a man"; "Shelley's nature is utterly womanish" (571–73). Kingsley's Shelley exposes a lurid anatomy of gender travesty:

> Not merely his weak points, but his strong ones, are those of woman. Tender and pitiful as a woman—and yet, when angry, shrieking and railing, hysterical as a woman. The physical distaste for meat and fermented liquors, coupled with a hankering after physical horrors, are especially feminine. The nature of a woman looks out of that wild, beautiful, girlish face—the nature. [. . .] Beatrice Cenci is really none other than Percy Bysshe Shelley himself in petticoats. (48: 572, 575)

To this pumper of muscular Christianity, it is hysteric Shelley and his doting readers who must answer for the present "spasmodic, vague, extravagant, effeminate, school of poetry" (574).[41]

In 1869, in a rematch of Shelley and Byron refereed by Alfred Austin (Poet Laureate after Tennyson), Byron prevails like old King Hamlet: "We may well say, 'he was a man'" (95), not the least for the "masculine" power of expression (113). What Austin delineated as Shelley's "feminine fault" of inarticulation

(113) was soon to morph into Arnold's impotent Shelley: that "beautiful and ineffectual angel, beating in the void his luminous wings in vain."[42] To Austin the feminine infection was epidemic: Tennyson, Trollope, and Swinburne; only Browning was manly.[43] *The Examiner* positively cheered the masculine "genius" of a "strange" new novel published in 1848. Though it found some "coarse and loathsome" excess, this was still a relief amid "the affectation and effeminate frippery which is but too frequent in the modern novel," and it was willing to hail "an author who goes at once fearlessly into the moors and desolate places, for his heroes" (22). "No *woman* could write *Wuthering Heights*," was the certainty of *Union Magazine* (287). If these readings of gender effects were as off as they had been for *Frankenstein* thirty years before, what mattered more was the scandal of female pens able to put out work more masculine than what was coming from men's pens.[44]

Austin himself was not happy about this female prowess. Disgusted by novel heroines "more animal and impassioned than the heroes" (102–3), he tracked the scandal back to a "fatally" taken "first wrong step—that of making women too conspicuous in life and literature":

> It is the feminine element at work when it has ceased to be domestic; when it has quitted the modest precincts of home, and courted the garish light of an intense and warm publicity. It is the feminine element, no longer in the nursery, the drawing-room, or the conjugal chamber, but unrestrainedly rioting in any and every arena of life in which an indiscriminating imagination chooses to place it. (104–5)

Breaking out of home, female elements spread havoc abroad. E. S. Dallas was already grumping in 1866 at the new women wrought by the "feminine influence" on literature. The ill was no mere "excess of refinement," but a riot of the "most unfeminine"; man's first Fall, he reminds us, issued from a woman's "masculine lust of power" twinned to a man's "feminine weakness of affection" (2: 296–98). Conjuring the specters of Burke's *Reflections* and Mathias's "*unsexed* female writers" (this was Polwhele's inspiration) who "instruct, or confuse, us and themselves in the labyrinth of politics, or turn us wild with Gallic frenzy" (Mathias 244), Austin indicts Romantic rioting as the crux of a social failure to control its "feminine element" (88). Fired by his own motives, he tells a story of the Romantic era that casts the threat of feminine rebellion into a social anarchy against which political constraints need to be ranged and exerted.

Polwhele's unsex'd women, Byron's re-sexed Baillie and Staël, Dallas's fable of gender-trouble in Paradise, Hazlitt's cross-sexed Macbeths, and the sex-travesty Blues—all relay gender transgression from literary sites to social-texts. However much the structures of official culture arrest imagination, these new arrays and arrangements vibrate into what Stephen Greenblatt calls a network of "negotiations," in which literature may "shape, articulate, and reproduce" culture through its own "improvisatory intelligence" ("Culture" 229). And "culture" is no monolith. If U. C. Knoepflmacher sees the Victorian era tuned to gender codes from which it produced "rich but one-sided myths" (94),[45] Romantic poetics were not unilateral. Byron casts a monstrous Empress Catherine in *Don Juan*, but rather admired the "masculine understanding" and "heroic boldness" of the historical personage (so Isaac Nathan reports): "'Catherine,' said he, 'possessed more real intrepidity than any woman of modern times: her struggles both in a mental and political nature were such as to astonish all Europe'" (*HVSV* 147). Even Coleridge could entertain new assignments of gender. He described Lessing's "female Friend, König" (later, wife) as "a woman of manly sense," and admired Agnes Ibbetson, a contributor to *Philosophical Magazine*, for a "rare Union of feminine fineness of Intuition with masculine energy," of "masculine intellect with all the woman's sense of Beauty." He regarded himself as having a "feminine" spirit or mind.[46] Back in 1808 he rued the very language of masculine representatives: "Quære—Whether we may not, nay, ought not, to use a neutral pronoun relative, or representative, to the word 'Person' [. . .] to express either Sex indifferently?"; "We sadly want—and that too alike in all the Languages, with which I am acquainted, a common gender in the pronoun adjective, his, her, and it—to agree with the word person, [. . .] and all words implying man or woman indifferently" (*CN* 3238, 3399).[47]

This tension between culturally ruled difference and indifferent implying is most legible in Romantic-era writing on the borderlines of gender, where figures appear in double exposures and the critical effects arise less from aberrations of definition than from strains in the definitional project itself. Look at the wry digression indulged in the midst of an unsigned essay about Hemans's installation as the premier "feminine" poetess of the day (*Athenæum*, 12 February 1831), her qualities to be summed "in one emphatic word, her *womanliness*" (104–5):

> Imagination says, that a poetess ought to be ladylike, claiming acquaintance with the Graces no less than with the Muses; and if it were not so, Imagination would conceive he had a right to be sulky. We appeal to any one who is imaginative. If, after sighing away your soul over some poetic effusion of female genius, a personal introduction took place, and you found the fair author a dashing dragoon-kind of woman—one who could with ease rid her house of a couple of robbers—would you not be startled? [. . .] Your understanding might in time be converted; you might bow at the very feet, and

solicit the very hand, the proportions of which at first inspired terror, but your Imagination, a recreant to the last, would die maintaining that a poetess ought to be feminine. (105)

Imagination here is but another name for Prescription in its most exalted mood, the shocked beholder of Jewsbury's contrarian cartoon.[48] But it's worth noting, too, Jewsbury's hesitation about the reverse, of female imagination not really capable of conceiving a dashing dragoon-kind of man. A couple of months later, she would use the trope of travesty to define the limits: women can't "pass the barrier of sex" to write like men and of male adventurers: "her smugglers, her murderers, her highwaymen, her seducers, her choice ruffians are, after all, *petticoated*," trailing the "drawing-room" fashioning that "she *cannot* shake off."[49]

Borderlines

What ought a poetess, or a poet to be? *Borderlines* arrays a chiasmus, two men, two women, each set to test "feminine" and "masculine." Each writer rewards concentration, each penetrates larger cultural questions, and together they develop a story of complex identifications and anxieties, struggles and accommodations. *Women* begins with Hemans, problematically revered and then, just as problematically, reviled as a "feminine" writer. Her complement is Jewsbury, admired as a "masculine" writer—a descriptive shorn of stigma but not free from the conflicts. *Men* reads Byron and Keats, customary bearers (respectively) of "masculine" and "feminine" male Romanticism. Hemans and Jewsbury are scarcely canonical today, and part of my project is to investigate what alterations occur and accrue when they play in the field of inquiry. While Byron and Keats are canonical familiars, my treatments are defamiliarizing, showing a canonicity configured by contradictions, whether in Byronic "masculinity" or in Keats's signature effeminate/feminine/feminist modes. Byron, the age's devilishly "masculine" poet-celebrity, produces in *Sardanapalus* a half-dandy/half-passioned meditation on masculinist culture and "effeminate" opposition. His most extravagant gender-play is *Don Juan*, where expectations of iconic masculinity fall immediately into parody and persistently into transvestite reversal. My chapters on Keats treat (first) his ambivalent fashioning of himself as a "manly" poet, then the gender of "Keats" as read or spun by others, from first reviews to recent views, from his day to yesterday. The career of "Keats" as a language of collective concerns sets the stage for my closing (if not concluding) stage of negotiation: "Sex in Souls?" With high stakes, this question persists today as "essence or construction?": is the soul as well as the body gendered? and is sex a predictor of gender?

My key figures—Hemans and Jewsbury, Byron and Keats—occupy the decades after Waterloo and before Victoria, but the contexts extend back to eighteenth-century formations and information, and forward to later eras of reception. In all sites, I approach literary aesthetics as historicized gender criticism, foregrounding a system of language, not only in doctrine but also in image, representation, and—in its widest play—a linguistically organized culture available for critical scrutiny, imaginative manipulation, political revision. The most potent sites are the wavering, arbitrary, and often traversable borderlines that vex and complicate the symbolic order. Here emerge the "masculine" woman and the male poet deemed "feminine" (or "effeminate"), cross-dressers of both sexes, transgressors of proprieties, or embodiments of sensibilities and social display, such as Keatsian "indolence" or Byronic theatricality, that resist coherent gendering.

My work on the borders has called for flexible approaches and sympathies. I'm sometimes asked if I deem Hemans "as good a poet as Byron or Keats"—challenged to prove that she is, or if not, then to say why anyone should care about her. Such a question, I think, is culturally over-determined. Aesthetic pleasures are various and variable, and can be historicized as well as experienced. While we prefer good to bad, we might recall that in the Romantic decades, Wordsworth's poetry was thought not good at all by judges such as Jeffrey; the poetry of Keats and Coleridge struck many as ridiculous; Shelley and Byron even planned on offending readers—not just with ideas but with aesthetic practice. There is profit in diversity. When Virgil Nemoianu asks, "Will the appreciation of Felicia Hemans be enhanced by the neglect of or contempt for Keats?" to sigh, "One can only shrug at such naiveties" (243), I want to put the case in a form less easy to shrug. A zero-sum economy reports only the limits of an academic term; it is irrelevant to liberal reading. And the idea of a canon is vital to the degree that it is mobile and variable. Whether Jeffrey's melancholy handicapping in 1829 (Rogers and Campbell for sure; maybe Hemans), or the long reign of the "Big Six" (three would have delighted Jeffrey, the others perplexed or even dismayed him),[50] or the new constituencies of the 1990s,[51] or the nationalisms gaining attention at the start of the twenty-first century, canon is no timeless monument.[52] Even on the durables, new perspectives continue to reshape understandings. "How can our appreciation of Keats be enhanced by not neglecting Hemans?" I want to ask, and add, "how can our appreciation of Hemans be enhanced by reading Keats (and others) along the borders of gender?"

Two Women

Our elder literary women were, in the spirit of their intellect, more essentially masculine; our younger ones are integrally feminine. [. . .] We have not, and are not likely to have at present, another Mary Wolstencroft.

— [MARIA JANE JEWSBURY], 'ATHENAEUM,'
28 MAY 1831

CHAPTER TWO

Felicia Hemans and the Stages of "The Feminine"

> As a woman, she was to a considerable degree a spoilt child of the world. She had been early in life distinguished for talent, and poems of hers were published while she was a girl. She had also been handsome in her youth, but her education had been most unfortunate. She was totally ignorant of housewifery, and could as easily have managed the spear of Minerva as her needle.
>
> —WILLIAM WORDSWORTH ON FELICIA HEMANS[1]

Discriminating the "Feminine"

Although Felicia Hemans worked for this end, it didn't help that "Mrs. Hemans" won fame as "The Poet of Womanhood," the title awarded in 1886 by *Queens of Literature of the Victorian Era* (263). Her friend Henry Chorley, a champion of women writers against male prejudice, spelled out the cultural logic when he ended his *Memorials* noting that "the woman and the poetess" were "too inseparably united to admit of their being considered apart."[2] Yet (as Chorley knew) Hemans's signature genre was scored by conflicts between ideals and lived social experience. Gazing at her widely exhibited (then posthumously canonized) portrait (fig. 2.1) she herself sighed, "oh! almost strange, / Mine imaged self!" (*To My Own Portrait* 25–26). What was strange?

> To see *thee* calm, while powers thus deep—
> Affection—Memory—Grief—
> Pass o'er my soul . . . (31–33)

No boast of creative reserves, these deep powers play as antagonists to serene

39

Figure 2.1 *Felicia Hemans*, engraved by Edward Scriven (1839) from the portrait by William E. West (1827). Alaric Watts, editor of the *Literary Souvenir*, commissioned West (famed for having "painted the last likeness ever taken of Lord Byron" and Teresa Guiccioli in 1822) for a portrait of Hemans for his gallery of "the living authors of Great Britain." In autumn 1827 at Hemans's home, Rhyllon, West rendered three images of this wistful, womanly cultural icon. He gave the last to her sister, Harriett, and it was engraved by Edward Scriven for the frontispiece of her *Memoir* of the poet in the first volume of William Blackwood's edition of Hemans (1839). Another one was exhibited in May 1828 in London at the Royal Academy, Somerset House, where Joanna Baillie went see it, writing in advance to Hemans (whom she had never met) that she expected none to be "more sought for and observed" (5 May 1828; *Letters* 1162).

self-possession. Such alienation (the self estranged from its image and popular reception) is not special to Hemans; but what sharpens her regard is that the qualities she indexes in the portrait—"calm," "peace," "quiet," and a "look" "serenely" still (29–38)—spell her culture's romance of "Woman." Were she Lord Byron, she might have flaunted the anomaly of self and portrait, made existential capital out of it. But it was the cultural capital that mattered: however estranging, her portrait epitomized "Woman" and served Hemans' home-economics, promoting her fame and her sales. And so the poet compelled to state her estrangement was also compelled not to publish it.[3]

Wordsworth's lightly irritated headnote (my chapter epigraph) pinned the gender anomaly: her pen replacing "her needle"—society's assignment, even if Hemans didn't own one.[4] "I think it as scandalous for a Woman not to know how to use a needle, as for a Man not to know how to use a sword," woman of letters Lady Mary Wortley Montagu said (*L* 3: 23). Hemans's disdain of the needle pricks the borderline between the poet of ideal femininity, "Mrs. Hemans," and the woman of sometimes contrary imaginings who invented her, promoted her, and tried to reconcile, or at least manage, her difference from her.

Such divisions issue not just from the alienated information of the ideal, but also from the shadow of devaluation. It is "not because we consider her the best, but because we consider her by far the most feminine writer of the age," said George Gilfillan, that he has made "Mrs. Hemans" the "first specimen" in his 1847 series in *Tait's Edinburgh Magazine* on *Female Authors* (14: 360). For "feminine writer," the ready synonym was "poetess," a keyword in the aesthetic apartheid that emerged in the 1820s as she-poets were proving popular and commercially potent. In 1802, the year Felicia Browne wrote her first poem, Wordsworth advanced the idea of "Poet" as "a man speaking to men." Looking back from the 1820s, Hazlitt called this a "levelling" muse,[5] and he satirized some of the consequences; but it is telling that he let the gender definition stand. Lecturing in 1818 "On the Living Poets," he kept to the hierarchy, condescending to "female poets" (Hannah) More, Baillie, and Barbauld: the first, "never read"; the second, a tedious didact who treats adult characters "as little girls treat their dolls—makes moral puppets of them"; the third, "a very pretty poetess" (identified by rhymes for children, not the polemics on the slave trade, commerce and imperialism). Rogers enters the list as virtual poetess, "a very lady-like poet": "elegant but feeble."[6] So when in the 1820s "Poetess" Hemans was winnowed from her more various Regency poetry and its gender-various reception,[7] to be installed as a woman speaking to women of "feminine" values, it was to double business bound. Distinct from the man of letters, a poetess radiated sentiments, effortless grace, domestic culture, and the lesser genres.[8] "The art of verse to her was like her harp and her sketch-book," wrote Arthur

Symons in 1909. He might as well have added "her needle." It was "not an accomplishment, indeed," not man's work, but hyper-differentiated: "It is difficult to say of Mrs. Hemans that her poems are not womanly, and yet it would be more natural to say that they are feminine" (*Romantic Movement* 295).

Symons's sifting of *feminine* from *womanly* is no casual mumbling, but tuned to an issue related to the genre apartheid of the 1820s: the use of "Mrs. Hemans" in reaction to the rights of "Woman." This was a key appeal across otherwise opposed precincts of male British letters. "She must have been no ordinary woman who won the admiration and friendship of men so dissimilar as Scott and Wilson, Heber and Whately, Wordsworth and Jeffrey," reflected Francis Espinasse in 1877 (295). What joined men so dissimilar was not just the admirable Mrs. Hemans, but the odious binary nailed by Anglican clergyman William Archer Butler at the close of an article he published in 1834 in *Dublin University Magazine*:

> Felicia Hemans has, indeed, approved herself a worthy interpreter of the inestimable feelings of the female breast, and woman in the pages (whether we regard the *subjects* of some, or the exquisitely feminine *spirit* which pervades all) is more truly vindicated than if her "rights" were proclaimed by a thousand Mary Wollstonecrafts. (183)

On this implied counterpoint *Queens of Literature* opened its long chapter on Hemans: "it is to be hoped that the girls of our own time will enrich their minds and elevate their characters by becoming the students of this graceful and essentially feminine poet" (261). The memoir in Warne's 1874 edition of Hemans urged its "lady readers" to study the "estimate of womanly powers" with which Francis Jeffrey had opened his 1829 essay on Hemans, because it serves, via Hemans, "to answer many of the vexed questions of the present day."[9] Its 1900 edition amplified the theme, ruing the fading popularity of Hemans's "essentially feminine" genius and ascribing this to a "lamentable change in the tone of modern society"—particularly its gender politics. "The age [the 1890s] that gave birth to the cry of 'Women's Rights,' and to the unfeminine imitators of masculine habits, was not likely to appreciate the voice of the *true* woman that spoke in Felicia Hemans" (xv-xvi), it sighed, longing for *true*, not *Blue*.

On this score, things hadn't changed much since Hemans's day, when the *Quarterly* could countenance her obvious "reflection and study" because "talent and learning have not produced the ill effects so often attributed to them; her faculties seem to sit meekly on her" (24: 130–31). "Strictly *feminine* in the whole current of her thought and feeling," Hemans pleased *Edinburgh Monthly* for not ruffling the "modesty" and "delicacy which belongs to the sex," for "scrupulously abstaining from all that may betray unfeminine temerity"—especially the "club of political warfare, and the sharp lash of personal satire" (3: 374–75). Hemans's ordering of the "feminine" reflected more than natural inclination; it testified to ethical consideration and restraint. It was impossible, said Gilfillan, to "open a page of her writings without feeling this is written by a lady. Her inspiration always pauses at the feminine point" (*Tait's* 14: 360). The scruple of "pauses" nicely blends the reflex of instinct and the flexing of instruction.

Feminine icon "Mrs. Hemans" emerged in its most positive formation in the first decades after Waterloo, as Britain was consolidating its international prestige and celebrating female service to this end. Hemans's "delicacy of feeling," crooned the *Quarterly* in 1820, is "the fair and valued boast of our countrywomen," all that is best in "an English lady" (24: 131). *Edinburgh Monthly* closed its 1820 review praising her for restoring "moral dignity" to poetry and "moral purity and elevation" to the national imagination (3: 383). Attentive to reception protocols, Hemans's sister took care to cite this praise early in her *Memoir* (33), and Chorley paid tribute to Hemans for anglo-feminizing the entire domain of poetry: "romance and chivalry" are rehabilitated, "clothed in a female form"; in her "female hands," the "homely domestic ballad" is purged of "the grossness, which, of old, stained its strength" (*CMH* 1: 137–38). He was echoing Jeffrey's statement of the British value in 1829: drawing her themes "from the legends of different nations and the most opposite states of society," Hemans adeptly preserved the local color while eschewing

> the revolting or extravagant excesses which may characterise the taste or manners of the people or the age from which it has been derived. She has thus transfused into her German or Scandinavian legends the imaginative and daring tone of the originals, without the mystical exaggerations of the one, or the painful fierceness and coarseness of the other—she has preserved the clearness and elegance of the French, without their coldness or affectation—and the tenderness and simplicity of the early Italians, without their diffuseness or languor. (*Edinburgh Review* 50: 35)

Blackwood's bruited Hemans's international triumph: the "pre-eminence" of her feminine poetry "has been acknowledged, not only in her own land, but wherever the English tongue is spoken, whether on the banks of the eastern Ganges, or the western Mississippi" (38: 96); Blackwood's 1839 edition of Hemans reprinted this praise (7: 290). Hemans stars as the virtual eponym of Frederic Rowton's *Female Poets of Great Britain* (1848). Her "*intensely* feminine" character is able "to represent and unite" the "peculiar and specific qualities of the female mind" as Great Britain was proud to display them (386).

Yet, for all the honors, what haunts about this peculiar specificity is a reflexive negative that in effect, if not in theory, subverts the praise. Even Chorley's praises have this aura, with a refraction through Anna Jameson, who "has rightly said that Mrs. Hemans' poems 'could not have been written by a man'":

> Their love is without selfishness—their passion pure from sensual coarseness—their high heroism [. . .] unsullied by any base alloy of ambition. In their religion, too, she is essentially womanly—fervent, trustful, unquestioning, 'hoping on, hoping ever'—in spite of a painfully acute consciousness of the peculiar trials of her sex.[10]

The "essentially womanly" is a perfection of absences, a purity bleached of intellectual vigor and psychological interest. Implying a "masculine" binary, Jewsbury's Hemans-coded "Egeria" makes the negative impression: "Other women might be more commanding, more versatile, more acute; but I never saw one so exquisitely feminine."[11] Chorley blithely quotes this as a measure for Hemans (*CMH* 1: 187), and it patterns *Blackwood's* obituary: the second paragraph begins by proposing Hemans as "perhaps [the] brightest ornament" of "our female literature," then dims the luster:

> To Joanna Baillie she might be inferior not only in vigour of conception but in the power of metaphysically analyzing those sentiments and feelings, which constitute the basis of human actions; to Mrs Jameson in the critical perception which, from detached fragments of spoken thought, can discriminate the links which bind all into a distinctive character;—to Miss Landon in eloquent facility;—to Caroline Bowles in simple pathos;—and to Mary Mitford in power of thought;—but as a female writer, influencing the female mind, she has undoubtedly stood, for some by-past years, the very first in the rank. (38: 96)

By the time the sentence gets to its main point ("but . . . "), it has all but translated Hemans's first-rank into inconsequence. So if, says the eulogist, "her poetry is intensely and entirely feminine—and in our estimation, this is the highest praise which could be awarded it:—it could have been written by a woman only" (96–97)—gender serves up a distinctly faint praise.

This detractive effect was possible because it was virtually unrecognized. (Blackwood had no problem giving the obituary essay the honor of first place in an appendix of critical praises.)[12] Even so, there is a legible impression of a critical unconscious, the praises often verging on transvaluation. When Jeffrey judged "the poetry of Mrs Hemans a fine exemplification of Female Poetry" (*Edinburgh* 50: 34), he meant a tribute; but from his very first sentence, "fine" sifts visibly negative refinements. "Women, we fear cannot do every thing; not even every thing they attempt," he opens, in that hallmark verdict that so pleased Warne's memoirist (32). The rest of the paragraph unrolls an array of negative incapabilities. "Women" are categorically, "naturally," deficient in certain powers. They cannot represent

> the fierce and sullen passions of men—nor their coarser vices—nor even scenes of actual business or contention—and the mixed motives, and strong and faulty characters, by which affairs of moment are usually conducted on the great theatre of the world. For much of this they are disqualified by the delicacy of their training and habits, and the still more disabling delicacy which pervades their conceptions and feelings; and from much they are excluded by their actual inexperience of the realities they might wish to describe—by their substantial and incurable ignorance of business—of the way in which serious affairs are actually managed—and the true nature of the agents and impulses that give movement and direction to the stronger currents of ordinary life. Perhaps they are also incapable of long moral or political investigations, where many complex and indeterminate elements are to be taken into account, and a variety of opposite probabilities to be weighed before coming to a conclusion. [. . .] Their proper and natural business is the practical regulation of private life, in all its bearings, affections, and concerns; and the questions with which they have to deal in that most important department, though often of the utmost difficulty and nicety, involve, for the most part, but few elements; and may generally be better described as delicate than intricate;—requiring for their solution rather a quick tact and fine perception than a patient or laborious examination. For the same reason, they rarely succeed in long works, even on subjects the best suited to their genius; their natural training rendering them equally averse to long doubt and long labour. (50: 32)

We don't need Wollstonecraft to audit the cultural stricture of "proper and natural" or the praise of "delicacy" as a deficit. Jeffrey himself says "disabling," and goes on to imply a tepid public taste in the appetite for Hemans: hers is a poetry to "allay the apprehensions of those who are most afraid of the passionate exaggerations of poetry" (34). She's no Byron; not even Shelley.

"Female Poetry" is a genre that Jeffrey means to differentiate from poetry per se, in order to cast a sorry eye on the immediate culture in which the male poets he admires—Southey, Keats, Shelley, Crabbe, Scott, Moore, Milman, Croly, Atherstone, Hood, "and a legion of others," not the least, "the blazing star of Byron" (50: 47)—are failing. In advance of Rowton, he claims cover as a friend to "female genius" and the female desire "to write for publication" (33–34), but this is all done with a sexual zoning of "the open field of literature":

> No *man*, we will venture to say, could have written the Letters of Madame de Sevigné, or the Novels of Miss Austin, or the Hymns and Early Lessons of

Mrs. Barbauld, or the Conversations of Mrs. Marcet. These performances, too, are not only essentially and intensely feminine, but they are, in our judgment, decidedly more perfect than any masculine productions with which they can be brought into comparison. (50: 33)

Jeffrey may sense gender as a performance, but his italics hold the line, with double import: a man will muddle masculine production by attempting genres "essentially" feminine, while a woman will only embarrass herself in attempting anything else. Mrs. Hemans, he cautions, needs to stick with "occasional verses" and not "venture again on any thing so long" as *The Forest Sanctuary* (47)—a brief epic that she herself put among "the best of her works" (*CMH* 1:123).

So when Jeffrey says of Hemans's poetry that it "may not be the best imaginable poetry, and may not indicate the very highest or most commanding genius" (34), he has specific protocols in mind. His *not*s are tied to what "it is," and this is an extremely "Female Poetry":

infinitely sweet, elegant, and tender—touching, perhaps, and contemplative rather than vehement and overpowering; and not only finished throughout with an exquisite delicacy, and even serenity of execution, but informed with a purity and loftiness of feeling, and a certain sober and humble tone of indulgence and piety. (50: 34)

Jeffrey's judgments shape and shade W. M. Rossetti's 1873 Prefatory Notice.[13] If "Mrs. Hemans," in "the deficiency which she, merely as a woman, was almost certain to evince" (16), may claim a "very honorable rank among poetesses," Rossetti's gender-rank (once again) depletes the honor:

One might sum up the weak points in Mrs. Hemans's poetry by saying that it is not only "feminine" poetry (which under the circumstances can be no imputation, rather an encomium) but also "female" poetry: besides exhibiting the fineness and charm of womanhood, it has the monotone of mere sex. (24)

Yet "Mrs. Hemans's poetry" was by this point a tendentious canon. "No Pythian enthusiasm fills the poet and compels us to forget her womanhood," sighed Agnes Mary Robinson in 1880, looking back in wonder at Jeffrey's day. "Fifty years ago few poets were more popular than Mrs. Hemans; her verses were familiar to all hearts," she began a headnote in Ward's *English Poets*. Here is a young scholar and poet who might have embraced Hemans as a precedent; instead she set her distance from a Hemans constituted in a mere dirge, ballad, and *Casabianca*. This little canon of "simple, chivalrous, pathetic" domestic lyrics, "sprung from a talent expressive but not creative" and "stamped with feminine qualities," was the "claim to remembrance," claimed Robinson; all the rest was "forgotten, and without injustice" (4: 334–35).[14] The "feminine" had occluded everything else, and this little remnant was damped, if not damned, with faint praise.

Hemans and a Woman's Life

"Mrs. Hemans" had succeeded, but with the shearing off of a larger and more various canon that even Jeffrey had at hand. He had on his desk *The Forest Sanctuary* and *Records of Woman*—the first a romance opening in a lurid Spanish Inquisition *auto da fé*, the second a chronicle of infanticides, suicides, war, blood feuds, tortures, murders, betrayals, and fatal heartbreak. From *The Domestic Affections* (1812), to *Tales, and Historic Scenes* (1819), to *The Siege of Valencia* (1823), across annuals verse and more than a few items in *Records of Woman* (1828), to *Songs of the Affections* (1830), Hemans's poetry of "Woman" traces its "feminine" ideal on a fabric of dark contradictions. Nineteenth-century ideologic tended to read the darkness as a peculiar Hemans melancholy, or a "feminine" excess that could be transvalued as patient suffering, forbearance, faith, and martyrdom. It was Christian heroinism. But Chorley, at least, intuited the counter-cultural vectors, a baseline despair about "the farewells and regrets of life" and "the finer natures broken in pieces by contact with a mercenary and scornful world."[15] Poet Rose Lawrence, a close friend of Hemans in later years, put gender into the equation, taking the abrasion as no peculiarity, but generic for any ambitious woman. "In the world, as it is called, it fared with her as it has with done with all other women of genius, from Madame de Stael, downward: she was frequently accused of heresy and schism, and several times regularly convicted of contumacy and non-conformity"—among the incitements, the way "her brilliant conversation rose above the level and conventional tone of society. Her pleasantry was not always genuine or happy" (*Recollections* 316–17).

What was genuine in this woman of genius was an oppositional sensibility, and a willingness to expose it. After holding fire for 25 pages, *Dublin Review* admitted its abhorrence at the unfeminine character of the poet in Chorley's pages: her theatricality, her swings of feeling about her fame, her satirical remarks on her fans and some acquaintances, and her "being a romp" (2: 272–73). Hemans had more going on than "Mrs. Hemans" let on. She knew she was a non-conformist on "Woman." In the view of proper "ladies," she guessed that she seemed an "altogether foreign monster, a <u>Poetess</u>" (*CMH* 2: 280). She liked Baillie for creating heroines "so perfectly different from the pretty '<u>un-idea'd</u> girls,' who seem to form the <u>beau ideal</u> of our whole sex in the works of some modern poets" (1: 96).[16] For giving women depth and dimension (an idea better than the ideal), she dedicated *Records of Woman* to Baillie. It is no coincidence that Hemans's own poetry and its reception cut to the core of several critical issues: women's writing in and against the grain of gendered culture; cultural determinations of aesthetic value then and now; how we define the poetry of the Romantic era; and (as the Victorians' "Mrs. Hemans" reminds us) how we define Hemans herself.[17] Not only is her poetry "never simply Victorian," proposes Tricia Lootens in a dazzlingly smart pioneering essay, but "where it is most Victorian, it is perhaps least simple" (239). In another ground-breaking essay a few years before, Stuart Curran detailed the alterity, and over the next decade, Hemans received fresh critical assessment and new places in the anthologies. This recovery of Hemans was no quaint project of antiquarian curiosity, dutiful sociology, or feminist pleading, but a sharpening interest in the way Hemans's mainstream themes exposed cross-currents, counter-currents and contradictions in the core and lore of the "feminine."[18]

Not the least of the influences was Hemans's own material history: her avid reading and liberal education, her failed marriage and her determined professionalism.[19] Felicia Browne was a prodigy, with substantive home-schooling by her mother, writing poetry by age ten and publishing by her teens. In her girlhood, her father left the family to seek a living in Canada, after his Liverpool business failed. He never returned, dying there in 1812, the year of Felicia's starry-eyed marriage to Captain Alfred Hemans, her brother's comrade in the Peninsular War. In the post-war economy, Captain Hemans found only brief employment, and in 1813 the couple, and a son, moved into Mrs. Browne's household. There was a fifth son on the way in 1818 when the captain left for Italy, never to return. Everyone said it was for his health (he was war-weakened and scarred) but the exit looks over-determined. For her part, Hemans may have found it hard to deal with the after-effects of a war that she (and the nation) had cheered as a romance of British chivalry rising against tyrant Napoleon.[20] Her romance of "the gallant patriots" in "the theatre of glory" (*CMH* 1: 31) was confronted with the reality of a bother and a husband who had suffered horrible ordeals. Meanwhile, the emergence of "Mrs. Hemans" as money-earning poet worked a further strain.[21] Jewsbury (her friend about ten years onward) had the impression that ex-Captain Hemans was unhappy living off his wife's revenue and unhappy that "wife" was a secondary role; an early memoir of Hemans cited his complaint that "it was the curse of having a literary wife that he could never get a pair of stockings mended," and later memoirists struggled to spin their separation.[22]

The collapse of the marriage left a strange wake of debris and potential. If the ideal of hearth and home summed in "Mrs. Hemans" was haunted by two broken marriages, there were material benefits for her. Now the sole support of five sons, Hemans determined to make a living by writing. Her domestic situation was an advantage. In her mother's home with adult siblings, and with no husband to require service and obedience, she was given time to read, to study, and to write—to be the breadwinner. Such "peculiar circumstances" (Chorley put it) constituted a career on a heterodox basis. Living "in a household, as a member and not as its head," she was excused from "many of those small cares of domestic life," as well as the large ones that fall to woman's weary lot.[23] Were Hemans typically burdened (Chorley surmised), she might have "fretted away her day-dreams, and, by interruption, have made of less avail the search for knowledge to which she bent herself with such eagerness." But what kind of knowledge? Chorley thinks that had Hemans more typical woman's cares, her poetry might have had "more of masculine health and stamen, at the expense of some of its romance and music" (*CMH* 1: 43)—the very terms of its "feminine" fame. Being more of a woman would have made her more masculine.

This strange, fleeting paradox—of a too-feminine poet needing masculine tempering by a stronger dose of woman's life—had another facet in the symbolic order of the domestic. However heterodox, Hemans's situation at home detoxified the broken marriage and "unfeminine" professional independence.[24] "Mrs. Hemans" gave conduct advisors such as Mrs. Sandford an icon of "domestic life" as the basis of woman's happiness and worth. Under "the maternal wing," Hemans seemed even an innocent child.[25] Focusing on Hemans, Gilfillan could say of all women (adapting Wordsworth's apostrophe to his "dear Girl"), "God is with them, when they know it not" (*Tait's* 14: 362). A dyspeptic Rossetti warmed to this "popular poetess" in her domestic sphere of "loving daughter" and "affectionate, tender, and vigilant mother" (15). Chorley reported the concordant literary tastes: she cherished Wordsworth (to other eyes, the poet laureate of undomestic solitaries and alienated visionaries) as the "true Poet of Home, and of all the lofty feelings which have their root in the soil of home affections"; "his gentle and affectionate playfulness in the intercourse with all the members of his family" refuted Byron-toned theories about "the unfitness of genius for domestic happiness."[26] Poetess of Home was Mrs. Hemans's public profile.

Hemans knew that the ideal was as frangible as it was cherished, and that her "feminine" fame was something of a strange fit. In one and the same letter she could insist, "there is <u>no</u> enjoyment to compare with the happiness of gladdening hearth and home for others—it is woman's own true sphere," then admit, "I am not at all well just now; I believe it is owing to the great fatigue I have had of late with my boys," then plead, "How very foolish [. . .] do not betray my weakness!" (*CMH* 1: 224). It is the frayed edges of the ideal on which recent critical attention has focused. All those hymns to "the enduring value of the domestic affections, the glory and beauty of maternal love, and the lasting commitment of a woman to her chosen mate," argues Anne Mellor, are conscious of fragile underpinnings. The poetry is "haunted by death and insubstantiality," comments Jerome McGann. Even Victorian anthology-favorites could show this. *Casabianca* links precious filial piety to horrific, pointless martyrdom; *England's Dead* ponders global empire as global graveyard: wherever you go in this world, "*There* slumber England's dead!" The array of "proper sentiments," "normative morality," and "the emerging stereotype of the pure, long-suffering female," are more than melancholy, proposes Cora Kaplan (unfolding Chorley's hint); it looks like a symbolic discipline of anger.[27] Hemans's true haunt and home was a shifting ground between counter-cultural critique and conduct-book compliance.[28] Across "Mrs. Hemans" fall the shadows of the Romantic era, scored with social and ideological conflicts. Not the least of these involved the reaction to a woman whose pen has won her fame. (fig. 2.2)

Hemans in the Scales

"Mrs. Hemans," wrote Wordsworth (in the headnote to *Extempore Effusion*), "was unfortunate as a Poetess in being obliged by circumstances to write for money, and that so frequently and so much, that she was compelled [. . .] to write as expeditiously as possible." If Hemans's professional discipline and determination embodied his worst nightmare about the commercial deformation of poetic vocation, the female embodiment was a further aggravation. He put this more frankly to a friend during Hemans's extended visit with him in the summer of 1830. While he "could say much very much in praise of Mrs Hemans," he sighed at her conversation, which "like that of many literary Ladies, is too elaborate and studied—and perhaps the simplicity of her character is impaired by the homage which has been paid her—both for her accomplishments and her Genius."[29] Hemans was an irritating sign of the incursion of the "Poetess" into the world in which homages to his own accomplishments and genius as "Poet" were sadly in arrears. In Wordsworth's elegy, tender as it is, she is coded as a "Holy Spirit, / Sweet as the spring, as ocean deep" (37–38). Coleridge, Lamb, and Crabbe are named, and Scott by epithet ("Border Minstrel"). Hemans is as easily decoded, but her translation into natural spirit marks a feminine difference from male poetic labor.[30]

Hemans's styling as a Literary Lady disrupted gender economy on two fronts: how women ought to behave, and how women ought to behave around

Figure 2.2 *Felicia Hemans*, Edward Smith's engraving from a miniature painted by Edward Robertson in Dublin, autumn 1831. At the height of her fame, but bereft of most of her family and living away from her beloved Wales, Hemans conveys the melancholy beauty that was the hallmark of her poetry. With her signature underneath, this engraving supplied the frontispiece of Henry Chorley's *Memorials of Mrs. Hemans,* the first posthumous memoir, published in 1836. Chorley called it "a faithful and graceful likeness" (2: 253).

male genius. What Wordsworth lacked, and couldn't conceive, was a measure of accomplishment for a woman whose "education had been [so] unfortunate" not only to make her a confident conversationalist but also to leave her "totally ignorant of housewifery" (as that headnote put it): she "could as easily have managed the spear of Minerva as her needle." The rueful mock-heroics about the warrior goddess are sharpened by the lore that even Minerva knew enough to serve as weaver for the gods. In the Wordsworth household, anyway, a woman managed "her needle" to sew for the family and to stitch the poet's manuscripts.[31] Hemans's truancy prompts him to remediate, first in person, then, as a likely consequence of that pedagogical failure, in the posthumous public headnote:

> It was from observing these deficiencies, that, one day while she was under my roof, I *purposely* directed her attention to household economy, and told her I had purchased *Scales*, which I intended to present to a young lady as a wedding present; pointed out their utility (for her especial benefit), and said no *ménage* ought to be without them. Mrs. Hemans, not in the least suspecting my drift, reported this saying, in a letter to a friend at that time, as a proof of my simplicity.

What a frustration to the poet who liked to regard himself as a teacher for the ages.

As that "letter" shows (Wordsworth had read it by the time he wrote the headnote),[32] Hemans not only got his drift, but turned it to her own little comedy of judgment:

> Imagine [. . .] a bridal present made by Mr. Wordsworth, to a young lady in whom he is much interested—a poet's daughter, too! You will be thinking of a broach in the shape of a lyre, or a butterfly-shaped aigrette, or a forget-me-not ring, or some such "small gear"—nothing of the sort, but a good, handsome, substantial, useful-looking pair of scales, to hang up in her store-room! "For you must be aware, my dear Mrs. Hemans," said he to me very gravely, "how necessary it is occasionally for every lady to see things weighed herself." (*CMH* 2: 141)

With a politely blinkered refusal of the poet's palpable design, she gamely converted his pedagogy into her own aesthetic property:

> "Poveretta me!" I looked as good as I could, and, happily for me, the poetic eyes are not very clear-sighted, so that I believe no suspicion derogatory to my notability of character, has yet flashed upon the mighty master's mind: indeed I told him that I looked upon scales as particularly graceful things, and had great thoughts of having my picture taken with a pair in my hand. (*CMH* 2: 141–42)

If Wordsworth hoped to instruct this wayward poetic daughter with the example of a brother poet's daughter, Hemans tips the scales against him by shifting the utile "things" into a theatrical prop for gracious posing as the goddess of judgment. Treating the patriarchal advice with wry alienation and camping with the faux Italian lament, Hemans's sketch shows just how right Jewsbury was about her capacity for witty prose.[33]

Yet it was Hemans herself who was the most severe detractor of "her accomplishments and her Genius," in the calculus of her domestic happiness. Far more devastating than her failed marriage was her mother's death, in January 1827.[34] It felt like her own death: "I have lost the faithful, watchful, patient love, which for years had been devoted to me and mine; and I feel that the void it has left behind, must cause me to bear 'a yearning heart within me to the grave;' [. . .] I now feel wearied and worn, and longing, as she did, for rest."[35] She was still cushioned, the home now managed by a brother and sister; but when this band was "scattered" by her brother's remove to Ireland and her sister's marriage, she was left in miserable independence. "Strange as it may seem to say," she sighed to Mary Russell Mitford in November 1828, "I am now for the first time in my life holding <u>the reins of government</u>—independent—managing a Household myself—and I never liked any thing <u>less</u> than "ce triste empire de Soi-même."[36] She was no matriarch.

Records of Woman, assembled in the months after her mother's death, is haunted by this alienation, with a poignant fantasy of restoration in *Madeline: A Domestic Tale*. Madeline's marriage is implicitly death as daughter. But Hemans's tale (preempting the desertions that she and her mother suffered) kills off the husband, to realize a double return. From under the overt lesson that the death spells to woman—"the part / Which life will teach—to suffer and be still" (61–62; the source of that Victorian adage)—emerges a compelling romance: the daughter is reborn when Mother comes to the rescue. In the last lines, Madeline sighs, "Take back thy wanderer from this fatal shore, / Peace shall be ours beneath our vines once more" (101–2). Echoing "fatal shore" from Wordsworth's *Laodamia* (Laodamia's husband was the first Greek to die on Troy's "fatal shore"), Hemans substitutes woman's marital life for the alien field of men's martial life. While nostalgia for childhood is a famous male Romantic sigh (Wordsworthian especially), the purchase of *Madeline* is to realize the female form of the wish.

Even fatal conclusions can seem paradisical this way. In the record of *Pauline*, the heroine perishes in the fire from which she attempted to save her child. Her heroic "strength" (61) springs, in the imagery of a military charge, from a mother's "deep love" (18):

>   there is no power
> To stay the mother from that rolling grave,
> Tho' fast on high the fiery volumes tower,
>   And forth, like banners, from each lattice wave.
> Back, back she rushes thro' a host combined—
> Mighty is anguish, with affection twined! (61–66)

In an essay in 1833 on noble and virtuous cases of "The Female Character," with warm praise of Hemans, *Fraser's* ascribed to "nature," all those "instances of female heroism, of devoted attachment, and of endurance of suffering," especially "love of offspring" (594–95). Hence the shock effect of another poem in *Records*. The eponym of *The Lady of the Castle* unnaturally abandons her daughter to become a king's mistress, and the poet conveys the scandal:

>   how shall woman tell
> Of woman's shame, and not with tears?—She fell!
> That mother left that child! (15–17)

The consequences are dire: in "grief and shame" (27), her husband seeks death in foreign wars, and her daughter grows up a "blighted spirit" (43). Years later, pale and poor, the Lady seeks her out. When her daughter fails even to recognize her and shrinks back, it's a death blow.

The extreme courses of these narratives report a deep investment in their ideals. At the same time, however, the catastrophes that shape nearly all Hemans's records betray an intuition not just of a frangible ideal, but of a phantasmic devotion that may be life-destroying for women. Across her career of writing, a world of women, in the very heart of domestic affection, turns desperate, violent, and self-destroying. No alien monsters, they are devoted lovers, wives, daughters, sisters, lovers, and sometimes artists, too, who expose an incoherent cultural mythology, and in their aggregate trace out a cultural unconscious of fragmented, dissonant awarenesses.

Such shadows darken the romance of *The Domestic Affections*, vexed Hemans-wise, by aesthetic effects in conflict with apparent argument. This volume-titler begins with by-the-book hymns to "home" as refuge from "storms of discord," from "war's red lightnings," the desolation of thrones, the destruction of empires (31–33), and all "rude tumultuous cares" (73):

> Gem of seclusion! treasure of the vale!
> Thus, far retir'd from life's tumultuous road,
> Domestic bliss has fix'd her calm abode,
> Where hallow'd innocence and sweet repose
> May strew her shadowy path with many a rose. (22–26)

In the world at large, the female figures are reciprocal nurturers, abstract muses for male action: Fame—"ev'ry life-pulse vibrates to her voice" (161–62); Freedom, on her "throne of fire" (165*ff*). The poem's design is to trace a continuity to domestic affection. The "aspiring eagle" of male Genius (166) really wants nothing more than to go home:

> soon, descending from his height sublime,
> Day's burning fount, and light's empyreal clime;
> Once more he speeds to joys more calmly blest . . . (171–73)

But the poem's aesthetics contest the exemplum: delaying this descent, the verse lingers in the splendors of Genius (159–72). The homeward track is as affectively reluctant as it is thematically calculated. When the rhyme for 173 is completed with "'Midst the dear inmates of his lonely nest!" (174), *lonely* slips the sense of "inmates" from cohabitants into co-prisoners.[37] No sooner is the nest gained (moreover) than it is fled, not in argument but in poetic drama:

> Thus Genius, mounting on his bright career,
> Thro' the wide regions of the mental sphere;
> And proudly waving, in his gifted hand,
> O'er Fancy's worlds, Invention's plastic wand;
> Fearless and firm, with lightning-eye surveys
> The clearest heav'n of intellectual rays!
> Yet, on his course tho' loftiest hopes attend,
> And kindling raptures aid him to ascend;
> (While in his mind, with high-born grandeur fraught,
> Dilate the noblest energies of thought;)
> Still, from the bliss, ethereal and refin'd,
> Which crowns the soarings of triumphant mind,
> At length he flies, to that serene retreat,
> Where calm and pure, the mild affections meet;
> Embosom'd there, to feel and to impart,
> The softer pleasures of the social heart! (175–90)

The "length" that is meant experientially is also a telling poetic effect: with the dilating syntax of *yet, while, still*, the rapturous phase before the pivot on *retreat* so temporizes, that retreat from bliss and triumphant soaring comes to seem a reluctant fall.

This hymn to home's serene retreat manages to index solitude, seclusion, loneliness, and a withdrawal from the world that seems a withdrawal from life itself—at least for the women in its "bower of repose" (77), whose labors paradoxically create and sustain it.[38] On the map of high argument, there is no place like home for the "exhausted," "oppress'd," "wearied pilgrim" of life (71–76): "To *thee* we turn, still faithful, from afar,/Thee, our bright vista! thee, our magnet-star!" (79–80). But even as *we* argues a general boon, the *thee* is female gendered.

Byron concedes as much in *Sardanapalus* (a play Jewsbury and Hemans knew), when slave Myrrha rebukes the king's condescension to the inconstancy of "woman's love":

> the very first
> Of human life must spring from woman's breast,
> Your first small words are taught you from her lips,
> Your first tears quench'd by her, and your last sighs
> Too often breathed out in a woman's hearing,
> When men have shrunk from the ignoble care
> Of watching the last hour of him who led them. (1.2.509–15)

"M.J.J." used these lines as the epigraph for one of the most idealizing, and most gender-heroic essays of *Phantasmagoria, Woman's Love* (1: 107). But Felicia Browne finds herself saying (in subordinate clauses, then in fuller meditations) that in a domestic bliss wrought by female care, the result for woman is asymmetrical. She must "conceal, with duteous art,/Her own deep sorrows in her inmost heart!" (291–92); "(Still fondly struggling to suppress *her own*)," the poet writes, the italics pressing against the parentheses (298). When the poet protests, again with italics, "But who may charm *her* sleepless pang to rest,/Or draw the thorn that rankles in her breast?" (343–44), the only answer is a "Faith" in an "Eden, freed from every thorn" (359–62): the transcendent hereafter (the only real freedom for slave Myrrha, too). The ideal of home, strained by what it must suppress and exclude, turns out for women to lie "Beyond the sphere of anguish, death, or time" (424)—beyond, that is, social and historical existence.

Nineteenth-century editors put *The Domestic Affections* with "Juvenile Poems," but the developing intuition is more prescient than juvenile: the teenage poet was sensing a socially wrought ideal so wearing on woman as to make her long for death as the only release. In 1825 Hemans wrote *Our Daily Paths* on a request from a friend that she discipline her signature melancholy ("dwelling on what was painful and depressing") by "giving more consolatory views of the ways of Providence, thus infusing comfort and cheer into the bosoms of her readers, in a spirit of Christian philosophy" (Blackwood's 1873 *Poems*, 370n). So she gets off a few game stanzas about the beauty to be discovered, even in life's darker paths. But it's those dark passages that prevail: "we carry our sick hearts abroad amidst the joyous things" (15). An epithet for women's domestic lot, "our daily paths" tacitly genders this "us." The final stanzas offer the requested consolation, but as with many of Hemans's poems of faith, despondency hovers as a spectral twin:

> . . . in our daily paths lie cares, that ofttimes bind us fast,
> While from their narrow round we see the golden day fleet past.
>
> They hold us from the woodlark's haunts, and violet dingles, back,
> And from all the lovely sounds and gleams in the shining river's track;
> They bar us from our heritage of spring-time, hope, and mirth,
> And weigh our burden'd spirits down with the cumbering dust of earth.
>
> Yet should this be? Too much, too soon, despondingly we yield!
> A better lesson we are taught by the lilies of the field!
> A sweeter by the birds of heaven—which tell us, in their flight,
> Of One that through the desert air for ever guides them right.
>
> Shall not this knowledge calm our hearts, and bid vain conflicts cease?
> Ay, when they commune with themselves in holy hours of peace,
> And feel that by the lights and clouds through which our pathway lies,
> By the beauty and the grief alike, we are training for the skies! (24–36)

The questions, rhetorically cast, verge on a real interrogation of the "knowledge" that is the usual balm. The "lesson" and the "training" seem more enforced than felt, while salvation in "the skies" shimmers as only the remotest of romances.

These bleak apprehensions seize almost all Hemans's stories of women, denaturalizing the assumed basis of female happiness. In *The Maremma* Bianca is not just figuratively but literally killed by domestic affection—or rather disaffection.[39] Her jealous husband has taken her and their child to Maremma to suffer a slow death from its pollutions, a betrayal by both nature and affection. If *The Domestic Affections* hails a female-nature as the type and ally of home values, here it is co-conspirator: "trust thou not her smile, her balmy breath, / Away! her charms but the pomp of Death!" (5–6)—the rhyme tightening the league of treason. No less than the husband, Nature "charm[s] us with seductive wiles" (20), a femme fatale to the female heart: "Where shall we turn, O Nature! if in *thee* / Danger is mask'd in beauty—death in smiles?" (21–22). Circe is the prototype (23), allied with a husband who conceals "the workings of each darker feeling, / Deep in his soul" (105–6), in fatal parody of the romantic ideal. "Affection's power" (108) is betrayed to "Affliction's own" (226). No training for the skies, the knowledge Hemans draws here is strictly mortal: "It is our task to suffer—and our fate / To learn that mighty lesson, soon or late" (227–28). Hemans's famous melancholy is this conformity to training, but a conformity that is restless, even rebellious.

Domestic Fates, Woman's Heroism

Such betrayals press Hemans to imagine women who won't suffer fate but rebel, and in forms that perversely parody domestic affection. This is a strategy, in Isobel Armstrong's terms, of turning "customary 'feminine' forms and languages" to "*analytical* account" (15). If Hemans's relentlessly fatal conclusions spell a poetics of resignation, they also issue a political report. One recurring issue, with a Hemans signature, is maternal infanticide in reaction to rotten husbands or invading armies.[40] These fatally driven mothers act from both domestic and political devotions. And if Hemans's idioms send the shock to exotic locales and sensational extremes, the displacements transparently come home.

The Wife of Asdrubal (in *Tales, and Historic Scenes*), though set in ancient Carthage, also plays in 1819, the Roman siege evoking Napoleonic sieges, the infanticide implying a desperate politics of domestic affection. In exchange for his safety, governor Asdrubal has secretly ceded the city to the invading Romans. Wife, sons, and a few patriots hold out in the citadel, and as conquest impends, they torch it and die. Just before this climax, his wife berates him from the heights, stabs their sons before his eyes, and hurls the bodies into the blaze. Hemans scripts this act as both a mother's indictment and a mother's love in time of war:

> thou, their sire,
> In bondage safe, shalt yet in them expire.
> Think'st thou I love them not?—'Twas thine to fly—
> 'Tis mine with these to suffer and to die. (57–60)

To voice such stark affection in a world of no separate spheres, Hemans (mother of five sons) embodies its agent in the supernatural surreal:

> But mark! from yon fair temple's loftiest height
> What towering form bursts wildly on the sight,
> All regal in magnificent attire,
> And sternly beauteous in terrific ire?
> She might be deem'd a Pythia in the hour
> Of dread communion and delirious power;
> A being more than earthly, in whose eye
> There dwells a strange and fierce ascendency. (15–22)

This "being more than earthly" gives Hemans a form through which to write, in terrific ire, against male power politics. A. M. Robinson's sigh of "no Pythian enthusiasm" (Ward's 4: 334–35) says more about the poems lost to Victorian eyes than what was missing in Hemans's imagination.

Putting an edge on the conventional she-gendering of city-states, Hemans allies it with the doomed Wife, then sharpens two critical points. Asdrubal will be feminized down to a trophy in a Roman "triumph," while his Wife, "triumphant" in "wild courage," blazes forth as a warrior:

> The dark profusion of her locks unbound,
> Waves like a warrior's floating plumage round;
> Flush'd is her cheek, inspired her haughty mien,
> She seems th' avenging goddess of the scene. (29–32)

In all these details—not the least, the ramping up of angry wife to divine avenger—Hemans casts an unsexed female with a vengeance:

> Are those *her* infants, that with suppliant-cry
> Cling round her, shrinking as the flame draws nigh,
> Clasp with their feeble hands her gorgeous vest,
> And fain would rush for shelter to her breast?
> Is that a mother's glance, where stern disdain,
> And passion awfully vindictive, reign? (33–35)

Is that a mother or Medea? In the spectacle of a woman whose towering form has become less (or more) than maternal, domestic affection turns political, angry, lurid, and fatal: "Behold their fate!—the arms that cannot save / Have been their cradle, and shall be their grave" (61–62). The maternal "arms" that kill usurp in affection the military arms will send all to the grave, anyway:

> Bright in her hand the lifted dagger gleams,
> Swift from her children's hearts the life-blood streams;
> With frantic laugh she clasps them to the breast;
> Whose woes and passions soon shall be at rest;
> Lifts one appealing, frenzied glance on high,
> Then deep midst rolling flames is lost to mortal eye. (63–68)

Almost lost in this gothic sensation is the shape of the political argument.

A few years on, however, Hemans will set wartime infanticide as a global destiny, and bring it closer to home. *The Suliote Mother* (1825) uses a scene that is only slightly displaced, just by decades, and in the European world. It is based on a famous event from 1803, in which Suli women, watching the Turkish army advance on their mountain fasthold, and with their men already lost to a failed defense, hurled themselves and their children into a chasm, to avoid rape, murder, or slavery.[41] Hemans writes this as a ballad of sublime female heroics:

> She stood upon the loftiest peak,

> Amidst the clear blue sky,
> A bitter smile was on her cheek,
> And a dark flash in her eye. (1–4)

Her last words sound a national anthem: "Freedom, young Suliote! for thee and me!" (40).

A heightened consciousness of the fatal binding of female freedom and female death informs the implicit historiography of *Records of Woman*. The singer of *Indian Woman's Death-Song* stands in a canoe rushing towards a cataract:

> Proudly, and dauntlessly, and all alone,
> Save that a babe lay sleeping at her breast,
> A woman stood: upon her Indian brow
> Sat a strange gladness, and her dark hair wav'd
> As if triumphantly. She press'd her child,
> In its bright slumber, to her beating heart,
> And lifted her sweet voice, that rose awhile
> Above the sound of waters, high and clear,
> Wafting a wild proud strain, her song of death. (7–15)

Her song is a Byronic anthem to freedom, extended to heroically extravagant fourteeners:

> Roll swiftly to the Spirit's land, thou mighty stream and free!
> Father of ancient waters, roll! and bear our lives with thee! (16–17)

But the inspiration is female gender-specific: Hemans's headnote indicates a woman "driven to despair by her husband's desertion of her for another wife." Thus while in the narrative frame "Father of ancient waters" is folk formula, on Hemans's rhetorical plane it indicts any patriarchal system licensed to betray a wife, cast her off, deem her worthless:

> And thou, my babe! tho' born, like me, for woman's weary lot,
> Smile!—to that wasting of the heart, my own! I leave thee not;
> Too bright a thing are *thou* to pine in aching love away,
> Thy mother bears thee far, young Fawn! from sorrow and decay.
>
> She bears thee to the glorious bowers where none are heard to weep.
> (36–40)

In a poem for which one epigraph is "Let not my child be a girl, for very sad is the life of a woman," it is Father-force that finally finishes off a woman's life.

In the *Death-Song*, the political protest is the rhetorical unconscious of the narrative, linked to the historiography of Hemans's headnote and epigraphs.

Back in 1819, in *The Widow of Crescentius* (*Tales*), she had written the protest right into the heart of the narrative, where the affections of a betrayed wife mobilize action in the political sphere. Widowed by the treachery of Otho III of Germany, Stephania bursts into the poem with the Hemans-semiotics of unleashed female anger: her "rich flow of raven hair / Streams wildly on the morning air" (1.107–8); her "wild and high expression" is "fraught / With glances of impassion'd thought" (145–46), a "fire within" (152). With a heart "vainly form'd to prove / The pure devotedness of love" (269–70), she gets revenge in multiple perversions of the feminine. She insinuates herself into Otho's court as minstrel-boy Guido, providing music to his troubled soul with divinely domestic nurture: "Of power to lull all earthly pain" (2.122). Hemans's cross-dressed threat—a diabolical replay of "Cesario" in Shakespeare's *Twelfth Night,* with a Byronic update (in Lootens's nice gloss, 244)—is a hidden agenda wrapped in the legible signs of the alienated, lethal Byronic rebel:

> oft his features and his air
> A shade of troubled mystery wear,
> A glance of hurried wildness, fraught
> With some unfathomable thought.
> Whate'er that thought, still, unexpress'd,
> Dwells the sad secret in his breast;
> The pride his haughty brow reveals,
> All other passion well conceals. (2.161–68)

Short a metrical foot, the last couplet is virtual *Corsair*.[42] But where the Byronic hero's private torment tends to be the chief action, Hemans gives Stephania's torment public, historical agency: the death of Otho. It is poison, another perversion of feminine nurture, that brings it about. Otho's agony unfolds in loving detail, launched by the wickedly parodic form of an anti-erotic sonnet-stanza:

> Away, vain dream!—on Otho's brow,
> Still darker lower the shadows now;
> Changed are his features, now o'erspread
> With the cold paleness of the dead;
> Now crimson'd with a hectic dye,
> The burning flush of agony!
> His lip is quivering, and his breast
> Heaves with convulsive pangs oppress'd;
> Now his dim eye seems fix'd and glazed,
> And now to heaven in anguish raised;
> And as, with unavailing aid,

> Around him throng his guests dismay'd,
> He sinks—while scarce his struggling breath
> Hath power to falter—"This is death!"   (2.235–44)

In an ensuing gloat of almost sixty lines, the poetry savors the poisoner's delight:

> And on the sufferer's mien awhile
> Gazing with stern vindictive smile,
> A feverish glow of triumph dyed
> His burning cheek, while thus he cried:
> "Yes! these are death pangs!—on thy brow
> Is set the seal of vengeance now!" (2.253–58)

The check on this extravaganza is the fatal bargain. Hemans ends the tale with Stephania's impending execution, and the effacement of her story in the pace of men's history:

> . . . o'er thy dark and lowly bed
> The sons of future days shall tread,
> The pangs, the conflicts, of thy lot,
> By them unknown, by thee forgot. (2.231–34)

This final rhyme echoes another unhappy woman's: "How happy is the blameless Vestal's lot! / The world forgetting, by the world forgot," sighs Pope's Eloisa (*Eloisa to Abelard* 207–8). Hemans's repetition implies a distinction without historiographic difference between the blameless vestal and the self-martyring assassin: both are unknown in a man's world. Hemans, the historian of woman, intervenes, putting Stephania in her *Tales, and Historical Scenes.*[43]

In *Records of Woman*, she dedicates herself, with a full armature of annotation, to recovering these lost, forgotten, or politically exiled histories. It is accomplished not by means of a master narrative such as Gibbon's *Decline and Fall of the Roman Empire* (which she read and used), but as Stuart Curran puts it, "in the specificity of lives, whose daily acts bear the burden of historical force."[44] Men scarcely mark the archive, except to break women's hearts, evoking the etymology of *record* as a recalling on the heart.[45] If Hemans deflects the full critical force of this totalizing by gleaning records from alien cultures and eras, *Woman* proposes to her English readers, as much as Wollstonecraft's *Rights of Woman* did, a categorical view.[46] Across the archive falls a common story: the failure of domestic ideals, in all cultural varieties, to sustain women's lives.[47] What Rossetti will disparage as the "monotone of mere sex" is inscribed in *Records* as a cultural fate of mere sex. That *Records* proved Hemans's most popular volume was not by force of this fatalism, however. It was her crafting of this fate into a stage of heroism, of ordinary women cast into extraordinary situations and finding uncommon resources—and this, not by turning into monsters, but by discovering innate courage (another punning on the core/*cor* of *Records*).

The title-page sets this key with an epigraph from *Laodamia*, one of the very few of Wordsworth's poems that Jeffrey was willing to call "classical and manly."[48] Hemans insists on a womanly heroism of the heart:

> ———Mightier far
> Than strength of nerve or sinew, or the sway
> Of magic potent over sun and star,
> Is love, though oft to agony distrest,
> And though his favourite seat be feeble woman's breast.

In *Rights of Woman* Wollstonecraft argued that a woman of rational sense will be "raised to heroism by misfortunes" (30). Reading *Shakespeare's Heroines*, Anna Jameson thought otherwise: "woman's heroism is always the excess of sensibility" (27). Hemans sets *Records of Woman* on a middle-ground of strength from sense and sensibility, and against any separate gender-sphering. Gertrude, heroine of a record subtitled *Fidelity Till Death*, sustains a husband under political torture with the "strength" of "high words . . . / From woman's breaking heart" (25–26). In a national crisis, the heroine of *The Switzer's Wife* (its epigraph from Jewsbury's *Arria*) discovers her "power" in the domestic and civic relations that are her identity:

> . . . she, that ever thro' her home had mov'd
>   With the meek thoughtfulness and quiet smile
> Of woman, calmly loving and belov'd,
>   And timid in her happiness the while,
> Stood brightly forth, and stedfastly, that hour,
> Her clear glance kindling into sudden power. (67–72)

Hemans makes this scene of crisis a stage to issue a political manifesto for female fortitude:

> Are we thus oppress'd?
> Then must we rise upon our mountain-sod,
>   And man must arm, and woman call on God! (76–78)

When Hemans has Werner (who is named) exclaim, "Worthy art thou . . . // My bride, my wife, the mother of my child! / Now shall thy name be armour to my heart," she imagines how a man might summon his domestic relations for his strength (101–4).

The political hesitation of Hemans's poetics of woman is the severe economy that fetters female fortitude to female self-sacrifice. The first Record, *Arabella Stuart* sets the terms. Imprisoned by James I to prevent marriage and issue, Arabella gambles with "male attire" (headnote) to escape to France with her secret husband. A series of mishaps returns her to prison, the site of her monologue. Arabella declares "my woman's spirit strong" (31); "my woman's heart / Shall wake a spirit and a power to bless, / Ev'n in this hour's o'er-shadowing fearfulness" (227–29). But the awakening is death-sentenced—and in the record of another heroine, Imelda, simultaneously. Discovering her lover murdered by her brother (their fathers are enemies), Imelda finds strength to die with him:

> Wo for young love! but love is strong. There came
> Strength upon woman's fragile heart and frame.
> There came swift courage! On the dewy ground
> She knelt, with all her dark hair floating round,
> Like a long silken stole; she knelt, and press'd
> Her lips of glowing life to Azzo's breast,
> Drawing the poison forth.   (*Imelda* 95–101)

A Byronic foil (perhaps an allusion) glints in this strength. In *The Corsair,* Medora's "long fair hair lay floating" over her pirate lover, who is trying to leave her, and will (1.470), while Imelda's "dark hair floating round" her lover's corpse (98) is set in a syntax of female determination. But this, too, is a distinction without a difference. As in *The Wife of Asdrubal* and *Arabella Stuart,* female heroics arise amid the political pathologies of men. In *Imelda,* it is a Romeo-and-Juliet-themed blood feud. This is no crisis of national principle (as in *The Switzer's Wife,* even *The Siege of Valencia*), just a degraded warfare in which female affectional strength is also female political impotence.

The daring heroine of *The Bride of the Greek Isle* is bound to no national cause either, just a culturally mapped traffic in women. To name the bride Eudora ("good gift") and to introduce her decked in jewels for transfer from "her father's hall" (28) to her groom is to figure woman as a commodity in a patriarchal economy that is the legitimate analogue of the pirate economy that abducts her for sale into slavery. The economic base was certainly what Hemans read in *Sardanapalus,* as her epigraphs from Byron's play make clear:

> Fear!—I'm a Greek, and how should I fear death?
> A slave, and wherefore should I dread my freedom?
>   * * * * * *
> I will not live degraded.

Untagged by speakers, these lines, even with ellipses, might seem to issue from one voice. You would have to know the play to know that this isn't the case: the first voice is a female Greek slave's, the second, her male owner's. They are meditating suicide, should a civil revolt succeed. Stripping the names from the claims, Hemans's epigraph equalizes what in Byron's play are the romantic pledges of politically asymmetrical, even diametrical, characters:

> SARDANAPALUS. ... dost thou fear?
> MYRRHA. Fear?—I'm a Greek, and how should I fear death?
> A slave, and wherefore should I dread my freedom?
> SARDANAPALUS. Then wherefore dost thou turn so pale?
> MYRRHA. I love.
> (1.2.478–81)
>
> SARDANAPALUS. Fate made me what I am—may make me nothing—
> But either that or nothing must I be:
> I will not live degraded.
> MYRRHA. Hadst thou felt
> Thus always, none would ever degrade thee.
> (1.2.627–30)

What caught Hemans's attention and gives the cue for the fatal revolt of her enslaved Greek Bride is the slave-owning monarch's refusal to live in the state he abides and adores in his lover. For him, suicide is preferable to exile or house arrest, an unacceptable loss of freedom. For the Greek sex-slave in exile, death, far from degradation, looks like an upgrade. As that supervisor of female writers, M. A. Stodart, recognized in one of her zigzags (a rare Wollstonecraft-like moment), gender is the political differential:

> How nobly does Dr. Channing, in his discourse against slavery, shew that man cannot bend to man *as man,* without being degraded by it! Alas! for poor woman, this servile degrading spirit tinctures the whole course of her training. (*Female Writers,* 28)

Hemans makes the woman's case through her aesthetic and figurative textures.

The primary figure is the paradise of girlhood. As in *Madeline,* female social fate, marriage, entails this paradise lost: "Will earth give love like *yours* again? / Sweet mother!" cries Eudora in farewell (73–74). Hemans pivots back to this love by aborting the marriage plot. The wedding is no sooner under way than pirate-slavers burst in, murder the groom and abduct the bride. Shifting the romance into heroic melodrama, Hemans stages a new bride-blazon for the "mother's gaze" (23), straining to see the pirate ship on a dark sea, and startled by a burst of flame:

>   It has taken the flag's high place in air,
>   And redden'd the stars with its wavy glare,
>   And sent out bright arrows, and soar'd in glee,
>   To a burning mount midst the moonlight sea.
>
>   . . . . .
>
>   . . . lo! a brand
>   Blazing up high in her lifted hand!
>   And her veil flung back, and her free dark hair
>   Sway'd by the flames as they rock and flare;
>   And her fragile form to its loftiest height
>   Dilated, as if by the spirit's might,
>   And her eye with an eagle-gladness fraught,—
>   Oh! could this work be of woman wrought?
>   Yes! 'twas her deed!—by that haughty smile
>   It was her's!—She hath kindled her funeral pile!   (195–98, 203–12)

As if kindled from the glances of Eudora's mysteriously resplendent eye, the fire dilates her meek femininity into a Byronic rebellion.[49] In Hemans's reading of Byron, the passion-driven, self-tormenting hero is a contingency of gender and culture that is open to substitution: a rebellious Corsair may be recast as a rebellious slave; a hero may pattern a heroine. With the investment of her own aesthetic energies, Hemans writes Eudora's revolt as an epiphany of female art, a work of woman wrought. The retaliatory blaze is a self-transformation from patriarchal gift into independent, eagle-gladness. Her formerly bound, bejeweled and braided hair and veiled face reappear, with the descriptive *free* (205), in the iconography of female revolutionary heroism.[50]

Byron's Myrrha is the pattern, heart-driven from slave-harem to battlefield:

>   her kindled cheek;
>   Her large black eyes that flash'd through her long hair
>   As it stream'd o'er her; her blue veins that rose
>   Along her most transparent brow; her nostril
>   Dilated from its symmetry . . .   (*Sardanapalus* 3.1.387–91)

No less than Byron, Hemans works the tacit contrasts of close affiliations: disheveled Cassandra's prophecy of Troy in flames, the virtual confession of murder in the way Gulnare (the self-liberated slave of *The Corsair*) "threw back her dark far-floating hair" (3.410); the male visionary erotics embodied in Shelleyan dream-maidens.[51] Without the taint of madness, homicide, or sexual ecstasy, Hemans orchestrates the report: "Man may not fetter, nor ocean tame / The might and wrath of the rushing flame!" (189) with cultural genetics ("Her blood was the Greek's, and hath made her free" (214) to cast Eudora for female liberation, escaping Man-fetters as the modern Promethea Unbound.

Yet nothing is more typical of Hemans than the death sentence on this symbolic drama and its seeming female apotheosis. The pattern of Staël's *Corinne* (female genius must die unhappy) was not just a cultural fad; it was Hemans's inner "feminine" calculus: the more rebellious a woman, the more vivid the aesthetic fireworks, the more necessary her death. In a perfection of the "feminine," the Bride's final fire is a marriage rite after all: a suttee, kin to the pyre on which Myrrha burns with the man she calls husband and master. In Hindi, *sati* (Englished as *suttee*) means *good woman*, the analogue of *Eudora*. When Hemans writes, "Proudly she stands, like an Indian bride / On the pyre with the holy dead" (215–16), the simile not only evokes the romance of the suttee as a second marriage, but also refuses the developing view of the rite as not merely anti-modern but an atrocity of (orientalized) patriarchal power.[52] It was outlawed by the Raj in 1829. A poem Hemans knew, Jewsbury's *Song, of the Hindoo Women, while accompanying a widow to the funeral pile of her husband,* sharpens the issue. A long epigraph from "Forbes' Oriental Memoirs" (1813) exposes the horror under the romance: the widow is a "living victim" who mounts the funeral pile, her limbs oiled, and "dressed in her bridal jewels, surrounded by relations, priests, and musicians"—the company not just celebratory but brutally necessary: "During the cremation, the noise of the trumpets and other musical instruments, overpowers the cries of the self-devoted victim, should her resolution fail her" (*devoted* carries the older sense of *doomed*).[53]

Writing in the mid-1820s, Jewsbury toned her *Song* as heroic tragedy; by 1831, just months before leaving for India, she had become an acerbic critic of the romanticized abomination, and said as much when she wrote a review in *The Athenæum* of Percy Ashworth's prize poem, *The Suttees:*

> Few have been the Suttees that have originated in simple love of the deceased, and unbiased desire to follow him;—independent of the extreme timidity and desolation of a Hindoo widow, many dark and extraneous influences have been known to cause her decision. In fact, by hundreds and thousands, the funeral pile has been gone to, merely as a fiery bed of refuge from a destitution and contempt that European women have no conception of. Thank God, these abominations are at an end. (643)

Hemans's *Bride* indulges the retro-romance for the sake of a glorious but impotent defiance. The Bride's blazing heroism is ultimately futile: "the slave and his master alike" escape from the ship, while she (like young Casabianca) "stands on the deck alone" (201–2). Her only triumph is a spectacular love-death.

Women and Fame

Still in the bookstores and on parlor shelves in Hemans's day was More's *Strictures*, advising that for a woman to enjoy her talents, or worse, to "exercise them as instruments for the acquisition of fame," was "subversive of her delicacy" (224).[54] The woman who lived her fame risked judgment as immodest, improper, degraded. Hence the anonymity, the pseudonyms, or the prefixing of a domestic "Mrs." in the published successes. Hemans trains her fascination with famous women into the containment of fatal narratives. In *The Last Banquet of Antony and Cleopatra* (in *Tales*), Cleopatra's power and pride occupy a stage of impending defeat:

> thou art by his side,
> In all thy sovereignty of charms array'd,
>   To meet the storm with still unconquer'd pride.
> Imperial being! e'en though many a stain
>   Of error be upon thee, there is power
> In thy commanding nature, which shall reign
>   O'er the stern genius of misfortune's hour
> And the dark beauty of thy troubled eye
> E'en now is all illumed with wild sublimity.   (52–60)

Yet for all the historical syntax of doom, the queen dazzles with imperial self-possession. Antony is the defeated one at this scene. And while Cleopatra's epithets, "enchantress-queen" (51) and "Proud siren of the Nile" (65), bear some taint, Hemans does not arraign a domestic truant. Her final salutation, "Daughter of Afric!" (72), hails a woman of global importance.

"Cleopatra" is a loaded sign, synonymous with the complication of fame and infamy, of pride and defeat, and synonymous, too, with "Antony and . . . " As a woman of fame without a partner, Hemans felt an economy of depletions. She was fixated on her tale of another "enchantress," this one "who, to win and secure the love of a mortal, sacrifices one of her supernatural gifts of power after another: [. . .] last of all, her immortality," and is "repaid by satiety—neglect—desertion." The "injurious influence" of this downward narrative forced her to abandon it, but it kept returning (*CMH* 2: 4–5).[55] The year after *Records*, she confided to a friend, "I have so often found a kind of relief in throwing the colouring of my own feelings over the destiny of historical characters, that it has almost become a habit of my mind" (2: 50–51). There is a poignant double-cross in *relief*: psychological therapy, and the aesthetic work (sculptural relief) that betrays it, casting characters as poet, their destiny as her almost-habit. *Habit* too plays double: unconscious tendency; costuming, the investment of art. In this "often-found" relay of characters and mind, the relief of writing exposes (raises) the feelings it would allay. The famous women of *Records of Woman* are a virtual relief-work of Hemans's uneasy self-measurings.

For her record of *the* woman of national fame—*Joan of Arc, in Rheims*—Hemans imports an epigraph from her own *Woman and Fame* (not yet published in 1828):

> Thou hast a charmed cup, O Fame!
>   A draught that mantles high,
> And seems to lift this earthly frame
>   Above mortality.
> Away! to me—a woman—bring
>   Sweet waters from affection's spring.

Staging this rejection in *Joan of Arc,* Hemans works to remediate this famed transgressor of the "limits prescribed to her sex" (so writes Hannah More, linking Joan with Amazon Queen Thalestris ["On Religion" 338]). She sets the record at the dauphin's coronation and its honors for Joan, to find the heart of a woman under the robes of triumph. Joan's "helm," the emblem of her fame, is transfigured into a halo around a "Woman" who shimmers in the cathedral as the angel in the house. Her military transvestism—as infamous as her heresy[56]–is all but effaced:

>   But who, alone
> And unapproach'd, beside the altar-stone,
> With the white banner, forth like sunshine streaming,
> And the gold helm, thro' clouds of fragrance gleaming,
> Silent and radiant stood?—the helm was rais'd,
> And the fair face reveal'd, that upward gaz'd,
>   Intensely worshipping:—a still, clear face,
> Youthful, but brightly solemn!—Woman's cheek
> And brow were there, in deep devotion meek,
>   Yet glorified with inspiration's trace
> On its pure paleness; while, enthron'd above,
> The pictur'd virgin, with her smile of love,
> Seem'd bending o'er her votaress.—That slight form!
> Was that the leader thro' the battle storm?   (17–30)

The female warrior shimmers into meek votress; and the "woman, mantled with victorious power" (36), this "Daughter of victory" (46), wants nothing more than to be restored as daughter of home. Echoing her epigraph, Hemans unfolds a syntax of restoration:

> And forth she came.—Then rose a nation's sound—
> Oh! what a power to bid the quick heart bound,
> The wind bears onward with the stormy cheer
> Man gives to glory on her high career!
> Is there indeed such power?—far deeper dwells
> In one kind household voice, to reach the cells
> Whence happiness flows forth!—The shouts that fill'd
> The hollow heaven tempestuously, were still'd
> One moment; and in that brief pause, the tone,
> As of a breeze that o'er her home had blown,
> Sank on the bright maid's heart.—"Joanne!"   (49–59)

Hemans sets the public cheer for Joan's "power" in elevations *(rose, high)* that prove a "hollow heaven." The "wind" of Man's acclaim is trumped by the "breeze" of home; the "deeper" dwelling of "one kind household voice" reverses the exaltations. What sinks into the heart is her home name, "Joanne!" not the title of fame, "Joan of Arc." When she recognizes her father and brothers, "She turn'd" (62), a physical pivot correlating a spiritual one: "She saw the pomp no more" (71) as "Her spirit turn'd" to heart and home (76–77).

Hemans writes this turn as "winning her back to nature" (81)—the real victory. When Joan removes the "helm of many battles" to let "her bright locks" fall (82–83)—sister of Spenser's Britomart—she could not be more feminine. Her loosened hair does not bode the liberated passions of the Wife of Asdrubal, Stephania, Eudora, the Indian Woman, or Maimuna (*The Indian City*). This daughter of victory is a prodigal daughter, begging for paternal (domestic and divine) restoration: "Bless me, my father, bless me! and with thee, / To the still cabin and the beechen-tree, / Let me return!" (85–87). In other histories, Joan is undone by male political treachery. In Hemans's record, she is undone by female fame, the unforgiving economy summed in the final lines:

> Oh! never did thine eye
> Thro' the green haunts of happy infancy
> Wander again, Joanne!—too much of fame
> Had shed its radiance on thy peasant-name;
> And bought alone by gifts beyond all price,
> The trusting heart's repose, the paradise
> Of home with all its loves, doth fate allow
> The crown of glory unto woman's brow. (87–94)

In the bad bargain of female fame, domestic paradise is forever lost. Hemans echoes Milton's elegy for Eve's first, and fatal separation from Adam: "Thou never from that hour in Paradise / Found'st either sweet repast, or sound repose" (*PL* 9.406–7).

Thus Hemans's self-measuring, at the height of her fame she looked back on "the comparative peace and repose of Bronwylfa and Rhyllon" (her childhood paradise) to sigh, "How have these things passed away from me, and how much more was I formed for their quiet happiness, than for the weary part of <u>femme célèbre</u> which I am now enacting!" (*HM* 176). Celebrity seems weary, stale, and flat and, however profitable, unreal, alien, empty. "Fame can only afford <u>reflected</u> delight to a woman," she tells Mitford; "How hollow sounds the voice of fame to an orphan!" (23 March and 10 November 1828; *CMH* 1: 159, 234)—as hollow as the cheers at Rheims. Hollow to the lovelorn, too. Hemans was haunted by Gibson's "statue of Sappho, representing her at the moment she receives the tidings of Phaon's desertion":

> There is a sort of <u>willowy</u> drooping in the figure which seems to express a weight of unutterable sadness, and one sinking arm holds the lyre so carelessly, that you almost fancy it will drop while you gaze. Altogether, it seems to speak piercingly and sorrowfully of the nothingness of fame, at least to woman. (*CMH* 2: 172–73)[57]

To Jewsbury, Sappho, "that lady of the lyre, two lovers, and leap" was "a great misfortune to after-poetesses" (*Athenæum* 236, 283). Hemans was her heiress. As if to supplement Gibson's silently expressive statue, she imagines *The Last Song of Sappho*, staging this poem at the moment of "desolate grace [. . .] penetrated with the feeling of utter abandonment" (headnote), just before that leap: "*Alone I come—oh! give me peace, dark sea!*" Sappho's leap bears none of the political resistance of the Suli mother or even the Indian Woman's protest against "woman's weary lot." Her voice speaks personal pain alone.

The Grave of a Poetess is Hemans's only record about a contemporary, and it is explicitly self-killing. Her "poetry has always touched me greatly from a similarity which I imagine I discover between her destiny and my own," she said of Mary Tighe (*CMH* 2: 212). Depleting the fame of the poetess, Hemans keeps Tighe's name out of the verse.[58] Even there, she says little about her poetry, beyond calling it a "light of song . . . shrined" in "woman's mind" (15–17), or rather, "a sorrow in thy song" (45). What fixes her imagination is a woman's delivery from the pains of life on "mortal ground" (49): "Now peace the woman's heart hath found, / And joy the poet's eye" (51–52).[59] Shifting her title's *Poetess* (the cultural capital) to "poet," then divorcing "poet" from "woman's heart," Hemans arrays the conflicts. Visiting the grave three years later, she "env[ied] the repose of her who slept there" (*CMH* 2: 211). The genre of woman and fame is what L.E.L. grasped in her reciprocal elegy, *Stanzas on the Death of Mrs. Hemans*, in which she gave Hemans the tribute of the repose she imagined for Tighe:

> Didst thou not tremble at thy fame,
>   And loathe its bitter prize,
> While what to others triumph seemed
>   To thee was sacrifice? (73–77)

L.E.L. hopes that Hemans's signature genre, the "sorrowful" song, will at last find the solace it seeks: "The hopes of which it breathes, are hopes/That look beyond the tomb" (43–44). This wasn't just Hemans's weary lot, she proposes, but what all poets suffer into song: "The meteor wreath the poet wears/Must make a lonely lot;/It dazzles, only to divide/From those who wear it not" (69–72). But as L.E.L. knew, the divisions for woman were also internal, an alienation not just from public dazzle but also from her own talents.

Hemans's hymns against female fame entered the record of her fame, with split reception among female poets. Sighing at L.E.L.'s elegy, Elizabeth Barrett was irritated by the infection of Hemans-melancholy ("the quick tears are in my eyes,/And I can write no more," are L.E.L.'s last lines). She answered in the next issue of *New Monthly Magazine* with *Stanzas Addressed to Miss Landon, and Suggested by her "Stanzas on the Death of Mrs Hemans."* Consigning Hemans to the grateful dead, her life of mourning at an end, she also gently parodies her signature anguish, urging L.E.L. not to "mourn, oh living one, because/*Her* part in life was mourning," and asking, "Would she have lost the poet's flame,/For anguish of the burning?" (25–28). Yet for all her wry impatience, Barrett was on the same page with Hemans's records of the strictures on female fame, especially for the artist. Chorley (an intimate friend of both) directly connected *Aurora Leigh* to one of the most famous of the *Records, Properzia Rossi*.[60]

Rossi is that familiar Hemans-alter ego, fatally lovelorn and alienated from her art: "Worthless fame!/That in *his* bosom wins not for my name/Th' abiding place it ask'd" (81–83). This final reckoning is forecast by the epigraph—unsigned and, like *Woman and Fame,* Hemans's own. *Properzia Rossi* is thus set in Hemans's professional genealogy:

> Have I not lov'd, and striven, and fail'd to bind
> One true heart unto me, whereon my own
> Might find a resting-place, a home for all
> Its burden of affections? I depart,
> Unknown, tho' Fame goes with me; I must leave
> The earth unknown. Yet it may be that death
> Shall give my name a power to win such tears
> As would have made life precious.

If the division of Fame and the unknown self may vex men too, Hemans's emphasis on the burden of affections is what makes this a record of woman. Giving a pattern to Tennyson's *Lady of Shalott*, Rossi hopes her art might serve her heart, as her proxy to her beloved Knight:

> Something immortal of my heart and mind,
> That yet may speak to thee when I am gone,
> Shaking thine inmost bosom with a tone
> Of lost affection;—something that may prove
> What she hath been, whose melancholy love
> On thee was lavish'd. (10–15)

Hemans keeps Rossi always aware that the fantasy of posthumous connection is only futile sublimation by another name: "It comes,—the power / Within me born, flows back; my fruitless dower / That could not win me love" (25–27). The counterpoint rhyme of "power" and "fruitless dower" captures the zero-sum economy. Rossi's final hope is not for immortal art, but (in another repeated rhyme [81–82; 118/121]) a collapse her "fame" into a "name" that one day may move the Knight to pained recognition: "*'Twas her's who lov'd me well!*" (128).

Yet Hemans's headnote to this record conveys a strangely discrepant intuition:

> Properzia Rossi, a celebrated female sculptor of Bologna, possessed also of talents for poetry and music, died in consequence of an unrequited attachment.—A painting by Ducis, represents her showing her last work, a basso-relievo of Ariadne, to a Roman Knight, the object of her affection, who regards it with indifference.

Rossi is cast into the relief as a later love-forsaken Ariadne, but Hemans closes with a hint that the Knight is a worthless dolt, more like Theseus than Rossi may realize. If it's not clear whether Hemans means pathos or satire, it is clear that she skewed her report of Jean-Louis Ducis's *La Sculpture de Properzia de Rossi* (exhibited in Paris in 1822) to a display of the Knight's "indifference." Ducis shows Rossi unveiling her Ariadne to a raptly adoring courtier, and makes Rossi herself look at this moment like a statue come to life, a Pygmalion romance for the 1820s.[61] Hemans forces art and heart into opposition, and implies that the man is not worth it.

Hemans's self-reflecting records are her most divided ledgers, especially on the question of artistic fame and lost love. The pedagogical designs of two late-career poems, *Corinne at the Capitol*, and *Women and Fame* (both written for popular annuals), are palpably strained by wayward aesthetic effects. The pedagogy of *Corinne* is a frame of cautionary epigraph and didactic final stanza:

> Radiant daughter of the sun!
> Now thy living wreath is won.
> Crown'd of Rome!—Oh! art thou not
> Happy in that glorious lot?—
> Happy—happier far than thou,
> With the laurel on thy brow,
> She that makes the humblest hearth
> Lovely but to one on earth! (41–48)

The epigraph is from Corinne *avant la lettre*, Madame de Staël:

> Les femmes doivent pense qu'il est dans cetter carrière bien peu de sorts que puissent valoir la plus obscure vie d'une femme aimée et d'une mère heureuse.[62]

That *femme* means both *woman* and *wife* is the stricture on Corinne's laurel crown.[63] Hemans's intertext is Staël's *Corinne, ou l'Italie*, the subtitle a crucial signifier. In the crowd enchanted by Corinne at the Capitol is Englishman Oswald Nelvil, who admits that at home he would have disdained such a woman, but "he did not apply any social conventions to Italy" (20); this is his exotic vacation, and he will jilt Corinne for a proper English wife. In place of Nelvil, Hemans arrays the gaze of an Englishwoman who can't avoid a final ambivalence:

> Thou hast gained the summit now!
> Music hails thee from below;—
> Music, whose rich notes might stir
> Ashes of the sepulchre;
> Shaking with victorious notes
> All the bright air as it floats.
> Well may woman's heart beat high
> Unto that proud harmony! (17–24)

The hesitant "well may" glances at the melancholy close of Staël's novel: Corinne jilted, fatally. Byron, for one, hated the implied moral, protesting to Staël herself how "dangerous it was to inculcate the belief that genius, talent, acquirements, and accomplishments, such as Corinne was represented to possess, could not preserve a woman from becoming a victim to an unrequited passion, and that reason, absence, and female pride were unavailing" (*BCB* 260); when his literate Italian mistress Teresa Guiccioli read his comment, she marked the margin. Byron was right about the danger. It was the novel's conclusion, far more than Corinne's dazzling debut, that impressed, possessed Hemans: "its close [. . .] has a power over me which is quite indescribable; some passages seem to give me back my own thoughts and feelings, my whole inner being."[64]

Yet between Hemans's headnote and her didactic coda falls not the shadow, but the electric romance of Corinne at the Capitol: genius, talent, acquirements, accomplishments. In the version published in the 1827 *Literary Souvenir*, the title-name is "Corinna," recalling the poet of Greek antiquity famed to have won five victories over Pindar for the lyric prize. In *Songs of Affections* Hemans sets her title to match that of *Corinne*, Book II, where, with Nelvil, we first see the modern Corinna, performing in all her glory.[65] Staël elaborates her triumph, giving all of "Corinne's Improvisation at the Capitol" and concluding in apotheosis: "No longer a fearful woman, she was an inspired priestess, joyously devoting herself to the cult of genius" (32). Hemans reports this apotheosis across 42 1/2 lines of glowing words: *fires, Joyously, festal, triumphs, glory bright, golden light, ascending, freedom, proudly, gemlike, summit, rich, music, victorious notes, proud harmony, thrilling power, tide of rapture, flush*, "the joy of kindled thought / And the burning words of song." That her moralizing coda can't sustain more than 5 1/2 lines is an exemplary Hemans-pattern of the conflict between cultural logic and aesthetic energy.

Hemans's repeated returns to this conflict never resolve it. Intertextually charged by an epigraph composed from the last four lines of *Corinne at the Capitol* (45–48, above), *Woman and Fame* is set to disparage fame against the durable nurture of "home-born love." "What is fame to a heart yearning for affection, and finding it not?" Hemans wrote in a notebook early in 1827, and stayed to answer: "Is it not as a triumphal crown to the brow of one parched with fever, and asking for one fresh healthful draught—the 'cup of cold water'?"[66] But *Woman and Fame* proves another poem at war with itself. Its lesson proceeds with a litany of cautions:

> Fame! Fame! thou canst not be the stay
>   Unto the drooping reed,
> The cool fresh fountain, in the day
>   Of the soul's feverish need. (25–28)

Nothing is more typical of Hemans than what she lets slip of Fame before, and in anticipation of, this final rejection:

> Thou hast a voice, whose thrilling tone
>   Can bid each life-pulse beat,
> As when a trumpet's note hath blown,
>   Calling the brave to meet. (13–16)

The effect of this thrilling voice is as subversive as Keats's poet realizing that mortal life, for all its transience versus art's "forever," is "breathing human passion" (*Ode on a Grecian Urn*). Hemans's *life-pulse* is as critical a concession as Keats's *breathing*, and although she tries to shore up her lesson ("A hollow sound is in thy song, / A mockery in thine eye" [19–20]), the Woman doth protest too much. Her last stanza can only turn away, not toward any alternative:

> Fame, Fame! thou canst not be the stay
>   Unto the drooping reed,
> The cool fresh fountain, in the day
>   Of the soul's feverish need;
> Where must the lone one turn or flee?—
> Not unto thee, oh! not to thee!   (25–30)

With no positive answer, only "not to thee," the question points to a no-Woman's land between the "record of one happy hour" at home (12) and a record of Woman obliquely romancing fame across her determined refusals.

A less famous Maria Jewsbury married, went to India (where her husband was posted as chaplain), and soon died in the cholera plague. Devastated by the news, Hemans attempted a curious consolation in imagining her friend's escape from a worse fate. Fresh from reading the *Athenæum*'s obituary, she wrote to a friend,

> With all my regret, I had rather, a thousand times, that she had perished thus in the path of her duties and the brightness of her <u>improving</u> mind, than become, what I once feared was likely, the merely brilliant creature of London life: <u>that</u> is, indeed, a worthless lot of a nobly-gifted woman's nature! (*CMH* 2: 314–15).[67]

She traced out these alternate paths more than once:

> How much deeper power seemed to lie <u>coiled up</u>, as it were, in the recesses of her mind, than was ever manifested to the world in her writings [. . .] the full and finished harmony never drawn forth! Yet I would rather, a thousand times, that she should have perished thus, in the path of her chosen duties, than have seen her become the merely brilliant creature of London literary life, living upon those poor <u>succès de société</u>, which I think utterly ruinous to all that is lofty, and holy, and delicate in the nature of a highly-endowed woman. (28 June 1834; *CMH* 2: 312–13)

Jane Williams would quote these sentences as a caution in *Literary Women* (378–79), but Hemans's emphases tell a more complicated tale. She pretends that the choice is between the path of duties and poor *succès de société*, but her deeper question is the fate of any "highly-endowed woman." The hyperbole of "a thousand times" in her wish for Jewsbury's life-unto-death as a dutiful wife does not suppress her admiration for Jewsbury's power of mind and her fascination with its coils of never-expressed energy (any more than the lesson of Corinne's misery eclipses the dazzle of her performance). In the glints of this latency, the alternative to the fatal path of duties is not hollow fame (that's easily disparaged), but something Hemans could not yet, in the binds and blinds of her cultural moment, fully imagine for a highly-endowed woman.

Writing about Jewsbury, she was writing about herself, especially that part animated by Jewsbury's enthusiasm, her rare company, her force of confirmation. What bonded the two was a commitment to "literary work and literary ambition" that each felt "free both to reveal in herself and recognize in the other" (Norma Clarke nicely perceives; 75). Jewsbury was one of the "very few indeed" to whom Hemans was "fully <u>unsealed</u>" (*CMH* 2: 314):

> my spirits have been depressed ever since the tidings of my poor friend's death arrived. I never expected to meet her again in this life, but there was a strong chain of interest between us, that spell of <u>mind on mind</u>, which, once formed, can never be broken. I felt, too, that my whole nature was understood and appreciated by her, and this is a sort of happiness which I consider the most rare in all earthly affection. (*CMH* 2: 313–14)

The romance of mind on mind, spelling a whole nature not limited to set forms, implies an alternative marriage, a bond of female affection free from the usual scripts of the "feminine."

Before she had been hailed (not without her bid) into the cult of the "feminine," the gender of Hemans's pen was less settled. She baffled the *British Review*'s radar with her unsigned *Modern Greece* (1817), its "high polish" and "classical" modeling seeming "the production of an academical, and certainly not a female, pen" (15: 299). But a decade on, the female pen was her hallmark: "Were there to be a feminine literary house of commons, Felicia Hemans might very worthily be called to fill the chair as the speaker—a representative of the whole body, as distinguished from the other estates of the intellectual realm," was Jewsbury's verdict, in an unsigned essay for the *Athenæum*, 12 February 1831 (104). Jewsbury's "Felicia Hemans" is distinctly feminine/not masculine; yet other views read the conflicts: "of genius struggling, if not borne down, under the pressure of worldly cares,—of a powerful mind strictly fettered, yet ever compelled to exertion,—of a brilliant and buoyant fancy restrained and overcharged by 'the aching weight' and heaviness of a wounded heart," was how another friend from the 1830s, Rose Lawrence, drew the portrait of Hemans (363). In the unsettled shifting between the spear of a Minerva and the careworn romance of the domestic affections abide Hemans's truest records as the "Poet of Womanhood."

CHAPTER THREE

The Generations of "Masculine" Woman

> It has been much the fashion, of late, to write and talk about women's minds, and to make comparative estimates of the power of female and masculine intellect—
>
> —M. J. J. PHANTASMAGORIA

In the comparative estimate of sex-masked M.J.J., the genders play asymmetrically, even ambivalently: female is sexed; but "masculine," as Maria Jane Jewsbury's heroes Macaulay and Wollstonecraft argued, is not for men only. As much was said of M.J.J. herself, from *Phantasmagoria* to her reviews for *The Athenæum* in the early 1830s, which she could write in the unmarked anonymity of the corporate voice, sometimes in a masculine character. She was one of the few women on editor Charles Wentworth Dilke's staff, the only unmarried one.[1] Thought a rare one, praised as "masculine," freighted with female-fated domestic cares for most of her life, burning with professional ambition, reluctant to marry, then suddenly married to a fatal course, and all the while reckoning with the toxic, irrepressible legacy of Wollstonecraft, Jewsbury zigzagged the borders, testing various authorial identities, some gendered, some not: "M.J.J.," poet "Miss Jewsbury," "Maria Jane Jewsbury" the "historian," or anonymous.[2]

Jewsbury's Difference

I first bumped into Jewsbury in the letters of William and Dorothy Wordsworth; she intrigued me because she intrigued them. Here was a professional female writer who didn't spark the antipathies to "literary ladies" that "Mrs. Hemans" irritated in the household. Jewsbury was often described as having a *masculine* mind and manner of writing. What did this gendering mean in the era of her career—the 1820s and early 30s—in light of, or rather, the shadows, of the derogatory cast for women in the anti-establishment politics of the 1790s? By the 1820s, the ghost of Wollstonecraft was all but vanquished in the cult of the "poetess"—that icon of "feminine" propriety. For better or worse, the "masculine" woman conjured this binary, and a favorite name was "Mrs. Hemans." It was after he dubbed "Mrs. Hemans" the "most feminine writer of the day" that George Gilfillan proceeded in his next installment of "Female Authors" for *Tait's Edinburgh Magazine* to honor "Mrs. Elizabeth Barrett Browning" as "the most masculine of our female writers" (ns 14 [1847]: 620). Jewsbury was the first Hemans binary: "It was scarcely possible to imagine two individual natures more strikingly contrasted," said Hemans's own sister, Harriett Hughes (in her memoir of 1839): "the one so intensely feminine, so susceptible and imaginative, so devoted to the tender and the beautiful; the other endowed with masculine energies, with a spirit that seemed born for ascendency, with strong powers of reasoning, fathomless profundity of thought" (*HM* 142).[3]

From the get-go, Jewsbury's wit flashed "not-feminine." Reading the *Manchester Gazette* in 1823, Alaric Watts was delighted by the "vein of humour" in her verses, a "rare quality in women's writings at that day" (Watts 1: 182), and he set out to encourage her talent. The result was a two-volume debut, *Phantasmagoria; or, Sketches of Life and Literature* (1825). Like his father, Watts Jr. liked the rare "virility of [. . .] humour" and "keenness of [. . .] intellect," especially "in the writings of women" (1: 184, 204). *Literary Chronicle* just assumed "M.J.J." was "he" (336: 673).[4] Though *Literary Magnet* had heard about "a young lady," it still wanted to register the non sequitur of the writer's sex and the writing's gender: "so nervous and masculine a character, that we should have supposed it to have proceeded from some experienced male writer" (239).[5] The "sketches of life and manners" might rank with the best of Washington Irving (235). Not only was the "character" of her writing "masculine"; it seemed male in information, physiological and experiential.

Masculine, in these measures, is the name of intellectual force and interest. Macaulay's *History of England*, said *European Magazine* in 1783, is "strong, nervous and eloquent, untinctured with the weakness of a female pen; and breathing sentiments of the most manly" (4: 330). In 1790, *General Magazine* praised the "masculine turn" of mind and pen: behold this "bold and nervous writer" (they said), full of "vigour and dexterity" and none of that "feminine [. . .] language of indignant passion" (543). M.J.J. endorsed this value mark, admiring the "masculine intellect" of Jane Taylor and Hannah More (*P* 1: 47–48) and the "masculine mind" of Kennava, a governor's wife who, during a siege of 1573, displayed a double endowment: "the foresight and self-possession which dignify man,—the ardour and self-devotion which characterise woman" (2: 38–39). In her unsigned essays for *The Athenæum*, M.J.J. continued to put a female purchase on "masculine," urging that smart girls be given a curriculum "in some degree sound, masculine, invigorating and comprehensive" so as to cultivate "grave, sound, masculine knowledge"—the adjectival company at once a positive credential and a sign of the negative feminine binary.[6]

This masculine goal was far from policy, however, and it trailed a history from the culture wars of the 1790s, in coalition with *Amazon, virago, monster,* even *man*.[7] Thus *Critical Review* (1792) justified its "ad hominem" on Wollstonecraft: "it means man or woman—either exclusively man, or those *manly females* who endeavour to imitate men" (2d ser. 4: 392). The *Anti-Jacobin*'s debut issue (1797) played it both ways, spoofing the "Muse of *Jacobinism*" not only as a masculine *she,* but a bad male drag act: "in whatever disguise she appears, [. . .] like *Sir John Brute* in woman's clothes, she is betrayed by her drunken swagger and ruffian tone" (1: 6)—*she* covering the Jacobin muse and the transvestite man in vulgar twinship. If, as Nicola Trott observes, "the moral, ideological and generic outrages of jacobinism all cohere in the image of a cross-dressing, transgressing, trans-sexing female" (36), Wollstonecraft's *Rights of Woman* issued a pre-emptive strike, not only refuting the "bugbear" of "the word masculine" (113) but proactively vindicating it.[8] For strong-minded women "hunted out of society as masculine" (144), she would polish the stigma into a badge of honor, while awaiting a "REVOLUTION in female manners" (341).

There were some successful turns by the end of the 90s. In 1798 Joanna Baillie, a writer who mattered immensely to Jewsbury no less than to Hemans, endowed her Wollstonecrafted satirist in *Count Basil* (Countess Albini) with a "mind" that "procures to her the privilege of man" in social esteem (2.4.114–15).[9] Yet a negative transvaluation was always potential, especially if it could involve Wollstonecraft. In some reviews today, with two centuries' hindsight, these shifts of *masculine* look like a mere recasting of old parts, the gender values still in place. In the 1790s, the gesture was conspicuously counter-cultural. Fordyce's *Sermons to Young Women* (1765; and still a best-seller in the 90s) bristled with cautions about "masculine women" raiding "the province of men," a territory he mapped out as "War, commerce, politics, exercises of strength and dexterity, abstract philosophy, and all the abstruser sciences" (1: 272). In a sentence that really irked Wollstonecraft (*VRW* 219–20), young women were lectured that "manly exercises are never graceful," that any "tone and figure [. . .] of the masculine kind, are always forbidding" (2: 224–25). Especially as a marriage prospect (warned the reverend), a "masculine woman must be naturally an unamiable creature": if she "throws off all the lovely softness of her nature, and emulates the daring intrepid temper of a man," she earns the judgment, "how terrible!" The "transformation [. . .] must ever be monstrous"—the unnatural twin to the "effeminate fellow" (1: 104). The masculine she is no borderventurer; this creature is beyond the pale.

The double bind of this monster-sighting for women was the uncomplimentary norm, as Macaulay and Wollstonecraft were quick to see in one of the touchstones: Pope's moral essay, *Of the Characters of Women*. The frequency with which its maxims got cited testifies to his shrewdness in attributing to a Lady the view that "Most Women have no Characters at all" (2), his boldness in spinning "Fine by defect, and delicately weak" (44) into a compliment (redeeming Adam's rant about woman as the "fair defect / Of nature" [*PL* 10.891–92]), and his summary "Picture of an esteemable Woman, made up of the best kind of Contrarieties." The faint praise was all too legible in the casting of "best kind" as a factory second: "Heav'n, when it strives to polish all it can / Its last best work, but forms a softer Man" (271–72). If "softer Man" may be a compliment to woman, it's still no proper man.[10] It is this degraded formation that Macaulay summons to the front line of polemic in her *Letters on Education* (1790). Gender language is not nature, she argues in the letter titled "*No characteristic Difference in Sex*" (XXII); it's a discourse. If in the social index, "the virtues of the males" turn out to have "displayed a bolder and more consistent picture of excellence than female nature has hitherto done," this is the accident of education and opportunity, reified in a linguistic norm:[11] "when we compliment the appearance of a more than ordinary energy in the female mind, we call it masculine; and hence it is, that Pope has elegantly said *a perfect woman's but a softer man.*" Macaulay is sharp on the force of contingency: accidents might be appealed to a common "rule of moral excellence for beings made of the same materials, organized after the same manner, and subjected to similar laws of Nature": we can do it Pope's way, or we can "we must reverse the proposition, and say, that *a perfect man is a woman formed after a coarser mold*" (204). (And how, she implies, should Pope's elegance be gendered?)

In the spirit of such reversals, and with a wish that Macaulay's intervention "might have been carried much farther," Wollstonecraft opens her essay on *Let-*

ters in *Analytical Review* (Nov. 1790; one of her longest), giving Macaulay the benefit of Macaulay. Upgrading Pope's view of the best woman as a softer man, Wollstonecraft advances a primary claim for Macaulay: this is a "masculine and fervid writer" with "very superior powers of [. . .] mind" (241; *W* 7: 309). *Rights of Woman* is punctuated throughout with a Macaulayan contempt of Pope's so-called "Moral Essay" on sexual character. "Men are allowed by moralists to cultivate, as Nature directs, different qualities, and assume the different characters" that passions give to individuals, while women "are to be levelled [. . .] into one character of yielding softness and gentle compliance" (*VRW* 219). It is this leveling, Wollstonecraft proposes, and not any "bold attempt to emulate masculine virtues," that deforms women, working in alliance with the Pope-puffed female culture of "indolence and vanity—the love of pleasure and the love of sway" (313)—an allusion to other lines in *Characters of Women* that don't even pretend to praise.[12]

Masculine Shows

No small project of *Rights of Woman* is a rehabilitation of the "masculine" woman, right from the start, against the grain of a culturally revered "femininity" that is mere "slavish dependence" by another name (111):

> from every quarter have I heard exclamations against masculine women; but where are they to be found? If by this appellation men mean to inveigh against their ardour in hunting, shooting, and gaming, I shall most cordially join in the cry; but if it be against the imitation of manly virtues, or, more properly speaking, the attainment of those talents and virtues, the exercise of which ennobles the human character, [. . .] comprehensively termed mankind;—all those who view them with a philosophic eye must, I should think, wish with me, that they may every day grow more and more masculine. (*VRW* 110)

This is more than a critique of gender-policing. It is a satire of man-show antics susceptible of female masquerade, paired to a proposal (and demonstration) of a rational measure for "masculine" to which women might aspire in a culture open to liberal exercise.

In the same year (1792) that Wollstonecraft was urging both men and women to "become more masculine and respectable" (*VRW* 113), Charlotte Smith was also analyzing system, protesting in her preface to her political novel *Desmond* the censure of women "as affecting masculine knowledge if they happen to have any understanding" (45). No wonder Wollstonecraft craved a republic of letters, linguistic and practical, in which genderings would not just be an open assignment, but would fall away. She paves the way by citing Macaulay as a case "of intellectual acquirements supposed to be incompatible with the weakness of her sex," then describing "her style of writing" as one in which "no sex appears, for it is like the sense it conveys, strong and clear." *Sex* means female sex (a standard locution), but Wollstonecraft refuses the implied binary: "I will not call hers a masculine understanding, because I admit not of such an arrogant assumption of reason" (*VRW* 231).

Mary Hays made the point with a satire on assumption. Heroine Emma Courtney, given free range of her father's library to indulge a passion for Plutarch's *Lives* as well as novels, has to suffer the censures of a man of fashion up on his Fordyce:

> "This lady reads, then"—said our accomplished coxcomb—"Heavens, Mr Courtney! you will spoil all her feminine graces; knowledge and learning, are insufferably masculine in a woman—born only for the soft solace of man! The mind of a young lady should be clear and unsullied, like a sheet of white paper, or her own fairer face: lines of thinking destroy the dimples of beauty; aping the reason of man, they lose the exquisite, *fascinating* charm, in which consists their true empire." (*The Memoirs of Emma Courtney* [1796] 57)

In Hays's lines of thinking, the true ape is this accomplished coxcomb. What is "masculine in a woman" is nothing more deviant than intellect.

Hays sharpens satire into polemic in *Appeal to the Men of Great Britain in Behalf of Woman* (1798). Against the Fordycing that "knowledge renders women masculine, and consequently disgusting," she wields a "two-edged sword" of rebuttal: not only is learning *not* deformative, but a masculine woman is not "infallibly disagreeable to the men" (172–73). Her binary for the "truly masculine" woman—that *she* "possessed of mental accomplishments" (178)—is not the oft praised lass of "essentially feminine" social accomplishments, but the man of no accomplishment at all. To refute the slandering of female intellect, she refreshes Wollstonecraft's he-man cartoon with a riff on the coxcomb's term of censure for pathetic aspiration, "aping": if a masculine woman is

> one who apes the exercises, the attributes, the unrestrained passions, and the numberless improprieties, which men fondly *chuse* to think suitable enough for their own sex—and which excesses to say the truth after all, chiefly distinguish their moral characters from those of women [. . .] such are masculine in the worst sense of the word. (*Appeal* 179–80)

Like Wollstonecraft, Hays plays male brands of gender into travesty. Making "masculine" a theater of apery in which a woman can suit up (be "suitable"), she slyly casts men into a by-the-book "feminine" character (fondly chosen, over-passionate, sex-distinguished by excess).

No less than Macaulay, Hays means to identify a linguistic system that is a contingency of culture and no rigid law of exclusion: that "firmness of character, and greatness of mind commonly esteemed masculine."[13] The linguistic custom is analogous, as even M. A. Radcliffe was willing to suggest in 1799, to costume: we "dress out" the "virtues and accomplishments of the sexes" in different manners "to suit a reigning taste" (*Female Advocate* 174). Though staying shy of systemic critique, she was willing to set *masculine* as a textual effect. While not every woman may possesses "the Amazonian spirit of a Wolstonecraft," she wrote in her Introduction, "unremitted oppression is sometimes a sufficient apology for their throwing off the gentle garb of a female, and assuming some more masculine appearance" (xi). Read in this fashion, Hays's "masculine woman" names no freak of nature but a performative impulse quite esteemable, and a formation not unmarriageable:

> If we are to understand by a masculine woman, one who emulates those virtues and accomplishments, which as common to human nature, are common to both sexes; the attempt is natural, amiable, and highly honorable to that woman, under whatever name her conduct may be disguised or censured. (*Appeal* 173–74)

Suspecting a male interest in restricting masculine license, Mary Robinson (using a pseudonym in 1799) focused on the policing, or in her word, policy:

> Prejudice (or policy) has endeavoured, and indeed too successfully, to cast an odium on what is called a *masculine* woman; or, to explain the meaning of the word, a woman of enlightened understanding. Such a being is too formidable in the circle of society to be endured, much less sanctioned. Man is a despot by nature; he can bear no equal, he dreads the power of woman. (*A Letter to the Women of England* 72)

Robinson traces the power play of policy; Hays mocked the foundational prejudice: "the present age furnishes examples enough, that women may be truly masculine in their conduct and demeanor, without wounding the delicacy of the men" (*Appeal* 180). She had in mind such prescriptions as Fordyce's: "men of sensibility desire in every woman soft features, and a flowing voice, a form, not robust, and demeanour delicate and gentle" (*Sermons* 2: 225); it's not just that "the character peculiar to each sex seems to require a difference" (1: 105), but that men of sensibility require a hyper-feminized difference in order to secure their character as "masculine."

Did Jewsbury finally enjoy the advantage of "no sex" for which these rationalist women were contending? Improving on the praise of M.J.J.'s masculine wit, Chorley was happy to admire her "great natural powers of reasoning" (in contrast to Hemans's poetic flights of fancy) without rushing to say "masculine" (*CMH* 1: 172). In other quarters, however, Jewsbury had to pass muster as a lady. At the meeting of *Noctes Ambrosianae* in *Blackwood's* December 1829 issue "Miss Jewsbury" was vetted by Shepherd (James Hogg, the Ettrick Shepherd) and Christopher North, the Ambrose-Tavern *nom de plume* of John Wilson.

> SHEPHERD. I often wush that we had some leddies at the Noctes. [. . .] Next time she comes to Embro', we'll hae the Hemans, and she'll aiblins sing to us some o' her ain beautifu' sangs. [. . .] wunna you ask Miss Jewesbury to the first male and female Noctes? She's really a maist superior lassie.
>
> NORTH. Both in prose and verse. Her Phantasmagoria, two miscellaneous volumes, teem with promise and performance. Always acute and never coarse——
>
> SHEPHERD. Qualities seldom separable in a woman. See Leddy Morgan.
>
> NORTH. But Miss Jewesbury is an agreeable exception. Always acute and never coarse, this amiable and most ingenious young leddy——
>
> SHEPHERD. Is she bonny? [. . .] I'm thinkin' Miss Jewesbury maun be a bit bonny lassie, wi' an expressive face and fine figure; and, no to minch the maitter, let me just tell you at ance, that it's no in your power, Mr North, to praise wi' ony warmth o cordiality neither an ugly woman nor an auld ane—but let them be but young and fresh and fair [. . .] pretendin' a' the while that it's their *genius* you're admirin'—whereas, it's not their genius ava, bu the living temple in which it is enshrined.
>
> NORTH. I plead guilty to that indictment. Ugly women are shocking anomalies, that ought to be hunted, hooted, and hissed out of every civilized and Christian community into a convent in Cockaigne. But no truly ugly woman ever yet wrote a truly beautiful poem the length of her little finger . . . (*Blackwood's* 26: 871–73)

Cockaigne, in Blackwood's-speak, is the Cockney realm of gender deformities like prancing Leigh Hunt and his ephebe Johnny Keats. By the 1820s, Lady Morgan had succeeded Wollstonecraft as gender fodder of choice. The age of chivalry is not dead for these ambrosial knights: female beauty is all; admiration of genius is either a front for lasciviousness, or of no consequence. Whatever *Phantasmagoria* may have performed or promised, the author must be a fine bonny lassie.

The standard of refinement, as Jeffrey's essay on Hemans in the same year shows, could easily sift female weakness. Jameson took this measure in 1832 at the start of *Characteristics of Women*, a Pope-ish title tuned to a refutation of Wollstonecraft:

> We hear it asserted, not seldom by way of compliment to us women, that intellect is of no sex. If this mean that the same faculties of mind are common to men and women, it is true; in any other signification it appears to me false, and the reverse of a compliment. The intellect of woman bears the same relation to that of man as her physical organization—it is inferior in power, and different in kind. That certain women have surpassed certain men in bodily strength or intellectual energy does not contradict the general principle founded in nature. (31)

The year before she had argued this case across political history, declaring in her preface to *Memoirs of Celebrated Female Sovereigns*, "the power which belongs to us, as a sex, is not properly, or naturally, that of the sceptre or the sword" (xiii). Reviewer Jewsbury lit into the unexamined contradiction:

> if Mrs. Jameson proves that women have no business to succeed to the sceptre, how will she prove that they have any right to wield the pen? Power is power; and the power of disseminating opinions is not much less valuable than that of holding a levee or opening parliament. There is sufficient prejudice undestroyed, without women, and women of mind helping its diffusion. (*Athenæum* 12, 211: 731)

Yet for all this acuity, Jewsbury had to concede the undestroyed prejudice in print and in life. It had ably survived the intrepid gender critiques and savvy reversals of the 1790s.

Even Wollstonecraft could not prevail over it, and found herself refeminized in reception as a condition of praise. In 1796, the *British Critic* welcomed her Scandinavian *Letters* for "joining to a *masculine* understanding, the finer sensibilities of a female": those polemics of "extensive information and considerable powers of reasoning" were "masculine"; *Letters* outs the feminine, "that delicateness and liveliness of feeling which is the peculiar characteristic of the sex" (602–3). It was a character even Hays and Godwin curated in posthumous spin: the "high masculine tone" of *Rights of Woman*, proposed Hays, was a "performance" of sometimes regrettable "coarseness," yet elsewhere "softened and blended with a tenderness of sentiment, an exquisite delicacy of feeling" (*Annual Necrology* 423).[14] Godwin's *Memoirs* also bracketed the polemic: if some phases had "a rather masculine" cast or a "rigid, and somewhat amazonian temper," this was a "performance" calculated to "repel" antagonists, a "character *pro tempore*" discontinuous with the "feminine" person known for "a luxuriance of imagination, and a trembling delicacy of sentiment, which would have done honour to a poet, bursting with all the visions of an Armida and a Dido"—those epic heroines who, for all their powers, kill themselves when abandoned by the men they love, as Wollstonecraft herself tried to do more than once. Not pausing over this retrovision, Godwin produces a "lovely" Wollstonecraft, engagingly "feminine in her manners" (75–76).

Such terms of engagement were hard to break. Forty years on, restlessly homebound Elizabeth Barrett could still put mind-forged manacles on the figure of "the literary woman." Having heard that formidable poet, playwright, and translator of Petrarch Lady Dacre (Barbarina Brand) was "a <u>woman of the masculine gender</u>, with her genius very prominent in eccentricity of manner & sentiment," and she sighed in relief to meet "much gentleness & womanlyness" (3 July 1838; *Letters to Mitford* 1: 80). How unlike Jewsbury's fantasy of a smitten reader finding the "fair author" of "some poetic effusion of female genius" to be "a dashing, dragoon kind of woman."[15] But Barrett was evolving, and one prick was an encounter with Jewsbury herself in the pages of her friend Chorley's *Memorials of Hemans*. Here was a woman of remarkable "individuality & power," she marveled in 1844 to Mitford (ibid. 2: 425)—"a woman of more comprehensiveness of mind & of a higher logical faculty than are commonly found among women"; she radiates "<u>working-power</u>" (1845; ibid. 3: 118–19). How should one measure the uncommon finding?

Masculine Woman, Female Writer

The gender of heterodox female genius would continue to challenge judgment across the century. Coventry Patmore was pretty sure in the 1880s what he meant (in the Coleridgean ideal of greatness) when he described Romantic-era male poets Keats, Shelley, and Clough as "feminine."[16] But he balked at contemporary female gender-bender Alice Meynell. His essay on her opens in the thick of, and never really recovers from, this quandary:

> At rare intervals the world is startled by the phenomenon of a woman whose qualities of mind and heart seem to demand a revision of its conception of womanhood and an enlargement of those limitations which it delights in regarding as essentials of her very nature, and as necessary to her beauty and attractiveness as a woman. She belongs to a species quite distinct.
> (*Mrs. Meynell* 118)

To concede a revisable "conception of womanhood" is, in effect, to set essential nature into a question about the nature of essentials. If Patmore evades the test by deciding that the "woman of genius" (120) is another "species," such taxonomy entails another question: is this species in alienation a gender deformity, or a sign of deformative pre-conception? The definitional crux traces out an essay of zig-zagging. On the one hand, Patmore liberalizes the borders, contending that Meynell is "not less but more womanly" in her "possession of qualities which are usually the prerogative of the ideal man." On the other hand, he holds the line with a Burkean sword: all "women of the grander type, who prefer their womanhood to the assertion of their right to a masculine attitude towards the world, have always had the world in worship at the feet of their greater and sweeter femininity" (118–19). The roiling about gender has genre stakes: no less than a qualification for the canon. The genius of Meynell's poems ultimately has a disqualifying gender, a betrayal of essence:

> they breathe, in every line, the purest *spirit* of womanhood, yet they have not sufficient force of that *ultimate* womanhood, the expressional *body*, to give her the right to be counted among classical poets. No woman has ever been such a poet: probably no woman every will be, for (strange paradox!) though, like my present subject, she may have enough and to spare of the virile intellect, and be also exquisitely womanly, she has not womanhood enough. (120)

The parenthetic drama makes a mystery of a prejudice. If Patmore is willing to speculate that "the hallmark of genius" is "the marriage of masculine force of insight with feminine grace and tact of expression" (122), the partners of "double-sexed insight" are the old gender forms (119).[17] Double-sexed genius is an exclusive he-purchase: a man may cultivate "femininity" of sensibility, even "femininity [. . .] such as no mortal lady has ever attained or ever will attain"; but the "truly masculine, whether in character or in art" is a quality "women and womanly artists never attain."[18] Species Meynell is a conceptual challenge, but not really a discursive one: "species quite distinct" turns out to be a distinction without a difference.

If Patmore senses without confronting contradictions, M. A. Stodart, the female writer of *Female Writers* (1842), was clearly embarrassed by the strange paradox of her title. She recovers on two fronts, both allied against the initiatives the 1790s. She will celebrate the feminine female and derogate the masculine *she*. Her standard for the first, is predictably, "Mrs. Hemans": "no amazon in literature, but a tender, a delicate, a sensitive woman," with "nothing masculine either in her mind or in her influence" (92). The negatives cue the other gender, heralded by Polwhele's favorite truant officer, Hannah More:

> Mrs. Hannah More in one of her letters, speaks of Mrs. Macaulay as having nothing of the woman about her, but as being only "a tolerably clever man," and this description seems to suit very well with all that we hear of this lady. She came booted and spurred to her public career; a free-thinker.
> (*Female Writers* 126)

Endorsing More, Stodart arraigns free-thinking, man-booted "Mrs. Macaulay" for "laying aside the amiable weakness of her sex" (127)—a knowing citation of the term of praise in Pope's *To a Lady* (44) that Wollstonecraft despised (misremembering his exact wording, but getting the gist and underscoring the political consequences). "It would be an endless task," she sighs,

> to trace the variety of meannesses, cares, and sorrows, into which women are plunged by the prevailing opinion, that they were created rather to feel than reason, and that all the power they obtain, must be obtained by their charms and weakness:
>
> "Fine by defect, and amiably weak!"
> And, made by this amiable weakness entirely dependent . . .   (*VRW* 178)

Mindful of Wollstonecraft, Stodart adds her to the indictment: she and Macaulay were "a pair of true Amazons," those "he-shes of literature [. . .] little likely to gain our affections" (127). Although Stodart could sound like Wollstonecraft in contending that women "have been too often delineated by those whose interest it was to keep them in subjection, and who aimed at this end by exaggerated accounts of their weakness" (25), she recoiled at an unsexing "Amazonian spirit." For women "to engage in any species of combat, even in an intellectual one," is to exercise a "masculine vigour and courage" that can only "derogate from female honour, and female dignity" (163). The gender economy is zero-sum, "masculine" depleting not just "feminine," but the biological base, "female." Even a woman that she admires, Lady Mary Wortley Montagu, makes her nervous: this "woman of remarkably strong intellect; a woman of almost masculine mind," who "unites the force of a male with the lightness of a female pen," ultimately proved "there was little of the woman about her," and so is "more a person to be feared and admired than loved" (108–13).

With a Romantic template, female writer Virginia Woolf anatomized the desexed woman writer with a kind of modernist abstraction. Musing on Coleridge's table-talking about the great mind as naturally androgynous,[19] she was prompted to theorize the genius of double-sexed minds. So she decided to "test what one meant by man-womanly, and conversely by woman-manly, by pausing and looking at a book or two." Yet what the books showed was a historical stage inhospitable to the female androgyne. When women make a bid for male territory (say, in Suffrage politics), men seem roused to "an extraordinary desire for self-assertion"—a defense of borders that lays "an emphasis upon their own sex and its characteristics which they would not have troubled to think about had they not been challenged" (*Room* 102–3). Female challenge provokes male definitional reactions, a concerted defense against sex-character incursions.

Despite Woolf's repeated insistence that "it is fatal for any one who writes to think of their sex, [. . .] fatal to be a man or woman pure and simple; one must be woman-manly or man-womanly," her explications of the argument make it vividly clear that only a woman writer would be moved to theorize an androgynous utopia.[20] This is because, on the historical page, it has been "fatal for a woman to lay the least stress on any grievance; to plead even with justice any cause; in any way to speak consciously as a woman," and have a claim to genius (108). Every time Woolf casts an ideal chiasmus of writerly androgyny with "porous" borders, she finds herself confronting material limits: "how much harder it is to attain that condition now than ever before" (102–3). Or, thinking back through the grandmothers of the Romantic era, just as hard as before. Contending with this impasse, Woolf's aesthetic utopia has seemed to some later theorists to enact a political retreat, or at best, a deconstruction of sex for male advantage, allowing "female" factors in the composition of male genius.[21] No less than Coleridge, Woolf trains her theory to this terrain, liberating men to be androgynous. When, however, it came to actual women, especially in men's political and aesthetic territory, Coleridge tended to be rather less liberal, and Woolf tended to be sarcastic about the cultural prohibitions.[22]

The diciest figure for a woman writer in the Romantic era is the gender-shifter, that "womanly-manly or manly-womanly" he-she who trumps essence with affect. While there may shimmer a broad, smooth, and easy passage from Wollstonecraft's rationalist brief for sexual moral capacity, to Coleridge's androgyny of genius, to Woolf's denatured writing, the infernal course, especially for women, was fast and durable. Wollstonecraft's theory of "*male* spirits, confined by mistake in female frames" (*VRW* 145) might solicit a liberal correction, but from another angle, the mistake could register a perverse, even scandalous deformation—the sort Jewsbury has Julia's friends in *History of an Enthusiast* fear: the unfeminine independence of "a second Mary Wolstonecroft" (143).

Everyone recognized Jewsbury's Enthusiast as a composition of her own gender conflicts.[23] For all her admired "masculine" energy, Jewsbury kept discovering (now with satirical wit, now with rueful melancholy) that a masculine woman might find no home outside the "feminine" sphere. Even her own liberal host, *The Athenæum,* wound up eulogizing her in normative praise, mourning the loss of "a bright ornament from the female literature" of England.[24] Sharp and industrious, smart and soulful, voraciously literate and set on "remodelling" *A Vindication of the Rights of Woman* "that it would not fail to become again attractive, and [. . .] useful,"[25] Jewsbury was never rid of the social logic that arrayed female literature as canonical ornament and arraigned the truants. This logic not only beset her; it could even possess her. In an unsigned review she published the year after *The History of an Enthusiast,* her compliment to

Mrs. S. C. Hall's *Sketches of Irish Character* as "very clever, lively and yet lady-like" turns suddenly into a legislative occasion:

> the epithet lady-like is meant in eulogy: a lady ought invariably to write as a lady. [. . .] She may reveal as much as she likes, or as much as she can, of the strong and active workings of mind, even of perverted mind, provided she does not pass the barrier of sex. [. . .] she may try to write like a man and be coarse, but she will not thereby manifest man's redeeming element—strength. We could name half-a-dozen superior female writers who have fallen into this erroneous ambition—that of endeavouring to write like men. (*Athenæum* 182: 262)

What, however, is the gender of this hectoring? Is it lady-like? Or does the strong-minded law-giving paradoxically pass the barrier of sex? It's the same question, within months, Jewsbury would put to Jameson's lecturing.

Among the female writers fallen into the erroneous ambition of endeavoring to write like men, Jewsbury knew she was not exempt; yet she was never absolutely sure that this was a fall into error. Recognizing and often feeling the tug of "feminine" ideals, she was also compelled to question, investigate, complicate, and ironize the definition, even to exercise the voice and style of "masculine" writing. The heyday of this counterform, she knew with acute regret, was the generation just prior to her own. The culture of her day was so different that it seemed to demand description as "feminine." Where did this starkly gendered history leave a writer of Jewsbury's genius, Jewsbury's estrangement?

CHAPTER FOUR

Woman's Life and "Masculine" Energy: The History of Maria Jane Jewsbury

"And what good would fame do you,—a woman?"
"It would make amends for being a woman—"

Jewsbury and the Stories of Women

So young Julia Osborne (heroine of *The History of an Enthusiast*) is quizzed by her best friend's father, and stays to answer (25). Hemans's signature genre was *Records of Woman*; Jewsbury's was becoming Histories of woman against the grain—and on the pulse of her own experience: "I think I could make a decent paper descriptive of the miseries of combining literary tastes with domestic duties," she sighed to Mrs. Watts, just as her career was taking off (30 Aug. 1824; Watts 1: 197). A new acquaintance of 1826, Dorothy Wordsworth, reported with acute sympathy her agon of ambition amid ceaseless, stupefying duties:

> Her Father[,] a wealthy man, became a Bankrupt when Miss J. was but 15 years old, and about the same time her Mother died and she was left at the head of a large Family. She has remarkable talents—a quickness of mind that is astonishing, and notwithstanding she has had a sickly infant to nurse and has bestowed this care upon the rest of her Brothers and Sisters, she is an authoress. [. . .] Phantasmagoria [. . .] shew[s] uncommon aptitude in discerning the absurd or ridiculous in manners. [. . .] most of the things [. . .] were written

in ill-health—Booksellers urgent—Children sickly so that she wrote in a sick room, and often sate up till three or four o'clock to enable her to do so.[1]

The pathos of remarkable talents bent to domestic obligations halted that champion of women writers, H. F. Chorley, in the midst of his *Memorials of Mrs. Hemans,* to give a "passing notice" to Jewsbury—a nearly twenty-page excursus in the genre of melancholy romance (1: 164–82). "Few have been more strenuous in the task of mental self-cultivation," he says as prologue to printing a letter to Hemans in which she recalls being "seized" in girlhood with "the ambition of writing a book, being praised publicly, and associating with authors" (165):

> I sat up at nights, dreamed dreams, and schemed schemes. My life after eighteen became so painfully, laboriously domestic, that is was an absolute duty to crush intellectual tastes.

The very energy of this discipline is a contradiction to any crushing:

> I wrote and wrote, and wrote. [. . .] I was twenty-one before I gained any desire for knowledge, as the natural road to the emancipation I craved. [. . .] My domestic occupations continued as laborious as ever. I could neither read nor write legitimately till the day was over. (*CMH* 1: 165–66)

"Emancipation" was no casual trope in a decade when the colonial question was the hot issue. It is etched at the top of Jewsbury's first paper in *The Athenæum* series "On Modern Female Cultivation" (28 Jan. 1832): "the rational estimate and education of women marks national progress or deterioration [. . .] in the emancipation of the understanding from prejudice, in the recognition of principles, and in the desire to ameliorate the human condition." On this estimate, she did not hesitate to challenge the glory that was Greece, the romance of her day: "Athens, in her palmiest state of literature and the arts, condemned the female citizens to ignorance, confinement, and obscurity" (65). Lucy Aikin had said as much, with a politicized riff on the *lot/forgot* couplet from *Eloisa to Abelard* that Hemans echoed at the close of *The Widow of Crescentius*. Like Jewsbury, Aikin is writing in the teeth of the romance of "illustrious" Athens:

> Thy wives, proud Athens! fettered and debased,
> Listlessly duteous, negatively chaste,
> O vapid summary of a slavish lot!
> They sew and spin, they die and are forgot. (*Epistles on Women* 3.98–101)

What if history focused on its fettered female characters?

The eponym of *The History of an Enthusiast* burns with "hope of self-emancipation" from "dull, dreary, and most virtuous domestic life," a prospect she focuses on becoming a writer (69). She might have been the latest chapter from the book of female biography, including the writers, that was Jewsbury's early project.[2] Yet Jewsbury's own history, chaptered in "the trials & employments of womanhood," had her thinking that the best story she could tell her younger sister was the necessity of religious resignation.[3] Thus she imagined the bliss of another literary woman who lived "from infancy under two influences, calculated to mature female intellect in the happiest manner—rural life, and domestic intercourse at once polished, intellectual, and affectionate." What this first essay (as far as I know) by a woman on Jane Austen describes, right at the outset, is an idyll of female intellect cultivated without female cost, either in happiness or public regard:

> For those who may doubt the possibility of engrafting literary habits on those peculiarly set apart for the female sex, and for those who may doubt how far literary reputation is attainable, without a greater sacrifice to notoriety than they may deem compatible with female happiness and delicacy, it is pleasant to have so triumphant a reference as Miss Austen. (*Athenæum*, 31 Aug. 1831, 553)

Jewsbury has more at stake than triumphant refutation of the doubters. When she goes on to say Austen "passed unscathed through the ordeal of authorship" (553), she is also registering her own history, and the differences tempered by it. Writing about "Literary Women," Jewsbury is also writing as a woman literate in the ordeals.

Austen may seem a sister of the pen (with a "peculiar forte" in "delineating folly, selfishness, and absurdity—especially of her own sex"); but Jewsbury suspects that the "benevolence of her temper, and the polish of her manners" was less a blessing of nature than a deformative discipline "set apart for the female sex." Of Austen, she imagines: "In society, she had too much wit to lay herself open to the charge of being too witty; and discriminated too well to attract notice of her discrimination." Jewsbury discerns self-division, self-alienation, even self-hatred in the practiced repression, as if Austen had "acted on the principle" of "one of her own heroines": "that 'if a woman have the misfortune of knowing anything, she should conceal it as well as she can.'" "Miss Austen" plays as antitype to Jewsbury: a writer of "unambitious temper," for whom "literature was a delightful occupation [. . .] not a profession." It is the temper (habit, or discipline) of her heroines: "Miss Austen seemed afraid of imparting imagination to her favourites"—afraid, that is, of writing the history of an enthusiast.[4]

Along the bias of this tacit interest, Jewsbury projects "Miss Austen" as converse. She had been reading Henry Austen's "Biographical Notice" (1817), by 1831 a keystone in the canonizing of placid, pious, proper Austen: "Though the frailties, foibles, and follies of others could not escape her immediate detection," says this brother, "she never uttered either a hasty, a silly, or a severe expression" (5).[5] It was from one of the novels prefaced by this notice, *Northanger Abbey*, that Jewsbury drew that heroine-principle, but with a weird refraction. In the novel, the advice about concealing knowledge is hardly straightforward; it is wry narrative satire about Catherine Morland not being up to speed with the Tilneys on picturesque aesthetics.[6] Eliding this fellowship of temper, Jewsbury reads a regime of feminine concealment, continuous with her hyperbolizing of Austen's rural situation into Wordsworthian other-worldliness. "So retired, so unmarked by literary notoriety, was the life Miss Austen led," that its best image is "A violet by a mossy stone / Half hidden from the eye" (553)—a figure for the maid of that little *Song* ("She dwelt among th'untrodden ways") radically antithetical to any urban, professional woman.

"Jane Austen" was not alone in this anti-typing. "Felicia Hemans" is Jewsbury's first article in the survey of "Literary Women" (*Athenæum*, 12 Feb. 1831), and while she says nothing directly detractive of her friend, Hemans proves another antithesis: "feminine," "ladylike" and "womanly"; absent of "satiric" wit, of "sparkling repartee, intellectual snap-dragon," no "dashing dragoon-kind of woman" (104–5). Jewsbury summons an unnamed American critic to put *manly* to what's missing: "Others have had more dramatic power, more eloquence, more manly strength . . . " (104). She had weighted similar syntax for Egeria, the Hemans-coded heroine of her own *History of a Nonchalant*: "Other women might be more commanding, more versatile, more acute; but I never saw one so exquisitely feminine," sighs the Nonchalant (193; Jewsbury writes in his first-person). Not only is Egeria's feminine perfection inverse to the intellectual energy Jewsbury knew in herself and read in the women who inspired her, but it's no professional resource. When the couple falls into financial straits and Egeria offers to put her talents to work, Jewsbury sets a double exposure. The indirect discourse that renders the husband's shock also works as a satire of his strictures:

> She made the proposition—is it needful to say that it was received and repelled with a vehemence almost amounting to anger?—live upon the money earned by a woman—that woman my wife—and that wife Egeria!—I could far sooner have died than permitted such a reversal of the order of nature, a desecration of my dignity and her softness. (198–99)

A "proposition" sounds unsavory, as if prostitution. Although in the *History*, the "order of nature" prevails when it turns out that Egeria is the one to die—not only proving her delicacy but effecting a repaired male bonding in the reconciliation of father and son—the ripple of irony to readers of the *History* remains a crucial effect.[7]

These oblique regards of Hemans and Austen are reports in alienation. Surveying the novels, annuals, and "the poetess" cult of her day, Jewsbury yearned for an earlier generation. "It would afford a subject for a long and not uninteresting article to point out the striking difference in the mind and writings of the literary women of thirty or forty years ago, and the literary women of the present time," she writes in an essay on Joanna Baillie, on the front page of the May 1831 *Athenæum*. The writing of the "elders" bristles with "nerve, simplicity, vigour," while the new novels, so full of "accomplishment, grace, brilliancy, sentiment, scenery poetically sketched," have little to "claim the name of genius." The new poetry follows suit: "fascinating tenderness, brilliancy of fancy, and beauty of feeling, stand in the place of sustained loftiness of imagination, and compact artist-like diction" (187: 337). This generational difference seems as stark as gender difference, and the trope serves just fine:

> Our elder literary women were, in the spirit of their intellect, more essentially masculine; our younger ones are integrally feminine—women of fashionable as well as studious life, women generally, who not only write books but abound in elegant accomplishments.
>
> We have not, and are not likely to have at present, another Mary Wolstencroft (we merely speak of her as having exhibited grasp of mind), another Mrs. Inchbald, another Mrs. Radcliffe—Joanna Baillie is their only representative; adding, to the power of mind which they possessed, that dignified play of fancy, that amplitude of calm, bold thought, and that "accomplishment of verse" which they possessed not. (337)

Wordsworth wrote of "Poets . . . sown / By Nature; Men endowed with highest gifts, / . . . / Yet wanting the accomplishment of Verse."[8] Jewsbury gives Baillie the men's endowment, and more: a positive accomplishment, with implicit Wollstonecraftian disdain (the parentheses reflects only an enduring notoriety) of the "elegant accomplishments" of female culture. Within a year (*Athenæum*, Feb. 1832), she will be satirizing "THE ERA OF ACCOMPLISHED WOMEN":

> Accomplishment is the intellectual shadow of an intellectual substance; it is not attainments, not science, not even knowledge in its simple form, but the combined phantasm of all; it is less a cultivation of understanding than a preparation for society, a fashioner of deportment, and a teacher of conversation. ("On Modern Female Cultivation" 79)

In such an era (Jewsbury sighs in the article of May 1831) Baillie might as well be dead:

her name [. . .] is not buzzed and blazoned about as very inferior names are; her works do not attain the honour of calf and gold in libraries where inferior works shine. [. . .] *we* feel vexed to see women of later date, and, however gifted, every way inferior to Joanna Baillie, written about, and likenessed, and lithographed, before HER. (337)

The snap-dragon alliterative poetic wit of "buzzed and blazoned, . . . likenessed, and lithographed," echoes in another Jewsbury genre: satiric poetry about women in the nexus of book-marketing and social buzz.

In *Athenæum* issues across early 1831, alternating with her essays on Hemans, Austen, and Baillie, Jewsbury published three masked "Lays" on fashionable female culture. The title of the first, *The Blue Belles of England* (26 Feb.), already spells a decline and fall from the great late eighteenth-century salons to contemporary ballrooms:

> It was a bitter spirit, not a biter,
> Who said a *bas bleu* had not dressing skill in her;
> I've sat beside a first-rate female writer,
> And really taken her for a first-rate milliner;
> So knowing was she about gauze and stuff,
> And if you mentioned books—in such a huff. (137)

With *skill in her* degraded to partnering with *milliner*, this *bas blue* is just a fashion-plate remnant of the brainy salons More had celebrated in *The Bas Blue* (1786). In the persona of male society-reporter, Jewsbury cuts the satire several ways. If this reporter wields no old slanders on the literary woman's sexual repulsiveness, the modern mode is merely frivolous. Admiring all "That may in female mind be elemental; / Whate'er the disposition, form, or line," our reporter scruples only on points of style: "excepting those that clash with *mine*." In the mask of a self-satirizing satirist, Jewsbury stands outside the whole she-culture to speak her own "masculine" difference.

She even indulges a parodic masquerade: "*I* am a blue, you'll note, / When I have on my best gilt-buttoned coat." Thus dressed for success among the chic she-blues, the "he" poet is an ace at buzz and blazoning. Filing a virtual essay on Literary Women, he rues that "Brunton and Austen" have fallen to Death, but he finds plenty to romance among "the living":

> [I] in my turn have been in love with each,
> And shall be oft again, if I survive.
> First with F.H., hearkening her Delos speech;
> Then reverenced her of "Montford," whose eye seems
> Pale, dim, and deep—a placid fount of dreams.

> I've had a penchant, but with strict propriety,
> For three more Mrs. H.'s—one in verse,
> And two in tales and sketches;—then for variety
> I gave the Ennuyée my heart to nurse;
> Then flirted in an "honourable" way
> With Mrs. N; then friendshipped with Miss J.
>
> And to Miss M., and to her cricket-bat,
> My heart hath also made itself a ball;
> And by Miss B. of "Churchyards" I have sat,
> Whose "Chapters" like the leaves of summer fall;
> In fact, as you may by this time discover,
> I've been a general literary lover.
>
> But to our *soirée*—there sits L. E. L. . . . (p. 137)

This she-culture is nothing so much as a dance-card for season.[9] The "friendshipped" "Miss J." may glance wryly at "Miss Jewsbury," a supplier to annuals such as *Pledge of Friendship* and *Friendship's Offering*.[10] The lay ends with a mock-envoi, a casting of fortunes on the market of desire:

> I'll not turn showman, and in love and charity,
> Without "encouragement," as writers say
> In a first preface;—if this gives you pleasure,
> Praise me, and I'll proceed when next at leisure. (p. 137)

The next lay (untitled, 19 March) doubles the gender-play. Its signature, "Sapphira," looks feminine (Sappho in sapphire-blue), but it's another cross-dressing. The poet is the he-satirist of *The Blue Belles,* now glad to report that the muses

> . . . promise "encouragement" unto the bard
>   Who gave to the blue belles a lay;
> For courtesy sake they with pleasure award
>   To him the green laurel and bay!
>   . . . . . .
> The Muses in conclave have called upon me
>   To answer Apollo, and show
> Their fondness for "blue belles" of ev'ry degree,
>   By *tying them with a bleu beau!*   (p. 185)

This crowning pun nicely ties up poetic compliment and savvy courtship, Jewsbury as male beau-bard charming the she-culture that as reviewer she finds alien and alienating. But not without ambivalence. In the last *Lay* of this series, *On Receiving a Bunch of Violets* (2 April), Sapphira protests, "I'm not a 'blue belle'—no," insisting that *"true blue"* is to be found only in nature, in a bouquet of "*blue* violets," and not in any anthology.[11]

On the borders of female writing and the literary scene in general, Jewsbury was finding her voice as a satirist of both, and finding a way to keep her balance amid the conflicts of her professional aspiration. If in 1832 Anna Jameson would tag the "female satirist by profession" as "an anomaly in the history of our literature" (*Characteristics* 7), Jewsbury's debut turn, *Phantasmagoria; or, Sketches of Life and Literature* did not stint to include some brutally hilarious satires on the culture of "author" in the 1820s, with such titles as *The Age of Books, A Vision of Poets, The Young Author, First Efforts in Criticism, Writing a Love Tale, The Miseries of Mediocrity.*

In *The Young Author,* M.J.J. writes as aspirant to the men-of-letters club in which the strong-minded Jewsbury herself would be a travesty, or an impossibility. Tracking a young careerist out "to *train* as a literary character," she spoofs all the craven calculations: "reading every new novel—sporting every new opinion—circulating the cant of the most common-place critics—and adopting the pet phrases of the worst periodicals" (*P* 1: 189). Nicely catching the cant of pretending to ironize cant,[12] she nails the gender games of male self-promotion into Author. The apprentice becomes adept at quoting "whole lines of Moore, and half lines of Byron," and at pegging "authors by their style." Out to please the female arbiters of the game, he graces any album handed to him with "original verses on those original subjects, 'Forget me not,' and 'Remember me'" (prototype of the parrot famed for singing "I gotta be me" in Woody Allen's *Broadway Danny Rose*).

He steeps himself in female society: the "oracle of the tea-table on every tea-table subject; and the arbitrator of all feminine disputes, respecting flowers and ribbons" (190). Success with the ladies makes him a ladies' man with a vengeance, an honorary blue-belle:

> The ladies [. . .] flattered him without mercy; some for his pretty face, and others for his pretty verses; whilst he, not to be outdone in folly and affectation, wrote acrostics for them, collected seals, invented mottos, drew patterns, cut out likenesses, made interest with his bookseller for the loan of the last new novel,—and proved himself, in all points, "a most inter*est*ing young man." (190)

In "full blown authorship," Young Author is happy to abjure the man in the interests of genius-fashion, cultivating "all those eccentricities and affectations by which *little* geniuses endeavour to make themselves appear *great*": displaying "nerves and sensibilities" and (M.J.J. shows how even Wordsworth's high ode can succumb to travesty) "'thoughts too deep for tears,' and 'feelings all too delicate for use'" (191; the second phrase is Coleridge's self-satire). It is not long before he graduates to melancholy genius, with a "little dry delicate cough" and "consumptive tendencies"—proving "more inter*est*ing than ever!" to the ladies. He curates his props and sets his scenery:

> my study:—a repository of litter and literature, studiously *dis*arranged for effect. [. . .] "my proofs" so *accidentally* scattered about the floor;—and letters from "my literary friends," left open on the table with so much *careless care;*— and the heaps of well-worn pens;—and the spattered inkstand;—and the busts of Milton and Shakspeare;—and the real skull stuck between bouquets of artificial flowers. (191–92)

He plays the role large, keeps late hours, disdains domestic life, boasts a spare diet of biscuits and wine (dosed by "the only intellectual beverage," coffee), and now that he is successful, scorns "feminine babble." All these displays are scripted (he records in notes-to-self) "'to make some sort of figure in life' [. . .] determined to distinguish myself in some way or other immediately" (1: 192–94). Patterning his figure on current fashions as well as Hamlet, Milton, Chatterton, Byron, Alfieri, Moore, Shelley, Keats (even critics Jeffrey and Z.), Young Author is happy to poach from successful women (Mrs. Radcliffe), even as he trades in fraternity-abuse of others. This former ladies' man ably switches to opportunistic misogyny:

> Parodied "Auld Robin Gray"; and gave the "Improvisatrice" a regular cutting up—perfectly infamous for a woman to write, and write well; ought to be satisfied with reading what men write. Shall make a point of abusing every clever book written by a woman. (195)

The first venue of this rant, the *Literary Souvenir,* thickens Jewsbury's satire with its intertext : the volume boasted three poems by "Improvisatrice" L.E.L. as well as a reverential poem (just before *The Young Author*) by W. L. Bowles on Anne Lindsay's famous ballad: "To Miss Stephens, on first hearing her sing 'Auld Robin Gray.'"

Writing a Love Tale (*P* 1: 219–31) treats the author as no more than an agent of points to be made, tuned to formula over-inspiration.[13] So, too, *First Efforts at Criticism* (1: 233–47), where a disappointed author determines to "become critical," and works up a portfolio. One sample gives a gender-honed abuse of *Love and Idleness, with other Poems, by Edgar Percival Clerimont,* ridiculing the poetic flutter with a snide allusion to Milton's nightingale: "'Love and Idleness, by Edgar Percival Clerimont!'—most musical, most melancholy!—Well, well,

Master Edgar did not intend to be read by men, that is clear.—His aim was to please the tea table" (235)—a Young Author, panned by a Young Critic trained on Z's *Blackwood's* attacks on Hunt. In a second sample, Young Critic plays generous patron, enjoining sympathy for this same poet's budding Shelleyan genius, his "fervent aspiring after the unattained and incomprehensible;—after those beauties which mock mortal eye-sight, and come to the longing spirit, in midnight dream and vision" (238). A try-out as drama reviewer mocks a hapless tragedy. Another sample promises skill in wresting big-gesture cultural criticism out of the thinnest of occasions—here, six dry treatises on subjects mathematical. Playing curmudgeon on the lack of respect for "the arithmetical knowledge of past ages," the critic growls:

> We will never sanction by our approbation the "projects," and "discoveries," and "new systems," which in this day of mad restlessness and innovation, are destroying that national energy, and national identity, which we possessed while adhering more scrupulously to the precedents of antiquity, and the wisdom of our ancestors. We are professed haters of every thing *new*. (246)

We are channeling Francis Jeffrey on *Lyrical Ballads*.

Whether or not Wordsworth caught the Jeffrey code, his habitual disdain of "literary ladies" was baffled by Jewsbury's sparkle, "the good sense, the vivacity, the versatility and the ease and vigour diffused thro' your very interesting volume"—he wrote to her in May 1825 about her gift of *Phantasmagoria*, adding that the "Critical Essays, and those that turn upon manners and the surface of life, are remarkable, the one for sound judgment, and the other for acute observation and delicate handling, without exaggeration or caricature."[14] By 5 August, he was happily sharing with Watts his "high opinion," and speculating about the career in the offing:

> It is impossible to foretell how the powers of such a mind may develop themselves, but my judgment inclines to pronounce her natural bent to be more decidedly toward life and manners than poetic nature. Yet it would not in the least surprise me if, with favourable opportunities for cultivating feelings more peculiarly poetical, Miss Jewsbury should give proof of capabilities for productions of imaginative enthusiasm.[15]

What did concern him was Miss Jewsbury's evident ambition, and he could not forbear advising her about the miseries of "Authorship" ("of even successful Authors how few have become happier Men"), and hoped she had some immunization from a sense of "female merit" in "the depth of your feelings and the loftiness of your conceptions" (4 May 1825; *LLY* 1: 343–44). Jewsbury remembered his moody concern, shared it with Hemans (who would hear similar instruction from him in 1830), and then rehearsed it all to his daughter Dora early 20 January 1829:

> I repeated some of his opinions on the pains & penalties of female authorship, & Mrs Hemans agreed to them, in the sober sadness that I do. [. . .] I cannot conceive, how, unless a necessity be laid upon her, any woman of acute sensibility, & refined imagination can brook the fever & strife of authorship. Do you remember your father's simile about women & the flowers growing in their native bed, & transplanted to a drawing room chimney piece? I wish I could forget it.[16]

Wordsworth may have been relaying the weight of cultural opinion into the sober sadness he visited on female authorship, but he was also smarting from his own wounds, and feeling protective.[17] Jewsbury continued to win him with a talent, energy and professional dedication to which his homiletics, as he was coming to realize, were unequal. He tried to interest *The Keepsake's* editor, Frederic Mansel Reynolds (who was courting him), in signing her up; and for her part, Jewsbury knew that Wordsworth thought her better than fodder for the annuals.[18]

By 1829 she had published *Phantasmagoria, Letters to the Young*, and *Lays of Leisure Hours*, and was working on *The Three Histories*. And in 1829, Wordsworth was reflecting her frustrations and promise in two poems inspired by her gift of a bowl of goldfish. *Gold and Silver Fishes in a Vase* casts an allegorizing glance. Writing of these enchanting beauties (in 1829, goldfish were exotic), Wordsworth closes with a comment on "mute Captives" (53), the poem's initial trope, in fact: life without liberty of expressive (poetic) exercise.

> The soaring lark is blest as proud
>   When at heaven's gate she sings;
> The roving bee proclaims aloud
>   Her flight by vocal wings;
> While Ye, in lasting durance pent,
>   Your silent lives employ
> For something more that dull content,
>   Though haply less than joy. (1–8)

This is no "fish fret not"; it's far more equivocal. The she-gendering of the naturally endowed, culturally frustrated singers has to imply Jewsbury. The notation of silent lives in "glassy prison" pent would linger, and stir again in her reply-poem, "The Gold & Silver Fish to their Poet,"[19] where literary conversation is the explicit tenor. With a bit of *Phantasmagoria* satire and touch of Thomas

Hood, Jewsbury's fish speak in the discourse of wry critic and whimsical Shakespearean poet—a wit able to take that image from sonnet 5, "a liquid prisoner pent in walls of glass,"[20] and transform it into a trope for the literary life:

> From the great globe wherein we dwell,
> And from our ocean undiminished,
> Your verses, having studied well,
> We do pronounce extremely fin-ished;
> And greater praise no fish can give . . .

Reversing Wordsworth, the globe is no prison, but an enfranchised stage, and sphere, of operation. An equal interlocutor, this is a voice that imparts Jewsbury's desire to be part of the world of letters and literary conversation, the circle she will find at the *Athenæum*. It's all done lightly and satirically, in a tone to make Wordsworth smile:

> And now we're gossipping, we & you,
> (The greatest always gossip best,)
> Say Bard when you have quite read through,
> Dear Lady Morgan, Typeland's pest,
> Will you inform us what you think
> Of Mrs. Jameson's new book?—
> "Loves of the Poets"—(needn't shrink)
> Her Ennuyée your fancy took.
> May it be properly admitted
> Into our club? May I propose?
> We hear tis elegant—brightwitted—
> From the commencement to the close.
> The Annuals were so full of passion
> They turned our water into blood,
> They really are not in our fashion,
> Though very much in them was good.
>
> . . . . .
>
> Dear Mr Wordsworth!—to return—
> I'm so ashamed—(now don't say finical,)
> I feel my back with blushes burn,
> Lest you should call our body cynical.
> Your verses—ah! how sweet the praise!
> Delighted us—(quite true these tales)
> We think you do deserve the bays,
> And know, like justice we have scales. . . .

Wordsworth retured a "Sequel" more serious. "Addressed to a friend," *Liberty* speaks obliquely, or in friendly code, of Jewsbury's aspirations and his too-anxious strictures. He means to liberate her from his worries about the strife of authorship, female in particular. The lovely fish in a "bauble prison" (15), where "they pined, they languished while they shone" (21), all denied the natural birthright (25) of freedom, seem like so many frustrated she-authors:

> I ask what warrant fixed them (like a spell
> Of witchcraft fixed them) in the crystal cell;
> To wheel with languid motion round and round,
> Beautiful, yet in mournful durance bound. (46–49)

These verses stand with the best of Wordsworth's ethical imaginations. Answering the warrant of fortune, he is happy (with just the briefest gender inflection) to give his blessing to Jewsbury's hopes of emancipation:

> Thus, gifted Friend, but with the placid brow
> That woman n'er should forfeit, keep *thy* vow;
> With modest scorn reject whate'er would blind
> The ethereal eyesight, cramp the wingèd mind!
> Then, with a blessing granted from above
> To every act, word, thought, and look of love,
> Life's book for Thee may lie unclosed, till age
> Shall with a thankful tear bedrop its latest page. (133–40)

Other than that wish for female placidity, *Liberty* is a gender-liberal epistle. "Life's book" is only part cliché. It is also a compliment to Jewsbury's vocation. Soon after, he decided to liberate the goldfish from the domestic prison, releasing them to a natural pool at Rydal Mount.

But the fish got washed away in a storm (Gillett liv), and this too must have seemed allegorical, though Wordsworth couldn't bring himself to write about it. The elegy he appended to *Liberty* when he published it in 1835 sighs only of an early closing of Jewsbury's life-book. Generously, tearfully, he writes that latest page:

> There is now, alas! no possibility of the anticipation, with which the above Epistle concludes, being realised: nor were the verses ever seen by the Individual for whom they were intended. She accompanied her husband, the Rev. Wm. Fletcher, to India, and died of cholera, at the age of thirty-two or thirty-three years. (*PW* I: 157)

The final sentence of this note—"In one quality, viz. quickness in the motions of her mind, she had, within the range of the Author's acquaintance, no equal"—is a nonpareil that Wordsworth does not think to qualify by "woman."[21]

Woman's Lot, Woman's Plot: The History of an Enthusiast

Jewsbury's desire to rehabilitate Wollstonecraft's *Rights of Woman* succumbed to her marriage, not only by interruption but also a seeming renunciation of the project: "She married, and therefore gave it up," Mrs. Elwood's correspondent reports, her conjunction pressing the sequence into ideological necessity.[22] In *Memorials of Hemans*, Chorley identifies the gender "prejudice," citing Jewsbury herself, the referent of the asterisk (1: 7–8):

> "If"—to quote one* who wrote eloquently in defense of, and apology for, her own sex—"we still secretly dread and dislike female talent, it is not for the reason generally supposed—because it may tend to obscure our own regal honours; but because it interferes with our implanted and imbibed ideas of domestic life and womanly duty."

Writing *we* and *our* in the mode of male cultural ventriloquy, Chorley means to render an enlightened apology. Though he has distanced himself from the argument "that genius is of no sex" (1: 6), he will refute the prejudice against female genius. No natural inevitability, "implanted and imbibed ideas" mark (Wollstonecraft-wise) the determinative work of culture (agriculture and diet), an ideology of nature.[23]

Chorley was probably more optimistic than Jewsbury however. Overdrawing the account in *The History of an Enthusiast*, he hasn't exactly quoted Jewsbury, but paraphrased on a bias passage in which she was rendering, with no little sarcasm, a sad analysis of "Man." Jewsbury uses no syntax of a reserved *If* that would suggest an embarrassed Polwhelean venom having to stew in secret by the 1830s. Chorley's shifts convey his hope that in 1836 such prejudice is "fading rapidly away" (*CMH* 1: 8), but just half a decade or so on, conflicted female author Stodart was feeling its still powerful grip:

> We are well aware that strong prejudice has existed against learned and even against literary women. This prejudice is first to be imputed to the natural and deeply-rooted selfishness, (with all respect be it spoken) of poor woman's lord and master. (*Female Writers* 2)

By Stodart's measure, what is natural is not womanly duty, but the male selfishness that dictates it.

Jewsbury sets *The History of an Enthusiast* in this double perspective, of a prejudice recognized and even theorized, yet still in force. Calling her fiction a "history," she reflexively foregrounds the fictions of "history," the historical conditioning of implanted ideas. In its narrative of women and genius, her critique is sometimes overt, sometimes felt by refractions that figure a debate, and sometimes grasped by ironic dissonance. Her most critical effect (as we shall see) is her decision to halt the Enthusiast's story at a threshold that refuses to perform what some influential critical stories today insist was the ideological project of nineteenth-century fiction: an imaginary resolution of the conflicts and contradictions of social existence.[24] Everything stays up in the air.

This effect may seem an unexpected sequel to *Letters to the Young* (1828), Jewsbury's sober tract on the incumbent duties of female life and the dangers of ambition. Yet *Letters* seems in didactic overdrive, as if disciplining insurgent energy.[25] How apt of Freud to see denial as qualified "negation": if *Letters* pleased the public (three editions), the Jewsbury sisters weren't taking its lessons to heart.[26] Not only did young Geraldine refuse Maria Jane's advice and become a professional writer, but Jewsbury revisited the question almost immediately in *The History of an Enthusiast*. What would it be like to be a woman with brains, energy, talent, money, and no material need to marry? *Enthusiast* tracks the fall of female genius with the popular formula of pride, vanity, melancholia, loneliness, and of course, heartache. Yet, the identificatory genre, "history," names a contingency that may not be inevitable.

By writing in the mode of "history," Jewsbury invites a discernment of cultural forces and formations at work in the conduct-plot of character, errors, suffering, punishments, and corrections. This invitation is issued right at the start with a featured paratext, an epigraph on the obverse of the title page. It is a lopped sonnet-stanza from Spenser's *Visions of the World's Vanities,* about an adventurous she-ship undone by antagonisms of the deep:

> Looking far forth into the ocean wide,
> A goodly ship, with banners bravely dight,
> And flag in her top-gallant, I espied,
> Through the main sea making her merry flight;
> Fair blew the wind into her bosom right,
> And the heavens looked lovely all the while,
> That she did seem to dance as in delight,
> And at her own felicity did smile;
> All suddenly there clove unto her keel
> A little fish, that men call Remora,
> Which stopped her course, and held her by the heel,
> That wind nor tide could move her thence away. (12)

Set as prelude to *The History*, Spenser's moral allegory tips into social allegory, an emblem of invisible cultural forces—little and local but pervasive and inevitable—thwarting splendid she-desire. Jewsbury scarcely needed his summary couplet: "Straunge thing me seemeth, that so small a thing / Should be able so great an one to wring."²⁷

Before getting to her heroine, Jewsbury's historian (a confessed, but not confessedly miserable, "spinster" with a vivid memory of her own "mischievous, romping, untidy, destructive" childhood energies [8–9]) indulges a reflection that Wollstonecraft might have cast:

> Except in the cases of supererogatory misdoings, there is a tacit toleration extended to boys; from their birth they have the benefit of sex; but this toleration is never extended even to the least naughty of girls. It is an understood thing, that from the cradle they *ought*, at all events, to be good. (8)

Then Julia bursts upon us: truant girl, avid reader, hemmed in by Grandmamma-orthodoxy on "young ladies" (19). Her "eccentricities" are her rebellion: she abuses her girly clothes, uses her bonnet to collect blackberries, rides without a saddle, and climbs trees—especially for clandestine trysts with Shakespeare. This is a "heathen" scandal to Grandmamma, but to Julia it opens a world of naughty maids and madams, from Juliet to Lady Macbeth.

As a local war-zone, juvenile Julia's enthusiasm signals doubly in this history: a rebel-imagination that spells embryonic genius; a female embodiment that bodes social misery. To prevent this last murmur, Grandmamma remands her to the aptly named Miss Shackleton's boarding-school to learn how to "be a good child" (13), and Julia survives the fettering by becoming (in the historian's sympathies) a secret Wordsworthian: "the spirit that actuated her as a child was now in stronger, and more concentrated, if also in more silent operation. Her mind was athirst for knowledge"; she is possessed by a "restless, questioning, dreaming power" that "made her draw inferences from every thing she beheld—that bade sounds and spectacles, however trivial, 'haunt her like passion'—that made nature a vague glory that she loved without comprehending—that excited high but unutterable longings after lovely but unimaginable things" (19). Drawing on the Wordsworthian lore of a boy's life (the quotation is from *Tintern Abbey;* other echoes involve the Wanderer's boyhood [*The Excursion,* Book 1]), Jewsbury gives the girl a purchase on this dreaming power—a little case in point for Wollstonecraft's conjecture about "male spirits, confined by mistake in female frames," but with no concession of mistake.

In this romance of girlhood, liberal fathers (Mr. Mortimer and Mr. Percy) are there to subvert maternal policing and be patrons of social legitimacy, each flashing a bit of Wollstonecraft. Neighbor Mr. Mortimer (Julia's Shakespeare-source) advises appalled Grandmamma to nurture the "born genius": "Julia has it; so resign yourself to the affliction, buy her books instead of trinkets—in a word, let her follow her bent" (21). He is happy to wield more cross-gendered poetry from the album of romantic boyhood to spell her genius: her "soft, dark, earnest spiritual eyes" (quoting, and adding "spiritual" to a description of a boy in Hemans's *Forest Sanctuary* 1.65) radiate "ardor and intelligence; 'a child of grace and genius'" (22; now riffing on the visionary Poet of Shelley's *Alastor* [690]). Rector Mr. Percy is no Revd. Fordyce: "Had his young friend been his own daughter, he would in a private sphere, and with the modifications rendered necessary by her sex, have given her the education of a boy." Forgetting about modification, he includes Julia in vacation-reading with his sons, all "admir[ing] the rapidity with which she apprehended, and the perseverance with which she pursued knowledge; and this, joined to her more than equivocal partiality for their sports, made them pay the great compliment of wishing she had been a boy" (44). In the world of such fathers and the sons they influence, Julia gets a boy's life, the sort of "masculine education" that Wollstonecraft was convinced produced women of "courage and resolution."[28]

In Jewsbury's historical fiction, however, this boyish girlhood is no first chapter of utopian reform. Even in this early idyll, there are cautions. For all his admiration of Julia over his "pretty idle baggage, Annette" (12), a "Miss Giddy-brains" (23), Mr. Mortimer senses peril in Julia's desires. On her burning for fame as a poet (24), he throws cold water drawn from the well of Jewsbury's encounters with Wordsworth's worries:

> Setting aside the ten thousand chances against a woman's achieving what shall permanently and honorably distinguish her, she will probably suffer great loss, certainly great trials, during her foray into the enchanted wood; even her genius will probably be like a chariot wheel, set on fire and consumed by the velocity of its own motion; then her health—her spirits—oh, you forget yourself, my dear child, make another choice. (25)

Jewsbury lets Julia keep her eyes on the prize: "I do, sir, as before—Fame" (25). To our ears, she may sound too pert-precocious (a Lisa Simpson for the 1830s), but what modifies this effect is the reminder of how extraordinary it would be for a girl to have this voice at all. For every prodigy such as Felicia Browne, there were legions of girls chastened of any thought of becoming anything other than wife and mother. It's a cultural knowledge that shades Julia even in the care of Mr. Mortimer. Jewsbury has him cite a cautionary para-history in this chapter's last word, a bit of sober wisdom articulated at life's end by one of history's more transgressive women:

Well, Julia, that may pass off as the wish of a young lady of fifteen, who knows little of herself, and nothing of the world; but just see here what a very, very distinguished woman has left on record, (Mr. Mortimer turned to the preface of Madame Roland's Impartial Appeal)—the only celebrity that can increase a woman's happiness, is that which results from the esteem excited by her domestic virtues. (26)

This seems like capital armature, a woman whose public life won a death sentence, whose last thoughts sound more like Hannah More and Mrs. Ellis than Wollstonecraft.

Yet this cautionary effect is complicated by the rather partial hearing of Roland's *Appeal to impartial posterity*.[29] In this celebrated prison tract, written in the shadow of Terror-execution, the "record" cited by Mr. Mortimer is not Roland's preface. It is from her friend Bosc's "Advertisement from The Editor," opening the *Appeal* with an appeal calculated, in 1795, to win sympathy for the frequently blistering record of political life and death in Roland's text:

> Citizenness Roland, the wife of a man of science, was persuaded, that the celebrity of a woman ought to be confined to the esteem arising from the practice of domestic virtues. On this account she always refused to publish writings, which would have procured her literary fame. (*Appeal* i)

Within the fictional design of the *History,* "Madame Roland" is summoned as a caution. But across the plane of Jewsbury's historical consciousness and the horizon of Wollstonecraft (a friend of Roland), the advice is ironized. The effect is to write Julia's enthusiastic girlhood as a paradise lost not to moral error, but to a social persuasion of no woman's land.[30]

As a document of a problem, Jewsbury's *History* is no smooth argument, but a record of conflict, its discourses shifting between object lesson and ironic critique, now sounding a fault in Julia, now in her social stars. As she becomes a young woman restless in domestic confinement, reading, dreaming, and longing for the "more brilliant sphere" of a gender-liberal "mental efforts" (69), Jewsbury allows her to romance, with full Shelleyan power, a history to ratify her enthusiasm:

> O that the illustrious dead might from the grave, speak to my spirit, make me the pupil of their ashes, and let me learn from their history how to tread the path that leads to fame! O that the spirit and presence of the past could breathe into me the breath of etherial and heroic life!—the spirit and presence of nature kindle within me its own boundless, glorious energy, its own grandeur of beneficence—its own silent triumph over all that can injure and debase! (46–47)

Yet just as often, the *History* betrays the conflicts of Jewsbury's own education in life. So while gender prescription gets treated to critical irony, enthusiasm is tainted with moral irony. Julia can scarcely invoke the muses of "history" before the *History* begins to seed verbal effects that do the work of parental disapproval. Its next paragraph is a prose Ode to Fame that heats enthusiasm into incipient disease—call it idolatry, call it egotism, call it obsession:

> Fame! what energy dwells in that one word—what power to kindle and exalt! I feel the hope of it, even now, the spirit of my spirit, the breath of my being, the life-blood of my life. I long for it, nay, as if it were a divinity—I pay it an idolatry—I feel that for it I could surrender ease, health, happiness, friends, fortune, keep long vigils through many years, and wait for its appearing as the watchman for the morning light. O Fame! let me not pass away unknown, a hidden rill in the world's might forest; lay me in the grave, if so be thou wilt, then build over me a monument—only come! (47)

The History of an Enthusiast is the accumulation of these shifting transvaluations. Whether or not Jewsbury needed the measure of moral pathology to indulge these spurts of *spirit, energy, power, breath, life-blood,* it is clear that the question is the historical meaning for the 1830s.

This historical meaning is also generated by the plot. At the point where a marriage-plot convention would tame a female enthusiast, *The History of an Enthusiast* hazards a career in the world—romanced as "the breathing world of society, where mind is king; for living intercourse with the great, the gay, and the gifted; for access at will to what is various and splendid" (97), or monitored as the shipwrecking deep. Julia is launched as a Jewsbury-laden test case: a young woman of independent means, off to London to try her talents and her enthusiasms. "I never met with any woman who possessed her powers of conversation," said another London celebrity and woman-of-letters, L.E.L., of Jewsbury herself.[31] Julia wins the world with her writing and her "brilliant energy in conversation" (78), and within six years she gains "a new, luxurious, and yet intellectual style of life; perfect freedom as regarded the regulation of her movements; the vivacity of youth not yet departed" (102–3). Shelleyan language endorses Julia "walk[ing] to her own apprehension, enveloped in light:—but emparadised in dreams of intellectual beauty" (103). The alliance with Shelley is a dicey gambit for any enthusiast, especially a female one.[32] But Jewsbury is willing to risk it, knowing that her allusion is not just to his *Hymn to Intellectual Beauty* but also to a text that he knew as well as Jewsbury did, Wollstonecraft's *Rights of Woman*, not in the least its indictment of the low esteem in which men hold a woman's "intellectual beauty" (160) and "those nobler passions that open and enlarge the soul" (113). In this passion, Julia becomes her epithet:

> Julia was the enthusiast. [. . .] She had her hours for study no less than for gaiety; and if she often preferred brilliant paradoxes to sound argument, it was more from caprice than deficient judgment. Her mind had wings, and she made it use them. (103–4)

Even so, we can trace Jewsbury's cautions in the defensive syntax, which sometimes tilts over into ironic supervision, as in this audit of Julia's "energy": "it yielded a delight that she never deemed less valuable because it was feverish, or less secure because it generally involved ambition" (103).

The harbinger is the epigraph for Chapter 13 (the site of the reports above), about delusion. It is a set of lines from "Coleridge's *Remorse*," a jaded woman disabusing a young girl of her dreams of urban splendor and court glamour: "So doth the ignorant distance still delude us! / Thy fancied heaven, dear girl, . . . / In its mere self a cold, drear, colorless void . . . "[33] Just about every other sentence in this chapter sprinkles caution over Julia's enchantment: if "the whole aspect and structure of the world" resembles "as yet a glorious, ever-moving pageant," "as yet" is a time bomb; and if "Society was her Cydnus," Cleopatra's river-stage flows into a fatal historical course (103–4). An earlier epigraph (for Chapter 8 [63]), calls back the poem that supplied the *History*'s master-epigraph, *Visions of the World's Vanity*: "Shortly within her inmost pith there bred / A little wicked worm, perceived of none, / That on her sap and vital moisture fed" (Stanza VII). The she-allegory is the same as that goodly ship's: splendor and pride undone by an unsuspected antagonist. The world's vanity comes home: "Novelty at length grew old; excitements ceased to be exciting [. . .] the shroud fell from the world, and revealed—death" (106). In this death, Julia begins to yearn for her past: first, Cecil Percy (the rector's son, a childhood crush, and bearer of the aborted marriage plot); then, her innocence: "she began as in early youth, again to live alone, to be to herself both law and impulse, and whilst mixing as usual in society, to have an inner and separate existence; but it was now the existence of sadness" (106). The skewed allusion to Wordsworthian childhood tracks the sorry fall. In "Three years she grew," "Nature" is "law and impulse" to her darling "Girl," and nurtures with "overseeing power / To kindle or restrain" (7–12). A few pages on Julia will say that "Nature" is lost to her, not only insufficient in itself but poisoned as a hope: "I deserted her once, and she does not, like Deity, call back her prodigals to her bosom" (112).

The *History* drives this alienated course into Chapter 14. "I am cured of ambition," Julia writes, five years on, to pastoral Annette: "I am not contented";

"I am inwardly, habitually unhappy," "exquisitely weary"; "books have lost their early charm," and "knowledge [. . .] seems only to open my eyes to fresh views of human crime and sorrow." Poetry has proven no vocation, but a disease that "imparts poison in an odour—slays with a jewelled scimitar"; it is a language of "exile—loneliness—desertion—change—suffering—remembered joy (which is pain)—love in its strength and beauty, but love also in its inevitable alliance with sorrow or satiety" (109–11). "Society" has become Milton's death, a "robed, and crowned, and sceptered skeleton," or Shelley's nightmare in *The Triumph of Life*: "an imperial pageant—a triumphant procession in which I am an actor;—well, if I wear a purple robe, I walk amongst the—chained: or call me a spectator only of the same procession" (111–12). Julia's fame is no triumph: "there was an accession of power, but a diminution of pleasure; there came the looking before and after, the labor of comparison, the dread of failure, the distaste of rivalry" (107). It's a melancholy Shelley channeled through Hamlet.[34]

If this were a man's story, such consciousness could launch a high Romantic idealism in disdain of mundane life, or with Byron's bravado, a grand existential torment (Julia will mock herself as "a deformed transformed" [119]).[35] Jewsbury sets this stage with a female difference when she has pastoral Annette write to Julia in her London whirl, as if she were reading the society pages of Byron's Years of Fame: "your *soirées* and *conversazioni,* and balls, and routs, and parties three of a night, and your very fine compliments from very fine people, and your introductions to distinguished, really distinguished people, and your visits to artists' studies and sculpture rooms: it is all very grand" (86). Jewsbury will not write Julia as this kind of heroine however, nor even very grandly alienated. Fame is merely degraded and decadent:

> fame (using the word in the mere popular sense) was become tangible, something to be seen, and felt, and understood; its etherial aspect was gone, it was [. . .] a common thing, the birth of common life. It might be calculated, weighed, measured, and debated upon; it consisted in being looked at with curiosity, in being talked and written about, and the materials that went to its composition were the notice of superiors, the homage of equals, the envy of inferiors and the hatred of rivals. (107)

Jewsbury is nothing if not critical about the alienation of fame, of the multiple agencies of writing, talk, looks, notice, homage, envy, and hatred. What she suppresses are the strictures more likely to doom female aspirants to this sense of merely decadent commodification.

But the question keeps prodding her attention. In March 1831, reviewing a volume of poetry by H. G. Bell, she pauses over *The Favourite Actress*, to wish that such a subject, the alienation of celebrity, were treated more often "in our imaginative literature":

> Such a woman, the idol of a day, if also a woman of feeling and reflection, stirs our deepest sympathy. [. . .] we must have a couple of verses:
>
>> The light of what the world calls fame,
>>   On woman's path a curse,
>> Than dull insensibility—
>>   Than thoughtless folly worse.
>> O why should I have ever sought,
>>   For what I value less
>> Than ev'n the saddest thought that haunts
>>   My spirit's loneliness!
>> Why stoop to court the vulgar crowd,
>> For what I scorn'd when once bestowed!
>>
>>   . . . . .
>>
>> I wish he saw my pale hot cheek,
>>   Not he alone, but all
>> Who scarce a little hour ago,
>>   Before the curtain's fall,
>> Beheld me in the glittering scene
>>   A form of smiles and light,
>> As if my heart could know no care,
>>   My day could have no night:
>> I wish they saw me now—for I
>> Am sick of this wild mummery!   (*Athenæum* 175: 151)

Here the etiology of sickness is a woman's curse. Chorley saw this in Hemans and called it "Melancholy." This is not the Keatsian aesthetic of achingly complex sensation that Julia romanced in her enthusiasm (65), but the preferred cultural diagnosis of female susceptibility.

It's not unreasonable for Norma Clarke to discern the anatomy of melancholy and the implied cure in Jewsbury's *Farewell to the Muse*.[36] Yet as with so many of Jewsbury's self-corrections, the farewell performance is a stylized act. For one thing, it was published in the *Literary Souvenir* for 1826 with two contradictory items: a strenuous *Remonstrance* by the annual's editor, and a poem blazoned on the "Contents" page with the signature of Jewsbury's recent fame: *To a Poet's Infant Child. By M.J.J., Author of "Phantasmagoria; or Sketches of*

Life and Literature" (xiii). Writing as poet, M.J.J. blesses a child destined to be another:

> Bright nursling of a Poet's love,
>   To thee by birth belong
> The Delphic shrine, the laurel grove,
>   The heritage of song;— (*Souvenir* 79)

True, this is a gender-heritage: "Thine, boy, shall be a nobler crest,—/ Thy father's Wreath and Lyre!" concludes the benediction signed "M.J.J." and dated, as if a historical record, "*August* 8, 1825" (80). But if this seems the witnessing of a succession by a she-angel in a male house of fame, wafting her blessings, the poem is also readable as rhetorical cross-dressing, an exercise in the voice of a paternal, patrilineal "Poet." No easier to peg is the performative gesture of the *Farewell*. Also signed "M.J.J." and also notarized, "*October 5th*, 1825" (381), it may register a cool reckoning, despite desire and endeavor, of inability. But far from presenting *Farewell* as a female capitulation, the venue of the *Souvenir* treats the sign-off as a genre exercise (kin to those of *Phantasmagoria*) to partner with a complementary one: *A Remonstrance/To the Authoress of the Forgoing "Farewell to the Muse"* (383). If it is now clear that M.J.J is she (the table of contents lists just a short title, *A Remonstrance*), this information proves no cue for strictures. The remonstrance could not be more encouraging, urging a farewell to the muse only in a farewell to life.

Even if the *Farewell* of 1825 had been sighed as an existential speech act, M.J.J. soon recanted and contradicted it with a raft of subsequent publications, including poetry.[37] The letter to the Wordsworths with the first draft suggests that renunciation was no intent at all. Jewsbury seems to have meant farewell only to the muse of poetess-poetry, sensing that it wasn't her strong suit. "I am tired of writing pretty verses," she sighs to Dora Wordsworth, 24 October 1826; "Admire my heroism. I really am going to read Geoffrey Chaucer." She's after a particular career, "not a Lake Poet, but a lake Prose."[38] By the spring, her family is giving her a room of her own, which she describes to Dora Wordsworth in all the glow of paternal support:

> My father is so delighted that he will procure the glass coverings himself, & beautifully will they ornament the chimney piece of my new & pretty writing room. My dear father has indeed spared no expense to fit up the house to as contribute to my comfort & pleasure. (1827; Dove Cottage WLMS A 10)

This is a better situation than Jane Austen's little writing table in the midst of the family parlor. Looking forward to a recovery from a protracted illness, by the summer, Jewsbury was energetically "planning what I <u>will</u> do if I get strong," and telling Dora of her "scheming & dreaming" (10 July 1827; WLMS A; Low 270). *The History of an Enthusiast* is still romancing the muse: the muse of poetry in an ironic key, and a passionate gamble with the muse of prose. "I only write verse to improve my prose," she insisted to Dora early in 1829.³⁹

In the improvements of the *History*, the by-the-book laments on fame, for all the knowing elaboration, prove equivocal. This double-step is clearly afoot, for example, in the way Jewsbury shifts her Enthusiast's first-person sighs over "what the world calls my genius and my fame" ("I am exquisitely weary," etc.) into third-person discourse, precisely to put critical pressure on the whole aspect and structure of the world in relation to woman's aspirations:

> Ah, what is genius to woman, but a splendid misfortune! What is fame to woman, but a dazzling degradation! She is exposed to the pitiless gaze of admiration; but little respect, and no love, blends with it. (112–13)

No small factor in this aspect and structure, Jewsbury insists, are the reception protocols: "as her delineations of emotion are presumed to emanate from her own experience, a desire is roused to discover her private history in her writings" (113). If Byron was only half in love with such effect, he had both male and aristocratic inoculation. A woman (Jewsbury is sorry to say) can only be degraded in the mutation of self into textual effect: "However much as an individual she may have gained in name, and rank, and fortune, she has suffered as a woman; in the history of letters she may be associated with man, but her own sweet life is lost"—lost not just in the equation of her writings with private history but lost to the public staging of everything. She is "a splendid exotic, nurtured for display; an ornament," a "jewelled captive—bright, and desolate, and sad" (113). Asking her own reader to see the chaining of "bright" to "desolate, and sad" for women in "the history of letters," Jewsbury turns the plot of her *History* into a critical meditation:

> This is her fate, these are her feelings, if her character predominantly possess the excellence of her sex. If it be otherwise, if that which should be womanly in her is worldly, if she be not so gentle as vain, at heart a creature of ambition rather than of affection, she will be less unhappy; but, alas, she will also be less worthy of happiness! (113–14)

Jewsbury may have Julia introject all this, to sigh, "what is to become of me? To neither class do I belong entirely, yet I partake in the nature of both!" (114). But obliquely screened in the total report on "woman" is a figure on the border between "worldly" and "womanly."

From the perspective of a character in "neither class," everything shifts. All those judgments "as regard the delight and glory of distinction to a woman" (114) and the doom of her genius on a worldly stage get pried away from unexamined "fate" and read as the effect of a received history—one that another historian might identify, and even protest:

> A *man* may erect himself from such a state of despondency; throwing all his energies into some great work, something that shall beget for him "perpetual benediction;" he may live for, and with posterity. But a woman's mind—what is it?—a woman—what can she do?—her head is, after all, only another heart; she reveals her feelings through the medium of her imagination; she tells her dreams and dies. *Her* wreath is not of laurels but of roses, and withers ere it has been worn an hour! (115)

Keats had faith that "Poesy . . . can tell her dreams," using the feminine to name a power perhaps not susceptible of, or to, male invocation.[40] Actual female existence, Jewsbury proposes in this reading lesson, offers no poet's laurel. Her allusions to Wordsworth's macro-myths are to gender-restricted redemptions: the male "despondency [said to have been] corrected" in *The Excursion* (Book 4) and the "perpetual benediction" that answers and redeems loss in the "Immorality" *Ode* (134). Man has the option of exercise to win the laurel; women have only the tribute of roses, good (as Wollstonecraft had said) for the hour of youth alone. Julia herself writes "the rose *must* die" (151), and Jewsbury's italics cast a critical protest.

By 1832, she would articulate (under the cover of anonymity) the cultural determinants for women, with an analogy to the education-denied "working classes." The argument of political constriction replaces the diagnosis of individual, or even gender-earned fever:

> The great misfortune [. . .] that lies in the path of highly-cultivated women, is the absence of active occupation for their mental energy, which, when combined with ambition, as it too generally is, lays waste and consumes them. Men have professions and offices; to them belong, of right and courtesy, all the activities and authorities of life. Authorship is the only accredited vent for a woman's intellect; and this, by obviating one evil, induces many others. The fever of unoccupied energy is quenched: but, by and bye, the worse fever of sensitive ambition, or ungratified longing after sympathy, arises, and her position in society becomes yet more false. (*Athenæum* 250 [11 August 1832]: 521)

Here fever is diagnosed in contingencies of gender and culture—of female mental energy, intellect, and ambition set in a system of male rights and authorities—without a community of female sympathy, or sympathy for female inclusion.

That author Jewsbury meant to ruffle the lore of female ambition as pathology is clear in the diagnostic scene in *The History of an Enthusiast*. Framed to evoke the turning point in the novel of female conduct—the arrest of error and a call for reform—it rejects the dose. Just after her lament about women as all heart, Julia is visited by old heart-throb Cecil. Not having seen her for several years, he is shocked to find no wreath of roses but "a sickly verdure, an unnatural bloom, [. . .] unsound at the core, withered at the root [. . .] with energies that only kindled their own funeral pile" (118)—as if her celebrity were a crime against nature. "I should not like a lioness for a wife," he sniffs (120), just before reporting his betrothal to some plain Jane. Later that day, Julia receives a letter from him "and a small bible—his own, and full of his own marks and observations" (127). But here's the swerve. Jewsbury does not give the reader this letter (as she had with Julia's and Annette's); she has the historian-narrator report it in ironizing paraphrase. The "reader" (a he-generic, or maybe specifically male) is hailed into its rhetoric:

> if he have scrutinized society, the character of man, and the condition of woman, he will be at no loss to guess its style of contents. She who is brilliant in mind, and gifted with the perilous gifts of genius, may receive the homage of saloons [*sic*], may be courted as a companion, and worshipped as a goddess; but for his help-meet, man chooses far otherwise. Beauty in connection with simplicity, or even "wonder-working, weak simplicity" alone, determines his choice. (127)

What the character of man will choose, Jewsbury makes clear, is not a woman like her, but "far otherwise"—the *beau ideal* of the "pretty, unidea'd girl" that Hemans, too, disliked (*CMH* 1: 96). The gloss of "wonder-working, weak simplicity" is from Hartley Coleridge's *Prometheus: A Fragment*, and as is the usual case with Jewsbury's intertexts, the context is important. Pitying the Titan's torment, the Sylphs offer to entreat Jove, hopeful of the "spell of unresisted power/In wonder-working weak simplicity/Because it is not feared," but Prometheus doubts the force of such "idle chirpings of imprison'd love,/That warbles freely in its cage" (*W* 301). Even if the imprint of this context in Jewsbury's *History* is faint, the tenor of male rule and sylph simplicity is clear enough in the historian's paraphrase of Cecil's principles of choice:

> Man does not secretly dread and dislike high intellect in woman, for the mean reason generally supposed—because it may tend to obscure his own regal

honors; but because it interferes with his implanted and imbibed ideas of domestic life and womanly duty. (127)

Chorley may have optimistically misremembered the syntax (*CMH* 16–17, above), but he was right to hear a critique of Cecil-scruples.[41] No mere relay of Cecil-speak, Jewsbury's discourse vibrates with irritation, sharpened with a Wollstonecraft edge on *implanted* and *imbibed.*

New Monthly Magazine caught the drift: glad to say that "In an age when female talent has been more cultivated than during any other, the powers of Miss Jewsbury have been deservedly acknowledged," it could view Cecil only as a deformation, one who "represses any feeling" for Julia "from an idea that her pursuits are inconsistent with the female character" (June 1830, p. 33). A few good men, Jewsbury's historian sighs in a survey of her times,

> there are, able and willing to do the justice of the heart (a very different thing from the justice of the head) to women distinguished by talent;—firm believers in their amiability, disciples of their gentleness, respecters of their independence, reliers on their friendship, trusters in their devotedness; but such men are comparatively rare, and their power of doing *heart*-homage to female genius, is no less a gift than the genius itself. (128)

Was Jewsbury thinking of Godwin's admiration of Wollstonecraft? This is the last word in this chapter (15), and she lets it stand a statement of male failure.[42]

It is Cecil, more than any other figure in the *History*, that spells the question with which Jewsbury contended. Early and late, his passionless placidity tags him as no big loss. When this "sweet, mild youth" (30) urges teenage Julia to cast away her "intense, dreamy, passionate" books and find happiness in reality, affection, home, and nature, Julia's tart resistance could make Oscar Wilde proud: "Your mind is dreadfully healthy, Cecil" (58). Jewsbury's introductory portrait of this monitor is a virtual set-piece of satiric equivocation:

> Reader, allow me to present to you Mr. Cecil Percy, just returned from his first term at ———— College, Oxford; the very reverse of a dashing youth; but one whom dashing youths find it better to avoid than to insult. He has no genius, but a thoroughly cultivated taste and understanding; he is warmly affectionate in his feelings, though wholly clear of impassioned or imaginative sensibility; has an inborn sentiment of reverence for the female character, but, as he has never been in love, he is less tender than respectful in his attentions to women. In short, reader, Cecil Percy is just the kind of young man you might (if a young lady) covet as a brother, be very happy with as a husband, though I do not feel quite certain that he will do for you as a lover. (38–39)

The staccato of *but* and *though* hits the limitations that become even more overt as Jewsbury goes on to spoof the romance novel, in which two such characters "must marry" (39):

> Cecil Percy is not brought forward as a hero [. . .]. The lovers of sense, principle, and reality, will perhaps be kind enough to like him as he is. He could, however, play on the flute, and he had a head of luxuriant, clustering, black hair. I mention these trifles to save him from the utter detestation of those who admire the Corsair style of excellence. (42)

Byron's dashing hero is tamed to a flute-playing drawing-room fashion-plate.

Cecil may live in Julia's imagination as a romance hero, but Jewsbury keeps her readers tuned to the misalliance of any enthusiast and this "cold and simple" nature, "more passionless" and "more subdued" in each return (117). Home for her grandmother's funeral, and longing for the "living" world of London, Julia is visited by her patron Mrs. Hervey, eager to draw her back to town. Jewsbury sketches a little parlor badinage, with Wordsworthian birds as the birdies. To Mr. Mortimer, Julia is like the Cuckoo, "A hope, a love, / Still longed for, never seen," or like the Skylark, "True to the kindred points of heaven and home." "All very fine," answers Julia, "but I would much rather be the same poet's 'wandering bird of Paradise.'"[43] When Mrs. Hervey chirps, "A far more poetical style of existence," Cecil can only grouse, "Is it equally feminine?"—sweetening the stricture with a "calm, grave, beautiful smile, that possessed such mysterious power over the character so opposed to his own" (99–100). Not only does Jewsbury ironize such power, but she even gives Julia an intuition, a wish that he were "a little more imaginative, a little more impetuous," more able to like "what is wild, or say anything silly" and let go of that "calm, grave, beautiful smile" (66). He seems cut from the same starchy cloth as the "Religious Novelists" satirized in *Phantasmagoria:* "miserably defective in the power of developing the passions and principles of human nature, [. . .] weak in talent whether inventive or descriptive—and lamentably deficient in vigour of thought, and strength of feeling" (1: 43). Sending Cecil off on a Grand Tour, Jewsbury refuses to cast Julia as homebound abject. She is positively liberated, embracing her books and solitary visions, quoting Shelley like mad (*Prometheus Unbound*), and yearning for society that young men of energy and imagination take for granted: "In two, perhaps three years, I may be placed in a more brilliant sphere—placed there by my own mental efforts! How earnestly do I labor towards that point; whilst a voice within me whispers—'Not in vain!'" (69).

Even her rueful reflection on the penalty, her non-candidacy for Mrs. Cecil Percy, implies a negative account. Despite her audit of a deficient capacity for "self-denial" and "daily self-content," Julia knows that union with Cecil "would not have made [her] abidingly happy" (158). Jewsbury has all along invited a different accounting, a transvaluation of what Julia calls incapacity into latent resistance. Cecil's wife is "full of simplicity; not endowed with genius," Julia writes to Annette, adding ruefully, "—but when did genius in woman win love from man?" Jewsbury's keywords make it clear that the damages could be reassessed in her favor, and against Cecil-adjudication. The fault is not in genius stars, but in the male constellations of value, Jewsbury suggests, amplifying the case via Hemans's most famously lovelorn artist:

> My gifts—let them now pass for ever from me, since they could not win the only affection I ever desired; and let the ambition that lured me on with the vain dream, that when the world praised me, *he* would lend a delighted ear [. . .] let all these perish, worthless, and evil, and vain, that could not win me love! (136)

"My soul's lofty gifts! Are they not vain?" cries Properzia Rossi; "my fruitless dower / That could not win me love"; "Worthless fame! / That in *his* bosom wins not for my name / Th' abiding-place it ask'd!"[44] *Properzia Rossi* (Hemans transparent) chimes with Julia's lament, to cast *History of an Enthusiast* as a critical chapter in female history. In the midst of that doleful letter to Annette, Jewsbury lets her heroine imagine a revolutionary alternative. "Literary enthusiasm is no more; but without literature as a profession, a void would be created in my heart," she sighs, imagining a world elsewhere: "except I were a Frenchwoman, thrown once more amongst Frondeurs and Girondists, I doubt the power of anything to fill abidingly" (114). Citizenness Roland returns, not as a conduct caution but as the ghost of a lost generation, kin to the era of Baillie and Wollstonecraft for which Jewsbury herself yearns.

The foil for Julia's plight between two worlds, one dead and one powerless to be reborn, may seem to be the idyll of Annette—the pattern drawn from *Corinne* (a proper sister who is loved).[45] But this idyll is no less a critical text than Cecil. The epitome of "quiet, domestic happiness" (129), Annette is a patent fantasy in a cultural imaginary and thus (Jewsbury hints) a little vacuous. Her epigraph for the chapter on Annette's paradise (16), again calling upon Hartley Coleridge (and again, with paratextual information), is to double business bound:

> Her being's law is gentle bliss,
>   Her purpose and her duty;
> And quiet joy her loveliness,
>   And gay delight her duty. (129)

This looks like an Ode to Annette, but its Coleridgean context betrays its sing-song inanity.[46] The "blissful being" seems ultimately other than human; so, too, the effect of Captain Egerton's happy appropriation of Shelley's *To a Sky-lark* to praise his wife (134).[47] It is better for bird-brained Annette to "*be* poetry" than to write it, says this doting husband (133), whose full name turns out to be "Captain Alfred Egerton" (a coterie glance at "Captain Alfred Hemans"?). He likes to call her "my good little woman" (139), a triple modification of possession, convention, and diminution. Julia, "brilliant—profound—full of information" (132), is a candidate for the laurel crown; Annette plays with her children under the "spreading laurel" at her cottage. Giving Julia an homage to Annette that is self-abjecting, Jewsbury can't resist a discursive plane scored with equivocation:

> what should you, sitting at ease in your elegant cottage, planting roses, teaching your two pretty children their ivory letters, or listening to your brilliant husband's conversation, without the slightest desire to be brilliant yourself—what should you know of a state of mind bordering on phrenzy? Farewell, and may you never know it! (138)

If myrtle cottage is bliss, it is also folly. It may figure a haven from the diseases of the world, but it is also an elegantly infantalized prison. What Julia knows is that she must "press" on with self-identifying actions: "I read, I travel, I observe, I reflect, I converse" (114).

"Unfeminine Style"

"I travel." Jewsbury's *History* enters the records of woman with an array of gender prescriptions refused: a refusal to expose her enthusiast as only vain and vacant, to pathologize her restless unhappiness, to recuperate her to womanly duty in domestic life, to invoke the death-sentence of fiction's popular pattern (Staël's Corinne, Jameson's Ennuyé). Jewsbury reinvests her heroine with some of her original spirit in a choice to quit England for Europe, traveling on her own as a "second Mary Wolstonecroft" (143).[48] This liberatory plot is seeded early on. When Cecil, about to embark on his Grand Tour, bids Julia farewell with a question, "what and where will you be a few years hence?" she replies: "You will find me Julia Osborne, wherever I am"—always herself and (not pathetically) unmarried. In the present tense, all she can do is suppress her rage at the divergent gender-courses: loath to express "a single good wish" to Cecil, "she put down her veil and turned away. By the time she reached home she had a violent head-ache, and retired immediately to her apartment" (61–62).

In the last chapters, Jewsbury releases Julia from veil, headache, and apartment, without (her physician is happy to say) having to report "the reason" to anyone's assent for what she "chooses." In "much greater dread of her staying at home," he has "advised" (Jewsbury sets this against female conduct advice) such travel (142–43). Naming this advisor "Dr. Morphinus," Jewsbury signals a needed reshaping anodyne, even an avatar of Morpheus, god of dreams (the sense of wasting addiction was much later). The physic will put a world of pain to sleep, and bring another, only dreamed of, to life: "abroad." "Foreign scenery is all I want," Julia herself says, her "want" speaking not only desire but also the lack of possibility in England (156). The gender of this desire is broadcast by "the full bloom of a three days' notoriety" when some "mad verses" by Julia appear in a London paper. Whether this flair of Byronic wit across 6 stanzas of couplet-capped, pentameter sexains is mad-verse by derangement or by rational anger, its gender effect is unarguable; "Most unfeminine style for a woman— dreadfully indecorous!" exclaims Julia's scandalized patroness (147), unable to keep from reiteration (153).

Jewsbury is the real stylist, writing out as Julia what might halt the pen of "Miss Jewsbury."[49] "What a strange thing, and how excessively improper!— well, the reviewers will certainly leave off their compliments about her womanliness," cries "good Mrs. ─────" (142–43). As Dr. Morphinus reads the preface, we sense Jewsbury's intimate identification: "talented pen—youthful *distinguée*—literary circles—profound passion—soul of no sex—versatile powers—beg to direct—fifteen thousand daily readers" (144). All Jewsbury's burning romance, but also her fever. "Do you know I feel quite sorry for Miss Jewsbury!" (wrote L.E.L. to a friend); "She has a thousand fine qualities, and talents of a very high order indeed; but she has all the exaggerating sensitiveness which I have observed in too many literary people, towards the opinions of those whose good word is valueless, and whose evil one is powerless for the same reason—neither are spoken of in sincerity" (Blanchard 1: 86).

Writing in the fiction of Julia's "Reply to a Letter of Advice," Jewsbury not only manages her sensitiveness, but even satirizes the pretense of sincere public concern. Julia's poetry challenges the "fearful" monitors of her fate, all so sure of "the right prescriptive / To whip with words, didactic and descriptive":

> And what if I remain in bed till noon?
>   And what if I say wise things and do mad ones?
> If better than this earth I like the moon,
>   And better than some good people, like bad ones? (144)

Mad, bad, not quite dangerous to know; this is the same glee with which, in a bit of satiric self-reporting, Jewsbury described herself just arrived "from the moon."⁵⁰ Like the *History* which produces it and the author who writes it, Julia's "Reply" does have its mood swings (now witty spoof, now rueful satire, now energetic recovery, now a sigh); but Jewsbury decides to end the verses, like the *History,* with a tone of forward-looking determination:

> But I shall drink my coffee I suppose,
>   And form with bread and butter a connection,
> Morning and evening—just as if no woes
>   Had ever of my spirit made dissection;
> The greatest harlequin on earth is sorrow,
> So now, my friend, farewell until to-morrow! (147)

The second mad verse, 24 more such sexains (also read aloud by the doctor), is another satire on the pain of female fame: a public "roused to discover her private history in her writings" (113). "Farewell after a Visit" (148–53) attracts interest with a promise of some "peeps into what [. . .] one may consider private history" (148). Alternately reluctant, determined, rueful, cynical, ironic, and elegiac, the farewell addresses the "little darling cabinet" that has been Julia's room of her own. The tones of affection might have been sighed to a lover, but it's no Farewell to the Muse. It is a valediction determined to forbid mourning, laced with Byronic spice:

> And then we get into our chaise and pair,
>   Filled with our luggage, selves, and constancy,
> For ten miles (if the scene's not very fair)
>   We think of what we've left; ten more, and we
> Begin to find that fancy yet can frisk it,
> And with we had remembered a dry biscuit.   (149)
>
>   . . . .
>
> And I would rather lose what I love here,
>   Be it man, woman, flower, or recollection,
> By swift translation to another sphere,
>   Than have it in the shape of retrospection;
> I hate all ghosts, but most, and without measure,
> The apparition of departed pleasure.
> And memory is mental indigestion;
>   You are not healthy if it much afflicts you;
> Hope, which is hunger, without any question,
>   By no means in your health so much restricts you;
> For never to be dainty is *her* cue,
> If turtle is not, blackberries will do.   (150)

Pragmatic and a tad jaded, these verses are not without hope, hunger, and enthusiasm, a romance of swift translation to some other sphere of reality.

Jewsbury's mixed review of the mixed genre of L.E.L.'s *Romance and Reality* (issued a year after *The Three Histories*) gives a report of her own way with romance as history, history as fiction. "To call it a novel is incorrect," she warns; it will satisfy "no lover of history and mystery, no demander of event and catastrophe, no old-fashioned believer in its being equally the duty of governments to put down plots, and of novelists to purvey them" (*Athenæum* 215: 793). While she hoped L.E.L. would some day be able "to conceive some *whole* in a strain of high mood, consecrated by high purpose, and crowned with high reward" (795), she already saw a "remarkable" talent, its "real and delightful occupation" emanating from a generic mix that cast off whole dictations to indulge "keen and varied observation and reflection": "essays, criticism, sketches of life, portraits living and dead, opinions on manners, descriptions of feeling," alternately in the provinces of "wit" and "poetic and moral feeling." This census sounds like nothing so much as a description of *Phantasmagoria*, theorized in the retrospect of *The History of an Enthusiast*, especially its last chapters.

The last chapter of Julia's history and mystery is a discursive mix of moods refusing generic government. Its scene is Julia's conversation, on the cusp of her actual farewell to England, with chivalric Captain Egerton, who has come to rescue her (he imagines) with a swift translation to Myrtle Cottage. Its signifying event is the Julia's refusal, in line with Jewsbury's refusal of conduct plots. "I *know* I shall be better as soon as I begin to travel," Julia insists, with a flush of health not only in the desire, but also in the escape from myrtle life-in-death. Writing a dire simile into the Captain's protest, "What possible enjoyment can you have in wandering about, like a woman belonging to nobody?" Jewsbury converts it to a positive experiential truth: "How else would you have me wander? I *am* a woman belonging to nobody," Julia declares (156). Her poetic "Farewell" had already refused the cliché diagnosis of broken-heartedness, with Byronic brio:

> That phrase "a broken heart," has had a run,
>   I like it not, it makes me think of china
> Broken, and by a monkey, ten to one;
>   And yet I really never could divine a
> Better—"ossification" would sometimes
> Best suit the fact—but then you see the rhymes! (152)

If the Captain sees Julia only as a "rational lunatic" (from the moon, again), Jewsbury puts this to new account. Across her wavering relapses into laments about the vanity of celebrity and lovelorn life, Jewsbury hints that domestic bliss would also be a hollow masquerade: "I must *seem* unreasonable, my kind, good friend; because you do not see the feelings and motives that actuate me, only the outward circumstances" (157).

The "ethics of imagination" conveyed to women by the novels of the day, Jewsbury would complain in her second *Athenæum* paper "On Modern Female Cultivation" (1832), consist only of "two great duties," "being beautiful, and being devoted," and "two great occupations," "loving and dying" (96). In *Enthusiast,* she puts her heroine in peril of this lore, precisely to feature her opposition. Of the syllabus of "Female Cultivation," Jewsbury asks, "has it done justice to, has it benefited WOMEN?" then renders an acid Wollstonecrafted verdict:

> We trow not. They have received from poetry and fiction lip homage and knee reverence, adulation, incense, every concomitant of idol-worship, with *only* the absence of fervent rational respect. The process of degradation has taken the semblance of adoration; compliments to their love have veiled contempt of their understanding. (*Athenæum,* 96)

From this theater of derationalized regard and progressive degradation, Jewsbury excuses Julia, and does not stint to fortify her with one last purchase on male-signed romance:

> I must be left to myself—I am so very, very weary. There are four lines written by one with whom, in many things, I can sympathise too well, and I repeat them to myself almost in my sleep—he is addressing the wind, and says
>
>> "O lift me as a wave, a leaf, a cloud;
>> I fall upon the thorns of life—I bleed;
>> A heavy weight of hours has chained and bowed
>> One too like thee, tameless, and swift, and proud."
>
> Julia closed the repetition of these lines with a sigh. "God bless you, and farewell once more, my friend; when I return I shall not, you know, be so very, very weary, so let me go now."
>
> Captain Egerton sighed also, but he relinquished her hand, and in a few moments was left in the room alone.   (*History of an Enthusiast* 160)

Closing in this transitional scene, Jewsbury releases Julia right on the borderlines, heading out in determined self-emancipation, on the wings of Shelley's *Ode to the West Wind*. Refusing to death-sentence the lovelorn heroine, Jewsbury leaves her future left untold—"life, my life is uncertain," is all Julia can say (159). What is certain is the frustration of life in England in 1830 for any female enthusiast. The historian lets Julia's enthusiasm, her ambitions and her desires, her alienated wit and her witty alienation, hang in the air "beyond the ending."[51]

What this recoil of exile and exclusion produces, no less for Hemans than for Jewsbury, is an imagination of a world elsewhere: call it the Continent; call it Heaven; or following Jerome Christensen, call it "anachronism": "signs out of time . . . performing a social movement without a social vehicle," and thus appearing "illegible according to what, in the Preface to *Lyrical Ballads,* Wordsworth calls 'pre-established codes of decision.'"[52] The dislocation operates as a "performative, historicizing trope that is compelling because of its insistently ethical and potentially political import" (208).

Maria Jane Jewsbury: M.J.J./Miss Jewsbury/Mrs. Fletcher

Unsettled by the structural suspense of the *History*'s close, some reviews supplied a corrective armature. *New Monthly,* for all its suspicion of passionless Cecil, was not about to issue Julia a license, and injected a stern moral: "the Enthusiast gives up every hope of happiness" and is "determined to retire and hide her sorrows in a foreign land" (233). Also wanting to tighten up a disciplinary design, Francis Espinasse hammered away on two fronts, a failure and a success: "while Julia, disappointed and solitary, is left to roam about the world in wayward idleness, the purposes and destiny of the authoress are expressed and foreshadowed in the happier finale of the heroine's successful rival for the love and hand of the hero" (329). Admonished Mrs. Ellis in her obituary on Jewsbury for *The Christian Keepsake* (edited by her husband, Revd. William Ellis), *History of an Enthusiast* gives a "most melancholy picture of the ceaseless conflict, the insatiable thirst for what is unattainable, and the final wretchedness necessarily attendant upon the ungoverned ambition of superior intellect, when associated with the weakness, natural dependence and susceptibility of woman" (32).

Yet other reviews not only did not subscribe to, but actively opposed, this view. The newly founded *Edinburgh Journal* wanted to point out a misfit between disciplinary design and the vitality of the author and her heroine. Hailing the author as "a woman of a very superior mind" (the very companion for which teenage Jewsbury wished), a woman whose "soundness of judgment, warmth of feeling, and liveliness of fancy" animate both her writings and her latest heroine, it regretted the moralizing narrative that "traces the career": "the lesson it seems to inculcate is, that the higher the genius, the less likely it is that happiness will be within the reach of the possessor" (270). The irony of *inculcate* is sharp: literally, oppressive trampling, and a synonym of *implant* and *impress,* it evokes Cecil's "implanted [. . .] ideas of domestic life and womanly duty" (127). *Literary Gazette* (impresario of the public romance of L.E.L.) also assayed a pernicious ideological coding in the "moral medicine":

> Julia, the heroine, is young, beautiful, rich, but, alas! a genius—a successful one—and consequently doomed to a life of mental misery, and an early death. Our great objection to this picture is its false groundwork. We neither can nor do believe that the possession of one of Heaven's noblest gifts is like that of the false fair—to be fatal. (24 April 1830, 271)

Although its protest that "poor Genius is blamed" for "the unhappiness [of] an unreturned attachment" may seem to hew to romance codes, there is good critical perception in describing the fettering of female genius to fatal misery as a "picture" with a "false groundwork" (an ideology). For the most part, reviews of *The Three Histories*, including the *Gazette*'s, hailed Jewsbury herself as talent boding still greater "power" and higher reaches of "genius."[53]

Writing as a literary woman about literary women, Jane Williams was as sensitive to the conflicts in genius-Jewsbury as Jewsbury was about Austen's self-discipline. Here is a "woman devoting herself [. . .] assiduously to domestic and family duties," yet so possessed of "secret aspirations" that she also devoted herself "to study," to a "course of literary compositions," and to forming "friendships with the principal authors and authoresses of the day" (373). And here, too, is the reflex of negative discipline: "Dreading, perhaps, to be instrumental in communicating doubt, or in eliciting presumptuous inquiry, her advice on theological and religious subjects tended rather towards dogmatism" (370). It's not that Jewsbury experienced doubt; it's that she didn't want to admit it in(to) social existence and social relations, and so she overcompensated. Thus, too, the discipline of her moodiness: "I am melancholy by nature, cheerful on principle," she wrote to a friend, an epigram that all biographies like to cite.[54] She said this just before she left England, not as Julia, belonging to nobody, but as Mrs. William Kew Fletcher, belonging to a brusque, unimaginative chaplain off to India, in the employ of the East India Company.

He was probably a model for the boat not taken in *The History of Enthusiast* (she knew him as early as 1826): Cecil Percy, appointed "to a chaplaincy in the East Indies" and India. Committed to delivering "the fruit of righteousness" that will save "the heathen part of the world" from its "wickedness," he is no less intent to save Julia from the evil of her genius: all her "motives, energies, youth, and enthusiasm" (he says in the assurance of solemn "TRUTH") are "vanities" that must be renounced for the sake of "the eternal future" (121–22). Just before turning thirty-two, spinster historian Jewsbury married a man whom she seems not to have loved, but was determined to admire. Hemans's sister, the wife of the chaplain who performed the marriage, wrote to Dora Wordsworth about the solemnities: "I must do her the justice to recount that she uttered the terrible 'obey,' with edifying distinctness." The date Jewsbury became Mrs. Fletcher, 1 August 1832, was the same as M.J.J.'s envoi to the reader of *Phantasmagoria*, seven years earlier: 1 August 1825 (2: 309).[55] The calendrics are no accident: Jewsbury meant to turn a page. She went off to India as a chaplain's wife, and within months died in the plague of cholera.

Hemans's letters, and later, the memoirs by William Cooke Taylor and Jane Williams, all read Jewsbury's marriage as self-correction, duty realized, and a martyr's death. Even as Taylor fixed her fame with a place in his *National Portrait Gallery of Illustrious and Eminent Personages*, he rendered a temper averse to such eminence:

> this worthy lady cheerfully sacrificed, to a sense of duty, her own peculiar tastes and inclinations, lest they should interfere with household cares; and so far did she carry her generous self-denial, that she never allowed herself to open a book in the evening til the children were gone to rest. (37)

He even hinted that the collapse of her health after *Phantasmagoria* was due to a distraction of "anxious interest" from domestic cares (37). In other Victorian sermons, Jewsbury learned too little, too late. Mrs. Ellis cited the *History*'s sigh on female genius ("Ah, what is genius to a woman, but a splendid misfortune! What is fame to woman, but a dazzling degradation!") to moralize about Jewsbury herself (*Christian Keepsake* 39). Although she concedes that "many and unkind things are said of literary women" (33) and recognizes "those flashes of genius, and that bursting forth of powerful intellect, by which [Jewsbury] was so strikingly distinguished from the more superficial writers of her day, and which gave promise of a degree of literary eminence which few women have attained" (38), her sympathy halts at the Enthusiast's "conflict": "elements of intellectual greatness are seldom allied to those of social and domestic happiness, especially in woman." No social production for Ellis, this misalliance is a natural guarantee: the "fervour" and "impulse of feeling connected with high mental capabilities" is "at variance in their nature with the repose, and too often with the loveliness, of the female character" (36). So, too, for all its sympathy for Jewsbury's struggles, Williams's *Literary Women* reads *The History of an Enthusiast* as the tale of "a selfish woman of genius, full of worldly ambition," who regards "her rare abilities and attainments merely as forming a lever to raise her into the sphere of fashionable distinction" and shallow "fame" (385).

Yet Espinasse, for all his moralism about the *History*, can't quite fix the case for Jewsbury. One the one hand, guessing the lure of a lioness life ("It is possible that in the social whirl of London so striking a woman, and one whose

Figure 4.1 *Mrs. Fletcher, late M. J. Jewsbury*, by G. Freeman, engraved by J. Cochran (1832). The slight tension in this image of Jewsbury posed with a book (or manuscript), looking more impatient than wistful in the festoons of feminine fashions and accessories, is apt: in 1832 Jewsbury accepted a husband unsympathetic to her literary vocation. Although she was determined as "Mrs. Fletcher" to stay true, she knew the cost: "Authorship is the only accredited vent for a woman's intellect; and this, by obviating one evil, induces many others. The fever of unoccupied energy is quenched: but, by and bye, the worse fever of sensitive ambition, or ungratified longing after sympathy, arises, and her position in society becomes yet more false," she wrote in an unsigned essay published 11 August 1832 in the *Athenæum,* ten days after her marriage.

conversation was so vivid, may have been visited by transient impulses of social ambition"), he has no trouble imagining (in the same sentence) it chastened "with that contempt for such aspiration which philosophy, religion, and sharp feminine insight into character could scarcely fail to engender in reflective moods and moments": "If there was in Miss Jewsbury's mind and heart any conflict of the kind, it ended." On the other hand, his sense of this ending wavers: that "Some traces of the struggle may perhaps be discovered" in *The Three Histories* (329) suggests irresolution—for Jewsbury and for Espinasse. What discipline does a recourse to religion engender anyway? M.J.J.'s essay on "Religious Novels" in *Phantasmagoria* satirized storytelling pedagogy, not only on the agenda but also, more fundamentally, with a sense of the indeterminacy of reading, which Jewsbury knew (on her own confession) was often "the art of skipping" over the plot put down:

> it may be very much doubted whether it is possible to *coax* human nature into the performance of any painful duty, or the surrender of any evil temper, however the medium which conveys the truth may be sugared, or however delightfully the hero, or heroine, may set us an example of performing the duty, or surrendering the temper in question. Besides, it is forgotten that the young, (and it is they who principally read these works,) are generally good adepts in the art of skipping (to use the school phrase) whatever parts may be too serious for their taste, and those, the very, and indeed the only parts, which can tend to their edification. (1: 46–47)

In this doubt, and in recollection of the ways of the young reader, Jewsbury intuits a paradigm for the end of *The History of an Enthusiast*. Is Julia diminished? Julia released? Julia banished? England banished? The open ending shapes a female negative capability, when a woman is capable of being in uncertainties, mysteries, doubts.

It has been in the paradigm of defeat, strangely, that Jewsbury's chief recent critics cast her story.[56] Monica Fryckstedt, though she wants to recover a forgotten writer of palpable promise thwarted by early death (177), plots a sorry life. Her chapters move through "Adolescence and Literary Debut" (179), the *Phantasmagoria* satires, the religious "Conversion" reflected in *Letters to the Young*, a rejection of fame, and the tepid, conventional *Lays of Leisure Hours*. *The Three Histories* is tuned accordingly, its flashes of talent, wit, and satire stamped out by *Corinne*-tragedy, with a moral lesson: realizing that her success "has been in vain" and that genius devoid of Christian faith is no genius at all, lovelorn Julia leaves for the Continent in search of "refuge" (452, 459). The cold lesson is what makes "the deepest impression" on Jewsbury, seems "basically" the case, "permeates her best writings," and shapes a "proper understanding" of Jewsbury for her readers (469–70). Even Fryckstedt's archival discoveries are mined to serve this account. Norma Clarke tweaks it slightly to propose a strategy of "appeasement" behind which Jewsbury continued to write (56–57); yet she patterns out abjection pretty much along the lines argued by Fryckstedt: the satiric spirit of *Phantasmagoria* and then its success bring on illness; the initiatives with Wordsworth fail and settle for friendships with his sister and his daughter; hence a farewell to the muse and the religion of humility reflected in *Letters to the Young* and its disciplinary sequel, *The History of an Enthusiast*.[57] Thus focused, Clarke elides the Phantasmagorian satires of *Enthusiast*, especially about what "Man" (in the pallid icon of Cecil Percy) thinks of "high intellect in women" (124; Clarke 84–86). What I like most about her account is her review of Fryckstedt's sense of the ending: Jewsbury's patent refusal of the standard menu of "sickness, retirement, domesticity, and death" becomes a platform from which to send her heroine "forward into an unknown, uncharted new life" (86). Clarke reads this charter right into the biographical sequel of Jewsbury's "masculine" career at *The Athenæum,* one that Mrs. Fletcher was determined to sustain as a foreign correspondent.

It's an irony of literary history that Jewsbury's unsigned essay on stay-at-home Austen found its credit cross-dressed. In 1833, on the occasion of Richard Bentley's republication of *Sense and Sensibility* in his Standard Novels series, Henry Austen added to his *Biographical Notice* of 1817 some "extracts from a critical journal of the highest reputation" (xi). The single source he indicates was actually a patchwork, consisting of a big (somewhat redacted) swath of Jewsbury's recent, unsigned essay in the *Athenæum*, and a final paragraph from an unsigned retrospect in the *Quarterly* by Richard Whately, published ten years earlier.[58] It was the Whately couverture that led G. H. Lewes, in 1859, to attribute the whole to him (*Blackwood's* 86:104)—a text including, ironically, Jewsbury's remark that Austen had won her readers well before her "éclat" in posthumous reviews, such as the *Quarterly*'s of 1821. Cross-dressed as he-critic Whately, Jewsbury's writing on Austen gained its credit and its fame.[59] How a woman may be heard under male cover, or what a man may say with a woman's words, becomes the extravagant experiment of Byron's transvestite adventures.

Two Men

Pray dispense me . . . from Mrs. Hemans. . . . No more <u>Keats</u> I entreat . . . there is no bearing the drivelling idiotism of the Mankin.

—LORD BYRON TO JOHN MURRAY, 8 OCTOBER 1820

You see what it is to be under six foot and not a lord.

—JOHN KEATS TO GEORGE AND GEORGIANA KEATS, 14 FEBRUARY 1819

I do think better of womankind than to suppose they care whether Mister John Keats five feet hight likes them or not.

—JOHN KEATS TO BENJAMIN BAILEY, 22 JULY 1818

Never, in English verse, has a man been seen who was so much a man and so much an Englishman. It is not man in the elemental sense, so much as the man of the world.

—ARTHUR SYMONS, ON LORD BYRON, 'THE ROMANTIC MOVEMENT,' 1909

CHAPTER FIVE

Lord Byron, *Sardanapalus*, and "Effeminate Character"

> I do think the preference of <u>writers</u> to <u>agents</u>—the mighty stir made about scribbling and scribes, by themselves and others—a sign of effeminacy, degeneracy, and weakness. Who would write, who had any thing better to do?
>
> —BYRON'S JOURNAL, 24 NOVEMBER 1813

Cultures of Effeminacy

The very culture that made Byron famous also struck him as symptomatic of a rampant disease: effeminacy. Was its most buzzed about poet thus contaminated? In 1821 Byron finally put the question to public reckoning with *Sardanapalus,* a self-conscious staging of "effeminate character" (*BLJ* 8: 128) in the exotic idiom of ancient Assyria.[1] Hazlitt had no trouble bringing the issue home, the following year, in his essay "On Effeminacy of Character." The palimpsest was transparent. "EFFEMINACY of character," begins his elaborate diagnosis,

> arises from a prevalence of the sensibility over the will: or it consists in a want of fortitude to bear pain or to undergo fatigue, however urgent the occasion. We meet with instances of people who cannot lift up a little finger to save themselves from ruin, nor give up the smallest indulgence for the sake of any other person. They cannot put themselves out of their way on any account. [. . .] They live in the present moment, are the creatures of the present

impulse [. . . .] beyond that, the universe is nothing to them. The slightest toy countervails the empire of the world. (*W* 8: 248)

What is remarkable is that despite the flagrant gendering of the disease, Hazlitt is not describing sexual activity, nor provoking the developing equation of effeminacy with the sexual corruptions denounced in such livid tirades as *The Ten Plagues of England*.[2] Hazlitt's scandal of evacuated manhood names something uncloseted and abroad, a character in the public threatening to model a public character. The icon was Sardanapalus, with Hazlitt training on a domestic brood the complaints that Byron scripted for the Assyrian king's frustrated allies as they watch the truant fumble the empire. "He must be roused. Alas! there is no sound/ To rouse him short of thunder," laments royal brother-in-law Salemenes (1.1.27–28). "Nothing but a miracle can rouse such people from their lethargy," writes Hazlitt, with the same verbal compass; "Will you rouse the indolent procrastinator to an irksome but necessary effort, by shewing him how much he has to do? He will only draw back the more for all your intreaties and representations" (250). The effeminate seems all too born for languid opposition.

"Such people" are one thing, but an "effeminate thing that governs" (2.1.95) raises the stakes from social decadence to national peril. This was the hot alarm of John Brown's mid-eighteenth-century *Estimate of the Manners and Principles of the Times*. Mindful of "the declining State of the *Roman* Republic" (78), Brown cries havoc for England: "We are rolling to the Brink of a Precipice that must destroy us" (15), sped along by a "*vain, luxurious,* and *selfish* EFFEMINACY" (66–67). "It is indulgence and luxury that effeminates us," lectures a conversant a few years on in Clara Reeve's *Progress of Romance* (1785) (2: 75). Coleridge echoed the gendering at the century's end to indict a degenerate body politic. *Fears in Solitude, Written, April 1798, during the Alarms of an Invasion* arraigns materialistic, corrupt, tyrannical Britons as a "selfish, lewd, effeminated race" (57).

As the verb-form suggests, *effeminated* is not just character, but cultural process. Wollstonecraft marked the erosion even where one might least suppose it, in "the present system" of military life: it was more a scandalous "school of *finesse* and effeminacy, than of fortitude" (*VRW* 283). Of boys spoiled into "vain and effeminate" men (*VRW* 299–300), of rich who "supinely exist without exercising mind or body" and so have "ceased to be men," and of "noble families" whose reek of "luxury and effeminacy" spreads the "contagion of restless idleness [. . .] through the whole mass of society" (*VRM* 11–12, 51–52), class-fed corruption was the culpable cause. With the hint of *finesse*, all this amounts to a home culture of *ancien-régime* "profligates of rank, emasculated by hereditary effeminacy," who earned a revolution in France (*VRM* 97).³⁰ That such republican invective could find agreement in conservative monitoring was not lost on the conservatives: a profligate aristocracy eroded the claim of hereditary privilege and gave themes to critics.⁴ After Waterloo, and with unrivaled British world power now on the horizon of expectation, monitors such as Hazlitt issued cautionary bulletins about a national relapse into the French-style effeminacy that enabled a revolution: "we laugh at the prophet of ill"; "we resent wholesome counsel as an impertinence" (*W* 8: 251).

But what of Byron in this plural, and in Byronic figuration? He was nothing if not shifty. In 1818, from abroad, he spoofed the sermonizers in *Beppo*, casting the Regency version of the effeminate *ancien régime*, its "dynasty of Dandies," into a mock-heroic of that *de casibus* genre in which Sardanapalus was a familiar: "how / Irreparably soon decline, alas! / The demagogues of fashion: all below / Is frail; how easily the world is lost," sighs the blasé poet (60), adding Napoleon to the club (Byron also drafted "Anthony," a mirror of Sardanapalus; *BPW* 4: 148). In perfect reflex, *Beppo* itself was indexed as a dangerous infection: traducing all that is "manly and true" (railed the *British Review*'s editor, William Roberts), it reflected the "denationalizing spirit" that, ever "since the late revolution in France," was fueling "a decay of that masculine decency, and sobriety, and soundness of sentiment, which, about half a century ago, made us dread the contagion of French or Italian manners." There was no better warning to England to "dread an amalgamation with the Continent" than decadent Byron himself, "dipped in the deepest die of Italian debauchery" (11: 329–30). Yet Byron was more prismatic than single-dyed, and the *British*'s outrage over a trifle such as *Beppo* also managed to register what was so charming about dandyism: its cheeky irreverence and counter-cultural play with masculinity as spectacle. It was social theater, performed by a "class / Of imitated imitators" (60) for a public whose shock, amusement, or envy could be counted on. This is the coding of Byronic Sardanapalus, on the dandy pattern Ellen Moers so nicely describes: "a Hero so evidently at the centre of the stage that he need do nothing to prove his heroism—need never, in fact, do anything" except radiate "superiority, irresponsibility, inactivity" (*The Dandy* 13). It was a class act flaunting an aristocratic charter.

"I liked the Dandies," Byron recalled when he had *Sardanapalus* in press; "I had a tinge of Dandyism in my minority—& probably retained enough of it—to conciliate the great ones—at four & twenty.————I had gamed—& drank—& taken my degree in most dissipations" (*BLJ* 9: 22). If the *British* read dissipated masculinity, dandy Byron tweaked bad-boyism with feminine flair. Meeting him in 1811, Isaac D'Israeli was shocked by a "fantastic and effeminate thing," "all rings and curls and lace"; "he looked more like a girl than a boy." Scrope Davies dropped in on the twenty-something lad late one night the same year to find him "in bed with his hair *en papillote* [. . .] acting the part of the Sleeping Beauty"—gender as practice and gender as theater. Busted, Byron copped to a nightly ritual: "I am as vain of my curls as a girl of sixteen."[5] Well into the manhood of his Italian years, Byron affected the "character" (so E. J. Trelawny reported) of the old dandy "vogue": "Byron, not knowing the tribe was extinct, still prided himself on having belonged to it; of nothing was he more indignant, than of being treated as a man of letters, instead of as a Lord and a man of fashion" (41). Leigh Hunt cattily etched the Sardanapalian gender-effects:

> He had a delicate white hand, of which he was proud; and he attracted attention to it by rings. [. . .] He often appeared holding a handkerchief, upon which his jewelled fingers lay embedded, as in a picture. He [. . .] had the remnant of his hair oiled and trimmed with all the anxiety of a Sardanapalus. (*Lord Byron* 156)[6]

This was 1828. Carlyle was soon at work on *Sartor Resartus*, stitching into it a ranting chapter on "The Dandiacal Body" that is exquisitely alert to the theatricality. The editor previews his presentation of Teufelsdröckh's anatomy with his own deft satire on this "Poet of Cloth": "A Dandy is a clothes-wearing Man"; "he lives to dress," asking only that "you would recognise his existence [. . .] as a visual object"; he "solicits [. . .] simply the glance of your eyes" (313–14). No incarnation of essential Man, the Dandy is a specular rhetoric, produced from same social grammar, in Carlylean logic, as "Poet"—a composition of style.[7] By the chapter's end, however, the satirical aim is visibly confused by a Byronic glamor. The editor can't quite fix the tone of Teufelsdröckh's own take on the Dandy, unsure whether it is "piercing vision," "satire," or just "blinkard," and he's at a loss as to its "Practical Inference" (323–24).

In the spectacle of Byron himself, flagrant gender effects proved just as slippery to judgment. Estimate Brown cited "the higher Ranks" for "effeminate Refinement" (153), but in those silver-fork novel fashions of the 1830s that irked Carlyle, Mary Shelley could give a liberal pass to her Lord-Byron-coded Lord Lodore: "Although essentially spoiled, he was not pampered in luxury. [. . .] he possessed none of those habits of effeminacy" evident in "our young self-indulged aristocracy."[8] In Byron's day Hazlitt argued the case: "Lord Byron is a pampered and aristocratic writer, but he is not effeminate, or we should not have his works with only the printer's name to them!" he said, closing his survey of effeminacy not with Byron, but with Keats's disturbingly lush style.[9]

Blackwood's Christopher North actually seethed at Hunt's anecdotes of Byron's effeminacy. "What if the Grand Signior did take the youthful Byron for a woman in disguise?"; "The mistake of that barbarian" is no proof "that his lordship had an effeminate appearance." With Popean acidity, he defended Byron by charging Hunt himself (a pet target in *Blackwood's* gender-sports) with "a Sporus-like effeminacy in the loose and languid language in which he drawls out his sentence into what he thinks the fine-sounding word Sardanapalus" (32: 393)—North evidently enjoying, under hunting cover, his own fine-sounding sentence.[10]

With the shimmer of Byronic license, *Sardanapalus* tests the possibilities for freedom of style—personal, political, and literary—within the structures of social experience; and Byron is willing to risk some undecidable estimates.[11] Casting its specular dynamics meta-theatrically, he puts *effeminacy* into a script that perplexes interpretation. While the term summarizes all that is pampered and luxurious, the play as a whole amasses disparate, often conflicting synonyms: sloth, self-indulgence, self-mystification, hedonism, eroticism, aristocratic privilege, devotion to women, political idealism, humanitarian compassion, oppositional critique. Byron tweaks the contradictions by playing the lexicon—*effeminate, feminine, manly,* and *unmanly*—across a fraught cultural syntax, not only in the Assyrian imaginary but also in the modern world.[12] The reviews bristled at the rifts and contradictions. To "receive lectures on social morality from the mouth of the effeminate King of Assyria," protested the *British* (Roberts again), doesn't just strain historical probability; it betrays "the best interests of society": the "ill-conceived and unnatural combination" of traits still adds up to an "effeminate prostitution of manners" (19: 72–73). Even Whiggish *Scots Edinburgh* objected to the gender logic, arguing that "the passion for effeminate enjoyments was never found in company with the love of humankind, or with reluctance to occasion human misery" (2d ser. 10: 103, 105). Such contradictions, set in a view of manners as a dialectic of individual style and cultural determination, went by another name in Byron's day: *Byronism*—an eponym by 1821 (*BLJ* 8: 114). Sardanapalus was legibly the latest, drollest, and most decadent presentation of a Byronic hero, that character type with an authorial template.[13]

What makes this hero more than just a serial installment is the intimate investment of its figural extremes with Byron's uneasy, fragmented self-reading as writer, social lion, erotic liberal and frustrated political activist. That murmur in 1813 over authorial celebrity as a sign of cultural "effeminacy, degeneracy, and weakness" (*BLJ* 3: 220) came only a year after the éclat of *Childe Harold* and only days after publisher Murray offered (so Byron records) "one thousand guineas for the 'Giaour' and the 'Bride of Abydos' [. . .] No bad price for a fortnight's (a week each) what?—the gods know" (3: 212). What other poets might have embraced as confirmation of vocational manhood, or at least "attaching that importance to authorship which many do," Byron disparaged for its difference from real agency: "Who would write, who had anything better to do? 'Action—action—action'—said Demosthenes: 'Actions—actions,' I say, and not writing,—least of all, rhyme" (3: 220). It is on a plan of actions to challenge, or anyway qualify, reports of effeminacy, degeneracy, and weakness that the poetry of *Sardanapalus* takes shape. Byron opens with a spectacle of "effeminacy" with a difference, marked by "latent energies, / Repress'd by circumstance, but not destroy'd" (1.1.11–12), and thus scripted for a rise into action:

> Baal himself
> Ne'er fought more fiercely to win empire, than
> His silken son to save it; he defies
> All augury of foes or friends. (3.1.312–15)

So the palace soldiers marvel at the king's belated, bold dash into battle, Byron-pumped with Shakespearean fuel—a bit of Prince Hamlet's delayed surge into action ("Not a whit, we defy augury"), and a whole fraternity of war-transformed silken sons in *Henry V*: "Now all the youth of England are on fire, / And silken dalliance in the wardrobe lies." Heroizing Sardanapalus, these cues for action also project Byron's longing for self-renewal through political crisis, his hero set forth to vindicate, even idealize, his "conception of his own character."[14]

The urgency is the uncertain fate of this conception for Byron in modern Italy. Unlike Sardanapalus's Nineveh, Ravenna was already under foreign domination and astir with intrigue and revolt. Byron was supplying money, advice, and collaboration.[15] In this respect, he was more like a rebel satrap than a decadent Sardanapalus. At the same time, his recreations with Teresa Guiccioli left this jaded dandy, facile rhymer, and politically defunct ex-pat Lord feeling a kinship with the king. Long before, he knew that he was susceptive of "softening in the presence of a woman" (*BLJ* 3: 246). And now, variously bored and amused by the social routines or Ravenna, and always restless as Teresa's boytoy (he was writing of Juan's harem travesty these same months), he wanted to harden up.

For an antidote, he was reading lives of heroes and longing for release from a "lifetime, more or less ennuyé"; the only cure for his "depressed spirits," he sensed, was an arousal by "Violent passions" (*BLJ* 8: 15). This seemed possible in Italy in early 1821, when the threat of Austrian invasion heated hopes of revolution.[16] By mid-January, Byron was caught up in the excitement and busily outlining a long-planned, defense-prone "tragedy of Sardanapalus":

Took the names from Diodorus Siculus, (I know the history of Sardanapalus, and have known it since I was twelve years old), and read over a passage in [. . .] Mitford's Greece, where he rather vindicates the memory of this last of the Assyrians.

Dined—news come—the <u>Powers</u> mean to war with the peoples. The intelligence seems positive—let it be so—they will be beaten in the end. The king-times are fast finishing. There will be blood shed like water, and tears like mist; but the peoples will conquer in the end. I shall not live to see it, but I foresee it. (*BLJ* 8: 26)

Yet this last Mosaic figure of prophecy without participation intuits the discontinuity between the politics of the play and the play of politics in Italy, each situating the end of king-times with a different, even opposite value.

Byron's journal becomes an imprint of this problem, a chronicle of hot purposes fissuring into lapses of faith and relapses into trivial business, of lethargy amid reading, scribbling, aimless activity, and the stir of ultimately futile Carbonari political intrigue:

<u>January 14th, 1821</u>   Turned over Seneca's tragedies. Wrote the opening lines of the intended tragedy of Sardanapalus. Rode out some miles into the forest. Misty and rainy. Returned—dined—wrote some more of my tragedy.

Read Diodorus Siculus—turned over Seneca, and some other books. Wrote some more of the tragedy. Took a glass of grog. After having ridden hard in rainy weather, and scribbled, and scribbled again, the spirits (at least mine) need a little exhilaration, and I don't like laudanum now as I used to do. [. . .] The effect of all wines and spirits upon me is, however, strange. It <u>settles</u>, but it makes me gloomy [. . .] and not gay hardly ever. But it composes me for a time, though sullenly.

<u>January 15th, 1821</u>   Weather fine. Received visit. Rode out into the forest—fired pistols. Returned home—dined—dipped into a volume of Mitford's Greece—wrote part of a scene of "Sardanapalus." Went out—heard some music—heard some politics [. . .] War seems certain—in that case, it will be a savage one. (*BLJ* 8: 27)

From this looming certainty he is distracted by a memory from 1814, reading a gazette with Tom Moore (off to "to dine with Earl Grey, the Capo Politico of the remaining whigs") and finding "a dispute" on their respective poetic merits. Calling up some of the references he was using to shape the voices of Sardanapalus's critics in the play, Byron sighs of himself:

there is <u>fame</u> for you at six and twenty! Alexander had conquered India at the same age; but I doubt if he was disputed about, or his conquests compared with those of Indian Bacchus. [. . .] The only pleasure of fame is that it paves the way to pleasure; and the more intellectual our pleasure, the better for the pleasure and for us too. (*BLJ* 8: 27–28)

Who would write, who had anything better to do?

> January 16th, 1821 Read—rode—fired pistols—returned—dined—wrote—visited—heard music—talked nonsense—and went home.
>   Wrote part of a Tragedy—advance in Act 1st with "all deliberate speed." Bought a blanket. [. . .] Politics still mysterious. (*BLJ* 8: 28)

He quotes Portia's instructing Balthasar to get things going for her transvestite intervention into Venetian civic affairs (*Merchant of Venice* 3.4.56). But he writes of a decadent transvestite and buys a blanket. Thus January is absorbed, and this is life: "am not in spirits to continue my proposed tragedy of Sardanapalus, which I have, for some days, ceased to compose," he moans on the 21st, aggravated by a reckoning: "To-morrow is my birthday [. . .] in twelve minutes, I shall have completed thirty and three years of age!!!—and I go to my bed with a heaviness of heart at having lived so long, and to so little purpose."

But the pattern holds: "Read—Rode—fired pistols, and returned. Dined—read. Went out at eight—made the usual visit" (he notes on the 23d); "Heard of nothing but war,—'the cry is still, They come'"—a rueful, mock-heroic quoting of Macbeth's news of his enemies' advance (5.5.1–2). "The Cari seem to have no plan—nothing fixed among themselves, how, when, or what to do. In that case, they will make nothing of the project, so often postponed, and never put in action" (*BLJ* 8: 31–32). They multiply and magnify his own vacillations. So he sketches a plan for his action:

> Came home, and gave some necessary orders, in case of circumstances requiring a change of place. I shall act according to what may seem proper, when I hear decidedly what the Barbarians mean to do. At present, they are building a bridge of boats over the Po, which looks very warlike. A few days will probably show. I think of retiring towards Ancona [. . .] if Teresa and her father are obliged to retire [. . . .] But my movements will depend upon the lady's wishes—for myself it is much the same.
>   I am somewhat puzzled what do with my little daughter, and my effects, which are of some quantity and value. [. . .] Half the city are getting their affairs in marching trim. A pretty Carnival! (*BLJ* 8: 33)

It's as if everyone had become Sardanapalus: "met some masques in the Corso—'Vive la bagatelle!'[17]—the Germans are on the Po, the Barbarians at the gate [. . .], and lo! they dance and sing, and make merry, 'for tomorrow they may die.' [. . .] The principal persons in the events which may occur in a few days are gone out on a <u>shooting party</u>," a "snivelling, popping, small-shot, water-hen waste of powder, ammunition, and shot, for their own special amusement" (33).

By February Byron's hope of transformation by "events" was fading, his mood-swings more intense: "What I feel most growing upon me are laziness, and a disrelish more powerful than indifference. If I rouse, it is into fury. [. . .] Oh! there is an organ playing in the street—a waltz, too! I must leave off to listen" (*BLJ* 8: 42–43). "Much as usual," he writes on the 14th:

> Wrote, before riding out, part of a scene of "Sardanapalus." The first act nearly finished. The rest of the day and evening as before. [. . .] Heard the particulars of the late fray at Russi, a town not far from this. [. . .] Another assassination has taken place at Cesenna,—in all about <u>forty</u> in Romagna within the last three months. (*BLJ* 8: 45)

He finished Act 1 of *Sardanapalus* that night. By the 18th he has thoroughly compounded the energies invested in the drama with those of the projected Carbonari revolt: "It is a grand object—the very <u>poetry</u> of politics. Only think—a free Italy!!! Why, there has been nothing like it since the days of Augustus" (*BLJ* 8: 47). But prospects pretty much washed out on March 7, when the Austrians defeated the Neapolitan army at Rieti.

The poetry of politics was becoming an ironic embarrassment. Byron wrote to Murray (on Bastille Day, no less), "I trust that 'Sardanapalus' will not be mistaken for a <u>political</u> play—which was so far from my intention that I thought of nothing but Asiatic history" (*BLJ* 8: 152).[18] It's either a coy protest or a transparently defensive disclaimer from one who for months had been romancing the "<u>poetry</u> of politics" on the pivot of "of": politics, distilled to its essence, as a vindication *of* poetry; politics as the grand subject *of* poetry. Yet even as Byron was insisting to Moore later in April that "no time nor circumstances shall alter my tone nor my feelings of indignation against tyranny triumphant," his activity amid "the present business" is chiefly writing, with a sigh of failure and a Shakespearean falling off:

> And now let us be literary;—a sad falling off, but it is always a consolation. If "Othello's occupation be gone," let us take to the next best; and, if we cannot contribute to make mankind more free and wise, we may amuse ourselves and those who like it. What are you writing? I have been scribbling at intervals. (*BLJ* 8: 104–5)

The dandy was still in vogue.

Staging Gender, Signifying Effeminacy

If Byron shifts about the politics of *Sardanapalus*, his staging of a politically gendered culture is as sharply etched as it is on the fields outside Shakespeare's Troy, where even Patroclus, the boytoy who keeps Achilles in his tent and from the field, can recite the party line: "A woman impudent and mannish grown / Is not more loathed than an effeminate man / In time of action" (*Troilus and Cressida* 3.3.217–19). In Byron's Assyria (knowingly set in this Shakespearean shadow as well as Cleopatra's Alexandria), if a man is not manly, he is effeminate; if a woman is not feminine, she is a monster. Of these polarities, *Sardanapalus* is a virtual primer. There are critical disturbances in the syntax, but it takes a crisis to release these into disarray, and it takes a war to produce a spectacular transformation. The crucible of emergency reflexively confirms the norm—its laws escapable, Byron lets himself intuit in his theatrical imaginary, only by a determined opting out of historical imperatives altogether.

On a frame of these imperatives the stage of Nineveh is set. On the feminine side are the harem, the king's "favorite," Greek slave Myrrha, and his sequestered, neglected queen, Zarina. On the masculine, a deep patriarchal field. The icon is Nimrod, "hunter-founder of [his] race" (4.1.179); the avatar is Salemenes, royal advisor and voice of empire; and the rhetorical circuit, "what all good men tell each other" (1.1.45)—all harsh critics of the king's effeminate "mode of life or rule" (1.2.246). Yet it matters, too, that the two women who are most important to Sardanapalus are not polar opposites to this masculine culture, no clueless domestic luxuriators. Mother of princes Zarina is mindful of dynasty. Myrrha, no less than Salemenes, begs the king to have a care for "thy past fathers' race, / And for thy sons' inheritance" (1.2.589–90). A "female Salemenes," a voice of "manly counsels," said Reginald Heber of her (*Quarterly* 27: 496).[19] Byron makes Salemenes the keynote speaker. "Oh that I could rouse thee!" he cries to the king (1.2.63), miming the choral voice of Shakespeare's Philo reporting Antony's fall into Egyptian luxury, and sounding the very verb—*rouse*—that sighed Byron's longings amid the idles of Ravenna:

> He must be roused. In his effeminate heart
> There is a careless courage which corruption
> Has not all quench'd, and latent energies,
> Repress'd by circumstance but not destroy'd—
> Steep'd, but not drown'd, in deep voluptuousness. (1.1.9–13)

With the etymology of "courage" in the effeminate "heart," Salemenes anatomizes (after Byron's heart) a prodigal lapse from a still legible grammar of manhood under wraps: alive, not quenched; latent, not absent; repressed, not destroyed;

deep-steeped, not drowned: "not all lost, even yet he may redeem / His sloth and shame, by only being that / Which he should be": one who would "sway his nations" and "head an army" rather than "rule a harem" (1.1.18–23).

But it is the scandalous default, with national destiny at stake, that calls up the ghost of Estimate Brown: the end of "thirteen hundred years / Of empire" impends as this king "sweats in palling pleasures" (1.1.7–8, 24; "in dreary dulled effeminacy," Byron first wrote),[20] and "Lolls crown'd with roses," while his "diadem / Lies negligently by to be caught up / By the first manly hand which dares to snatch it" (34–36). In the king's looming legacy as "nothing but a name," Salemenes whispers a rhyme to the cause, "sloth and shame" (16–19); "all the nations" that "thy father left / In heritage, are loud in wrath against thee," he will warn, ringing another (frequent) chime: this "king" as "a nothing" (1.2.98–102). The prophet of this "nothing" is no man. As "femininely garb'd" as his harem (the gender-adverb was revised from "glitteringly"), Sardanapalus is a travesty, "scarce less female" (1.1.42). Heralding the entry of "The grandson of Semiramis, the man-queen" (43), Salemenes's disparaging syntax lets "man-queen" point both to the *he* and the *she* (Spence 60). The *he* scandal is clinched by the advent, cued for readers by Byron's stage direction at the top of Scene 2:

> *Enter* SARDANAPALUS *effeminately dressed, his Head crowned with Flowers, and his Robe negligently flowing, attended by a Train of Women and young Slaves.*

One can read the punning of *Flowers* into *flowing*, recall Shakespeare's Antony's swooshing onto the stage of Cleopatra's palace (a fatal political omen), or remember Milton's Samson lamenting the "foul effeminacy" of his sensuous "slavery" to Dalila (407–19).[21]

These effeminates are all orientalized.[22] Yet in the ever-readiness of gender-terms to broadcast crisis, Byron returns a home language. Writing in 1830, Coleridge invoked laws of gender as if these descended from a metaphysics of pure opposites that "suppose and require each other." "The feminine character is *opposed* to the masculine; but the effeminate is its *contrary*."[23] In such a regime, a "monarch subject to his slaves" (1.1.47) is no figure of liberal reform, but a spur to revolt. But even the rebels feel degraded by the "woman's warfare" of overthrowing a "king of concubines" (2.1.59, 82):

> To have pluck'd
> A bold and bloody despot from his throne,
> And grappled with him, clashing steel with steel,
> That were heroic or to win or fall;
> But to upraise my sword against this silk-worm . . . (2.1.83–87)

Bearing Pope's contempt of Sporus—"that Thing of silk" (*Arbuthnot* 305)—this silk-worm is a cancer on the monarchy. "Better bow down before the Hun, and call / A Tartar lord, than these swoln silkworms masters!" a conspirator in *Marino Faliero* hisses of such "unmanly creeping things"; "The first at least was man, and used his sword" (2.2.114–117). "The she-king, / That less than woman," sneers Assyrian conspirator Arbaces (2.1.48–49). From Estimate Brown to conductrix Stodart, the unmanly man gets no credit as a gender-liberal. He is only a silky grotesque: "when a man displaces himself by frivolity and folly from his rank in the creation," warns Stodart, "he does not take his standing with the excellent of the subordinate sex, but with quite the lower members."[24]

To refute such a downgrade and the slander of having turned the scepter "into a distaff," "king of distaffs" Sardanapalus (2.1.344) tries to enlist he-man Hercules, scorned for loving "a Lydian queen" (1.2.324–30) and sporting her distaff. Anyone up on the mythology would see a hand under-played: Queen Omphale enslaved Hercules, forcing him into female dress and she-tasks of spinning and weaving, while she took on his lion skin and club.[25] Even Myrrha won't endorse the appeal, likening her king's "effeminate arts" to Hercules's shame "in wearing Lydian Omphale's / She-garb, and wielding her vile distaff" (3.1.219–22). Sardanapalus's abuse of patriarchal trophies seems merely contrary rather than politically honed. He parties in the "hall of Nimrod" and uses "Nimrod's chalice" to toast Bacchus (1.2.635, 160), a deity he blithely Sardanapalizes for his in-house critics: his renown is not his conquest of India, but "the immortal grape" (166–74)—a legacy "better . . . than Nimrod's huntings, / Or my wild grandam's chase in search of kingdoms / She could not keep when conquer'd" (3.1.5–7). Sardanapalus means to condescend to his grandam, but as with Omphale, her name has its own signifying power. The legendary "man-queen" is foil to a "she-king." "Semiramis—a woman only," chides Salemenes in the voice of public history, led "our Assyrians to the solar shores / Of Ganges" and returned "like a *man*—a hero; baffled, but / Not vanquish'd" (1.2.126–30). When Arbaces, abashed by Sardanapalus's noble pardon, murmurs, "Semiramis herself would not have done it," his co-conspirator Beleses tags him a "Sardanapalus! / I know no name more ignominious," and he piles it on: "the *pardon'd* slave of *she* Sardanapalus," the italics scoring the metrical stress (2.1.368–73, 404).

With such conversations Byron canvasses a regime quick to applaud violence as manly, and to scorn reluctance as effeminate, each cheer and sneer sounding the totalizing logic. And he sets Sardanapulus outside, as Byronic critic—a wry, ironic heterosexual, who flaunts "effeminate character" as a style of refusal. The character is also Byron's patent refusal of the degenerate effeminate, transvestite, man-and-woman-loving libertine transmitted down through the centuries from Diodorus Siculus:

He lived the life of a woman, and spending his days in the company of his
concubines and spinning purple garments and working the softest of wool, he
had assumed the feminine garb and so covered his face and indeed his entire
body with whitening cosmetics and the other unguents used by courtesans,
that he rendered it more delicate than that of any luxury-loving woman. He
also took care to make even his voice to be like a woman's, and [. . .] to pursue
the delights of love with men as well as with women; for he practised sexual
indulgence of both kinds without restraint. (1.425–27)

Byron gives this "Story" as his Latin source, and asks Murray to have it "translated—as an explanation—and a note to the drama." In the dramatic context, however, it is more foil than gloss.[26]

Byron knew the legion scandals, refreshed in Lemprière's popular *Classical Dictionary* and featured in Lydgate's *Fall of Princes*. Under the title, "How vicious Sardanapalle kyng of Assirie brent himsilff and his treso*ur*," Lydgate portrays a king of base appetites, raging intemperance, and perverted manliness (2.2234–338). His "Sardanapalle" is "Most femynyne off condicio*un*" (2237):

> Off fals vsage he was so femynyne,
> That among women vppon the rokke he span,
> In ther habite disguisid from a man.
> And off froward flesshli insolence,
> Off alle men he fledde the presence
>
> . . .
>
> . . . at the laste God off veray riht
> Displesid was with his condicio*u*ns,
> Because he was in euery manys siht
> So femynyne in his affecciouns. (2243–47; 2283–86)

No serial repetition of this famous deviant, Byron's Sardanapalus breaks the link of *effeminate* and *homosexual* to release *effeminate* (it is telling that Louis Crompton doesn't even mention him in his study of homoerotic Byron) as the discourse of counter-cultural critique.

A keyword in this critique is *soft*. It is famed for the Genetic-Miltonic ontology: "For contemplation hee and valor form'd, / For Softness Shee," we hear of Eden's originals (*PL* 4.297–98). In key, Hannah More's *Strictures* set the character of women in the mold of "softness and refinement," of hearts "naturally soft and flexible" (231, 238). To Salemenes, Sardanapalus's love of "soft hours" (1.2.8) is the effect of "the softening voices / Of women, and of beings less than women"—no men, with no excuse (1.1.30–31). When Arbaces hesitates in the first revolt, Beleses despises that "spirit shrunk / Into a shallow softness"

(2.1.397–98); even Myrrha feels "fallen" in "loving this soft stranger" (1.2.653). At the same time, Byron sets *soft* against such disparagements. When Sardanapalus muses on Salemenes' "severe . . . / Hard" temper, contrasting himself as "softer clay, impregnated with flowers" (2.1. 522), *softer* tenders no fault, but an alternative valuation, one that could extend (as Byron knew) even to *effeminate*.[27] Zarina recalls the king's being ever "soft of voice and aspect, / . . . not austere" with her (4.1.241–42).

It is kingship rather than softness that is the deformation. To Myrrha's address of Sardanapalus as "Lord—king—sire—monarch," Byron has him feel "a chill" in his "heart, a cold sense of the falsehood / Of this my station" (1. 2443–49). This alienation sponsors Sardanapalus at his most Byronic pitch of sarcasm. When Salemenes cites Semiramis's heroic retreat to Bactria "with but twenty guards" (1.2.130–31), he snaps back,

> And how many
> Left she behind in India to the vultures?
>
> . . .
>
> Is *this* glory?
> Then let me live in ignominy ever.   (1.2.131–32, 138–39)

In the same tone, he volleys the contempt of an "ungrateful" people who "murmur"

> Because I have not shed their blood, nor led them
> To dry into the desert's dust by myriads,
> Or whiten with their bones the banks of Ganges;
> Nor decimated them with savage laws,
> Nor sweated them to build up pyramids,
> Or Babylonian walls. (1.2.227–32)

Byron mirrors his refusal of traditional measures of Sardanapalus in the hero's own refusal of dynastic determinations. In opposition to "masculine" imperatives, the humanitarian plays effeminacy to reassign, even resignify the gender force—so seductively that professional critics have been eager to file *amici curiae*. Sardanapalus is "guilty in his indolence and contempt for his subjects" but "admirable in his pacifism and humanity," says Spence. Or not even guilty: this is no "indolent wallower in voluptuousness, but a contemplative character whose inaction was owing partly to his humanitarian hatred of war and violence and partly to his contempt for the ends of worldly ambition and the lust for power," urges Marchand; he is "not effeminate" but "humane."[28]

This is an impressive effect in the reactionary post-Waterloo years, when he-man muscle was keyed to national security.[29] Yet the deepest problem of effeminate character in *Sardanapalus* is not the doom of humane vision in a world of hawks and power-lusters (that's the romance), but the situation of "Sardanapalus's golden reign" (4.1.517) on a rather dark material base—that's the political unconscious. However oppositionally theorized and practiced, the king's policy looks rather less liberal in a world of slaves, peasants, and powerless women, all serving his every new pleasure. When he protests of his nominal marriage to Zarina, "I married her as monarchs wed—for state" and even fancies his superiority to what draws a "peasant to his mate" (1.2.213–16), Byron's counterpoint rhyme of *state* and *mate* (noticeable in blank verse) strains the distinction. On the stormy night of the revolt, when Myrrha reminds the king how "awful" it is "for those who have / No palace," he sighs: "That's true, my Myrrha; and could I convert / My realm to one wide shelter for the wretched, / I'd do it" (3.1.39–43)—a remark Byron lets hang between Lear-epiphanics, compassionate conservatism, and disingenuous selfishness. The address to "my Myrrha" involves the question: an affectionate embrace, but also a reminder that she is property. When Byron has her say that love has made her half-forget this, he also has her admit that "shackles worn like ornaments no less / Are chains" (3.1.190–96)—a sentiment that might have been scripted by Wollstonecraft as she was reading about Sophy in *Émile*.

The critical question is whether the language of slavery is being tuned for the ironizing work sounded by *manliness* and *effeminacy*. Slave Myrrha is the star of a sentimentality of gender that synonymizes her heroism with subjection and degradation:

>   —King, I am your subject!
> Master, I am your slave! Man, I have loved you!—
> Loved you, I know not by what fatal weakness,
> Although a Greek, and born a foe to monarchs—
> A slave, and hating fetters—   (1.2.496–500)

Byron evades this triple alliance of King, Master, Man to romance the lover: "My eloquent Ionian!" dotes Sardanapalus (1.2.516). More than once, the play lets stand the contradiction of a political vision signified by effeminacy and the political subjection of the ideal female.[30] Thus reviewer Heber, having just admired Myrrha's manly counsel, has no trouble imagining "her talents, her courage, and her Grecian pride [as] softened into a subdued and winning tenderness by the constant and painful recollection of her abasement as a slave in the royal haram; and still more by the lowliness of perfect womanly love. [. . .] No character can be drawn more natural than hers."[31] What he calls "natural,"

Wollstonecraft tagged a "prevailing opinion" purveyed by male "prejudice" and "prescription," to naturalize the wrongs of woman. The fault of Sardanapalus is cast as hedonism or dreamy utopianism, but not masculinism, royal complacency, or slave-owning. It's difficult to gauge the ironies. British colonial slavery was still legal in 1821, and Byron was for abolition.[32] That some of Sardanapalus's slaves (Myrrha) are Greek, as Hemans saw, is politically resonant: Greece was still enslaved to the Ottoman empire in 1821, and Byron was an activist for liberation. So to give Sardanapalus a world of slaves and, amid this oppression, even an unreflective sigh on himself as a "slave"—pleading excuse to "wronged Zarina," he calls himself "the very slave of circumstance / And impulse" (4.1.330–31)—may be to expose shallow self-pity.[33] Yet it is a measure of Byron's desire to keep his hero sympathetic that the slave-trope remains uncriticized inside the play, and by seductive extension, unremarked by most readers. The liberty with this trope may reflect Byronic as well as Sardanapalian self-interest. Contemporaries ably, even wryly, read the scene with Zarina, a patent addition to the sources, as a legible code for long estranged Lord and Lady Byron, scripted with his noble regret and her noble forgiveness.[34]

Yet if this pity-me plea was Byron's agenda, it is oddly countered by the pointing of his opening scenes with references to another selfish, wronging husband, the widely despised George IV.[35] The political jabbing was irresistible. If the "hardship" of writing "in these times," Byron grumbled to Murray, is that one cannot "speak of kings or Queens without suspicion of politics or personalities" (in *Sardanapalus* he insists, he "intended neither"; *BLJ* 8: 152), he knew that for any minimally alert Briton in 1821, Salemenes's opening grievance, "He hath wrong'd his queen" (1.1.1), would prompt a lusty cheer in the house. Queen Caroline sparked a wildfire of partisan sympathy when the king brought charges of adultery for her (Byronic) escapades in Italy and then subjected her to a theatrical two-month trial from late August to early November 1820.[36] Byron amplified the cue with the king's first words, "Let the pavilion . . . / Be garlanded, and lit, and furnish'd forth / For an especial banquet" (1.2.1–3), as if inspired by an invitation to George IV's notorious revels at Brighton Pavilion, especially after his estrangement from the queen.[37] "Nothing was ever half so magnificent," Moore marveled of one gala; "It was *in reality* all that they try to imitate in the gorgeous scenery of the theatre" (J. B. Priestly 40). In the orientalized theater of *Sardanapalus*, conceived in the wake of the public's first admission, in 1821, to gape at the Pavilion's splendors, Byron taps the spectacle of luxuries that were as exclusive as they were generally taxed. Begun in 1787 and elaborated over the next decades at a total cost of £70,000, the Pavilion was conspicuous for its expense, its rich interiors and furnishings, its lavish galas. The defeat of Napoleon may have clinched the prestige of the British monarchy among the restored European powers, but its royal extravagance, fed by taxpayers in hard times, was weakening its prestige at home. Versailles epitomized the synonymy of "effeminate & royal" to Percy Shelley (Mary Shelley, *Journals* 133), and Brighton Pavilion orbited in this solar system.

If these extra-textual jibes served Byronic political sport, they could only detract from the hero in the play's internal economy. The ricocheting of texts and contexts—Sardanapalus's slave-owning against Byron's abolitionism; a king who claims humanitarian concern for the citizenry taxed for his luxury; an errant husband who is no less manipulative than sorry—puts at risk sympathy for the Assyrian king, sympathy for his idealism, sympathy (even) for his Byronism. Sardanapalus's self-praised "disposition / To love and to be merciful, to pardon / The follies of my species, and (that's human) / To be indulgent to my own" (1.2.275–78) is also a disposition, arrayed in parallel syntax, to rationalized selfishness. In this configuration of "effeminacy," a romantic refusal of debased worldly imperatives licenses indifference to capable government.[38] And dandyism was the template. "As a social, even political phenomenon, with repercussions in the world of ideas," dandyism, Moers remarks, was "the invention of the Regency, when aristocracy and monarchy were more widely despised" than ever before in English history. "What the utilitarian middle class most hated in the nobility was what the court most worshipped in the dandy [. . .] the epitome of selfish irresponsibility" (*The Dandy* 12–13).

This default is as deep in Byron's characterization of Sardanapalus as any latency of courage. On the verge of defeat, he sounds his self-mythologizing anthem, "To me war is no glory—conquest no / Renown" (4.1.506–7), without recognizing the slips in his old sweet song:

> I thought to have made mine inoffensive rule
> An era of sweet peace 'midst bloody annals,
> A green spot amidst desert centuries,
>
> . . .
>
> . . . Sardanapalus' golden reign.
> I thought to have made my realm a paradise,
> And every moon an epoch of new pleasures. (4.512–14, 517–19)

With its too-convenient premises of revelry or tyranny, regal self-idealizing pretends to political idealism. It is "selfishness admirably drawn," said Heber, but it is also bad civic faith: "he affects to undervalue the sanguinary renown of his ancestors as an excuse for inattention to the most necessary duties of his rank; and flatters himself, while he is indulging his own sloth, that he is making his people happy." The self-regard that (G. W. Knight puts it) "masquerades as conscience" is the signature rhetoric (Peter Manning argues) of the Byronic protagonist who moves "not towards self-knowledge but towards self-revelation"; "Byron's most impressive achievement" is to expose "the problematical motives beneath unimpeachable sentiments."[39]

Focused on the psychological motives that play into social defenses, Manning also illuminates one more aspect of the effeminate masquerade, and this a self-knowing one: the king's reflexive intuition that the sanguinary renown of his ancestors is not just a cultural heritage, but a heredity of blood. This arousal, too, impends in what Salemenes urges:

> if they rouse me, better
> They had conjured up stern Nimrod from his ashes,
> "The mighty hunter!" I will turn these realms
> To one wide desert chase of brutes . . . . (1.2.372–75)

Here the epithet is caustic disdain, but it is soon a simile: "he look'd like Nimrod," remarks one conspirator of Sardanapalus's anger (2.1.352). In this aspect, the Coleridgean notion of effeminacy as a culturally disruptive "contrary" looks like a discipline of a contrary within.[40] Watching but not knowing his nightmare of this blood-heritage, Myrrha worries, with that keyword, "who knows / From what I rouse him?" (4.1.16–17). "All the predecessors of our line / Rose up, methought, to drag me down to them," Sardanapalus soon tells her (175–76).

To have Sardanapalus possessed by this lineage even as he defies its augury is to expose his deep allegiance to its gendered polarities. Byron's analysis is shrewdest in his understanding of how even cultural critique may reproduce cultural grammar. The inner Nimrod is one trace; an affection for feminine orthodoxy is its necessary twin. Hence Sardanapalus parries Salemenes's flashing of the shaming foil of manly Semiramis: rather than venture with "twenty guards," she "had better woven within her palace / Some twenty garments" (1.2.134–35). With less of an edge, this is Byron's view, too. As he was writing the play, reading Mitford, and probably recalling Rousseau's *Émile*, he mused on the "convenient" ancient Greek system of sequestering women: "Present state, [. . .] artificial and unnatural. They ought to mind home" and not be "mixed in society [. . .] read neither poetry nor politics" (*BLJ* 8: 15)—not, that is, cross into man's pursuits.[41] Because women "have not seen enough nor felt enough of life," he wrote to Moore during the year of his marriage to a very literate Lady Byron, they "(saving Joanna Baillie) cannot write tragedy." He cites two other exceptions, both of horrific power: "Semiramis or Catherine II. might have written (could they be unqueened) a rare play" (*BLJ* 4: 290). There is no range between the ideal *ought* of sequestration and the monstrous liberty that lets women rival men, in politics or rare playwriting.

In Byron's rare play, Semiramis figures only as misogynist grotesque. Jewsbury, for one, thought Byron had missed a good opportunity with this legend:

> Semiramis [. . .] whose life and history combined the Asiatic extremes of blood and luxury, horror and magnificence, would have afforded Byron even a more powerful dramatic subject than Sardanapalus; but it is strange that no English writer has produced anything original concerning the female representative of "the mighty hunter."[42]

For Byron's purposes, this female form presses too close a complement to Sardanapalus, a man of magnificence and luxury whose aversion to bloody history, though it jabs at Nimrod, is magnetized by the female representative. In his theater of imagination, her transgression is super- and un-natural: Semiramis is, semi-punningly, a "semi-glorious human monster" (1.2.181). Writing this figure of horror lets Byron put Sardanapalus into military action with a difference. On this customary masculine proving ground, his king holds to, even liberates, "effeminate" character. Myrrha's dazzled report that he "springs up" and "rushes from the banquet to the battle, / As though it were a bed of love" (3.1.221–24) conflates the traditional antagonism of these passions. When a palace officer marvels, "the king fights as he revels!" (213), Byron's comparative *as* almost suggests simultaneity. "He dallies with Bellona as her bridegroom— for his sport and pastime," Jeffrey (or Hazlitt) writes in the *Edinburgh Review;* "the spear or fan, the shield or shining mirror, become his hand equally well" (36: 424).[43]

How different is the transformation of an earlier Byronic effeminate, Selim in *The Bride of Abydos* (1813). A political threat to his powerful uncle, he is kept from masculine hunt and battle, confined to the harem, and scorned as "effeminate." In perfect reciprocity, his revolt is signaled by an escape from the harem and advertised by his re-manning of dress:

> His brow no high-crown'd turban bore,
> But in its stead a shawl of red,
>   Wreath'd lightly round, his temples wore:—
> That dagger, on whose hilt the gem
> Were worthy of a diadem,
> No longer glitter'd at his waist,
> Where pistols unadorn'd were braced.
> And from his belt a sabre swung . . . (2.132–39)

This over-the-top phallic fashion is not the pattern for haremite Sardanapalus.

In a scene that he assured Murray had "historical" precedent and was "natural in an effeminate character" (*BLJ* 8: 128), Byron has Sardanapalus call for that shining mirror Jeffrey mentions, to preview himself in battle drag:

> [*looking at himself*]. This cuirass fits me well, the baldric better,
> And the helm not at all. Methinks, I seem
>   [*Flings away the helmet after trying it again*]
> Passing well in these toys; and now to prove them. (3.1.163–65)

Byron wanted a note on "the Latin passage from Juvenal upon Otho—(a similar character who did the same thing)."[44] Same, yes, but *similar* is a tad evasive. Homosexual Otho committed suicide after a military defeat, and Juvenal treats his mirror phase with the kind of contempt voiced by the satirists of Sardanapalus—deriding his behavior, in the same run of lines, against Semiramis and Cleopatra in battle.[45] As a genre, moreover, mirror scenes are in analogical oversupply. One of its scandals (as Byron knew) is Shakespeare's famously castigated effeminate, Richard II, crushed by "insults and injuries, which his own misconduct had provoked, but which he has not courage or manliness to resent," so Hazlitt wrote in 1817 (*Characters* 178–79). The Ricardian reflection in Byron's play is the Indian provenance of Sardanapalus's mirror: a spoil from Semiramis's victory over effeminate Eastern luxury. What moderates this stigma in the Assyrian scene is Byron's campy theatricality. No less than Juan arrayed in "effeminate garb" and pleased at the "perfect transformation [. . .] display'd" (*Don Juan* 5.76, 80), Sardanapalus preens for display, or in his punning, "passing well" for the character at hand—not just "passing" inspection, but also the archaic sense of "in a surpassing degree; . . . exceedingly, very" (OED). This flagrantly stylized self-regard may show something "natural in an effeminate character"; but it is also performatively (Byronically) ironizing: iconic masculinity styled as yet another masquerade.

Byron had double-played the question before in *The Giaour*, where the eponymous hero thunders into the tale in a towering Satanic rage, "Swift as the hurl'd on high jerreed" (251). To this hyper-manly, flamboyantly phallic advent, Byron added a strangely burlesque note:

> Jerreed, or Djerrid, a blunted Turkish javelin, which is darted from horseback with great force and precision. It is a favourite exercise of the Mussulmans; but I know not if it can be called *manly* one, since the most expert in the art are the Black Eunuchs of Constantinople.

What is the law of gender if "manly" arts can be exercised by the emasculated? Or by women? "It seems it is the custom here for the boats to be manned by women," Byron writes in half amusement, half amazement (to Augusta) of a hired tour of the Lake of Brientz (*BLJ* 5: 103). In the theatrical terms he summons for the oscillations of play and epiphany as the king heads off to battle, Heber intuits a masquerade: "Sardanapalus displays the precise mixture of effeminacy and courage, levity and talent which belongs to his character" (*Quarterly* 27: 500).[46]

This character is etched against the tradition represented by Surrey's sonnet, in which the "Assyryans king" on the battlefield is mere effeminated incompetence:

> In warr that should sett pryncelye hertes afyre
> Vanquyshd dyd yeld for want of martyall arte.
> The dent of swordes from kysses semed straunge,
> And harder then hys ladyes syde his targe;
> From glotton feastes to sowldyers fare a chaunge,
> His helmet far above a garlandes charge.
> Who scace the name of manhode dyd retayne,
> Drenched in slouthe and womanishe delight . . . (3–10)

Byron's battlefield does not stage this fiasco.

Yet neither is it Heber's laboratory of precise mixing. The war is a whirl, where customary signs of gender alchemize into things rich and strange. Sardanapalus's effeminacy is not so much revoked as propelled into a spectacular configuration of "silk tiara and his flowing hair" (3.1.205), scarcely distinguishable from Myrrha, waving a sword over her "floating hair and flashing eyes" (384). And she shimmers into further confusions. In this chiastic resexing from Coleridge's *Kubla Khan* ("His flashing eyes, his floating hair!"), does she evoke the Revolutionary icon of "Victory herself" (399)? or Semiramis Rediviva? or inspired madness? Whatever the template, the most significant, most troubling revelation is of a female no less violent than the masculine models Sardanapalus would escape. Byron has the king sense this complication in answering Myrrha's urging of swift reprisals for the first conspiracy:

> Myrrha, this is too feminine, and springs
> From fear—
>
> . . .
>
> I have observed your sex, once roused to wrath,
> Are timidly vindictive to a pitch
> Of perseverance, which I would not copy. (2.1.584, 586–88)

Yet the model is not sex-specific. "He must be roused"; "if they rouse me": Sardanapalus's perception of feminine arousal to wrath not only troubles his policy of effeminacy, it also challenges the logic of gender difference as a master-trope of social understanding and self-fashioning.

The king's preferred name for female wrath up to this point had been "Semiramis," but because her motive was empire, not love, she could be alienated as monstrous: "ghastly beldame!/ Dripping with dusky gore, and trampling on/The carcasses of Inde—away!" (4.1.31–33). Myrrha is trouble precisely because her aspect is so "feminine": she is "the chief charm and vivifying angel of the piece," says Jeffrey/Hazlitt; "a beautiful, heroic, devoted, and etherial being," using her "influence" to "ennoble as well as to adorn" the king. Her very extravagance is a "heroism of the affections" (*Edinburgh* 36: 426). When the battle does not send her "herding with the other females,/ Like frighten'd antelopes" (3.1.377–78), but shows her as one of the new-"made warriors" (386), the effect on Sardanapalus is not horrifying. It is so erotically mesmerizing as to launch a new blazon:

> her kindled cheek;
> Her large black eyes, that flash'd though her long hair
> As it stream'd o'er her; her blue veins that rose
> Along her most transparent brow; her nostril
> Dilated from its symmetry; her lips
> Apart; her voice that clove through all the din,
> As a lute's pierceth through the cymbal's clash,
> Jarr'd but not drown'd by the loud brattling; her
> Waved arms, more dazzling with their own born whiteness
> Than the steel her hand held, which she caught up
> From a dead soldier's grasp; all these things made
> Her seem unto the troops a prophetess
> Of victory, or Victory herself. (3.1.387–99)

To Salemenes, the new dazzle is most impressive for reactivating the old Sardanapalus:

> [*aside*]   This is too much.
> Again the love-fit's on him, and all's lost,
> Unless we turn his thoughts. (3.1.400–402)

Magnificently militant, the female body is still fit to love, love, love.[47]

The problem is an emergent female "too much": violent love. When Sardanapalus sees Myrrha on the field "like the dam/ Of the young lion, femininely raging" (3.1.378–79), he confronts something natural in a *feminine* character (Semiramis is "grandam" [3.1.6]). When he muses that "femininely meaneth furiously,/ Because all passions in excess are female" (3.1.380–81), the drive to definition does not dispel the vexation to logic: the revelation of female fury undoes the differential by which the effeminate king had been fashioning self-regard and justifying his civic policy. Byron wrestled mightily with the she-language in these lines, writing and rewriting their signs.[48] But the question only deepens in the nightmare he gives Sardanapalus during a respite from the battle. Not staged, this trauma is vividly related to Myrrha, as if she were its discovering muse. It is of a "horrid kind / Of sympathy" with dynasty at its most archetypal: "the hunter" Nimrod and "the crone" Semiramis (4.1.124–25; 132), the hunter queerly passive, the crone a ghastly embodiment of imperialism and sexual aggression. More awful yet, the crone displaces, or stands in for, Myrrha.[49] The chiming of *Myrrha* within the syllables of "Se*mira*mis" spells the uncanny latency:

> In thy own chair—thy own place in the banquet—
> I sought thy sweet face in the circle—but
> Instead—a grey-hair'd, wither'd, bloody-eyed,
> And bloody-handed, ghastly, ghostly thing,
> Female in garb, and crown'd upon the brow,
> Furrow'd with years, yet sneering with the passion
> Of vengeance . . .   (4.1.102–8)

In this figure, hyperbolically demonized over and against other available accounts of Semiramis, Byron exposes the error of gender-oppositions.[50] The deepest horror of this she-thing is its effacement of what, exactly, "femininely meaneth"; the garb is the only sign of "female" amid the host of "crowned wretches, / Of various aspects, but of one expression" (114–15).

The other exception, of sharp peril to an effeminate who still cherishes male priority, is that Semiramis leers "with . . . lust" (4.1.108).[51] Her sexual aggression feels like predation:

> Ay, Myrrha, but the woman,
> The female . . . she flew upon me,
> And burnt my lips with her noisome kisses   (4.1.148–50)
>
> . . .
>
> . . . she still
> Embraced me, while I shrunk from her, as if,
> In lieu of her remote descendant, I
> Had been the son who slew her for her incest. (4.1.155–58)

This harpy, categorically *woman/female*, is the nightmare of what it is to give the bed of love and the battlefield the same passions. So effectively does Semiramis subsume "masculine" aggression that men become redundant: she is a "homicide and husband-killer" (4.1. 180). Neither the feminine nor the erotic is an escape from violence, and so Sardanapalus's oppositional self-fashioning is canceled: "Then—then—a chaos of all loathsome things / Throng'd thick and shapeless: I was dead" (159–60). He awakes to cry, "Where am I?" (34).

In this nightmare of history, there is no refuge in male ancestors. Nimrod may draw admiration to his "noble aspect" and court allegiance—"The hunter smiled upon me" (4.1.133–34)—but Sardanapalus's habitual revulsion plays out as a fantasy of rejection: as he "grasp'd" Nimrod's hand, "it melted," and Nimrod "vanish'd" into "nothing but / The memory of a hero" (144–46). This disappearance, repeated in his father's reticence ("he, / I know not why, kept from me" [177–78]), leaves the dreamer simultaneously alienated from patrilineal dynasty and horrified at female power. Nimrod himself seems most frightening in an aspect of female monstrosity, his "serpent hair" (91) turning Sardanapalus to "stone" (122); to launch this Medusan suggestion, Byron canceled *falling* for *serpent* (ms T). So intimately does he involve Sardanapalus's sense of gender with his alienation from empire that the condensation of horrific empire into a monstrous woman comes with a figural logic. Cast into the phantasmic and the demonic, Semiramis lives in this nightmare; but thus exiled, she is spoken of no more.

Gender Formations, Gender Theatrics

This purging allows Byron to attempt in the remaining scenes one final reordering of sexual and political priorities. His Preface may even predict this in the stated preference for "the more regular formation of a structure, however feeble, to an entire abandonment of all rules whatsoever" (viii). Byron means dramatic rules—the "unities" as a universal "law of literature"—but the play implies social structure as well. Jeffrey/Hazlitt sensed this in dismissing Byron's summoning of "law" as "mere caprice and contradiction":

> He, if ever man was, is *a law unto himself*—"a chartered libertine";—and now, when he is tired of this unbridled license, he wants to do penance within the *Unities!* This certainly looks very like affectation. (*Edinburgh* 36: 422–23)[52]

Byron's return of the libertine to law is more than dramaturgy, however; it is also a social decision.

This is the latent allegory of the last acts. In a culture of gendered polarities, the terms of conservative restoration are already in place, even as the empire crumbles.[53] When the king's eagerness for the final fray prompts Salemenes to remark that he sounds "like a young soldier," he replies, "I am no soldier, but a man," opposing "soldiership" not, as before, with effeminacy, but with masculine pride (4.1.565–67). If this is a hero with "masculine and feminine tendencies in irreconcilable conflict" (Spence 69), masculinity fortifies the last lines of defense. Taking leave of his soldiers, Sardanapalus urges, "Let's not unman each other" (5.1.401). When he fears that losing his sons "may / Unman my heart" (4.1.210–11), the verb is reproof. In the farewell to Zarina, he takes caution not to "grow womanish again" (4.1.396), or soft:

> I must learn sternness now. My sins have all
> Been of the softer order—*hide* thy tears . . .
> . . . let me not behold them; they unman me
> Here when I had remann'd myself. (4.1.397–403)

Byron wrote *renerved*, then revised to *remann'd*, his own coinage.[54] Circumstances may unman, but *re-man* is always a reflexive verb, a self-shaping. The consolidated man-verbs bolster a fresh concern for patrilineage. Diodorus reports that Sardanapalus had both daughters and sons (1.439); Byron hones a male line. His king regrets leaving to "crownless princes" the paltry heritage of a "father's sins": "all earth will cry out thank your father! / And they will swell the echo with a curse" (4.1. 281–82, 289–90). Zarina assures him they will know only "what may honour / Their father's memory" (277–78), and Salemenes, always voicing public history, gloats that the rebels will

> Have miss'd their chief aim—the extinction of
> The line of Nimrod. Though the present king
> Fall, his sons live—for victory and vengeance. (4.1.377–79)

Filial fire burns in the king's last words. Just before torching his "fathers' house" to keep it from spoil (5.1.208), he cries, "Adieu Assyria! / I loved thee well, my own, my fathers' land" (492–93).

Complementing this re-manning is a refeminized Myrrha, ready for "the woman's [part to die] with her lover" (5.1.372–73) and caressed by Sardanapalus's suggestion that if she feels any "inward shrinking," he'll love her all the "more, / For yielding to [her] nature" (414–17).[55] Refusing freedom, she chooses a suttee, doing "for love, that which / An Indian widow braves for custom" (466–67) and quite exempt from suspicion of "the childish helplessness of Asian women" (2.1.590). To Hemans, this was a distinction without a difference in a world of male priority, and she exposed the political base of the fantasy in *The Bride of the Greek Isle*. But it is Byron's operatic superstructure that stirs the enduring critical romance, of Myrrha's suicide as a "*Liebestod*" and worthy "apotheosis."[56] He gives the cue with the "frankincense and myrrh" (details not in Diodorus) that he has Sardanapalus summon for the pile (5.1.280).[57] The epiphanic Christianizing involves another transformative mythology: myrrh is the shrub into which Myrrha in *Metamorphoses* is changed, delivered from the agony of delivering Adonis, the issue of paternal incest.[58] Byron was as horrified by this fable as Sardanapalus was by the reciprocal nightmare of the incestuous mother.[59] The Myrrha of *Sardanapalus* is a project of revisionary refinements. There is no incest, only the ennobling passion of a woman standing by her King, Master, Man.

Refeminized Myrrha supports and mirrors (her name half-puns)[60] the play's even more ostentatious revisionary refinement: Sardanapalus's emergence not just as a man but as a gentleman. Diodorus's king, after sending "much of his treasure" away with his children (1.439), brutally enforces his waning power, closing himself, his remaining "gold and silver as well as every article of the royal wardrobe," and his "concubines and eunuchs in the room which had been built in the middle of the pyre," then consigning everything "to the flames" (1.441). This infamous selfishness was still the strong tradition, the inspiration (for instance) for Delacroix's lurid *Mort de Sardanapale* (Salon de 1827). Byron's Sardanapalus is a paragon of chivalry: he ensures the escape of his wife and sons and the safety of his harem; he frees his slaves and "all the inmates of the palace, of / Whatever sex" (5.1.257–59), and (like Shakespeare's defeated Antony) he distributes his treasure to his soldiers. He "preserves frankness and generosity to the last," cheered the *Examiner* (23 Dec. 1821; 809). It is a short step from such idealizing to a final play at aesthetic transcendence, the suicide pyre, again with a conspicuous swerve from the precursor texts.

Byron plots his king's exit from genetic and cultural heritage alike with a determined self-cancellation, and by this, evaporates the question of gender in this deed—one notoriously unsettled in literary tradition. To Lydgate the suicide was "Mor bestial than lik a manli man" (2.2319); in Surrey's caustic sonnet, it was a last bid: the king "Murdred hym selfe to shew some manfull dede" (14). In Byron's day, *Scots Edinburgh* sourly cited a female model: no Antony, "he shewed himself no ways superior to Cleopatra" (10: 103). Yet Cleopatra, a flamboyant drag act on the Shakespearean stage and never more theatrical than in her stagey death, is a canny gloss. Byron drops the curtain with Sardanapalus stage-managing a transcendence of imminent political defeat. As the flames subsume plot into spectacle, immediate history, with its entanglements of gender and empire, is canceled. In the early scenes, forgoing the demands of office, the "king" had rendered himself "a nothing" in public eyes (1.2.103). In the final scene, he reclaims and transvalues this nullity: "Adieu, Assyria! / . . . now I owe thee nothing" (5.1.492–95).[61] With this quitclaim, Byron gives the hero one last act of self-fashioning, projecting his death from "too material being" (425) into a spectacle of universal mythology:

> ... the light of this
> Most royal of funereal pyres shall be
> Not a mere pillar form'd of cloud and flame,
> A beacon in the horizon for a day,
> And then a mount of ashes, but a light
> To lesson ages, rebel nations, and
> Voluptuous princes. (5.1.436–42)

Simultaneously redeemed is the historical record, and in Byron's script, Sardanapalus's first thought for his tomb: "Eat, drink, and love; the rest's not worth a fillip" (1.2.252)—a sentiment Aristotle deemed "*fit for a hog.*"[62] Byron leaves this most Byronic hero stage-managing the ages, confident of prevailing over the mighty stir of other agents:

> Time shall quench full many
> A people's records, and a hero's acts;
> Sweep empire after empire, like this first
> Of empires, into nothing; but even then
> Shall spare this deed of mine, and hold it up
> A problem few dare imitate, and none
> Despise—but, it may be, avoid the life
> Which led to such a consummation. (5.1.442–49)

Yet if Sardanapalus gets this farewell self-review (the "consummation" half-ruefully punning the perfect climax into the fire), the reception of *Sardanapalus* was more vexed. The hero and playwright became (no less than Cleopatra) texts for other agents.

During the months he was writing *Sardanapalus*, the author was in play back in England, where the "London Managers" trading on his name were staging *Marino Faliero* against his will and over his protests. Evoking the plot of *Sardanapalus*, Byron railed against the unauthorized staging as a "usurpation," insisting to everyone that *Marino* was "not for the Stage" (*BLJ* 8: 22, 116–34). "I claim my right as an author to prevent what I have written from being turned into a Stage-play," he protests to Murray (8: 90). In a further irksome irony, his agency was not just usurped but shammed: "The Milan paper states that I brought forward the play!!!" he fumes to Murray, to Moore, to Hoppner, and whoever else would listen; "I opposed the representation," but it "continued to be acted—in spite of Author." Waxing Sardanapalian, he rages, "I would have flung it into the fire rather than have had it represented" (8: 116–19).

That authority could so elude "Author" exposes a force field with other powers of production. The question of Byron's Sardanapalus was not if it would be imitated but how, especially in its complex test of effeminate character. *Blackwood's* went for satiric deflation:

> But the sot whom his subjects had rated a zero,
> Bravely fights, and then dies in a blaze like a hero! ("Critique" 459)

Byron must have liked this rhyme-chime because he retuned it the next year for British national hero Wellington:

> But though your years as *man* tend fast to zero,
> In fact your Grace is still but a *young Hero*. (*Don Juan* 9.2)

This is Byronism at its best, returning the volley with interest.[63] As for *Sardanapalus*, the partisan *Examiner*, merely noting the king's "effeminate and inactive life," was happy to recommend the play for its very Byronism: an original, "highly spirited" "sketch" of an amiable and generous sensualist whose finest moments are his satires "against priestcraft" and "sabre sway" (809). Other reviews just purged the king's effeminacy or read effeminacy transformed. Long before Marchand, Jeffrey/Hazlitt saw Byron producing "Epicurean philosophy": its hero "is not an effeminate, worn-out debauchee," but a "sanguine votary of pleasure, a princely epicure" who "enjoys life [. . .] and triumphs in death; and whether in prosperous or adverse circumstances, his soul smiles out superior to evil" (*Edinburgh* 36: 424). The 1833 *Works* gave this view the privilege of a long note at the top of the play (13: 65–66). In the *Quarterly*, Heber, whose half-brother Richard would flee to the Continent in 1826 after being outed as homosexual (Crompton 357), contested the old slanders; but he, too, marginalized the experiment with effeminate character:

> the dissipation and effeminacy of Sardanapalus (however they may be alluded to as the original cause of the revolt) in no way [. . .] can be said to accelerate his end, or materially to influence his fortunes. He is offered to our attention as a young king, fighting gallantly in his first battle, erring (if he errs) from excess of courage, not of carelessness, and overpowered by irresistible violence and treachery. The peculiarities of his character are, so far as the plot is concerned, incidental and ornamental only. [. . .] hardy and martial monarchs would have fallen like the silken prince of Nineveh. (27: 493)

In going on to say that the slanders are the discourse of "triumphant enemies" (494), Heber verges on marking gender as a political determination; but he finds it more agreeable to treat the experiment as a peculiar, and ultimately neglible ornamentation.[64]

In happy complicity, the theater of *Sardanapalus* featured spectacle, especially the final blaze. William Charles Macready's staging in 1834 tried for the apocalyptic sublime, modeling the last scene on John Martin's epic painting *The Fall of Nineveh*. Charles Kean's hit staging of 1853 halved the script and placed its bet on sensation, including fireworks and a cast of hundreds. Charles Alexander Calvert's 1875 foray unabashedly treated the play as a showpiece: "The play is a poem over the heads of the people, but the 'conflagration' will make it a *financial* success," he assured everyone.[65] In this commercial éclat, the king's effeminate character was simplified, reduced, depotentiated.[66] Both Macready and Kean even cut the mirror scene, a revision that seemed to bother only G. H. Lewes, who fumed at Kean's bowdlerizing:

> he must know the plain meaning of plain English words, and therefore is it astounding to see him not only carefully evading any representation of the effeminate voluptuousness and careless indifference of Sardanapalus, but also uttering the words in tones directly contrary to the sense. Thus, when the sword is placed in his hands, he gives it back, with the remark that it is too heavy, and the remark, instead of expressing effeminacy, he utters as if it were a stolid assertion of a matter of fact! How Byron would have fumed could he have heard his intention thus rendered! Charles Kean omits the detail which Byron laid so much stress on, viz., Sardanapalus calling for the mirror to arrange his curls before rushing into battle. (252)[67]

Fancifully embellishing the scene that he misses (maybe with Phillips's famous portrait of Albanian-clad "barbered" Byron in mind), Lewes is aware of the stakes, guessing that since Kean "also omits to give *any* indication of the effeminacy, he, perhaps, instinctively felt that detail would raise a titter!" for a Victorian audience to be sated with "weary pomp" (252, 250).

The suppression of feminine detailing was not absolute, however. If Byron has the king give his story as "a problem few dare imitate, and none / Despise" (5.1.447–8), the gender dare stayed in play. Reversing the boy-impersonations of Shakespearean Cleopatra, Mrs. Shaw-Hamblin donned title role at New York's Bowery Theatre in 1854.[68] "The man's inscrutable," marvels Altada of Sardanapalus's transformation from "silken son" to fierce warrior. "Not more than others," replies Sfero; "All are the sons of circumstance" (3.1. 319–20). This is less an answer than the question: what makes a man scrutable? a revelation of essential masculine depth in emergency? a cultural contingency? a generative circumstance? a matter of performance? As the curtain falls, the character that challenges imitation is delivering himself to a conflagration that imitates a transcendence of ideology, including the ideology of transcendence itself. And in the midst, the problem of what's "natural in an effeminate character" retains its daring and conflicting strains of definition.

CHAPTER SIX

Gender as Cross-Dressing in *Don Juan*: Men & Women / Male & Female / Masculine & Feminine

When the poet of *Don Juan* Canto XIV exhorts abolitionist William Wilberforce to teach all tyrants "that 'sauce for goose is sauce for gander,' / And ask them how *they* like to be in thrall" (83), the adage hints at a sexual politics, too, in the apposition of tyrant with the gander-gender.[1] But it is male thraldom that proves the warmer concern—no less so for Byron, especially in the arena in which this was most likely, the domestic affections. "Indeed I do love Lord [Holland]," he assured Lady Blessington in 1823, the year Canto XIV saw print, in prelude to this sigh:

> though the pity I feel for his domestic thraldom has something in it akin to contempt. Poor dear man! he is sadly bullied by *Milady;* and, what is worst of all, half her tyranny is used on the plea of kindness and taking care of his health. Hang such kindness! say I. She is certainly the most imperious, dictatorial person I know—is always *en reine.* (*BCB* 11–12)

Hereby hangs the general tale of *Don Juan*: the ganders get better sauce, with Byron's wit the seductive co-conspirator in keeping females in thrall. For all her wry and canny critiques of male privilege, even Virginia Woolf (after an evening of enervation with Katherine Mansfield's *Bliss)* had to agree with her father about "the able witty mind of [Byron's] thoroughly masculine nature" in *Don Juan,* and she welcomed his decidedly "male virtues."[2]

That Woolf was "ready . . . to fall in love" with the poet of *Don Juan,* and felt a "superb force" in his letters is connected to the way both archives reflect a liking for women cut of Lady Holland's cloth.[3] Taking a breath after his grumble about her imperious behavior, Byron tenders a sympathetic, even an exculpatory, supplement: if the Lady is always *en reine,* this stance, "in her peculiar position, shows tact, for she suspects that were she to quit the throne she might be driven to the antichamber" (*BCB* 12). Admiring the Lady's skill on the field of her endeavors, the home front and its theater of social warfare, Byron not only cheered her self-possession, but felt a twin in her rejection of "cant" (in her case, on female propriety).

Lady Holland and Lady Blessington are Lord Byron's social test-cases: like him, they are aristocratic nonconformists not in thrall to what the world expects; unlike him, they live in a world in which a man's domestic thraldom is the exception that proves the rule. They are continuous with the women in the textual imaginary of *Don Juan* who exercise power, in figures from enthralling to appalling, for self-interest and against male autonomy. Writing *Don Juan,* Byron turns again and again to the arbitrary grants of gender, to find both fun and serious reflection by vexing, sometimes unfixing, the sign-systems of difference—nowhere more so than in an array of transvestite forms. No less than in *Sardanapalus,* the gender-play with "feminine" and "masculine" proves shifty. When power is at stake, the poet of *Don Juan* may appeal to customary patterns of privilege: male, aristocratic, European. Yet across the cantos, these patterns can unfold into a complicated, often contradictory, patchwork of unpredictably vibrant effects. A heightened awareness of the artifice of gender generates a critical energy along the unstable edges.[4]

One edge is a homoerotic frisson, which I want to trace out a bit before turning to the hetero-play that would register with Byron's widest readership. Like the campy hetero-effeminate that fronts the gender-play of *Sardanapalus,* the cross-dressings of *Don Juan* wink at the subculture, subtexted in code words ("boy") and substitute figures. This is a poem, comments G. Wilson Knight, that romances the "almost feminine beauty in its hero" (*Oracle* 268). Dancing like "swift Camilla" (14.39), Juan is a boyish goddess, by turns a confection for male bemusement and gazing as well as for female doting and desire. Byron stages him to refresh and recover the homosexual appeal of the female-garbed boys in Shakespeare's theater[5]–or in an even more private code, the young man romanced in the she-guise of Byron's Thyrza lyrics.[6] The gender drift was not invisible in nineteenth-century reception. On the heels of the 1821 cantos (including Juan's career as harem-girl), there appeared a fantasy supplement, *The Sultana: or, A Trip to Turkey*. In its reconception, Haidée doesn't die of lovelornness, but dons boy-garb to go off in search of kidnapped Juan. She catches harem-eunuch Baba's attention on the docks of Constantinople with a sad song, hoping he'll bring her to court as a minstrel:

> Alas! he's gone, ah! never more
>   He'll come his love to save.
> And I must mourn, his loss deplore,
>   Until I find a grave. (p. 19)

As a she-lament ("They tore me from my love away"), this is sighing by the book. But sung by "a likely lad" cruising the docks in Turkey, the proto-Wildean effusion looks like erotic liberty of the kind England had to keep closeted, or drive into exile.[7]

Byron's most self-invested figure under wraps in *Don Juan* is Canto XIV Lord Henry Amundeville, a Regency aristocrat with an Abbey and a hetero-flair that has the look of a coterie-legible act. For all his macho broadcasts—he's a "handsome man," famed "in each circumstance of love or war" to have "preserved his perpendicular" (71)—there is a static of estrangement: he kisses Lady Adeline "less like a young wife than an aged sister" (69). There is "no connubial turmoil:/Their union was a model to behold,/Serene, and noble,—conjugal, but cold" (86). The latest epitaph on Byron's marriage, the couplet also models a code of "truths . . . better kept behind a screen" (80), the screen not only disguising but advertising a secret. "But there was something wanting on the whole—/ I don't know what, and therefore cannot tell—" the poet demurs (71), then proposes that "undefinable '*Je ne sçais quoi*'" that led Helen to prefer what Byron did, a "Dardan boy" (72). It is with a coy rhyme-pairing of *perplexes* and *sexes* that the poet plays out this Continental affectation of mystery:

> There is an awkward thing which much perplexes,
>   Unless like wise Tiresias we had proved
> By turns the difference of the several sexes:
>   Neither can show quite *how* they would be loved. (14.73)

It is the phantasm Tiresias who not only experiences sexual difference, but does so beyond the binary of just two sexes, with something like homoerotic knowledge.

Taking up her Byron, Woolf made a socially activated Tiresias the star of her utopian fable *Orlando* (1928). Although Orlando's biographer rehearses the argument for identity as fabrication—"it is clothes that wear us and not we them. [. . .] they mould our hearts, our brains, our tongues to their liking" (188)—on the question of "the difference between the sexes," she tends more toward a philosophy of clothes as authentic language:

> Clothes are but a symbol of something hid deep beneath. It was a change in Orlando herself that dictated her choice of a woman's dress and woman's sex. (188)

Woolf's radical twist is on that "something hid beneath." Translating out of monster-mythology Byron's hint of "the difference of the several sexes" in one body, she proposes this fluidity as "a dilemma" for normative humanity:

> Different though the sexes are, they intermix. In every human being a vacillation from one sex to the other takes place, and often it is only the clothes that keep male or female likeness, while underneath the sex is the very opposite of what it is above. Of the complications and confusions which thus result every one has had experience. (189)

Woolf's modernist gesture is to theorize dress-coding as a social regulation imposed on a more various, always vacillating sexuality. Byron's Georgian initiative is to intermix the clothes for complications and confusions in social experience.[8] As in Woolf, there are homosexual threads; and in Byron's own adventures, clothes may have been the least of it. "He associates with wretches who seem almost to have lost the gait & phisiognomy of man, & who do not scruple to avow practices which are not only not named but I believe seldom even conceived in England," a dismayed Percy Shelley wrote of Byron's Italian forays in 1818.[9] This is a body-language in which both were literate, even if it wasn't speaking its name.

In this chapter, I focus on heterosexual names and conceivings because the generally legible symbolism was more effectively situated, to use Natalie Davis's words, "to make statements about social experience and to reflect (or conceal) contradictions within it."[10] The prime symbol is dress. Thus in 1796, the *Monthly Magazine* deployed the sign system against Wollstonecraft's argument in *Rights of Woman* "that philosophy is of no sex": she might as well as said "that the creatures, hitherto called men and women, ought to wear a common dress" (182). In 1798 two advocates for respectable female employment summoned the trope against male preemptors. In *Reflections on the Present Condition of the Female Sex* Priscilla Wakefield ridiculed men in jobs that should be women's as "a brood of effeminate beings in the garb of men" (153)—clothes not at all making the man. Mary Anne Radcliffe went further in *The Female Advocate, Or an Attempt to Recover the Rights of Women from Male Usurpation*, deriding the "unmanly" usurpers, then imagining the travesty if women were to refuse to deal with them: the "effeminate traders" would be forced into "tragic-comic farce, to effect the business under the disguise of gown and petticoat," impersonating the females they've usurped.[11] This imposture could earn even sexual reassignment. Mary Hays terms the traders a "she-he gentry" (*Appeal* 201), the situation remaking the man.

Declining polemical rancor, *Don Juan* entertains such fashions with a savvy critical sense of travesty as gender critique.[12] The chief star is the poem itself, its "great power," said Hazlitt (with a transvestic trope in the wings) deriving from "the oddity of the contrast[s]":

> From the sublime to the ridiculous there is but one step. You laugh and are surprised that any one should turn round and *travestie* himself: the drollery is in the utter discontinuity. ("Lord Byron" [1825] 161)

Don Juan, the hero with a difference, is the meta-trope of this operation. The sole instance *travesty* in all Byron's poetry is the "odd travesty" of Juan's compelled disguise, "femininely all array'd" (5.74, 80) for hiding in a harem—a critical figure through which not just Juan, but the entire social structure of "feminine," is exposed as an array, not nature but a stylizing manageable by either sex. The poet can mock himself for a feminine style, likening his meaning-gathering to Ruth gleaning (13.96), or dubbing himself "a male Mrs. Fry" (10.84). The proactive female complement is "her frolic Grace—Fitz-Fulke" adventuring in "sable frock and dreary cowl" (16.123). There is also an epicene blur: Juan is "handsome" (1.54, 5.9) and so are the *she*s: Empress Catherine (9.63); the "handsome paramour" for which a Sultan lusts (6.91); Julia with her "handsome eyes" (1.60).[13]

Don Juan is book you can't tell by its cover, the sign of the legendary rake honored more in the breech than the observance. In a kind of incipient transvestry Juan often gets lost in she-fabrics: in Canto I he is smothered in Donna Julia's bedding, with the sole "masculine" signifier the fashion of his empty shoes (1.181); in Canto II, he comes back from the dead to be covered by Haidée's and Zoe's clothes. Even the body is dubious text. The poet gives him to us as "feminine in feature" (8.52), "a most beauteous Boy" (9.53), with a capacity for dancing away "like a flying Hour" (14.40). To the internal observers, the gender is double. Donna Julia's maid beholds a "pretty gentleman" of "half-girlish face" (1.170–71); Haidée dotes on "a very pretty fellow," his "cheek and mouth" like "a bed of roses" (2.148, 168)—a blazon a sonneteer might array for a lady love. In Juan's debut in Empress Catherine's court, the very "Man" has to be surmised:

> ... slight and slim,
> Blushing and beardless; and yet ne'ertheless
> There was a something in his turn of limb,
>   And still more in his eye, which seemed to express
> That though he looked one of the Seraphim,
>   There lurked a Man beneath the Spirit's dress. (9.47)

Byron arrays the *a*-rhymes so that the gender signifier *him* is just a verbal ghost in "Seraphim."[14] Even Salemenes had more confidence about the man that might be roused from Sardanapalus.

If the drag theatrics of Sardanapalus signified artistocratic license, Don Juan opened a liberal franchise for gender-play. Well after their affair incinerated, Caroline Lamb turned up as a Byronic Don Juan at a masquerade at Almack's in 1820 (earning a report in the *Morning Chronicle*).[15] Petite, epicene, lad-like, she may even have patterned Byron's slender, pretty "stripling of sixteen" (1.83). If Juan is "active . . . as a page" (1.54), Caro activated page's guise in her erotic intrigues with Byron, donning it for portraits and discreet visits to his rooms, knowing that in addition to its cover, it turned him on with its boy-miming and the proto-Woolfian riff on the theatrical fluidity of sexual identity (fig. 6.1).[16] This was the Byronic pattern for clandestine visits, one lover being passed off by Byron as "my brother Gordon," and young men being mistaken for girls in drag. Touring the Levant in 1810, dandy Byron himself was mistaken by the Grand Signior as a woman strategically touring in lord's disguise—an effect of indulgence in sartorial frills that were feminine even by dandy-standards, with no abatement in Byron's Italian days, as everyone remarked.[17]

Such clothesplay tunes fashion-fun with transgressive energy. "The woman shall not wear that which pertaineth unto a man, neither shall a man put on a woman's garment: for all that do so *are* abomination unto the LORD," went the old Deuteronomic law (22: 5). Divine abomination was the discourse that preserved the social register from confusions. "I have met with some of these trulls in London so disguised that it hath passed my skill to discern whether they were men or women," complained William Harrison in 1587 (channeling Shelley in 1818).[18] Phillip Stubbes devoted no small part of his *Anatomie of Abuses* (1583) to the body social, with an appeal to natural law: "Our Apparell was given us as a signe distinctive to discern betwixt sex and sex, & therefore one to weare the Apparel of another sex is to participate with the same, and to adulterate the veritie of his owne kinde."[19] For Stubbes, this *signe* is no proto-Saussurean arbitrary signifier; it is a "given" verity, a scripture. Yet it is telling that, in his

Figure 6.1 *Lady Caroline Lamb in Page's Costume,* by Thomas Phillips (1814). This portrait in a favorite guise was displayed in Phillips's studio next to his portrait of Byron in his Albanian get-up. With curly light-colored hair, fair complexion, and boyish physique, Caroline Lamb mirrored Byron's lost beloved, choirboy John Edleston: "very thin, very fair complexion, dark eyes, & light locks" (*BLJ* 1: 123). Adding to this advantage, "Caro" flaunted the sexual titillation of pageboy livery.

script at least, other wordings slip out. Stubbes's fear that women who "weare apparel assigned onely to man" are ready "as wel [to] chaunge their sex, & put on the kinde of man" and "verely become men indeed" means to denounce unnatural perversion.[20] But "put on the kinde of" may be a little more than kind, allowing a theatricality of everyday life that follows no assignment. This put-on flashed in the pronoun-switching titles of that famous 1620 pamphlet debate, *Hic Mulier; or, The Man-Woman* and *Haec Vir; or, The Womanish Man* (*hic* is masculine; *haec* is feminine). No wonder the same year saw King James ordering the clergy to sermonize against she-transgressors (at least).

Always a shrewd reader of Byron, and never more so in spite, Caro Lamb tweaked the semi-opaque disguise of *Don Juan* (Byron was transparently the author of unsigned Cantos I–II) to spoof this mode of outlaw performativity. In *A New Canto* (1819)—her textual masquerade of *Don Juan*—she voices this complaint about the "rigour" of French prosody:

> Their prim cesuras, and their gendered rhymes,—
> Mine never could abide their statutes critical,
> They'd call them neutral or hermaphroditical. (XIX)[21]

In French (she and Byron knew), *genre* denotes *gender* and *genre*. *Don Juan* is outlaw to both. It introduces the hero in a declension of feminine rhymes: *new one/true one/Juan,* later repeated for an actual she, *Julia/truly a/newly a* (2.208).[22] Pegged to both social and linguistic legislation, the decree of Jacques Derrida's *La Loi du Genre, Ne pas mêler les genres,* names the orthodoxy and its instability: "As soon as genre announces itself, one must respect a norm, one must not cross the line of demarcation, one must not risk impurity, anomaly or monstrosity"—the melee at once proving and provoking the law (224–25). Lamb's wry coupleting of *statues critical* with *hermaphroditical* nicely collates the legal artifice with the abjected anomalies, anticipating Derrida's French generics and recalling Stubbes's scandal of female cross-dressers as "*Hermaphroditi,* that is, Monsters of bothe kindes, half women, half men" (73).

If Byron's star cross-dressers ironize gender borders, other figures traingulate into "third sex" mixings: fops, epicenes, eunuchs, "*She* Men" (rhyme-paired with *women;* 14.31), and the "black old neutral personage / Of the third sex" (5.26) who designs Juan's Turkish travesty. These figures are not switched signs. They are deformations of the sign system, outside the law, potentially despicable. Baba may be a bit of queer theorist *avant la lettre,* but without a Byronic endowment, a third sex quickly translates into unsexed and, as with Polwhele's unsexed female, into moral reprobate. In the Dedication to *Don Juan,* "intellectual eunuch Castlereagh" (11) is cut to an "Emasculated" *It* (15), the neuter revised from *he*. Castlereagh's political ally, Poet Laureate Southey, "quite adry, Bob" (3), gets into the poem proper as a degraded cross-dresser: "turncoat Southey" (11.56; cf. *Vision of Judgment* 97). He falls not to gender travesty but to the opportunism of no man: a fellow "turncoat" poet performs in Haidée's court in the company of "Dwarfs, dancing girls, black eunuchs" (3.78).

Old Patterns, Common Threads

Byron's repetitive scenes of women with power turning their worlds to chaos is the reflex of an orthodoxy credited by satiric wit. Disorder brews when Julia cuckolds her husband and makes a boytoy of Juan, or when Haidée, her father absent, runs the island on her erotic desires. It is by exploiting legends that subvert patriarchal claims to Norman Abbey that Duchess Fitz-Fulke sets in motion her designs on Juan. And these are the lighter cases, in which Juan's sexual curiosity is complicit. There is only acid reflux in the way Sultana Gulbeyaz's "imperial, or imperious" sexual appetites "thr[o]w a chain o'er" men (5.110). Empress Catherine, the "'teterrima Causa' of all 'belli'" (9.55), is a rampant monstrosity of political power and lust.[23] Queen Elizabeth so perverts eros with power that she "put[s] a favourite to death," a "vile, ambiguous method of flirtation" (no coital "death") that disgraces "her Sex and Station" (9.81).[24] "Hatred" is a spider-woman with a "hundred arms and legs" (10.12). Even when "woman" escapes such extreme figurings, it is only towards chaos:

> What a strange thing is man! and what a stranger
>   Is woman! What a whirlwind is her head,
> And what a whirlpool full of depth and danger
>   Is all the rest about her! Whether wed,
> Or widow, maid, or mother, she can change her
>   Mind like the wind . . . (9.64)

Man may be strange, but woman is trebly "stranger": stranger than he, a stranger to him, and estranged from the systems that ensure the security and coherence of his world.

In this stanza a Byronic reflex of irony does pluck the rhyme chord *stranger/danger/change her* with exclamations that camp the melodrama. This gender text is so knowingly hyperbolized that it all but conjures (decades and a continent away) Ambrose Bierce crafting *The Devil's Dictionary*:

> *Curiosity*, n. An objectionable quality of the female mind. The desire to know whether or not a woman is cursed with curiosity is one of the most active and insatiable passions of the masculine soul.

This is one of Bierce's best entries, wryly self-ironizing, cheerfully deconstructive about gender difference. Byron can ride this kind of groove in *Don Juan*, but its larger field has more than few reactionary plots, where female force earns a put-down.

Take Juan's tutelage by women. "Juan's education is his experience with women," writes Peter Manning, meaning not only the serial affairs of "that useful sort of knowledge/Which is acquired in nature's good old college" (2.136), but also female domestic education.[25] This is a college of culture more than of nature, in which Juan is a miserably feminized subject: mother-shaped and reined, trained on dame books and bowdlerized (*emasculated* was a current synonym) texts, managed like a miss for marriage-marketing, primed as a commodity. From this kind of reduction Byron's narrative extricates its hero with a vengeance. Donna Inez's regime falls with the mere onset of puberty, and after this farce, women of power (sexual, social, economic, political) are subtly tainted, overtly demonized, publicly humiliated, killed off. Those with political or economic power earn grotesque cartoons. Uppity "ladies intellectual" are nastily put down, doomed to be "unwed she sages" (12.30) or cut with ridicule: "Men with their heads reflect on this and that—/ But women with their hearts or heaven knows what!" (6.2). Their claim to "sober reason" is so tenuous that it's impossible, the poet smirks, to know what "can signify the site/ Of ladies' lucubrations" (11.33–34).

Subject to his sharpest lash are that old target, the Blues,

> . . . that tender tribe, who sigh o'er sonnets,
>   And with the pages of the last Review
> Line the interior of their heads or bonnets . . . (11.50)

They read what men may read, but with a trivializing difference. Even Juan, "who was a little superficial," can impress "this learned and especial/ Jury of matrons" with no more than a light Continental style, "Which lent his learned lucubrations pith,/ And passed for arguments of good endurance" (11.51–52), earning an extra pass for his buoyantly undeluded charade. As for women of more substance, "'Tis pity learned virgins ever wed/ With persons of no sort of education," the poet muses early on, his line-cut flirting with a more radical prophylactic. The fun of the stanza's famous punch-line rhyme, "Oh! ye lords of ladies intellectual,/ Inform us truly, have they not hen-peck'd you all?" (1.22), has to be purchased in a pact about she-smarts as torture to men. The "hen-pecked husband," comments Ian Donaldson, is a ridicule set against the norm (14)—the ghost in Byron's phrasing "lords of ladies," and part of why the couplet gained cultural life as a virtual English law of gender. In *Le Bas Bleu*,

Lady Blessington has Lord Avondale cite it to a young friend, cautioning that "an intellectual wife" promises "inglorious thraldom."[26]

In actual law, the master-trope of marriage was *coverture:* a wife clothed by and effaced under a husband's legal cover. Byron knew Blackstone's *Commentaries on the Laws of England* (1765–69), which gave "the very being or legal existence of the woman" as "suspended during the marriage," "incorporated and consolidated into that of the husband: under whose wing, protection and *cover*, she performs every thing"; she is "therefore called in our law-french a *feme-covert*." A precedent was *Magnae Britannia Notitia* (1716): "Her very necessary apparel, by the law, is not her's in property." Patterning the clothes-trope, an Elizabethan homily advised, "Let women be subject to their husbands and they are sufficiently attired."[27] Such incorporation struck Wollstonecraft as not just "an absurd unit" but a social, legal, and moral evacuation: "considering him as responsible, she is reduced to a mere cypher" (*VRW* 282–83). But coverture persisted well into the nineteenth century.[28] Thus it was proactive female cross-dressing, under no husband's cover, that Hazlitt equated with all sorts of infractions. In the same essay in which he praises Byron's ability to "travestie himself," he calls on female transvestitism to index what bothers him about Byron's problematic transgressions. Hazlitt does not "wish to see the Muses drest out in the flounces of a false or questionable philosophy, like *Portia* and *Nerissa* in the garb of Doctors of Law"; released from simile-work, these characters were just as irksome in their own roles, neither "a very great favourite with us."[29]

On the she-pages of Byron's "Eastern tales" of 1813–14, the law of gender falls quite hard. In *The Giaour,* Leila's escape from the harem in "likeness of a Georgian page" (456) to join her lover is reversed by a fatal capture and endorsed by transcultural male-bonding.[30] The man she loved admits that the man she betrayed did "but what I had done / Had she been false" (1062–63). Rivals in love, enemies in nation and creed, they can agree on this. In *Lara,* mysterious page Kaled at first seems a gender-puzzle: while his hand is "So femininely white it might bespeak / Another sex, when matched with that smooth cheek," this might also bespeak high birth and better days rather than woman; moreover, there is "something in his gaze, / More wild and high than woman's eye betrays" (1.574–79). Yet for any reader pausing over *might* and literate in the gender-codes of strong devotion and the disguised-page tradition (as old as Sidney's revised *Arcadia*), there is no ultimate mystery; the "secret" is "but half-conceal'd" (2.515). When, at Lara's death, Kaled faints and some try to revive the lad, "baring to revive that lifeless breast," the feint is up: the "sex confest."[31] The poet has just blurted as much: "that *he* lov'd! Oh! never yet beneath / The breast of man such trusty love may breathe!" (2.512–17). Popular reception had no trouble reading gender by the book. *Eclectic Review* was unflapped, wanting only to sift the travesty for Kaled's "most womanly attachment [. . .] to her master,—unfeminine only in its origin and in the degree of the passion,—most womanly in its disinterestedness, secrecy, and truth" (397). "The Page is still a Woman," sighed Anne Savage in her essay on Kaled in *Heath's Book of Beauty for 1847* (205): "With unobtrusive grace Kaled wins upon us, even in her masculine attire, for she still pays homage to the sex whose station and prerogative she abjured" (204).[32] The relief that dare not speak its name is that Kaled is not a boy-lover, that the gesture to Eastern sites is haremized rather than sodomized.

If Byron was working more than one code,[33] in the overt romance, the she-pages abide on the same page with the female forms that the poet of *Don Juan* loves to praise, all obedient to laws of "nature." Haidée and Zoe shower Juan with "soft attentions, / . . . of female growth" (2.123). The Sultana who would force Juan into sex-slavery is a woman still, baring "the fault of her soft sex" first in rage, and then in tears (5.136). Nowhere, in fact, does "the sex" receive so natural an imprimatur in *Don Juan* as in the tears that choke she-command:

> . . . her sex's shame broke in at last,
> A sentiment till then in her but weak,
> But now it flow'd in natural and fast . . . (5.137)

The crowning couplet to this stanza enforces the political corrective: "she felt humbled—and humiliation / Is sometimes good for people in her station." This is because (so the poet lectures us about an earlier event of she-tears) "nature teaches more than power can spoil"; "female hearts are such a genial soil, / For kinder feelings, whatsoe'er their nation" (5.120). Byron's draft shows that he was after a correction of social power by nature: under the sway of kinder, genial tears, the Sultana "forgot her station" and (elsewhere) can be mocked as a "Poor Girl" (*BPW* 5: 279, 284).

If these correctives seem overdriven, this is because Byron knows that the good old college of nature is coeducational, and among the things it teaches women is the art of acting natural. If "women shed and use them at their liking" (5.118), are their tears "nature" or costume? Gulbeyaz knows that her "grand resource" against Juan's obstinacy is to "cry of course" (5.139). The rhyme winks at the act, and at the start of the next canto we find the poet lecturing us (his text is Gulbeyaz) on how "Kisses, sweet words, embraces, and all that" are a kind of dress, "put on as easily as a hat, / Or rather bonnet, which the fair sex wear, / Trimmed either heads or hearts to decorate" (6.14). Not so literate about trim, let alone tears, Juan finds his obduracy "Dissolved like snow before a woman crying" (5.141).[34] What of men's tears? Juan's "burst into tears" for lost

Haidée (5.117), far from discrediting his manliness, confirms it, because this is no art. Men's tears are agon, and by this torture (the poet says on behalf of them all) one knows the difference: "A woman's tear-drop melts, a man's half sears"; "To them 'tis a relief, to us a torture" (118). When one of a shipwrecked crew (Canto II) "wept at length," it was "not fears / That made his eyelids as a woman's be," but the thought of his "wife and children" (43).

The contrast to these natural tears is a world of female shams in power plays against men. Mimicking the operatics of a diva caught just *post flagrante delicto*, the poet camps,

—Oh shame!
Oh sin! Oh sorrow! and Oh womankind!
How can you do such things and keep your fame,
Unless this world, and t'other too, be blind?
Nothing so dear as an unfilch'd good name! (1.165)

Yet there is an air of real protest in compact with what Iago (for all his treachery) proposes to Othello, should Desdemona's chastity come into question: "he that filches from me my good name . . . " (3.3.159). Rumors of sexcapades had filch'd Byron's good *name* into unwanted *fame*, and a likely resentment of the female art of having it both ways must have spurred his addition of *shame* to the rhyme. Being "circumspect" is a matter of "apparel," he has the poet remark of women in general (14.56), and of the epitome, Lady Adeline:

she acted right;
And whether coldness, pride, or virtue, dignify
A Woman, so she's good, what does it signify? (14.57)

Good is no term of virtue; it's a theater review. Lady Adeline shows how any woman may, with a "little genial sprinkling of hypocrisy," become one of the "loveliest Oligarchs of our Gynocrasy" (12.66). Byron liked this feminine rhyme, recalling it to advise all who would "take the tone of their society" to "wear the newest mantle of hypocrisy, / On pain of much displeasing the Gynocrasy" (16.52). Hearing of women's aversion to *Don Juan,* he ascribed it to his refusal to play in their dress: "it took off the *veil:* it showed that all their d——d sentiment was only an excuse to cover passions of a grosser nature. [. . .] it showed and exposed their hypocrisy" (*HVSV* 452). "The women hate every thing which strips off the tinsel of Sentiment—& they are right—or it would rob them of their weapons," he said to his publisher Murray in 1820 (*BLJ* 7: 202). He cheers the poem that "strips off this illusion" as his counter-attack, defying "the wish of all women to exalt the sentiment of the passions—& to keep up the illusion which is their empire" (*BLJ* 8: 148).

Yet nothing is more typical of *Don Juan* than the vibration of these differentials along a web of affiliations. The poet's rhyme-matchings are kin to the pleasure-principle of women's dabbling in "match-making" (15.31). Byron had a kinship for their social theatrics. "He was all *couleur de rose* last evening," Princess Caroline said of him in 1814 (*HVSV* 78), using the term the poet would apply to the coquette: that "amphibious sort of harlot, / '*Couleur de rose*,' who's neither white nor scarlet" (12.62). Even in more heartfelt matters, their arts are undecidable. Juan's first lover, Donna Julia, seals her farewell letter to him with a "motto, cut upon a white cornelian": *Elle vous suit partout* (1.198); and the poet lets us wonder if this is just she-sentiment, even cant. But Byron knew better, having taken it from a heart-shaped cornelian given to him by his college passion, choirboy John Edleston, whom he called "my *Cornelian*."[35] What of Byron's tears? "Talking one day of his domestic misfortunes, as he always called his separation from Lady Byron" (writes Lady Blessington), he "dwelt in a sort of unmanly strain of lamentation on it, that all present felt to be unworthy of him."[36] Does *unmanly* read imprudent self-indulgence, or a kind of she-theatrics? Byron casts "Dissimulation" as *she*, but he does so in a stanza whose theme is how "men" dissimulate "their thoughts of worst or best," by "Making the countenance a masque of rest, / And turning human nature to an art" (15.3). The liberal gender of such art is conceded by his rhyme in Canto XII (66), which completes *hypocrisy / Gynocrasy* with *our Aristocracy*—as if women's arts were the pattern of general class success.

This is not cross-dressing, but cuts of the same cloth. When the poet says, "Now what I love in women is, they won't / Or can't do otherwise than lie, but do it / So well, the very truth seems falsehood to it," it is a favorable contrast to "politicians and their double front, / Who live by lies, yet dare not boldly lie" (11.36). In a world corrupted by the cant of "Truth," she-lies are honest. Fronted by "women," Byron's poet can even defend "a lie" as "but / The truth in masquerade," the deconstructive shadow of any "fact" (11.37). A writer may be distinguished (but not really differentiated) only by a willingness to theorize the masquerade: "if a writer should be quite consistent, / How could he possibly show things existent?" the poet protests near the end of Canto XV (87), his next stanza arguing that even the intents of "Truth" must "cut through such canals of contradiction, / That she must often navigate o'er fiction" (88). While this "Truth" has she-agency, it's looking increasingly like livery for Byronic poetry. Canto XVI begins with a reprise this last rhyme, with the poet praising his muse as "beyond all contradiction / The most sincere that ever dealt in fiction" (2). Does *beyond* mean surpassing, or refuting the charge altogether? The signature term for this versatile sincerity emerges in this same canto: *mobility*.

Byron introduces this signature with several she-markings, starting with its star, Lady Adeline as social queen. Juan is the least generous of her beholders:

> when he cast a glance
> On Adeline while playing her grad role,
>   Which she went through as a dance
> (Betraying only now and then her soul
>   By a look scarce perceptibly askance
> Of weariness or scorn), began to feel
> Some doubt how much of Adeline was *real,*
> So well she acted all and every part
>   By turns with that vivacious versatility . . . (16. 96–97)

Byron wrote this act from some female templates: Lady Blessington, and Staël's celebrated performing poet and conversationalist Corinne.[37] But rather than launch a gender rant in the mask of Juan's doubt about Adeline's authenticity, he interpolates that parenthetical gloss. Not in Juan's ken, it is a comment from poet to reader, a kind of aside about Adeline beside herself, either subverting the soul of her social performance with that look, or exposing her very soul as alienated (the double-play of *betraying* is a very Byronic touch). Byron takes stanza 97 away altogether from Juan's glance, and has the poet read the spectacle directly to us. It is remarkable that he does so not only with sympathy, but without insistent gender-assignment:

>   . . . that vivacious versatility
>   Which many people take for want of heart.
>   They err—'tis merely what is called mobility,
>   A thing of temperament and not of art,
>   Though seeming so, from its supposed facility;
>   And false—though true; for surely they're sincerest,
>   Who are strongly acted on by what is nearest. (16.97)

Byron also supplied a paratextual note:[38] "French, 'mobilité' [. . .] It may be defined as an excessive susceptibility of immediate impressions [. . .] and is, though sometimes apparently useful to the possessor, a most painful and unhappy attribute." While here, too, he may be remembering *Corinne,* the sympathy sounds personal.[39] If it's not possible to know, exactly, the degrees of acting or being acted on, what can be known, by Byron (if not Juan), is that mobility is gender-mobile. He admitted "the abundance of this quality in his own nature" as well as its peril to a perception of "consistency and singleness of character" (reports Moore). The poet of *Don Juan* may be sure that a "feminine Caprice" inspires women's "indecision,/Their never knowing their own mind two days" (6.117–19) and that it is "ladies' fancies" that are "rather transitory" (10.9), but Byron proves the complication. The "mobility of his nature is extraordinary, and makes him inconsistent in his actions as well as in his conversation," Lady Blessington remarked; "Byron is a perfect chameleon, taking the colour of whatever touches him. He is conscious of this, and says it is owing to the extreme *mobilité* of his nature, which yields to present impressions." She was so <u>perplexed</u> with the "mass of heterogeneous evidence" that she found it "most <u>difficult</u> to draw a just conclusion" of Byron's character (the underscores are by Teresa Guiccioli, living with Byron at the time).[40] And Juan, forever a new one in every canto, turns epic heroism itself into a perfect chameleon play—well in advance of Woolf's hypertheorized Orlando.

Moving from *she* to *they* in stanza 97, Byron skirts *he,* and more particularly, *I*—however implicit these applications. By the next stanza, however, he is setting mobility beyond psychology and reading it, as Jerome McGann proposes, into a general structure of relations with an audience, one that takes its pattern from "the artist's life" ("Mobility" 38–40):

> This makes your actors, artists, and romancers,
> Heroes sometimes, though seldom—sages never;
> But speakers, bards, diplomatists, and dancers,
> Little that's great, but much of what is clever . . . (16.98)

George Ridenour thus sees Adeline's mobility of a piece with "that growing urbanity Byron has so praised in his hero himself: 'The art of living in all climes with ease.'" Ridenour regards this art (he's quoting Canto XV.11) as Byron's answerable style "Amidst life's infinite variety"—a kind of "conversational facility" linked to the art of the "Improvisatore" (15.19–20), of the sort Staël endows her urbane Corinne.[41] But the nod to Corinne and the Shakespearean allusion cast a shadow that Ridenour doesn't measure. Corinne's mobility is a loveless boon, and Cleopatra's arts of "infinite variety" (*Antony and Cleopatra* 2.2.235–36) involve the transvestitism that bodes Antony's fall: in one improvisation, she "put [her] tires and mantles on him," and "wore his sword Philippan" (2.5.22–23). A military trophy thus toyed and disgraced spells the scandal as well as the fun of Eastern/Byronic masquerades—the world that prompts Hazlitt's lament over "the effeminate character of Mark Antony."[42] Thinking of Byron's relations with his audience, *The Champion* looked at the structure of weariness and scorn that McGann describes, to find the travesty not at all droll, just degrading:

> *She would and She would not,* is a pleasing comedy, when performed by a lovely woman, but a change of gender converts it into a farce. Allowances are due to

the caprices of genius,—but is it worthy of a man of genius to be perpetually claiming them?

The reference to Colley Cibber's play, featuring a young woman who dons soldier's garb to follow her lover, shows how gender-switching can turn pathos into ignoble farce.[43] And Byron likes to designate "caprice" as "feminine" (6.119).

Critical Accounts

In these mobile poetics of mobility, Byron's regard of female arts can cut both ways. One of the edgiest cases is that farewell letter he scripts for Julia to send to Juan. The theme is gender-fate:

> "Man's love is of man's life a thing apart,
>   'Tis woman's whole existence; man may range
> The court, camp, church, the vessel, and the mart,
>   Sword, gown, gain, glory, offer in exchange
> Pride, fame, ambition, to fill up his heart,
>   And few there are whom these can not estrange;
> Man has all these resources, we but one,
> To love again, and be again undone." (1.194)

"Where did you learn all these secrets?" Shelley asked Byron when he read this "masterpiece" of a "love letter," adding "I should like to go to school there" (*L* 2: 198). The answer is that Byron's school has two curricula, women's texts of the heart (Staël) and his own heart, reading these in sympathy. It's not too many stanzas on from Julia's letter that his poet is singing this theme about his own past heart (now disciplined, perhaps not the better for it):

> No more—no more—Oh! never more, my heart,
>   Canst thou be my sole world, my universe!
> Once all in all, but now a thing apart . . . (1.215)

If this poet is one for whom love is a thing apart, he admits that he once had Julia's anatomy of gender: his heart was once a she-heart, his whole existence. Julia's letter is the creditable voice of Byronic melancholy, she-styled.[44]

From Donna Julia forward, the Byronic hero that starred in the Regency gains a female form. It may be that in boyish Juan and the wry narrator of *Don Juan* the Byronic hero flickers into parody. But its romance burns in the heroines: Julia, lovelorn and exiled to life-in-death (with whom widow Mary Shelley strongly identified);[45] Haidée, lovelorn unto madness and death; Adeline, "playing her grand role" in "weariness or scorn" (16.96), even mysterious, inscrutable

Aurora Raby. The poet of *Don Juan* may "want a hero," but the author of *Don Juan* wants a (Byronic) heroine. Alfred Austin exposed this regendering when, a half a century on, he recalled Julia's words as a Byronic chant of manly independence from the "female element" in culture. Byron "never shirked dealing with sexual passion and sentiment," but

> he was not for ever harping upon it.
> "'For Love is in man's life a thing apart;
> 'Tis woman's whole existence,'"
> he sings; and he proved the truth of the first line, as far as he was himself concerned, by his *Cain*, his *Manfred*, his *Childe Harold*, and most of his dramas. (95)

Byron proved this truth in just as many works in sympathy with the female lament. In one mood swing, he declared to Lady Blessington that it was only through knowing women that men had any sense of what "purity and goodness" could be: "even though she may lapse from virtue; she makes a willing sacrifice of herself on the altar of affection, and thinks only of him for whom it is made," while men were bearers of "evil" into their lives (*BCB* 196). The poet of *Don Juan* may "want a hero," but author Byron wants a Byronic heroine giving all for love.

Julia's letter registers more than Byron's sympathy with the female heart, however. It also fronts a critique of female social fate, credited with swaths of Austen and (again) Staël, and even the poet himself, who in the next canto is willing to say, "man, to man so oft unjust, / Is always so to women" (2.199–200).[46] At the end of the century, lesbian feminist Frances Power Cobbe recalled Julia's letter to comment on a happy life without marriage, "albeit I have gone through life without that interest which has been styled 'woman's whole existence'" (*Life* 1: 3). "Men think of themselves alone, and regard the woman but as an object that administers to their selfish gratification, and who, when she ceases to have this power, is thought of no more, save as an obstruction," Byron himself admitted to an "incredulous" Lady Blessington, adding, "I have a much higher opinion of your sex than I have even now expressed" (*BCB* 196). Teresa Guiccioli underlined this last sentence, too.

It was the poem's seeming sympathy with Julia that launched her letter from romance into political controversy. Byron set the stage by having his poet introduce the letter as a virtual set piece, a "copy" he happens to have (1.191) and is willing to show (the original, we learn in Canto II, did not survive).[47] The first reviews treated it as if it were a promiscuous position paper, hotly debating Julia's erotic self-determination and subsequent lament, sometimes with surprising alliances across political lines, sometimes with surprising twists. Writing in 1822 for *Edinburgh Review,* Francis Jeffrey (usually given to praise Byron) took offense at "this shameless and abandoned woman address[ing] to her young gallant, an epistle breathing the very spirit of warm, devoted, pure and unalterable love—thus profaning the holiest language of the heart, and indirectly associating it with the most hateful and degrading sensuality" (450).[48] Meanwhile *Blackwood's,* though it despised Byron for "brutally outraging all the best feelings of female honour, affection, and confidence" and "brutally, fiendishly" wounding Lady Byron "with unhallowed strains of cold-blooded mockery" (Donna Inez), so admired the "beautiful letter" that it could not forbear giving four of its six stanzas (1.194–97) ("Remarks" 5: 514, 517). The most liberal view was Leigh Hunt's critique of the social fate visited on commodity-wives. Julia merely "gives way to her natural feelings, and is unfaithful to her marriage vows, the example (observe) being set her by this very husband's intrigues with *Juan's* mother," he notes acidly, going on to contend:

> Lord Byron does no more than relate the consequences of certain absurdities. If he speaks slightingly of the ties between a girl and a husband old enough for her father, it is because the ties themselves *are* slight. [. . .] stupid and selfish parents will make up matches between persons whom difference of age or disposition disqualifies for mutual affection. [. . .] *Julia,* the victim of selfishness and "damned custom," is shut up in a convent [. . .] but even that was perhaps pleasanter to her than living in the constant irksomeness of feigning an affection she could not feel. (*Examiner* 618: 701)

Such reactions suggest why some women *did* like the poem.[49] Murray's Tory *Quarterly* understood the peril, warning in 1820 that "that the most dangerous writer of the present day finds his most numerous and enthusiastic admirers among the fair sex; and we have many times seen very eloquent eyes kindle in vehement praise of the poems, which no woman should have read" (24: 131). The news in 1823 from Galignani's bookshop in Paris that Byron was happy to relay to John Hunt (his publisher after Murray grew reticent) was "that of all my works D Juan is the most popular [. . .] especially amongst the women who send for it the more that it is abused" (9 April; *BLJ* 10: 146).

With a fresh sense of this popularity among women, Byron tunes Canto XIV (1823) to reprise the 1790s critiques of sexual politics and policy. Back in Canto XII, the poet was savagely satirizing the "male loss of time, and hearts, and bets / Upon the sweepstakes for substantial wives" (36) (the substance being their fortunes). Canto XIV seems in key. The poet starts out jauntily, surveying the great world of "beauties brought to market by the score; / Sad rakes to sadder husbands chastely taming" (18), and it is not long before he is refreshing old anti-feminist lore:

> Alas! Worlds fall—and Woman, since she fell'd
>   The World (as, since that history, less polite
> Than true, hath been a creed so strictly held)
>   Has not given up the practice quite. (14.23)

But in the very next line, the poem starts to sound like a versified *Rights of Woman*:

> Poor Thing of Usages! Coerc'd, compell'd,
>   Victim when wrong, and martyr often when right,
> Condemn'd to child-bed . . . (14.23)

Byron is even willing to forgo the temptation to be bawdy, and let the verb "penetrate" rebuke that old trope of men as skilled readers of women:

>   as to women, who can penetrate
> The real sufferings of their she condition?
> Man's very sympathy with their estate
>   Has much of selfishness and more suspicion.
> Their love, their virtue, beauty, education,
>   But form good housekeepers, to breed a nation. (14.24)

This is a poet who owns a he-complicity in the "she condition" and who is compacting with she-critics. Wollstonecraft (or early Barbauld) could have been the muse of his next stanza:

> The gilding wears so soon from off her fetter,
>   That—but ask any woman if she'd choose
> (Take her at thirty, that is) to have been
> Female or male? a school-boy or a Queen? (14.25)

How closely this accords with Barbauld's warning to women back in 1772:

> In beauty's empire is no mean,
> And woman, either slave or queen,
> Is quickly scorn'd when not ador'd. (*Song V* 16–18)

Wollstonecraft quoted these lines in *Rights of Woman* to gloss the specious "power" of beauty (171). That "ev'ry Lady would be Queen for life" was the old lore from Pope's *To a Lady* (218)—the epistle that irked Macaulay, Wollstonecraft, and Hays.[50] Byron guesses that any woman would prefer the lowly lot of school-boy ("ploughboy" in a draft) to that of even a sovereign female.

Yet it is just as revealing that such genuine sympathy can recoil into the fashions of the prevenient order. In the very next stanza of Canto XIV, his poet is apologizing for "Petticoat Influence," deeming it "a great reproach, / Which even those who obey would fain be thought / To fly from, as from hungry pikes a roach" (26).[51] The redress is man-show leering, Regency style, on the "mystical sublimity" of petticoated female bodies (26–27).

The politics of gender are never stable. When Hazlitt writes, "Lord Byron makes man after his own image, woman after his own heart; the one is a capricious tyrant, the other a yielding slave" ("Byron" 154), he cannily gives Byron's heart to the female gender, the she-condition. "I am easily governed by women," Byron protested to Medwin; even flighty Caro Lamb "gained an ascendancy over me that I could not easily shake off. I submitted to this thraldom long" (he said) and was "regularly installed into what the Italians call *service*" (*MCB* 216). "Strange as it may seem," he recalled of Lady Oxford, married and forty, "she gained (as all women do) an influence over me so strong, that I had great difficulty in breaking with her, even when I knew she had been inconstant to me" (*MCB* 70). He claimed he was only being "true to Nature" in his poetry "in making the advances come from the females" (*MCB* 165). The naturalizing is less interesting than Byron's recourse to it to rationalize his enchantment. Discerning Lady Byron in Donna Inez, *Blackwood's* charged in August 1819 that Byron treated women with cold contempt; Byron's protest to Murray may be disingenuous, but it was a story that had come to feel like a truth: "it may be so—but I have been their martyr.—My whole life has been sacrificed to them & by them" (*BLJ* 6: 257).[52]

In *Don Juan* this sacrifice is routinely staged as one of male dress. As male-garbed Duchess Fitz-Fulke invades Juan's chamber for a sexual conquest, he is starkly *en dishabille*:

> he was undrest,
> Saving his night gown, which is an undress;
> Completely "sans culotte," and without vest;
> In short, he hardly could be clothed with less.   (16.111)

Undrest and alone, Juan is iconic she-vulnerability: the gazed-upon, scantily clad maid (Madeline in Keats's *The Eve of St. Agnes*); the menaced ingénue in the gothic genre ("apprehensive of his spectral guest") of Byron's staging. Undress unmakes the man. "Sans culotte" is no French revolutionary fashion statement against effeminate aristocratic style, but more in line with (if less acidic than) the *Anti-Jacobin* cartoon of Godwin unmanned by Wollstonecraft:

> Her husband, sans-culottes, was melancholy,
> For Mary verily would wear the breeches—

God help poor silly men from such usurping b———s.
(*Vision of Liberty* XV)

In this panting semiotic, "sans-culottes" is sans-manhood.

Juan undrest is always Juan nearly unmanned. He is "half-smother'd" (1.165) in Julia's bedding as she hides him from her husband's posse, from which he flees "naked" into the night (1.188). Washed up naked, half-dead on the beach, he is captured by Haidée's gaze (the hetero-homoerotics on display in Ford Madox Brown's image; fig. 6.2), then reborn as her dress-up toy: Haidée "stripp'd her sables off" to make his bed, and for covers she and Zoe "gave a petticoat apiece" (2.133). Petticoat influence survives the clothes in which Haidée later "dress'd" Juan: the apparel of those "very spacious breeches" does not proclaim the man. Or it does another: absent patriarch Lambro (2.160). For both Julia and Haidée, Juan is always a "boy"—so too his charm for Empress Catherine's "preference of a boy to men much bigger" (9.72). Byron lightly exacerbates the crisis by letting all these women seem much bigger. Julia is of "stature tall," with "handsome eyes" (1.60–61). Haidée is "Even of the highest for a female mould" (2.116). Protecting Juan from Lambro's wrath, she "threw herself her boy before; / Stern as her sire" (to sharpen the point, Byron revised *calm* to *stern*); "She stood . . . stern, she woo'd the blow; / And tall beyond her sex"; "She drew up her height," and "with a fix'd eye scann'd / Her father's face"; "How like they look'd! the expression was the same"; "their features and / Their stature differing but in sex and years" (4.42–45). In this mirroring, Haidée and sire differ less from each other than both from boy Juan—his cast throughout this episode (2.144, 174; 4.19, 38). In a shrewd extrapolation of this logic, *The Sultana* gives Haidée not only a "boy's disguise" (10) for tracking Juan to Turkey, but also male economic power: intent to "purchase his liberty" (19), *Sultana*-Haidée bribes the guards to let her onto the slave ship, bribes the captain with her jewels, and plans to use her remaining wealth in Turkey to "obtain me every where interest and friends, and should I find my Juan, will throw off his chains, and make our union blest with affluence" (10). Not just clothes, but money makes the man.

The comic romance of *The Sultana* casts the edgier economy of *Don Juan* into relief. "Juan nearly died" in Julia's chamber (1.168). It's a fatal she-sea, just about to "suck him back to her insatiate grave" (2.108), that releases him to Haidée's isle. Rebirth as Haidée's treasure imperils not only Juan's manhood but, implicitly, his life in the world: Haidée's doting eyes are raven-fringed, "black as death" (2.117).[53] The threat is perpetual: Juan is "half-kill'd" by Lambro's squad (4.74), and his Turkish travesty wins a Sultana's death warrant; ravenous Catherine all too soon reduces the "beauteous" boy to "a condition / Which augured of the dead" (10.39). So, too, in his first brush with Fitz-Fulke's back-from-the-

Figure 6.2 *The Finding of Don Juan by Haidée,* by Ford Madox Brown (1873). Exhausted on the beach after surviving a shipwreck and near starvation, naked Juan seems less buff than the Greek maid leaning over him while Haidée gazes on. "And, like a wither'd lily, on the land / His slender frame and pallid aspect lay, / As fair a thing as e'er was form'd of clay" (2.110).

dead Black Friar-drag ("sable frock and dreary cowl"; 16.123), a she-comparison of freaked-out Juan to Medusa is no empowerment; he seems more like one of the Gorgon's unmanned, petrified victims:

> . . . Juan gazed upon it with a stare,
> Yet could not speak or move; but, on its base
> As stands a statue, stood: he felt his hair
> Twine like a knot of snakes around his face;
> He taxed his tongue for words, which were not granted . . . (16.23)

The next morning they both look death-"pale" (16.31) and, in a canto Byron didn't live to finish, there is a morning-after pallor of an apparently longer encounter, with Juan looking ever more "wan and worn," and her Grace scarcely better, "pale and shivered" (17.14). A manuscript scrap indicates the agenda: "The Shade of the/Friar/The Dth of J" (*CPW* 5: 761n). To relinquish the gender grammar, even in farce, is to court a death sentence. If Juan's defaults are culpable, the women pay the fuller wage: all save the Duchess are humiliated; Julia is doomed to convent life-in-death; Haidée is bereft, prisoned, demented, pregnant, dead.

And yet, for all this sorting out, the power of *Don Juan*—both its popularity and its scandal—emanates from Byron's critical perspective on these ordering schemes.

Double-Cross-Dressing

Back in 1705, Mary Astell complained that when male historians "condescend to record the great and good Actions of Women," they usually give "this wise Remark":

> That such Women *acted above their Sex*. By which one must suppose that they wou'd have their Readers understand, That they were not Women who did those Great Actions, but that they were men in Petticoats![54]

In order to sustain the habit of equating great and good actions with the male sex, extraordinary women get classed as cross-dressed men. Astell knows that in this wry reflection on the figure of women acting "up" lies a more serious proposal: that "men," too, are defined by how they act, and a man in petticoats is no figure of greatness. In the two episodes of cross-sex cross-dressing in *Don Juan*, Byron stages a theater of mobility with these genres in play. Even as the narratives draw comic energy from their dress-reversals and structural dislocations of power, the fate of manhood in the new formations remains a nagging question. What is a man in a petticoat?

This wasn't theory for Byron. It was life as Teresa Guiccioli's Cavalier Servente, rehearsed in that "*service*" to Caroline Lamb. In the Italian culture of young wives and husbands much older, the *Servente* is a wife's socially tolerated "escort." Byron was capable of a wry perspective on the business. Here was a system of fathers minding daughters as goods, "shut up in a convent till she has attained a marriageable or marketable age," to be sold preferably "under the market price" (that "portion of his fortune [. . .] fixed by law for the dower") to a suitor of riches or rank. Eligible bidders were sometimes older than father. La Guiccioli was married off in her teens to a rich noble of fifty or sixty (*BLJ* 6: 107, 173). The pathos is that "objections are seldom made on the part of the young lady to the age, and personal or other defects of the intended, who perhaps visits her once in the parlour as a matter of form or curiosity," because marriage Italian style was a better deal than life-sentence to a convent. The daughter "is too happy to get her liberty on any terms," and her husband to get "her money or her person." "There is no love on either side," Byron observed of this unhappy, corruptible, and "preposterous connexion" (*MCB* 22).[55]

When, however, Byron reacted to his part in the system, the terms shift in direct correspondence to his degradation. Not only did a distinction between "*Cavalier Serventeism*" and that "prostitution, where the women get all the money they can" in loveless business "contracts" seem a bit moot (*MCB* 22), but serventism seemed less dignified than the frankly managed business. Teresa may have been a "Woman on the Market" in Luce Irigaray's terms ("they always pass from one man to another" [171]); and Byron may have enjoyed male privileges, in their crudest forms: "He allows fathers & mothers to bargain with him for their daughters" (said P. B. Shelley in disgust in 1818), a practice "common enough in Italy" but still distressing to "an Englishman" (*L* 2: 58).[56] But in Italy Byron was also a commodity: his service and trophy value (a "fetish object" of power-display [Irigaray 183]) was part of the Italienne culture of boy toys. "The *k*night-service of the Continent, with or without the *k*," is "slavery," he groused to Medwin (*MCB* 73–74). In Italy, Staël's Nelvil complains to Corinne, it almost seems "que les femmes sont le sultan et les hommes le sérail" (*Corinne,* bk. 6, ch. 3, p. 157). Unlike England, "the polygamy is all on the female side," Byron chimes in, the "strange sensation" of this degradation exacerbated by his "effeminate way of life" in Italy (June 1819; *BLJ* 6: 226, 210).

Having just ranted to Murray in April 1819 about not castrating the first two cantos of *Don Juan*—"I will have none of your damned cutting & slashing" especially to please "le femine"—(*BLJ* 6: 105–6), he swooned in first love to Teresa. She was already calling him in public "Mio Byron," having known him scarcely a week, and busily arranging his life. "I should not like to be frittered down into a regular Cicisbeo," Byron sighed to Hobhouse; but it was an elegiac case: "What shall I do! I am in love—and tired of promiscuous concubinage" (6: 108). By June he was helpless: "The Lady does whatever she pleases with me" (6: 162); he was "completely <u>governed</u> by" her—"every thing depends upon <u>her</u> entirely" (164). And by August he was a slave: "this Cisisbean existence is to be condemned.—But I have neither the strength of mind to break my chain, nor the insensibility which would deaden it's weight" (214).

In Juan's Turkish episode, Byron sets out to govern in poetry what he can't manage in life. Polygamy gets put back on the male side, and sexual property is female: the Sultan has a harem of 1500 and four wives (one of them Gulbeyaz). "Turks and Eastern people manage these matters better," he thought (reflecting on the "fatal" fall of his "*beau idéal*" in his experience with worldly women); "They lock them up, and they are much happier"—*they* and *them* gender-sorted at least in Eastern stages (*MCB* 73; cf. Iley 2: 237).

Not under such tight management, *Don Juan* finds an escape clause is cross-dressing. While Juan in drag is a farce, the genre doesn't dispel the critical effect: the denaturalizing and theatricalizing of gender as an "act."[57] Well before Joan Riviere was theorizing "Womanliness as a Masquerade" (1929) and Luce Irigaray raising the stakes by identifying "the *masquerade of femininity*" as a production for the male marketplace of desire ("Questions" 133–34), Byron staged the question with Juan's protests that he is not "in a masquerading mood" for this "odd travesty" (5.73–74). No "perfect transformation," Juan's feminine masquerade is "display'd" in a form that all but makes the Wollstonecraft case: the artifices to which females are routinely trained. His costuming and coaching "to stint / That somewhat manly majesty of stride" (5.91), a dressing down for him, is every woman's schooling for success. Byron had intuited the master-trope of feminist critique. "I don't mind drag," Gloria Steinem put the case plain; "women have been female impersonators for some time." "Is drag the imitation of gender, or does it dramatize the signifying gestures through which gender itself is established?" asks Judith Butler in her preface to *Gender Trouble* (x).[58]

The artifices that gender critics theorized and Byron recognized are politically invested by the harem site. This was a male Romantic trope for erotic paradise, a beau-idealizing with which Byron collaborated when he made the enslaved heroine of *The Giaour* "Circassia's daughter" (505). "For my part," Rousseau crooned in *Émile*, "I would have a young Englishwoman cultivate her agreeable talents, in order to please her future husband, with as much care and assiduity as a young Circassian cultivates hers, to fit her for the Haram of an Eastern bashaw." The English is Wollstonecraft's text in *Rights of Woman* (208), the translation not only a convenience but also a point about the translation of ideology, whatever the other national antagonisms. Keeping the woman French rather than rendering her English, Macaulay had cited the same passage in a "Letter on Education" that began: "Though the situation of women in modern Europe, [. . .] when compared with that condition of abject slavery in which they have always been held in the east, may be considered as brilliant; yet if we withhold comparison, and take the matter in a positive sense, we shall have no great reason to boast of our privileges." This, because the privileges coincide "with a total and absolute exclusion of every political right" (210).[59] Refusing the orientalizing, Macaulay and Wollstonecraft set the harem as a trope for patriarchal system per se. It is no less the project of English culture, Wollstonecraft acidly remarks, to form girls into creatures "only fit for a seraglio" (*VRW* 113, cf. 138).

Yet for all this troping and travesty of she-training, *Don Juan* is most Byronic in its side-lining of the wrongs of woman for the wrongs of a feminized man.[60] Byron even thought to up the ante by having the Sultana "carry [Juan] off from Constantinople" (*MCB* 164), sex-switching the usual ravishment. Fronting Byron's embarrassment about women's ways with him, haremized Juan is shocked (shocked!) to find himself eyed as sexual "property" by an imperious woman: "a glance on him she cast, / . . . merely saying, 'Christian, canst thou love?'" (5.116). "A man actually becomes a piece of female property," Byron grumped of his service to La Guiccioli (*BLJ* 7: 28); "the system of *serventism* imposes a thousand times more restraint and slavery than marriage ever imposed" (Blessington, *BCB* 180; Teresa didn't mark this comment). He felt particularly taxed by "the defined duties of a Cavalier Servente, or Cavalier Schiavo"—i.e., slave (*BLJ* 7: 195). It was virtual reverse *couverture*:

> "Cavalier Servente" is the phrase
>   Used in politest circles to express
> This supernumerary slave, who stays
>   Close to the lady as a part of dress.
> Her word is the only law which he obeys.
>   His is no sinecure, as you may guess;
> Coach, servants, gondola, he goes to call,
> And carries fan, and tippet, gloves, and shawl. (40)

Byron first wrote *gentleman*, then decided on *slave*. It's not just that a Servente carries his lady's accessories, but that he is one of these, "stays / Close to the lady as a part of dress" (40)—the punning and sliding of *who stays* ("whose stays") reinforcing the complaint. Byron never developed his plan to extend Juan's travesties into the "ridicules" of this Italian role (*BLJ* 8: 78), but he gives the lad an audition with the Sultana and then the Empress, when he compares "the actual and official duties" of "the Imperial Favourite's Condition" to those of a "Cavalier Servente" (9.51–52). When he later described Juan's "station" as that of "man-mistress to Catherine the Great" (*MCB* 165), the compound spells the cost: degraded to woman's property, Juan is regendered.[61]

This status is not exactly a new one. Secreted from patriarchal notice, he is Julia's boytoy and Haidée's pet: "her bird," "her own, her ocean-treasure" (2.168, 173), "her beautiful, her own" (4.58), and always "her boy" (2.174, 4.42). Rather than a radical transformation, slavery is the disenchanted variation: "chain'd, so that he cannot move, / And all because a lady fell in love" (4.51). If erotic thrall hazards a loss of male social identity (Antony, too, a "slave" to "Love" [2.205]), material slavery confirms it. The "boy" Juan (5.13), an "odd male" (figuratively no less than numerically), gets paired for the slave-mart with an "odd female" in an allotment in which everyone else is linked "Lady to lady," "man to man" (4.91–92). His gender in this odd couple—the female is as "handsome" as he (4.95, 5.9)—falls to operatic theatricality: he keeps company with a strange soprano who occasions "some discussion and some doubt" among the vendors if she "might be deem'd to be male" (4.92), and a castrato of the "*third* sex" (4.86). Juan soon finds himself (again) in a she-place, leered at and for sale. His "intended bidder" eyes him more intently than "lady e'er is ogled by a lover" (5.26), like a woman whom "wealth[y] lust / Buys . . . in marriage" (2.200). The gender-trade is completed when it turns out that the purchaser is a powerful she, by whom he will be "eyed . . . o'er and o'er" (5.107). Byron joked to Lady Melbourne on the eve of his marriage to the first woman he expected to "govern" him, "I shall become Lord Annabella" (*BLJ* 4: 229). Like "Man-Queen" in *Sardanapalus*, the self-titling double-names his subjection and her command.

Juan's slavery is more Byronic yet in its trace of the subjection of authors to the market and its female arbiters. At the end of Canto IV, the poet abandons the slave ship to muse on authorship and its love of "fame." This, too, is a self-correction: "Byron's vanity, or to give it a milder, and, perhaps, more appropriate term, his love of fame," Iley reports, "was excessive" (2: 355). *Don Juan* doses love with savage critique. A patently fickle she, "fame is but a lottery, / Drawn by the blue-coat misses of a coterie," *blue* now the tone of an entire she-ensemble of courted readers.[62] The winners are gender-contaminated, a "ball-room bard, a foolscap, hot-press darling" (4.109). The figures are cut from Byron's cloth: "a ball-room bard—a *hot-pressed* darling," he recalled his life in 1812 (*MCB* 214). By 1814 he had come to despise "authorship" as a "sign of effeminacy" (*BLJ* 3: 220), and by 1819 he disdained the suit for public "Estimation": "I have never flattered their opinions," he rages to Murray; "Neither will I make 'Ladies books' 'al dilettar le femine e la plebe'—I have written from the fullness of my mind, from passion—from impulse—from many motives—but not for their 'sweet voices'" (*BLJ* 6: 105–6), he sneers in echo of Shakespeare's *Coriolanus* (2.3.111). He talks the talk, protesting the integrity of motives, mind and passion, independent of the idols of the marketplace.[63] In other letters to Murray, he scorns "the bookmaking of women," both the commodity "*She* book" and the economic gamble (September 1820; *BLJ* 7: 183).

Yet as with the disdain of fame or the edginess about mobility, Byron concedes a onetime complicity, even a she-style—"that false stilted trashy style which is a mixture of all the styles of the day" (182). Medwin thought Byron was still out "to captivate all the ladies" (*MCB* 214), hearing him say that he "was more pleased with the fame my 'Corsair' had, than with that of any other of my books. Why? for the very reason because it did shine, and in *boudoirs*. Who does not write to please the women?" (206). When in 1822 Shelley lamented the truckling to the "vulgar" and "the ephemeral demand of the day" in Murray's urging of Byron "to resume [the] old 'Corsair style, to please the ladies,'" Byron conceded his part, but with an escape clause: "Murray is right, if not righteous: all I have yet written has been for women-kind; you must wait until I am forty, their influence will then die a natural death, and I will show the men what I can do" (Trelawny 35–36).

Byron's sensitivity to the choice between selling oneself to womankind and showing men what a man can do (an emerging rhetoric for the self-constituting male writer in the nineteenth century) registers in Juan's Turkish career. The Sultana's "blue eyes" (5.116) link her "passion and power" over Juan to those "Benign ceruleans of the second sex" who "make the fortunes of all books" (4.108), the latest avatar of the fickle goddess herself. Such slavery is on the poet's mind in his return to enslaved Juan at the close of Canto IV: "But to the narrative: the vessel bound / With slaves to sell off in the capital" (113). Before it is clear that "the vessel bound" is a slave ship and not a book, and that the capital is Constantinople and not London, a common market terminology seems to cover feminized human slaves ("deck'd . . . out in all the hues of heaven" for "sale" [114]) and the hot-press darlings drawn in a lottery run by women. No wonder, then, that Byron devises renewed expressions of male power.

The agenda is cued by Juan's steadfast integrity: Byron allows him the dignity of protesting to his buyer, "I'm not a lady," of worrying about his reputation if "it e'er be told / That I unsexed my dress," and of declaring, "my soul loathes / The effeminate garb" (5.73, 75–76). It is only Baba's threat that petulance will leave him with more unsexed than dress that effects nominal compliance. Lordly male character abides. Juan "stood like Atlas" before the Sultana, refusing the command to "kiss the lady's foot" (102): "rather than descend / To stain his pedigree," he hews to the Castilian custom that "commands / The gentleman, to kiss the lady's hands" (104–5). Opposing abasement with chivalric courtesy is the polite correction. A slap more political comes in Juan's public refusal of the Sultana's "imperial" advance:

> . . . he was steel'd by sorrow, wrath, and pride:
> With gentle force her white arms he unwound,
>   And seated her all drooping by his side.
> Then rising haughtily he glanced around,
>   And looking coldly in her face, he cried,
> "The prison'd eagle will not pair, nor I
> Serve a sultana's sensual phantasy. . . .
>
>   . . .
>
>   Love is for the free!
>
>   . . .
>
> Whate'er thy power, and great it seems to be,
> Heads bow, knees bend, eyes watch around a throne,
> And hands obey—our hearts are still our own."   (5.126–27)

In the mask of enslaved, cross-dressed Juan, Byron sings liberation, its theme continuous with his refusal of Teresa's urging a love interest for *Sardanapalus*: it "could scarcely exist in the social state of inferiority in which woman was placed in ancient civilization" (*HVSV* 247). He was repelled by modern atrocities, and helped rescue a thirteen-year-old girl kidnapped by Kurdish mountaineers for sale at a bazaar, "whence Constantinople is supplied with *women*, like *beasts of the field*, from a *cattle* market." Byron hid her "in boy's attire" and hoped to return her to her parents (Iley 3: 123–26). Yet *Don Juan* is not only less consolidated on this liberal thinking, but self-conflicted by its tug of male self-interest. As Elaine Showalter remarks about *Tootsie*, "'feminist' speeches" by a man in drag (here, on the job market) "are less a response to the oppression of women than an instinctive situational male reaction to being treated like a woman" ("Critical Cross-Dressing" 138).

An allied male reaction, also *Tootsie* and also Byron, is to diffuse political import into cliché or farce. "This was a truth to us extremely trite," the poet yawns at Juan's protest (5.128)—*us*, the men who've heard it all, already, for whom Juan's passion is no great matter. The episode then plays out as farce, the genre of choice for male transvestitism in literary and theatrical tradition. Questions of female subjection are translated into camp and parody.[64] The Englishman who befriends Juan in the slave market gives the cue with a jesting riff on

Laertes' caution to Ophelia—"Keep your good name"—and Juan plays along: "'Nay,' quoth the maid, 'the Sultan's self shan't carry me,/ Unless his highness promises to marry me'" (5.84). When the Sultan takes a shine to his beauty, Juan shows his skill at feminine mimicry: "This compliment . . . / . . . made her blush and shake" (5.156). When Baba forces him into "a suit/ In which a Princess with great pleasure would/ Array" (5.73), the genre, and gender, turn into a queer-eye drag act:

> sighing, on he slipp'd
> A pair of trowsers of flesh-colour'd silk,
> Next with a virgin zone he was equipp'd,
> Which girt a light chemise, as white as milk;
> But tugging on his petticoat he tripp'd . . .
>
> And, wrestling both his arms into a gown,
> He paused and took a survey up and down. . . .
>
> . . . Baba found
> So many false long tresses all to spare,
> That soon his head was most completely crown'd,
> After the manner then in fashion there;
> And this addition with such gems was bound
> As suited the *ensemble* of his toilet . . .
>
> And now being femininely all array'd,
> With some small aid from scissars, paint, and tweezers,
> He look'd in almost all respects a maid,
> And Baba smilingly exclaim'd "You see, sirs,
> A perfect transformation here display'd." (5.77–80)

The spectacle "see, sirs" is wryly rhymed with its device, "tweezers." Byron took the pattern of this transformation from female models: Lady Mary Wortley Montagu's "habit" during her residence in Turkey with her ambassador-husband [fig. 6.4], and its imprint on Haidée at festival: "Her orange silk full Turkish trowsers"; "azure, pink, and white . . . her chemise"; "Her hair's long auburn waves," "starr'd with gems" (3.70, 72, 73). Vanished from *Don Juan,* Haidée is resurrected as a virtual Donna Juanna. The poet's pronouns—"Her shape, her hair, her air, her every thing" (6.35)—cheerily abet, miming the *blazon* of Baillie's enchanted Count Basil on Princess Victoria ("Her form, her face, her motion ev'ry thing" [1.2.123]) and the common fount, Shakespeare's besotted Troilus on "fair Cressid" ("Her eyes, her hair, her cheek, her gait, her voice" [1.1.54]). Of Juan's regendering the poet explains in an aside,

Figure 6.3 *Byron in Albanian Dress*, by Thomas Phillips (1813). Not only its theatrics, but the ensemble's conspicuous luxury delighted Byron: "the most magnificent in the world, consisting of a long <u>white kilt</u>, old worked cloak, crimson velvet gold laced jacket & waistcoat . . . so much gold they would cost in England two hundred" guineas, instead of the 50 he paid in Albania, he reported to his mother in 1809 (*BLJ* 1.227 and 231).

> (I say *her*, because
> The Gender still was Epicene, at least
> In outward show, which is a saving clause)   (6.58)

Byron plays the grammatical sense of *epicene*, nouns designating both genders, into the theatrical one, female characters played by male actors. He's already epicened Juan's easy fit into the odalisques "all clad alike; like Juan, too"; "They formed a very nymph-like looking crew" (5.99); "His youth and features favour'd the disguise" (115), and

> no one doubted on the whole, that she
> Was what her dress bespoke, a damsel fair,
> And fresh, and "beautiful exceedingly."   (6.36)

The phrase in quotes further cross-dresses Juan as Coleridge's Geraldine in damsel guise (*Christabel* [1816] 1.66), like Juan, ready to vamp. Shelley joined this fun at least: "The Don Juan is arrived," he wrote of a yacht he commissioned; "nothing can exceed the admiration she has excited, for we must suppose the name [. . .] given her during the equivocation of sex which her godfather suffered in the Harem" (16 May 1822; *L* 2: 421). The convention of she-ship, covered with a male name, is recast as a male in she-drag.

Across these transformations, the poem called *Don Juan* stays true to the "manly" genre. Juan's feminine array ultimately bodes no unsexing. In a "labyrinth of females" (6.57), a seraglio of "a thousand bosoms there / Beating for love as the caged birds for air," Juan "in his feminine disguise" (6.26) emerges as a newly potentiated male. No prisoner of sex, he now wields the gaze, "ogling all their charms from breasts to backs" (6.29). His masculinity remains so intact that "Although they could not see through his disguise, / All felt a soft kind of concatenation, / Like Magnetism, or Devilism" of attraction (38) to "Juanna," and want "her" in their beds. Juan's dress proves the indirection by which to find directions out; as the only phallus in the harem, he gains a world of sexual opportunity.[65] Juan's conquest of the East is a conquest of drag. Clothes make the man.

So much so, that Juan himself stages his next masquerade; and here, gender-play, rather than abject travesty, is the flagrant trope. In an outrageous drag act, Juan makes his debut in Catherine's court, (cross?)-dressed as a military dandy. His couturist is she "Art" (9.44):

> . . . in a handsome uniform;
> A scarlet coat, black facings, a long plume,
> Waving, like sails new shivered in a storm,

> Over a cocked hat in a crowded room,
> And brilliant breeches, bright as a Cairn Borme,
>   Of yellow cassimere we may presume,
> White stocking drawn, uncurdled as new milk,
> O'er limbs whose symmetry set off the silk.   (9.44)

This is right out of the book of Byron's Eastern masquerades. "For ceremonial occasions abroad" (reports Doris Langley Moore of the he-artist of this scene), Byron "had a cocked hat with plumes, and a scarlet suit embroidered with gold which was the full dress uniform of an aide-de-camp."[66] Offering a similarly gaudy Albanian outfit (famous from Thomas Phillips's 1813 portrait; fig. 6.3) to Margaret Mercer Elphinstone for a masquerade the same year (*BLJ* 4: 112–13), Byron was the wry impresario of a layered transvestite spectacle: a Regency "Beauty" decked out as an Albanian dandy, and a female impersonation of Phillips's "Byron."

Behind this Byronism in masquerade are long-standing psychological investments that pay off in male power plays. The psychological matrix is described by Otto Fenichel and Robert Stoller, who both read male transvestitism as a fantasy of phallic-woman (169).[67] Stoller proposes that the transvestite man believes in "the biological and social 'inferiority' of women, and also know[s] that within himself there is a propensity toward being reduced to this 'inferior' state" (215)—a reduction legible in Juan's "feminine" characteristics and serial enslavements. But it also goes in reverse, to become the motor for his phallic luck. The male transvestite, goes Stoller's argument, fantasizes himself a phallic woman, either to counter his feminine tendencies or to assert a superior presence in relations with strong women. The prototype for this strong figure, moreover, "has actually existed in his life—that is, the fiercely dangerous and powerful woman who [. . .] humiliated him as a child": mother, whom the male transvestite at once identifies with and supersedes (Stoller 215). This story may seem a myth of male-theorized, male-centered psychoanalytic lore, but for this very reason it illuminates Byron's gallery of imperious women: Juan's mother Donna Inez, the Sultana and Empress Catherine; and their prototype, the first Catherine, the "Mrs. Byron furiosa" of Byron's letters (*BLJ* 1: 93–94)—her character etched in an escalating series of Byron-rants written at about Juan's age (in 1805–6) to a half-sister Augusta (not Catherine's child):[68]

> In former days she spoilt me, now she is altered to the contrary, for the most trifling thing, she upbraids me in a most outrageous manner. [. . .] she flies into a fit of phrenzy upbraids me as if I was the most undutiful wretch in existence. [. . .] Am I to call this woman mother? Because by natures law she

has authority over me, am I to be trampled upon in this manner? [. . .] Am I to be eternally subjected to this caprice! I hope not, indeed a few short years will emancipate me from the shackles I now wear. (1: 54, 56)

I have never been so <u>scurrilously</u> and <u>violently</u> abused by any person, as by that woman, whom I think, I am to call mother. [. . .] such is my mother; <u>my mother</u>. (1: 66)

this female Tisiphone, a name which your <u>Ladyship</u> will recollect to have belonged to one of the Furies.——[. . .] my tormentor whose <u>diabolical</u> disposition [. . .] seems to increase with age, and to acquire new force with Time. [. . .] No Captive Negro, or Prisoner of war, ever looked forward to their emancipation, and return to Liberty, with more Joy, [. . .] than I do to my escape from maternal bondage. [. . .] I have escaped the Trammels or rather <u>Fetters</u> of my domestic Tyrant Mrs Byron. (1: 74, 75–76, 79)

Wresting authority from nature's law Byron casts Juan-the-phallic-woman to address (and redress) a psychic grievance in the form (Stoller puts it) of "a better woman than a biological female."[69]

Because the female dictating Juan's travesty is a Sultana, the shift into phallic woman plays out more than a psychic grievance. Noting transvestic sanction "at carnival times, at masquerade parties" (186), Stoller touches on the liberatory latency. As Byron could discern from his own carnivalizing, transvestic play was risky business for the status quo ante. Contesting the regard of carnival as "a safety valve" for "conflicts within the system" that preserves "the basic order," Natalie Davis argues that festive and literary inversions of sex roles could excite "new ways of thinking," and so undermine assent, especially through "connections with everyday circumstances outside the privileged time of carnival and stage-play" (130–31, 142–43). Carnival could even provide the strategies. Aware that women were deemed irrational, and so given some license for misbehavior, men who wanted to act up cross-dressed. Female clothes and titles could even energize and "validate disobedient and riotous behavior," Davis proposes, citing transvestite rioting in Britain from the 1450s to the 1840s (147–50). The market-women's march on Versailles in October 1789 involved "men in the disguise of women," reports Paine (*Rights of Man* 299). Scott's *Heart of Midlothian* (1818) staged the Edinburgh Porteous Riots of 1736, spearheaded by transvestite "Madge Wildfire"—a "stout Amazon" in the sorority of "bold and bloody" Empress Catherine, a "modern Amazon" (9.70; 6.96). Byron knew all this and more. An opponent of capital punishment for frame-breaking, he was well aware of "General Ludd's wives,"

Figure 6.4 Lady Mary Wortley Montagu, frontispiece in *The Letters and Works of Lady Mary Wortley Montagu* (1887). Montagu caught Byron's interest in 1817 (*BLJ* 5: 276), and by 1818 he was enjoying her letters (6: 64), wherein she gives a famous report of her "Turkish habit" to her sister: "a pair of drawers, very full, that reach to my shoes and conceal the legs more modestly than your Petticoats. They are of a thin rose colour damask, brocaded with silver flowers, my shoes of white kid leather, embroidered with gold. Over this hangs my Smock of a fine white silk Gause, edged with embroidery. This smock has wide sleeves, hanging half way down the arm, and is closed at the neck with a diamond button; but the shape and colour of the bosom very well to be distinguished through it. The Antery is a waistcoat made close to the shape, of white and Gold Damask, with very long sleeves falling back and fring'd with deep Gold fringe, and should have diamond or pearl buttons. My Caftan of the same stuff with my Drawers is a robe exactly fitted to my shape and reaching to my feet, with very long strait falling sleeves. Over this is the Girdle of about 4 fingers broad, which all that can afford have entirely of diamonds or other precious stones" (April 1817; *L* 1: 326).

two men in women's clothes who led a loom-smashing, factory-burning riot at Stockport in 1812.[70]

If Juan in she-garb is obliquely masculinized by these affiliations, he gets a direct boost from Byron's determined reduction of the Sultana to a woman after all. Her "mixture" of "half-voluptuousness and half command" (5.108) resolves into the body beautiful: "Her presence was as lofty as her state; / Her beauty of that overpowering kind" (97); "Her form had all the softness of her sex" (109). The poet derides her "self-will" and everything "haughty" in her, capping his critique with relief that "She was a sultan's bride, (thank Heaven, not mine)" (111). Outwitted, she collapses into a caricature of a woman scorned. Not outwittable, just escapable, Empress Catherine gets degraded by slander. While her sexual appetites match Byron's, she earns contempt as "the greatest of all sovereigns and w———s" (6.92), a word Byron spelled out in his manuscript (*BPW* 5: 327), and over which his friend Douglas Kinnaird paused to question the unfair play:

> why call the Katherine a whore? She hired or whored others—She was never hired or whored herself—why blame her for liking fucking? If she had canted as well as cunted, then call her names as long as you please—But it is hard to blame her for following her natural inclinations. [. . .] I looked for more liberality from you—You must not turn against rogering—even tho' you practice it seldomer.[71]

Kinnaird tweaks Byron with an illiberalism of geese and ganders, of not being able to imagine a natural woman with political power. The culpability of the Sultana in commanding Juan's sexual surrender or of the Empress's in hiring it, moreover, is not something Byron cares to impose on men who seize women's bodies: Canto XIII makes crude jest of geriatric rape. After the sack of Ismail, some seventy-year-old virgins are raped, while "widows of forty" were "heard to wonder in the din / . . . 'Wherefore the ravishing did not begin!'" (8.130, 132). To whom is this *Playboy* humor "very funny"? Mary Shelley refused to fair-copy the couplet about the old virgins.[72] The guys at *Blackwood's* (July 1823) managed to have it both ways, lamenting the "leering and impotent [. . .] loinless drivelling [. . .] where the poet (the *poet!*) is facetious at the state of females during the sack of a town*"—letting this asterisk point to a pageful of objectionable text (stanzas 128–34), with this loinless apology: "it is a pity to reprint such things, but a single specimen here may do good by the disgust for the whole which it must create" (4: 89). Disgust or gusto? Let the reader decide.

*I almost think that the same skin
For one without—has two or three within*
                    —the poet of *Don Juan*, on himself (17.11)

Even skin seems dress, as if nature were no guarantee. The degraded formation is the Poet Laureate who "turn'd his coat—and would have turn'd his skin" (*The Vision of Judgment* 97), but this does not exorcise all the turns of *Don Juan*. One of its most liberal forms, in league with erotic adventure, is Duchess Fitz-Fulke. Lustful woman with purchasing power is rebuked in the Sultana, and the lustful she with political power is travestied in the Empress. But a designing woman with social and theatrical savvy (a Byron in drag) opens the question for another hearing. The Duchess's turn as Friar-ghost recalls Byron's own donning of friar-robes for fraternity fun at his abbey (*BLJ* 7: 231), and then a masquerade at Almack's in 1814 (Marchand, *Biography* 459), as well as the adventures of Caro Lamb, who showed up in his rooms "in the disguise of a carman" (Byron recalled to Medwin). "My valet, who did not see through the masquerade, let her in," and when "she put off the man, and put on the woman [. . .] Imagine the scene!" (*Byron* 216–17). Detoxified of Caro, Fitz-Fulke's "man" is an extravagant fantasy. Like a female author wrapped in a male pseudonym, the Duchess dresses for success. She is Byronism cross-gendered, a modern woman, sexually self-possessed, socially adept, out to manipulate the system of representation to advantage.

No less than Caro, restless female readers grasped the emancipatory lure of male guising—*genius* by another name. In 1833, *The Athenæum*'s "Paris Correspondence" (2 February) outed "George Sand" as a cross-dressed "young lady, who, some years back, distinguished herself at the age of thirteen, by an indomitable wish to escape from her parents and seek out Lord Byron"; and in true Byronic fashion, Sand became "answerable for works that do more honour to her genius than her delicacy" (74). She-men in *Don Juan* are cast for contempt or hapless farce; but she-transvestites, driven by will, desire, and imagination, dress up to move up and move out. In a Gynocrasy confined to gossip, social intrigue, and strategic hostessing, the Duchess dons male garb for sexual adventure. Her gender-game takes its cue from masquerade-culture, in Venetian streets and London assembly rooms, in all its transgressive frisson, with an extra libertine thrill in the clerical garb.[73] Scolds such as Thomas Gisborne warned of masquerades giving "scope for unbounded licence of speech and action [. . .] in one promiscuous assemblage" (152–53). But Lady Mary Montagu got the dynamic in the alterity of Turkey, where women go out only in complete covering. It looks like repression, but isn't: "This perpetual Masquerade gives them entire

Liberty of following their Inclinations without Danger of Discovery" (to her sister, 1 April 1717; *L* 1: 328). All these sites, Terry Castle proposes, flirted with "female sexual freedom, and beyond that, female emancipation generally." And in the eighteenth-century novel, masquerade episodes stage a "symbolic theater of female power," where women usurp not only male dress but also men's "social and behavioral 'freedoms'."[74]

Fiction is no more a containment in Castle's story than the masquerade is in Davis's. Novelists indulge "the scenery of transgression while seeming to maintain didactic probity. The occasion gets a moralizing frame, yet its representation permits the novelist, like the characters, to role-play, to cast off the persona of the moralist and turn instead to the pleasures of intrigue."[75] Byron implies even more: masquerading is not just a fictional theater, and not just the carnival binary of the norm; it is its very fabric. The Duchess is kin to all those "Historians, heroes, lawyers, priests" who put "truth in masquerade" (11.37), some of whom (lawyers and priests) at least, have dress habits (those robes and frocks, those wigs and gowns) that flirt with gender-borders. If masquerade episodes introduce "a curious instability into the would-be orderly cosmos of the eighteenth-century English novel" (writes Castle), the cross-dressings of *Don Juan* reflect an entire world, as Anne Mellor puts it, of "abundant chaos; everything moves, changes its shape, becomes something different"[76]—and nowhere more so than in the encounter left open-ended at Byron's death.

In the last few stanzas of fragment-Canto XVII, Byron resumes the business of Juan:

> Our Hero was—in Canto the Sixteenth—
>   Left in a tender Moonlight situation,
> Such as enables Man to show his strength—
>   Moral or Physical;—on this occasion
> Whether his virtue triumphed—or at length—
>   His Vice—for he was of a kindling Nation—
> Is more than I shall venture to describe—
> Unless some Beauty with a kiss should bribe.— (12; ms.)

Byron arrays the *ors*—moral *or* physical; virtue *or* vice—but only to perplex the definitions and alignments, and not the least, the outcome. He enters the game himself, refraining or relenting only in the seduction of a she-Beauty, the muse of intrigue. With male coyness and female arts thus perplexed, Byron's poet will say only, "I leave the thing a problem, like all things" (17.13). In effect, he's pleading the case of the she-epistle he had spoofed in Canto XVIII:

> The earth has nothing like a She epistle,
> And hardly heaven—because it never ends.

> I love the mystery of a female missal,
> Which, like a creed, ne'er says all it intends. (13.105)

This is a fair enough description of the poem that *Don Juan* has become, the gender of the generic mode of unending. Between the whim of Beauty's bribe and the determination to leave the thing a problem, falls a canceled draft of a she condition, this one in the poet's sensation:

> ~~But Oh! that I were dead—for while alive=~~
> ~~=Would that I neer had loved=Oh Woman=Woman=~~
> ~~All that I writ All that I write or wrote can neer revive~~
> ~~=To paint a sole sensation=though quite common=~~
> ~~Of those in which the Body seemed to drive~~
> ~~=My Soul from out me at thy single summon~~
> ~~Expiring in the hope of resurrection=~~[? sensation]

"Expiring in the hope of resurrection" (or maybe "sensation") dangles as a modifier of all things, and contradictorily: *sensation, Body, Soul, me*. The unwritten rhyme for *resurrection* might be already syllabled: maybe *erection*; maybe *insurrection*. But this last word, aptly, is not certain. Is it "sensation" once again?[77] If so, then the destined partner might be *elation*, or *creation* or *recreation*. The subtle punning of *soul* surrender to *sole sensation* is set in a syntax that cannot say with certainty whether the summons will lead to the consummation devoutly to be wished, or leave the sensationalist expiring in the mere hope of it. This is a radically Byronic idealism, and a radically Byronic indeterminacy, a hope in a suspense that forestalls expiration.

Instead, Byron turns from the jokey mystery about Juan's strength and length to theorizing the "problem" as the nature of "all things." Yet the crossed-out stanza survives as a textual ghost, to expose a re-experiencing and repression of the perplexities of writing and sensation, of lust and love, body and soul, pleasure and damnation, of knowing better and doing it all over again—and in capitals, Woman and Man. This is, after all (first of all), the poet who courted his wife with a boast about living by sensation alone: "the great object of life is Sensation—to feel that we exist—even though in pain—it is this 'craving void' which drives us [. . .] to intemperate but keenly felt pursuits of every description whose principal attraction is the agitation inseparable from their accomplishment" (6 Sept. 1813; *BLJ* 3: 109). Quoting Pope's Eloisa ("No craving void left aching in the breast"), he is inhabiting a man's imagination of a woman's imagination of what it is like to lose oneself in the sensation of love—and here implying to Annabella Milbanke that this is what will fill the void for him:

> Oh happy state! when souls each other draw,
> When love is liberty, and nature, law:
> All then is full, possessing, and possess'd,
> No craving void left aking in the breast . . . (*Eloisa to Abelard* 91–94)

If the masculine tradition is famed for writing "Woman" as other, *Don Juan* expires in negotiation. It may forever array the binaries of "masculine" and "feminine," but it is restlessly driven by pursuits of every description—all in the erotic liberty that writes, and rewrites, "nature's" laws. Not the least are the cross-dressings of Byron's imagination, which transmit his intrigues with, and within, the borderlines of gender.

CHAPTER SEVEN

Keats and Gender Acts: "Had I Man's Fair Form"

> You see what it is to be under six foot and not a lord.
>
> —KEATS TO HIS BROTHER AND HIS SISTER-IN-LAW, VALENTINE'S DAY, 1819

> He says he does not want ladies to read his poetry: that he writes for men.
>
> —RICHARD WOODHOUSE TO KEATS'S PUBLISHER, SEPTEMBER 1819

Boy John

What is man's fair form, and how is it performed? For Keats at the outset of his career, the question—bearing social credit as well as vocational credibility—was tied to the gendered grammar of Wordsworth's audition and answer in the 1802 Preface to *Lyrical Ballads:*

> What is a Poet? To whom does he address himself? And what language is to be expected from him? He is a man speaking to men: a man, it is true, endued with more lively sensibility, more enthusiasm and tenderness [. . .] than are supposed to be common. (751)

No less critical than this confident address of the "Poet" to a male rhetorical community, however, is the immediate unsettling by qualifications (those *mores*) too akin to "feminine," and then further, and repeatedly, by poems at odds with what might be expected from a man.[1] It wasn't too long past, after all, that Thomas Gisborne's *Inquiry into the Duties of the Female Sex* (1796) had

205

given the "native worth of the female character" in a blazon of "sympathising sensibility" and "dispositions and feelings of the heart" (22–23).

Pace Mackenzie's *The Man of Feeling* (1771), a transfer to men of feeling was too proximate, and no credit.[2] That literary culture was implicated compelled careful desynonymizing from some quarters. Writing "On the Slave Trade" in 1796 for *The Watchman*, a periodical for "Men of Letters" (5), Wordsworth's collaborator-to-be derided the thrill to "the fine lady's nerves" as she "weep[s] over the refined sorrows" of fictional characters amid indifference to real atrocity: not only is "Sensibility not Benevolence," railed Coleridge; but "by making us tremblingly alive to trifling misfortunes, it frequently prevents it, and induces effeminate and cowardly selfishness" (139). As this *us* admits, he is sensitive to his own leaning, and the defense is legible in his sonnet of the same year "To The Rev. W. L. Bowles." The soothing "soft strains" of Bowles's poetry are sufficiently culpable to get a fortification into "manliest melancholy."

Some two decades on, Keats was unsure which readers would validate him as "a Poet," but he hoped it would be the rising generation: literate, urbane, unencumbered by old-school prerequisites (class credentials, university education), and open to modern, eclectic, enthusiastic experimentalism—a "style" seeking notice as "vivacious, smart, witty, changeful, sparkling, and learned,—full of bright points and flashy expressions that strike and even seem to please by a sudden boldness of novelty" (so *Scots Edinburgh Magazine* admired it).[3] But novelty is risky. The counter-cultural Wordsworth of 1802 had suffered derision as puerile, and would for some years more. If the Wordsworth of 1817 was less vulnerable, he was also less similar: he had grown to man's estate with the epic gesture of *The Excursion*, with a post-Waterloo Tory temper, and a philosophical discipline—all giving him a decent claim to the title of England's premier Poet (the un-Byron). Wordsworth could read acclaim for his "dignified purity," "noble compositions," and "patriarchal simplicity" in the same issue of *Blackwood's* (October 1817) that launched Z's campaign against "The Cockney School of Poetry" (headmaster Hunt, star pupil Keats). The gender-information of opposite Keatsian gush and its poetic effects was in Z's cross-hairs.

Even friendlier notices of Keats's debut with the 1817 *Poems* had to navigate a gender maze. *Scots* was willing to bet that this "very young man" "might succeed" in "the truest strain" of modern poetry: "manly singleness of heart, or feminine simplicity and constancy of affection,—mixed up with feelings of rational devotion, and impressions of independence spread over pictures of domestic happiness and social kindness" (254, 256). Even so, what Wordsworth had tried with equivocal success to invest in a man-of-feeling's poetry, Keats was displaying in decided excess: elements "too fond," "straggling and uneven," with "inlets of vulgarity" and "indolence" (256). And then there were strains "worthy only of the Rosa Matildas whom the strong-handed Gifford put down" (257).[4] The risk of such experimental, or maybe just accidental mix-ups, would play out more harshly in Z's voice, buzzing at Huntian political insurgency. The man in the mask of Z, John Gibson Lockhart, was university-educated (Glasgow, Oxford), and a muddying of the community of university men speaking to university men was what he saw in Keats, a poet catering to uneducated classes and irregularly educated women, for whom his affected literariness and eclectic learning might look creditable.[5] Keats's flaunted outsider boyishness struck just this self-proposed difference from culturally endorsed forms of manhood. Attacking the inept "boy" was one resort, but qualified: a boy (as *Scots* ventured) could still mature. So Z also mined a foundational flaw, exposing it in those good old categorical binaries to manly: *feminine, effeminate*. If the former was not necessarily a stigma in 1818, the latter assuredly was.

My next chapter is about the ways "Keats" magnetized this discursive field. My interest here is the pressure on Keats's poetic theory and practice, and on the social existence that impinged on both. In his own anatomy, "Mister John Keats five feet hight" was "under six foot and not a lord"—i.e., lacking Byronic immunization (*L* 1: 343; 2: 61). Keats felt the gender diminution acutely. In some moods of writing he could play it to parodic performance and speculative review, indulging, even camping up, tendencies describable as feminine. But in other phases of writing, he bristles at being a feminized object of view and judgment, or casts feminine figures as fell opponents of manly self-possession and professional self-definition. About actual women he is just as unfixed—by turns, adoring, sympathetic, defensive, or hostile (especially about their claims as readers, writers, and arbiters). What makes a man of achievement, especially in poetry, was a question Keats worried as well as worked as he circulated in a post-war, Regency England where "masculine" was a figure, or figures, under construction and in debate, and upon which he reflected frequently from points of difference. In the press of surging poetic genius, adolescent uncertainty, social anxiety, and cultural prejudice, Keats's overall syntax of gender proves more zigzag than linear, his narratives keyed less to definitive horizons than to variable borders. Nowhere are these effects more vivid than in that Keatsian signature for poetic temper, "Indolence," to which I turn later on.

It may seem a long way from Z's gender put-downs to Keats's gradual, then confirmed twentieth-century honors as a hero of receptivity and indeterminacy, hailed for a "camelion" sympathy, even self-annihilation, in refusal of the "egotistical sublime"; for speculation instead of fixed reasoning and palpable designs; for a mode of "intensities" that make no claims "beyond the Moment."[6] In the disinclination of his own age to read these qualities into manly power, Keats would press for review. Those "who have proper self Men of Power" (he proposes to Benjamin Bailey, November 1817) are distinct from "Men of Genius," who operate without "individuality, any determined Character" (*L* 1: 184). Within weeks, he would be equating the character of this Genius to "Negative Capability," an aesthetics of "uncertainties, Mysteries, doubts, without any irritable reaching after fact & reason" (1: 193). These formulations have become so canonical for Romantic, more specifically, Keatsian strength, that their original gender-markings are almost worn from view, and it's unsettling to encounter them. Yet these are not accidental, not insignificant. Twentieth-century women of letters would take up negative capability and self-effacement as terms of "feminine," even "feminist" consciousness,[7] but the Keatsian syntaxes are a caution. These principles, which typically get stated in male homosocial exchanges and disquisitions (as Keats's letters show), do not align with any oppositional "feminine" mode: Keats typically resorts to the old gender binaries to reinforce the manliness of the new forms. The poetry he is writing in the heat of this thinking, moreover, rehearses to the point of obsession scenes of gender crisis, where female power threatens male autonomy, or a man feels pumped with power by mastering a woman.

Such complications are the reflex of the risks Keats knew he was taking with established gender capital. To theorize "Men of Genius" as categorically without "individuality, any determined Character" was (after all) to evoke a famous feminine figuring of "no character": "Most Women have no Characters at all," Pope begins *To a Lady, of the Character of Women*. While he attaches the aphorism to the Lady, it has his endorsement from the get-go (1–2). His headlined Argument is that "the Characters of *Women*" as "contradistinguished from the other Sex," are "more inconsistent and incomprehensible." A footnote reiterates: "their particular Characters are not so strongly mark'd as those of Men, seldom so fixed, and still more inconsistent with themselves."[8] Always energized by going up against Pope, Keats transvalues "no Character" for male Genius. Within a year he would be defining his own "poetical Character" in a litany of *no*—"no self," "no character," "no Identity"—and affiliating the negatives with creative "speculation" (*L* 1: 387). These formulations stay focused on "Men": men's thinking, men's writing, men's operation in the world. To preserve the masculine legitimation, Keats keeps women out of the picture, except as effects of male "cogitating" (Ops or Imogen; 1: 387). Negative capability forms a "Man of Achievement," and it is Shakespeare who is the model (not Katherine Philips, Ann Radcliffe, Mary Tighe—all of whom Keats read and liked). It is "Adam's Dream" prior to the advent and event of Eve-complications that is his ideal of "Imagination" (*L* 1: 185; *PL* 8.309–11), and his extended simile of life as a "Mansion of Many Apartments" turns out to be a gender-fable as much as a genetic one: the "Chamber of Maiden-Thought" matures by becoming masculine in both agency and object; among the effects that thinking is "father of," Keats says, "is that tremendous one of sharpening one's vision into the heart and nature of Man" (*L* 1: 281–82).

When Keats thinks of women as forces in his world, he radiates defensive antipathy. Clubbing with the men, he hates the Blues, hates not just their learning but their pretenses to authority from it: "Women, who having taken a snack or Luncheon of Literary scraps, set themselves up for towers of Babel in Languages sapphos in Poetry" (his included) at the cost of "real feminine Modesty" (*L* 1: 163). Real women don't eat Keats. Modesty is no saving grace; it just earns softer contempt. The "generallity of women," he writes in October 1818, just after he met the love of his life, Fanny Brawne, "appear to me as children to whom I would rather give a Sugar Plum than my time" (*L* 1: 404). Reading Keats's confessed "tendency to class women in my books with roses and sweetmeats,—they never see themselves dominant" (*L* 2: 327), his worldly friend Charles Brown saw a strange bedfellowing with Byron.[9] Faded the sight of Macaulay, Wollstonecraft, and Hays on womanchild as cultural deformation.[10] A long-standing rite of passage into manhood was exactly this kind of corporate satire, especially on women who could compete with or even judge an aspiring man of letters— or, on another axis of power, might enthrall the man in love.

And Keats was both. When Arnold read his letters to Fanny Brawne, he was repelled by the love swoons, the want of "character and self-control" ("John Keats" 205). What saved Keats for him was an imprint of devotion to something higher than this passion, even a steeling against it. This was "no character" with a vengeance, "character passing into intellectual production": a "severe addiction [. . .] to the best sort of poetry affects him with a certain coldness" (Arnold imagines), "as if the addiction had been to mathematics, towards those prime objects of a sensuous and passionate poet's regard, love and women" (212). Keats actually cultivated this coldness, as intellectual discipline, and as implicit fortification against the gush of a man of feeling, or sensation: "should you observe any thing cold in me." he advises "dear Bailey" (22 November 1817), he should not put it

> to the account of heartlessness but abstraction—for I assure you I sometimes feel not the influence of Passion or Affection during a whole week—and so long this sometimes continues I begin to suspect myself and the genuineness of my feelings at other times—thinking them a barren Tragedy-tears. (*L* 1.186)

But abstraction from passion, both in the letter and in the psychological relay it reports, was also a connection to passion, as Keats knew.

The very next sentence in the letter to Bailey, "My brother Tom is much improved," is the proximate agony (Tom never stayed improved for long), the pain behind the coldness. Arnold's thermometer takes a no less complex measure of cold self-control. He was reading that "Sugar Plum" put-down and Keats's contempt of "the offence the ladies take" at his poetry (*L* 2: 327). With his own tacit investments, he is glad to see Keats's self-described "yearning passion for the Beautiful" trumping the yearning for women: "as he himself truly says, the master-passion is not a passion of the sensuous or sentimental man, is not a passion of the sensuous or the sentimental poet. It is an intellectual and spiritual passion." It is (Arnold is relieved to think) no human passion at all, but an orientation to a "mighty *abstract idea* of Beauty" or "*principle of beauty*" (213).[11] It's worth remembering what Arnold omits: that Keats declared this "yearning Passion [. . .] for the beautiful, connected and made one with the ambition of my intellect," in the same journal-letter in which he snickered at the Reynolds sisters' ordinary looks, admired Jane Cox for a theatrical beauty that was blessedly indifferent to his prospects, and felt he would "never marry," never be domesticated—all just weeks before he was captivated by one Miss Brawne.

The degree of defense in Keats's disdain of women and erotic passion helps explain his solidarity with learned misogynist patter, man-show rallies armed with classical satire. One of his first poems took a line from "Terence's *Eunuch*, Act 2. Sc. 4"—"What wondrous beauty! From this moment I efface from my mind all women"—to set as the epigraph for a petition for "some drug design'd / To banish Woman from my Mind" ("Fill for me a brimming Bowl" 3–4). A design (or designer drug) against this peril to self-possession becomes a Keatsian reflex: "'Tis vain—away I cannot chace / The melting softness of that face," he cries in the same poem (13–14)—*melting* covering the enraptured poet no less than the agent, Woman.

The incurable romance with poison is the gender-story that possesses Keats from boyhood to final days, from first poetic declarations to the acid catastrophes of *Lamia*. "I have not a right feeling towards Women," he confessed to Bailey in summer 1818, in a remarkably candid diagnosis:

> I am striving to be just to them but I cannot—Is it because they fall so far beneath my Boyish imagination? When I was a Schoolboy I though[t] a fair Woman a pure Goddess, my mind was a soft nest in which some one of them slept though she knew it not—I have no right to expect more than their reality. [. . .] When I am among Women I have evil thoughts, malice spleen. [. . .] I must absolutely get over this—but how? The only way is to find the root of evil, and so cure it "with backward mutters of dissevering Power." That is a difficult thing; for an obstinate Prejudice can seldom be produced but from a

gordian complication of feelings, which must take time to unravell and care to keep unravelled—I could say a good deal about this but I will leave it in hopes of better and more worthy dispositions—and also content that I am wronging no one, for after all I do think better of Womankind than to suppose they care whether Mister John Keats five feet hight likes them or not. (*L* 1: 341–42)

The ravel of interwoven narratives is revealing. Even as Keats recognizes his own puerile fictions and their social impossibility, he can't help but resent a disappointed "Boyish imagination." There are only negative incapabilities in his story: what "cannot" be managed, gotten over, unraveled, all framed by the young-manly imagination of Womankind's disdain of Mister John Keats in a Boyish body. This complication of feelings—part pride, part prejudice—calls up two gendered fables. Keats abjectly reads himself as Milton's imprisoned Lady in *Comus*, her "stony fetters fixt and motionless," indissoluble without her enchanter's wand "revers't, / And backward mutters of dissevering power" (816–19). Keats is she, and powerless. The second fable does identify the power, but it is not a self-identification. Facing the famously raveled Gordian knot, Alexander does not stoop to unravel; he whips out his sword and boldly severs it, a prefiguration of the "Great" conqueror.

Keats's Boyish ravel involves a vocational self-reading, and the strands were ones he himself despised as all too "smokeable," a word implying male group ridicule, pained further by his own aim of it at women: "Women with few exceptions—the Dress Maker, the blue Stocking and the most charming sentimentalist differ but in a Slight degree, and are equally smokeable" (*L* 2: 18–19). That he was displacing into this Popean sorority a bit of self-smoking is clear in his attachment to that she-saturated genre, "Romance." Its Spenserian trials remote by centuries, the modern genre was synonymous with sentiment and daydreaming. Keats did have a certain conceptual sympathy with the view Mrs. Sandford would posit in *Woman*: romance as opposition to the "vulgar, and cold, and dull, and monotonous reality" of "common sense alone" (142). But it was under the sign of Hunt that he worked this out, and under the sign of Hunt that the critical force attenuates. Early in January 1818, having consummated and fallen out of love with a 4,000–line affair titled *Endymion: A Poetic Romance*, Keats tried to wean himself and grow Shakespearean, sitting down to read *King Lear* once again. He wrote a (now famous) sonnet on the discipline, casting and casting out "Romance" as a dangerous muse, a golden-tongued, fair-plumed Syren. But for all the determination, the sonnet sings an ambivalent, uncertain farewell, and by the end of the year, Keats had defaulted on the masculine test, unable to complete the epic project called *Hyperion*.

What he could complete were new romances. He hoped to save himself from the old siren song by ironizing, even satirizing the illusions of "old Romance" (a discourse in both *Isabella* and *The Eve of St. Agnes*),[12] and by flaunting worldly knowledge. But the fault of *Isabella*, he groaned to Richard Woodhouse just as he was giving up *Hyperion*, was that it was still "mawkish."[13] He didn't want to publish it at all: it was "too smokeable," exposing "too much inexperience of life, and simplicity of knowledge": in a camelion imagining of himself as "a reviewer," he judged it "A weak-sided Poem" that "will not do to be public." He thought even *St. Agnes* open to a "good deal" of this "objection" (*L* 2: 174), despite the urbane eroticism of calculated seduction and sexual heat he had worked at—so well that his publisher John Taylor, with an eye on "Decency & Discretion" and "the suffrages of Women," was provoked to see if some chaste revision could be coaxed out of Keats (*KC* 2: 96–97). To this circumspect Tayloring (Woodhouse was distressed to report back) Keats reacted with Byronic contempt:

> He says he does not want ladies to read his poetry: that he writes for men— & that if [. . .] there was an opening for doubt what took place, it was his fault for not writing clearly & comprehensively—that he shd despise a man who would be such an eunuch in sentiment as to leave a maid, with that Character about her, in such a situation [. . .] and all this sort of Keats-like rhodomontade. (19 September 1819; *L* 2: 163)

Keats pumps up and runs with the male pack that would "despise a man" failing the seduction, would even revoke his claim to manhood. Channeling the reviewer-discourse that has eunuchized him, he directs it against those who would design him into a "ladies" poet. In order to stay publishable, Keats cooled the sexual heat, but he kept the "Change of Sentiment" in his newly grotesque final stanza, glad that its cold bath had upset Woodhouse. "I apprehend he had a fancy for trying his hand at an attempt to play with his reader, & fling him off at last," Woodhouse sighed to Taylor, noting a "'Don Juan' style of mingling up sentiment & sneering."[14]

But was this masculine writing? For all the canny craft, these new romances still looked like figurative women, their arts penetrable by a superior male reading, and their delusion synonymous with deficiency: "Women must want Imagination," Keats proposed to Bailey, the month before he confessed to those gordian complications, just as he was learning of harsh comments about him in *Blackwood's*.[15] If Keats was sure of "no objection of this kind to Lamia" (*L* 2: 174), it was because he had taken extreme measures, debasing everyone, everything, every attitude.

The counterpart of Lycius in his source-tale in Burton's *Anatomy of Melancholy* (which he appended to the end of *Lamia*) is Keats's near twin, "a young man twenty-five years of age."[16] Keats honed him to front an assault on romance, shifting him from vulnerable swooner in Part I into a "cruel," "perverse," tyrant in Part II (69–81). "Women love to be forced [. . .] by a fine fellow—<u>such as this</u>," he assures Woodhouse, full of the male-club swagger (*L* 2: 164). Yet this fine fellow dies of disenchantment the instant that Lamia, the embodiment of "Romance," is destroyed by Apollonian penetration—this collapse despite Keats's having scoured the *Anatomy* for choice items of preemptive defense. He was so pleased with one stretch of misogyny, housed in the same part and section as the story of Lycius, that he copied it out for George and Georgiana. It's a counter-blazon of "such errors or imperfections of boddy or mind" an admiring Lover will overlook in his Mistress.[17] "There's a dose for you—fine!!," he cheers; "I would give my favou[r]ite leg to have written this as a speech in a Play: with what effect could Mathews [a stage comedian] pop-gun it at the pit!" (*L* 2: 191–92). The performative aggression, armed with right script, is more potent than any favorite piece of anatomy. Yet Keats's postscript to this "Feu de joie" tells another tale: "This I think will amuse you more than so much Poetry" (2: 192), his earnest vocation after all. He already knew "that the man who redicules [*sic*] romance is the most romantic of Men—that he who abuses women and slights them—loves them the most" (19 February 1819; *L* 2: 67).

The extremes of *Lamia* are generated not only by this double-mindedness, but also against another gender-imprint on Keats's disdain for his "too smokeable" poems: female success in a genre with which some other romances, two in the *Lamia* volume, flirted. "I shall send you the Pot of Basil, St Agnes eve, and if I should have finished it a little thing call'd the 'eve of St Mark,'" he tells George and Georgiana early in 1819, adding, "you see what fine mother Radcliff names I have—it is not my fault—I did not search for them" (*L* 2: 62). Even as he disclaims the Radcliffe names as inadvertence, a joke about a commercial venture he half-disowns as a chance matriarchal affiliation and no serious patriarchal venture, it's clear that he's raiding what he affects to mock.[18] Keats's publishers certainly longed for such a bright female star: James Hessey, writing to Taylor about the advance sale of Maria Edgeworth's *Patronage* in 1814, reports that her publisher "printed 3000 and could deliver only half what were subscribed for," sighing, "When shall we pick up a Miss Edgeworth?" On a list that hosted Keats, and over the years, Clare, Lamb, De Quincey, Hazlitt, Landor, Hood, and Coleridge, their stars were Jane Taylor ("Twinkle, twinkle, little star") and her mother Ann Taylor.[19] Radcliffe's potency was an embarrassment to Keats, and he knew it—knew it enough to know what was to be gained by reducing her sublime scenery to bawdy boy-banter with brother poet John Hamilton Reynolds. Hence this report from a vacation:

> loosen your Braces—for I am going among Scenery whence I intend to tip you the Damosel Radcliffe—I'll cavern you, and grotto you, and waterfall you, and wood you, and water you, and immense-rock you, and tremendous sound you,

and solitude you. Ill make a lodgment on your glacis by a row of Pines, and storm your covered way with bramble Bushes. Ill have at you with hip and haw small-shot. (March 1818; *L*1: 245)

With phallic-lite brio, Keats pop-guns Radcliffe's scenic markers into verbs of erotic aggression, a mock egotistical sublime. But was this Boyish fun an augury for the manhood of the poet?

Across all these reports, moreover, fell the shadow of one potent man of achievement in literature, signified in the Spenserian stanzas of *St. Agnes* and the ottava rima of *Isabella*. Just before listing these romances to George and Georgiana, Keats wrote, "I was surprised to hear from Taylor the amount of Murray the Booksellers last sale—what think you of £25,000? He sold 4000 coppies of Lord Byron" (*L* 2: 62)—that is, *Childe Harold's Pilgrimage, Canto the Fourth,* the latest canto of his romance epic, published to sensational success in April 1818.[20] Having this news from his own publisher must have been painful to the poet who had just given up on his epic, the genre into which his eager prospectus of late 1816, *Sleep and Poetry,* had projected the "nobler life" (123) that would prove "strength of manhood" (163): "I have not gone on with Hyperion," Keats reports (*L* 2: 62). Back in 1777, in *Essays for Young Ladies,* Hannah More characterized the mode of those "lofty bards who strung their bolder harps to higher measures" as "the sublime, the nervous, and the masculine," and distinguished the sexes: "women are fond of incident, men of argument"; women excel in "regions of romance, and in that fashionable species of composition" (*W* 6: 264–65). In 1798, Revd. Polwhele was only too happy to cite these distinctions in the final footnote to *The Unsex'd Females* (36). This gendering was still a critical measure in 1817, and it was Keats who was unsexed.

Unmanning the Poet

In the vogue of sentiment and romance still flourishing in the Regency, the vocation of poet courted questions about the gender of the poet, fanned by the growing influence of female readers and "femininity" on men's writing. The dispirit of the age was this "effeminizing sensuality," said *Blackwood's* in 1824 (162). A sonnet Keats wrote in 1814 showed that even Byron's blush in this market was unexpended, notwithstanding the epic heroics of *Childe Harold* and the pirates and murderers, rebels and revolutionaries of his Eastern tales. It was to all his still cherished love-me-tender lyrics that a teenage Keats swooned:

> Byron, how sweetly sad thy melody
>   Attuning still the soul to tenderness
>   As if soft Pity with unusual stress
> Had touch'd her plaintive Lute . . . (1–4)

Had this sonnet appeared when it was written, in 1814, it would have chagrined the poet who had shown himself of sterner stuff in *English Bards and Scotch Reviewers* (1811).[21]

While the branding of effeminate from 1818 on was a *Blackwood's* franchise, Byron had fired the irons in this best-selling satire.[22] Avenging an anonymous attack in the *Edinburgh Review* on his debut volume, *Hours of Idleness* (1807), he was also performing a self-correction from the culture where he had lately sung.[23] *English Bards* arraigns a world of unmanly poets. Lewis traces "chaste descriptions . . . / To please the females" (265–66). A "simple WORDSWORTH" sings a she-coded lay: "as soft as evening in his favourite May" (231–32), and a "childish prattle" (887) is chimed by "brother COLERIDGE" (900). Bowles, Coleridge's manliest melancholic, fares even worse. He is the "Prince" of that "soft idea" of "Sympathy," the "first, great oracle of tender souls" (321–26): "with thee our nursery damsels shed their tears" (339). As these "whining powers" wane for the damsels (341), "LITTLE" takes up the slack. This is he

> Who in soft guise, surrounded by a choir
> Of virgins melting, not to Vesta's fire,
> With sparkling eyes, and cheek by passion flushed,
> Strikes his wild Lyre, whilst listening dames are hushed . . . (277–80)

The syntax of 279 wickedly blends the poet into his listening dames: its preposition is for either, or both. In a cartoon that Z would refresh, Lord Byron points gender satire with contempt of class aspiration. The rusher of the modern bardic fraternity is a cobbler whose talents can cheer only "the vulgar," the "ladies," the multitudes, and the shallow:

> When some brisk youth, the tenant of a stall,
> Employs a pen less pointed than his awl,
> Leaves his smug shop, forsakes his store of shoes,
> St. Crispin quits, and cobbles for the Muse,
> Heavens! how the vulgar stare! how crowds applaud!
> How ladies read, and Literati laud! (747–51)

The vulgar pen is a soft tool, no match for these sharp couplets (its pen quicker to skewer the hapless mechanic than endorse any payment for trade in his goods and services). What Byron cares to call to account is the new democracy of Poesy, a travesty of learned letters:

> Let Poesy go forth, pervade the whole,
> Alike the rustic, and mechanic soul:
> Ye tuneful cobblers! still your notes prolong,
> Compose at once a slipper and a song;

> So shall the fair your handiwork peruse;
> Your sonnets sure shall please—perhaps your shoes.
> May Moorland weavers boast Pindaric skill,
> And taylors' lays be longer than their bill!
> While punctual beaux reward the grateful notes,
> And pay for poems—when they pay for coats. (771–80)

This farce, pointed with Popean zeugmas, would get just as nasty an edge in Z's "Cockney School" papers, the keyword summing offenses of gender, class, and political insurgence.

The target of Z's first papering was Keats's champion Hunt, and Keats knew he was on deck. It appeared October 1817, just months after *Poems* was published, and just as he was finishing *Endymion*, his new bid for fame.[24] Keats picked up *Blackwood's* to find himself epigraph-rhymed into a farce as "The Muses' son of promise":

> Our talk shall be (a theme we never tire on)
> Of Chaucer, Spenser, Shakespeare, Milton, Byron,
> (Our England's Dante)—Wordsworth—HUNT, and KEATS,
> The Muses' son of promise; and of what feats
> He may yet do. (2: 38)

In the paper proper, Z ridicules Hunt's pretense to this canon, his bid for fame feminized to travesty his desires, his professions, his affectations, and his ultimate misfiring:

> One feels the same disgust at the idea of opening *Rimini*, that impresses itself on the mind of man of fashion, when he is invited to enter, for a second time, the gilded drawing-room of a little mincing boarding-school mistress, who would fain have an *At Home* in her house. Every thing is pretence, affectation, finery, and gaudiness. The beaux are attorneys' apprentices, with chapeau bras and Limerick gloves—fiddlers, harp teachers, and clerks of genius: the belles are faded fan-twinkling spinsters, prurient vulgar misses from school, and enormous citizens' wives. The company are entertained with lukewarm negus, and the sounds of a paltry piano forte. (2: 39)

Aware that Hunt had gendered his embrace of a two-year jail sentence rather than compromise political principle—he would "act like a man" and "suffer any extremity rather than disgrace myself by effeminate lamentation," Hunt declared in the final sentence of his first "Political Examiner" from prison (7 Feb. 1813, 83)—Z inverts the gendering and degrades the political courage into vulgarity. Hunt's presumption in dedicating *The Story of Rimini* (substantially drafted in prison) to Lord Byron earns a mock-epic simile on the clueless, politically impotent social pretender amid her tawdry social text. Every thing is insipidly feminine, feminizing, unmanning. *The Satirist, or Monthly Meteor* had put the cartoon in play in the first sentence of a review of Hunt's poetry back in 1814: "We were always of the opinion that Mr. Leigh Hunt, the Editor of the Examiner, was a very silly fellow: in politics, a drivelling man-milliner; and in literature, an empty coxcomb" (14: 327). Z inflates this parlor effeminate to disarm any shade of political potency. Like the man-manque cobbler of *English Bards* in his "lofty [. . .] pretensions" and "vulgar taste" (2:38), this is an impotent fool damned by the praise of a too fit audience:

> He would fain be always tripping and waltzing, and is sorry that he cannot be allowed to walk about in the morning with yellow breeches and flesh-coloured silk stockings. He sticks an artificial rose-bud into his button hole in the midst of winter. He wears no neckcloth, and cuts his hair in imitation of the Prints of Petrarch. (2: 39)

This may be standard issue for a dandy, but in the Regency fashion regime, it was an aristocratic license only. A Malvolio, or any "vulgar man [. . .] perpetually labouring to be genteel" (39), is a smokeable sham. In a later installment, Z would pause over Haydon's "foppery of having his hair curled over his shoulders in the old Italian fashion" (3: 520), and *Blackwood's* would smirk at "Mr. John Keates" performing "without a neckcloth, according to the custom of Cockaigne" (6: 239).[25]

The satires mean to gatekeep what Baudelaire saw emergent in 1862 (and the *fin de siècle* would confirm): dandyism as "a new kind of aristocracy," determined not by class or wealth but by intellectual flair (28). Z's Regency discipline is to bruit a travesty of canonical fathers (Petrarch) and tar class aspiration with suspect sexuality. Classing Hunt's "low birth and low habits," Z reminds his readers, "All the great poets of our country have been men of some rank in society, and there is no vulgarity in their writings." This rank protects itself from pretenders with the innuendo of suspect sexuality: "In his verses [Hunt] is always desirous of being airy, graceful, easy, courtly, and ITALIAN," Z mocks, highlighting ITALIAN to imply not-English, mincing, not manly:[26] he "is always on the stretch to be grand" (*Blackwood's* 2: 39–41). *Stretch* is slang for self-stimulating promotion in place of legitimacy. *London Magazine and Monthly Critical and Dramatic Review* would write Keats into the act: in a poetry of "intolerable affectation" and "seldom natural," Keats "says nothing like other men, and appears always on the stretch for [. . .] originality." Sneering at the "trash" eroticism of "Jack Keats or Ketch or whatever," Byron summed it to Murray as "the *outstretched* poesy of [a] miserable Self-polluter of the human Mind."[27]

The over-determination of this gender-contempt marks the embrace by Z's manly canon of 1818 of the poets Byron mocked in *English Bards:* Z's Wordsworth exemplifies that "patriarchal simplicity of feeling"; Z's Moore ("Little") is a "thorough gentleman." Z's Byron (*pace* the scandals of 1816) upholds the standard: this "most nobly-born of English Patricians" must feel only insult at Hunt's dedication of *Rimini,* as if he were a "*peer*" (40–41). Z carried his epigraph over to the next Cockney School Paper (November 1817, a savaging of *Rimini;* 2: 194). Then a "Letter from Z. to Leigh Hunt, King of the Cockneys" (*Blackwood's* May 1818) heralded the abuse of Keats. It was "in that magnificent chamber of yours at Lisson Grove," Z smirks at Hunt, that the

> amiable but infatuated bardling, Mister John Keats, slept on the night when he composed his famous Cockney Poem in honour of
> "Him of the rose, the violet, and the spring,
> The social smile, *the chain for freedom's sake,"*
> and other mighty masters of the lyre . . . (3: 197)

If Z's italics remind readers of Hunt's jail time for "abuse of [his] sovereign" (197), the jab at Keats is not even this complimentary: a bardling is too puny for outrage; he's just a gushing apprentice, a Mister but no master. "Hunt is a small poet, but he is a clever man. Mr Keats is a still smaller poet, and he is only a boy" (Z will soon say; 3: 522)—a mere epiphenomenon of Hunt. Z's inset verse is from Keats's sonnet praise of Hunt, "Great spirits now on earth are sojourning," and his scene is Hunt's library, reported by Keats at the end of *Sleep and Poetry* (both in *Poems*). Clearly forecast is the Hunting of Keats in Z's fourth Cockney paper, August 1818–its epigraph pared to the lines on "KEATS" (now all in caps). Z spots "good Johnny Keats" in a "rising brood of Cockneys" trying to be Hunt, one of the "uneducated [. . .] fanciful dreaming tea-drinkers" in the circle (3: 520–21). On reading the sentences about himself in "Letter from Z," Keats ruefully punned the magazine into "Endinburgh" (*L* 1: 294).[28] While Z didn't "end" Keats's career, he would imprint it for a century.

What his self-congratulatory sarcasm missed was Keats's own ironizing of the whole industry of masculine self-making, especially the making of a modern poet.

Performing the Poet: Keats's Debut

Keats's debut in *Poems* radiates a rhetoric of gender. It blazons a genealogy of literary fathers (Homer, Chaucer, Chapman, Spenser, Shakespeare, Beaumont and Fletcher, Milton, Wordsworth), a rhetorical circuit of "brother Poets" (*To George Felton Mathew*) and a local fraternity (Haydon, Hunt, the poet's brothers and friends), along with a bid for male bonding via a stock in trade of feminine figures: "artless daughters," "Ladies," blushing maids, and sporting nymphs. Yet even as *Poems* rushes this fraternity of song, its poetics conspicuously tune its male poet to feminine kinds of pleasure, feminine forms of enchantment, and more than a few feminine rhymes. The publishers, the Olliers, thought it worth advertising *Poems* ("By John Keatts") in *The British Lady's Magazine.* What makes *Poems* a "Cockney" venture, in a counter-cultural rather than degraded sense, is Keats's ironic plays on his visibly enchanted desire for masculine credit and male canonizing. His figures of gender are strangely, presciently, undecided in alignment, especially on questions of pleasure, desire, and reception.

Take the capstone, *Sleep and Poetry.* Where Z reads ridiculous boyish infatuation I see a parade, frequently verging on parody, of Keats's poetic measuring against mighty and less mighty masters. Vocation, the calling to the career, is the self-conscious subject, a casting call relayed into audience and audition. Aware of the stakes, Keats hedges enthusiasm with stagey affectation. He cuts a figure of the poet that is knowingly styled and stylized:

> O Poesy! for thee I hold my pen
> That am not yet a glorious denizen
> Of thy wide heaven—Should I rather kneel
> Upon some mountain-top until I feel
> A glowing splendour round about me hung,
> And echo back the voice of thine own tongue?
> O Poesy! for thee I grasp my pen
> That am not yet a glorious denizen
> Of thy wide heaven . . . (47–55)

Wielding "that mighty instrument of little men" (so Byron called the poet's pen in *English Bards* [10]), Keats heightens a theatricality that verges on dissociation, putting ironies in the fire of desire.

The conspicuous excess is a denaturing into style that bears a critical and crucial effect, however. It is the reflex of Keats's awareness that however much his pen is pointed for vocational manhood, it is drawn to the pleasures of females styles and forms of leisure, to female sites of recreation and fantasy, and to female culture of commonplace books:

> a bowery nook
> Will be elysium—an eternal book
> Whence I may copy many a lovely saying
> About the leaves, and flowers—about the playing
> Of nymphs in woods, and fountains; and the shade
> Keeping a silence round a sleeping maid. (63–68)

About playing the young master is never wrong. He writes "about," as focus and as location, a world that is very Fragonard—artificial, luxurious, female, effeminizing.

Keats knows that no eternity is forever. ⌐"The danger in beauty," argues Frances Ferguson, "is that its appearance of weakness does not prevent its having an effect, which is always that of robbing us of our vigilance and recreating us in its own image." The sublime is the Burkean antidote: to the degree that "the beautiful has been joined with physical and political entropy, issuing in death," the sublime calls up labor, "exciting the passions of self-preservation" (*Solitude* 52).⌋ This wasn't written about *Sleep and Poetry*, but it could have been. With a grand narrative in the wings, Keats reproduces just this sequence, first by assigning his bowery book to a merely temporary, consciously temporized pleasure (a Chamber of Maiden-thought), then projecting a masculine accomplishment:

> Then the events of this wide world I'd seize
> Like a strong giant, and my spirit teaze
> Till at its shoulders it should proudly see
> Wings to find out an immortality. (81–84)

What makes *Sleep and Poetry* a drama of rather than a dramatization of aspiration is its rhythm of hesitation: this poet keeps retracing the plan, the tracing becoming the tale.

In another turn of the verse, life becomes "the reading of an ever-changing tale" about maidens and schoolboys (91–94). No giant shoulders after all, just nymphs' white shoulders; no seizing, just a teasing bite. The only masculine spirit is adolescent, glad animal movements to

> Catch the white-handed nymphs in shady places,
> To woo sweet kisses from averted faces,—
> Play with their fingers, touch their shoulders white
> Into a pretty shrinking with a bite
> As hard as lips can make it: till agreed,
> A lovely tale of human life we'll read. (105–10)

"Women consider how things may be prettily said," said More, introducing *Essays for Young Ladies* (*W* 6: 264). With his pen on this pulse, Keats means to sober up his vision of pretty Poesy with a tragic turn, an intent to move on that he maps with a sharply split couplet:

> . . . in the bosom of a leafy world
> We rest in silence, like two gems upcurl'd
> In the recesses of a pearly shell.
>
> And can I ever bid these joys farewell?

> Yes, I must pass them for a nobler life,
> Where I may find the agonies, the strife
> Of human hearts . . . (119–25)

Yet for all its mimetic splitting, the couplet 121–22 holds affection, *shell* lingering to echo in the anticipated *farewell*. This formal ambivalence is magnified by the designated harbinger of nobler things, that glorious charioteer: while he is projected as Apollonian visionary, among the "Shapes of delight, of mystery, and fear" (138) he summons, the most legible of all is "a lovely wreath" not of laurel, but of girls, girls, girls, "Dancing their sleek hair into tangled curls" (149–50). Z found it absurdly easy to dismiss the higher ambitions of *Sleep and Poetry* as sheer effeminacy, "very pretty raving" from "a boy of pretty abilities" (*Blackwood's* Aug. 1818; 3: 520, 522). Even a reflexively sympathetic Amy Lowell had to admit that "manhood in this poem is mere vision" (1: 222).[29]

It matters, however, that this is only the poem's latest, not last vision. It is a phase of a drama that tests out a visionary arc, discovers its very pretty raving, lets it go, and gathers the remains to pivot another test. As the vision collapses into a "sense of real things . . . doubly strong" (157), Keats doubles back, using the very language of estrangement for a rhyme track toward a potent manly posture in the social real, a poet-critic set to spar with Z:

> I will strive
> Against all doubtings, and will keep alive
> The thought of that same chariot, and the strange
> Journey it went.
> Is there so small a range
> In the present strength of manhood, that the high
> Imagination cannot freely fly
> As she was wont of old? (159–65)

As the charioteer and his unreadable script recede, the stage is cleared for the strife of the poet-critic with his own world, a *range* literally distilled in the wake of the visionary *strange*. In this line of witty strife, Keats rehabilitates the girlish feminine of the visionary gleam into a vigorous feminine (the Imagination of old), and then, from this antithetical critical stance, rebukes the enervated manhood of present esteem. With Z implied, Keats hints the effeminacy of establishment poetics, reading this as the issue of a "scism / Nurtured by foppery and barbarism" (181–82). And with *English Bards* implied, the Keatsian critic sets the neo-classicals into the terms that Byron's satirist had wielded against the insurgents: now it is the neo-classicals who are the impostures, a "thousand handicraftsmen" in "the mask / Of Poesy" (200–201).

In embattled league with rising young poets, Keats deliberately courts the combat. More than any other stretch of *Sleep and Poetry*, this estimate struck home with male readers. Haydon praised the bold "flash of lightening that will sound men from their occupations, and keep them trembling for the crash of thunder that <u>will</u> follow" (in *KL* 1: 125). In another cheer for "Young Poets," Hunt dubbed *Sleep and Poetry* the "best" in the volume, especially its "impatient, and as it may be thought by some, irreverend assault" (*Examiner* 13 July 1817, 443). On another front, Byron never forgave Keats for the barbs on Pope.[30] Z retaliated by shifting the genre from heroic to mock-heroic, unmanning the upstart: this "long strain of foaming abuse against a certain class of English Poets [. . .] with Pope at their head" is the signature of "ignorant unsettled pretenders," the "raving" of "flimsy striplings" not qualified to evaluate, let alone pretend equality with "other *men of power*" (*Blackwood's* 3: 520). Keats had already discounted such esteem in that letter to Bailey (November 1817), and his friend and fellow Young Poet Reynolds reinvested the slap as a badge of merit, assuring Keats that the "overweening struggle to oppress you only shews the world that so much of endeavour cannot be directed to nothing. Men do not set their muscles, and strain their sinews to break a straw" (14 Oct. 1818; *Letters of Reynolds* 12).

Yet if Keats's poet-critic is hot for combat, the Keatsean poet exercises an internal check, a half-subversion into a vision of poesy as noble feminine restraint:

> 'Tis might half slumb'ring on its own right arm.
> The very archings of her eye-lids charm
> A thousand willing agents to obey,
> And still she governs with the mildest sway. (237–40)

This female sway is charged with a female offices of the kind Hemans described in *The Domestic Affections*, "To sooth the cares, and lift the thoughts of man" (247). The poet's inspiration is co-feminized: "As she was wont, th' imagination / Into most lovely labyrinths will be gone" (265–66). It may be that the hegemony is one of "poet kings / Who simply tell the most heart-easing things" (268–69), but the total figure is a he-poet with she-imagination. None of this is a sure point and resting place is reasoning, however. It's a zig prone to zag. Breaking out a new paragraph, Keats emerges from the lovely labyrinth battling for this vision, with more reception-baiting:

> Will not some say that I presumptuously
> Have spoken? that from hastening disgrace
> 'Twere far better to hide my foolish face?
> That whining boyhood should with reverence bow
> Ere the dread thunderbolt could reach? (270–74)

Eclectic answered by refusing the invitation and just reviewing its discourse: such lines "shew that he is indeed far gone, beyond the reach of the efficacy either of praise or censure, in affectation and absurdity" (2nd ser. 8: 272). Keats was on a roll, however, pleased at "speaking out what I have dared to think" (300), though unsure if this spelled madness or martyrdom: "should I / Be but the essence of deformity" (297–98; one of only two "I" rhymes in *Poems*).[31] The poetry that had romanced a lovely labyrinth now twins itself to architect Daedalus's reckless son:

> Ah! rather let me like a madman run
> Over some precipice; let the hot sun
> Melt my Dedalian wings, and drive me down
> Convuls'd and headlong! (301–4)

The new poetry enacts what it describes, running its lines in a meta-poetic excess of enjambment, setting *run* and *down* to fall into blank spaces, and daring censure for these flagrantly romantic, non-Augustan couplets. *Sleep and Poetry* doesn't resolve the tonal indeterminacy of such over-the-top moments: brave risks, campy extravagance, smokeable excess, or anxiety of impotence?

From this welter of male forms—whining boyhood, foolish excess, boyish nymph-pursuit, acolyte ardency, humble awe, heroic aspiration, battling ardor—Keats seeks relief by scanning the "friendly aids" to "brotherhood" in Hunt's library (316–17). Yet the hoped-for aids instead give back the poem's composition of disparate gender stylings: "an inventory of the art garniture of the room," as Cowden Clarke put it (*Recollections* 134). On view are "bards who sung / In other ages—cold and sacred busts" (356–57); "fauns and satyrs taking aim / At swelling apples with a frisky leap" (361–62); "a train / Of nymphs" (364–65); "Sappho's meek head . . . half smiling down / At nothing" (381–2), "Great Alfred's too, with anxious, pitying eyes," and "Kosciusko's worn / By horrid sufferance—mightily forlorn" (385–88); enthralled Petrarch "start[ing] at the sight of Laura," unable to "wean / His eyes from her sweet face" (389–91); and finally, the female "face of Poesy," which, Keats says, "overlook'd things that I scarce could tell" (395)—among the things of muted supervision, the paradoxically "sleepless" (400) poet of *Sleep and Poetry*.

It is apt that Keats ends his dreaming of poetic and gender allegiance with no telling into a clear idea, but instead, in lines that withhold, or parody, patrilinear security:

> And up I rose refresh'd, and glad, and gay,
> Resolving to begin that very day
> These lines; and howsoever they be done,
> I leave them as a father does his son. (401–4)

When Amy Lowell exclaims, "Was ever so boyish and inconsequential an ending?" (2: 226), she also gives the syntax of a real question. It is not possible to tell *howsoever*, especially with the last line in such verbal ambiguity: to write that a poet leaves his lines "as a father does his son" may be the standard *envoi*—go little son. But *leave* is not just bestowal; it's also a term of abandonment, and outside the syntactic analogy it bears Keats's consciousness of his own fatherless transition into manhood. At the close of his debut (*Poems* puts a gothic 𝔉𝔦𝔫𝔦𝔰 on this last page), Keats scarce can tell how much a literary son may depend on any father.

It is telling, however, that another idealizing simile for inspiration, also an awakening, involves a startled son, a remote father, and an emergent feminine: "The Imagination may be compared to Adam's dream—he awoke and found it truth" (*L* 1: 185). Found it in the form of a beloved who precipitated a fall. Among the exceptions that Jack Stillinger admits to his view of *Poems* as devoted to "dealing with the question of Keats's career as a poet" are the untitled sonnets of erotic vexation, "Woman! when I behold thee" and "Had I a man's fair form," and one titled *To a Friend who sent me some Roses* ("Order" 13). I want to propose that these, too, are vocational, entering the question of gender into Keats's conception of his career as a poet. And all tell rather strange and strained stories, effecting what Judith Butler calls a "kind of gender performance" that enacts "the performativity of gender itself," yielding "parodic displacement" and sometimes, "parodic laughter" (*Gender Trouble* 139).

To a Friend is extravagantly performative. Its back-story is a little indeterminate: is this a quarrel between the poet and a friend, quelled by roses?[32] Or is it a campy affectation of a quarrel, done with extravagant humor? Whatever the discourse, the old knightly strife survives only in a simile for the poem's early morning scene, "when anew / Adventurous knights take up their dinted shields." The poet had been out smelling the wild musk-roses,

> But when, O Wells! thy roses came to me
>   My sense with their deliciousness was spell'd:
> Soft voices had they, that with tender plea
>   Whisper'd of peace, and truth, and friendliness unquell'd. (11–14)

In modern chivalry, flowers and tender poetry may bind men, too, Keats suggests—Wells's roses spelling the sense, Keats returning a fine spell of words. The risk of this romance, even in a campy mode, is the scent of queerness that Alexander Smith's article on Keats in *Encyclopædia Britannica* sniffs: "the whole 'Cockney School'" was characterized by "effeminacy and puerile sentimentalism. [. . .] They wrote sonnets to one another, sent one another bouquets of roses and baskets of fruit, they wreathed crowns of ivy and placed them on one another's foreheads" (56).

The heterosexual romances in *Poems*, both more hyperbolic and more generic, dote on this discourse as a poetic credential. "Heavens, how desperately do I adore/Thy winning graces," a sonneteer says to categorical Woman, mindful of the masculine tradition;

> to be thy defender
> I hotly burn—to be a Calidore—
> A very Red Cross Knight—a stout Leander—
> Might I be loved by thee like these of yore. ("Woman!" 10–14)

But for all the ardor, the tone of his hot-burning infinitives is undecidable: is it nostalgia, or a smokeable mimicry of what Keats imagines women want, tempered for male reception by the patent anachronism of the models: Spenser's knights, Marlowe's Leander? What does not seem in question is the power of Woman (even paradoxically) "meek, and kind, and tender" (9). A poem Keats withheld from *Poems—On a Leander Which Miss Reynolds, My Kind Friend, Gave Me*—tells even by its title: Leander is no stout hero, but a wee gem (from William Tassie's popular line) for female purchase and kind gifting.[33] In fable, gift, and sonnet, he is reduced to a little spectacle of death from love, and the poet's call is to "all sweet maidens" (1) to witness this "victim of your beauty bright" (6). "Sinking away . . . / Sinking bewilder'd," this "young Leander toiling to his death" (9) is any young poet's worst nightmare:

> O horrid dream—see how his body dips
> Dead heavy—arms and shoulders gleam awhile:
> He's gone—up bubbles all his amorous breath. (12–14)

The last word is the rhyme for *death* (9), Leander's heroism a heavy purchase, and his translation into a gleaming gem, a shallow grace. One who loses breath in bubbles, all for love, is a dubious model for any poet who would woo female readers with his own amorous breath.

When knights appear in *Poems*, they are similarly sapped. They are no sweet lady's "stout defender" (*Specimen of an Induction* 13–16), nor any model from which the present state of manhood might draw strength. They are patent fictions, archaic figures, antiques to be doted on by the poet and offered to doting book-buyers. Like the odist's Psyche in 1819, they are a faded hierarchy, and though too late for antique vows, still available for style. Yet even as Keats produces these decadent ornamentations, the stylizing gets a critical sheen beyond the merely ornamental. The conscious antiquing projects a self-conscious, modern perspective on old authority, viewed in a range of attitudes, from fair to silly, from sentimental to satirical. Keats has the knights of *Poems* cut figures for manhood as a smokeable performance.

Calidore, for instance. His debut in *Calidore, A Fragment* is not as Spenser's knight, by a long stretch, though there are some attractive affiliations for the Keatsian poet of 1817. Spenser's Calidore, both a "gentle" man and a pattern "to fashion a gentleman" ("Letter of the Authors"), exhibits "Courtesie," a form of manhood as synecdoche for social coherence and harmony, in chivalric service to the nation, epitomized (Burke knew this) in its "soueraine Lady Queene" (Book VI, Proem 6). With "gentlenesse of spright / And manners mylde," a "comely guize withall, / And gracious speach," Spenser's Calidore endears himself as much to "mens hearts" as to ladies' (*FQ* VI.i.1–2). His definition is indisputably manly:

> Nathlesse thereto he was full stout and tall,
> And well approu'd in batteilous affray,
> That him did much renowne, and far his fame display. (VI.i.2)

Keats's is a Calidore with a difference, more boy than man, more young poet than young knight:

> Young Calidore is paddling o'er the lake;
> His healthful spirit eager and awake
> To feel the beauty of a silent eve,
> Which seem'd full loth this happy world to leave;
> The light dwelt o'er the scene so lingeringly. (1–5)

Allott (36n1) hears in line 1 an echo of the opening of *The Faerie Queene:* "A Gentle Knight was pricking on the plaine." The syntax has to be a parody. Keats means "paddling a boat," but there is a slip-sense of Calidore as a glad animal paddling around in a romance bath. Spenser's sentence continues in the heroic mode: "cladd in mightie armes and siluer shielde, / Wherein old dints of deepe wounds did remaine, / The cruell markes of many a bloudy field" (I.i.1). Keats's Calidore has nothing to do with these marks and the career they report. Instead,

> the sharp keel of his little boat
> Comes up with ripple, and with easy float,
> And glides into a bed of water lillies. (19–21)

His world is a "bowery shore" (26), disturbed by nothing more mighty than a "trumpet's silver voice" (55); his company is not knights of chivalry, but damsels who make him giddy:

> What a kiss,
> What gentle squeeze he gave each lady's hand!
> How tremblingly their delicate ancles spann'd!

> Into how sweet a trance his soul was gone,
> While whisperings of affection
> Made him delay to let their tender feet
> Come to the earth. (80–86)

The gush of exclamations is no Spenserian pricking of the metrical line. The feet of Keats's line 84 are tender indeed: *affection* is drawn out into four syllables, with a silent pant in place of the tenth beat. *What a kiss* completes a rhyme, absurdly, with *threatening portcullis* (79)—a fortification suspended in a cockney-rhyme partnering that verges on hudibrasis. The king of the Cockneys himself, Hunt, was amused by the pairing.[34] These "prank rhymes," Greg Kucich suggests, dose romance with a parody, injecting an "intrusive familiarity, or casual intimacy, with sources of cultural authority" (Cockney 129).

Like *Sleep and Poetry*'s young poet, Young Calidore is a prospect. His telos in the social semiotic seems to be "brave Sir Gondibert" (122), a very Spenserian Red Cross knight, the maturity of the "aspiring boy" (128).[35] In Keats's vocational code, this "far-fam'd" senior (122) is the inspiration for any "healthful spirit eager and awake" (2), possessed by "large-eyed wonder, and ambitious heat" (127). It is winning of Keats to cartoon this too obvious interest: Sir Gondibert is a man of such "stature tall" (112)

> that the waving of his plumes would be
> High as the berries of a wild ash tree,
> Or as the winged cap of Mercury. (113–15)

The fashionable plume may be the great elevator, but it is to a height similed by boy Mercury. This rhyme triplet has two Keatsian heirs, one in fashion, one in rhyme. In *The Eve of St. Agnes* "young Porphyro, with heart on fire / For Madeline" (IX), finds his way to her chamber in style, "brushing the cobwebs with his lofty plume" (XIII). Hapless Endymion is the heir in rhyme. Having dreamt of a moon-goddess, he wakes next to his "delicious lady," a palpable and panting Indian Maid. This may be a "state perplexing" for him, but it gives his by-now fed-up fabler a cue for farce:

> He who died
> For soaring too audacious in the sun,
> When that same treacherous wax began to run,
> Felt not more tongue-tied than Endymion. (*Endymion* 4.441–44)

The hero is tongue-tied, but the rare triplet trips off the poet's tongue with deft sarcasm.[36]

If this seems a defensive tack, Keats is not innocent of the psychology. When in December 1818 he first tells George and Georgiana of his captivation by Fanny Brawne—"beautiful and elegant, graceful, silly, fashionable and strange we [h]ave a li[ttle] tiff now and then" (*L* 2: 8)—it is just before he gives this report, one of his most elaborate self-satires:

> I am to be invited to Miss Millar's birthday dance [. . .] I shall be the only Dandy there—and indeed I merely comply with the invitation that the party may no[t] be entirely destitute of a specimen of that Race. I shall appear in a complete dress of purple Hat and all—with a list [of] the beauties I have conquered embroidered round my Calv[es.]

Keats plays at gender, imagining a flirtation in a "camelion" mimicry of the female fuss of fashion. In this beautiful, elegant, silly, strange, and fashionable spectacle, he also mocks himself as Regency dandy and lady-killer, wearing the text of his success as frivolous finery. The fabric of sharp satire is usually woven with serious thread, however, and here it's a subtext of poetic suits. Keats jokes that as a Dandy, he "shall be obliged to shirk a good many" Misses (*L* 2: 8). Just two months earlier, Woodhouse had sought to disarm the *Quarterly*'s ridicule of *Endymion* by reducing it to Dandyism, assuring Keats that it will scare away only those "'Dandy' readers, male & female, who love to be spared the trouble of judging for themselves" (21 Oct. *L* 1: 378). In the Dandy theater that Keats projects in December, he mocks their spare taste and layers it with a stylized self-objectification that blithely assumes the female position Laura Mulvey maps out in her analysis of sexualized spectatorship:

> In a world ordered by sexual imbalance, pleasure in looking has been split between active/male and passive/female. The determining male gaze projects its fantasy onto the female figure, which is styled accordingly. In their traditional exhibitionist role women are simultaneously looked at and displayed, with their appearance coded for strong visual and erotic impact so that they can be said to connote *to-be-looked-at-ness*. (436)

The pleasure in looking is inseparable from the politics of the world, and for a small poet in this position, if he is not a celebrity (Byron), the erotic impact may be in doubt. But a worldly and theatrical temper might parody the fantasy and redress imbalance with meta-theatrical power.

Keats's text of the poet as dandy, only a text and not anything he ever enacted, is a highly mediated jokiness about how boys become men, and what kind of men. It is not at all clear that Calidore's destiny is Sir Gondibert, a "man of elegance, and stature tall" (112), that he is cut out for anything more than paddling, ankle-gazing, and swooning. Gondibert looks more like his antithesis: he greets the boy with a "mailed hand" (126), and commands all ears to rapture. His speech is "brimful" of "knightly deeds, and gallant spurning," stories of "how the strong of arm / Kept off dismay, and terror, and alarm / From lovely woman" (143–46). Calidore, true to his name, is "burning / To hear" more (142–43), sitting among the entranced damsels. All attention is on Gondibert, who tells a tale of chivalry with "such manly ardour" that erotic success is secure: "each damsel's hand" gets a warm kiss between syllables (147–48). *Calidore, A Fragment* breaks off just a dozen lines on; but Keats's decision to include it in his debut volume suggests his desire to stage an adolescent subjectivity that is eager, yet not exactly sure of its determinations and definitions.

The other knight in Keats's repertoire, his most famous, is a rehabilitated Calidore, not only burning but wielding a burning gaze: Porphyro in *The Eve of St. Agnes*. The poet salaciously addresses the strategist secreted in Madeline's chamber (and the implied male reader): "Now prepare, / Young Porphyro, for gazing" (XXII). The young man obliges with pornographic ardor: "Stol'n to this paradise, and so entranced, / Porphyro gazed upon her empty dress, / And listen'd to her breathing" (XXVIII). But as determined as he is (more than Apollo, he is Keats's first and only "fore-seeing" hero), he is not all of a piece.[37] Not only is his rakishness played for laughs (his operatic arrival, that plume), it is also compromised by its pulse of passion. Eyeing Madeline, he grows "faint" (XXV), his arm is "unnerved" (XXXII) as he slips into her bed, and on the verge of seduction he buckles: "upon his knees he sank, pale as smooth-sculptured stone" (XXXIII). Keats's fascination with the male gaze is gender-conscious not so much in terms of endorsing active male/passive female as for reflecting the instability of this array of power.

When Keats's scenes of conquest involve the potency of "Poesy," the suits to this "coy muse" (*To George Felton Mathew*) are imprinted with negatives not yet negatively capable. A valentine in *Poems* with a generic, and thus categorically laden, title *To * * * * * **, sets the double investment of erotic and poetic success:

>   Had I a man's fair form, then might my sighs
>   Be echoed swiftly through that ivory shell
>   Thine ear, and find thy gentle heart; so well
>   Would passion arm me for the enterprize:
>   But ah! I am no knight whose foeman dies; (1–5)

Without creditable physical form, male passion is disabled, for all its ardor.[38] Even "fair form," as a qualifying figure, is trouble: it is a Regency cliché for female beauty.[39] Keats used it in this sense in "Fill for me a brimming bowl" ("the fairest form / That e'er my reveling eyes beheld"), and would again: "fair the form / I floated with," the dreamer of Francesca murmurs (*A Dream*); it is Lamia's "fair form" that is assailed by Apollonius (*Lamia* 2.248); and dearest Fanny Brawne who entrammels Keats with "so fair a form" (1 July 1819; *L* 2: 123). Even with the projection of a potentiated male form, the courtship of *To * * * * * ** is a limpid pledge to "dote upon thee,—call thee sweet," with "spells, and incantation" gathered in the pallid light of a female moon. Doting, moreover, evokes the kind of feminine sentiment that George Keats recalls of their mother's "doting fondness for her children" (*KC* 1: 314). With a "camelion" poetic a little too adept at filling the fair form it courts, what Keats's sonnet concedes, without making it its theme, is its poet's difference from the socially validated figure of manhood. It is not his words that denote him truly so much as his body, a traditionally female semiotic.

To hear "my size" ruefully sounded in "my sighs" might be thought a stretch, even for Keatsian punning, did not his sober friend Woodhouse measure it: "the author has an idea that the diminutiveness of his size makes him contemptible and that no woman can like a man of small stature" (Sperry, "Woodhouse" 148). He may have caught the *ize* of the rhyme partner (*enterprize*); certainly he knew Keats's abject sense of his body-text. Keats's expressions almost always take this text, without the immunizations of class or other exhibitions of prowess, as a sign of a failure almost fated. *Poems* is populated with men of stature tall such as Sir Gondibert, epic figures such as "stout Cortez . . . with eagle eyes" (*On first looking into Chapman's Homer*), and Haydon, the champion of "the great man's fame" and himself "a stout unbending champion" of "stedfast genius, toiling gallantly" (*Addressed to Haydon*). Yet this volume opens with a small-man's poem that begins, in the poet's voice, "I stood tip-toe upon a little hill." It was at once a joke for his friends, and a parody of the Wordsworthian or egotistical sublime:[40]

> What visionary powers of eye and soul
> In youth were mine; when, stationed on the top
> Of some huge hill—expectant, I beheld
> The sun rise up . . . (*The Excursion* 4 [1814] 110–13)

In the poem that "I stood tip-toe" seeded, *Endymion*, Keats even shifts the tip-toe figure to a she. The hero beholds a statue "on light tiptoe divine, / A quiver'd Dian" (2.261–62). Tip-toe Keats is not so awesome. Just weeks after *Endymion* was published, he joked to the Jeffrey sisters about his impact on Hampstead society, "I being somewhat stunted am taken for nothing" (*L* 1: 291). More than any of his contemporaries, Keats marks the exception to Virginia Woolf's oft-quoted statement that women serve "as looking-glasses possessing the magic and delicious power of reflecting the figure of man at twice its natural size" (*Room* 35). In love with Fanny Brawne, Keats laments to her of his having a "body too small for" for his mind (*L* 2: 275).

The first image he gives George and Georgiana of her begins with a self-measuring: "Miss Brawn? she is about my height" (*L* 2: 13). Two months on, he reports a painful social correlative:

> I have not seen M[r] Lewis lately for I have shrunk from going up the hill—M[r] Lewis [and] M[rs] Brawne [. . .] talked about me—and I heard that M[r] L Said a thing I am not at all contented with—Says he "O, he is quite the little Poet" now this is abominable—you might as well say Buonaparte is quite the little Soldier—You see what it is to be under six foot and not a lord—There is a long fuzz to day in the examiner about a young Man who delighted a young woman with a Valentine. (14 Feb. 1819; *L* 2: 61)[41]

Had Keats known that the successful young amant was Charles Lamb (61n8), another sub-six-footer, he might have taken cheer; but here he is "tender of being insulted" by the measure (he confesses to Bailey; *L* 2: 341). A little Poet is not the professional peer of little Soldier Buonaparte or the social peer of little Lord Byron, and not a candidate for the "long fuzz" (however mocking the term) in the papers publishing a lover's success. Hazlitt made the point about Byron's stature in an essay published after Keats's death, "On the Aristocracy of Letters" (*Table-Talk*, 1821–22):

> His Lordship [. . .] towers above his fellows by all the height of the peerage. If the poet lends a grace to the nobleman, the nobleman pays it back to the poet with interest. What a fine addition is ten thousand a year and a title. (*W* 8: 209)

Keats is the poignant contrast: "The poet Keats had not [the] sort of protection" that accrues to a poet "sheltered by rank" (211). In September 1819, with the play on which he and Brown had been laboring (*Otho the Great*) seeming destined for stillbirth, Keats writes his frustration in another rueful reflection on stature: "Were it to succeed," he says, "it would lift me out of the mire," redeem a "reputation," that "is continually rising against me. My name with the literary fashionables is vulgar—I am a weaver boy to them—a Tragedy would lift me out of this mess" (*L* 2: 186). In *The Fall of Hyperion*, on which he was also working, the would-be poet next to Moneta looks "like a stunt bramble by a solemn Pine" (1.292–93). In Keats's erotic imagination, the women loom literally large, as the Pre-Raphaelite painters surely understood.[42]

Apollo has fallen out of *The Fall*, and the crisis is not unrelated to the epic display of man's fair form, an anti-Keats (for all the parallels of poetry and medicine) imprinted with a strong visual and erotic impact. In his memoir of 1828, Hunt admitted that Keats's tendency to "poetical effeminacy" had conceived an Apollo who, even in the transformation into a god, "suffers a little too exquisitely among his lilies" (419). When *Hyperion* was first published, Hunt was at once franker and more elliptical, pausing at "something too effeminate and human in the way Apollo receives the exaltation which his wisdom is giving him. He weeps and wonders somewhat too fondly" (*Indicator* 44: 350). It's a strange and striking linkage, that *effeminate and human,* strained by the *too:* Keats writes of a body "enkindled," "Trembling," shaking with "wild commotions," "flushed limbs," "fierce convulse," and "golden tresses" in "undulation round his eager neck" (3.121–35). He had even tried writing this ravishment into feminine mythography:

> ~~Roseate and pained as a ravish'd nymph—~~
> Into a hue more roseate than sweet-pain
> Gives to a ravish'd Nymph ~~new-r~~ when her warm tears
> Gush luscious with no sob.[43]

But he knew Apollo was no nymph. Queer theory *avant le lettre* understood the uses of feminine sculpting to license a homoerotic gaze. "Apollo is portrayed in the sculptures with a feminine—sometimes extremely feminine—figure," remarks Edward Carpenter about the semiotic (35), and Winckelmann's writings about the Apollo Belvedere are a locus neoclassicus of male erotic fascination. What struck Hunt as effeminate about Apollo may have less to do with the substitution of fondness for fortitude than with the intensity of Keats's description of a ravished male body—one that implicates the reader/gazer in the flushes and kindling, the tremblings and commotions. Not for nothing did W. C. Courthope cite the "effeminate notion of Apollo" as the reason for the poem's sudden halt (*Liberal Movement* 184). What both he and Hunt sense is not just a breach of decorum (a god should not act thus) but a breach of gender: a man should not act thus, not look thus. Nor should a manly poet purvey such imagination.

The poem's witness to Apollo is self-possessed goddess Mnemosyne: not just no prospect for seduction, but sublime power embodied in female form. "During the pain Mnemosyne upheld / Her arms as one who prophesied," while Apollo shrieks in ecstasy (3.133–35). The erotic form of this possession, staged for gazing—most scandalously to Victorian readers (as we shall see in the next chapter)—is in *Endymion*'s spectacle of Adonis in the Bower of Venus:

> ... on a silken couch of rosy pride,
> In midst of all, there lay a sleeping youth

> Of fondest beauty, fonder, in fair sooth,
> Than sighs could fathom, or contentment reach:
> And coverlids gold-tinted like the peach,
> Or ripe October's faded marigolds,
> Fell sleek about him in a thousand folds—
> Nor hiding up an Apollonian curve
> Of neck and shoulder, nor the tenting swerve
> Of knee from knee, nor ankles pointing light;
> But rather giving them to the filled sight
> Officiously. Sideway his face repos'd
> On one white arm, and tenderly unclos'd,
> By tenderest pressure, a faint damask mouth
> To slumbery pout; just as the morning south
> Disparts a dew-lipp'd rose.   (*Endymion* 2.392–407)

This is a set piece of "embarrassment"—not only for Endymion (430) but also, as Christopher Ricks proposes, for the (male) reader. Endymion's encounter with this luxuriously sleeping body is a set lesson about male subjection to doting divinity. But the lesson may overproduce. In Adonis's body, filling sight with traces of physical contours and breathing life, Karen Swann reads an unembarrassed Keatsianism: that serial form of luscious boys—"mute, self-enclosed, and infinitely seductive, all officiously displayed to the filled sight."[44] No regal she-poesy of "might half slumbering" (*Sleep and Poetry* 236), these feminized boys are poems themselves.

What sort of reader of "man's fair form" is capable of staging its strange as well as standard attractions? of voicing a young man's desires, but also registering the cultural formation and information? What but an inchoative "Man of Genius" whose greatness is the absence of "any determined Character"? The critics who scorned Keats as no man but mere boy were not ready to credit the genius of this indeterminacy, the incipient theorizing of male adolescence that would, after Romantic "childhood," become the haunt and main region of Victorian fiction.[45] "Knowing within myself the manner in which this Poem has been produced," Keats says in his Preface to *Endymion,* he gives the terms, in a tone of abject irony: "inexperience, immaturity, and every error denoting a feverish attempt, rather than a deed accomplished." All this emanates from what he maps, as few paragraphs on, as a "space of life between, in which the soul is in a ferment, the character undecided, the way of life uncertain, the ambition thick-sighted: thence proceeds mawkishness, and all the thousand bitters"—effects, he readily concedes, apparent to "men who are competent to look, and who do look with a zealous eye, to the honour of English literature." Yet this space between, the scene of Keats's most stretched out romance of glamorous, half-silly, half-brilliant youth, is not just the terrain of adolescent psychology; it is also an intuition of Keats's mature poetics: his famously unsettled closures, his poetics of suspense and deferral, his character of "no Identity," and, of course, his "negative" capability. Not the least of the venues for the space of life between is Keats's romance—variously temperamental, experimental, performative, ironic—with the genders of indolence.

What Is the Gender of Indolence?

Wordsworth wrote his first lengthy prose treatise, Preface to *Lyrical Ballads*, so he claimed at its outset, to protect his experiment in a poetics of feeling (always prone to ridicule as unmanly) from "the most dishonorable accusation which can be brought against an Author, namely, that of an indolence which prevents him from endeavouring to ascertain what is his duty, or, when his duty is ascertained prevents him from performing it" (*LB* 743). If indolence is a culpable, self-canceling dishonor, Keats is doubly fascinating both for performing it, and refusing to publish the performance. The most volatile character of Keats's self-definition is that attractive camelion named "Indolence." Its shifting genders, played etymologically against pain (*in+ dolens*, not feeling pain) and experientially against "Ambition," chart the erratic course of Keats's part defensive, part earnest, part bold, part parodic story of poetic desire.

The key texts are private letters and drafts of unpublished poems tracing a set of speculations, for friends and family, on male postures of passivity and receptivity. An early site is an elaborate meditation in a letter to Reynolds, 19 February 1818, on that lovely flirtation with oxymoron, "diligent Indolence" (*L* 1: 231–33). It seems to require (inspire) a double-sexed language:

> Now it appears to me that almost any Man may like the Spider spin from his own inwards his own airy Citadel—the points of leaves and twigs on which the Spider begins her work are few and she fills the Air with a beautiful circuiting: man should be content with as few points to tip with the fine Webb of his Soul and weave a tapestry empyrean. (232)

Across this circuitry of speculation play swift counter-changes of gender: a "Man" thinking the way a she-Spider spins; a Citadel, the defense-work of men, transforming into a tapestry-making, the labor of women; then the resorption of this female art as a metaphor for Man's soul, and this compromised by a spelling of "Webb" that recalls Cornelius Webb, the poet credited by Z for the verse featured in the "Cockney School" epigraphs pointed at Keats.

From his double-sexed spider figure of diligent work and play, Keats moves into double-gendered figures of delicious, if not exactly diligent, indolence, where the sex-roles are in doubt:

> It has been an old Comparison for our urging on—the Bee hive—however it seems to me that we should rather be the flower than the Bee—for it is a false notion that more is gained by receiving than giving—no the receiver and the giver are equal in their benefits—The f[l]ower I doubt not receives a fair guerdon from the Bee—its leaves blush deeper in the next spring—and who shall say between Man and Woman which is the most delighted? (232)

This question in another old comparison. Blake played with it in a notebook:

> What is it men in women do require
> The lineaments of Gratified Desire
> What is it women do in men require
> The lineaments of Gratified Desire

If Blake's politics of sexual liberty are strained by visionary schemes of masculine power,[46] in this quatrain at least, he plays equally. "Here are two supposedly antithetical questions, perhaps flung at each other by a more subtle Zeus and Hera," remarks John Hollander; "Yet they have the same answer" (50) and are pegged to questions in the same measure.

Keats comes at the question not only by perplexing giving and receiving (Blake fudges with the ambiguously active/passive *require*), but also by complicating the gendered lore of passivity and activity. The syntactic alignment of the question that brings "Man and Woman" into his equation challenges the "old Comparison": resisting the chiasmus that aligns Man with the active, giving Bee, Keats sketches a parallel in which Man mirrors flower, and in this passive delight radiates supermanly self-possession:

> Now it is more noble to sit like Jove tha[n] to fly like Mercury—let us not therefore go hurrying about and collecting honey-bee like, buzzing here and there impatiently from a knowledge of what is to be arrived at: but let us open our leaves like a flower and be passive and receptive—budding patiently under the eye of Apollo and taking hints from eve[r]y noble insect that favors us with a visit. (232)

Nobly, divinely "passive and receptive," even in the "female" position of being gazed upon by Apollo (who himself is imaged as maternally doting), male passivity is floral and Jovian at once. We can see why Margaret Homans would argue that Keats thus appropriates the "passive female position" for "masculine power and pleasure."[47] Yet Keats's identification is ultimately not with this Jovian power. It is with a suspect indolence whose only remedy may be this Mercurial boy-buzziness: "Now I am sensible all this is a mere sophistication, however it may neighbour to any truths, to excuse my own indolence—so I will not deceive myself that Man should be equal with jove—but think himself very well off as a sort of scullion-Mercury or even a humble Bee—"(233).[48]

In early 1818 the she-spider's spinning is beautiful work, but in the more bitter mood about business that was Keats's in late summer 1819, the spider and indolence are both demeaned, and the gendering gets nasty. Resolving to remedy a life he thinks is becoming viciously "idle minded"—"I have not known yet what it is to be diligent," he tells Brown—he determines to write "for whoever will pay me" (*L* 2: 176). The same day, 22 September, he writes to Charles Dilke:

> Even if I am swept away like a Spider from a drawing room I am determined to spin—home spun anything for sale. Yea I will traffic. Any thing but Mortgage my Brain to Blackwood. [. . .] It is fortunate I have not before this been tempted to venture on the common. [. . .] [I] am confident I shall be able to cheat as well as any literary Jew of the Market and shine up an article on any thing. (*L* 2: 179)

This spider is now confederate with marginalized, despised workers: woman as whore, trafficker and commoner, a fancy cheat who earns a dose of anti-Semitism. Its world is not empyrean, but a repetition in a darker tone of the more often quoted remark in this trope, from March 1818, in which Keats, in a "very sceptical" temper, describes "Poetry itself" as a commodity with no use value: "As Tradesmen say every thing is worth what it will fetch [. . .] being in itself nothing" (*L* 1: 242–43). This proto-Marxist trope is still cast for imaginative desire, here called a creatively "ardent pursuit." By late 1819, the ardor has become a cynical shining of whatever one can spin for market desire, and at the cost of self-authorizing masculine independence. The prostitute and the Jew spell this degradation, and if these figures do nothing for Keats's hopes, the sordid boon at least is to ally him with a Byronic contempt of "prostituted muse and hireling bard" (*English Bards* 182).

Between these extremes, a spring 1819 ode "On Indolence" and some comments on its inspiration by a "temper indolent and supremely careless" reveal more flexible gender play. In a letter of 19 March 1819 (*L* 2: 78–79), Keats describes his indolence as a "state of effeminacy," but not carelessly. It's a morning-after story, of nursing a black eye from a cricket game with the guys the day before, and he camps up the gender codes of this hangover with melodramatic scenery:

> My passions are all alseep from my having slumbered till nearly eleven and weakened the animal fibre all over me to a delightful sensation about three degrees this side of faintness—if I had teeth of pearl and the breath of lillies I should call it langour—but as I am† I must call it Laziness.
>
> †especially as I have a black eye

Keats's footnote may be a reflex of male defensiveness (so Homans reads it); but if so, its sign of potency is not dominant, either in this scene or in the ode. Is "all alseep" a punning slip of a pen bereft of passion? Keats goes on to describe a happy relaxation of his usual toiling and spinning about "Poetry," "Ambition," and "Love"—an array he genders as "a Man and two women" (in order? Keats says "no one but myself could distinguish in their disguisement").

The ode itself is only half-indolent, however, vexed by that "difference between an easy and uneasy indolence" Keats had posed to George and Georgiana the day before the game (17 March; *L* 2: 77). While the odist speaks in urbane disdain of "the voice of busy common-sense" (40), the bee-buzzing of the mind in its diligent working of poetic form hasn't forgotten those "three figures" of habitual desire. They don't die into effeminate indolence, as in the letter, but face the poet in challenge, and with new gendering:[49]

> to follow them I burn'd
> And ached for wings because I knew the three:
> The first was a fair maid, and Love her name;
> The second was Ambition, pale of cheek,
> And ever watchful with fatigued eye;
> The last, whom I love more, the more of blame
> Is heaped upon her, maiden most unmeek,—
> I knew to be my demon Poesy. (23–30)

In the letter-scene of 19 March, "Poetry" had no pull; but here "my demon Poesy" simmers, the siren of everything Z despised as vulgar sensuality. The answer to effeminate indolence is no masculine imperative but a "Maiden most unmeek." The rapt sonneteer of 1817 wants woman "meek, and kind, and tender" ("Woman!" 3, 10). The poet of 1819 says, in effect, this muse of unmeekness I acknowledge my own.[50] And what of that admitted binary of Indolence, Ambition? Brown's busy writing "affronts my indolence and Luxury," Keats sighed the previous summer (*L* 1: 344); but now Ambition is enervated, a pale visionary, like the Knight-at-arms in *La Belle Dame*. While in the next turn of the urn and its ode, all three subjects fade from desire, it is Ambition that seems more actively banished. Love is left a folly or a mystery, Poesy holds no joy, but Ambition is ridiculed: "poor Ambition—it springs / From a man's little heart's short fever-fit" (33–34).

Now all this belittling may be mere sophistication. "I am more frequently now, contented to read and think—but now & then, haunted with ambitious thoughts," Keats writes to his brother and sister-in-law in September 1819 (*L* 2: 209). Telling a female friend in June 1819, "the thing I have most enjoyed this year has been writing an ode to Indolence," he confesses both a healthy disenchantment and a damning defeat: "I have been very idle lately, very averse to writing; both from the overpowering idea of our dead poets and from abatement of my love of fame." Within a sentence, he is punning *averse* into self-ridicule, "a versifying Pet-lamb" (*L* 2: 116). The rare value of indolence is that decided "advantage in the body overpowering the Mind" (*L* 2: 79), especially its store of other men's (other women's) achievements.[51] Indolent Keats can ironize the master desire that joins Poesy, Ambition, and Love: "love of fame."

That letter on "diligent Indolence" (*L* 1: 231–33) is woven into this romance of disengagement, with deceptively casual references to Milton's famously ambivalent meditation on "Fame" in *Lycidas:*

> Fame is the spur that the clear spirit doth raise
> (That last infirmity of Noble mind)
> To scorn delights, and live laborious days. (70–72)

Deceptively casual, because Milton's text is an intensity of Keatsian ambivalences. Milton's lament that "the fair Guerdon we hope to find" is thwarted by she-fate, a scissors-wielding "blind Fury" who cuts life short (73–76), is a gender-trope of antagonism that Keats could endorse. He cast Mary Shelley into the instrumental role: "Tell her to procure some fatal Scissars and cut the th[r]ead of Life of all to be disappointed Poets," he joked to Hunt, just weeks after the debut of the 1817 *Poems* (*L* 1: 140). Milton takes comfort in a redemption by male deities: the assurance of the god of poets himself, Phoebus (a Keatsian devotion, too), that immortal fame will be pronounced by the "perfect witness of all-judging Jove" (82). Yet the parenthesis of line 72 (That last infirmity . . .), interrupting what might otherwise be a manly motto to live by, is a rueful check; and the oscillation imprints Keats's defense of indolence. Using Milton's phrases, Keats affects a refusal of fame-devoted labor. A flower doesn't hope; it just "receives a fair guerdon from the Bee" and blushes deeper the next spring for it, the syntax unlinking "fair guerdon" from labor for fame, attaching it to pleasure, then apposing it to a serenely sitting Jove (*L* 1: 232), who is not all-judging, just soaked in "noble" delight. At the same time, however, these echoes are so consciously revisionary that they vibrate as the reaction formation of a lingering romance, an infirmity of mind not entirely cured.

Leaving medicine for poetry, Keats courted fame with the best of them. In *Poems* he cheered Hunt's "fame" and "the great man's fame" (Sonnets III and XIII), and exclaimed to Hunt while he labored on *Endymion*, "What a thing to be in the Mouth of Fame!" (*L* 1: 139). In a draft of its Preface he admits "a love of fame"; and he didn't mind all the prophesies and appreciations his friends and well-wishers voiced for his debut volume.[52] Yet the final event of the *fame* in *Poems* is a punctuation of irony. Its scene is that summary survey of Hunt's library:

> Round about were hung
> The glorious features of the bards who sung

> In other ages—cold and sacred busts
> Smiled at each other. Happy he who trusts
> To clear Futurity his darling fame! (*Sleep and Poetry* 355–59)

The elder bards have achieved both fame and triviality: nameless, their laurels fade to Regency decor, their singing into a dead, self-enclosed audience for one another. The sarcasm is of a piece with Byron's assessment in *Don Juan* two years later (1819): "fame" is but "To have, when the original is dust, / A name, a wretched picture, and worse bust" (1.218). Richard Abbey (guardian of the Keats estate) liked to needle Keats with this satire (*L* 2: 192), but it was redundant: "O smile among the shades, for this is fame!" was the toast Keats offered on a visit to Burns's cottage in the intervening summer of 1818 ("This mortal body"), aware of the vulgar fame this Scotch bard was never so lucky to enjoy in his lifetime. The irony is both sadly enchanted and disenchanted: fame is the unknowable future, or if won now, then more surreal rather than real.

The great man's fame, Keats was coming to guess, is a compound whose instability is not just the idea of "fame," but the idea of a "great man," a gender-figure that turns out to be most legible in parody and travesty. When Reynolds defended *Endymion* after the *Quarterly*'s savaging, he took the occasion to sift fame from popularity, feminizing the latter:

> There is not one poet of the present day, that enjoys any popularity that will live; each writes for his booksellers and the ladies of fashion, and not for the voice of centuries. Time is a lover of old books, and he suffers few new ones to become old. Posterity is a difficult mark to hit, and few minds can send the arrow full home. [. . .] The journey of fame is an endless one; and does Mr Rogers think that pumps and silk stockings (which his genius wears) will last him the whole way? Poetry is the coyest creature that ever was wooed by man: she has something of the coquette in her; for she flirts with many, and seldom loves one. (*Examiner*, 12 Oct. 1818, 648–49)

Evoking Keats's casting of poesy as a "coy muse" (*To George Felton Mathew*), Reynolds sets masculine "Time" as the true lover, won by masculine endeavor: skilled archery, epic journeying. Poets of fashion (Rogers) degrade themselves with feminizing dress for success, all the more pathetic in suit of a heartless she-flirt. Rogers was acidly unmanned in the same year by Hazlitt, who cut this "very lady-like poet" on the pattern of Z's Hunt: his "glittering cover of fine words" is a "tottering, wriggling, fidgetty translation of every thing from the vulgar tongue, into all the tantalizing, teasing, tripping, lisping *mimminee-pimminee* of the highest brilliancy and fashion of poetical diction" (*Living Poets* 293). To woo the coquette, he has become one.

Yet for all this public security against popular failure, Keats's private accounts remain unsettled. In the fashion of a "a Poet," he said to Haydon in December 1818, "I feel in myself all the vices of a Poet, irritability, love of effect and admiration" and a tendency, when "influenced by such devils," to "say more rediculous things than I am aware of" (*L* 1: 414). Also "rediculous" was the "Man in love" (2: 187). In August 1819, when love was not just a trope or a spectacle, but a passion felt in the self for the girl next door, Keats wrote to his publisher, seeking another advance on the prospect of success in the literary world that, he frankly admits, he looks upon "with hate and contempt." The ready synonym for this hateful siege of contraries is "the love of a woman." If he chose (Keats assures Taylor), he could be "a popular writer"; but he will refuse the bid in order to nurture "finer things": "I equally dislike the favour of the public with the love of a woman—they are both a cloying treacle to the wings of independence" (2: 144). The rhetoric is tortured between self-respect and self-subjection, and a knowing exactness about the term of comparison. "Ask yourself my love whether you are not very cruel to have so entrammelled me, so destroyed my freedom," he protested to Fanny Brawne in July, blaming her (2: 123). Back in April, he had put the question to himself, in a self-discipline that was set, in the voice of poet, against the love of a public and the love of a woman. The exercise was two sonnets "on Fame," written at about the time of *Ode on Indolence*—not for publication, just self-sobering (2: 104–5).

Both put Fame into a degraded courtship. "I know not why Poetry and I have been so distant lately I must make some advances soon or she will cut me entirely," Keats jokes in the same journal-letter in which he copied out these sonnets (13 March 1819; *L* 2: 74). To "cut" is to refuse notice, an action particularly associated, in the wake of Lord Byron's ostracizing after his separation from Lady Byron in 1816, with the power of women as arbiters of social life and death.[53] Keats's preemptive poetic strike is to cut Poetry. The sonnets address a fraternity of suitors of worldly fame, urging a divorce from the what is only, in Milton's words, "glistering foil / Set off to th' world" (79–80). Beginning "How fever'd is that ~~Man misled~~," *On Fame* diagnoses by measures of gender: in the ardent pursuit of fame, a man corrupts his integrity, robbing "his fair name of its maidenhood" in the gambits of commodity. It is a feminizing self-spoiling, "as if the rose should pluck herself / Or the ripe plumb finger its misty bloom." Keats knowingly tunes these images to his recent resentment of being reviewed, reading his love of fame into witless complicity with reviewer-molesting: setting oneself to be "fingerable over by Men," he said to Haydon, 22 December 1818 (*L* 1: 415), remembering Woodhouse's rage, two months earlier, about the *Quarterly*'s reviewer having "laid his finger of contempt" on the "beauty" of

Endymion (*L* 1: 379). This humiliating submission of self to market recalls even the awkward petitions for credit with publishers. "I must endeavour to lose my Maidenhead with respect to money Matters," he wrote to Taylor and Hessey in June 1817, gender-cartooning the self-sale: "I am a little maidenish or so—and I feel my virginity come strong upon me—the while I request the loan" (*L* 1: 147–48). A month before, in the same suit, he could at least manage a mock-epic of manly exploit: "I am extremely indebted to you for your liberality in the Shape of manufactued rag value £20 and shall immediately proceed to destroy some of the Minor Heads of that spring-headed Hydra the Dun" (1: 145).

Having to seek, accept, and not disappoint the faith of a loan, Keats is exquisitely sensitive to the gender allegory, the close proximity to hireling bard and prostituted muse. In a second sonnet of April 1819, *Another on Fame*, he distributes this self-commodifying into a heterosexed scenario, with the degraded object cast as a female-gendered fame-fetish that self-respecting men might well disdain. The call of Fame is reduced to the flirtation of a tarty girl—by turns "coy," doting, teasing, jilting, maddening, responsive, but in sum not worth any man's suits of woe (*L* 2: 105). Female changeability is no camelionism, just promiscuity, an incapability of character in a world of commodity. "Reviews have enervated and made indolent mens minds—few think for themselves," Keats complained in February (2: 65). In a pose of jaded sophistication, his sonneteer plays out a self-possessed counter-courtship.[54] Keats weans himself with the further reminder that the fair guerdon, even if won, might yield nothing more than fame as a "versifying Pet-lamb" (2: 116). Was he remembering that pretty creature for a little maid's doting in Wordsworth's *The Pet-Lamb* (a poem he ridiculed to George and Georgiana the same month)? The poet of *Ode on Indolence* casts this pet as the end of any fame-seeking: "I would not be dieted with praise, / A pet-lamb in a sentimental farce" (53–54). Yet this lamb, as Keats knew, was twin in impotence to that "milk-white lamb that bleats / For man's protection" in "Woman!"—with a contagion for the man who might imagine the relation of the sexes in this cartoon.[55]

Keats's spring 1819 rejections are accompanied by no retrenchment of masculine self-identification, however, nor even the promise of better, more manly work that he voiced the year before in the self-lacerating Preface to *Endymion*, a failure chastened by "the Memory of great Men" and a disdain of "Mawkish Popularity" (9 April 1818; *L* 1: 266–67). Hazlitt opened his lecture on the living poets with a bracing dismissal of "the idle buzz of fashion, the venal puff" of "popularity" from genuine fame, which he described in man's terms: "the very spirit of a man surviving himself in the minds and thoughts of other men" (283). Keats endorsed this integrity, but not without lingering division.

In February 1820, in desperately ill health, he tells Fanny Brawne of an old dialogue of the mind with itself:

> "If I should die," said I to myself, "I have left no immortal work behind me—nothing to make my friends proud of my memory." [. . .] Thoughts like these came very feebly whilst I was in health and every pulse beat for you—now you divide with this (may I say it?) "last infirmity of noble minds" all my reflection. (*L* 2: 263)

In this now rueful allusion to Milton's anthem, Keats both recognizes the romance of immortal work as a last infirmity of manhood, and feels it as the lifepulse of young ambition. And more: it is the romance that may redeem a heart desperately in love. For Keats, loving a woman is never more than a heartbeat from courting fame, not as a division, but as a synonym.

Writing to Brown, always the adept lover, in August 1820, about his latest bid, the *Lamia* volume, Keats laments that its sale, like that of his previous efforts, has been "very slow, though it has been highly rated," and he had heard of probable cause: "the offence the ladies take at me." He wanted to sift this report and claim independence: "On thinking that matter over, I am certain that I have said nothing in a spirit to displease any woman I would care to please" (*L* 2: 327–28). The reciprocal is not to care to please, to maintain manly freedom from whatever ladies may think, require, or requite. What of actual women, especially ones who might care to please Keats? Here's a conversation that might have surprised and disturbed him:

> Don't suppose I ever open my lips about books before men at all clever and stupid men I treat too ill to talk to at all. Women generally talk of very different things—Don't you or do you admire Don Juan? perhaps you like the serious parts best but I having been credibly informed that Lord B. is not <u>really</u> a great poet, have taken a sort of dislike to him when serious and only adore him for his wit and humour. (Edgcumbe 39)

This woman who won't open her lips about books among men chats away to her female friend, confessing that—*pace* credible (probably male) authority—she rather likes a poem Keats despised, *Don Juan*. "[M]y dear Keats did not admire Lord Byrons poetry," Fanny Brawne more directly reports in a later letter to her correspondent, Fanny Keats (Edgcumbe 63). Byron is a constant shadow in the configuring of Keats, for better or worse, as a "feminine" poet; and female readers played an important part in the gender-shift.

CHAPTER EIGHT

Gendering Keats: "The Character Undecided, the Way of Life Uncertain"

> the old ideal of Manhood has grown obsolete, and the new is still invisible to us, and we grope after it in darkness, one clutching this phantom, another that; Werterism, Byronism, even Brummelism, each has its day.
>
> —[THOMAS CARLYLE], "CHARACTERISTICS,"
> 'EDINBURGH REVIEW' DECEMBER 1831

> It has been said that his poetry was affected and effeminate. I can only say that I never encountered a more manly and simple young man.
>
> —BARRY CORNWALL ON KEATS 1877

Radiating from Keats's own alternately passionate and satirical, always ambivalent course through gender forms, readings of Keats come bearing the question of gendering him and his kind of imagination. Everyone who knew or wrote about him confronted a perplexity, in his poetry, in his physical presence, and in the disturbing effects of both. That he did not fit the figure of culturally empowered manhood—in literary style and sensibility, in body and face, in class origin, and in the sentimental legend of his death—magnetized "Keats" for larger concerns about gender and poetry: was he *puerile? boyish? unmanly? effeminate? feminine? manly? virile? androgynous?* Channeling anxieties about

243

men feminized by sensibility and sensuousness, by aestheticism and romance, by passion and poetry, these questions bear on the "inner Keats" in men edgy about, even outwardly obliged to reject, what Keats and Keatsian aesthetics stirred up, called forth. Charges of effeminacy, defenses of his manliness, affection for "feminine" qualities, briefs for liberal gender values, speculations on mental androgyny: these were not only Keats-causes or even symptoms of general culture wars; they were also private concerns that needed a Keats to front them—or found in Keats a legible, and often unsettling syntax.[1] Not just a poet, Keats was also a language.

A symptom of the effect was the sweat to distinguish "feminine" from the deformations of "effeminacy." Back in the 1760s Revd. James Fordyce, wishing for female culture to improve crude male behavior by "a sort of assimilating power," hastened to clarify: "I do not mean, that men [. . .] will become feminine," only "that their sentiments and deportment will contract a grace" (*Sermons* 1: 23). This contract halts at any "effeminate" production: the man who, "destitute of every manly sentiment, copies with inverted ambition from the sex," turning himself into "an object of contempt and aversion"—no less "monstrous" than the "masculine woman" (1: 104–5). In 1835, the author of *Woman: As She Is and As She Should Be* was still monitoring "effeminacy" in men under female influence, especially in the new fashion of "supine and excessive softness of manners" (20, 28). Hence (around the same time) Coleridge's desynonymizing: some kind of "feminine—not *effeminate*, mind—is discoverable in the countenances of all men of genius."[2]

Shelley could weather such a discovery, and Byron, by force of Byronism, could even risk extravagances of effeminacy. An *effeminate* Shelley, however, was inadmissible: if "the mind of Shelley was essentially feminine, some would say fastidious in its delicacy" (tendered an essay in an 1847 *New Monthly*), his behavior was "the least effeminate of men, so far as personal and moral courage were concerned" (289). Whatever Shelley was, however eccentric and delicate, whatever Byron was, however dandy or ungentlemanly, whatever his Sardanapalus paraded and masqueraded, "not effeminate" was the verdict. Not so for Keats, whose readers charged him with effeminacy from a manifold of overdeterminations—not the least because many found it a necessary defense against sympathy, even a secret identification, with the signs. The gender-language roiling the culture in which Keats wrote, published, and was reviewed, stayed with "Keats" for a century after his death, and would play again, more favorably but no more securely, in twentieth-century gender criticism. Registering pressures at the borderlines, "Keats" emerges as a concentrated sign for the border itself.

COCKNEY (OED)

noun: *"A child that sucketh long"; a mother's darling; pet, minion; "a child tenderly brought up"; hence a squeamish or effeminate fellow* . . .

A derisive appellation for a townsman, as the type of effeminacy in contrast to the hardier inhabitants of the country.

One born in the city of London, strictly one born within the sound of Bow Bells; used to connote the characteristics in which the born Londoner is supposed to be inferior to other Englishmen.

One of the "Cockney School"; a nickname for a set of 19th cent. writers belonging to London, of whom Leigh Hunt was taken as the representative.

adjective: *effeminate, . . . Pertaining to or characteristic of the London Cockney.*

Even as the article on Keats at the end of the century in *Encyclopædia Britannica* (by Alexander Smith) conceded that "political animosities" had inflamed Keats's Regency reception, the uninflected report that "the whole 'Cockney School'" was a hothouse of "effeminacy and puerile sentimentalism" (56) confirmed a gender lexicon. First, then indelibly, attacks on Keats tracked a field of Cockney practices linked to gender detractions: district frippery, pretentious aspiration, and flaunted suburban counter-culture that real men of letters could disdain. Where Brown's *Estimate* of 1757 eyed effeminacy as a scandal in the "higher Ranks," the higher ranks of the Regency, mindful that an effeminate *ancien régime* had been cited for the French fall, deflected the charge to class pretenders. From its inaugural moment, the Cockney School was a no-man's land. Tagging Keats an ephebe of the "Cockney School of Politics, as well as the Cockney School of Poetry," Z showed his own school spirit with hooting ridicules of effeminacy, puerility, vulgarity, and the bantling eagerness "to lisp sedition." He set the stage for Keats with other farcical insurgents, female and class pretenders to the letters: "farm-servants and unmarried ladies" now fancy themselves poets; "our very foot-men compose tragedies, and there is scarcely a superannuated governess in the island that does not leave a roll of lyrics behind her in her band-box." Keats joins the farce with a "prurient and vulgar" imagination, insulting class and gender gentility with a purloined aristocratic license for erotic play. If Keats's aesthetics signified class aspiration and anti-establishment insurgency, the remedy was to emasculate the poet.[3]

With relentlessly condescending nomenclature, Z strips Keats of all manly claims and patrilineage. The parody of praise in the reiterated epithet, "The

Muses' son of promise," echoed in the diminutives of "boy," "Mr John," "good Johnny Keats." The little name stuck, not only in *Blackwood's* but well beyond, and across the century, with an implicit nod to Z's cartoon.[4] In the immediate wake, Byron termed the "under School" affectations and corruptions "shabby genteel," and amplified the sexual slurs.[5] His letters to Murray (part owner of *Blackwood's*) tacitly assume Z's contempt, to sniff at a Keats "spoilt by Cockneyfying and Surburbing," prone for puerilizing put-downs: "Johnny Keats's piss-a-bed poetry"; the "drivelling idiotism" of a "Mankin"; the "Onanism of Poetry"; and in his literary styling, "a tadpole of the lakes." Byron tweaked "Johnny" into a pattern for all "the English Johnnies who had never been out of a Cockney workshop before."[6] Insults also derided the patronym.[7] Byron hissed to Murray his disgust at the *Edinburgh*'s "praises of that little dirty blackguard KEATES" (now the name of camp-follower and street-boy)—a sequel to Z's summary advice in 1818 to this "young Sangrado" to go back to the apothecary shop, another site of dubious reputation.[8] *Blackwood's* meanwhile boasted of its patent on *Cockney* as a byword for sexual immaturity, effeminacy, social inferiority, and lisping sedition. "The nickname we gave," crowed its Preface of 1826, "has become a regularly established word in our literature"; "Lord Byron, while patronizing the sect, called them by no other title than the Cockneys" (19: xvi).[9] On Z's initiative, *Blackwood's* hosted running jokes on Cockney rhymes, any absurd couplet credited to Keats.

Irritated by class clubbing, Hazlitt protested, using Keats to front his own polemics. Any aspiring author, he snipped in *London Magazine* (June 1820), had best be "a noble-man, or rich plebeian, [. . .] it is name, it is wealth, it is title and influence"; "This is the reason why a certain Magazine praises Percy Bysshe Shelley, and vilifies 'Johnny Keats.'"[10] Z retorted that it was "audacious insolence to say, that we praise Mr Shelley, although we dislike his principles," because he is protected by wealth, "and, *vice versa*, abuse Hunt, Keats, and Hazlitt, and so forth, because we know that they are poor men" (Sept. 1820; *Blackwood's* 7: 686). Hazlitt didn't buy it, and pressed the issue again in *London Weekly Review* 1828, this time including Byron (whose aristocratic airs never endeared him): "Pray did it never strike you that Lord Byron himself was a *cockney-writer*, if descending from the conventional to the vernacular is to be so?" (*Don Juan*, to which *Blackwood's* had warmed, was nothing if not vernacular.) Hazlitt hit the other end of the discursive span, too: "Can you tell me if the phrase 'grandeur of the glooms' [. . .] is Keats's or Byron's: if it belong to the one, you will allow it is damnable, if to the other, highly commendable?"[11]

Oddly, it was Hazlitt's project of buffing up the man of letters that gave an imprimatur to "effeminate" Keats—a judgment that could not be set aside as

Blackwood's tarring of a Cockney. Keats is the summary example in that essay "On Effeminacy of Character" (1822): "I cannot help thinking that the fault of Mr. Keats's poems was a deficiency in masculine energy of style." And for Hazlitt, style is character: "Effeminacy of character arises from a prevalence of the sensibility over the will," his essay opens, then elaborates: "every sensation must be wound up to the highest pitch of voluptuous refinement, every motion must be grace and elegance." The excess is decadent. Because "the whole of their existence, every moment of it, must be made up of these exquisite indulgences," these voluptuaries "live in a luxurious, endless dream, or 'Die of a rose in aromatic pain!'"[12] Everything reeks of an "effeminacy of style" that is "all florid, all fine," a poetic junk-food that "cloys by its sweetness, and tires by its sameness." The posterboy of this deadly satiety is "Keats"—too ready to "die a death/Of luxury" (*Sleep and Poetry* 58–59). That Hazlitt doesn't call it "Cockney" hardly matters. Keats, like a lovely ingénue, "had beauty, tenderness, delicacy, in an uncommon degree, but there was a want of strength and substance," a "want of action, of character"; "youth, without the manhood of poetry," "soft and fleshly, without bone or muscle," "none of the hardy spirit or rigid forms of antiquity." All lax and lacks, this uncommon degree is no avant garde, but a caution to an era when the manliness of poetic vocation had to be argued against a bevy of poetesses. In his own feminine-pitched genre, *Elegant Extracts from Chaucer to the Present Time* (1824), Hazlitt writes the prefaces to extract the man. Chaucer has "strong manly sense"; Denham's "forte is strong, sound sense" and "unaffected manly verse"; Cowper shows "fine manly sense" (*W* 9: 236, 238, 242,). Only Keats is without "manly strength and fortitude" (244–45).

Against contemporaries, Keats fared no better. It was Byron's haremized, but never really depotentiated Don Juan at which *Blackwood's* bragging Preface of 1826 winked to cartoon Keatsian wants as abjection: "he outhunted Hunt in a species of emasculated pruriency, that, although invented in Little Britain, looks as if it were the product of some imaginative Eunuch's muse within the melancholy inspiration of the Haram" (19: xxvi). Desiring without potency, Keats is only pathetic. Other innuendoes hiss deviancy. Z hints that Hunt's narcissism, immorality, and dubious sexuality (the indictment of Z's previous papers) fastened on Keats as a mirror for "the holy contemplation of [his] own divine perfections, and there 'perk up with timid mouth' 'and lamping eyes,' (so you have it) upon what to you is dearer and more glorious than all created things besides."[13] Behind this mirror beckons the boy-darling of Cockney School degeneracy. Such "socio-sexual revulsion" (Matthews's phrase, *KCH* 35) also simmers in Byron's naming of "blackguard" boy hustlers as "Keatses." To call Keats "boy" could even evoke the female impersonators of the English Renaissance stage, "boy" there (and thence) code for a homoerotic confection—as Wilde's *The Portrait of Mr. W. H.* makes clear.[14]

The class thrust of the put-downs comes into clearer view in the way gender, even in extravagant forms, plays out for Byron and Shelley. If Byron was luxurious, even Hazlitt wouldn't call him effeminate. Carlyle saw him "faithfully and manfully struggling, to the end," the epitome of "spiritual manhood" ("Goethe" 243). To Arthur Symons, Byron's imagination was defined by its "manly quality": "Never, in English verse, has a man been seen who was so much a man and so much an Englishman. It is not man in the elemental sense, so much as the man of the world" (*Romantic Movement* 249, 255). When Byron gets called "unmanly," it is class-coded: "un-gentlemanly," indecent, but not effeminate. If the case of Shelley was less a lock, it still was not as open (and shut) as Keats. The Cockney School "opinions" in *The Revolt of Islam* might have courted a gender slur, but Lockhart (Z) exempted Shelley by "the privileges" of innate "genius" (*Blackwood's* 4: 475–76). It is puerile Keats whom he trots out to caution a still salvageable Shelley: "whatever his errors may have been," Shelley "is a scholar, a gentleman, and a poet; and he must therefore despise from his soul the only eulogies to which he has hitherto been accustomed—paragraphs from the Examiner, and sonnets from Johnny Keats. He has the power to select better companions" (482). Lockhart does it for him.

Charles Kingsley's derision of Shelley as odiously "girlish," weakly "feminine" and "utterly womanish" (*Fraser's* 48: 572) might seem to twin Z's Keats, but the aim was otherwise, trained on the Shelley of infidel potency, whose political passions demanded containment. And while Shelley's dangers were readable as or translatable into gender degeneracy (Eric Clarke argues), there was always a positive track alongside, assimilating feminine/effeminate effects into a charming, refined androgyny—a trope that came much later for Keats, and then (as we'll see) with more psychological than public capital, and in a transparently defensive discourse.

A careful spin on Shelley's feminine figure weaves the text of Trelawny's famous recollection, in 1858, of his first acquaintance with the poet:

> Swiftly gliding in, blushing like a girl, a tall thin stripling [. . .] I could hardly believe as I looked at his flushed, feminine, and artless face that it could be the Poet. [. . .] was it possible this mild-looking, beardless boy, could be the veritable monster at war with all the world?—excommunicated by the Fathers of the Church, deprived of civil rights by the fiat of a grim Lord Chancellor,

discarded by every member of his family, and denounced by the rival sages of our literature as the founder of a Satanic school? (26–27)[15]

This "feminine" poet is calculated to temper the Tory-pressed "Shelley": that anti-patriarchal infidel and political rebel. Keats never cut such a figure.

Other configurations of Shelley keep feminine to a juvenile phase, a "girlishness" from a boyhood in retirement with sisters, said Thomas Medwin (*Memoir* [1832] 472), echoed by Edward Dowden (5–6), and W. M. Rossetti: "girlish Shelley" disdained "boyish sports from shyness and delicacy" (*Memoir* xxxvi). Girly Shelley, moreover, could be transvalued into moral refinement, "a pure and virgin mind" shocked by schoolboy coarseness (Medwin 472), or tuned politically, rising in "unquenched indignation against the outrages of the fagging system" (Rossetti, xxxvi). Blending delicacy and outrage, W. R. Greg conveys feminine Shelley into just this leonine heroism:

> Poor Shelley—gentle, tender, ethereal [. . .] delicate as a woman in his organization, sensitive as a woman in his sympathies, loathing all that was low with a woman's shrinking, detesting all field-sports as barbarous and brutal. [. . .] His blood boiled fiercely as that of the strongest at the bare idea of injustice and oppression, and [. . .] in such a cause he was as brave as a lion, and would take any odds. (131–32)[16]

Gentle man Shelley also had cover, like Byron, as a gentleman and a ladies' man. Oxfordian Shelley, "growing towards a man's estate, was strong, active, and tall," Rossetti put it; if the figure was "slight" and "his features small, and in some sort feminine," the estate is clear: "He was a finished gentleman, and as Mr. Hogg emphatically puts it, 'a ladies' man'—the elect of dames and damsels. And certainly Shelley repaid the preference without stint" (*Memoir* xliii).[17]

It was in Keatsy faults, and links to Keats, that Shelley seemed effeminate.[18] Kingsley blames both for the rise of unmanliness, and fall from "the nobler and healthier manhood" and "manful possession" of earlier poets (*Fraser's* 48: 453, 456). Coventry Patmore's *What Shelley Was* mirrored his *Keats:* a "beautiful, effeminate, arrogant boy," then a man "almost wholly devoid of the instincts of the 'political animal,' which Aristotle defines a man to be" (70–71). If he could grant an aesthetic license to this effeminacy, other critics cited Shelley's elegy for Keats, *Adonais*, as low point, its "unmanly wailing," said *Cornhill*, an indictment of both; the "contempt" of Byron for Keats's fabled collapse from bad reviews was "more to the purpose" (34: 558). Even Rossetti conceded that Shelley's wailing had brought him "dangerously near the confines of feminine sensibility, rather than virile fortitude" (*Adonais* 126).

"Poor Keats"

Without question, *Adonais* was the single most decisive nineteenth-century document in the lore of Keats's unmanliness. The gender cut of its argument wasn't invented out of whole cloth, however. The pattern was inadvertently set by Keats's lifetime defenders. Writing for the *Alfred* in October 1818, Keats's friend Reynolds assailed the *Quarterly*'s abuse of Keats as "lower than man would dare to utter to female ears"; honorable criticism, he scolded, ought to "chuse its objects from the vain, the dangerous, and the powerful, and not from the young and the unprotected" (118). Linking Keats to kinder, gentler female culture, Reynolds wrote him, in effect, into a Burkean scandal of ungallant male ravishers. It didn't help that Hunt (liking the lunge at the *Quarterly*) reran the article in the next *Examiner*, giving wider circulation to this vulnerable, implicitly feminine Keats. That Reynolds had also hailed Keats as a "young and powerful" poet, pulsing with "solitary vigour" and "sinewy" thought (118, 121–22), scarcely registered in the developing story. *New Monthly* did its part by comparing the *Quarterly*'s "laborious attempt to torture and ruin Mr. Keats" to its attack on Lady Morgan, "one of the coarsest insults ever offered in print by man to woman" (14: 306).[19]

Mindful of these stories and hot to avenge his own insults from the *Quarterly*, Shelley used his preface to *Adonais* to cast Keats as fragile flower and bullied boy:

> The genius of [Keats] was not less delicate and fragile than it was beautiful; and, where canker-worms abound, what wonder if its young flower was blighted in the bud? The savage criticism on his *Endymion* which appeared in the *Quarterly Review* produced the most violent effect on his susceptible mind. The agitation thus originated ended in the rupture of a blood-vessel in the lungs; a rapid consumption ensued. [. . .] the poor fellow seems to have been hooted from the stage of life.

To this prefatory indictment of boy-abuse, the poem itself adds the delinquency of Urania, Milton's muse:

> . . . thy youngest, dearest one has perished,
> The nursling of thy widowhood, who grew,
> Like a pale flower by some sad maiden cherished,
> And fed with true love tears instead of dew.
>
> . . .

> The bloom, whose petals, nipt before they blew,
> Died on the promise of the fruit, is waste;
> The broken lily lies . . . (VI)

She-nurtured, broken flower-Keats is a poor boy, the Muse's neglected son of promise: "Where wert thou mighty Mother, when he lay, / When thy Son lay, pierced by the shaft which flies / In darkness?" (II). Shelley gives Keats a redemption by, and in, a better mother, Nature:

> He is made one with Nature. There is heard
> His voice in all her music, from the moan
> Of thunder to the song of night's sweet bird . . . (XLII)

In this double-sexed music, Keats's thunder seems as feminine as Philomel's music. Charles Brown placed XLII and XLIII ("He is a portion of the loveliness / Which once he made more lovely . . . ") as the epigraph for his *Life of John Keats*; then H. B. Forman set the lines from Stanza II on the title-page verso of Keats's letters to Fanny Brawne, to suggest a death wrought no less by love-longing than by reviewer-shafting. By mid-century, it was no astonishment for *Chambers' Cyclopedia* to open its article on Keats with the story of fatal reviews.[20]

Hazlitt, too, found it convenient to unman Keats to settle his own scores with the press. In his tirade against Gifford's attack, reporting that "Mr. Keats died when he was scarce twenty!" ("Mr. Gifford" 267), he enhances the melodrama by arraigning the venom, repeating Shelley's trope of the "serpent" press in his essay on the "Aristocracy of Letters" (1821–22). No less than Shelley's self-interested figures, Hazlitt's prove a dubious boon, sympathetically tendered, but with antithetical effects. With "no pedigree" (Hazlitt put it), Keats could offer reviewers only "'the fairest flowers of the season, carnations and streaked gilliflowers,'—'rue for remembrance and pansies for thoughts'—they recked not of his gift, but tore him with hideous shouts and laughter, 'Nor could the Muse protect her son!'" The quotations install Keats in a gallery of Shakespearean maids: Perdita holds the first bouquet; fatally deranged, pitied Ophelia the second. Nor does the feminizing of the reviewers as hysterical bacchantes (via Milton) redeem Keats's masculinity; it just echoes Shelley's trope of Urania's failure of her fatally vulnerable poet-son—a slight misquotation of Milton too aptly converting *defend* to a more flutteringly maternal *protect*.[21]

This effect haunts almost any defense of "Poor Keats." Said Hazlitt in another *Table-Talk* essay, the reviewers' abuse "proved too much" and "stuck like a barbed arrow in his heart":

What was sport to the town was death to him. Young, sensitive, delicate, he was like

"A bud bit by an envious worm,
Ere he could spread his sweet leaves to the air,
Or dedicate his beauty to the sun"—

and unable to endure the miscreant cry and idiot laugh, withdrew to sigh his last breath in foreign climes. ("On Living to One's-self" *W* 8: 229–30)

The inset verse (Romeo's father on his lovesick son) blazons Keats's incapability: Romeo is famously unmanned by love.[22] The parallel proved prophetic when Keats's letters to Fanny Brawne appeared. Swinburne, flaunting a disdain of Keats to repel similar charges on his own character, sneered that "a manful kind of man or even a manly sort of boy, in his love-making or in his suffering, will not howl and snivel after such a lamentable fashion" (*W* 14: 297). When Keats does not play as a subject for feminine doting, he is a scandal of feminine weakness. Dr. Johnson "was no man to be killed by a review," said Carlyle in 1828, before dismissing "the whole of Keats's poetry" as "weak-eyed maudlin sensibility" (*Burns* 277).

While Keats still drew breath, *Blackwood's* affected an apology in September 1820 for its rigor, scarcely restraining the snidely effeminizing innuendos:

> we are informed that he is in a very bad state of health, and that his friends attribute a great deal of it to the pain he has suffered from the critical castigation his Endymion drew down on him in this magazine. If it be so, we are most heartily sorry. [. . .] had we suspected that young author, of being so delicately nerved, we should have administered our reproof in a much more lenient shape and style. (7: 686)

Frailty, thy name is Keats. When Byron heard from Shelley that "Young Keats [. . .] died lately at Rome from the consequences of breaking a blood-vessel, in paroxysms of despair at the contemptuous attack [. . .] in the Quarterly" (*L* 2: 284), he was incredulous:

> is it <u>actually</u> true? I did not think criticism had been so killing [. . .] in this world of bustle and broil, and especially in the career of writing, a man should calculate upon his powers of <u>resistance</u> before he goes into the arena.
> (*BLJ* 8: 103)

Assured by Shelley that it was all "too true" (*L* 2: 289), Byron was one of the first to stage a farce, in a stanza of *Don Juan* (1823) that gained an influence (by wide circulation) equal to, if not greater than *Adonais*. Of this poet "killed off by one critique," Byron marvels:

> 'T is strange the mind, that very fiery particle,
> Should let itself be snuffed out by an Article. (XI.60)

He first wrote "weakly Mind" (*BPW* 5: 483), then decided to let the couplet's feminine rhyme make the point. The memorable epigram relayed Shelley's myth into a riot of allusions. Even on a different subject (for instance, *Blackwood's* on Alexander Smith in 1854), "snuff'd out by an article" always recalled Keats. As late as the 1870s, *Cornhill* was mocking "the soul which let itself be snuffed out by an article" and suggesting that *Adonais* could be excused only "on the theory that poetry and manliness are incompatible, that a poet is and ought to be a fragile being, ready to [']Die of a rose in aromatic pain'"—refreshing the Pope cartoon of extreme sensibility that Hazlitt had summoned to gloss effeminacy of character.[23]

If the marriage of poetry and manliness wouldn't admit the impediment of Keats, female culture answered with a warm embrace. To say that for "some women readers, the story of Keats's supposed extreme weakness had a sort of attraction" is to risk understatement.[24] *Ladies' Companion* wrung tears for the poet who "burst a blood vessel on reading a savage attack" on *Endymion* in the *Quarterly*, "and died in Rome as a consequence" (Aug. 1837, 186). She-biographers made the victim a fetish. F. M. Owen crowned her study with *Adonais* XLIII ("He is a portion of the loveliness . . . "). A century on, Dorothy Hewlett titled her biography of Keats *Adonais*, and took lines from Stanza 1 for her epigraph. On hostile tongues, "Poor Keats" was contempt or mock pity; in Byron's mouth, disdain; in Hazlitt's, pity and regret; in the Keats circle, a polemical bond.[25] But in female sighing, "Poor Keats" issued a call to be the "mighty Mother" whose absence *Adonais* had indicted. *Victoria* closed its article in high maternal rage:

> What shall we say of the malicious, the utterly brutal criticism, the hand of the cloddish boy tearing the myriad-hued fragile butterfly to fragments! No words can express the loathing every honest educated Englishman must feel for the ruffian tasks which inaugurated a long career of prosperity for the two Quarterlies. (67)

The butterfly is the binary of the masculine figures: cloddish boys, *Quarterly* ruffians, and chivalric Englishmen called to defense. Keats does not survive as a man. The "poor young poet [. . .] savagely used by the censors of literature," cries Mrs. Oliphant (141), echoing Shelley's rage at the "savage criticism," and finding the "fluctuations of this bitter drama [. . .] heart-rending": "the poor sick lad" (145). Amy Lowell is wrenched to exclaim, "Poor little shaver, so pitiably unable to cope with his first great sorrow" (1: 14), and to vilify the first reviewers as "first-class cads," "ruffians at heart without a spark of decent feeling" (2: 80, 82).

From Mrs. Sandford's anatomy of "the female mind" as "constitutionally less stable than that of man" (*Woman* 35) to Thomas Gisborne's caution in his best-selling *Inquiry into the Duties of the Female Sex* (1796) that "the acute sensibility peculiar to women" is "liable to sudden excesses [. . .] sometimes degenerat[ing] into weakness and pusillanimity" (34–35), one had ready templates for the Keats "pierced by the shaft" of reviews, or in another desire, by Cupid's arrow. Admiring biographer Sidney Colvin had to concede the "weakness" of the poet's "helpless and enslaved submission of all the faculties to love" (99). Even Gilfillan, with a tender regard for "boy" Keats, did not help with the refinement that Keats's "great defect" was "the want, not of a manlike soul or spirit, but of a man-like constitution" ("John Keats" 385). The fables of Keats's suffering bore poison fruit, a female-marked pathology exceeding even tuberculosis.[26] Keats had become the language of, the story of, a manifestly marginal relation to man's estate, and if women, especially women of letters, could identify with this dissolution, that was part of the problem.

We cannot estimate the relation of Keats to his predecessors and successors without also estimating the state of manners, knowledge, religion, and politics in his age.
—W. C. Courthope, *National Review*, September 1887

That "Keats" was more than Keats—the confusion of the age, poetry and the age, the parts played by men and women—is clear in the interventionist agenda of R.M. Milnes's long-awaited biography (1848). Out to re-man Keats from the cartoon of the first reviews, of Shelley's mythology, and of Hunt's recruitments, Milnes frankly introduced a Keats of moral discipline, "earnestness," "self-command and self-direction," of "strong will, passionate temperament, indomitable courage, and a somewhat contemptuous disregard of other men." It was the frank agenda: "I had to make prominent the brave front he opposed to poverty and pain—to show how love of pleasure was in him continually subordinate to higher aspirations." Yet the polemic also refreshed the charges. If Keats's "poetic faculty," Milnes concludes, "confines within manly affections and generous passions a nature so impressible that sensual pleasures and sentimental tenderness might easily have enervated and debased it" (2: 107), the syntax overrides the confines. The reception of Milnes's case continued to press the question. *Edinburgh Review* described a poet in whom the "passive part of intellect, the powers of susceptibility and appreciation" shaped no masculine confines but "a feminine mould": "masculine energy" in Keats seems to have "existed deficiently, or had not time for its full development." When Carlyle heard from a friend of his interest in Milnes's *Keats*, he read it back as a discredit to his manliness: "That shows you to be a soft-horn!"²⁷ Keats was the differential by which men assured themselves, and others, of their own hardy manly fiber.

Milnes had more to contend with than the trajectory from Z's serial zingers to *Adonais*. Keats was being marketed to women as a kind of honorary *she*. "Albion's maidens [. . .] Will cherish thy sweet songs!" predicted the epigraph of *Pocket Magazine*'s article on Keats in 1821 (II: 333), itemizing the promise: "the purity and refinement of his manners, and the general tenderness of his heart," "delicate taste and refined inclinations" and "uncontroulable and unlimited sympathy with all kinds of suffering"; a "heart [. . .] peculiarly formed for the endearments of love and the gentle solaces of friendship" (335). If by 1831 Sandford's *Woman* would declare "Gentleness is, indeed, the talisman of woman" (16), *Pocket* had already pocketed Keats. In the 1830s, *The Young Lady's Book of Elegant Poetry* found a place for *To Autumn* (314–15), and *The Ladies' Companion* offered reminiscences from George Keats, along with a clutch of lyrics. Keats had already entered the ladies' companion culture of the annuals, via Thomas Hood's *The Gem*.²⁸ Publisher John Taylor may have worried in 1819 about offending ladies' delicacy with *The Eve of St. Agnes*, but ladies turned out to be doting Keatsians. In 1854, *The Boy's Second Help to Reading* left out boyish Keats, while *The Girl's Second Help to Reading*, airing "such passages as referred specifically to the high duties which woman is called up to perform in life," happily offered three stanzas on *The Eve*'s Madeline at prayer (32–35), the same George Gilfillan cited in 1845 to admire Keats's way with dresses: "No poet describes dress with more gust and beauty," he sighed; "Its every line wears *couleur de rose*," a shade that made him "curious" about the "elegant effeminacy" of "Keats' mind" ("John Keats" 383). In her *Shelf of Old Books* (1894) Mrs. Fields featured a plate of the "I stood tip-toe" manuscript, climaxing in the poet's nymphish effusion, "Ye ardent marigolds!" (43).

As with *Adonais*, the flourishing she-cult was a mixed boon, one more force of unmanning. In 1820 the *Guardian* condescended even to the determinedly tough-minded *Lamia* volume as a mere toy: the poems were like "the sweets of *Woman's Will—a Riddle*," the enigmatic passages akin to the riddles in "the last Ladies' Diary," an annual of entertainments.²⁹ Half a century on, in 1870, *Victoria Magazine*, out to remedy the view of women as mere "lumps of maudlin feeling, or centres of excited nerves" (3), all but undercut the goal with an essay titled superlatively "Keats—The Daintiest of Poets."³⁰ Its epigraph was "Glory and loveliness have passed away," the first line of Keats's sonnet dedicating the 1817 *Poems* to Hunt, describing the world of old mythology, full of "nymphs soft-voiced and young, and gay," that Hunt has refreshed and Keats means to keep fresh. *Victoria*'s epigraph shifts the line to Keats himself. So it no wonder that in disdain of those who "worship" Keats as "the poet of 'Light feet, dark violet eyes, and parted hair, / Soft dimpled hands, white neck, and creamy breast,'" Arnold verges on regendering Keats ("Keats" 207). He's quoting Keats's nymph-raptured poem of 1817, "Woman! when I behold thee." But like *Victoria*'s epigraph, his syntax makes the attributes seem the poet's own: Keats the she-nymph. *Endymion*—the hero and the poem—was a durable female favorite, and lavishly feminized. Dubbing Keats "essentially a worshipper of beauty" (57), *Victoria* hailed the romance as "ever cherished reading for youthful pilgrims on the flowery road of poesy" (59). Pilgrim Frances Mary Owen bestowed a long Neo-platonic explication in an "attempt to make others love" Keats as she does (v). Publishers rallied to please material tastes with elegant parlor-table editions.[31] And in the 1880s, Mrs. Oliphant's *Literary History* was busy fashioning Keats into a Victorian parlor woman:

> He turned from the confusions of his own age, which he had neither strength nor inclination to fathom [. . .] not robust enough for political strife, or to struggle as his contemporaries were doing with noisy questions about the Regent's morals or manners, or the corruptions of the state. It was so much easier and more delightful to escape into the silvery brightness. [. . .] poetry had become his chief object in life. Those whom life endows more abundantly with other interests may play with their inspiration, feeling towards that divine gift as, according to Byron, men do toward a scarcely stronger passion—
> "Man's love is of man's life a thing apart,
> 'Tis woman's whole existence."
> This was the case of Keats in respect to the heavenly gift. [. . .] In poetry his was the woman's part—(137–38)

With no apologies, Oliphant's Keats, even in high aspiration, is twinned to Donna Julia. This was mythology doing the work of gender sociology.

Just a few years on, in 1877, Coventry Patmore published an essay on Keats that was premised on a gender sorting "into two distinct classes" of sensibility, as easily discerned as Mrs. Sandford's classifications of sexual character.[32] Although he concedes "a border-line at which they occasionally become confused," about Keats he was certain:

> In the first class, which contains all the greatest poets, with Shakespeare at their head, intellect predominates. [. . .] Such poets are truly spoken of as masculine. In the other class—in which Keats stands as high as any other, if not higher [. . .] the beauty and sweetness, is the essential, the truth and power of intellect and passion the accident. These poets are, without any figure

of speech, justly described as feminine (not necessarily effeminate); and they are separated from the first class by a distance as great as that which separates a truly manly man from a truly womanly woman. (61–62)

Patmore insists "no sort of disrespect is intended"; but if the distance separating the genders of male poets is no less than that between a "manly man" and a "womanly woman," the feminine man is not necessarily uneffeminate, either.

This kind of Keats overproduces, however. If the not truly manly poet was a figure by which true men could know their difference, it was also a worry, a sign of something that couldn't be securely differentiated, or quarantined. Specters and spectacles of effeminacy spooked literature and the arts, because this was the culture suspected of corrupting men—not just making them feminine, but actually promoting the unmanly. When in 1853 Kingsley condemned the age as effeminate, he cited among the symptoms (and causes), the poetry of Keats. Its "passionate sensibility" epitomized the threat to "the sound heart of the English people" being posed by "the effeminate frivolity which now paralyses our poetry as much as it does our action."[33] The peril was no less dire to modern England than to *ancien régime* France. Echoing Kingsley and recalling Brown's *Estimate*, W. C. Courthope diagnoses the national crisis. Keats's "vivid intensity," he writes, "reflect[s] certain tendencies of modern civilization—its softness, its luxury, its *ennui*" (a French reminder), and demonstrates how "in the absorbing pursuit of ideal beauty, men forget [that] this kind of lotus-eating takes the life out of patriotic sentiment, and the pith and manliness out of the national idiom" (*Keats' Place* 24). As in the decadence of Rome (it wasn't too much to suggest), the sapping of manly strength from the men of England boded the end of civilization.

The Kingsley-map of eroded manliness, with warnings of shipwrecks on Keats-imprinted Tennysonian Lotos-Land, was not absolute in an age which found islands of tolerance, even indulgence, for manly tears. But Keats was not their occasion. It was, chiefly, Dickens. In a culture of sentiment that Wilde could only parody, the men of England famously wept over the deaths of Little Nell and Paul Dombey. No less than Frances Jeffrey confessed to Dickens himself, "I could not *reserve* my tears. [. . .] they flowed and ebbed at your bidding," and about the death of Paul Dombey, "Oh, my dear, dear Dickens! [. . .] I have so cried and sobbed over it last night, and again this morning; and felt my heart purified by those tears, and blessed and love you for making me shed them" (*Life* 2: 391, 406). The Dickens-exception confirmed the normal discipline.[34]

And even in the Dombey decade of the 1840s, Carlyle was promoting "Great Men, their manner of appearance in our world's business," and their place in that "divine relation" that "unites a Great Man to other men" (as his inaugural lecture on heroes put it; 1–2). Feminine qualities were allowed, but only with manly governance. So when Carlyle praises Dr. Johnson in terms that Mrs. Ellis might use to advise the wives of England—"was there ever soul more tenderly affectionate, loyally submissive to what was really higher than he?"—he also stresses the "rugged pride of manhood and self-help," his "nobleness and manfulness" (179). And if Giotto's portrait of Dante's "most touching face" shows "softness, tenderness, gentle affection," this is matched, in "sharp contradiction," by true grit: "protest, and life-long unsurrendering battle, against the world" (86). When Carlyle proposes "The Hero as Poet," it is a poet set above the merely "beautiful verse-maker" by his "power of intellect" (84), a distinction reinforced with a vigorously phallic vocabulary. Like the old Prophets, the heroic Poet "penetrate[s]" into "the sacred mystery of the Universe" (80); Dante "pierces [. . .] down to the heart of Being [. . .] seizes the very type of a thing" with "fiery emphasis and depth" (92)—none in that Keatsian realm of "unrealities,—clouds, froth. [. . .] there was no footing for them but on firm earth" (178). It is definitional overdrive, remarks James Eli Adams, "charged with the energies and anxieties of masculine self-legitimation" (1).[35]

The fraught social logic and psychological stresses in post-Romantic manhood get channeled through Keats, with disciplinary pressure. To Courthope, Keats shows how the "pursuit of mere Beauty of Form [. . .] involves a relaxation of all the nerves and fibres of manly thought, the growth of affectation, and the consequent encouragement of all the emasculating influences that produce swift deterioration and final decay" (*Liberal* 194). The beauty-chaser's body—its slack nerves and fibers, its growth of affectation, its receptivity to anti-masculine influence—is at once its own autopsy and a sign of cultural decadence. Courthope is referring to Keats's "struggle to get absolutely free from the world of sense," but even Keats's sensuousness was a caution. Byron was sensual, but always in masculine sexual adventure; Tennyson was luxurious, but also brooding and philosophical; Keatsian luxury was just puerile, even infantile. Rossetti complained of an "affected or self-willed diction" tending "to the namby-pamby" (*Life* 206), and Smith summed *Endymion* as a "style of babyish effeminacy about 'plums / Ready to melt between an infant's gums'" (*Britannica* 56). This poetry is actually from the spectacle of sleeping, embowered Adonis, which embarrasses even Endymion (2.430, 450–51), but Smith won't buy any irony, and chalks up all "these and lines of a similar nauseous sweetness" to Keats. Carlyle thought Keats "wanted a world of treacle" (Allingham 205), and his wife Jane guessed that he had already raided the dessert trolley. Refreshing Z's compote of class and gender, she opined that *Isabella* "might have been written by a seamstress who had eaten something too rich for supper and slept on her back" (Allingham 310). Her trope was trading on "seamstress" as a synonym for prostitute, with a Cockney-paper trail in its code of "desire, of emulation, and of excess."[36] In this manifold of class and gender (if the seamstress were a poet, she'd be Keats), Keats the sweet-maker, the sweet-taker, is too conspicuous, childish, appetitive, excessive, all the while failing to produce or consume anything of substantial value. Yeats depicted him in 1919 as a schoolboy addict, "With face and nose pressed to a sweet-shop window / . . . / Shut out from all the luxury of the world, / The coarse-bred son of a livery-stable keeper" (*Ego Dominus Tuus* 55–61). Although he sees a connection between Keats's exclusion ("his senses and his heart unsatisfied") and his "luxuriant song" (58–62), the portrait gets its force from Victorian disgust. Keats was the sign of an unseemly desire.

Advocating a modern adult literary culture that would be "neither puerile nor feminine, but virile," Swinburne exiled Keatsian desire to no-man's land. Stoking his revulsion at the love letters, he despised the poetry as "some of the most vulgar and fulsome doggerel ever whimpered by a vapid and effeminate rhymster in the sickly stage of whelphood." Calling up the lines *Blackwood's* had ridiculed in 1818—Endymion's call to Cynthia as a "known unknown *from whom his being sips such darling* (!) *essence*"—he sneered (the italics and exclamation are his) that such "nauseous" phrases "make one understand the source of the most offensive imputations or insinuations levelled against the writer's manhood."[37] As in Hazlitt's indictment, Keats-rapture is a story of body, soul, and desire in effeminate default. Meaning conduct as well as poetry, Patmore decides that in Keats "the man had not the mastery. For him a thing of beauty was [. . .] the supreme and only good he knew or cared to know" (a parody patching the opening of *Endymion* to the close of *Ode on a Grecian Urn*), and so Keats didn't know "the manly virtue of the vision of truth." Hopkins argued with Patmore about the equation of Keatsian "sensuality" with the "feminine" (the "fault" was the excess); but he had to admit that Keats strains the case: "It is impossible not to feel with weariness how his verse is at every turn abandoning itself to unmanly and enervating luxury!"[38]

When *National Review* praised Tennyson for the "reflective gift of the mature man" and called Keats an "impulsive, original, and refined boy" (9: 390), Keats was doubly unmanned: not only versus the mature man but also by feminine descriptives. He could have been one of the misses whom conduct-manualists chastised for "habits of frivolousness, and trifling enjoyment" (Gisborne 34). Easy enough was the fit with Hannah More's "women": "they do not so much generalise their ideas as men, nor do their minds seize a great subject with so large a grasp"; they want "steadiness in her intellectual pursuits," while the male "will most certainly attain his object by direct pursuit, by being less exposed to the seductions of extraneous beauty" (*Strictures* 234–35). "I like a person who knows his own mind and sticks to it; who sees at once what is to be done in given circumstances and does it," Hazlitt declares, advocating this "manly firmness and decision of character" at the top of that essay on effeminacy that found Keats wanting (248). Half a century on, Rossetti remarks at the close of his generally dyspeptic biography of Keats, that in most of the poems one hears "an adolescent and frequently a morbid tone, marking want of manful thew and sinew and of mental balance" (*Life* 208). In Louis Étienne's view, Keats exposes an "absence d'une énergie virile. [. . .] il manquait de force et de substance" (69.1: 298).

Everyone saw this lack in Keats's heroes, "pining away for love" just like the maidens: "They might all be of the same sex; the men are as effeminate as the women," said Courthope, his simile relaying "that supine and feminine impressibility which Keats supposes to be the mark of the poetic character" ("Keats' Place" 14, 16). Courthope could accept this in female form: "the absorbing grief of Isabella [. . .] awakes strong sympathy," he remarks, quoting the stanzas about her doting on the head of her murdered lover (*History* 6: 341–42). But in male embodiment, such absorption was repellent, pathological. Only "physical debility," Courthope proposes, can explain Keats's "unblushingly-avowed preference for the feminine over the masculine motive of composition," his elevating "the emotion of an ideal love-scene" over "human *action* of any kind" (*Liberal* 181–82). As *Pocket* put it back in the post-war era of 1821, "He was not bold or brave enough to encounter the struggles of life, and he shrunk instinctively from the conflict" (335). By the war year 1914, Léonie Villard could assume a consensus on "the weakness and effeminacy" of Keatsian lovers, including even passionate Porphyro, exposed by sinking and fainting (87).

Behind this anatomy is a genealogy, from Spenser's knights to Milton's Samson, of men enslaved by passion and unmanned for action, reeling in spiritual degeneracy.[39] Even a partisan Colvin concedes "a touch, not the wholesomest, of effeminacy and physical softness" in Keats's heroes: "the influence of passion" is apt to "fever and unman them quite" (99)—a sentence Patmore was too happy to quote ("Keats" 63). In an age when Ruskin sorted man from woman by "his rough work in open world" and a necessary "encounter" with "all peril and trial," an arena in which he is "*always* hardened" (*Of Queens' Gardens* 98), soft, weak Keats, casting heroes in his own image, fell short.

Keats's signature genre, Romance (as he feared), was symptomatic. Courthope saw none of the "masculine method" defining Homer, Aristophanes, Horace, Virgil, Dante, Shakespeare, and Milton: "All these men faced Nature in a masterful spirit, making imagination the servant of religion and reason," while Keats failed at the "masculine style required for the drama, the epic, or even for a stirring tale of sustained romantic action" (*Keats' Place* 24, 16, 21). "Unaffected by the social influences of his age" (*History* 6: 323), Keats was "blind or indifferent" to "the actual strife of men" (*Liberal* 193). Hopkins, though agreeing with Arnold about "the true masculine fibre in Keats's mind" (it had "the distinctively masculine powers in abundance, his character the manly virtues"), saw the spirit of Romance as the undoing: unlike Wordsworth, Byron, Shelley, "and even Leigh Hunt," who all took up such "great causes, as liberty and religion," Keats "lived in mythology and fairyland the life of a dreamer" (238). Disputing the equation of unworldliness with effeminacy, William Howitt tried to argue the growth of power, "vigour and acumen" in the poetry and poet: in an "iron age of murderous criticism," Keats "manfully defended himself." But Howitt nearly undid his case in hailing Keats as one of the "swift and resplendent messengers" of "life issuing from the infinite heaven," for which "neither ours nor any other history can furnish a specimen more beautiful" (425). For this specimen, only italicized English would do for Étienne: "Il manque de cette *manliness* dont le premier effet est de sortir du rêve stérile et de la plainte efféminée, d'accepter ce qu'elle ne peut [pas] changer et d'en tirer le meilleur parti possible" (298).[40] This view was so consolidated by the post-war 1920s that Jack Lindsay took the very pulse of Keats's poetry as a desire to see life "through the miasma of romance [. . .] a feminine feebleness" (9).

The most impassioned case for Keatsian aesthetics was argued by Wilde. In his Oxford commonplace book, he read Keats's (and Swinburne's) "effeminacy and languour and voluptuousness" as "characteristics of that 'passionate humanity' which is the background of true poetry" (Ellman 42), and he went public with a lecture: "all things are not fit subjects for poetry. Into the sacred house of Beauty the true artist will admit nothing which is harsh or disturbing, nothing about which men argue." At its head he placed Keats, whose "unerring sense of beauty, and whose recognition of a separate realm for the imagination" rendered him "the pure and serene artist, the forerunner of the Pre-Raphaelite school."[41] While such honors answered Victorian detractors, they also magnified the question. Was Keats the avatar of a new aesthetic manhood, or did his conscription force the terms into contradiction?

Dante Gabriel Rossetti hoped to set the masculine ethos of the Brotherhood against what he regarded as feminine style favored by the Royal Academy. Ruskin broadcast the claim, deriding the Academy for sponsoring a system "of which the main characteristic was the pursuit of beauty at the expense of manliness and truth" (354). Arthur Benson's biography of Rossetti (English Men of Letters, 1904) stressed the "masculine individuality" of the Pre-Raphaelite ethos (20). But the reception, both of painting and poetry, did not always accede. P. T. Forsyth (1889) ejected Burne Jones from "the masculine order of art" for a too "feminine sensibility" (54–55). "I hate the effeminacy of [Rossetti's] school," declared Browning; "the men that dress up like women,—that use obsolete forms, too, and archaic accentuations to seem soft" (*Dearest Isa* 336). This alarm was famously sounded in 1872 by Robert Buchanan in *The Fleshly School of Poetry*, warning of a threat to the male "body social" by "the singers of the falsetto school [. . .] male, female, or other" (5–7). Naming names—chiefly Rossetti and Swinburne but also Keats—as a types of "falsetto voice" (12), and citing Rossetti for "effeminacy" (84), Buchanan sharpens literary criticism, on the whetstone of *Blackwood's*, into a weapon for the culture wars.[42]

It wasn't just the feminine in men that he arraigned, but also this homosocial erotic, and it all swirled around Keats as something between masculine/feminine. Wilde's "Keats" is typecast for male as well as female love: young, beautiful, doomed—the perfect subject, the perfect object, for aesthetic rapture. The extravagant spectacle of affection Wilde staged in *Glykypikros Eros* ("Flower of Love"; 1881) blatantly claimed Keats for homoerotic culture, a figure though which men could communicate and celebrate their passions:

> Keats had lifted up his hymeneal curls from out the poppy-seeded wine,
> With ambrosial mouth had kissed my forehead, clasped the hand of
>   noble love in mine.

"I thought of him as of a Priest of Beauty slain before his time; and the vision of Guido's St. Sebastian came before my eyes as I saw him at Genoa, a lovely brown boy, with crisp, clustering hair and red lips, bound by his evil enemies to a tree and, though pierced by arrows, raising his eyes with divine, impassioned gaze towards the Eternal Beauty of the opening Heavens," so Wilde imagined "this divine boy." A martyr raped by reviews, Keats was to be redeemed by poetic love.[43]

Manliness is distinct from height and bulk
—Charles Brown, *Life of John Keats*

Wilde's erotics are the latest and lushest in a history fixated on Keats's physical form, which was not quite normative. The first defenses of Keats's manliness, keyed to the Gisborne credentials of "robustness of constitution" and physical difference from the female (20), pump Keats up. Seething at *Blackwood's* slanders on Keats's manliness, Brown insisted to Milnes that although Keats "was small in stature," he was "well proportioned, compact in form, and, though thin, rather muscular;—one of many who prove that manliness is distinct from height and bulk" (*KC* 2: 57–58). This was the way he sketched Keats 1819, as a Regency buck, with a bit of poetic cast (fig. 8.1); and in his ekphrasis, Milnes buffed the portrait (1: 7). But this was not the only "Keats" abroad. Hunt's "Mr. Keats" (housed in his popular *Lord Byron,* 1828) was a jumble of gender signals, zig-zagging from the young-manly, to the limits of young-unmanly:

> He was under the middle height; and his lower limbs were small in comparison with the upper, but neat and well-turned. His shoulders were very broad for his size. [. . .] Every feature was at once strongly cut, and delicately alive. If there was any faulty expression, it was the mouth, which was not without something of a character of pugnacity [. . . .] the chin was bold, the cheeks sunken; the eyes mellow and glowing; large, dark and sensitive. At the recital of a noble action, or a beautiful thought, they would suffuse with tears, and his mouth trembled. In this, there was ill health as well as imagination, for he did not like these betrayals of emotion; and he had great personal as well as moral courage. His hair, of a brown colour, was fine, and hung in natural ringlets. (407–8)[44]

What were "these betrayals"—emotion per se, or emotion at odds with noble feelings? Hunt was enchanted, the he-contours of his "Keats" blurring even more in his portrait for Gorton's *Biographical Dictionary* (1828), doting on the "remarkably beautiful hair curling in ringlets" (242). The "Keats, with young tresses and thoughts" at his *Feast of the Poets* (1832) seems chaste in comparison. Reading Hunt, H. W. Mabie thought some manly retrofitting was needed for "John Keats: Poet and Man": "A strong, virile, sensitive nature evidently" (170).

What of Keats's voice? Benjamin Bailey thought it "sweet-toned," deeming this "'an excellent thing' in *man,* as well as 'in woman'"—his italics liberalizing Lear's cherishing of Cordelia's voice.[45] In tune, Haydon recalls Keats reciting the "exquisite ode to Pan [. . .] in a low, half chaunting, trembling tone" and the *Ode to a Nightingale* with "a tremulous undertone [. . .] extremely affecting!" (*Diary* 2: 378, 318). Brown fixates on Keats's lips: whenever he "spoke, or was in any way excited, the expression of the lips was so varied and delicate" (*KC* 2: 57). Reading these reports, Milnes decided that he had to man Keats with a "deep grave voice" (*Keats* 1: 245). Colvin followed suit, giving Keats a "rich and low" voice; in conversation it had "an eager but gentle animation" (47) without "the tears [or] the broken voice which are indicative of extreme sensibility" (20). Milnes fortifies Keats at the outset with anecdotes of boyhood scrappiness and seeming destiny for military glory. But if the fortifying was meant to contain the beauties; it also seems, by its safety, to license rapt attention: "His eyes, then, as ever, were large and sensitive, flashing with strong emotions or suffused with tender sympathies" (1: 7). "Keats" was emerging as a code of sentimental description by which men could express and communicate a love for intellectual, feeling-shaped male beauty.

Later biographers keep retracing the figures. J. R. Lowell dispassionately repeats Hunt's array (241), while Colvin strains the extremes into a nearly heterogeneous marriage of opposites:

> A small, handsome, ardent-looking youth—the stature little over five feet; the figure compact and well-turned, with the neck thrust eagerly forward, carrying a strong and shapely head set off by thickly clustering gold-brown hair; the features powerful, finished, and mobile; the mouth rich and wide, with an expression at once combative and sensitive in the extreme. (46)

W. M. Rossetti hangs the feminine details on a more emphatically masculine port:

> Keats had an unusually small head, covered with copious auburn-brown ringlets. [. . .] his lower limbs also were small beyond the due proportion for his broad-shouldered and generally alert and vigorous-looking, though by no means tall, frame. His eyes were large, blue, and sensitive: his mouth likewise was singularly sensitive, combined with a certain pugnacious look of the full under-lip. ("Sketch" xi)

Cowden Clarke purges the feminizing details to render a butch Keats: "He was, withal, compactly made and well-proportioned [. . .] active, athletic, and enduringly strong—as the fight with the butcher gave full attestation" (155; cf. 143–44), or his Byronic enthusiasm for prize-fighting (145). David Masson, with a cheer for pugilistic Keats (a foil to feminine and ethereal Shelley), went over the top, giving him a "thick torso" and "a deep, grave voice" (9) emanating from a mouth that had "altogether a savage pugilistic look" (4).[46]

In excess of mere documentary duty, every account dwells, blazon-like, on the shape of the face, the size and hue of the eyes (hazel? black? brown? blue?), and the quality, style, and even shade of the hair (brown? auburn? brown-gold? red? lighter than Titian red? golden red? sunset-red?).[47] Colvin even supplies an Appendix with a scholarly note to settle questions about the exact color of Keats's hair and eyes (221). Along with Hunt's rhapsodies, there is Bailey recalling that Keats's "hair was beautiful—a fine brown, rather than auburn," and adding dreamily, "if you placed your hand upon his head, the silken curls felt like the rich plumage of a bird" (*KC* 2: 268). Mrs. Procter, whom Milnes cites for a "feminine acuteness of perception" (1: 103–4), recalled Keats's hair falling "in rich masses on each side his face" (*KC* 2: 158). Keats's eyes draw attention, often linked to exquisite emotion. George said that they "moistened, and his lip quivered at the relation of any tale of generosity or benevolence of noble daring, or at sights of loveliness or distress" (*KC* 1: 325). Haydon at least lends a divinity to shape this end: Keats's "eye had an inward look, perfectly divine, like a Delphian priestess" (*Autobiography* 1: 251). Colvin quotes them all (46). Severn makes the deity male: the "intensity of Keats's eager glances when he was keenly excited or interested" was "like the hazel eyes of a wild gipsy-maid in colour, set in the face of a young god"). Another simile is all man: "a peculiarly dauntless expression, such as may be seen on the face of some sea-men" (Sharp's *Life*, qtd. in Parson 15).

As the move from eyes to expression suggests, Keats's whole face called up the gender question. It lacked "the squareness of a man's," Mrs. Procter said on meeting him in 1818; it was "more like some womens faces I have seen [. . .] so wide over the forehead and so small at the chin" (*KC* 2: 158)—a gendering corroborated by Bailey when he read it in Milnes's *Keats* (1: 103): "It is in the character of the countenance what Coleridge would call *femineity*," he remarks, eliding Coleridge's desynonymizing of *feminine* and *effeminate*.[48] "He bore [. . .] much beauty of feature and countenance. The contour of his face was not square and angular, but circular and oval," he reports, adding authoritatively, "this is the proper shape for a poet's head" (*KC* 2: 268). Rossetti's *Sketch* seems less fanciful when, after usual notes about the small head, ringlets, and "feminine" contour, he insists that the sum is "eminently virile and gallant" (xi). Still bothered by the want of "manly thew and sinew" in the poems (206), his biography gives the poet's face the best masculine claim that litotes can manage: "The whole aspect of the face is not greatly unlike Byron's" (128). Scholar Donald Parson decides that the face was "oval, rather than square and masculine" (*Portraits* 116), his asymmetrical syntax evoking the elided gender. Another weirdly androgynous image, reminding some of George Eliot (fig. 8.2), is the fancy of Mary Newton, whose father Joseph Severn is often accused of effeminizing Keats with his 1817 picture of a fat-faced dreamer (fig. 8.3).

Severn's was the best known image. After Milnes used an engraving of it for his frontispiece, it became the popular choice for editions, biographies, and critical studies.[49] The reception of the portraits is as gender-fraught as the recollections. Bailey thought Severn could have done more to capture Keats's "peculiar sweetness of expression," while Severn worried that his *Keats* was too "Byronized."[50] A "masculine" rival by William Hilton (a friend of Keats's publisher, Taylor, and Severn's rival at the Royal Academy) was painted in 1830, then engraved for Taylor and Walton's 1840–41 edition of Keats's *Poetical Works* (fig. 8.4).[51] Hilton had done a chalk sketch in 1819–20 (fig. 8.5), a face with

Figure 8.1 Sketch of John Keats by Charles Brown (1819). During a working vacation on the Isle of Wight, summer 1819, Keats's friend and housemate did this pencil sketch, rendering Keats as roughly fashionable, handsome, virile, contemplative. This "Keats" was not known before the twentieth century.

Figure 8.2 Sketch of John Keats attributed to Mary Newton, Joseph Severn's daughter. Sometimes compared to George Eliot, this is among the images derided by defenders of Keats's masculinity.

Figure 8.3 Miniature of John Keats by Joseph Severn (1818), exhibited at the Royal Academy in 1819, and later given by Keats to Fanny Brawne. Endorsed by Keats's sister and his friends, and used by R. M. Milnes for an engraved frontispiece of *Life, Letters, and Literary Remains* (1848), this image prevailed in nineteenth-century memoirs and editions.

Figure 8.4 Based on Severn's 1818 miniature, this image was rendered many years after the poet's death by William Hilton, a close friend of Keats's publisher (after 1818), John Taylor. Although it appears in some of Taylor's editions of the 1840s, it did not become popular until the twentieth century.

Figure 8.5 Engraved by Charles Wass, from a lost chalk sketch by William Hilton, probably drawn in 1819 or early 1820, this image seemed to Joseph Severn to make Keats "a sneaking fellow," and admirers of Severn's various Keatses despised it. Even so, it was used for the frontispiece of an edition of Keats's poems published by Taylor and Walton in 1840–41.

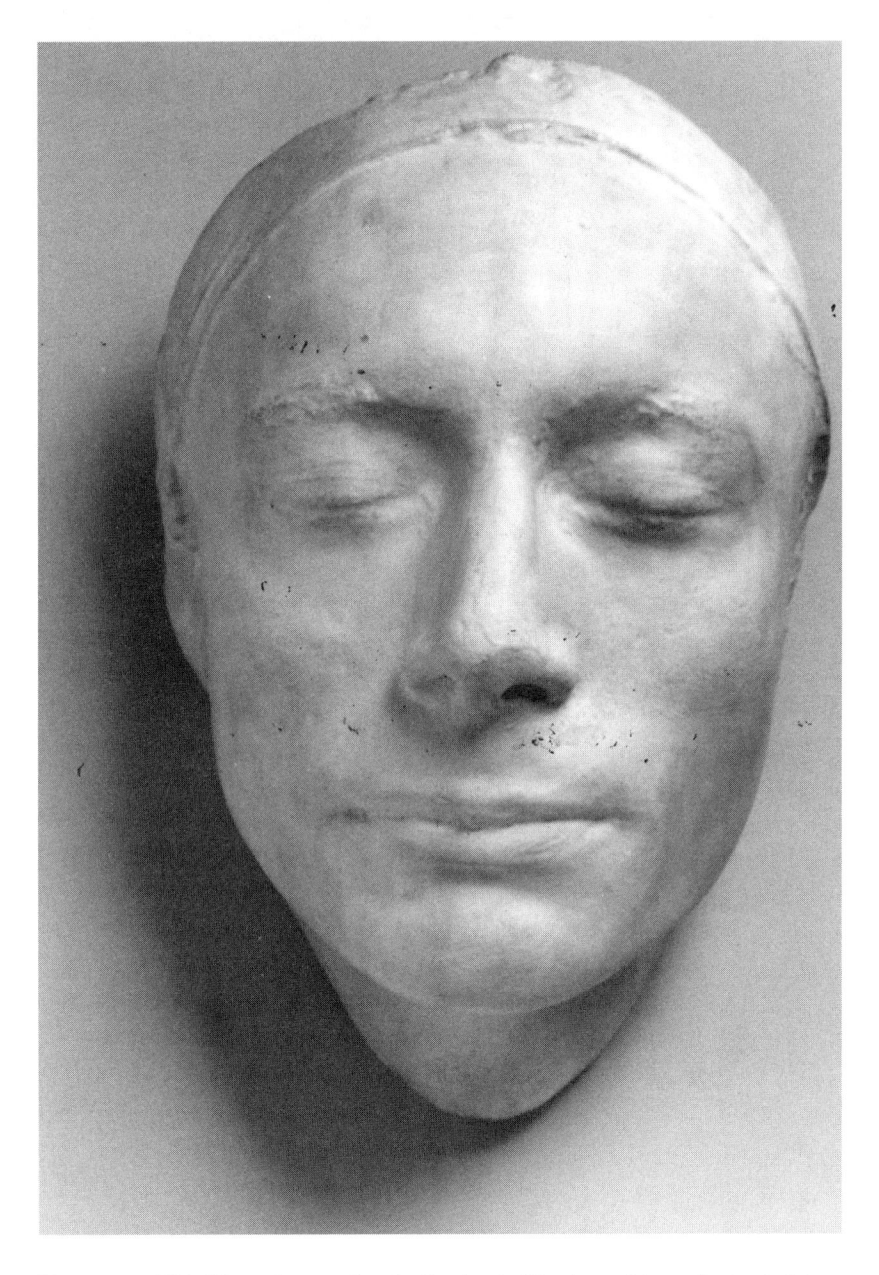

Figure 8.6 This life mask was taken by Benjamin Haydon at his studio in 1816, in preparation for his image of Keats in the crowd of *Christ's Entry into Jerusalem*.

Figure 8.7 Benjamin Haydon's chalk drawing of Wordsworth was done during his visit to London, in January 1818, when he was almost forty-eight, and when Byron's Regency style was not only vogue, but the emerging iconography for "poet." "With respect to the Drawing I did of your head," Haydon wrote to Wordsworth, "I am happy to tell you, it met with universal public approbation—and was considered by a great many as the best sketch I had ever made of any one" (*LMY* 2: 577).

small eyes and a firm chin that Severn loathed (*KC* 2: 329). Tweaking Severn, Hilton's portrait took the pose of Severn's *Keats* and applied the sterner features of Haydon's life mask of 1816 (fig. 8.6): the face is less fleshy and more elongated, the brow is lower, the cheek bones more pronounced, the jaw line firmer, the mouth less full, the chin stronger, the hair less curly and fussy, the eyes a little smaller, less wide-spaced and doe-like, the gaze a little less dreamy and more directed, and Severn's fastidious neckwear made over into a more rakishly Byronic accessory, like that sported by Haydon's Wordsworth (fig. 8.7).[52] Even so, that *Victoria* could warmly recommend Hilton's *Keats* to its readers as a "most interesting and agreeable picture of the poet in all his boy-like beauty" (15: 59) shows the degree to which a chastened Keats still eluded secure masculine definition, could even depict "the daintiest of poets."

Gender was character. The Galignani memoir set Keats's "political sentiments" as "manly and independent," taking a cue from Hunt, who introduces Keats's poetry in *Lord Byron* with the sonnet on Chapman's Homer, "a remarkable instance of a vein prematurely masculine." Conceding some later "poetical effeminacy," Hunt ascribes this to "ill health," insisting that Keats "was aware of this contradiction to the real energy of his nature, and prepared to get rid of it."[53] His article in Gorton's, limning a "very manly, as well as delicate spirit," praises Keats's "manly submission" to his final sufferings (241–42). Years later, Hunt is still harping on the "masculine [. . .] beauty" of the early poetry and, like everyone else, citing the "manly acknowledgement" of "youthful faults" in the Preface to *Endymion* (*Imagination* 285–86). Milnes out-hunted Hunt in the manly "impression," introducing a "noble nature perseveringly testing its own powers, of a manly heart bravely surmounting [. . .] hard experience" (*Keats* 1: 2). He stressed the "plain, manly practical" character anchoring the rich imagination, and the "bodily vigour" clearly "signalised" by his "severe drubbing [of] a butcher, whom he saw beating a little boy, to the enthusiastic admiration of a crowd of bystanders" (74). In Milnes's story, boyhood pugnacity and "skill in all manly exercises" (1: 6) prefigure the way mature Keats, "at the mention of oppression or wrong, or at any calumny against those he loved," would rise "into grave manliness at once," seeming "like a tall man" (1: 73), Sir Gondibert reborn. In summary, he cites George Keats's retort to the review "gladiators" that his brother "was the very soul of courage and manliness" (2: 44; cf. *KC* 1: 285).

Guessing that had Keats been spared love and disease, he might have realized higher "character and virtue," Arnold cited George Keats's testimony, recalling "manliness" as its first term (9: 207–8). Keats was getting rehabilitated as a subject for male admiration. Milnes's report of his "manfully and eloquently"

(1: 120) remonstrating with Reynolds over the Preface to *Endymion* (he printed it; 121–26) warmed the *Times*' reviewer to the "simple and masculine strength" of its "honest declaration" (3). *Edinburgh* speculated that "when the poetic mood was not on him," Keats's "heart was full of manly courage" (428). Bailey grabbed his pen to thank Milnes, again and again, for vindicating "the <u>manliness</u>" of Keats: "His <u>manliness</u> was the principal feature of his character"; "He had a soul of noble integrity"; "Indeed his character was, in the best sense, manly," he assures him (*KC* 2: 259, 261, 274). Colvin made sure to include Bailey's letter in his "English Men of Letters" biography of Keats (211)—the first after Milnes's—and to echo him on the "spirit of manliness and honour" (6) even in the boy. The poetry may be effeminate, but the poet was not. Masson's article of 1860 referred to Keats's "pugnacity" three times in its first paragraph (1).

While Smith's article for *Britannica* (1887) hit some old notes—"fopperies of style" and "effeminacy" in the early poems (56–57) and the "hysterical bursts" and "passionate tenderness" of the schoolboy—it began with the Keats brothers as a gang of "strong pugilistic tendencies and general fierceness of disposition. They fought with every schoolfellow who felt inclined to gratify them; and when no foe was procurable they supplied the deficiency [. . .] by fighting with one another" (55). Sports were a virtual index of manly prowess for Victorian readers, continuous with military character. Battling John matures over the course of Smith's article, growing into a Victorian sage, a letter-writer of "practical sense, clear judgment, a considerable knowledge" and "strong intellect," and, after *Endymion*, a poet of "strength" and "terrible power" (57). This is also Mabie's story, keyed not to the premature manliness of the sonnet on Chapman's Homer, but to the mature equanimity of the man after the drubbing of *Endymion* in the reviews of 1818: having applied his "own domestic criticism" with far more pain than what the reviews "could possibly inflict," Keats was ready to write it off as an ambitious failure and go forward with what he had learned, so he said in a plucky letter to his publishers (*L* 1: 374). Glad to have these "strong, clear-sighted words" to wave in the face of the popular legend, Mabie praised the "robust sense, courage, and virility." Such words

> were never written by a victim of stupid criticism or by a sentimental weakling. They show Keats not only resolutely holding to his ideals, but still possessed of that dauntless pluck which earlier ran to than excess of pugnacity on the playground. (162)

Yet in the story of pugnacious boy as father to the virile man, and the man as example to other men, the negatives of "victim" and "sentimental weakling" testify to terms still in play.

In re-manning Keats, the verdict is baffled by lingering questions and contradictions. Arnold admired the "flint and iron" of Keats's "attitude towards the public"—"that of a strong man, not of a weakling avid of praise, and meant to 'be snuff'd out by an article'" (*John Keats* 210–11)—but he couldn't break the spell of *Adonais* (he even had to quote it to refute it), nor the scandal of the love letters. Milnes didn't quite know how to spin Keats's gordian complication of feelings about women. Proposing "the peculiar action of a high imagination on the ordinary relations of the sexes," he seems unconvinced himself, sensing that Keats's "most delicate and wonderful" insight about "a Poet's heart" also forecast how "one intense affection" would come "to absorb his entire being, and to hasten by its very violence, the calamitous extinction against which it struggled in vain" (1: 172–73). Hence W. M. Rossetti's retraction: his "Sketch" of 1872 seconds Bailey in thanking Milnes for having dispelled "once and forever" and, "to the deep satisfaction of all who value manliness as a portion of the poetic character," the fable of Keats killed by harsh reviews (xi–xii); but his biography reopens the case:

> Because he thrashed a butcher-boy, or was indignant at backbiting and meanness, we are not to credit him with an unmingled fund of that toughness which distinguishes the English middle class. The English middle-class man is not habitually addicted to writing an "Endymion," an "Eve of St. Agnes," or an "Ode to Melancholy." (206)

Genre and style retain an indictment that biographical evidence cannot adequately answer.

Other biographers tried to secure Keats's manliness by skipping the middle-class measure and declaring him a gentleman—a sign of the ideological fusion, well after *Blackwood's* had left the field, of effeminacy and vulgarity. Recall Mrs. Carlyle's condescension to the author of *Isabella* as a seamstress, Swinburne's linking of the "vulgar" verses to an "effeminate" character (*W* 14: 296–97), and Courthope's lament about "vulgar and sensual imagery" (*History* 6: 335). In Keats's love letters, Arnold can see only the "unmanning grasp of mortal disease," its chief symptom an "abandonment of all reticence and all dignity," in the infection of "the merely sensuous man, of the man who 'is passion's slave'" (*Keats* 206)—what Hamlet implies of himself, when he says that Horatio is never thus enthralled (3.2.73–74). Not just unmanly, this is unclassy, exposing "something underbred and ignoble, of a youth ill brought up, without the training that teaches us that we must put some constraint on our feelings and upon the expression of them." And for all the passion about the "Creed of Love," the love letters show someone not man enough to love in a mature, honorable way: "It is the sort of love-letter of a surgeon's apprentice which one might hear read out in a breach of promise case, or in the Divorce Court," one "badly bred and badly trained" who will appeal only to "the badly bred and badly trained" (206–7). "The snobbishness under the calumny proves where the stricture really lies," Amy Lowell shrewdly remarks (2: 125). Yeats's image of Keats as the "coarse-bred [variant: ill-*bred*] son of a livery-stable keeper" (*Ego Dominus Tuus* 370) assumes what oft was thought.

Hunt, for whom such origin was a virtual credential, spins a proto-Yeatsian romance: "Mr. Keats's origin was of the humblest description." Tory editorialist Saintsbury nobly set aside "origin" to insist that "there was not a touch of vulgarity" about Keats, while Milnes gave him a class make-over, revising Cockneyisms and regularizing grammar, syntax, spelling, punctuation; deleting bawdy wordplay and references to sex, drinking, and sensuous indulgence.[54] He also assured readers that Harrow, Lord Byron's school, "had been at first proposed" for Keats's education but proved "too expensive" (*Keats* 1: 4). *Sir* Sidney Colvin also floated the Harrow balloon, then a noble defense of Enfield: "of good repute," displaying "the finest style of early Georgian classic architecture," and sited in a district "especially affected by City men of fortune for their homes" (4). But reinventing a classy Keats was a transparent romance, and critics on both sides of the Atlantic lampooned such efforts "to create [Keats] a gentleman by brevet" (219), in J. R. Lowell's wry phrase.[55] What was just as apparent was the need to create a Keats that answered to, and could shape, current questions of manly self-definition, in psychology no less than in sociology.

If Keats had not existed, the Victorians would have had to invent one.
—George Ford, *Keats and the Victorians*

Even as "Keats" was shaping up as a force-field of gender prescriptions under duress, some of the most vigilant police were uncertain of their own composition, and moreover, were susceptible to being read, with Keatsian gloss, as feminine, even effeminate. Alexander Smith worried Kingsley in this figure: it is only "where he forgets for awhile Shelley, Keats" that he is "terse, vivid, sound, manly" (48: 454); *Blackwood's* remanded Smith to the Spasmodic School, finding only one sonnet both "manly and pathetic" (75: 348–49). Ever didactic, notably dysfunctional Ruskin was a casebook of gender pathology.[56] Swinburne was the star of Buchanan's Fleshly School of "sickliness and effeminacy" (70). Linking him to Keats in 1867, Étienne said that both "manquer de virilité" (306); to clarify, he provided a generous translation of Hazlitt's "On Effeminacy" before closing his review with an exhortation to all English poets: "Soyez virile!" (317).

It was just the year before that *Spectator* recoiled at an "unmanliness" in Swinburne so "suffocating" as to require a gender-limbo: "Mr. Swinburne is both unmasculine and unfeminine. He is unmanly or effeminate, [. . .] morally the same thing" (1229). Following suit, *Edinburgh Review* judged the poetry "not virile or even feminine, but epicene," framing the indictment with an allusion to *Ode to a Nightingale:* reeking of "luxurious abandonment and corrupted passion," Swinburne's poetry "smell[s] of 'all the sunburnt south.'"[57] Patmore fared no better. *Blackwood's* reviled his "slip-slop vulgarities" and the male-romantic lineage: this "is the life into which the slime of the Keateses and Shelleys of former times has fecundated!" He was a devolutionary nadir: "the weakest inanity ever perpetrated in rhyme by the vilest poetaster of any former generation, becomes masculine verse when contrasted with the nauseous pulings of Mr. Patmore's muse" (56: 342 and 331).[58]

In these exposures, Keats begins to look less like an abject and more like a secret mirror. Hazlitt, the public monitor of effeminacy and Keats's surplus of sensuous verse, was a private scribbler of Keatsian swoons. On a blank leaf of *Endymion*, he writes, "I want a hand to guide me, an eye to cheer me, a bosom to repose on," swearing "to live and die for" the right woman (*W* 9: 114). As the note and its *Endymion*-site suggest, Keats gives a language to these hushed passions and desires. Keats confronted Hopkins with a welter of sensuality that he couldn't quite define as "masculine," or heterosexual anyway (James Najarian argues, 100–107). He is no less problematic for Arnold, in the way his sensuous enthusiasms evoked a self denied, "a version of his early self, the dandified poet whom he tried to live down" (73). The unmanning love for Fanny Brawne alarmed Arnold as an omen of post-Oxford heterosexual destiny. He and Clough bonded in queer contempt of this sequel to the fleeting romance of young manhood in academe: "Farewell, my love, to meet I hope at Oxford."[59] And in another aspect of truancy from Victorian manhood, Arnold sensed that Keats already had a claim at Oxford: Clough's Keatsian temper, an impressibility and irresolution that impressed critics such as Patmore as deficient in "masculine power."[60] In some of the letters in Milnes's *Keats*, Arnold could read a virtual twin in Clough, and wrote to Clough about Keats's lacking the patience to see that he must have "an Idea of the world in order not to be prevailed over by the world's multitudinousness." To such perils Arnold himself was not immune, especially when he read Keats. From Milnes he copied out Keats's remarks about the adversities of Burns's life ("Poor unfortunate fellow!") as a secret moment of meditating on the "true" suggestion that "out of suffering, there is no dignity, no greatness; that in the most abstracted pleasure there is no lasting happiness."[61] Keats let one think such thoughts.

Keats in love was the magnetic language for Arthur Symons. In the midst of lamenting Keats's erotic passions as a killing disease, *Romantic Movement* meanders into this meditation on the decentering, unmanning force of passion:

> Have you ever thought of the frightful thing it is to shift one's centre? That is what it is to love a woman. One's nature no longer radiates freely, from its own centre; the centre itself is shifted, is put outside one's self. Up to then, one may have been unhappy, one may have failed, many things may seem to have gone wrong. But at least there was this security: that one's enemies were all outside the gate. With the woman whom one loves one admits all one's enemies. Think: all one's happiness is to depend upon the will of another, on that other's fragility, faith, mutability. [. . .] That, or something like, it may well have been Keats's consciousness of the irreparable loss and gain which came to him with his love. (300–301)[62]

It may well have been, but are we still talking about Keats?

Informing all these private sympathies with Keats at his most vulnerable, most dreamy, or most sensuous were latent testings of new definitions of manhood. When Buchanan arraigned the "intellectual hermaphrodite[s]" of the Fleshly School, he meant monstrosities; but there were other compounds to consider. For all his devotion to Keats's manliness, Milnes thought of himself in mixed terms. In 1837 he writes to a friend, "I was thinking to-day that the thing I was intended for by Nature is a German woman. I have just that mixture of *häusliche Thatigkeit* and *Sentimentalität* that characterises that category of Nature. I think Goethe would have fallen in love with me." Taking a Coleridgean pattern, Patmore contended that "the spirit of the great poet has always a feminine element." To D. G. Rossetti, "the supreme perfection" in art is that "point of meeting" where male and female beauty "are most identical." So, too, Keats. Hunt's Romantic Keats is "manly and gentle"; Colvin's Victorian Keats is "conspicuous alike for manly spirit and sweetness," and *fin de siècle* Henry van Dyke, disputing Patmore's assignment of "feminine," asks for a better conclusion: "extreme sensitiveness is not an exclusive mark of femininity; it is found in men as often as in women."[63] Keats was one place to find this and talk about it.

Alongside Cockney/Effeminate Keats, there tracks a "Keats," first in private reflection, then in public theorizing, as the name for a sensitivity, even a genius, that sustains, demands, and determines new understandings of gender. At the century's end, Mabie's "Keats" is no exile, but a configuration of gender in the template of (male) genius: "Through this virile and manly nature, energetic and assertive to the verge of pugnacity, there ran a deep vein of sentiment; and combined with this vigorous health of mind and body, there was that extreme sensitiveness [. . .] which goes with a high imaginative genius" (143).

Yet for all this redemptive anatomy, the touchstone words, *verge of, deep, extreme, high*, expose a combination prone to fracture, with the constituent parts available to rewriting into the old grammars.

How can the woman be thought about outside of the Masculine/Feminine framework, other than as opposed to man, without being subordinated to a primordial masculine model?
—Shoshana Felman, "Woman and Madness"

Substitute *feminine man* for *the woman* in this question, and you'll see how much the primordial masculine model affects men, too. Substitute *Keats*, and you'll appreciate his force in conveying the question well into modernism. To J. C. Shairp, Keats-poetics are "destructive of true manliness" (43); to Sir William Watson, the "infantine prattle and babble" of his letters, shamed further by the "profound and powerful spirit" of Charlotte Brontë's letters (44), expose an "incontinent gushiness which is neither manly nor properly boy-like, but simply hobbledehoyish" (40). Symons wasn't sure how to add it all up. "Keats had the courage of intellect and the cowardice of nerves," he began the essay in *The Romantic Movement* (298). Though he recognized "something feminine" and "decadent" (305), he proposed a cultural contingency: "all that swooning and trembling of his lovers, which English critics have found so unmanly, would at all events be very much at home in French poetry" or the "frank subtlety of expression" in Elizabethan poetry (305–6). Others went for direct defense. Mabie located the problem not only in hostile critics but also in the fervent worshippers: those "feeble brethren" poets who pity him to pity themselves; and in his readers, all those "sentimental hangers-on at the court of poetry." The problem is not in Keats but in his stardom: "Instead of the real Keats, virile, manly, courageous, well-poised, and full of noble ambitions, the world has fashioned for itself a weakly, sentimental, sensuous maker of over-ripe verse, without large ideas of his art, and sensitive to the very death under the lash of a stupid and vulgar criticism" (138–39). Saintsbury, not content just to refute the charges of effeminate and unmanly, promoted Keats to "a captain and leader of English poetry," giving this "manly Englishman" a prime patriarchal credential: he is "the father [. . .] of every English poet born within the present century" (89–91). Leon Vincent urged readers of *Atlantic Monthly* to look for the "virile intellectual health" of "the real man" not in the poetry, but in the letters, which give a "refreshing" view of "the masculinity of this very robust young maker"

(399–400). In the same issue, Kenyon West used biographical lore to sketch a scrappy Keats of "strong and manly" character (909).

Is this modern progress, or is it the old effect of Keats bearing gender questions into new senses of self and culture? In 1927 Stephen Vincent Benét decided to characterize an anomalous member of John Brown's fearless raiders in the image of an almost Wildean Keats:

> There is only one whose air seems out of the common,
> Oliver Brown. That face has a masculine beauty
> Somewhat like the face of Keats. (*John Brown's Body*, 34)

If this poetry of masculine beauty sounds revisionary, the old values keep their grip in academe. The problem with the nineteenth century's "sensuous and hypersensitive Keatses," proposes John Jones, is not error, but a partial truth that traces out in defensive reactions (35). In the 1930s Douglas Bush is glad to see the "masculine and classic style of the sonnet on Chapman" recaptured in *Hyperion* after a lapse of "luscious, half feminine" poetry in "I stood tip-toe," *Sleep and Poetry*, and *Endymion* (88). In the 1940s, George Ford concedes Keats's "effeminate phrases" (141), while H. N. Fairchild cites the "manly" Preface of *Endymion* (3: 465), and J. R. MacGillivray insists on "Keats' perfectly masculine nature," evident in his "intellectual energy," his "courage and sense of humour, his developing emotional restraint [. . .] far more strict than that of Hunt or Haydon" (xiii). Having to note a "tendency toward effeminate gushing about the delights of 'poesy' and suburban 'leafy luxuries,'" and an occasional "jaunty vulgarity" in the poems of 1815–16 (a link of class and gender, without Z's bile), MacGillivray emphasizes the "masculine and classical influence" of Cowden Clarke in early autumn 1816, and (again) the sonnet on Chapman's Homer (xv). In the 1950s Lionel Trilling devotes four pages of a preface to Keats's letters to their manliness (21–25), and in a related essay celebrates Keats's "mature masculinity" ("the essence of his being") in terms of "an ideal that implies a direct relationship to the world of external reality, which, by activity, it seeks to understand, or to master, or to come to honorable terms with; [. . .] it implies fortitude, and responsibility for both one's duties and one's fate, and intention, and an insistence upon one's personal value and honor" (24).

Even as Keats's passions licensed the inner Keats in nineteenth-century male poets, so Keats's "development" gave men in academia an argument about modern heroism, modern genius. It was W. J. Bate's *John Keats* (1963) that introduced me to the gender polemics: his assiduous amassing of documents to confirm Keats's "virility" and "manly" character;[64] his insistence on the "virile, penetrating idiom" and "masculine strength of language" of the sonnet on Chapman's

Homer (85); his ardent defense of Keats's manly character and bitter attack on Severn's effeminate Keatses (112–16)—all this seemed to me over-invested, until I learned more about Bate and the history of debate. In 1963, too, Aileen Ward stage-set her *John Keats* with the threat of military invasion that hung over England in 1803, embellishing Milnes's report about a military uncle: "In this time of mobilization and suspense, John Keats confronted an anxious future of his own—the traditional first trial of manhood in England. He was to be sent away to [. . .] the Clarke academy at Enfield," which had trained his uncle, "a lieutenant in the Marines" who fought in Camperdown in 1797. "From the time of his first encounter with the world," she argues, "life was to seem a test of whatever fortitude he could bring to it" (1–3). Ward's little Iliad wields a virtual masterplot of gender heroics, with Keats conquering the "half-effeminate idiom into which his early poetry had been lured" and achieving the "real nature as it is revealed in his letters—masculine, energetic, straight-forward" (180–81). Both she and Bate rerun the debates about the portraits. Ward rues the "effeminacy" of Severn's Keats: it falsifies "the lean masculine strength" of the life-mask (89). Bate, deriding Severn's own "limp" character, credits Hilton's "much manlier" image, also "closer to the life mask" (113), showing "the strength, resoluteness, the masculine good sense that almost everyone found so abundant" in Keats (116).[65] To be a Keatsian was not to be a soft-horn.

Twentieth-century Keats is a borderline at which gender binaries play into composites or new combinations. Noting Coleridge's theory of the androgyny of the "great mind," Woolf included Keats in her canon of male writers responsive to "the woman part of the brain."[66] But it wasn't until Trilling's *The Opposing Self* that Keats is explicitly theorized this way; and in this figure, the analogy of Shelley, or rather Edward Carpenter's Shelley, proves a help. Both Carpenter and Trilling advance the prime binary not as masculine/feminine, but as self/culture: Carpenter's Shelley and Trilling's Keats bring an "intense and adverse imagination" to the "unconscious portion of culture" (Trilling x). Calling his essay on Keats (with a nod to Carlyle) "Poet as Hero," Trilling sees Keats earning this credit from a queer exploration of "complex and difficult" cultural strata (24). Keats is willing not only to identify male "passivity" as a "female principle," but also not to "shrink from experiencing" it, embracing it as "half of his power of creation" (28–29).[67] Old languages of "feminine" linger, but are used now to contest old codes of male. Christopher Ricks's *Keats and Embarrassment*, meaning to improve on Trilling (97), admires an "unmisgiving largeness of mind" in Keats that allows even those infamous "slippery blisses" (no "simple infantilism or sensation") to register a "purified and liberated" sensationalism (89, 104–5, 89): Endymion's "drunken" swoon "from Pleasure's nipple" (2.868–69) instances one of the trusting pleasures of adult love. This imagination of a "full pleasure comparable to the infant's" is audaciously mature (106). Ricks makes Keats a hero of the pleasures that the nineteenth-century prosecutors arraigned against his manliness.

From another theoretical quarter, another revisionary adventure was developing. This was the promotion of half-feminine Keats to feminist Keats. In 1983, echoing his remark that "axioms in philosophy" need to be "proved upon our pulses" (*L* 1: 279), Elaine Showalter described feminist-women's theories of women's writing as "theories proved on our own pulses" (*Raritan* 147). Out to trump he-feminists such as Terry Eagleton, she called up a Keatsian epistemology. Around the same time, in some incidental remarks in *Women Writers and Poetic Identity*, Margaret Homans proposed that Keats's class origins and lack of classical education shared "certain aspects of women's experience as outsiders relative to the major literary tradition" and its "masculine" practices, and she was interested in Adrienne Rich's designation of negative capability as a female aesthetic. Thinking of Nancy Chodorow's work on woman's "so-called 'weak ego boundaries,'" Rich had suggested that this might "be a negative way of describing the fact that women have tremendous powers of intuitive identification and sympathy with other people." When Barbara Gelpi remarked, "John Keats had weak ego boundaries," Rich took the cue: "Negative capability. Exactly. Any artist has to have it."[68] Soon after, Erica Jong, writing on Rich, made Keats's language a feminist badge: "feminism *means* empathy. And empathy is akin to the quality Keats called 'negative capability'—that unique gift for projecting oneself into other states of consciousness."[69] Feminist Keats is doubly feminized: not only is he "an honorary woman" (as Homans puts it); he also serves that female position of mediating relations, here not between men, but between women.[70]

Yet for all this revision of old slanders, old formations still seem in place. The "minds of women are more pliable" than those of men, said Mary Hays back in 1798 (*Appeal* 43). A few decades on Mrs. Sandford advised women of the distinctly female charm of "forgetting one's self, and sympathising with others" (7); "to be agreeable, a woman must avoid egotism" (9). Thus it was an easy step for Hopkins to dispute Patmore's feminine Keats and then cheer Patmore's antipathy to "Women's Rights, very perhaps cruelly plainspoken."[71] This is even rather Keatsian. Rich and Jong (for all their "radical" critique of patriarchy) miss the male definition of negative capability ("Man of Achievement") and never note that Keats's attitude toward women of genius, and views, and achievement,—I mean that sort of which Woolf, Rich, Gelpi, and Jong are members—was hostile.[72]

The problem of "feminist" Keats was redressed by Homans herself in a provocative lecture in 1986 (published 1990) that traced out his "resentment of [women's] real and imagined power over him" and a "compensatory wish to assert his own masculine authority" (*SiR* 29: 368). Macho Keats received an even stronger articulation in another essay published in 1990, when Marlon Ross argued that *Hyperion* (whose hero, recall, even Hunt thought effeminate) enacted Keats's desire "to assert not just [his] coming into *manhood* but also his coming into discursive power" with the "rituals which define poetic maturity in terms of patriarchal culture." What earlier defenders admired as the manly/manful/masculine manner of the Preface to *Endymion*, Ross read as an audition for patriarchal culture in a calculated "patrilineal discourse."[73]

In the gender-critique of Romanticism that played out at the end of the twentieth century, Keats looked like he was destined for identification as one of the macho gang. Yet in the face of this developing story, Grant Scott contended that the aesthetic thinking was less determinate and determinably sculpted (112), and his colleague at UCLA, Anne Mellor, decided to rehabilitate the nineteenth century's effeminate Keats into a feminist-minded "ideological cross-dresser," a man prone to "occupying the position of the woman in life [as caretaker] or in discourse, or by blurring the distinction between genders."[74] Although this Keats is unarguably entangled in the sexism and misogyny of his historical moment, his ultimate evolution, argues Mellor, with her eye on the posthumously published *Fall of Hyperion*, was toward female self-identification. Facing Moneta and aching to see what her brain "enwombed" (1.276–77), the poet discovers his power in her "pregnant tragic consciousness," and this is, by implied equation,

> what is ultimately for Keats the appropriate relationship between female and male in poetic discourse: that of goddess/mother/muse to human/son/poet, a relationship that sustains the role of humble submission and dependency Keats has everywhere adopted in relation to feminine creative power. (*Romanticism & Gender* 185)

Sifting into a finer feminist tone Z's abuse of "The Muses' son of promise; and what feats / He may yet do," Mellor also shows what Keats may do for a feminist genealogy of Romanticism.

Each reading of Keats, whether received or recalibrated, confronts a text as complex and elusive in its gender as it is compelling in its genius. The contradictions and controversies played out in Keats's poetic imagination and letters, and perpetuated in affection and reception, resist stable resolution, or find in this field only grounds prone to dissolution. In the essay that supplies the epigraph for this section, Shoshana Felman asks, "how can thought break away from the logic of polar opposition?" (4). Keats's play on, and at, the borderlines of gender so challenges polar logic that even as he provokes its terminology—*masculine, feminine, effeminate, patriarchal, feminist*—he compels reflection on the stakes, then and now, not only in literary history, but also in our attempts to take the critical measure of that history.

Body and Soul

I do not mean it an injury to women, when I say there is a sort of Sex in Souls. [. . .] the Soul of a man, and that of a Woman, are made very unlike. [. . .] The virtues have respectively a masculine and a feminine cast.
    —'THE TATLER,' 1710

Souls are of no sex, any more than wit, genius, or any other of the intellectual faculties. [. . .] the soul may have as fair and ample a chamber in the brain of a woman as of a man.
    —'BIOGRAPHIUM FEMINEUM,' 1766

from the education, which [women] receive from society, the love of pleasure may be said to govern them; does this prove that there is a sex in souls?
    —MARY WOLLSTONECRAFT, 'A VINDICATION OF THE RIGHTS OF WOMAN,' 1792

Is it true what is so constantly affirmed, that there is no Sex in Souls?—I doubt it—I doubt it exceedingly.
    —S. T. COLERIDGE, 'NOTEBOOKS,' 1808–1819

There is a sex in our SOULS as well as in their perishable garments.
    —S. T. COLERIDGE, LETTER (TO A LADY), 'THE FRIEND,' 1809

CHAPTER NINE

Sex in Souls?

Soul Talk

Quaint as soul-talk may seem now, it permeated Romantic culture. Metaphysically privileged, it pulled everything into its orbit. If you spoke of education (political, aesthetic, moral), excoriated slavery or consoled the enslaved, assessed the spiritual cost of commercial wealth, anatomized poetry or the poet, sooner or later you were talking about soul. Soul-talk was also gender-talk, usually tacit. In Wordsworth's *Immortality Ode* on the soul's doom by "her earthly freight" (VIII), the feminine imports more than Latin's *anima*. It is fraught gender ideology: the hero is a "growing Boy" (68), and masculine God is the true home of his soul, only temporarily regendered by a Mother-minded, imprisoning Earth, out "To make her Foster-child, her Inmate Man, / Forget the glories he hath known, / And that imperial palace whence he came" (VI). Even when Keats revises this Platonism to conjecture an existential "system of Spirit-creation" in which "*Soul*" figures as "Intelligence destined to possess the sense of Identity," gaining it in the heart-pains of worldly experience, the genders hold ground.

Keats does remap Wordsworth's gender-antagonism of foster-mothering and true fathering into a view of mortal suffering as a vital mother to the existential soul, "the teat from which the Mind or intelligence sucks its identity." Yet the telos is patrilinear: "As various as the Lives of Men are—so various become their souls, and thus does God make individual beings, Souls, Identical Souls of the sparks of his own essence" (*L* 2: 102–3). Whether Wordsworthian prison-matron or Keatsian suckler, the feminine subserves a male soul-story. If female soul has a role, it is usually in a scenario of muse-courtship, a marriage-plot for male creation. About the male priority, Hazlitt was transparent: "I would have her read my soul," is his advice for any romantic prospect; "she should know what I am, as if she were another self." He states this desideratum in the same paragraph of "On Great and Little Things" that hisses his "utter aversion to *blue-stockings*," and declares, "I do not care a fig for any woman that knows even what *an author* means" (*W* 8: 236).

Notwithstanding its transcendental key, soul-talk vibrated with temporal import for gender identity: its essentialism, its bases and superstructures, its forms of social existence, its marking or obscuring of foundational borderlines. I conclude *Borderlines* with the Romantic signings of soul as the pervasive, historically resonant, socially contingent, poetically magnetic language through which basic questions of sex and gender-shift play their highest stakes.

What happens if the gender-map of Keats's existential theology of soul is set into a female narrative? Here, for one, is that great theorist of androgynous soul, Woolf, talking about Wollstonecraft's soul, in comparison to what animates Austen's controlled wit:

> If Jane Austen had lain as a child on the landing to prevent her father from thrashing her mother, her soul might have burnt with such a passion against tyranny that all her novels might have been consumed in one cry for justice. ("Mary Wollstonecraft" 169)[1]

Woolf's view of soul-making is as existential as Keats's, but it is a political forging in paternal violence, rather than a general heart-suffering. If some soul-sexers urged a complementarity that (as *The Tatler* put it) was no "injury to women," Wollstonecraft (for one) saw a history of injury: sexing the soul was just a heartbeat from erasing the female soul and praising only the body beautiful. Her contemporary, Burke trumped the question with the premise that "one half of the human species [. . .] have not souls" at all. This report on Burke is from *A Vindication of the Rights of Men*.[2] *A Vindication of the Rights of Woman* takes as its premise the dignity of a "capable" female soul (185).

"Surely," Wollstonecraft urges, "she has not an immortal soul who can loiter life away merely employed to adorn her person, that she may amuse the languid hours" of men (137–38). Refusing praises that would "deprive us of souls, and insinuate that we were beings only designed [. . .] to gratify the senses of man when he can no longer soar on the wing of contemplation" (126–27), she insists that it cannot be "philosophical to think of sex when the soul is mentioned" (145). The issue is no mere abstract philosophy; it is of direct import to the sorry practices of female education. It is an insult to "the immortality of the soul" to deny a woman "the perfectibility of human reason," contends Wollstonecraft: "can that soul be stamped with the heavenly image, that is not perfected by the exercise of its own reason?" (167). Sighing at the contrary cultural lore, she neatly satirizes the logic: "If they told us that in a pre-existent state the soul was fond of dress, and brought this inclination with it into a new body," one would have to dismiss this as "a rant." It is with "that Being who impressed [. . .] on my soul" the falsity of any "sex to morals" and gave "sufficient strength of mind to dare to exert my own reason" that she will keep faith (147). Punning her soul into her reasoning, she marshals a series of "Animadversions" on received wisdom.[3] A hundred years earlier, Mary Astell had used the idea of the convent to propose a female academy of the soul, tracing out the social (if not yet a political) logic.[4] Over the century, "soul" would become a way to pose the political question: a politics of eternity at odds with temporal politics. "MERCIFUL Father!" Mary Hays protested at the end of the 1790s: "thou who hast in thy wisdom formed the sexes with souls so nearly alike,—can it displease thee, that they should by nearly equal means, strive to emulate thy attributes, and arrive at the perfection of virtue?" (*Appeal* 176–77). With an epigraph on the title-page, Mary Robinson's *Letter to the Women of England* blazoned the question with a *we* that was not gender-set: "Wherefore are we / Born with high Souls, but to assert ourselves?"[5]

In a poetic tribute written fresh on the heels of *A Vindication of the Rights of Woman* and *A Historical and Moral View of the French Revolution,* an unabashed fan of Wollstonecraft, John Henry Colls, featured this discourse in his summary praises:

>   . . . superior to each mean control,
> She shows her native dignity of soul,
> Runs the bright course her kindred should have ran,
> And throws the tyrant's fetters back to man.
> Thus WOLLSTONECRAFT, by fiery genius led,
> Entwines the laurel round the female's head;
> Contends with man for equal strength of mind,
> And claims the rights estrang'd from womankind. (143–150; pp. 18–19)

In the nice tuning of his angrily anti-Pope couplets, Colls has *soul* conquer *control*, and in this impetus partners *mind* with *womankind*.[6]

In the 1830s, Jewsbury boldly raised the discursive soul-stakes at the outset of her series "On Modern Female Cultivation": ancient Hebrew theocracy joined spirit and politics, giving "women political consideration, by allowing them to inherit property in default of sons, and practically proved that souls are equal, by making them occasionally the recipients of the prophetic spirit, and instruments of divine government" (*Athenæum* 223: 65). The widely despised antithesis to this consideration is Milton's Eve, a material formation of softness and sweet attractive grace. "I cannot comprehend his meaning, unless" (Wollstonecraft says in a sly critique of Milton's theology for Eve) "in the true Mahometan strain, he meant to deprive us of souls" (*VRW* 126). This is the theme infused by her daughter Mary Shelley into the "Mahometan" inset tale of Safie in *Frankenstein*. Having been taught by her own mother, a Christian Arab harem-slave, "to aspire to higher powers of intellect," and having (after her mother's death) seen enlightenment-era Paris with her father, Safie sickens at the prospect of "being immured within the walls of a harem, allowed only to occupy herself with puerile amusements, ill suited to the temper of her soul, now accustomed to grand ideas and a noble emulation for virtue" (98; II.6). "If woman be allowed to have an immortal soul," contends Wollstonecraft, "she must have, as the employment of life, an understanding to improve [. . .] or she was born only to procreate and rot" (*VRW* 180). The appeal to soul is not only an argument in itself, it is also an implicit refusal of the dictations of an unenlightened age.

In this respect, soul turns against the assignments seemingly guaranteed by nature, a difference that mattered even to conservatives such as Hannah More. Her *Essays for Young Ladies* (1777) had no argument with sexing the embodied mind: "The mind in each sex has some natural kind of bias," and "the happiness of both depends, in a great measure, on the preservation and observance of this distinction" (266)—a sentence that anti-Wollstonecraftian Revd. Polwhele was happy to brandish in *The Unsex'd Females* (36–37). But when the terms shift from mind to soul, distinctions become less firm, or even negligible. Just a decade on, in 1786, More celebrates blue-stocking culture precisely for the way its salons treat the souls of all as equal, in effect unsex'd:

> In taste, in learning, wit or science,
> Still kindled souls demand alliance:
> Each in the other joys to find
> The image answering to his mind.
> But sparks electric only strike

On souls electrical alike;
The flash of intellect expires,
Unless it meet congenial fires. (*The Bas Bleu* 358–65)

The witty rhymes—*science-alliance, find-mind, strike-alike*—nicely mime the converse of souls. Even so, the unwitting general signifier *his* remains unanswered. Wollstonecraft's electric move was to expose she-soul as a social formation, then to propose "that the few extraordinary women who have rushed in eccentrical directions out of the orbit prescribed to their sex, were *male* spirits, confined by mistake in female frames" (*VRW* 145). Her italics hit the theoretical crux: does the extraordinary woman have a he-soul in a she-body, or should the anatomy of gender itself be the question?[7] What mortal hand or eye frames this asymmetry?

It isn't Nature, Wollstonecraft contends, with a radical refutation of culturally induced gender difference: women "have been drawn out of their sphere by false refinement, and not by an endeavour to acquire masculine qualities" (*VRW* 129). Such soul-based theory, with its rational defense of "masculine" as a female claim, was far more provocative than our two centuries of historical distance may realize. So incensed was American Federalist Benjamin Silliman that he was driven to sexual slanders (over rational argument) to discredit her view:

> MARY Woolstonecraft, a female philosopher of the *new school* [. . .] indignantly rejects the idea of a sex in the soul, pronouncing the sensibility, timidity and tenderness of women, to be merely artificial refinements of character, introduced and fostered by men, to render sensual pleasure more voluptuous. [. . .] but unfortunately the practice of her life was at war with her precepts. [. . .] In short, polluted as she was by the *last crime* of woman, MARY stepped forth as the champion and reformer of her sex; she wished to strip them of every thing feminine, and to assimilate them, as fast as possible, to the masculine character. (Letter II; 22–23)

To propose "the idea of a sex" as an artifice rather than a certainty was to set off a foundational tremor. Wollstonecraft had released the idea that a male soul in a female frame was no monstrosity; the monstrosity was the deformative effect of the prescribed orbit. While Silliman could read only a scandal, exclaiming that a "virgin [female] soul" would "shrink back at the contemplation of a female soul *unsexed*," virtually "a man in female form!" (23), his broadcast couldn't help but give the new precepts a hearing.[8]

Even Coleridge wasn't sure. Normative gender forms were critical to his romance of sexed souls, a spiritual communion on the model of natural procreation. The body's "yearning to compleat itself by Union" impels him to ask, "Is there not a Sex in Souls?" and stay to answer: "Were there not [. . .] throughout, in body & in soul, a corresponding and adapted Difference, there might be addition, but there could be no combination" (12 March 1811; *L* 3: 305). Union of difference is a famous Coleridgean signature, endorsing his theory of "poetic Imagination" as a power that "brings the whole soul of man into activity," balancing or reconciling "opposite or discordant qualities" (*BL* 2: 15–16). Yet just as significant as this primary figure of "the whole soul of man" is the emergence of feminine creative agency in Coleridge's discussion:

> "Doubtless," as Sir John Davies observes of the soul (and his words may with slight alteration be applied, and even more appropriately to the poetic IMAGINATION.)
>
> > Doubtless this could not be, but that she turns
> > Bodies to spirit by sublimation strange,
> > As fire converts to fire the things it burns,
> > As we our food into our nature change.
> >
> > From their gross matter she abstracts their forms,
> > And draws a kind of quintessence from things;
> > Which to her proper nature she transforms
> > To bear them light, on her celestial wings. (*BL* 2: 17)

This verse is drawn from Davies's popular *Nosce Teipsum: Of the Soule of Man and the Immortalitie Thereof* (1599)—its subtitle echoed in Coleridge's "whole soul of man." As Coleridge knew, what is gendered along with categorical *Man* is the strange spiritual agency of the dictum *Nosce Teipsum* (Know Thyself). Davies's opening stanzas call it "my soul," an "inward self" so mysterious as to require (for the inquiring male poet) an opposite, feminine gendering ("her own form") as the name for his not-knowing, "ignorant both what she is and where."[9]

Female spiritual agency is not limited to these male metaphysics of mystery. It also shapes some counter-imaginations of female commerce that linger in Romanticism, especially for women. Astell was thinking of how, in retreat from the whole world of man, female friendship might become soul-mating: one might look into "the Soul of [a] beloved Person, to discover what resemblance it bears to our own"; two women "of a sympathizing disposition, the *make* and *frame* of whose Souls bears an exact conformity to each other, and therefore one wou'd think were purposely design'd by Heaven to unite and mix," might enter "into an holy combination to watch over each other" (100).[10] The encompassing man's world still held to hetero-hierarchy, but this structure did not necessarily lend succor to male Romantic imaginations. Their inscriptions of gender difference do not always serve the "spousal verse" celebrated in Wordsworth's Prospectus to *The Excursion* (57). Even in this marriage plot, the image of "the Soul" as "an impulse to herself" (12) intuits a potential rebel from the cause or, more radically, the intractable otherness of creative power and its alien sources.[11] Meanwhile, female Romantics, as eager as Wollstonecraft to affirm the dignity of a woman's soul, had to struggle against the force of official tradition to conceive new terms. Must women who refuse the prescribed orbit become that alien formation, "*male* spirits, confined by mistake in female frames"? Or might the alienation of the extraordinary woman—the *un*prescribed orbit—be a situation from which to query the very idea of a sex in the soul?

Michel Foucault has famously marked the nineteenth century as the crux when homosexuality gets transposed from "the practice of sodomy onto a kind of interior androgyny, a hermaphrodism of the soul" (*History of Sexuality* 1: 43). Romantic-era women, inspired by eighteenth-century predecessors, were already contending for a soul decorporalized from sexual determinism—a critical genealogy for Foucault's story, as well as a complication to its male lineage.

The Soul of Man

To the marriage of sexed souls, what could possibly admit impediment? Marriage plots are set to serve male needs and desires. By "spousal verse," Wordsworth means what his soul can "produce" from the union of the "intellect of Man" to "this goodly universe" (Prospectus 52–54). Keats's spousal verse, *Ode to Psyche*, has in mind a similar arrangement with its courtship of Cupid and the figure of soul itself, his Psyche true. But the best laid schemes of muse and man go oft awry. In the protracted agon at the outset of *The Prelude*, pressured by a conscious aversion of the "honorable" toil in epic that would confirm "manhood now mature" (1.653), Wordsworth resorts to gender difference not to bode happy nuptial, but to configure psychological crisis:[12]

> my soul
> Did once again make trial of her strength
> Restored to her afresh; nor did she want
> Eolian visitations; but the harp
> Was soon defrauded, and the banded host
> Of harmony dispers'd in straggling sounds
> And, lastly, utter silence.   (1805; 1.102–8)

When Wordsworth represents the spectacle of his soul struggling for inspiration and failing, he writes of she-failing, partly owned as "my," yet gender-alienated in the prospect of defeat.[13] Still feeling the grip of epic imperative, Wordsworth will aim at a male "Poetic" soul, marking its "feminine" form as a phase of primitive nurture: pastoral, maternal. His "Conclusion" thus sets the kind of love imaged by "the Lamb / And the Lamb's Mother" as "human merely"; it is a "divine" love that his "brooding Soul" seeks (13.154–65).

This is the familiar rap on Wordsworth, realizing vocation and identity by managing, subordinating, even conquering the feminine.[14] Yet it's only part of what *The Prelude* shows—and it is at odds with the strange feminizing of "higher" verse. "This love more intellectual" ("spiritual" in D, XIV: 188) needs the "moving soul" of an "Imagination" that is synonymous with "absolute strength / And clearest insight, amplitude of mind, / And reason in her most exalted mood" (13.166–170).[15] In the domain of Imagination, Wordsworth is willing to imagine the feminine as the trope for power that is never quite under masculine governance, but operates as mysterious inaccessibility. The crisis of vocation that climaxes in Book 1's actual compositional inception, "Was it for this?" (incorporated later at 1.272), plays out on this grammar of potentiated male gendering. The question stirs memories of a boy's soul in subordination, impressed by supernatural powers and by feminine "Nature," both deemed formative in a generic "mind of man" (1.352). When "soul" returns to the verse from its career in the "crisis" narrative as a struggling feminine, it is de-feminized and supercharged by self-constituting apostrophe: "Thou Soul that art the Eternity of Thought!" (430).[16] In Book 2 the poet amplifies the new-won confidence: "by the regular action of the world / My soul was unsubdu'd," he now can say (2.380–81), and even claim service "from Nature and her overflowing soul" (416). But is this exclusively masculine self-possession?

"Nature herself seems [. . .] to take the pen out of his hand, and to write for him with her own bare, sheer, penetrating power," said Matthew Arnold of this poet.[17] Nothing is more innate to the flow of this pen than the way it keeps marking a feminine soul with its own claims of authority—claims that by Book 2 come to seem foundational to the psycho-biography itself. Tracing "the progress of our being" back to the "Bless'd . . . infant Babe" whose "soul / Claims manifest kindred with an earthly soul" in the vital presence of the mother's body ("arms," "breast," "eye"), the poet "conjectures" the bond to nature and the world (2.237–43). The next time the word *soul* appears in his verse, the bond has been broken (the mother has died), leaving the memory of a boy with a solitary she-soul, impressed by, haunted by, yearning for its lost kindred:[18]

> the soul,
> Remembering how she felt, but what she felt

> Remembering not, retains an obscure sense
> Of possible sublimity, to which,
> With growing faculties she doth aspire,
> With faculties still growing, feeling still
> That, whatsoever point they gain, they still
> Have something to pursue. (2.334–41)

Impelled by the gender of its object, the boy-soul in pursuit of the sublime is no Burkean "he," but "she." And in its romance of access—a sense of "the latent qualities / And essences of things" now "strengthen'd with a superadded soul, / A virtue not its own" (344–48)—feminine soul figures what is not known or possessed: the *vir* in that "virtue not its own" bears a pun of this alienation.

In a Wordsworthian mood, Shelley tries to manage his ambivalence about the feminine by lifting it out of "Nature" and into a supernatural (for him, erotic rather than maternal) sublime. The Poet-hero of *Alastor* pushes the agenda into a radical rejection of feminine "Nature," and an antithetical romance of a visionary female soul. Yet the ultimate business of *Alastor* is to contemn both, casting the feminine as the site of every frustrated desire, every false hope. The first hint is in the framing narrative. Opening in an impassioned call to "Earth, ocean, air, beloved brotherhood!" (1), the frame-poet bonds his "soul" to his "beloved brethren" (16). It is only with latent suspicion that he can name the anterior power of generation, "our great Mother":

> If our great Mother has imbued my soul
> With aught of natural piety to feel
> Your love, and recompense the boon with mine . . . (2–4)

"Mother" may admit a debt, but "If . . ." harbors a question about the nurture.[19]

The latent doubt is more audible in its context of allusion, the tentative surmise of the last lines of the epigraph Wordsworth had just recently affixed to the most famous male-centered soul-story of the age, *Ode: Intimations of Immortality:* "And I could wish my days to be / Bound each to each by natural piety."[20] The doubt of natural piety intensifies in the next invocation Shelley writes for the *Alastor* frame-poet, this to a Mother whose knowledge is as untraceable as it is sought after:

> Mother of this unfathomable world!
> Favour my solemn song, for I have loved
> Thee ever, and thee only; I have watched
> Thy shadow, and the darkness of thy steps,
> And my heart ever gazes on the depth
> Of thy deep mysteries. (18–23)

This is a muse with a difference, the antagonist to poetic power and self-possession alike. Even as she provokes "obstinate questionings" (26)—another allusion to the story of Wordsworth's *Ode,* the soul's restlessness in nature—she withholds "the tale / Of what we are" (28–29). From this binding of eternal foundation and temporal frustration, Shelley projects the antithetical visionary quest. But it is only to find that the visionary feminine soul is another frustration. It is of primary significance in *Alastor* that this plight is not so much sequentially generated as inwrought from inception, and the revenge will be to deny the feminine any value at all.

This pivot is the Poet's dream of his soul-mate, a veiled maid shimmering as epipsyche (149 *ff*): "Her voice was like the voice of his own soul" (153). Shelley intuits that a sexing of souls works a saving grace from narcissism, deflecting the hint of self-reflection into procreative desire. This is a legible motive in his essay fragment *On Love*, which is saturated with self-duplication. Love "thirsts after its likeness"; it is a "conceiving" not from a corresponding and adapted difference (Coleridge), but from "a mirror whose surface reflects [. . .] a soul within our soul" (48).[21] Gender difference holds the line against sterile narcissism—that mere addition that is no combination (Coleridge, again). This is also the purposeful logic of Shelley's iconic soul-romance, *Epipsychidion*: a poet's yearning for a "soul out of my soul" (238). Yet in all these texts, the soul-sexing may not perform, may even betray, the generative work it is set to do: the warmest soul-mate in *Epipsychidion* is a self-reflecting soul-sister. "Spouse! Sister!" the poet calls to his desire (130), projecting their paradise of "Soul" on the pattern conceived by a "wise and tender Ocean-King" for "his sister and his spouse" (477–92).[22]

In this faltering into alter-egoism, fatal vacancy looms. The theme-phrase of *Epipsychidion*, "soul out of my soul," is set in a telling syntax. It is an unanswerable question: "Whither 'twas fled, this soul out of my soul" (238). It is only in the "echoes of an antenatal dream," Shelley concedes, that a soul out of the soul can be "a soul within the soul" (455–56), and it is only in the "soul" of Elysian fantasy that two souls may be "inseparable, one" (539–40). Across the poem's dreamscape, the poet's words shape a soul-verse of thwarted desire:

> The winged words on which my soul would pierce
> Into the height of love's rare Universe,
> Are chains of lead around its flight of fire.— (588–90)

It is a short step from frustration to resentful antagonism. This is the soul-story of *Alastor*.

The *Alastor* plot is set as the dream-maid dissolves and the poet wakes on a cold hillside of *ubi sunt:* "Whither have fled . . . ?" (96). The "dark flood" that obliterated the epipsyche leaves nature vacant and the poet soul-sick to death. Nature's dearest haunts prove as "soul-dissolving" (453) as the supernatural dream; and the course of "following his eager soul" (311) is a fatal enchantment. That its impulse is also within—"Obedient to the light / That shone within his soul, he went, pursuing" (492–93)—vexes high argument into a torture for the embodied soul:

> While day-light held
> The sky, the Poet kept mute conference
> With his still soul. At night the passion came,
> Like the fierce fiend of a distempered dream,
> And shook him from his rest, and led him forth
> Into the darkness.—As an eagle grasped
> In folds of the green serpent, feels her breast
> Burn with the poison, and precipitates
> Through night and day, tempest, and calm, and cloud,
> Frantic with dizzying anguish, her blind flight
> O'er the wide aëry wilderness: thus driven
> By the bright shadow of that lovely dream,
> Beneath the cold glare of the desolate night,
> Through tangled swamps and deep precipitous dells,
> Startling with careless step the moon-light snake,
> He fled. (222–37)

"As an eagle grasped" (227 *ff*) stages a grammar of reversed expectations. Unfolding across the enjambment, the syntax seems to set *eagle grasped* as subject and predicate, with an impending direct object: the Poet's passion, even as it takes control of him, has eagle-energy. Yet in a wicked turn of line, we find that this eagle is no grasper, but is itself grasped as serpent-prey—in the simile, the fierce fiend in possession of the poet's soul. The grammatical reverse carries a gender reversal: the poet is a defeated she-eagle, the emblematic negative (in 1814) of Napoleonic triumph.[23]

To feminize the Poet's possessed soul amid nature's torments is to crave the release, the consummation devoutly to be wished, from everything feminine. The deepest logic of *Alastor* becomes a metaphysical devaluation of anything gendered feminine—or, to put the real case, a feminine gendering of anything metaphysically devalued, summed in the last lines as "Nature's vast frame, the web of human things, / Birth and the grave, that are not as they were" (719–20). The frame-poet leaves his brethren with a scene of mother-nature as a vast array of spiritual absences, and with elegiac desire inscribed entirely by and for men: a dyad of a poet and his male epipsyche, the lost Poet.[24] *Alastor* concludes in this solidarity of masculine spirits with one another, and against all powers gendered, in protective anticipation, as feminine.

Tuned to Shelleyan narratives of dissolution, Keats tells soul stories in a lusher tone, a "soul . . . lost in pleasant smotherings" ("I stood tip-toe" 132). In theory, as Woodhouse discerns (and explains to Keats's publisher), Keats's poetics of "no Identity" (*L* 1: 387) are soul excursions: "The highest order of Poet" is one

> able to throw his own soul into t̶h̶e̶ any object he sees or imagines, so as to see feel & be sensible of, & express, all that the object wo^d see feel & be sensible of or express—& he will speak out of that object [. . .] He lives for a time in their souls or Essences of ideas. (*L* 1: 389)

Woodhouse is explicating poetic power of the highest order, but both he and Keats are aware of the fatal bargain of this soul-loss, however willed, in lived experience—a loss Keats tracks initially in his heroes, then in self-invested speakers, then in self-identified speakers. "The soul is in a ferment," explained the poet of *Endymion* in a self-tasking Preface. Dream-rapt with the moon, the hero sighs of a "dazzled soul / Commingling with her argent spheres" (1.594–95) and senses a plot "to knit / My soul with under darkness" (701–2). From beginning to end, his soul is devoted to the feminine, in the shape of deities or mortals or of both. Keats intuits the role of genre in the genders of soul lost and found. In *Ode to Psyche,* the primer of the story, he suspends narrative (too prone to arcs of pursuit and loss) for a genre that can rest in, and arrest, passionate petition: the ode. The courtship is deftly liminal: evoking the Coleridgean idea of sex in souls, the odist invites feminine soul into his working brain, to be seduced and made creative. In "allegorical meaning," Morris Dickstein proposes that Psyche figures more as "mind or soul than as beautiful girl" (199); but in Keatsian psychology, the sex matters—especially for an imagination whose inspirations, as Marjorie Levinson suggests, tend toward autoerotic figures (*Keats's Life* 27). In an earlier romance, Keats had warmly figured poetry as "the deed / That my own soul has to itself decreed" (*Sleep and Poetry* 97–98). By revising this self-stimulation as a heterosexual romance, he may claim the deed fulfilled on the analogy of male erotic potency.

Yet the map of *Ode to Psyche* subtracts as much as it imagines. The mind that builds a fane for Psyche to find Love, leaves that a prospect amid an "untrodden region," "dark-cluster'd" in "shadowy thought" (51–67). The hero of a romance Keats would concoct a few months on exposes the defensive aggression behind the tenuous enchantment. Emparadised with his psychic enchantress, Lycius tells Lamia how he wishes "to entangle, trammel up and snare/Your soul in mine, and labyrinth you there" (*Lamia* 2.52–53). This desire seems kin to the erotic caginess of *Ode to Psyche*, but on the arc of Lycius's fate (this is a narrative), its bravado is set for a fall. In Keats's later, last stories of soul-courtship, a male soul in peril before feminine power dooms to ruin the body of a male poet.

Even the stasis of an ode cannot fend off the existential peril. The quiet love-bower of *Ode to Psyche* shifts in *Ode on Melancholy* to the "sovran shrine" of "Veil'd Melancholy" (26), the goddess who commands a "wakeful anguish of the soul" (10) and self-surrender: "his soul shall taste the sadness of her might, / And be among her cloudy trophies hung" (29–30). In Keats's most desperate scenes of the soul, his private poems to Fanny Brawne, no sacrifice may suffice. His beloved may not "prize [his] subdued soul"—a noun revised from *heart* (*To Fanny* 49). "O, let me once more rest / My soul upon that dazzling breast!" he begs her ("What can I do?" 48–49). In "I cry your mercy," the petition to this hyper-infused female object of desire—"O, let me have thee whole,—all,—all—be mine!" (5)—chimes its term of frustrated plenitude, *whole*, in muted internal rhyme with the unavailing female *soul*, and casts an all-all-or-nothing result: "Yourself—your soul—in pity give me all, / Withhold no atom's atom or I die" (9–10). In this man's story of collapsing self-possession, the woman's soul is a vital nurture, and gender difference renders it as alien as it is essential.[25]

For this unmanned soul, Byron strangely turns out to be the liberal template, by force of theorizing, as the foundational existential deformation, any soul pent in earthbound clay. In his "human soul," said John Wilson, reviewing *Childe Harold's Pilgrimage, Canto IV*, "in his feelings, his passions, his musings, his aspirings, his troubled scepticism, and his high longings after immortality, his eagle-winged raptures, his cold, dull, leaden fears, his agonies, his exultation, and his despair,—we tremble to think unto what a mysterious nature we belong" (*Blackwood's* 3: 216). Wilson is not sanguine about the material fallout:

> Of the danger resulting from such poetry to souls of fine aspirations, but unsteadfast wills,—to souls where passion is the only or chief impulse, and where there is a tendency to hold cheap, and in derision, the dull duties of ordinary life, and at the same time not strength sufficient to grasp and master the objects of a more ambitious existence,—to such souls (and they are numerous among the youth of Britain,) that poetry is most fatal which [. . .] renders reason itself subservient to the senses. (3: 217)

The antidote is the old soul-story: the rebellious Byronic he-soul must be "elevated by [a] communion" with "nature in the sinless happiness which she has created, sanctified, and blest against violence and decay." It is Wordsworth's spousal verse, Wilson proposes, that Byron needs to take to heart, to discover therein terms of "penance, means to have fitted and disposed his soul for the reception and love of [. . .] lofty and universal truths" (3: 218).

Yet the marriage plot of taming the rebellious Byronic soul to Wordsworthian she-redemption sighs a rather dull end to Wilson's conspicuous enchantment by "the haunted darkness of the human soul" that he cherishes in *Childe Harold*, a darkness of "more awful interest than the mere halo round the brow of a poet" (3: 216). In the romance of Byronic soul, women, too, could find an interest, especially where passion is the throbbing pulse.

She-Souls

If Romantic men write a poetics of soul that is also a poetics of gendered agons, what happens when the writer is a woman?

> We can see the man of high poetic genius delighting in the wide-rolling ocean, as it heaves its yeasty waves, in dark resistless might beneath a frowning sky; his soul is strengthened to hold high converse with the elements, and with the spirits which his magician-wand calls forth from the vasty deep.

So wrote a woman, M. A. Stodart, on her way to sorting out (Rowton-wise) female difference (89). This plan notwithstanding, it is her pen that gives this rapture of male genius, that converses with the language of Shakespeare and Milton. Even though it's an ironic moment in Shakespeare (Hotspur satirizing Glendower's boast of power; *1 Henry IV* 3.1), in remembering the power, the author of *Female Writers: Thoughts on Their Proper Sphere* (*proper* as decorum and distinction) erupts, for a moment, into she-soaring with the enthusiasms of a man's soul.

By contrast, Jewsbury decided to headline the pivotal Chapter V of *The History of an Enthusiast* (1830) with the usual she-restraints, an epigraph endorsed with a didactic signature:

> As far as human soul may be let loose
> From impositions of necessity,—
> Forgetting oft, in self-willed fancy's flight,
> All human ties that would enchain her dreams
> Down to a homelier bliss; and loving more
> The dim aerial shadow of this life,
> Even than the substance of the life itself.
> PROFESSOR WILSON[26]

This is the John Wilson who fell for Byron's dark soul. In this image of necessity, the errant, "self-willed" soul that would forget constraints is feminized. Such frustration may be a universal case, but its feminine figuring matters, both in the run of lines in *An Evening in Furness Abbey* (230–36), the source of the epigraph, and in the import for the *History* at hand. When passionate Julia refuses ties to home, she earns a pass to no-woman's land. With no analogous penalty, Professor Wilson's loosening is a phase of youthful wandering that is just slightly, not egregiously, truant:

> wandering thus
> In ignorance of the future of my life,
> Nor caring, wishing, hoping, fearing aught
> Beyond the pregnant present—each wild day
> A world within itself, my griefs and joys
> All at my own creation and command,
> As far as human soul may be let loose . . .   (*Evening* 224–30)

And so forth, into the epigraphic verse. Although alienated wandering did ensue, by the present moment of fond recollection, paradise has been found at home:

> . . . it has pleased high Heaven to crown my life
> With such a load of happiness, that at times
> My very soul is faint with bearing up
> The bless'd burden. . . . (271–74)
>
> . . .
>
> How changed my state from what it was of yore,
> When 'mid an hundred homes no home had I
> Whose hearth had power to chain me from the rest! (324–26)

In this story of soul-salvation, Wilson indulges the paradox of burdens as blessings. Even so, the "chain" of that happy home is an arresting figure, in sympathy for just a moment with the impositions of necessity that culture puts on the female soul. It matters that Wilson comes to this state having had the freedom to do and be otherwise. Jewsbury's heroine knows only the chains. Nodding to Wollstonecraft on the "specious slavery which chains the very soul of woman" (*VRW* 281)—namely, female social fate—Julia, yearning for the wide world, can write only satirically of "home" ties as "fetters to our souls" (*Enthusiast* 149).

Answering Professor Wilson, Jewsbury has Julia raid a more liberal store of male-signed soul-poetry. Girl Julia revels in Shakespeare, the poet who seems (said Hazlitt) "to pass from one [character] to another, like the same soul successively animating different bodies."[27] She is cautioned of the penalty by Cecil

Percy, that unsoulful friend from her girlhood: "your having wholly, and all at once, plunged your spirit into an intellectual fountain of emotion, of which Goëthe and Schiller, Petrarch and de Staël, and Shelly [*sic*], and a dozen others, are the presiding spirits, will be productive of more loss than gain" (59). To this "grave, old-gentlemanly, discouraging glance" (60), Julia retorts with a customized revision of the soul-song of Ocean goddess Asia that closes Act 2 of *Prometheus Unbound*:

> "My soul is an enchanted boat,
>   Which, like a sleeping swan, doth float
> Upon the silver waves of *their* sweet singing.
>   And each doth like an angel sit
>   Beside the helm conducting it,
> Whilst all the winds with melody are ringing.
>   It seems to float, ever, for ever,
>   Upon that many-winding river,
>   Between mountains, woods, abysses,
>   A paradise of wildernesses!
>
>   . . .
>
>   And we sail on, away, afar,
>   Without a cloud, without a star,
> But by the instinct of sweet music driven." (*Enthusiast* 59)

Julia's italicized *their* shifts the referent of Asia's *thy* (a voice in the air) to the voices of her books, the feeders of her intellectual soul. Her wording not only refutes Cecil, it also bends Shelley's script (Asia is devoted to Prometheus) to her own ends: a story of female desire not devoted to the needs of men in crisis. Not long after, Julia is imagining a "communion of spirit" with a male epipsyche, an idea (she says) that "seems to give my soul wings" (*Enthusiast* 64). Soul for Cecil is merely the admonisher of "the eternal future": renounce "the gay and gorgeous life you lead," he scolds Julia; "entering that solemn chamber of the soul wherein conscience sits enthroned as judge, dare to ask yourself whether you are fulfilling the great end of existence" (122). Nothing could be further from the declaration of another "history," *Biographium Fæmineum,* that "the soul may have as fair and ample a chamber in the brain of a woman as of a man." Keeping a fair and ample prospect open, Jewsbury writes a sarcastic, counter-patriarchal response for Julia: "What more, father Cecil?" (122).

It is the other Percy in the *History*, Percy Shelley, who proves her soul-mate. Even (especially) in defeat, Shelley endows all enthusiasts with claims to poetic power, power felt in epochs of political and social struggle: "The soul of

Adonais, like a star, / Beacons from the abode where the Eternal are" (*Adonais* LV).[28] Julia's last turn to Shelley is to his self-cast image as martyr to the immediate hours, in devotion to higher sympathies. Weary of a world that has "paralyze[d] all the finer functions of the soul," and blasted all hope of regaining the "child-like surrender of the soul to fresh and vigorous impulses" (*Enthusiast* 114–15), Julia sighs the poetry of Shelley's abjection, sighs, too, the "enchain[ed] dreams" of Professor Wilson's verse. But it also through Shelley's inspired West Wind (recall) that she casts her soul beyond the bounds of English propriety.

In a culture mad for marriage-plotted novels, Jewsbury's poetics of the female soul register a world of conflicts. Unsettled by this latent but legible critique of the cultural present, Mrs. Ellis sounds its report, when she conspicuously recasts the soul-narrative of the *History* into a negative exemplum, constraining its transgressions and reinvesting the surplus spiritual capital into the paradigm of corrective trial. Writing of Jewsbury's real-life domestic burdens (including the care of several younger siblings), she has to exert a syntactic discipline on what she senses might matter to a woman's soul—and clearly matters to any credentialed male Romantic soul:

> Yet at the same time, that there burned within her soul the unquenchable fire of a genius too powerful to be extinguished by the many cares of her arduous life, so fearful was she of being absorbed by any selfish pursuit, that she made it a point of conscience never to take up a book, until all her little charge had retired to rest for the night. (34)

In the frame of moralizing, Ellis can concede a burning in some female souls, as long as it is contained by a discipline that can deny itself the pleasure of its heat.

Hemans may seem to be more congenial to the likes of Mrs. Ellis, since her poetic fame is the embrace of the female soul as a domestic soul. She was this figure in Jewsbury's day and for decades after, epitomizing the "ethereal purity of sentiment, which could only emanate from the soul of a woman"—so Jeffrey wrote in that canonical essay on Hemans published in 1829, the year before *History of an Enthusiast* appeared (*Edinburgh Review* 50: 37). Twenty years on, Rowton was tuning his note on Hemans's soul in *Female Poets* to the same gender scale:

> her works are to my mind a perfect embodiment of woman's soul:—I would say that they are *intensely* feminine. The delicacy, the softness, the pureness, the quick observant vision, the ready sensibility, the devotedness, the faith of woman's nature find in Mrs. Hemans their ultra representative. (407)

Rowton is happy to offer Hemans not just as a reflective representative *of* woman, but also as an exemplary representative *to* women. Elizabeth Barrett, as unorthodox as Jewsbury, certainly felt this force, and refused its pull. "I admire her genius—love her memory—respect her piety & high moral tone," she sighed in 1842 to Mary Mitford (who warmly admired Hemans); "But she always does seem to me a lady rather than a woman, & so, much rather than a poetess—her refinement, like the prisoner's iron . . enters into her soul."[29]

Yet Hemans chafed against the iron, her restlessness all the more compelling for its emergence in the mainstream rather than from angry depths or remote frontiers. Jewsbury understood this, and read the prisoner's iron not in Hemans's propriety, but in the "pains & penalties of female authorship": "Her fame has gilded <u>her</u> chain, but it has not lost its clank," she wrote to Dora Wordsworth in 1829 (WLMS A 17). If Barrett's impression of soul-refinement is true to much of Hemans's poetry,[30] so is her simile, "the prisoner's iron." Often, and passionately, Hemans writes of "woman" (rather than "lady") in prisons that will either kill her soul or provoke its defiance. Adversity presses on two soul-fronts: a darkened domesticity, and recurring fantasies of release, rebellion, or violent retaliation. The soul of Eudora in *The Bride of the Greek Isle,* one of the *Records of Woman* (1828), makes its debut as a site of trouble, a mysterious surplus for "woman":

> . . . the glance of her dark resplendent eye,
> For the aspect of woman at times too high,
> Lay floating in mists, which the troubled stream
> Of the soul sent up o'er its fervid beam. (15–18)

In the earlier *New Monthly Magazine* text, Hemans put a capital *W* to "woman" to signal gendered soul-trouble (and the affiliation to the "Records of Woman" series). If eyes are the windows of the soul, Hemans gives Eudora's soul a double-sexing, female and Byronic—the latter via "troubled stream," a signature of the Byronic hero. It is a direct citation of the iconic avatar, chained Titanic sufferer Prometheus:

> Thou art a symbol and a sign
>   To Mortals of their fate and force;
> Like thee, man is in part divine,
>   A troubled stream from a pure source;
> And Man in portions can foresee
> His own funereal destiny. (*Prometheus* 45–50)

Hemans's initiative for the female soul is to convert Byron's Man in Titanic/

Oedipal strife into Woman in emergent conflict with patriarchal social fate. If Eudora's impending marriage to "her soul's affianced" (37) seems to melt away "the cloud, on her soul that lay" (81), her soul-trouble foresees the funereal destiny that overtakes the marriage plot.

A utopia of double-sexed souls was how *Dublin University Magazine* cast Hemans's imagination: "She created for herself a world of high-souled men and women, whose love" was "a deep o'er-mastering stream, strong, steady, and unbroken" (10/56, 135). Yet it is revealing that *Dublin* imposes worldly distinctions of gender even in this ideal world of high souls: "the MEN" are famed for courage and fortitude; "the WOMEN" "sing hymns of passive worship" or "rush amid the spears and receive the wound meant for a sterner heart," or, following the conduct lore, submit "to bear uncomplaining agonies—and above all! to wait long, long days for the deceiver who will not return, to know the deadly sickness of a fading hope, and at last to dedicate a broken heart to him who has crushed it!" (135–36). About this run of infinitives (and I haven't quoted all of them), it is difficult to say whether the *Dublin* is describing a high soul or fated ordeal.[31]

The question haunts even Hemans's iconic early poem, *The Domestic Affections* (1812), which over the course of its elaboration manages to expose a terrible economy for woman's soul. Synonymous with female soul, domestic affections restore the souls of world-weary men, and in this solace evoke the ultimate home for the souls of all. This is woman's highest calling, her true work:

> Her angel-voice his fainting soul can raise
> To brighter visions of celestial days!
> And speak of realms, where virtue's wing shall soar
> On eagle-plume—to wonder and adore!
> And friends, divided here, shall meet at last,
> Unite their kindred souls—and smile on all the past.   (301–6)

These unities, kindred and divine, include woman. In celestial days to come, gentle spirits will "sooth her soul,/With soft enchantments and divine control," and be the "sweet guardians" that will "watch her sacred rest,/When slumber folds her in his magic vest" (395–98). Yet how peculiar these terms of salvation: being cared for, soul-soothed rather than charged with soothing others. This is the redemption not just from general "bonds of clay" (416) but specifically from woman's weary lot. *The Domestic Affections* closes in an image of an "Elysian clime" where women's souls at last gain what the worldly domestic sphere gives men, a final (punning) "consoling":

> Yes! in the noon of that Elysian clime,
> Beyond the sphere of anguish, death, or time;

> Where mind's bright eye, with renovated fire,
> Shall beam on glories—never to expire;
> Oh! there, th'illumin'd soul may fondly trust,
> More pure, more perfect, rising from the dust;
> Those mild affections, whose consoling light
> Sheds the soft moon-beam on terrestrial night;
> Sublim'd, ennobled, shall for ever glow,
> Exalting rapture—not assuaging woe! (423–32)

If teenage Felicia Browne (not yet "Mrs. Hemans") does not theorize gender asymmetry in *The Domestic Affections*, she surely reflects it, and nowhere more sharply than in these last words, where sublimation is worked across a double negative for woman's soul in the world.

Unlike women constrained at home and gaining rapture only in the next world, men (young Felicia was sure) had the wide theater of this world for their souls. "You know not what an <u>enthusiast</u> I am in the cause of Castile and liberty: my whole heart and soul are interested for the gallant patriots," she wrote to her aunt in 1808, when her brother was fighting in Spain, only to add, "though females are forbidden to interfere in politics" (*CMH* 1: 31). About the glory of warfare this is naive (her brother and future husband were being ravaged by the ordeals), but the gender prohibition was real. The proper, lifeless syllabus for a girl's heart and soul is the lesson treated in one of her most popular poems, *Evening Prayer, at a Girls' School* (first published in the female-marketed *Forget Me Not* [1826]). Putting in a female frame Gray's ode on the boys of Eton College, Hemans superimposes her adult melancholy: "in those flute-like voices, mingling low, / Is woman's tenderness—how soon her woe!" (23–24)—*woe!* echoing the last word of *The Domestic Affections*. The refrain "Therefore pray!" comes increasingly to sound like cold comfort. "Her lot is on you," the poet says more than once to the girls, as her verses descend into a rueful, almost bitter litany of the trials and frustrations that await the female soul:

> Her lot is on you—silent tears to weep,
>   And patient smiles to wear through suffering's hour,
> And sumless riches, from affection's deep,
>   To pour on broken reeds—a wasted shower!
> And to make idols, and to find them clay,
> And to bewail that worship—Therefore pray!
>
> Her lot is on you—to be found untir'd,
>   Watching the stars out by the bed of pain,
> With a pale cheek, and yet a brow inspir'd,

>   And a true heart of hope, though hope be vain;
>   Meekly to bear with wrong, to cheer decay,
>   And, oh! to love through all things—therefore pray! (25–36)

If prayer speaks the soul, the lesson here is that the girls' memory of these vespers will be their only soul-nurture, "a sweet dew to keep your souls from blight" amid all that "Earth will forsake" (40–41).[32] So, too, in *Woman on the Field of Battle* (in *Songs of the Affections*) love is a "trust / Woman's deep soul too long / Pours on the dust!" (53–60). Nothing could be bleaker than identifying the soul itself as the conveyer of trust to dust—an annihilation redeemed only when, as Felicia Browne intuited in the same rhyme in *The Domestic Affections,* "th'illumin'd soul may fondly trust, / More pure, more perfect, rising from the dust" (427–28).

In *Records of Woman,* Hemans sets the betrayal as a categorical grievance of "Woman" across history and culture, with a common indictment of men. In *Indian Woman's Death-Song,* a discarded wife commits herself and her daughter to a suicidal canoe borne by the "Father of ancient waters" (16). Lamenting that she has "faded from [her husband's] soul, as fades a moonbeam's trace" (21), she hopes for deliverance to soul-healing:

>   Some blessed fount amidst the woods of that bright land must flow,
>   Whose waters from my soul may lave the memory of this wo. (32–33)
>
>   And where the soul shall find its youth, as wakening from a dream,—
>   (42)

The soul of a woman, Hemans lets herself say through this exotic voice, is driven out of this world by gendered tyrannies, propelled to death by the Father of ancient waters. Her only hope is to be borne to, and reborn in a world elsewhere, across the divide of death.

If women are provoked to more immediate political retaliation (rather than sigh for spiritual oblivion and rebirth), in Hemans's records this proves a distinction without a difference. Maimuna, a Muslim widow on a pilgrimage to Mecca, erupts in violent passion when Brahmin children slay her son for wandering onto their holy ground (*The Indian City*). Imaging her grief as a soul in submission—"Her soul sat veil'd in its agony" (109–12)—Hemans makes the transformed soul the site of political reaction:

>   And what deep change, what work of power,
>   Was wrought on her secret soul that hour?
>   How rose the lonely one?—She rose
>   Like a prophetess from dark repose!

> And proudly flung from her face the veil,
> And shook the hair from her forehead pale,
>
> . . .
>
> And said—"Not yet—not yet I weep,
> Not yet my spirit shall sink or sleep,
> Not till yon city, in ruins rent,
> Be piled for its victim's monument." (121–25, 133–36)

Hemans invests this anger with Shelleyan poetic power, realized rather than merely dreamily epipsychic, in the call for "Moslem war" (146):

> Maimuna from realm to realm had pass'd,
> And her tale had rung like a trumpet's blast.
> There had been words from her pale lips pour'd,
> Each one a spell to unsheath the sword. (161–64)

Rather than unsex this emergence, Hemans romances a female heroic:

> . . . her voice had kindled that lightning flame;
> She came in the might of a queenly foe . . .
>
> . . .
>
> Her eye's wild flash through the tented line
> Was hail'd as a spirit and a sign,
> And the faintest tone from her lip was caught,
> As a Sybil's breath of prophetic thought. (170–71, 175–78)

Such a flash shows why Jewsbury praised Hemans's ability to "combine power and beauty" (*Athenæum* 171: 104). But just as telling is the female fate of "Vain, bitter glory" (179). Wrung with "the yearning left by a broken tie," the bereft mother turns sickening "from her sad renown, / As a king in death might reject his crown" (183–86), and soon makes good on the analogy with her own death, allied to the vanquished city rather than the victors.

The summary image is of a she-soul imprisoned in a doomed, besieged city:

> Slowly the strength of the walls gave way—
> *She* wither'd faster, from day to day.
> All the proud sounds of that banner'd plain,
> To stay the flight of her soul were vain;
> Like an eagle caged, it had striven, and worn
> The frail dust ne'er for such conflicts born,
> Till the bars were rent, and the hour was come
> For its fearful rushing thro' darkness home. (187–94)

The simile gains effect from its regendering of Byron's famous analogy, in *Childe Harold III,* of the pent he-soul as a caged falcon:

> But in Man's dwellings he became a thing
> Restless and worn, and stern and wearisome,
> Droop'd as a wild-born falcon with clipt wing,
> To whom the boundless air alone were home:
> Then came his fit again, which to o'ercome,
> As eagerly the barr'd-up bird will beat
> His breast and beak against his wiry dome
> Till the blood tinge his plumage, so the heat
> Of his impeded soul would through his bosom eat. (XV)

Only the vehicle, the impeded falcon-soul, is doomed in Byron's analogy. The tenor, Harold, "wanders forth again" (XVI). Not that he, "Self-exiled" (XVI), is ever free from torment; but the heroic existential wandering is something Hemans recognizes as a "Man's" freedom. In the record of Woman, Maimuna's caged soul has a last "fitful gust" (206) in yearning for death, and gains its longed-for release only then.

It is heroic action that Jewsbury gives female soul in *Arria,* but her master-narrative is just as death-bound.[33] Imprisoned with husband Pætus, Arria urges him to die with honor "by his own right hand." He is "in soul and strength subdued" by his fetters, so it's up to the "woman high" to summon her soul "to teach *him* how to die" (123).

> Ages, since then, have swept along;—
>   Arria is but a name,—
> Yet still is woman's love as strong,
>   Still woman's soul the same;—
> Still soothes the mother and the wife,
> Her cherished ones 'mid care and strife:
> *It is not painful, Pætus*—still
> Is love's word in the hour of ill. (124)

The italics are Arria's last words, her name the inner literals of "m*arria*ge." Whether in heroic or in melancholy tempers, the heroism of "woman's soul" that is continuous with "Woman's Love" is the reiterated subject of celebration throughout the volumes of *Phantasmagoria,* nowhere more so than in the ringing conclusion of an essay bearing the title "Woman's Love:"

> to manifest a faith which never fails, a patience that never wears out, a devotedness which can sacrifice, and a courage which can suffer;—to perform

the same, unvarying, round of duties, without weariness,—and endure the same unvarying round of vexations, without murmuring;—to requite neglect with kindness, and injustice with fidelity;—to be true, when all are false,—and firm, when all is hopeless;—to watch over the few dear objects of regard, with an eye that never sleeps, and a care that cannot change;—to think, to act, to suffer, to sacrifice, to live, to die, for them, their happiness and safety,—These are Woman's true triumphs;—this, this, is WOMAN'S LOVE.[34]

Offering an essay in 1833 on noble and virtuous instances of "The Female Character," *Fraser's* measured the occasional "exalted heroism of a woman's soul" as a departure from nature: "excited by love, religion, patriotism, parental affection, gratitude, pity" to "powerful" exertion, "a female can divest herself of the retiring gentleness of her nature" (594–95). This is "extraordinary," *Fraser's* said. But Jewsbury spans the gap between the quotidian domestic and ordinary heroism, and insists, via her roll of infinitives, that these triumphs are characteristic and universal; the historical agency and result are mere contingencies.

Summoning Roman models, Lucy Aikin's *Epistles on Women* (1810) refutes sex-determined soul-stories, and presses a Wollstonecrafted claim that, in the sublime text of "Virtue," genders vanish and "Souls have no sex":

> See there the ghost of noble Portia glide,
> Cato to lead, and Brutus at her side!
> Souls have no sex; sublimed by Virtue's lore
> Alike they scorn the earth and try to soar;
> Buoyant alike on daring wing they rise
> As Emulation nerves them for the skies.
> See Paetus' wife, by strong affection manned,
> Taste the sharp steel and give it to his hand. (Epistle III, *Epistles* 57)

Yet as arresting as the claim of "no sex" is the final adjective for earthly Arria (named only as Paetus' wife): *manned*.[35] This may be a Wollstonecraft purchase on the adjective, or it may be a contradictory concession that for a woman, to unsex the soul is really to claim a man's soul.

This is not Hemans's venture. Strong affection always womans the soul, even in the figure of the ambitious female artist. The modest (also basic) case is the eponym of *The Sicilian Captive* (1825). As she sings of her lost home, her "soul grew strong" from the inspiration (40), and Sicily's "soul flow[s] o'er [her] lips again" (52). The inspiration is killing: "Doth not thy shadow wrap my soul?" (43). When, recalling the "sweet sounds" of Sicily, the captive exclaims, "the soul to hear them faints in dreams of heaven away!" (66), the denouement is fated. At her song's close (also the poem's last lines) we learn, "She had pour'd out her soul with her song's last tone; / The lyre was broken, the minstrel gone!" (83–84).

The more conflicted cases, in representation and in female reception, were keyed to the novel that Hemans, Jewsbury, and Barrett all studied with care: the age's premier story of female fame, soul-sorrow and heartbreak, Staël's *Corinne*. Its heroine—the Queen of Enthusiasts—laments, "il y a dans mon ame des abîmes de tristesse dont je ne pouvais me défendre qu'en me préservant de l'amour." <u>C'est moi</u>, Hemans wrote next to these sentences.[36] Hemans's Corinne is Properzia Rossi, for whom artistic power is no compensation for a lovelorn "aching soul." The opening lines of Hemans's epigraph give the cue:

> ————Tell me no more, no more
> Of my soul's lofty gifts! Are they not vain
> To quench its haunting thirst for happiness?

The unhappiness of lofty gifts is a stock Romantic measure for the pains of genius. "One dream of passion and of beauty more!" Rossi cries for her art, "And in its bright fulfillment let me pour / My soul away!" (1–3). Like the Sicilian Captive, who pours her soul into her song, Rossi synonymizes self-consuming and self-realizing. Where is the pressure of gender-fate? A male poet may invoke some feminine blessing to nurture and complete his masculine soul (or, if not, to suffer slander as the gender of every bafflement to such desire). The female poet enjoys no reciprocal arrangement. Her yearning soul is doomed to cultural alienation (Jewsbury's Enthusiast has to leave England for the sake of her soul) or, as Hemans keeps imagining, the alienation of life itself.

Yet even in the midst of rendering this miserable she-economy, Hemans pauses for an alternative imagination. In Rossi's voice, she writes a romance of the soul's lofty gifts working along with, rather than against, the heart. Feeling a "power" of inspiration, Rossi greets it "proudly" (25) and with a sense of immortal creation: "I shall not perish all!" (28)

> The bright work grows
> Beneath my hand, unfolding, as a rose,
> Leaf after leaf, to beauty; line by line,
> I fix my thought, heart, soul, to burn, to shine,
> Thro' the pale marble's veins.   (29–33)

Rossi's sculpture of Ariadne is her mournful epipsyche, and Rossi herself is this mirror for Hemans, all relaying a trans-historical sisterhood of the lovelorn. Even so, the interval of artistic work, inspired by united "thought, heart, soul," sets out a different psychic economy, of the "aching soul" (68) transformed by the bright work of art.

One of Hemans's last poems, a sonnet written in 1834 in failing health, elevates and identifies with this moment in Rossi's history. The soul of *Design and Performance* is given entirely to artistic inspiration and labor, and it is not gendered. Its frustration is not of any domestic affection, but of mortality itself:

> They float before my soul, the fair designs
> Which I would body forth to Life and Power,
> Like clouds, that with their wavering hues and lines
> Pourtray majestic buildings:—Dome and tower,
> Bright spire, that through the rainbow and the shower
> Points to th' unchanging stars; and high arcade,
> Far-sweeping to some glorious altar, made
> For holiest rites:—meanwhile the waning hour
> Melts from me, and by fervent dreams o'erwrought,
> I sink:—O friend! O link'd with each high thought
> Aid me, of those rich visions to detain
> All I may grasp; until thou see'st fulfill'd,
> While time and strength allow, my hope to build
> For lowly hearts devout, but *one* enduring fane!

Where Coleridge imagined sexed souls, Hemans's design revises the gendering that grants only men's souls the force of desire and the romance of power. She accomplishes this in part by a textual marriage to male imaginings. There are strains of Shelley's *Ode to Liberty,* both its soul-story ("My soul spurned the chains of its dismay, / And in the rapid plumes of song / Clothed itself, sublime and strong" [5–7]) and its visionary architecture: "a city such as vision / Builds from the purple crags and silver towers / Of battlemented cloud" (61–63). There is a calm revision of the climax of *Epipsychidion* ("I pant, I sink, I tremble, I expire!" [591]). There are echoes of Wordsworth: "Earth has not any thing to shew more fair: / Dull would he be of soul who could pass by / A sight so touching in it's majesty: // . . . towers, domes" (*Composed Upon Westminster Bridge*); and a subdued version of the heart-swelling vision given to his despondent Solitary ("Clouds of all tincture, rocks and sapphire sky, // . . . composing thus . . . // . . . that marvellous array" [*Excursion* 2.854*ff*]). If Romantic men court an external soul with a sensation of alien inspiration, Hemans creates with other texts of soul. Her sonnet is intertextual soul poetry.

In the decade that Hemans died, Wollstonecraft's argument against sex in souls had come to seem unconvincing to her daughter Mary Shelley:

> My Mother had more energy of character—still she had not sufficient fire of imagination—In short my belief is—whether there be sex in souls or not—that the sex of our material mechanism makes us quite different creatures—better

though weaker but wanting in the higher grades of intellect.—(11 June 1835; *L* 2: 246)

Yet if Shelley defers the question of sexed soul, feeling more forcefully the determinism of the material body ("essentialism" by another name), back in 1816–17 she fronted a male character, Robert Walton, to inhabit these higher gradations. Writing to a sister whose name shares Mary Wollstonecraft Shelley's initials, he tells Margaret Walton Saville of feeling, on the verge of his adventures, "a steady purpose,—a point on which the soul may fix its intellectual eye" (*Frankenstein* 8).[37] Shelley did not revise this sentence in the 1831 text. As a female conception of male visionary venture, Walton's polar orientation of soul corresponds to Hemans's and Jewsbury's imaginations of soul-worlds elsewhere (call it North Pole, call it Heaven, call it Europe), all in effect a critique of the quotidian world of soul-shackled woman.

Transmigrations

Already in the making in the early 1830s was another figure of design and performance, Sand's Lélia, whose extravagant refusal of a conventionally feminine soul inspired the reviewer for *Athenæum* (a publication notably hospitable to women writers, including Jewsbury and Barrett) to strip Sand of any claim to soul: this is "a monster, a Byronic woman—endowed with rich and energetic faculties, delicate perceptions, rare eloquence, fine talents, but no heart—a woman without hope and without soul."[38] Inadvertently published in this scandal was something Hemans and Mary Shelley were on the verge of imagining and Jewsbury was clearly feeling, if not yet theorizing, on her pulses: the knowledge that women, too, could embrace the romance of alienation, by disdaining the "soul" assigned to them as the gendered bearer of cultural hope.

Arguing that "English feminine training" is antithetical to the "long experience [in] the meannesses of the world" that is a "necessary qualification for a great writer," an essay in *London Review* in 1864 titled "Literary Women" hit the same measure of Sand's aberration. To become the "greatest female author living" she had to undergo "a defeminizing process":

> How much has George Sand given up to gain her literary crown. She has simply abandoned the distinctive characteristics, not to say the distinctive mission, of her sex. She has gratified her genius by immolating to it her instincts and her nature. [. . .] though literary women amongst us would be horrified if they were told that George Sand was a type of themselves, she is a beacon that points out the rocks and shoals [. . .] in the direction of which most of them are sailing. (329)[39]

This radical caution hatches an unpremediated visionary phoenix-myth for women, of sex incinerated and reborn in the new formation of "George Sand"—a herald of a no-woman's land beckoning literary women, perhaps not horrified at all, to new directions.

This is a direction towards which some late Romantic women would sail, full-souled: "Beth was a poet herself—& there was the reigning thought—No woman was ever such a poet as she wd be," writes Barrett in an autobiographical tale etched with soul-gendering: "when she grew up she wd wear men's clothes.... One word Beth hated in her soul ... & the word was 'feminine.' Beth thanked her gods that she was not & never wd be feminine."[40] If Beth's Romantic-era sisters were less obstinate, their questionings are a critical legacy, opening the possibility not only of rejecting the feminine in the soul, but of finding new gods to thank for this ungendering.

Four years before eloping with Robert Browning, Barrett imagined herself into a cross-dressed Byronic adventure, a Childe Barrett's Pilgrimage. Impatient with needlework, and excited by a pre-teen encounter with *Rights of Woman,* "through the whole course of my childhood, I had a steady indignation against Nature who made me a woman, & a determinate resolution to dress up in men's clothes as soon as ever I was free of the nursery, & go into the world 'to seek my fortune,'" she recalled to Mary Russell Mitford, adding "'<u>How</u>,' was not decided; but I rather leant towards being poor Lord Byron's PAGE" (*Letters to Mitford* 2: 7). If, as Angela Leighton remarks, "Byron's entourage of would-be girl pages was a large one" (*Writing Against* 82), some women just wanted to be Byron, be Byron by claiming Byronic soul. In 1844 Barrett's sonnet *To George Sand: A Desire,* with no intuition of the monster to be hatched by *London Review* twenty years on, celebrates a woman who breaks out of the feminine with a double-sexed soul:

> Thou large-brained woman and large-hearted man,
> Self-called George Sand! whose soul, amid the lions
> Of thy tumultuous senses, moans defiance
> And answers roar for roar, as spirits can. (1–4)

In French parole, *man* and *Sand* chime and answer. A twin sonnet, *To George Sand: A Recognition,* seems to recant, asking Sand if she can "deny / Thy woman's nature with a manly scorn" (1–2), and suspecting that a "woman's voice" and "woman-heart" "Disprov[e] thy man's name" (6–11). But if this projects biology as destiny, it's not the last word. The sonnet ends imagining a salvation like the one that closes *The Domestic Affections*: "Till God unsex thee on the heavenly shore / Where unincarnate spirits purely aspire!" (13–14). This is the final borderline, past which borders are no more.

Reference Matter

Texts

When possible, I follow lifetime editions, listed in Works Cited. For Keats's posthumously published poems, I follow either an authorial holograph, or Stillinger's edition, but (with reference to his appendices) I restore the variants he modernizes.

Because my argument is historically situated, I approximate the texts as they would have been read in their first eras of reception, and so I have not standardized or modernized typography, orthography, or punctuation, unless indicated. The only exception is quotation-mark convention, which is modernized.

For ms. texts, particularly letters, I cite standard editions, for my readers' convenience. But I also convert editorial interventions back to original scriptive events: thus, italics are underlines; brackets that indicate canceled text are strike-throughs; spelling is not interfered with, if the sense is clear.

Full details on all references appear in Works Cited. Speculations about authorship are indicated with "?"

Abbreviations

When the author is evident, I use standard abbreviations, without clutter to indicate the author. Hence: *CW* for *Collected Works,* or *W* for *Works* (when there is only one edition); *L* for *Letters; PW* for *Poetic Works; PrW* for *Prose Works; P&P* for *Poetry and Prose.* More specific abbreviations are listed below. Titles of journals are abbreviated according to the Master List of Periodicals in the (Modern Language Association) *MLA International Bibliography.* Full information for all texts appears in Words Cited.

BCB	Lady Blessington's *Conversations of Byron,* ed. E. J. Lovell
BCH	*Byron: The Critical Heritage,* ed. A. Rutherford
BL	(Coleridge) *Biographia Literaria,* ed. J. Engell & W. J. Bate
BLJ	Byron's *Letters and Journals,* ed. L. A. Marchand
BPW	Byron's *Poetical Works,* ed. J. J. McGann
BW	Byron's *Works* (John Murray, 1833)
CMH	Chorley's *Memorials of Hemans*
CN	Coleridge's *Notebooks,* ed. K. Coburn
HM	Hughes, *Memoir of Hemans*
HVSV	(Byron), *His Very Self and Voice,* ed. E. J. Lovell
KC	*The Keats Circle,* ed. H. E. Rollins
KCH	*Keats: The Critical Heritage,* ed. G. M. Matthews
KL	Keats's *Letters*
LB	Wordsworth, *Lyrical Ballads,* ed. J. Butler and K. Green
LEY	Wordsworths, *Letters, Early Years,* ed. E. de Selincourt and C. L. Shaver
LLY	Wordsworths, *Letters, Later Years,* ed. E. de Selincourt and A. G. Hill
LMY	Wordsworths, *Letters, Middle Years,* ed. E. de Selincourt, M. Moorman, and A. G. Hill

MCB	Medwin's *Conversations of Byron,* ed. E. J. Lovell
NAL	New American Library
OED	Oxford English Dictionary
P	Jewsbury, *Phantasmagoria*
PL	Milton, *Paradise Lost*
RR	*The Romantics Reviewed,* ed. D. H. Reiman
RW	Hemans, *Records of Woman*
TT	Coleridge's *Table Talk,* ed. C. Woodring
VRM	Wollstonecraft, *Vindication of the Rights of Men*
VRW	Wollstonecraft, *A Vindication of the Rights of Woman,* ed. L. Macdonald and K. Scherf

Notes

Chapter One

1. Wollstonecraft, Letter 1, *Letters Written During a Short Residence* (1796); *W* 6: 248. Blessington, *Conversations of Lord Byron*, 2 and 10 April 1823 (Lovell, ed. 11 and 13).

2. The thesis of Terry Eagleton's "Ideology and Literary Form" (114) is echoed by Mary Poovey's "Ideology as Style": social acts and aesthetic self-expression are so fully "informed at every level by ideology" that "style" is always "ideology as it has been internalized and articulated by an individual" (*Proper Lady* xii-xiii). Jerome McGann's *Romantic Ideology* includes even gestures of critical opposition: however much aesthetic production may reflect and reflect upon social formations (he contends), these formations so thoroughly saturate primary observation that critical opposition is illusory (12–13). Judith Butler concurs with her deconstruction of the binarism of free will and determinism, arguing that construction "is the necessary scene of agency," the formation through which it is "articulated and becomes culturally intelligible" (147).

3. I concur with William Galperin's view of the question, indicated by the double-play title of his study, *The Historical Austen*: the historicism that would make Austen's work answerable to social or political contexts fails to appreciate "the degree to which the novels are just a much a context in themselves, where matters of history" are in play (1).

4. My discussion and quotations are drawn from Greenblatt's arresting Introduction to *Renaissance Self-Fashioning*, especially 4–5.

5. Important critiques at this phase include Margaret Homans, *Women Writers and Poetic Identity* (1980); Alan Richardson, "Romanticism and the Colonization of the Feminine" (1988); Marlon Ross, "Romantic Quest and Conquest: Troping Masculine Power in the Crisis of Poetic Identity" (1988), and *The Contours of Masculine Desire* (1989); Stuart Curran, "The 'I' Altered" (1988), and Anne Mellor, "On Romanticism and Feminism," in *Romanticism and Feminism* (1988), and *Romanticism & Gender* (1992).

6. For a nuanced discussion, see William Keach, "Romanticism and Language."

7. Wollstonecraft's *Vindication of the Rights of Men* (1790) involves questions of gender. In *Rights of Woman*, the word *prescription* first appears in her dedication to Talleyrand (103) and plays, with *prevailing* and *prejudice* (first paired at the opening of ch. 1

[117]) throughout the polemic. For gendering in the British debates on the Revolution, see Claudia L. Johnson, *Equivocal Beings* 1–30.

8. Invested with classical authority and deeper historical origins, the female iconography, argues Lynn Hunt, implied "the rejection of paternalist or patriarchal models," especially the king (31).

9. Both works were cited by the National Assembly in its unanimous declaration of honors: "Il sera élevé à l'auteur d'Émile et du Contrat social une statue portant cette inscription: 'LA NATION FRANÇAIS LIBRE A J.-J. ROUSSEAU.'" In the 1790s, "educational schemes and political schemes went hand in hand" in both England and France—nowhere more than in Rousseau (Chandler 98–99). In feminist polemic, Rousseau was "an object lesson in the danger of trying to abolish the tyranny of rank without sweeping away the tyranny of sex along with it" (Johnson, *Equivocal* 32).

10. Rousseau, in *VRW* 205. Wollstonecraft uses William Kenrick, *Emilius and Sophia; or, A New System of Education* (1762; 1763). My quotations of *Émile* follow *VRW* unless otherwise indicated.

11. "La liberté civile et politique est, pour ainsi dire, inutile aux femmes et par conséquent doit leur être étrangère. Destinées à passer toute leur vie renfermées sous le toit paternel, ou dans la maison maritale, nées pour une dépendance perpétuelle depuis le premier instant de leur existence jusqu'à celui de leur trépas, elles n'ont été douées que de vertus privés. [. . .] Une femme n'est bien, n'est à sa place que dans sa famille ou dans son ménage. De tout ce qui se passe hors de chez elle, elle ne doit savoir que ce que ses parents ou son mari jugent à propos de lui apprendre" (qtd. Tomalin 155; my translation). In *Essai sur l'admission des femmes au droit de la cité* (1790) Condorcet urged equal education and civil status for women; Talleyrand's report to the Constituent Assembly in 1791 advised equal education only to the age of eight, after which girls would learn domestic skills at home. Schools for girls were established in 1880, and female suffrage in 1944.

12. Conservative *citoyennes* declined to "dress in a costume [which] they respected but which they believed was intended for men" (Levy 200).

13. See, in order, Levy & c 214–17; Woshinsky 1; Joan Scott 115; Levy & c 219–220. This report is all the more remarkable given Corday's famously dignified comportment at her trial and execution. For an account, see Schama, *Citizens* 737–41; and Blakemore, *Crisis* 204–6.

14. My translation: "une *virago* [. . .] sans grâce, malpropre, comme le sont presque tous les philosophes et beaux esprits femelles [. . .] vint-cinq ans [. . .] dans nos moeurs, presque vieille fille, et surtout avec un maintien homasse et une stature garçonnierre. [. . .] Sa tête était farcie de livres de toute espèce. [. . .] cette femme s'était jetée absolument hors de son sexe; quand la nature l'y rappelait, elle n'éprouvait que dégoût et ennui; l'amour sentimental et ses douces émotions n'approchent plus du couer de la femme qui a de la prétention au savoir, au bel esprit, à l'esprit fort, à la politique des nations, qui a la manie philosophique et qui brule de se mettre en evidence. Les hommes bien pensants et aimables n'aiment pas les femmes de cette espèce" (Tomalin 152–53).

For Revolution-decade French feminism, see Levy et al. Tomalin studies the effect of French feminism in the 1790s and the Terror on Wollstonecraft (ch. 13), and Poovey reads the effects of the revolution on British views of gender, especially the paradoxes of traditional definitions (30–35).

15. Michelle Callender points out that Wollstonecraft turns a simultaneity of events—the crowd-thronged arrival of the dauphiness and a fire in Place Louis XV—into a cause-and-effect narrative of femme-fatalism (375).

16. *French Revolution* 424–26. In *Rights of Men,* Wollstonecraft paused over this sentence to suggest that the "abominable deformity" Burke excoriates may reflect only a difference in education and class between "the great and small vulgar" (67–68). It is not even clear, suggests Claudia Johnson (*Equivocal* 39), what Burke means by "abused shape": a ready female vehicle for hellborn evil? a denaturing of vile women into mere form? the abuse of female form by men rioting in female garb? Gender reversal is at least readable; but in the mixed mob's rioting, humanity itself seems effaced.

17. In the outer regions of Hell, host to "harpy-footed Furies," "all life dies, death lives, and nature breeds, / Perverse, all monstrous, all prodigious things, / Abominable, inutterable, and worse / Than fables yet have feigned, or fear conceived" (*PL* 2.596, 624–27).

18. For an account of gender in eighteenth-century Britain, especially the cult and culture of sensibility, see G. J. Barker-Benfield, ch. 3, "The Question of Effeminacy" (104–53).

19. Tom Furniss, 195–96. To Furniss, Wollstonecraft merely reorganizes "the old order's ideology of destined or natural hierarchies" for "a different political and economic interest" (209). To Steven Blakemore, she is simply "inverting the sexual clichés" (*Intertextual War* 28). The call for the "bourgeois woman's entry to the 'masculine' domain of the rational" leaves intact the Rousseauvian gender system, argues Caroline Franklin ("Juan's Sea Changes" 63). Yet defamiliarizing inversion is a usual first step in revolutionary critique; moreover, its work is hardly complete, except in some quarters of academia.

20. "Mary Wollstonecraft," *Annual Necrology* 422.

21. So report John Claiborne Isbel and Simone Balayé in *Madame de Staël: Écrits retrouvés* (1994–95); I'm indebted to Caroline Franklin for this information (*Mary Wollstonecraft* 221n21).

22. Quotations are from *VRW* 113, 316, 126–29, 111, 172. Poovey draws on conduct-book authority, especially for the literate middle class. But as Wollstonecraft's ironies indicate, such governance was not absolute; in the hands of Jane Austen, Fordyce is subjected to no little contemptuous satire (e.g., *Pride and Prejudice,* vol. I, chap. 14).

23. Quotations are from *VRW* 127–28, 232, 212, 134, 214, 217, 219; see also 110, 129, 256.

24. Even reinforced, to contain insurgency; see *Émile*: "To cultivate the masculine virtues in women and to neglect their own is evidently to do them an injury"; "when they try to usurp our privileges [. . .] they fall below their own level as women instead of rising to the level of men," while "effeminate" men are merely "foppish manikins who are a disgrace to their own sex and to the sex which they imitate" (Foxley 327–28).

For the modeling of female reading in eighteenth-century Britain on oppositions of "masculine and feminine, public and private, world and home," see Kathryn Shevelow (10). For the constitutive work of gender in literary criticism, see Laura Runge (3 and following).

25. For a pioneering discussion of Meiners in relation to "the woman question," see Caroline Franklin, *Byron's Heroines* (see her index for page references).

26. December 1790 (543), reviewing Helen Maria Williams, *Letters Written in France, in the Summer of 1790*. Channeling British affection for the revolution though a voice of personal enthusiasm, *Letters* opens, "I arrived at Paris," and uses "I" five more times in its first paragraph.

27. Young Polwhele met More in 1777, the year she published her *Essays*. For the sentences he assembles in his footnote, see More *W* 6: 264–66.

28. The reviewer was John Wilson Croker, later scourge of Keats's *Endymion* (1818). The disciplinary rhetoric, William Keach comments, sounds more appropriate to Croker's office as Secretary to the Admiralty ("A Regency Prophecy" 569–70). Murray's remark (which Keach cites) is recorded by Henry Crabb Robinson, who hoped the poem had been written "more in sorrow than in anger." For the "disheartening and dastardly tone in it which even I, with all my love for her, could not excuse," he found the discipline excessive, "a very coarse and even blackguard review [. . .] which, many years afterwards, Murray told me he was more ashamed of than any other article" (Morley 1: 64).

29. Elizabeth R. Montagu's was the most famous, attended not just by women but also by David Garrick, Edmund Burke, and Sir Joshua Reynolds (see Sylvia Harcstark Myers, *Bluestocking Circle* 6–11). Another regular was Benjamin Stillingfleet, who sported the blue worsted stockings customary among working and lower-middle classes for informal or home wear. Black silk was the formal male attire; white silk for business or casual aristocratic posing (see *Portrait of John, Lord Mountstuart* [1763] by Jean-Étienne Liotard, and *Portrait of John Chetwynd Talbot* [1793] by Pompeo Batoni). "Such was the excellence of his conversation," said James Boswell of Stillingfleet, "that his absence was felt as so great a loss, that it used to be said, 'We can do nothing without the *blue stockings*'; and thus by degrees the title was established" (*Life of Dr. Johnson* [1781] 462). More's *Bas Bleu* (more than 220 octosyllabic couplets) takes its title, says her Advertisement, from "the mistake of a foreigner of distinction, who gave the literal appellation" to some friends he had heard called "the Blue Stockings" (*W* [1834] 5: 314).

30. For the constraints on publishing women and the conflicts registered by Hemans and Jewsbury, see Norma Clarke, *Ambitious Heights*, ch. 1 and ch. 2; and Poovey, *Proper Lady*.

31. For Keats, see *L* 2: 139; also 2: 19. For Hazlitt, see "On Great and Little Things" (1821; *W* 8: 236). For Byron, see Medwin, *MCB* 19–20. Montagu's advice, and her sad report of knowledge as deformation, focused Austen's satire in *Northanger Abbey*, which caught Jewsbury's attention (see my Chapter 4, pp. 94–95, and n6 [p. 336]).

32. If Sanford and More credited their pens against blue ink, Gilfillan credits his blue-bashing by despising the "trite, vulgar, and limited" conduct-tract "idea of Woman"

that would censure even Shakespeare's imagination: "What could [Mrs. Ellis] have said of Juliet? How would she have contrived to twist Beatrice into a pattern Miss? Perdita! would she have sent her to a boarding-school? or insisted on finishing, according to the Hannah Moore [sic] pattern, the divine Miranda?" (361)—all inferior to Hemans's poetry of female passions. For a sharp tracing of Gilfillan's gender ideology, see Angela Leighton, *Writing Against* 28–30.

33. He described some *Elegiac Stanzas* addressed to Coleridge as "effused" rather than "composed," the "mere pouring out of my own feeling"; other poems "sprung" forth as "Effusions rather than Compositions" (*LMY* 1: 219, 2: 284). His best-known poem of this type is *Extempore Effusion on the Death of James Hogg* (Hemans would enter the necrology).

34. Lindop ed., *Confessions* 31 and 238n. One site De Quincey would have known was Coleridge's remark in *Biographia Literaria* (1817) that "in the elder poets [. . .] from DONNE to COWLEY, we find the most fantastic out-of-the-way thoughts, but in the most pure and genuine mother English" (*BL* 1: 23)—an implicit genealogy for the rare Mrs. De Quincey.

35. In *Paradise Lost* Book 2 "the whole of the speeches and debates in Pandemonium" have "a decided manly tone in the arguments and sentiments, an eloquent dogmatism, as if each person spoke from thorough conviction" ("On Shakespeare and Milton" 129).

36. See Elaine Showalter, *A Literature of Their Own* 17. Woolf saw this veiling as sociology linked to psychology: "It was the relic of the sense of chastity that dictated anonymity to women even so late as the nineteenth century. Currer Bell, George Eliot, George Sand, all the victims of inner strife as their writings prove, sought ineffectively to veil themselves by using the name of a man. Thus they did homage to the convention [. . .] that publicity in women is detestable" (*A Room One's Own* 52).

37. More's use of Galatians proves more progressive than closet Wollstonecraftian Stodardt's citing of the same text: dropping the key first negative ("in Christ Jesus, there is male nor female," so she quotes the apostle), she argues that the differences of power are "not in kind but in degree," with the female mind "weaker, feebler, fainter" (16).

38. For sensibility and Romantic-era women poets, see Stuart Curran, "The 'I' Altered" 195–203. If in the eighteenth-century cult of sensibility, men of feeling raided the "feminine" to enhance male subjectivity (Alan Richardson, "Colonizing" 16–21), the venture was increasingly risky. For the effects in *Lyrical Ballads*, see my "Wordsworth and the Language of (Men) Feeling."

39. Long despising the "puling childishness" and lack of "manly sense," Jeffrey bars Wordsworth and Coleridge from this higher order (*Edinburgh Review* 12: 133, 137). But it was Wordsworth who said that "all good poetry is the spontaneous overflow of powerful feelings" (Preface to *Lyrical Ballads*; *LB* 744), and whose *Essay Supplementary* to the Preface of 1815 called poetry a mode of treating things "as they seem to exist to the senses, and to the passions" (*PrW* 3: 63). In 1817, Coleridge (also with Shakespeare in mind) defined the true poetic image as one "modified by a predominant passion; or by

associated thoughts or images awakened by that passion" (*BL* 2: 23). Jeffrey may still be tweaking the Lakers by finding this female poet more able in their mode than they; but it is more likely that his terms of praise confirm the prestige of this mode, his own antipathy notwithstanding.

40. Ricks's edition of Tennyson (1424) cites a late notebook entry: "men should be androgynous and women gynandrous, but men should not be gynandrous nor women androgynous."

41. For "Christian manliness" and Kingsley, see Norman Vance, *Sinews of the Spirit.*

42. *Byron* (1881), *W* 9: 237. At the close of his review of Dowden's *Life of Percy Bysshe Shelley* (1886) Arnold repeats the judgment, citing Trelawny's lush description and Italicizing "and ineffectual" (*Nineteenth Century,* Jan. 1888; *Essays in Criticism, Second Series,* 1895).

43. The devotion of Swinburne and Tennyson to a "feminine muse," Austin laments, exposes the "prominent tendencies" of the day (78). Tennyson is not "manly very often, and never conspicuously"; "feminine is the proper word" (79)—inferior even to Shelley and Keats, whom Austin did admire (*The Cenci,* even *Endymion*): see *Poetry of the Period* 6, 17, 20, 28, 279.

44. *The Union* specified its logic: the characters are "of the most wicked and repulsive stamp; There is [. . .] no apparent shrinking of the writer from the fiends whom he has conjured up" (287). For Emily Brontë and masculine effects, see Mellor, *Romanticism & Gender* 186–208. The assumption that "Ellis Bell" was male was nearly unanimous. For similar surmises on the author (unnamed) of *Frankenstein* (1818), see *Blackwood's* (Walter Scott), *Edinburgh Magazine,* and the *Quarterly* (Croker).

45. Rowton's anatomy is one proof. The Poet Laureate's chastisement of aspiring novelist Charlotte Brontë is another: "Literature cannot be the business of a woman's life, and it ought not to be," lectured Robert Southey in March 1837; the more she is "engaged in her proper duties, the less leisure she will have" for literature, even as recreation (Gaskell 102–3).

46. I quote from *CN* 377, 4842; H. J. Jackson, 589n26; *CN* 430, 4250.

47. January and September, respectively. Kathleen Coburn notes that the second entry is a rare instance of Coleridge's "forgetting that he has already made a memorandum in another note-book and writing it again." For the connection of Coleridge's meditation on linguistic gendering to his aesthetic ideal of androgyny, see Jean Watson.

48. Jewsbury's interest in Wollstonecraft convinces me that she is tacitly reversing the play of expectation in a well-known passage in Godwin's *Memoirs* on the contradiction between the "person" and "the temper" of the writing: "In the champion of her sex, who was described as endeavouring to invest them with all the rights of man, those whom curiosity prompted to seek the occasion of beholding her, expected to find a sturdy, muscular, raw-boned virago; and they were not a little surprised, when, instead of all this, they found a woman, lovely in her person, and in the best and most engaging sense, feminine in her manners" (76).

49. *Athenæum* 182: 262.

50. Though he praised the "rich melodies of Keats and Shelley" and worshipped "the blazing star of Byron," Jeffrey thought them all headed for "oblivion" (*Edinburgh Review* 50: 47).

51. Treating "Romanticism" as a relative culture inside a wide and various era, many of us use the label for its history and prestige. See, for instance, Mellor, *Romanticism & Gender* (210–11). Developments in the 1990s include Carol Wilson and Joel Haefner's *Women Writers in the Age of English Romanticism* (1994), Paula Feldman and Theresa Kelley's *Romantic Women: Voices and Counter-Voices* (1995), Stephen Behrendt and Harriet Linkin's *Approaches to Teaching British Women Poets of the Romantic Period* (1997) and *Romanticism and Women Poets* (1999). Classroom texts also evolved. Duncan Wu's *Romanticism, An Anthology* (1994) included 29 women in brief selections (about 10 percent of 1,100 pages), followed in 1997 by a groundbreaking anthology, *Romantic Women Poets*, also the year Paula Feldman published *British Women Poets of the Romantic Era*. David Perkins developed a second edition of his long-reigning classroom standard *English Romantic Writers* (1995), giving a bit over 100 of 1,340 pages to women. Anne Mellor and Richard Matlak made their point not only with a de-Romanticized *British Literature 1780–1830* (1996), but also with the devotion of 50 percent of its pages to women's writing. Peter Manning and I edited *The Romantics and Their Contemporaries* for *Longman Anthology of British Literature* (1998–2006) with selections from about 20 women. Catching up, the 7th edition of the Norton (2000) gave women almost 25 percent of its expanded "Romantic Period" (now over 1,000 pages), much of it claimed by *Frankenstein*. A slimmer 8th edition (sans *Frankenstein*) reduces this to about 20 percent

52. The Keats canon expanded in 1848 with R. M. Milnes's *Life, Letters, and Literary Remains*. After his death, the Shelley canon was winnowed, for a century at least, to produce an ethereal, depoliticized visionary. "Wordsworth" was revised by the surprise of *The Prelude* in 1850; and as Wu observes, "more new Wordsworth poems have been published since 1974 than in the first thirty years of his life" (*Romantic Women Poets* xxvii). And for Byron-biography (his life is as canonical as the poetry), every new decade brings forth a new one, each puffed as a radical revision.

Chapter Two

1. Prefatory Note to *Extempore Effusion on the Death of James Hogg* (*PW*, ed. de Selincourt and Darbishire 4: 461).

2. *CMH* 2: 355. He gave the pattern in the last of his "Personal Recollections": moving from *woman* to *poetess*, Chorley proposed that "in Mrs. Hemans, these two beings were so closely intertwined, that it may appear superfluous, and is almost impossible to treat or think of them separately" (*Athenæum* 402: 527).

3. First printed in *Poetical Remains* (1836), quoted in Chorley's review. In the 1839 *Works*, West's portrait is cited in a footnote to the poem (6: 149).

4. Not much had changed since the *Monthly Review* disputed Wollstonecraft's critique in *Rights of Woman* of recreational needlework as mind-numbing, and of paid

needlework as abject: "It does not appear to us to be necessary, in order to enlighten the understandings of women, that we should prohibit the employment of their fingers in those useful and elegant labours of the needle, for which, from the days of Penelope, they have obtained so much deserved applause" (ns 8: 208–9). The *us* and *we* (against the female *they/their*) can only be a masculine assumption.

5. "Mr. Wordsworth," in *The Spirit of the Age* 191.

6. "On the Living Poets" 290–92. Hazlitt gets cover from his admiration for "the female writers of the present day" who may "thank the Gods for not having made them poetical": Inchbald, Radcliffe, Burney, and (unnamed) Mary Lamb (289–90).

7. In Regency reception, argues Stephen Behrendt ("'Certainly not . . . '"), Hemans could even be praised for departing from conventional "feminine" poetry.

8. So Rufus Griswold gives the map in his popular anthology, *The Female Poets and Poetry of America* (1863): "It does not follow, because the most essential genius in men is marked by qualities which we may call feminine, that such qualities when found in female writers have any certain or just relation to mental superiority. The conditions of aesthetic ability in the two sexes are probably distinct, or even opposite" (16). Anne Mellor tracks the discourse of "poetess" from the Romantic era into recent transvaluations, which save the anatomy but don't condescend to it. In the counter-tradition of the "Female Poet," to which she assigns More, Baillie, Smith, and Barbauld, she does not include Hemans ("The Female Poet and the Poetess" 261–62).

9. Prefatory Memoir xxiv, referring to *Edinburgh Review* (Oct. 1829).

10. *CMH* 1: 138. Chorley first published these comments in an essay in the *Athenæum* 395 (392), later excerpted in Blackwood's 1839 *Works* (7: 297).

11. Egeria (*The History of a Nonchalant*, in *Three Histories* 193) set the icon. Hughes quotes the character, citing its Hemans-basis (*HM* 143–44); so does Chorley ("somewhat idealized" but mostly "faithful"; *CMH* 1: 187–89); Gilfillan calls Hemans "Egeria" (*Tait's* 14: 361, 363); Jane Williams cites Egeria as "obviously true" for Hemans (*Literary Women of England* 479–80); W. M. Rossetti's Prefatory Notice takes the description as documentary (22–23), as does *Queens of Literature* (a "description of Mrs. Hemans"; 277–78).

12. 1839 *Works* 7: 287–91, credited to "Delta" (*Blackwood's* Δ), *nom de plume* of David Macbeth Moir, who helped edit these volumes.

13. Jeffrey's essay was lavishly excerpted in Blackwood's 1839 *Works*, whose editors (Hemans's son, sister, and Moir) praised this "admirable critique" for "acumen, [. . .] taste, and elegance," including all but its last paragraph, about which poets will endure (5: 317–26; see also Blackwood's 1873, 440–42). Warne's 1874 edition, recommending Jeffrey's first paragraphs to its "lady readers," also quoted the opening paragraphs on Hemans (xxiii).

14. "Of the seven volumes of her collected works," declared Symons of the 1839 Blackwood's *Works*, "not seven poems are still remembered, and these chiefly because they were taught, and probably still are, to children"; among these, *Casabianca, The Graves of a Household,* and *The Homes of England* (*Romantic Movement* 293).

15. *CMH* 1: 43–44. Despite its contempt of the candor of Chorley's *Memorials*, *Dublin Review* echoed the sentiment, impatient with the gloomy "monotony" of "moral" thematics: "The futility and mortality of all things furnish her constant theme" (257).

16. Echoing Dr. Johnson's impatience with a friend who would leave good male society "to go and sit with a set of wretched *un-idea'd* girls" (*Boswell's* LIFE OF JOHNSON, ed. Osgood 61). My thanks to Claudia L. Johnson.

17. In 1991 Virgil Nemoianu brandished Hemans to warn 1980s canon-liberalizers of the backfire of a "feminine literature" full of "acquiescence, formalized harmonies, and translations of obsolete ideologies"—"*par excellence* the domain of conservatism": Hemans is "a repository of and tireless extoller of the values of family, tradition, stability, religion, and hierarchy" (240); Tricia Lootens also comments on Nemoianu. Though Jennifer Breen's *Women Romantic Poets, 1785–1832* was issued in 1992 to remedy "long-neglected achievements," it mentions Hemans only briefly (xii), represents her with two dull Victorian favorites (a short dirge of pieties on a child's death and a reverential *To Wordsworth*), dismisses her in the notes as "chauvinistic, sentimental, and derivative," and mocks her: "She was an admirer of William Wordsworth's poetry but he did not reciprocate this admiration." So little did Breen care about Hemans that she gave her source with a glaring error (Rossetti's Preface "1810"). Her inability to advance Hemans beyond Ward's Victorian *English Poets* or the 1906 *Oxford Book of English Verse* (it included one short dirge [721]) was not ruffled by the 1993 *Norton Anthology of English Literature*, which cast Hemans with minor "lyric poets" (2: 863) linked by a Victorian sampler: *The Landing of the Pilgrim Fathers, Casabianca*, and *England's Dead*. As late as 1995 Germaine Greer's *Slip-Shod Sibyls* despised Hemans as a poet of "quaintness and insipidity" (60), recalled only "if at all" for *Casabianca*. With factual errors and research limited to a Victorian preface (92–94), Greer exposed an ignorance not only of new discussions but also of Hemans's canon (e.g., 144; not even getting the title of the volumes right [262, 509]). For a review of Hemans's reception, see my introduction to *Felicia Hemans*.

18. Important sequels to Curran's essay ("The 'I' Altered") include Marlon Ross's *Contours* (1989) and Norma Clarke's *Ambitious Heights* (1990). For the classroom revival, see Mellor and Matlak's *British Literature 1780–1830*, Perkins's 2d edn. of *English Romantic Writers*, Feldman's *British Woman Poets of the Romantic Era*, Wu's *Romanticism: An Anthology* and *Romantic Women Poets: An Anthology*; *Longman Anthology of British Literature*, a (tellingly) inaugural position in Leighton and Reynolds's *Victorian Women Poets*, and (at last) a dozen pages in the *Norton Anthology*'s 7th edn. (The 8th edn., 2006, adds three more poems.)

19. Though Chorley thought that Hemans's letters, no less than her poetry, gave a "fair picture of her mind in all its *womanliness*" (*CMH* 1: 139), his publication of letters contradicting this image caused *Dublin Review* to lament the "vain and gossiping details [. . .] little better than the tattle of a pair of sentimental milliners" (249), and *Dublin University Magazine* to suppose that such letters "might become positively injurious to her fame;—the caustic observations on her visitors and lamentations of overpowered *lionship*" (40). Chorley did not include any of Hemans's correspondence with her

publishers, assessing market tastes, negotiating fees, and so forth. For these, see Feldman, "The Poet," and my *Felicia Hemans*.

20. She wrote to her aunt in 1808, "my whole heart and soul are interested for the gallant patriots," and expressed her pride that her brother "is at present on the theatre of glory; and I hope he will have an opportunity of signalizing his courage, and of proving an honour to his family and an ornament to his profession" (*CMH* 1: 31).

21. George Browne's regiment was ravaged in the retreat at Coruña in 1809: "He is in most miserable plight, for he has lost all he possessed in the world, and is worn to a skeleton," his mother reported (Nicholson 12). Felicia was still in the romance: "Deeply as I feel for the sufferings my dearest Brother must have endured, still I can hardly regret that he has received a wound in so glorious a cause, and as a trophy of so brilliant a victory; it will ever be his pride that he has bled in the service of his Country" (ibid. 13–14). George returned at the end of the year, wounded and disillusioned, but was coerced by his mother to resume his military career rather than risk the "horrors" of failing in "mercantile undertakings," as his father had (19). He survived the catastrophic battle of Albuera (of nearly British 60,000 troops, 13,000 died).

22. *A Short Sketch of the Life of Mrs. Hemans* (1835) 32; cited by Wu, *Romantic Women Poets* 489. Chorley implies that only "literary pursuits" made her decide "not to leave England" (*CMH* 1: 42). Hughes insists the separation was initially and merely "a tacit conventional arrangement" and that the ensuing "years of absence, and consequently alienation" were "painful" to Hemans, with only "secondary consolation" in "the growing popularity of her writings" (*HM* 30). Warne's memoirist tendered a connection: "literary success was followed, it is to be feared, by domestic inquietude; for it was in 1818 that her husband left her" (xx). Rossetti speculates for a full page (14) about the marriage, the real "motive" of the Captain's departure, and the bearing of Hemans's fame on the separation. For the awkward discourse, see Ross, *Contours* 252.

23. Poet Lydia Sigourney indexed the heterodoxy: "her freedom, for many years, from those cares which usually absorb a wife and mother"; her "prolonged residence under the maternal wing"; her "shelter[ing] from the burden of those cares which sometimes press out the life of song" (xi-xii).

24. "There is, indeed, something unfeminine in independence," warns Mrs. Sandford; "It is contrary to nature." Rather than "acting the amazon," a "really sensible woman feels her dependence"; "her weaknes[s] is an attraction, not a blemish"; "like children," the more women "show their need of support, the more engaging they are" (*Woman* 2–5, 14–15).

25. See Norma Clarke 48. Despite its long tenure, the imagery of "the maternal wing" still appealed to Sigourney (xi), Hughes (52), and the memoirist for the Warne edition (xxi).

26. *CMH* 1: 174; 2: 115. Chorley then has Hemans citing Wordsworth: "It is not because they possess genius that they make unhappy homes, but because they do not possess genius enough; a higher order of mind would enable them to see and feel all the beauty of domestic ties" (119–20).

27. Mellor, *Romanticism & Gender* 124 (see 124–43); McGann et al. "Literary History, Romanticism, and Felicia Hemans" 228. Lootens brilliantly traces out the conflicting awarenesses in the patriotic and domestic poetry ("Hemans and Home"; see also Mellor 135–42); Kaplan reads the melancholy as a symptom of conflicts felt to be resolvable only beyond history, beyond mortal life (*Salt* 93–95).

28. Curran's shift of evaluation reflects the expectation. In 1988, he could trace in the iconic Victorian "poetess, celebrating hearth and home, God and country in mellifluous verse that relished the sentimental and seldom teased anyone into thought" some "darker strains": "a focus on exile and failure, a celebration of female genius frustrated, a haunting omnipresence of death" ("The 'I' Altered" 189). But five years onward, with further reading into other women's poetry, he adjusted the account: Hemans now seemed "the creator and enforcer of [an] ideological control masking itself as praise for feminine instinct and female duty," the emerging "broadly cosmopolitan, democratic, and liberal consensus" of the 1820s ("Women Readers" 190).

29. Letter to George Huntly Gordon, early August 1830; *LY* 2: 311.

30. Wordsworth's stanza became canonical: Gilfillan closed his essay on Hemans with it (363); so did Warne's memoirist (xxiv).

31. Hence, Dorothy Wordsworth: "still at work at the Pedlar, altering & refitting" (13 Feb. 1802); "I stitched up the Pedlar" (7 March 1802); *Journals* 67, 75. Thanks to Carol Shiner Wilson for the observation about Minerva.

32. Chorley first published this letter in "Personal Recollections" (27 June 1835, p. 495).

33. *To the Author of the Excursion and the Lyrical Ballads* appeared in *Literary Magnet* (April 1826), then in *Records* as *To Wordsworth*. Jewsbury's essay on Hemans for *Athenæum* (1831) suggests that had she tried prose, "it would be characterised by some [qualities] that in poetry cannot well appear:—wit, for instance." Jewsbury treats delicately with gender, going on to say that "female wit differs as much from a man's, as Cœur de Lion chopping the iron mace by a single blow of his straight ponderous sword, differed from Sultan Saladin severing the down pillow with his thin shining scimitar" (104). For her tact and tactics with gender, see Ross, *Contours* 244–45.

34. The "affections of daughter and mother were more dominant and vivid in [her] than conjugal love," Rossetti thought (Prefatory Notice 14).

35. *HM* 100. The internal quotation shows Hemans using her own poetry to word this heartache: the male speaker of *The Forest Sanctuary* is longing for the voices of his lost home.

36. Chorley prints a version of this letter (*CHM* 1: 231–35). I quote the ms.; see my edition of *Felicia Hemans* 501.

37. OED does not list the prisoner-sense for the nineteenth century, but it is emergent in a poem Hemans knew well, Wordsworth's Great Ode, where "Shades of the prison-house begin to close" on nature's "Inmate Man" (the soul in its mortal life) (66–84).

38. "Wordsworth might have been the poet of home, but he was not expected to

contribute towards home affections through the divine drudgery of sweeping and cleaning," Norma Clarke remarks dryly of the gender differential (*Ambitious Heights* 74).

39. 1839 *Works* 3: 129–39. The poem is based on a confession in Dante's *Purgatorio* Canto 5.

40. Kathleen Hickock reports that Hemans stands out among nineteenth-century English writers in featuring maternal infanticide (26).

41. Sir Henry Holland's *Travels in the Ionian Isles, Albania, etc., during the years 1812 and 1813*, issued in 1819 by Hemans's publisher, John Murray, was her likely source. During the Russo-Turkish war in the 1790s, the Suliotes, an Albanian Christian tribe, held out for thirteen years in their mountain fasthold against Ali Pasha's troops; in 1803, with conquest imminent, the remnant of the tribe leapt from a precipice, the women throwing the children down first.

42. For example, "And oft perforce his rising lip reveals / The haughtier thought it curbs, but scarce conceals" (1.205–6).

43. Hemans was also mindful of more proximate histories, the English Enlightenment canon-making collections that excluded women. This was not just the effect of male supervision per se, argues Greg Kucich, but of management by middle-class, professional men of letters, such as Dr. Johnson, whose implied (sometimes stated) binary was aristocratic patronage, a world increasingly caricatured as effeminate ("Gendering the Canons" 99–100). The emphasis on masculine independence excluded female poets from the "sons of imagination" (so Alexander Chalmers described the canon in his preface).

44. "Women Readers, Women Writers" 191. Gibbon's epic history supplies material for Hemans's *Modern Greece,* and paratexts throughout *Tales, and Historic Scenes* (including *The Widow of Crescentius*).

45. Records of "the heart's social and domesticated relations" write a feminine, sometimes feminist, historiography in the Romantic era, Kucich argues, including *Records* in this project, with antecedents in Macaulay and Hays, and collateral in Shelley and Jameson ("Mary Shelley's *Lives*" 206). See also Lootens 241–47.

46. "my woman's heart / Shall wake a spirit and a power to bless" (*Arabella Stuart* 227); "could this work be of woman wrought?" (*Bride of the Greek Isle* 210); "man must arm, and woman call on God" (*Switzer's Wife* 78); "Give . . . love's kind words to woman!" (*Properzia Rossi* 81), "woman's breaking heart" (*Gertrude* 26); "woman's fragile heart and frame" (*Imelda* 96); "woman's weary lot" (*Indian Woman's Death-Song* 36); the high "price" for the "crown of glory unto woman's brow" (*Joan of Arc* 91–94); "all that woman's heart had dared and done" (*Pauline* 80); "a woman's heart," "a woman's broken heart" (*Juana* 28, 52); "Such hours are woman's birthright" (*Costanza* 81); "A sculptur'd woman's form, / Lovely in perfect rest" (*The Queen of Prussia's Tomb* 8–9).

47. In *Records of Woman*, observes Clarke, all the husbands "are dead or dying or untrue" and there are "no happy women" (*Ambitious Heights* 80). Each Record, notes Wu, concludes with either the heroine's death or her lover's (*Romantic Women Poets* xxii).

48. Jeffrey, *Edinburgh Review* 40 (1824), 81. The epigraph is Laodamia's protest to her husband's shade (86–90).

49. The Corsair debuts "leaning on the brand, / Not oft a resting-staff of that red hand" (1.131–32); his first utterance is an order to sharpen his "boarding-brand, / And give its guard more room to fit my hand" (1.163–64); in prison, he laments his "worthless hand / That might have better kept so true a brand" (2.483–84). Hemans's blazing brand blends these associations with the "flaming Brand" with which Archangel Michael's Seraphim squadron destroys Eden (*PL* 12.643).

50. The genealogy involves Medusa's snake-locks, Eve's wanton ringlets, and Burke's epitome of French revolutionary violence in female hellions. In a splendid essay on Victorian tropes, Elisabeth Gitter writes: "When the powerful woman of Victorian imagination was an angel, her shining hair was her aureole. [. . .] when she was demonic, it became a glittering snare, web, or noose"; it always conveyed magical agency: "her gleaming tresses both expressed her mythic power and were its source" (936; cf. 943).

51. Part of this aura is the erotic visionary maid dreamed by the Poet of Shelley's *Alastor*: "her outspread arms now bare, / Her dark locks floating in the breath of night, / Her beamy bending eyes, her parted lips / Outstretched, and pale, and quivering eagerly" (177–80).

52. Parliamentary papers and the press issued reports that could not be written off as mere propaganda for the Raj. In 1827 *London Magazine* carried an article ("Hindoo Widows") filled with eye-witness accounts of brutal enforcements, at odds with "enlightened Christian government" (541). Its report of nearly 3,000 widow-burnings between 1820 and 1824 was widely broadcast. If a few widows were willing, resisting all dissuasion, and while Raj policy tolerated local practices, these considerations could not quell a view of the rite as barbaric, superstitious, violent, and degrading. In 1828 (the year Blackwood published *Records*), *Blackwood's Edinburgh Magazine* railed against "the abomination" (23: 161–62). For some appalling reports, and the sati in nineteenth-century British literature as the icon of female oppression, see Sophie Gilmartin.

53. Jewsbury's *Song* appears in *Literary Souvenir* (1825), then *Phantasmagoria* (2:131–34).

54. Hemans regarded fame as a poison charm for men, too, if the cost was domestic life. In *The Siege of Valencia*, whose governor lets his hostage sons be murdered rather than dishonorably forfeit Valencia (the pattern of Asdrubal), his wife taunts him with a hollow future: "in your utter desolation, turn / To the cold world . . . and bid it quench / Your soul's deep thirst *with fame!* immortal *fame!*/Fame to the sick of heart!" (1.489–93).

55. In his "Personal Recollections" for the *Athenæum*, Chorley gave this report more of an edge with "ingratitude" and its devastating effects: "To secure the love and constancy of a mortal suitor, a beautiful enchantress is represented as resigning one spell of power after another—last of all, her immortality; and is repaid by satiety—ingratitude—desertion. So strongly and painfully was Mrs. Hemans excited by the progress of the story, that her health and spirits began severely to suffer, and the tale was, therefore abandoned" (402: 528–29).

56. Her trial made much of her transvestism; see Garber, *Vested Interests* 215–17.

57. Chorley (*CMH* 1: 290) reports that Hemans adored Franz Grillparzer's *Sappho* (Germany, 1819), which climaxes in Sappho's suicide of love-despair over boatman Phaon—as did Pope's rendering of Ovid's 15th epistle, *Sappho to Phaon* (1707) and Mary Robinson's *Sappho and Phaon* (1796).

58. She is indicated in a footnote only by an epithet: "the author of Psyche."

59. With this Record, Hemans adds to the lore of Tighe's death as a caution to female ambition. "I heard much of her unhappiness was caused by her own excessive love of admiration and desire to shine in society, which quite withdrew her from Hearth and Home and all their holy enjoyments, and that her mother, standing by her deathbed passionately exclaimed—'My Mary, my Mary, the pride of literature has destroyed you'" (quoted by Clarke, *Ambitious* 50–51).

60. In both, Chorley saw a problematic "moral" on "the insufficiency of Fame and Ambition, be either ever so generous, to make up for the absence of Love:—a class-vindication wound up by an appeal against class-separation"; Chorley regretted to "see the agony more clearly than the remedy" (*Athenæum*, 22 Nov. 1856, 1425).

61. See Grant Scott, for both the picture and a sharp commentary ("Fragile Image" 43).

62. "Women have to realize that there is in this career [the ambition for *gloire*—celebrity, glory] very little of the sort of value in the most obscure life of a beloved wife and a happy mother" (*De l'influence des passions* [1796], in the chapter "De la vanite" [1.3; pp. 103–4]). *Songs of the Affections* misprinted "sorte" for "sorts," the correct reading of *Literary Souvenir* (1829), 189.

63. Translating *femme* as *woman*, Madelyn Gutwirth sees Staël submitting her "restive, ambitious, egocentric" nature to a "propitiatory self-flagellation" (252–53) that thwarts such Wollstonecraft-analytics as "La nature et la société ont déshérité la moitié de l'espèce humaine; force, courage, génie, indépendance, tout appartient aux hommes" [Nature and society have disinherited half of the human species; strength, courage, genius, and independence all belong to men] ("De l'amour de la gloire," *De l'influence des passions* 1.4, 129–30; Gutwirth 253).

64. *CMH* 1: 304; Chorley also published this remark in his third "Recollections" (*Athenæum* 402: 529). For the ambivalence of Hemans's *Corinne* in relation to the energetic celebration of Staël's chapter, see Leighton, *Writing Against* 30–34.

65. Published in France in 1807, *Corinne* was quickly translated into English. Hugely popular, especially with women (including Hemans, Austen, Shelley, Jewsbury), it went through 40 editions in the nineteenth century (Kadish 15). As "*the* book of the woman of genius," Ellen Moers remarks, its myth was "both inspiration and warning" (*Literary Women* 262)—a doubleness, as we'll see, also registered in Jewsbury's *Enthusiast*. For the impact on nineteenth-century English and American writers, see Moers, "Performing Heroinism: The Myth of Corinne" (ibid. 263–319).

66. *HM* III; quoting Jesus to his disciples, "whoever shall give to drink unto one of the little ones a cup of cold water only in the name of a disciple, verily I say unto you, he shall in no wise lose his reward" (Matt. 10: 42).

67. The news, forecast by rumors and a cessation of letters from Jewsbury and none from her husband, was slow to reach England, not confirmed for over nine months. *The Athenæum*'s obituary appeared 21 June 1834. Hemans's sad letters were written soon after.

Chapter Three

1. Leslie Marchand, *The Athenaeum: A Mirror of Victorian Culture* 171–72. Other women (notably Elizabeth Barrett) followed, both as regular contributors of original work and as reviewers.

2. For two foundational studies on the plights of intellectual woman, see Mary Poovey, *The Proper Lady and the Woman Writer*, on the force of gender propriety; and Deirdre David, *Intellectual Women and Victorian Patriarchy*, on the way three women defied the prejudice.

3. The comparison proved durable. Jane Williams's *Literary Women* repeated it verbatim, without citation, as if an established consensus (370).

4. M.J.J. courted the impression. In the first publication of one sketch, *The Military Spectacle* (*Literary Souvenir* 1825), M.J.J. sighed, "Ah, happy days! once more, who would not be a boy?" (a sentence deleted in *Phantasmagoria*).

5. This obsolete sense of *nervous* is "muscular, vigorous": the OED's first four definitions pertain to it (see, e.g., *General Magazine* on Macaulay, below). Branching from the physiological base, the denotation of hypersensitivity was concurrent: in *Sense and Sensibility*, Austen writes of Marianne's "most nervous irritability" (2.7; Johnson, ed. 127).

6. "On Modern Female Cultivation—No. III" (25 Feb. 1832, 129); "No. IV" (11 Aug. 1832, 521). I accept Norma Clarke's case for Jewsbury's authorship.

7. For a succinct account of women in the late eighteenth-century public sphere, see Anne Mellor's introduction to *Mothers of the Nation*.

8. Nicola Trott's essay gives a sharp report on the career of this cartoon.

9. Peter Duthie (*Plays* 17n1) reports the rumors of male authorship floated after the unsigned publication of *Plays on the Passions*: brother Matthew Baillie, Scott, actor John Philip Kemble. The *Introductory Discourse* especially seemed a "masculine" document. Jewsbury thought so (see p. 96, above) and so did Byron; but the first published comment on her "masculine" power I've been able to discover is the *Quarterly*'s he-she praise of her in the 1840s as "the mistress of a masculine style of thought and diction," with admiration of *Plays on the Passions* for "masculine force of mind" (*Quarterly* 67: 437, 441).

10. The misogyny of this Epistle, Laura Brown argues, serves a poetics of difference (101–7): "by their eminently transparent, clearly despicable characterlessness," women "shore up the notion of a stable, morally determinate identity for men" (106). For Wollstonecraft's serial antagonism to Pope, see my essay "Wollstonecraft Among the Poets."

11. "Though a woman, she is possessed of that bold and masculine spirit, which aims at the grand and sublime," said an "Admirer of the Fine Arts" of Angelica Kauffman's image of Achilles' despair over the death of Patroclus (*London Chronicle*, 4–6

May 1775, 429). In 1817, Leigh Hunt's praises of "a lady of what is called a masculine understanding, that is to say, of great natural abilities not obstructed by a *bad* education," linked gender to social system in a signature Wollstonecraft way (the "lady" was daughter Mary Shelley; *Examiner* 5 Oct. 1817, 626n).

12. "In Men, we various Ruling Passions find, / In Women, two almost divide the kind; / Those, only fix'd, they first or last obey, / The Love of Pleasure, and the Love of Sway. / That, Nature gives" (207–11). In a footnote Pope allows some forces beyond what nature gives ("This is occasioned partly by their *Nature,* partly by their *Education,* and in some degree by Necessity"), but he declines to trace a cultural anatomy into the tradition of misogynist satire.

13. Hays uses this phrase in writing about how, depending on motive, men will allow women a "masculine" character, then "endeavour to affix" a character of "universal weakness"; the contradiction, "at variance with nature, with reason, and with common sense," exposes the incoherent interests of the prevailing system (*Appeal* 56–57).

14. She had made the same point in *Monthly Magazine:* Wollstonecraft was "no less distinguished by admirable talents and a masculine tone of understanding, than by active humanity, exquisite sensibility, and endearing qualities of heart" (4 [1798]: 232).

15. *Athenæum* 172: 104. See pp. 33–34 above, for the full fantasy.

16. "Keats" 61, "Clough" 88, "Shelley" 70. Patmore even used "effeminate" for Shelley without damnation—a move beyond Coleridge's desynonymizing from "feminine" (see Chapter 8, below).

17. So, too, even as Edward Carpenter argues in 1925 for Shelley's visionary projection of mental androgyny, he leaves old norms in place: this "new type of human being" has "the feminine insight and imagination to perceive the evil" and "the manly strength and courage to oppose and finally annihilate it" (19).

18. "Keats" 62, 64. "We alone can write 'classics,' even of the feminine order," he adds (64). With this all male, confidently colonizing *we,* Patmore is particularly exercised by the competence of Barrett Browning, the veiled reference of this remark, expressly stated in "Meynell": her poetry does not strain "to rival man's work, as Mrs. Browning's does" (121–22).

19. *Table Talk,* 1 Sept. 1832 (2: 190–91).

20. Woolf cites Coleridge with a caution: "when he said that a great mind is androgynous," he did not mean that it "has any special sympathy with women [. . .] takes up their cause or devotes itself to their interpretation"; and while "Shakespeare's mind" is "the type of the androgynous, of the man-womanly," this does not imply what he "thought of women" (*Room* 102–3).

21. Although Toril Moi sees Woolf deconstructing "the death-dealing binary oppositions of masculinity and femininity" (13), Woolf limits the geniuses of mental androgyny to men (including Coleridge and Keats; *Room* 102, 107) and limits "writer" to male pronouns. For a woman, argues Elaine Showalter, Woolf's theory of androgyny is an aesthetic flight into "the sphere of the exile and the eunuch," in evasion of actual female political and social experience (*A Literature* 288, 285).

22. For the complications of Coleridge and androgyny, see the essays by Jean Watson and H. J. Jackson. For male-authored androgynous ideals in Romantic poetics, see Diane Hoeveler.

23. See Jewsbury herself (qtd. *CMH* 1: 171); Chorley, *CMH* 1: 7–8; Hughes, *HM* 142; and later, Ellis 32; Williams, *Literary Women* 370.

24. 21 June 1834, 473. Without explanation, Norma Clarke credits this unsigned notice to Chorley (22n40); but the *Athenæum* index doesn't. Moreover, Chorley's statement in *Memorials* that he has permission to quote from the letters by Jewsbury in this notice (1: 169) suggests an author other than himself.

25. Reported by Mrs. Elwood, in a note to a chapter on "Mrs. Mary Wollstonecroft [*sic*] Godwin" quoting "remarks from the pen of a well-known living writer" (2: 153). I owe this reference to Joanne Wilkes (116 and n20). Neither she nor Elwood identify this writer, but I suspect it's Barrett Browning.

Chapter Four

1. To Catherine Clarkson (the wife of abolitionist Thomas Clarkson), 1 April 1826, some eight months after the publication of *Phantasmagoria; LLY* 1: 434–35.

2. Gillett xviii. In 1820, G. R. Gleig, having asked teenage Jewsbury to contribute to his Library of General Knowledge, was sorry to respond to her proposal for a volume of "Female Biography" that Sir Egerton Brydges already had this assignment; "I should have been better pleased to entrust it to a woman of genius" (xviii–xix). The series on "Literary Women" that Jewsbury inaugurated for *The Athenæum,* about ten years later, bears this early interest.

3. Unpublished letter; quoted by Fryckstedt (195). This sister is Geraldine Jewsbury (1812–80), later a novelist at the forefront of new ideas about women (for brief comments, see Showalter, *A Literature,* and for a sustained account, see Norma Clarke, *Ambitious Heights*).

4. All quotations are from p. 553. Jewsbury is polite: "Jane Austen" opens in sorrow that this "interesting and gifted woman" is no longer "among the living," and closes in a sigh over the "chasm" left by her death (553); but there is an important critical angle that anticipates Gilbert and Gubar's feminist critique of Austen as a figure of "self-division," caught in a contradiction between "ladylike submission" and aspiration as a writer (*Madwoman* 155).

5. This account is a strategic fiction: Henry was motivated by a curatorial care, giving cues for the appreciations already taking shape in such influential journals as the Tory *Quarterly Review,* and eager to disarm suggestions that Austen in temper was similar to the sharp-tongued bitches of her novels.

6. Against Catherine's feeling "heartily ashamed of her ignorance," Austen's narrator applies this gloss: "A misplaced shame. Where people wish to attach, they should always be ignorant. To come with a well-informed mind, is to come with an inability of administering to the vanity of others, which a sensible person would always wish to avoid. A woman especially, if she have the misfortune of knowing any thing, should

conceal it as well as she can. [. . .] I will only add in justice to men, that though to the larger and more trifling part of the sex, imbecility in females is a great enhancement of their personal charms, there is a portion of them too reasonable and too well informed themselves to desire any thing more in woman than ignorance" (1: 14 [p. 90]).

7. In the rhetorical plane, Jewsbury's satire is also a coterie comment on Captain Alfred Hemans's reported discomfort in living off the income of his wife's talents.

8. *The Excursion* (1814) 7 (1.81–84). In another front-page essay, the next month, Jewsbury aligns the accomplishments of female and working-class writers. Challenging the term "UNEDUCATED POETS," she argues that the only *un-* is the lack of institutional imprimatur and connections; moreover, those "who have reached true distinction in literature" have "generally been men and women of *dis*advantages [. . .] who worked for themselves, fagged out their own diplomas, and fought their own way to estimation"— the struggle providing an education superior to that of "the 'accomplished scholars' [. . .] who know everything that everybody has said in books, and who know nothing more" ("Poetry by the People" 369).

9. Austen died in 1817, novelist Mary Brunton in 1818. In addition to Baillie (famed for *De Monfort*), Landon (L.E.L.), and Hemans (F.H.; Mrs. H.; Jewsbury knew that her publisher William Blackwood was urging her to try some tales and sketches), the nods are to Caroline Norton (Mrs. N.), a celebrated beauty and writer whose flirtation with Lord Melbourne, fanned by her husband for his advantage, would lead to a suit of adultery; Anna Jameson, whose *Diary of an Ennuyée* (1826) was so popular that (like Staël and *Corinne*) her heroine became her epithet; Miss M./Mary Russell Mitford, whose rural tales secured her fame with a serial publication in *Lady's Magazine* (from 1819) and then in a 5–volume collection, *Our Village* (1824–32); and Caroline Bowles, whose stories, *Chapters on Churchyards*, appeared serially in *Blackwood's* in 1829.

10. "Miss Jewsbury," a frequent poet in the *Athenæum* and in *Blackwood's*, published over 70 poems in the annuals, including 3 in *Friendship's Offering* (1830 and 1831) and 2 in the 1828 *Pledge of Friendship*.

11. *Spring Lays. On Receiving a Bunch of Violets* (*Athenæum* 179: 217). In *Blue-Stocking Revels; or, The Feast of the Violets*, Leigh Hunt proposed that "violet" replace the stigma of "blue," and with a clarifying sentiment about gender aberration, both male and female: "I hereby ordain, that in future the word / Be confined to the masculine, vain, and absurd"; "all real women, . . . / . . . / . . . the true breathers of sweets, / Take their name from the queen of the sylvan retreats;— / . . . / The violet,—charmer of all that light on it. / 'No Blue,' 'twill be said, 'is the she who so bears her'" (Canto III, near the end; 1884 *Poetical Works*, 130).

12. OED: "professional jargon"; "a stock phrase that is much affected at the time, or is repeated as a matter of habit or form"; "phraseology taken up and used for fashion's sake, without being a genuine expression of sentiment." Fashioning a hero is a matter of "cloying the gazettes with cant," said Byron (*Don Juan* 1.1). In *Northanger Abbey* (Jewsbury knew it so well that it might count as an allusion), Austen's narrator abuses the cant of condescending to the novels: "'I am no novel reader—I seldom look into

novels—Do not imagine that *I* often read novels—It is really very well for a novel.' Such is the common cant" (I: 5 [p. 25]).

13. The love tales in *Phantasmagoria* are in the neighborhood of these ironized mechanics. "A love tale I never shall write," Jewsbury assured Mrs. Watts; "The moment I begin to cogitate over the proper materials I feel an irresistible inclination to laugh. With one or two exceptions, I never have read a love-tale without seeing its ludicrous side" (30 Aug. 1824, Watts 1: 196). The wit of *Phantasmagoria*, both risible and serious, is to set a genre in variable perspectives.

14. *LLY* 1: 343. Jewsbury had sent him a gift copy and had dedicated the volume to him. He was cooler to the poetry, but liked even the sentimental tales, especially *The Unknown*, which Dorothy Wordsworth also admired (ibid.; and 1: 405). The reply was no routine courtesy. Keats sent Wordsworth his 1817 *Poems*, with more than one praise of Wordsworth; but the pages remained uncut at Wordsworth's death.

15. *LLY* 1: 377. These praises were warmed by Jewsbury's solicitous attention to his poetry, as well as her efforts to secure a publisher for him during a decade of cool, even cold prospects. Learning, during a summer visit, of Wordsworth's frustrations with Murray and Longman, she burned a letter off to Watts, asking him to approach the firm of Hurst and Robinson (publisher of *Phantasmagoria* and *The Literary Souvenir*). Wordsworth is writing to Watts to thank him for his interest, and to bring him up to speed. He even invited him to visit, offering to converse "upon certain principles of style, taking for my text any one of your animated poems," maybe those in the *Souvenir*, which "I read with no little admiration" (1: 377)—no little offer, given Wordsworth's general contempt for annual-poetry. Watts did his best for Wordsworth (*LLY* 1: 439) but the collapse of Constable early in 1826 rippled through the entire trade, including Hurst and Robinson, and Wordsworth had to return, hat in hand, to Longman on the terms he initially refused. Jewsbury worked to keep his poetry before the public in her own writing, with frequent quotations and allusions, some tagged, but many not, as if to treat Wordsworth as a recognized national idiom.

16. Here and hereafter, WLMS refers to manuscripts in the Dove Cottage archives, Grasmere, England. With some accidental variants, this letter is also in Gillet, *l*.

17. For speculation about Wordsworth's depressive affect on Jewsbury (and Hemans), see Norma Clarke 61–69.

18. For the letter to Reynolds (c. 27 Jan. 1829) urging his attention to Jewsbury see *LLY* 2: 13, and to Jewsbury about this overture, as well as its unlikely success, 2: 27.

19. 9 Dec. 1829; WLMS 50.

20. I thank the ears of Ronald Levao and Jeff Dolven for hearing this echo.

21. Eric Gillett, writing the first twentieth-century memoir, tells a story of pathos, concluding with Wordsworth's public appreciation (lxvii), an accolade that set Jewsbury's nineteenth-century reputation (while it lasted). Chorley quoted Wordsworth (*CMH* 1: 167), so did Hughes (*HM* 142), and even Jane Williams's more disciplinary story managed to cite it (*Literary Women* 379). Espinasse quotes the whole note, and

comments, "This is high praise from one so little given as Wordsworth was to public acknowledgment of the merits of his contemporaries" (338).

22. *Memoirs* 2: 153; lost thereby was the chance "to do Mrs. Godwin justice for her real benevolence, her ardent zeal, and her unflinching resolution, without adverting to the fallible points of her arguments, or the weakness and suffering which belonged to her conduct and experience." Mrs. Elwood herself had closed the essay proper in a question: "It is to be lamented that Mary Wollstonecroft, whom nature, when she so lavishly endowed her with virtues and talents, evidently meant should be a bright pattern of perfection to her sex, should, by her erroneous theories and false principles, have rendered herself instead, rather the beacon by which to warn the woman of similar endowments with herself, of the rocks upon which enthusiasm and imagination are too apt to wreck their possessor. If error even in a Mary Wollstonecroft could not be overlooked, what woman can hope to offend with impunity against the laws of society?" (2: 152). Elwood deflects blame by using a correspondent to re-open the question, via Jewsbury. The faintness of Wollstonecraft's imprint in the 1830s registers in the misspelling of her name as well as the misstatement of the title of her most important work as "Rights of Women" (throughout).

23. The word *imbibe* threads through the argument of *Rights of Woman*, implicating toxin with nurture. Men are scarcely aware of the "prejudices which they have imbibed" (*VRW* 118), and women are formed by "early imbibed notions" (145) internalized as natural inevitability: "confined to trifling employments, they naturally imbibe opinions which the only kind of reading calculated to interest an innocent frivolous mind, inspires" (330).

24. The line about literature bringing about "the ideological resolutions of real contradictions" descends from Terry Eagleton's *Criticism and Ideology* (110ff).

25. "When you leave school you become a member of society, and as such, the duties of society devolve upon you" (*Letters* 140). She then auditions the protest of the young aspirant—"'I am convinced,' was her language, 'that my ambitious motives are wrong, but I feel that without them I should be miserable, and lose all power of exertion"—in order to prick these "principles" as "meanness and weakness," the "building" of a "little Babylon," and to skewer the sequel in the form of Julia's melancholy: "Would you then be some sparkling wit, or admired poet, or erudite scholar, who, having wholly sought his own glory, and wholly received his reward in this life, has nothing further to expect?" (162–65). In an actual letter to Geraldine, she advises her, "Achieve genius how you will," but recognize that "if undevoted to God, the jewel is not without a flaw. Cultivate your mind how your please—but remember the intellect of an angel finds no resting place but in God" (undated; Fryckstedt 495).

26. Freud, "Negation," *Standard Edition* 19: 236. There was a second edition of *Letters* in 1829 and a "revised and enlarged" third in 1832. Not only does the lecturing concede a resistant ambition, but as Margaret Reynolds suggests, it emerges from a contrary recognition: that sickness, though seeming a reproof of ambition, actually afforded Jewsbury freedom to read and write, excusing her from the demands of "domesticity

and marriage market" (27). Jewsbury managed to write and publish quite a lot of work and, as her letters to Dora Wordsworth show, she was full of plans on her recovery.

27. For Jewsbury's readers, the epigraph is all the more potent for revisiting the cautionary allegory of enthusiasm as a ship setting forth in *To My Own Heart* (in *Lays of Leisure Hours*, 1829). In this poem, it's all error, even primal sin: "within thee burned th'enthusiast's fire, / Wild love of freedom, longings for the lyre;—/ And ardent visions of romantic youth, / . . . / Aspirings nurst by solitude and pride, / Worlds to the dreamer, dreams to all beside; / . . . / And aimless energies that bade the mind / Launch like a ship and leave the world behind. / But duty disregarded, reason spurned, / Knowledge despised, and wisdom all unlearned, / Punished the rebel who refused to bow, / And stamped SELF-TORTURER on th' enthusiast's brow. // No earthly happiness for such, / . . . / And such wert thou . . . " (44–61; p. 180).

28. *VRW* 197; in her list of rare examples are "Sappho, Eloisa, Mrs. Macaulay, the Empress of Russia, Madame d'Eon": lesbian poet; transgressive scholar; scholar called masculine; ruler deemed a monstrous travesty of the feminine; and transvestite diplomat (Charles de Beaumont, Chevalier d'Eon [1728–1810]), legally declared female in 1777.

29. See, e.g., More, *Strictures* ch. 14; Mrs. Ellis advises the daughters of England that "an attempt at display is always disagreeable, and even brilliancy will not atone for it" (*Daughters* 7). Brilliant, forthright, politically principled Girondin Citoyenne Roland was guillotined November 1793, just days after de Gouges. Her *Appeal to Impartial Posterity* was written in prison and published in Paris in 1795 (*Appel à l'impartiale postérité, Par La citoyenne Roland*); radical London bookseller Joseph Johnson issued the English translation. Bosc's sentences read: "La citoyenne Roland, épouse d'un savant, étoit convaincue que toute la célébrité d'une femme doit se borner à l'estime que lui attire l'exercise des vertus domestiques. Aussi s'est-elle toujours refusée aux publications qui auroient pu lui donner un réputation littéraire" (iii).

30. The ironized use of Roland here contrasts with her presence in the last of Jewsbury's papers, "On Modern Female Cultivation—No. IV" (*Athenæum* 250: 521–22), which tries to rein in the enthusiast's energies, first to the duty of influencing others, then to the regulation of the affections, and finally for no more than armature against ennui. It is this last cause that brings Mme Roland on stage, as its instructor (522).

31. This was a lengthy postscript to her essay, "On the Character of Mrs. Hemans's Writings," *New Monthly Magazine* 44: 432. Quoting L.E.L. in *Literary Women* (378), Jane Williams adds that Jewsbury's "society was much courted; and in London, as well as among her numerous acquaintance in various parts of England, her brilliant conversation confirmed and increased the reputation won by her writings" (373).

32. See also Clarke 86. Sincerely "sceptical" and "eccentric," Shelley was so reviled for his heterodoxy that "it became suspicious to quote, and dangerous to admire him," Jewsbury said in an unsigned defense of Shelley in *The Athenæum* 194: 456). Shelley was still a scandal, notwithstanding the rehabilitation of atheist revolutionary into sympathetic idealist in Mary Shelley's edition of 1824, with support in 1829 from various pieces in the *Athenæum*. Jewsbury urged readers to set aside any distaste for Shelley's "metaphysical

subtleties and moral mistakes" in order to enjoy "the remaining mass of his true, pure, beautiful poetry,—poetry instinct with intellectual life—radiant, harmonious, strong." It is not necessary to endorse his "political and religious opinions" to see the poetic "genius," she insists, and she castigates a public unwilling to sift the evidence (456–57).

33. Thus Lady Sarolta, in mountain exile from a usurped court, rebukes young Glycine's dreams of the "earthly heaven" of a "royal court." Jewsbury misremembers her source as the aptly titled *Remorse;* she is actually copying from *Zapolya* (Part II; I.i.48–52), the same scene that supplies the epigraph for Chapter IX (70).

34. "We look before and after, / And pine for what is not: / Our sincerest laughter / With some pain is fraught; / Our sweetest songs are those that tell of saddest thought," wrote Shelley (*To a Sky-Lark* 86–90). No less than Shelley, Jewsbury evokes Shakespeare's star melancholic, Hamlet, who muses in his last soliloquy that although man was created with "such large discourse, / Looking before and after," it fusts in him unused (4.4.36–39). In the 1802 Preface to *Lyrical Ballads,* Wordsworth equates this capacity with poetic power, but it is the Shelleyan link with misery that Jewsbury transfers to Julia. *The Triumph of Life* was published in 1824; Jewsbury, an avid reader of Shelley, knew this as well as any of his poetry.

35. *Enthusiast* 119; Byron's *The Deformed Transformed* was published in 1824.

36. Clarke doesn't address the *Literary Souvenir* site, only a republication in *The Poetical Album* (1828–29). Reading Jewsbury as pent by Wordsworthian gender strictures, both she and Reynolds see *A Farewell* as a "renunciation," conveyed to Wordsworth in the humility of one who realized her lack of talent "to be among the poetic great" and now "knew her place" (Clarke 67); having "learnt the womanly qualities of renunciation, self-abasement and humility," she is "a classic of the kind discerned by Gilbert and Gubar as gendered by 'anxiety of authorship'" (Reynolds, in Leighton and Reynolds 27). These accounts elide Wordsworth's layered concern for Jewsbury: his warm admiration of her prose, his depression about his own unpopularity, and his not inaccurate sense of the climate of reception for female ambition.

37. In various annuals alone, she published a half dozen poems the very next year. For a census see Boyle's *Index* 1: 152–54.

38. I'm grateful to Dennis Low for telling me about this letter (WLMS A 8; transcribed in Low 266) and for his sharp discussion of the import (266–68).

39. 20 Jan. 1829; WLMS A 17.

40. Keats's resonant phrase is from the "Induction" to *The Fall of Hyperion: A Dream* (1.8), not published until 1856.

41. Clarke does not allow any irony, and even represents, via a patched sentence from Cecil's actual rebuke (*Enthusiast* 120), all these sentences as his rebuke (84).

42. Clarke's attribution of these sentiments, too, to Cecil also seems questionable.

43. Jewsbury must have quoted from manuscript, and so pre-advertised the verse before it was actually published in 1832. This is a bird, Wordsworth says, of "Perpetual flight, unchecked by earthly ties," the last word the rhyme partner of "Paradise" (*Morning Exercise* 35–36).

44. *Properzia Rossi* epigraph 2–3; 26–27, 81–83. That Hemans's *Records* was on Jewsbury's mind is confirmed by her use of lines from another its poems as the epigraph to Chapter XV (116).

45. This betweenness is reflected by the Blackwell anthologies: Wu's *Romantic Woman Poets* omits Jewsbury (but not L.E.L., born after her); Reynolds and Leighton put her in *Victorian Women Poets,* featuring the poems of corrected enthusiasm: *To My Own Heart, A Farewell to the Muse,* and *A Summer Eve's Vision.* By Blackwell lights, Jewsbury is not only not "Romantic," but qualifies as honorary "Victorian" in conformity to Victorian strictures.

46. The source, *To Somebody,* is actually rather bitter, beginning with a male poet's double-edged statement of difference: "I BLAME not her, because my soul / Is not like her's—a treasure / Of self-sufficing good,—a whole / Complete in every measure" (33). And he proceeds to issue the blame he pretends to abjure: "Those winsome smiles, those sunny looks, / Her heart securely deems, / Cold as the flashing of the brooks / In the cold moonlight beams. // Her sweet affections, free as wind, / Nor fear, nor craving feel; / No secret hollow hath her mind / For passion to reveal. // Her being's law is gentle bliss," etc. (*Poems* p. 34). The bliss is ignorance, the serenity so passionless as to seem the perfection of nature at its chilliest.

47. Captain Egerton recites a pastiche of 26–30, 76–80, and the last two stanzas (96–105).

48. Female novelists valuing feminine propriety, argues Elaine Showalter, addressed the contradiction of their professionalism with plots in which the heroine's aspirations for an independent life are "undermined, punished, or replaced by marriage" (*A Literature* 22). If, as Rachel Blau DuPlessis argues, the conflict of romance and quest (the plots pointed, respectively, to marriage or death) is the pattern in nineteenth-century women's fiction (1–19) from which twentieth-century writers shape a "critical dissent" (5), Jewsbury was already at it.

49. The pentameter *ababcc* (the pattern of a Shakespearean sonnet sestet), called the "Venus and Adonis stanza" (from Shakespeare's poem), was a popular form for Renaissance complaints. Hemans used it in *Evening Prayer at a Girls' School,* that tonally ambiguous regard of female fate published just a few years before Jewsbury's *Histories,* in 1826.

50. In *Kent's Bank Mercury,* a family newspaper written from her vacation with the Wordsworths, Jewsbury listed among the "Fashionable Arrivals": "*M.J.J. from the Moon,*" bearing just the material essentials, "her coffee-pot and Writing-box"—all staged with whimsy about her ambitions and eccentricity in 1825, when no queen was likely for the throne; "the vagaries of this singular being have formed the subject of conversation in the circle of the court for some time past. Her majesty's known predilection for oddities however sanctions the report that she is about to become the Poet Laureate with one alteration in the customary remuneration. A Butt of Coffee is to supersede the Butt of Sack" (Gillett, ed. 102).

51. This is the appealing title of DuPlessis's study of how twentieth-century women

writers delegitimate "romance as trope for the sex-gender system." If narrative conveys ideology, "writing beyond the ending" releases it from "conventional structures of fiction and consciousness about women" (ix–x).

52. *Romanticism at the End of History* 26. The site is the Advertisement of 1798 (*Lyrical Ballads & c* 739), not the Preface of 1800.

53. *Edinburgh Journal* hoped for more to come (270). From *The Three Histories*, the *Literary Gazette* guessed an "author possessing higher powers than the actual work developes" (24 April 1830, 271); the *Athenæum*, greeting a "striking talent," sensed "a store of wealth yet unfolded" (131: 258); *New Monthly*, recalling the "powers" evident in previous work and admiring the still "higher style" here, felt confident "that Miss Jewsbury has not even yet attained the highest point to which her genius will lead her" (30 [1830]: 233).

54. See, in order of publication: *Athenæum* 347: 473; Chorley, *Memorials of Hemans* 1: 171; Williams, *Literary Women* 381; Gillett xxxiii, lxv.

55. Clarke's alert observation (159); for Harriett Hughes's letter to Dora Wordsworth, see Howard Vincent, ed. 98.

56. I state these reservations with respect. Having read about Jewsbury in Chorley, then Gillett's edition, I was excited by the work of Monica Fryckstedt and Norma Clarke. I'm also indebted to Joanna Wilkes's essay on Jewsbury's authorial self-fashioning (and fashions of "author"), and Dennis Low's work in the Dove Cottage archives.

57. Clarke draws a psychosomatic logic from the sequence of success and sickness (70–74), but as Low argues, this *post hoc ergo propter hoc* can be challenged by Jewsbury's noticeably sustained enthusiasm for writing.

58. The sentences from Jewsbury's essay in *The Athenæum* (553–54) constitute 75 percent of Henry Austen's "extract" (xi–xiii); a paragraph from Whately's essay (359–60) follows. Both excerpts are unattributed, except by that single vague citation. The incorporation of Jewsbury and Whately was perpetuated in reissues of Bentley's edition through 1854, in collected editions of Austen until 1869, and in editions based on Bentley's up to the 1880s.

59. I'm grateful to Wilkes (112–13) for noticing the unmarked use of Jewsbury's "Jane Austen" in Henry Austen's 1833 "Memoir," and then in Lewes's essay where, via Henry Austen's collation, it is all attributed to Whately (see Lewes 99–100, 102–4).

Chapter Five

1. "I remember Lord Byron's mentioning, that the story of Sardanapalus had been working in his brain for seven years before he commenced it" (E. J. Trelawny, in *W* [1833] 13: 196).

2. For a generous quotation and sharp discussion of this mid-eighteenth-century pamphlet, see Andrew Elfenbein, *Romantic Genius* 9–12. In the vein of Hazlitt, Linda Dowling distinguishes the republican discourse of *effeminate* from modern gender categories. The term expresses a "classical republican anxiety" over national destiny: evoking "a vanished archaic past in which the survival of a community was sustained in an

almost metaphysical as well as a practical sense by the valor of its citizen soldiers," *effeminacy* names both "civic enfeeblement" and "monstrous self-absorption" (5–8). In a similar key, G. J. Barker-Benfield notes "the widespread use of the term" in the eighteenth century as traditional ideas of manhood, "bound up with classical and warrior ideals," were receding in emergent capitalist culture (104); see ch. 3. But Elfenbein is right to nail the emergent gender-slur: *effeminacy* was the term of deviance for the "monstrous and indecent," "defiling and unnatural," "abominable" revels that the tract broadcasts (10).

3. See also her judgment of "emasculated by pleasure" in *Letter on the Present Character of the French Nation* (1793, pub. 1798; *W* 6: 445). This retrospect amounts to a revision of Brown's sense that the French had a special sanction: "the ruling Manners of the *French* Nation" ("as *vain* and *effeminate* as our own, and the very Archetype from which our own are drawn") did not affect "their national *Capacity*" and "public *Virtue*," he said in 1757 (135–37), while "our *effeminate manners* and *Defect* of *Principle* have weakened the national Capacity, and the Spirit of Defence" (142).

4. For a succinct discussion of this issue during the 1790s, especially in the anti-Jacobin novel, see M. O. Grenby 155–60. Dorothy Wordsworth reports a conversation on this theme in the Wordsworth household in late 1800: "the manners of the rich—Avarice, inordinate desires, & the effeminacy unnaturalness & the unworthy objects of education" (*Grasmere Journal* 23). "The Victorian notion of the English national character—energetic, disciplined, dutiful and above all manly—is not really a Victorian invention," remarks Marilyn Butler; "It is one of the more lasting products of Britain's intermittent eighteenth-century war with France for world domination, which ended with the anti-French alliance victorious on the field of Waterloo" ("John Bull's" 281).

5. D'Israeli is quoted from Cline 142; Davies, *HVSV* 42.

6. Although Hunt does note "tastes of a more masculine description," especially in the athletics of swimming and riding (157), his memoir is threaded with slurs of effeminacy, answering Byron's tweaking him in these terms. Byron "was as acute as a woman" in his "care about rank and titles" (45); his person tended "to fat and effeminacy" (151); he was prone to "old-womanish" superstitions (144), while his sister "had by far the greater judgment" and "the more masculine sense" (139). Hearing Hunt "dabbling on a piano-forte," Byron jabbed *Blackwood's*-style, snipping that "lovers of music [are] effeminate," while Hunt marked the absurdity of this "objector to effeminacy," sitting around in his "wealth, with rings on his fingers, and baby-work to his shirt," having "just issued, like a sultan out of his bath" (127–28).

7. Studying the alliance of literary and social logic in Victorian constructions of masculinity as performance, James Eli Adams reads *Sartor*'s Chapter X as proposing two forms of emasculation in the dandy: a default on a life of "manful" action, and a surrender of autonomy in the "appeal to an audience for his very identity" (24; see 21–26).

8. *Lodore* 81. Carlyle satirizes "Fashionable Novels" as the "Sacred Books" of the Dandy "sect" (316–17). For a sharp discussion of the Byron-coding of the silver-fork world of novelists Bulwer-Lytton and Benjamin Disraeli (Isaac's son), see Andrew Elfenbein 208–19.

9. *W* 8: 254. Hazlitt's tone is tricky. David Bromwich observes Hazlitt's sympathy with Byron's liberal politics and admiration of his genius in simultaneous irritation at Byron's self-will, egotism, and aristocratic pride (326–34). Anonymity is no easier to signify. If Hazlitt denotes a manly risk in controversial, legally actionable work, anonymity could also seem (as it did even to Byron) unmanly evasion. To later editions of *English Bards and Scotch Reviewers*, "contrary to the advice of my friends, I affixed my name," he said; "it was more manly not to deny it" (*MCB* 144). About his publisher's moaning about piracies of *Don Juan*, he snapped, "If he had put John Murray on the title-page, like a man, instead of smuggling the brat into the world, and getting [. . .] a printer and not a publisher, to father it, who would have ventured to question his paternal rights?" (*MCB* 168).

10. North implies Pope's cartoon of Nero's Sporus: "one vile Antithesis. / Amphibious Thing!"; "Fop at the Toilet, Flatt'rer at the Board, / Now trips a Lady, and now struts a Lord" (*Epistle to Dr. Arbuthnot* 325–29).

11. I paraphrase McGann's view of *Childe Harold* as an epic that tests "the question of personal and political freedom" in "oppressive and contradictory circumstances." Byron sensed that "the most personal and intimate aspects of an individual's life are closely involved with, and affected by" the social and political context ("The Book of Byron" 261). For the fluid uses of effeminacy, see Alan Sinfeld, ch. 2

12. McGann nicely calibrates the "double historical perspective" by which Byron issues a "series of symbolic historical and political meditations on current European ideology and politics" ("Book" 266, 262); although doesn't list *Sardanapalus*, it qualifies. Nineveh, argues Marilyn Butler, plays less as an Eastern site than as a "shadow-world" or parodic "other" of London in 1821 that satirizes any Orientalist displacement of "the feminine element" ("John Bull's" 284, 292).

13. "Such a character, luxurious, energetic, misanthropical," proposes Heber, is Byron's signature (*Quarterly* 27: 494). All "one individual," said the *Edinburgh* of the array; "the same varnish of voluptuousness on the surface—the same canker of misanthropy at the core" (though he found Sardanapalus rather more good-humored and amiable) (36: 420, 424). Whether in "self-caricature" or in "self-betrayal," notes Butler, "the king's frivolity, rebelliousness, effeminacy, cross-dressing and debauchery" are legibly "authorial" ("John Bull's" 285–86). Sardanapalus is "a representation, half-mocking, half-indulgent, or even self-admiring," of Byron's own "sensuality and politics," comment McGann and Waller (*BPW* 6: 611); the character's "odd compound of indolence and courage" reflects Byron's "contradictory ideas and impulses," Margaret Howell suggests (61).

14. Samuel Chew, *Dramas* 113. See *Hamlet* 5.2.220; *Henry V*, chorus before 2. 1–2.

15. For the flux of events and Byron's shifts with the revolutionaries, see Marchand, *Portrait* 336–43, and Lansdown, who also discusses the Ravenna journals for these months (140–50).

16. For an account, see Marchand, *Portrait* 338.

17. Byron revives the bitter charade of self-resignation in his satire of 1811, *Hints from Horace:* "Yes, Friend! for thee I'll quit my Cynic cell, / And bear Swift's motto 'Vive

la Bagatelle!' / Which charmed our days in each Aegean clime, / As oft at home, with Revelry—and Rhyme" (341–44). Bagatelle is a table-game like pool; Dr. Johnson observes that this was Swift's favorite motto.

18. 1833 *Works* prints Byron's disclaimer, with excerpts from the letters and journal of early 1821 (13: 55–56).

19. This assessment was reprinted in 1833 *Works* 13: 69.

20. Ms T; *BW* prints the reading (13: 67). For MS readings see *BW* 13 and *BPW* 6.

21. For Antony, see: *Flourish. Enter Antony, Cleopatra, her Ladies, the Train, with Eunuchs fanning her (The Tragedy of Antony and Cleopatra* 1.1, at 10)—the triumvir in retinue of ladies and eunuchs. For Samson: "I yielded, and unlock't her all my heart, / Who with a grain of manhood well resolv'd / Might easily have shook off all her snares: / But foul effeminacy held me yok't / Her bondslave . . . " (407–11), and so he finds himself "effeminately vanquish't" (562).

22. Shelley's Frankenstein, in relapse from "manly" scientific studies, finds solace "in the works of orientalists": "Their melancholy is soothing, [. . .] How different from the manly and heroical poetry of Greece and Rome" (I: 5, p. 51).

23. *Constitution* 24. He is defining the "essential difference between *opposite* and *contrary*": "Opposite powers are always of the same kind, and tend to union, either by equipoise or by common product."

24. Stodart 17; cf. Fordyce's eighteenth-century advice that "an effeminate fellow," who, "destitute of every manly sentiment, copies with inverted ambition from [the female] sex," can only be "an object of contempt and aversion" (1: 104–5).

25. "Hercules is represented by the poets as so desperately enamoured of the queen that, to conciliate her esteem, he spins by her side among her women, while she covers herself with the lion's skin, and arms herself with the club of the hero" (Lemprière's *Mythology*).

26. Byron to Murray, *BLJ* 8: 128–29. Murray put the passage in the 1833 *Works* (3: 64); it wasn't in the 1823 volume.

27. "Well we know your tenderness of heart, / And gentle, kind, effeminate remorse," says Buckingham, in public, to Richard III, who has refused the crown, "loath to depose [his] brother's son" (*Richard III* 3.7.208–10). If OED cites this as a use of *effeminate* "without implying reproach: Gentle, tender, compassionate," it neglects context: at this point in *Richard III* the adjective is ironic to the point of cynical, the language of a calculated charade for the public.

28. Spence 60; Marchand, *Portrait* 342, *Byron's Poetry* 103. M. K. Joseph describes an "enlightened ruler" (116) and G.W. Knight hesitates only about an "unpractical" bent (*Oracle* 225). To Martyn Corbett, "his ironic scepticism, his valour, his generosity, idealism and magnanimity" make him "the most admirable, noble and memorable of Byron's heroes" (115); "The pity of this tragedy is the world losing, partly because it cannot comprehend, and partly because Sardanapalus is incapable of realising, the splendid humanity of his vision. For all his faults, he towers above the rest. He is to Nineveh as Hamlet is to Elsinore" (98). To John Farrell, Sardanapalus suffers "the total

failure of anyone, friend or enemy, to comprehend the utopian majesty for which he stands" (164). If the king has a fault, "it is that he is too good for a world that loves war, glory, and the exercise of power," proposed McGann in the Vietnam-1960s; he "exposes the folly of such ideas, and counters with his own political philosophy," resolving "the conflict between power and pleasure" in "perfect self-possession" (*Fiery Dust* 233, 239); protests such as "I loathe all war, and warriors; / I live in peace and pleasure: what can man / Do more?" (1.2.529–31) confirm him as one of Byron's "forms of the human sublime" (236). Whether McGann's later regard of *Fiery Dust* as uncritically absorbed "in Romanticism's own self-representations" (*Romantic Ideology* 37–38) would apply to this view is a question. The power of the romance is clear.

29. See McGann: "Sardanapalus is an antitype of the European monarchs"; his leniency in Acts 1 and 2 "contrasts with the eagerness of early nineteenth-century regimes to repress and punish dissent" (*BPW* 6: 610).

30. Myrrha qualifies for the romance; Byron wrote to his mother in 1809 of the lot of women as hard "labourers" in "warlike" Albania: "treated like slaves, beaten &, in short complete beasts of burthen, they plough, dig & sow, I found them carrying wood & actually repairing the highways." Though here, too, he strained for romance: their lot is "no great hardship in so delightful a climate" (*BLJ* 1: 228–29). For *Sardanapalus* and questions of slavery, and of slavery as a trope for women's social status, see Malcolm Kelsall, "Slave-Woman in the Harem."

31. *Quarterly Review* 27: 496; rpt. 1833 *BW* 13: 69–70.

32. He can't imagine visiting the new world, where slavery is in the social fabric: "there is no freedom—even for Masters—in the midst of slaves—it makes my blood boil to see the thing.—I sometimes wish that I was the Owner of Africa—to do at once—what Wilberforce will do in time—viz—sweep Slavery from her desarts—and look on upon the first dance of their Freedom." (Hear the echo of Wollstonecraft's polemic in the 1790s on the denial of "civil and political rights" to women: "They may be convenient slaves, but slavery will have its constant effect, degrading the master and the abject dependent" [*VRW* 103–4; cf. 167]). Byron distinguished chattel slavery from "political slavery," which is "men's own fault—if they will be slaves let them!" ("Detached Thoughts" [1821–22], *BLJ* 9: 41), but he did not address women's subjection. Back home, the British press continued to expose the brutalities of chattel slave trade: one horrifying report appears in the *Edinburgh* issue in which *Sardanapalus* is reviewed (36: 34–52). Thanks to Jerry McGann for conversation on the various aspects of this question; see also his remarks in "Hero" 158n6.

33. Terms of slavery, voiced 42 times, most often name the social caste, usually in relation to Myrrha. Free men summon the language in contempt of weakness or abasement. Far from being a material slave, Sardanapalus is Assyria's principal slave-owner, and appropriates the descriptive variously to revile traitors and enemies, to despise a restless and complaining populace, and finally to himself, to excuse his own failings. See also Johnson's "*sang-froid*" shrug in the slave-market of *Don Juan*, Canto V (also written in 1821): "Most men are slaves, none more so than the great, / To their own whims and

passions" (5.25)—though here, at least, the trope is bravely summoned over and against the material fact. In purely aesthetic terms, Byron put himself in the chivalrous Burkean trope of willing subjection, when he dedicated *Sardanapalus* to Goethe as "the homage of a literary vassal to his liege-Lord."

As for "circumstance" as the master: this, too, was Byronic sentimentality, Sardanapalus's self-excuse repeated almost verbatim in a conversation with Lady Blessington in 1823. "'We are all the creatures of circumstance,' [said] Byron; 'the greater part of our errors are caused, if not excused, by events and situations over which we have had little control; the world sees the faults, but they see not what led to them'" (*BCB* 172–73). Byron thought this the antithesis of "cant," but the self-serving may make it only a more mystified version of it.

34. A memoir of 1825 not only caught the "strong [. . .] congruity" with Byron's domestic circumstances, but advertised it with a header, SCENE APPLICABLE TO LORD BYRON'S FAMILY AFFAIRS (Iley 2:53–58). Heber thought the fussing about infidelity so historically and culturally irrational for Assyria (1833 *BW* 13: 160n) that it had to come from elsewhere. James Hogg implied the domestic reference in a comment also printed in 1833 *BW*: "In many parts of this play, it strikes me that Lord Byron has more in his eye the case of a sinful Christian that has but one wife, and a sly business or so which she and her kin do not approve of, than a bearded Oriental, like Sardanapalus, with three hundred wives and seven hundred concubines" (13: 78). E. H. Coleridge ably read the domestic palimpsest (*BW* 5: 82n). See also McGann, *BPW* 6: 611, and "Hero" 144–49, where he sees the domestic allegory eluding Byron's management to expose Byron's "petty self-deceptions and justifications" (147).

35. See McGann's incisive account of this self-contradicted, anti-heroic heroic ("Hero," esp. 154–55): that Sardanapalus masks both Byron and George IV forces Byron "to reflect himself in the guise of the last, and most contemptible, of the English Georges" (155). A precedent for the use of Sardanapalus to shame a contemporary monarch is Surrey's sonnet, "Th'Assyryans king," which editor Emrys Jones sees as "a covert allusion to Henry VIII" (*Poems* 127).

36. Hemans's brother Thomas Henry Browne was part of the crown's espionage on the queen in Italy. Siding with the queen, Byron tried to supply evidence on her behalf. For her escapades and the trial, see J. B. Priestly 268–80; Roger Sales reports the political circus (178–86), as does Anna Clark, who shows how popular sympathy for the queen was manipulated against both the government and the royalty (49). For more on Browne, including Byron's hatred of him (though he didn't know the Hemans connection), see Nanora Sweet, "The Inseparables."

37. Byron's disclaimers seem disingenuous, meant to tweak Murray's Toryism: "Queen—& pavilion occur—but it is not an allusion to his Britannic Majesty—as you may tremulously [. . .] imagine"; "I have made Sardanapalus brave (though voluptuous as history represents him) and also as amiable as my poor powers could render him.— So that it could neither be truth nor satire on any living monarch" (*BLJ* 8: 126–27). E. H. Coleridge marks the contemporary references (*Works of Byron* 5: 15n1); see also

Woodring 189. Anyone reading the newspapers in 1820, "especially the gossip items, must have felt at home in the Assyrian court, with its king in marital trouble, beset by criticism and scandal, overgiven to throwing parties in an (oriental) pavilion," remarks Marilyn Butler; no less than Sardanapalus, King George preferred "the woman's world of the salon or pavilion to the increasingly weighty burdens of empire" ("John Bull's" 292).

38. See Daniel Watkins on the struggle between equally flawed social philosophies: if Sardanapalus's hedonism is a protest "against the ideology of the society he is born to rule," hedonism is only irresponsible ("Byron's History Plays" 806–7).

39. Heber, *Quarterly* 27: 494–95 (rpt. 1833 *BW* 13: 66); Knight, *Oracle* 254; Manning, *Byron* 133, 128. For Allen Perry Whitmore, the case is not even problematic: the king who will not "forbear the banquet," "nor forbear the goblet; / Nor crown me with a single rose the less; / Nor lose one joyous hour" (1.2.308–13) is a devotee of pleasure who despises his rebellious subjects "because they inconvenience him": his pacificism is based more on "a selfish wish to be free of responsibility than on any real concern for his people" (72).

40. Effeminacy is a tactic to escape "the heritage of violence he fears in himself" (Manning, *Byron* 128); he senses "something bloody and cruel in his nature" that he would hold in check (Whitmore 73).

41. See Rousseau, *Émile*: "When the Greek women married, they disappeared from public life; within the four walls of their home they devoted themselves to the care of their household and family. This is the mode of life prescribed for women alike by nature and reason" (tr. Foxley 330).

42. *Athenæum* 187: 338; reviewing a translation of Raupach's play about Semiramis, *The Daughter of the Air: A Mythic Tragedy.*

43. Jeffrey had assigned this review to Hazlitt, who wrote his remarks on *Sardanapalus* in haste amid divorce proceedings and sent it to Jeffrey, who revised so thoroughly (adding his own remarks on *Cain* and *The Two Foscari,* with which it was published) that he regarded the essay as his work. I am indebted for this information to Hazlitt scholars Stanley Jones (321) and Duncan Wu, "Talking Pimples" (164–65).

44. *BLJ* 8: 128. 1833 *BW* (13: 132) was the first edition to print Juvenal's *Satire II* 99–103, along with Gifford's rendering into English heroic couplets: "This grasps a mirror—pathic Otho's boast / (Auruncan Actor's spoil), where, while his host, / With shouts, the signal of the fight required, / He view'd his mailed form; view'd, and admired! / Lo, a new subject for the historic page, / A MIRROR, midst the arms of civil rage!" (translating 99–103). *Satire II* is about homosexuality. Juvenal, with a misogynist disgust of heterosexuality, was actively homosexual, and the active partner. "Pathic," translating *pathici,* is the recipient male; the OED gives Gifford's translation among its citations. The term is so arcane and obsolete that even Crompton missed this passage.

45. Here, for comparison to Gifford's decorum, is Peter Green's twentieth-century translation of the fuller passage of Juvenal's contempt of the pathics at cult parties in Rome: "Here's another clutching a mirror—just like that fag of an Emperor / Otho,

who peeked at himself to see how his armour looked / before riding into battle. A heroic trophy *that* was, / fit matter for new annals and recent histories, / a civil war where mirrors formed part of the fighting kit! / To knock off an imperial rival *and* keep your complexion fresh / demands consummate generalship; to camp in palatial / luxury on the battlefield, *and* give yourself a face-pack / argues true courage. No Eastern warrior-queen / (say the archer Samiramis [*sic*]), not ill-starred Cleopatra / aboard her flagship at Actium matched such behaviour" (99–109).

46. This, too, was quoted in 1833 *BW* (13: 134).

47. So, too, the Maid of Saragoza in *Childe Harold's Pilgrimage*. Though "all unsex'd" in battle, a "more than female grace" (1.54–55) preserves the fame of "Spain's maids": "no race of Amazons, / But form'd for all the witching arts of love" (57).

48. See Ms. T (*BPW* 6: 84): ~~And / and I say / most femininely for furiuosly Holding most excessive rage for~~ a / ~~And I say femininely for~~ And femininely meaneth furiously / [. . .] all passions in excess as are female

49. The linking, argues Caroline Franklin, is an anxious vision of how Myrrha could change in the catalyst of violence (*Byron's Heroines* 215). It is dramatically enforced on Sardanapalus's awakening, when Semiramis "is suddenly replaced by the real apparition" of Myrrha (McGann, *Fiery Dust* 231).

50. Guercino's *Semiramis Receiving Word of the Revolt of Babylon* (1624) depicts a self-possessed dark-haired beauty; Byron knew Guercino's work and perhaps this painting. More recent, specifically literary antecedents are Lemprière's *Dictionary* and Voltaire's popular play *Sémiramis*. Although Lemprière refers to the scandalous accusations (her conspiracy in the death of husband Ninus; the "unnatural" passion for her son and occasional impersonation of him; her "licentiousness" and dallying with hunky soldiers whom she then put to death "that they might not be living witnesses of her incontinence"), he stresses "her uncommon beauty," her sound advice and "prudent directions," her civic responsibility, and her establishment of Babylon as "the most superb and magnificent city in the world" (666–67). Voltaire's Sémiramis is a sympathetic, tragic figure: as haunted as any Byronic hero by her sins; her guilt a "dreadful malady" that weakens her grip on the "reins of empire" (149); beset by base manipulators and longing for death. The incestuous desire that Byron portrays in the dream is cast by Voltaire as innocent (Sémiramis does not know her son, and thinks he is the agent of restoration promised in the prophesies), and she welcomes his unwitting murder of her as "the fate I merited" (224).

51. Caroline Franklin notes her affinity to Empress Catherine in *Don Juan*; for both, sexual and imperial aggression mutually stigmatize one another (*Byron's Heroines* 215–16).

52. 1833 *BW* appends the remarks to the preface (13: 60–61). The paradox "chartered libertine" alludes to Archbishop of Canterbury's mildly sarcastic marveling at party-Prince Hal's emergence as a charismatic king: "when he speaks, / The air, a chartered libertine, is still" (*Henry V* 1.1.48–49). Hazlitt summoned the phrase describe Byron's

love of shocking his public, forcing them "to admire in spite of decency and common sense" (*Lord Byron* 168).

53. Paul Elledge reads a conflict of "effeminate emotionalism" and "rigorous intellectualism and combativeness" that finds resolution when, "after verifying his manhood through spirited participation in military engagements," Sardanapalus enacts a "fusion of [his] equally strong masculine and feminine impulses" (119–21)—an echo of G. W. Knight, who sees a hero who can "fuse man's reason with woman's emotional depth" (*Oracle* 247). Insisting on the social context, Diane Hoeveler demurs, seeing an exposure of "the impossibility of androgyny in a society that ultimately values only the masculine characteristics of aggression and power" (163); "neither the manly woman nor the womanly man" has a place amid such "radically polarized and then institutionalized sexual identities and roles" (167).

54. *BPW* 6: 101n. For Byron's priority with the gender-verb, see OED R.2 (418), which cites *Marino Faliero* 3.2.500, "Re-man your breast"—the reproof of a conspirator to Doge Faliero in a play that puts in critical perspective the ideology of manly honor. Byron originally wrote "Bear with yourself" (*BPW* 4: 383). I owe to Jack Cragwall's sharp reading my next remark about the reflexive form of the verb—as well as good conversation about both these plays.

55. "Appropriately enough, as Sardanapalus moves closer toward the reconciliation of his masculine with his feminine impulses," argued Elledge in 1968, "Myrrha's role as 'masculine' counterpart diminishes in importance, and the Greek slave assumes her proper place as a subservient, deeply affectionate companion" (121). Whether or not we accede to this notion of "proper," we can see how Byron's designs elicit it.

56. See (among legions) McGann, *Fiery Dust* 230; Corbett 112. Only Peter Manning ironizes the mythology, to observe "a male fantasy of the absolute dependence of women on men for their identity" (*Byron* 131).

57. Byron was familiar with the namesake link, having asked Murray in June 1820 to send him "<u>tincture</u> of Myrrh" (*BLJ* 7: 113). Frankincense is Homeric as well as Christian. Heber points out a reference in *The Odyssey* to the happy isles of afterlife, where "departed warriors" enjoy "altars steaming with frankincense" (1833 *BW* 13: 149n).

58. See 10: 2.84–99. Tormented by incestuous passion for her father, Myrrha insinuates herself into his bed. When, after several encounters, he unmasks her, she flees to a foreign land and begs the gods for relief as she labors in the birth of their child; they change her into a myrrh tree.

59. The year of Byron's birth, Alfieri produced *Mirra* (1788), whose heroine commits suicide at the mere confession of her desire (her torments echoing Voltaire's guilt-haunted Sémiramis):

Sleep everlastingly forsakes my pillow;
Or dreams, with horrid images of death,
Give greater martyrdom than sleepless nights:
I do not find, throughout the day or night,
A moment's peace, repose, or resting place.

Yet nothing in the shape of human comfort
Do I presume to covet; death I deem,
Expect, solicit, as my only cure.   (3.2; Bowring, *Myrrha*, 2: 338)

Byron may have read the play, and he did see it in August 1819, with no little gender trouble. "I am not very well today," he wrote Murray; "Last night I went to the representation of Alfieri's Mirra—the two last acts of which threw me into convulsions.—I do not mean by that word—a lady's hysterics—but the agony of reluctant tears—and the choaking shudder which I do not often undergo for fiction" (*BLJ* 6: 206). He was spooked for "a fortnight" (217)—maybe not a lady's hysterics, but the hysterical repression of his own incestuous liaison with his half-sister. At one point he thought to name Myrrha "Byblis," a lass in *Metamorphoses* Book 9 with a passion for her twin brother; see *BW* 13: 70n. Mary Shelley admired the tragedy so much that she undertook a translation; see her journal 9 April 1815 and 14 September 1818 (*J* 74, 226). Byron's friend Bowring seems to have relied silently on Charles Lloyd's 1815 translation.

60. With an American (Mir-rah) rather than a British ear (*My*-rah), Jerome Christensen glosses *Myrrha* as the punning *mirror* of masculine Sardanapalus, "a figure equal to her image of him" and "swayed by that example of the sovereign self" (*Lord Byron's Strength* 280–81).

61. The echoes of *nothing* extend to Byron's complaint in his Preface that his "private feelings" about not staging his plays seem to "stand for nothing." Against this "nothing," the "nothing" that Byron writes for Sardanapalus indulges a highly theatrical self-authorizing. David Erdman argues that Byron cherished hopes of theatrical success and issued statements such as those of the Preface to rationalize any failure ("Byron's Stage Fright").

62. So reports Diodorus, quoted in the 1833 *BW* 13: 64. In the lifetime publication, Byron himself supplies a note to the lines in 1.2 (*Sardanapalus & c* 171–73) in the form of a long quotation from Mitford's *History of Greece* (1818) 9: 311–13.

63. Though Byron rhymes *hero/ zero* two other times in *Don Juan* (3.110; 11.56), this is the only couplet rhyming, here or anywhere in Byron's poetry.

64. He "had, indeed, no unfavourable groundwork, even in the few hints supplied by the ancient historians, as to the conduct and history of the last and most unfortunate of the line of Belus. Though accused, (whether truly or falsely,) by his triumphant enemies, of the most revolting vices and an effeminacy even beyond what might be expected from the last dregs of Asiatic despotism, we find Sardanapalus when roused by the approach of danger, conducting his armies with a courage, a skill, and, for some time at least, with a success not inferior to those of his most warlike ancestors [. . .] and seeking his death with a mixture of heroism and ferocity which little accords with our notions of a weak or utterly degraded character" (27: 494). 1833 *BW* included these comments in a long quotation from Heber's review at the end of the play (13: 195).

65. Calvert, in Howell 81, with details of stage history; Weller gives a short report, *BPW* 6: 583–85. The phrase "apocalyptic sublime" is the title of Morton Paley's book, which discusses Martin's productions in this genre. Weller cites *Athenæum* (12 April

1834) to instance the general recognition of the influence of Martin's *Fall of Nineveh* (late 1820s) on Macready's staging. Hemans's disappointment even with Martin's *Fall*, her wish for "something more of gloomy grandeur" to "have been thrown about the funeral pyre," suggests why Byron stopped just short of this event. It "should have looked more like a *thing apart*," she said, "almost suggesting of itself the idea of an awful sacrifice. Perhaps it was not in the resources of the painter to do all this; but the imagination, *mine* at least, seems to require it" (*CMH* 2: 82).

66. After Macready, Kean mounted productions in 1838 and 1853, cutting the scenes bearing on effeminate character (Howell 67, 75). See also Martin K. Nurmi's report of Kean's 1838 production (a likely prototype for the later, sensational success): Kean cut text on gender ideology (e.g., "all passions in excess are feminine"), on Myrrha as a "complex and noble character," and on Semiramis as foil to Sardanapalus's effeminacy (see esp. 8–11).

67. The sword-refusing remark to which Lewes refers is: "A heavy one; the hilt, too, hurts my hand. / (*To a Guard*) Here, fellow, take thy weapon back" (2.1.194–95). In the production at Yale (1990), the actor took neither of these options (matter of fact; matter of effeminacy), but camped up the swordplay and the remark, as if to tweak the palace critics.

68. See Howell 80; Odell also reports this (6: 366), and notes that Shaw-Hamblin had also "impersonated the prince" in a staging of Act 3 of *Hamlet* in December 1836. This was part of a farewell benefit to help finance her suit of slander against an actor who had approached her husband with reports of her marital infidelity while she was performing in England (4: 142)—a kind of modern-day Queen Caroline.

Chapter Six

1. Parenthetical references to *Don Juan* are in arabic (canto.stanza), to *Beppo* by stanza, and other poems by line number. Mss. texts are cited from McGann's *BPW*, unless otherwise indicated.

2. 7 Aug. 1918; *Writer's Diary* 2–3.

3. Not only was he impressed that Lady Holland was "not vindictive" about a nasty note on her in *English Bards, and Scotch Reviewers*, but (Byron marvels to Lady Blessington), "I suspect I owe her friendship to it." The note was "we know from good authority, that the manuscripts are submitted to her perusal—no doubt for correction" (attached to line 541 in the 4th edition [1811], 44; see also *BPW* 1: 410n). Referring to her relations with Lord Holland, both the note and its anchor-line, "Reforms each error, and refines the whole" (line 559 in 1st edn.), comments McGann, wink at Lady Holland's divorce from her first husband and her illegitimate son by Lord Holland, scandals on which many women refused her acquaintance. "The first dispute I ever had with lady Byron," recalled Byron, "was caused by my urging her visit Lady [Holland]" (*BCB* 12).

4. Leslie Marchand comments on the heterosexual hierarchy (*Biography* 330), and Louis Crompton notes a similar aristocratic preference in Byron's homosexual liaisons (*Byron and Greek Love* 239–40).

5. Wilde conjectured such investment in Shakespeare's she-boy roles: "there must have been in Shakespeare's company some wonderful boy-actor of great beauty, to whom he intrusted the presentation of his noble heroines," for whom "he created Viola and Imogen, Juliet and Rosalind, Portia and Desdemona, and Cleopatra herself" (*The Portrait of Mr. W. H.* 42, 41). Viola, Imogen, Rosalind, and Portia exploit the double-sex allure by cross-dressing back into masculine garb, and even Cleopatra imagines her theatrics travestied by some boy-actor. In societies proscribing same-sex love, boy-dressed girls afforded "surreptitious romance," remarks Crompton (210).

6. Knight, *Oracle* 268. In *Lord Byron's Marriage*, Knight reads Byron's Cambridge passion, choirboy John Edleston, as the masked referent of "Thyrza" (30–38). Francis Jeffrey at least was convinced that these poems of "great beauty and feeling" were "elegies in honour" of the lady lamented in *Childe Harold's Pilgrimage II*.95–96 (*Edinburgh Review* 19 [1812]: 475). Crompton comments on this guise and on Byron's heterosexed translations of Greek and Latin homoerotic lyrics (94, 105–6, 177–78).

7. For the "surreptitious" homoerotic romance afforded by boy-clad girls, see Crompton 210.

8. Working from Shoshana Felman's notation of transvestism as a "travesty of travesty," Mary Jacobus uses Woolf's fable to read gender as a textual production, susceptible to travesty and exchange, with "no 'proper' referent, male or female, only the masquerade of masculinity and femininity" (Felman, "Rereading Femininity" 28; Jacobus, *Reading Woman* 3–4, 15). Judith Butler reads cross-dressing, drag theatrics, and heterosexual stylizing in homosexual relations as postmodern parodies of "the notion of an original or primary gender identity" (137).

9. *L* 2: 58. Mary Shelley kept these sentences when she published P. B. Shelley's letters in 1840 (*Essays, Letters* 2: 119).

10. Davis 127. For the deconstructive, fantasy-producing force of cross-dressing, see Marjorie Garber *Vested Interests*.

11. Radcliffe 50, 56, 59, 76, 108, 122, 59.

12. *travesty*: *trans* + *vestre* (to clothe); OED cites Don Juan's harem travesty.

13. No less than Lord Holland's "handsome" son (*BCB* 10), Byron liked "a handsome healthy woman, with an intelligent and intelligible mind, who can do something more than what is said a French woman can only do, *habille, babille, and dishabille*" (*BCB* 162; perhaps with a sense of her own inclusion, Teresa Guiccioli underlined this remark).

14. I owe this observation to Jack Cragwall.

15. Don Giovanni was sometimes a transvestite role in English pantomimes (Peter Graham 70, citing M. Wilson Disher 48). Keats reviewed one at Drury Lane December 1817 for the *Champion* (4 Jan. 1818).

16. Henry Blyth speculates that Lamb's attraction was her androgyny: "intensely feminine," and yet "half a boy" (90); for her masquerade as Byron's Don Juan, see *BLJ* 7: 169 and Marchand, *Biography* 840; for her pageboy antics, ibid. 341.

17. For the anecdotes, see Marchand, *Biography* 156; *MCB* 67; Hunt, *Lord Byron* 156–57.

18. Harrison 147. Jean Howard, citing Harrison, gives an informative report on the Renaissance polemics about social and theatrical cross-dressing; see also Garber, *Vested Interests* 25–32.

19. Stubbes 73. All those efforts in early modern tracts to control the cross-dressed woman, Jean Howard proposes, reflect an unstable gender system (425) and a felt threat to hierarchy and subordination (418); see her bibliography (419n3), and also Phyllis Rackin and Catherine Belsey.

20. Stubbes 73. For the Renaissance anti-theatrical tracts voicing fears of effeminization worked by dress, especially in the theater, see Laura Levine (121–22).

21. Credited to Lamb by Margot Strickland (*The Byron Women* 212–16), Peter Graham (*Don Juan and Regency England*), Duncan Wu, *Romantic Women Poets* (2d edn., 649) and "Appropriating Byron," James Soderholm, "Lady Caroline Lamb" (32); but disputed (without explanation) by Paula Feldman, *British Women Poets of the Romantic Era* 363.

22. To Jerome Christensen's observation of the fate of *Juan* for feminine rhyme (*Strength* 96–97), may be added a post-Miltonic disdain of rhyme. It "has something effeminate it its jingling Nature, and emasculates our *English* Verse," declared John Dennis in the early eighteenth century. He despised "Soft and effeminate Rhyme" as "the very Reverse" of "manly, and powerful, and noble Enthusiasm" (*Works* 1: 379; 2: 169). Editor E. N. Hooker (1: 430n4) cites a similar view in Felton's *Dissertation on Reading the Classics* (1715).

23. Implied by Byron's truncated apostrophe is the first word in Horace's "cunnus teterrima belli / causa" (a cunt the most dreadful cause of war; *Satires* 1.3.107–8). Byron's farce-tyrant pales against the "evil Principle impersonated" cast by Coleridge in 1796: "I never dared figure the Russian Sovereign to my imagination under the dear and venerable Character of WOMAN—WOMAN, that complex term for Mother, Sister, Wife!" he exclaimed, with a litany of the abuses: "the poisoning of her husband," "the libidinous excesses of her private hours," and "the desolating ambition of her public life" and its numerous military atrocities (*Ode to the Departing Year,* note to line 40, ms. 40 [*Poems* 162–63]). For the "perfectly feminine" binary, see a later note, ca 1827, quoted by H. J. Jackson (580 and n9).

24. Byron chimes with conductrix Stodart, who set Elizabeth on a zero-sum gender scale: "The masculine powers of her nature triumphed; the woman failed" (28). Cecil Lang, who cheers the "revolutionary" force of *Don Juan* in "transferring sexual aggression to the female figures," still wants to tag them "sexual predators," reserving for men only an "assertion of sexuality" (152–53).

25. *Byron and His Fictions* 180. Manning's reading of Byron's mother-smothered boyhood for "the effects of environment on character" may be extended to gender character, masculine and feminine.

26. p. 240. That Blessington was a Lady intellectual reflects a self-alienating confirmation of the popular currency of Byron's epigram. E. J. Lovell cites her conviction

that no union "can be happy in which the woman has more strength of mind than the man," and that "the most painful and humiliating epoch in the life of a woman" has to be the discovery "that *he* on whom she has anchored her hopes of happiness is deficient in intellect" (*BCB* 31; the sources are, respectively, *Desultory Thoughts and Reflections* and her confessional novel of 1833, *The Repealers*).

27. *Commentaries* bk. 1, ch. 15 (1: 442). For Byron's reading, see *BP* 5. *Magnae* 192–93; cited by Linda Colley 238, 404n3. "Homily Against Excess of Apparell," *Certain Homilies* 330; cited by Kathleen McCluskie (113).

28. Citing Blackstone, Sandra Gilbert and Susan Gubar make coverture a master trope in the fiction of Jane Austen (who decided more than once not to marry): her rational heroines inhabit a "cover story" that conforms to the ideology of man's world ("Jane Austen's Cover Story," *Madwoman* ch. 5; esp. 154–55).

29. "Lord Byron" 164; *Characters* 273. Hazlitt's bristling at Portia and Nerissa registers a key effect: even though their garbed intervention at court does not "dismantle the sex-gender system," the theatrics by which they "successfully assume masculine positions and authority" expose prerogatives "based on custom, not nature" (Jean Howard, "Crossdressing" 433).

30. While *Georgian* refers to Caucasia, "Georgian page" may cover Caroline Lamb's English masquerades. The inspiration for Leila's guise may even have been her pageboy cover for an elopement with Byron (planned and intercepted) the summer before he wrote *The Giaour*.

31. That *the sex* means "female" reflects the simultaneity of a gender system with gender difference. The preferred view of the essentially female-hearted, crossed-dressed she-traveler is given by *Fraser*'s essay, "The Female Character" (May 1833): "There are, in the annals of warfare, several instances of females, impelled by feelings of the sincerest affection, disguising themselves in the apparel of the other sex, and following their lovers, or their husbands, through battle and through bloodshed, till they either perished or triumphed with those they loved" (7: 595).

32. Said another contributor to *Heath's* of Kaled's probable avatar, harem queen Gulnare (who murders the Pasha and liberates the Corsair from certain execution), though "extravagant and unfeminine" (158), she is redeemed by "the return of her woman-nature" (160): her shame, her passivity, and her submission on realizing the Corsair's dismay, once he is safe, at her murder. No woman, Baillie speculated caustically of Byron, "would satisfy him but the grovling devotedness of a ~~Gulnare~~ gulnair" (to Scott, 22 Oct. 1817; *L* 375); Baillie seethed at Byron's behavior in marriage, writing this just months after the separation.

33. Byron either half-confessed or theatricalized an oblique confession of this import to his wife. Speaking of "allusions to himself" in his poems, she said, "He said of 'Lara,' 'There's more in *that* than any of them,' shuddering and avoiding my eye'" (Milbanke, *Astarte* 20).

34. *Don Juan* casts she-sentiment as a covert "quest for power," with tears as weaponry, argues Anthony Vital (287), noting the reverse of *Hours of Idleness*, where women

are a static "'pre-text,' a group of signs dawn from the repertoire that defined eighteenth-century femininity" (278).

35. See *BPW* 5: 680 and *BLJ* 1: 124. Byron compared his passion for Edleston ("I certainly <u>love</u> him more than any human being") not only to male pairs Pylades and Orestes, Nisus and Euryalus, Jonathan and David, but also to the celebrated "Ladies of Llangollen" (*BLJ* 1: 124–25), lesbian Irish aristocrats (one related to Caroline Lamb), who dressed as men and lived together for fifty years in Wales. For the cultural fascination they sustained without adverse judgment, see Garber 143–46.

36. *BCB* 33. Like Medwin, Blessington is not always reliable. For her fictionalizing and Byron's theatricalizing for her amusement, see Soderholm, *Fantasy* ch. 5. Even so, her reports, like Medwin's, are part of the "Byron" lore, and many are corroborated.

37. For Blessington, see Lovell *BCB* 57–59. For the comparison to Corinne, see Ridenour, "Mobility and Improvisation," *The Style of* DON JUAN 162–66.

38. In *Don Juan: Cantos XV and XVI* (London: John and H. L. Hunt, 1824), this note is set at the back of the volume (p. 129); see *BPW* 5: 769 for the full text. On the manuscript, however, reports Doucet Fischer of the Pforzheimer Library, it is written up the inner margin and then across the top of the same page. Though an afterthought, it was perhaps not too much after, since the ink appears to be the same (correspondence, 8 Sept. 2003). The placement as endnote produces a delayed encounter for the reader, at odds with the impression of immediate supplement given by the ms.

39. Corinne describes her arts of "conversation animée" and "improvisation": "Je ne me laisse point astreindre à tel ou tel sujet, je m'abandonne à l'impression que produit sur moi l'intérêt de ceux qui m'éncounter" [I don't let myself be bound to this or that subject; I abandon myself to the impression made on me by the interest of those who encounter me]; bk. 3, ch. 3; Staël 84–85. She relates this to *mobilité*: "la gaieté, la mobilité ne me servent qu'en apparence: mais il y a dans mon âme des abîmes de tristesse" [gaiety, *mobilité* serve me only in appearance: but there are in my soul abysses of sadness]; bk. 4, ch. 6; Staël 126. This last passage impressed Hemans (*CMH* 1: 304n).

40. Moore, *Life of Byron*, in *BW* 6: 237; Blessington, *BCB* 47, 71–72. Blessington could not have appreciated the irony that Keats, whom Byron ridiculed for unmanliness, designated his own "poetical Character" as a "camelion": a liberal imagination bound by "no self" and "no character" (*L* 1: 386–87–first published 1848 in Milnes, *Life, Letters*). The same trope occurred to P. B. Shelley when, writing to Byron, he compared the language that "clothe[s]" *Don Juan* to "a sort of cameleon under the changing sky of the spirit that kindles it" (22 Oct. 1821; *L* 2: 358).

41. Ridenour, "Mobility and Improvisation."

42. *Characters* 71. M. R. Ridley notes that the sword is the one "which triumphed in the overthrow of Brutus and Cassius at Philippi" (*Antony and Cleopatra* p. 68n23).

43. *Champion*, 11 Feb. 1816, 45; referring to Byron's broken promises to his public amid the separation scandal of 1816. See also Christensen, *Lord Byron's Strength*, 92–93.

44. George Barnefield, guessing a repressed homosexual Shelley, summoned the same phrase: "He was by nature liable to the warmest impulses of affection—often

towards others of his own sex, and he felt Love as a woman feels it: it was 'his whole existence'" (61).

45. On hearing of Byron's death, she wrote to Teresa Guiccioli, "Non ha detto il caro Byron se stesso (egli che conobbe al fondo il cor femenile) che tutta l'esistenza d'una donna dipende dall'amore . . . ?" [Did not dear Byron himself say (he who knew to the depths the female heart) that the whole of woman's existence depends on love . . . ?]; *L* 1: 419.

46. Following Hobhouse's notes, Marchand (*Don Juan* 465) and Pratt (4: 45) cite *De l'influence des passions* (1796)—"L'amour est la seule passion des femmes . . . L'amour est l'histoire de la vie des femmes; c'est un épisode dans celle des hommes" (1.4: "De l'amour" p. 150)—and *Corinne* bk. 18, ch. 5 (which Byron paused over): "Que les hommes sont heureux d'aller à la guerre, d'exposer leur vie, de se livrer à l'enthousiasme de l'honneur et du danger! Mais il n'y a rien au dehors qui soulage les femmes; leur existence, immobile en présence du malheur est un long supplice" [How happy men are in going to war, risking their lives, giving themselves to enthusiasm for honor and danger! But there is nothing in the outside [world] to console women; their existence, immobile in the presence of unhappiness, is one long agony]. Marking the first sentence in Guiccioli's Italian translation, Byron wrote "No.—No" in the margin (*BP* 222–25). Whether he meant protest or sympathy, his arrest is apparent. Alaric Watts quoted the passage from *Corinne* in the *Literary Gazette* (24 Feb. 1821, 123) to charge Byron with plagiarism, a kind of textual transvestism.

McGann suggests that Murray, who published *Persuasion* (1818), may have sent Austen's novel to Byron not long before this passage was written (*BPW* 5: 680). "We certainly do not forget you, so soon as you forget us," says Anne Elliot to Captain Harville on the difference between men's and women's love; "It is, perhaps, our fate rather than our merit. [. . .] We live at home, quiet, confined, and our feelings prey upon us. [. . .] You have always a profession, pursuits, business of some sort or other, to take you back into the world immediately, and continual occupation and change soon weaken impressions" (2. ch. 11).

47. I'm indebted to the West Virginia Seminar in Criticism, 2003, for noting this detail.

48. As late as 1975, Bernard Blackstone could refuse any "compassionate sigh for poor woman" in Julia's letter, discerning instead "a vampire threat to the whole structure of masculine, rational values painstakingly built up through the civilized centuries" (299–300)—and perhaps intuiting the opening to non-heteronormative interests such as Cobbe's.

49. Caroline Franklin relates the secular, relativist view of sexual morality in *Don Juan* to tracts on "the woman question" (*Byron's Heroines* 101–21) that Byron owned: Ségur's *Women: Their Condition and Influence in Society* (English trans. 1803) and Meiners' *History of the Female Sex* (English tr. 1808).

50. Upon Pope's "principle," Hays comments, "men have formed a standard, to which they would willingly reduce the whole sex" out of self-interest: they "model them

[. . .] after their own fashion; to suit their passions and prejudices" (*Appeal* 31–32). Pope's line about Queenly ambition was a hot reference. More's *Strictures on Female Education* (1799) invoked his shudder at "a whole Sex of Queens!/ Pow'r all their end" (*Epistle* 220) in order to take Wollstonecraft to task: it is not just the "woman vain of her beauty" who "'would but be Queen for life'" but also "the public-spirited wit"—that modern "she who is vain of her genius" and "contends for the equality of pretensions," who "struggles [. . .] to enthrone 'a whole sex of Queens'" (227).

51. Manning (*Byron* 247) notes the twin of Englishwomen as unholy "Fishers for men" (12.59).

52. Margaret Homans is measuring legendary Byronism more than Byron in declaring that "the men are even bolder, the ladies even more beautiful and passive, in Byron than in life" (*Women Writers* 8). This account doesn't tally the bold beauties in *Don Juan* (Julia, Haidée, Gulbeyaz, Fitz-Fulke), Zuleika in *The Bride of Abydos,* Gulnare in *The Corsair,* Myrrha in *Sardanapalus*; and it elides the relapses of men such as Corsair Conrad and beautiful, passive Don Juan.

53. For the involvement of Haidée with death, see Peter Manning: "Enveloping protection becomes suffocation, and what were only undertones in Juan's affair with Julia become prominent" (*Byron* 186).

54. To Ruth Perry (25) I owe this reference to *The Christian Religion, As Profess'd by a Daughter of the Church of England* (London, 1705; p. 293). Astell's status as gentlewoman, Perry remarks, "gave her a sense of entitlement" that she could exercise against sexist hierarchy (24).

55. See also More's *Life of Byron,* which casts Italian mothers as bawds: Count Guiccioli's "great opulence rendered him an object of ambition among the mothers of Ravenna, who, according to the too frequent maternal practice, were seen vying with each other in attracting so rich a purchaser for their daughters, and the young Teresa Gamba, then only eighteen, and just emancipated from a convent, was the selected victim" (1832 *Works* 4: 144).

56. Mary Shelley deleted this report in her edition of P. B. Shelley's letters.

57. For a pioneering essay on how Byron's poetics of defamiliarization "indicate the effects of sexual subordination" that has come to seem natural, see Katherine Kernberger.

58. Steinem's remark is noted by Garber (65), citing Anthony Calnek, *The Hasty Pudding Theatre: A History of Harvard's Hairy-Chested Heroines* (New York, 1986; 95). "*All* women cross-dress as women when they produce themselves as artifice," Marjorie Garber proposes (49); adds Judith Butler, "drag implicitly reveals the imitative structure of gender itself—as well as its contingency" (137–38).

59. For Rousseau, see *Émile,* Book V ("Sophy") (374). Wollstonecraft reviewed Macaulay's *Letters* for *Analytical Review* in 1790. In 1797, Mary Hays was still rebuking Rousseau's syllabus (*Monthly Magazine* 3: 193). For the specious orientalizing of harem slavery, see Alan Richardson, "Escape."

60. *Lara* even troped "Slavery" as a she-tyrant (2). On the power politics of Selim's haremizing in *The Bride of Abydos,* see Peter Manning, *Byron* 40.

61. Cecil Lang calls Juan Catherine's "male whore," specifying *male* to state the scandal (158).

62. "They made me without my search a species of popular Idol—they—without reason or judgement beyond the caprice of their Good pleasure—threw down the Image from it's pedestal," Byron ranted to Murray in 1819 (*BLJ* 6: 106). The male writer's "fantasy of self-creation and self-government," argues Sonia Hofkosh, had to confront the purchasing power of women (*Sexual Politics* 37). Byron's scorn of the professional writer as effeminate, no man of letters, tunes the blue-stocking mockeries of *Beppo*. The virulence of the attack, argues Peter Manning, reflects the fear of a male self "rendered precarious by the power of the woman-dominated society" in salons, in the culture of *cavaliere servente,* and the audience of women readers ("Nameless" 151–55).

63. The satires on sentiment in *Don Juan,* argues Anthony Vital, reflects the concern that writing poetry is un-aristocratic and un-manly (269, 273). Malcolm Kellsall sees *Don Juan* still vulnerable: the English cantos, flirting with the genre dominated by women, the novel, courts a correlative "domination of men by women: the Gynocrasy," a "transfer of power from the poet's Muse to the female salon" already registered in Canto IV's blue-stocking stanzas ("Byron" 171). For the psycho-cultural dynamics of Byron's female readership, see Andrew Elfenbein 59–74.

64. Jane Stedman distinguishes the Elizabethan convention of boys in serious female roles from the later transvestite theatrics of farce and grotesque parodies (20); "the actor must be seen as a bad parody of femininity" (Straub 127).

65. A comic opera by J. B. Buckstone, *A New Don Juan!* (1828), has Juan entering a London boarding school disguised as a girl (Chew, *Byron in England* 41). Byron's friend, the resourceful Colonel Mackinnon, who "disguised himself as a nun in order to enter a Lisbon convent" (*The Reminiscences of Captain Gronow* [1862] 85–86; *HVSV* 612n39), supplies a fantasy sequel to Juan's disrupted romance with Julia.

66. "It was an admissible dress for peers being presented at foreign courts, and certainly it had a tremendous effect on certain pashas in Albania and Turkey" ("Byronic Dress" 5). Citing 9.43–45 and Moore's report, Cecil Lang reads a masked reference to Byron: like Juan, Byron piqued the sexual interest of a sixty-something potentate (Ali Pasha), who doted on his physical beauty (158–61).

67. Fenichel 169. This kind of transvestite, elaborates Stoller, is essentially butch, reveling the phallus under wraps, and getting a big charge "in revealing that he is a male-woman" (176–77). It is worth noting how Stoller can substitute ideology for science: a father "overly loving and 'maternal' to his small children" earns judgment as "effeminate," as does a man "oversolicitous to other people and thrillingly responsive to the universe of art" (179); feminization is always humiliating (185).

68. For the literary imprints of Byron's relationship with his mother, see Manning, *Byron* 23–55, 177–99. To Jack Cragwall I owe the note on the name *Catherine*.

69. Stoller, 177. Citing Stoller and Davis, Gilbert and Gubar argue that transvestite episodes in modern literature, sensitive to emerging social issues, recoil into restored and revitalized male authority (*Sexchanges* 333–35). Showalter invokes Stoller to describe the male feminism of the 1980s as a cross-dressed "phallic woman"—the male establishment usurping and in effect marginalizing the feminism it seems to endorse ("Critical Cross-Dressing").

70. For the Stockport riots, see E. P. Thompson 567; for the riots in Scott, see chapters 6 and 7. Byron said he had read all of Scott's novels "at least fifty times" (*BLJ* 8: 13); for *Midlothian*, see *BLJ* 9: 87, 10: 146, 11: 46. Byron's maiden speech in the House of Lords opposed the Frame-breaking bill (specifying a death penalty), his bitter *Ode to the Framers of the Frame Bill* was anonymously published a few days later in the *Morning Chronicle*.

71. Letter to Byron, 15 Oct. 1822; ms. in John Murray Archives; transcribed by Jane Stabler in *Byron* 182–83, to whom I am indebted for this reference.

72. For her refusal, see Steffan and Pratt 3: 177. Byron used such "wit" in 1813 in *The Devil's Drive:* as a town is besieged, "an old maid, for years forsaken," asks one invader, "pray are the rapes beginning?" (Stanza 9). It is Andrew Rutherford who deems the *Don Juan* stanzas "very funny," though he regrets Byron's "flippant treatment of the rapes" (178–79). Even McGann tries to have it both ways, viewing these stanzas as an extreme of unassimilable nihilism, but willing to amuse an audience by rehearsing them ("Discussion," *Byron and Romanticism* 136–37).

73. At the masquerades, the religious garb gave an extra transgressive thrill to the transvestic fun (Garber, *Vested* 219).

74. "Eros and Liberty" 164. G. J. Barker-Benfield notes that eighteenth-century writers, from political critics to sentimentalists, worked the masquerade as a master-trope for a "corrupt and duplicitous 'world'" (185).

75. Colley (242) reports the prohibitions of female cross-dressing at Edinburgh assemblies. Commenting on the institutionalized disorder of the masquerade, Castle discerns a double effect, a "voluptuous release from ordinary cultural prescriptions" and "a stylized comment on them." The sexual reversals may even have contributed "to incipient feminist sentiment in the late eighteenth century" ("Eros" 159, 175). Juliet Dusinberre reads similar effects in female cross-dressing on the dramatic stage (231–71). At the very least, women could perform the compelling male roles—famously Byron's acquaintance Sarah Siddons. See also the essays by Jane Stedman and Frank Wadsworth.

76. Castle, "Carnivalization" 909, 912, 904; Mellor, *English Romantic Irony* 42.

77. Nicholson, from whose edition I quote the stanza, reads *resurrection* (171–72); McGann, whose reading of the last word I put in brackets, reads *sensation* (*BPW* 5: 660n). In a correspondence with me about this, McGann said that he thought the scrawl too brief for "resurrection," even though the word scans better; returning to the ms., he now also feels uncertain about the reading of "in."

Chapter Seven

1. See my essay "Wordsworth and the Language of (Men) Feeling."
2. For the aura of effeminacy in *The Man of Feeling*, see Barker-Benfield 144–48; see also Sinfeld, ch. 3.
3. 2d ser. 1, 256. See also *Monthly Magazine*'s praise of "a revelry of the imagination and tenderness of feeling, that forcibly impress" (248).
4. Poetic satirist and former editor of *The Anti-Jacobin*, William Gifford was now editing the Tory *Quarterly*. "Rosa Matilda" is Charlotte Dacre, acolyte of the Della-Cruscan poets who drew Gifford's satires of the 1790s, *The Baviad* (1791) and *The Maeviad* (1795). She attracted Byron's ridicule in *English Bards, and Scotch Reviewers*: "The lovely ROSA'S . . . / . . . strains, the faithful echoes of her mind, / Leave wondering comprehension far behind. / Though Crusca's bards no more our journals fill, / Some stragglers skirmish round their columns still" (1811, 4th edn.; 737–40); the text in McGann's *BPW* is the suppressed 5th edition, which Keats is less likely to have known than the 4th, which my subsequent quotations follow.
5. Z's identity was unknown to Keats and his circle; Hunt guessed it was John Scott. Haydon and, later, De Quincey suspected "Christopher North" (John Wilson). See Keats, *L* 1: 217 and n7.
6. All oft-cited phrases: see for the key sites *L* 1: 186, 192, 224, 386–87.
7. I address the feminist use of these formulations in the next chapter.
8. The categorical declaration, argues Ellen Pollak, is "the *not man* that by opposition gives identity (gives 'character') to man" (*Poetics* 111).
9. Charles Brown in 1841, *KC* 2: 79. "Give a woman a looking-glass and a few sugar-plums, and she will be satisfied," said Byron to Medwin (*Conversations* 73; 1824, 101). Brown probably read Medwin's popular book (15 editions by 1842, the year Brown died). If not always reliable, Medwin is corroborated here by Iley (2: 337), and in any event, helped shape "Byron" for the nineteenth century.
10. Macaulay cites Chesterfield's contempt: "'Women,' says his Lordship, 'are only children of a larger growth. [. . .] A man of sense only trifles with them, plays with them, humours and flatters them, as he does an engaging child; but he neither consults them, nor trusts them in serious matters'" (*Letters on Education* 209). The contemptible figure is a routine punctuation in Wollstonecraft's *Rights of Woman*, e.g., "The little artless tricks of children, it is true, are particularly pleasing and attractive; yet, when the pretty freshness of youth is worn off, these artless graces become studied airs, and disgust every person of taste" (187). Mary Hays's *Appeal* condenses this discourse into a cartoon deformation: "PERPETUAL BABYISM" (97).
11. Arnold's italics, from Keats's journal letter of October 1818 to George and Georgiana (the entry of the 24th; *L* 1: 404), and from a letter to Fanny Brawne, February 1820, after his first severe hemorrhage, in which physical debility and the shadow of mortality were making a cruel futility of erotic passion (*L* 2: 263). To Arnold, the dominance of Keats's aesthetic passions over the erotic configured a "'sensuous,' 'masculine,' and yet not quite heterosexual" being—a screen on which Arnold could test some of his own questions; for this analysis, see James Najarian 98–99 (from whom I quote).

12. See my chapter on this mode in *Questioning Presence*, and the discussions to which it is indebted, especially by Robert Kern and Stuart Sperry.

13. 19 Sept. 1819; *L* 2: 162. Insisting that *Isabella* has "none of that sugar & butter sentiment, that cloys & disgusts," Woodhouse guessed that Keats's distaste was the result of a review in a temper "more sobered & unpassionate" than the mood of writing: "that which comes upon us where any thing of great tenderness & excessive simplicity is met with when we are not in a sufficiently tender & simple frame of mind to bear it: when we experience a sort of revulsion [. . .] from the sentiment or expression" (ibid.). Keats's *mawkish*, Christopher Ricks suggests, usually signals "that he is near to things that are urgent for him because his truest imaginings are involved and also that he knows how necessarily open to ridicule is his refusal to ridicule" (146). Keats could remember Jeffrey's scorn of Wordsworth's poetry for "maukish affectations of childish simplicity" (*Edinburgh* 20 [1812]: 438). The coding as feminine consolidates over the century. In 1869, Alfred Austin cited female influence, especially on such Keats-marked poets as Tennyson, for the "mawkish commonplace domesticities" that had eclipsed "the grand, the heroic, and the manly" ("Mr. Swinburne" 79, 95).

14. Keats may not yet have read *Don Juan*, but he knew about it. Its shifts of sentiment and satire in the treatment of Julia and especially of the shipwreck dismayed many reviewers. For the draft-stage of *St. Agnes* that alarmed Keats's publishers with its clear representation of "all the acts of a bonâ fide husband" (Woodhouse to Taylor; *L* 2:163), see Jack Stillinger, *Reading* 'The Eve of St. Agnes" 26–28, 144. Stillinger is famous for initiating a reading of *St. Agnes* with respect to this aggressive Keatsian temper ("The Hoodwinking of Madeline").

15. 10 June 1818; *L* 1: 293. Keats means female simple-mindedness; he is echoing Hazlitt's echo, in the midst of a misogynist paragraph in *The Examiner* ("The Round Table," no. 7; 12 Feb. 1815), of an observation "by an ingenious writer of the present day, that women want imagination" (108). The relay from one man to another reports and reinforces a consensus. *Blackwood's* had just published "Letter from Z. to Leigh Hunt, King of the Cockneys," about which more soon.

16. See *Lamia & c* 45–46. Burton's source is the fourth book of Philostratus's *De vita Apollonii;* Keats uses the paraphrase in *Anatomy* Partition 3 ("Love-Melancholy"), Section 2 ("Heroical or Love Melancholy"), Member 1 ("His pedigree"), subject 1, which includes a catalogue of witches that have had "carnal copulation" with mortals.

17. *Anatomy*, Partition 3, Section 2 (see note above), Member 3: "*Symptoms or signs of Love-Melancholy, in Body, Mind, good, bad &c.*" The categorical relation, in Burton's anatomy of Love-Melancholy, of this passage to the one on which Keats bases *Lamia* is yet one more sign of the close, nearly reflexive relation in Keats psychology between a proneness to fatal enchantment and the pleasures of misogynist satire.

18. See Margaret Homans's important discussion in "Keats Reading Women" 360.

19. Hessey, 18 Jan. 1814, cited by Chilcott (22); for the Taylors' sales, chiefly of Ann Taylor's advice manual and novels, and daughter Jane's novels, see Chilcott 41, 67–68, 178, 207. Keats bought Jane Taylor's *Essays in Rhyme* for his sister in September 1817 (*L* 1: 155).

20. Keats may have been thinking of the news in *Monthly Magazine,* February 1818, that the advance sales of *Childe Harold IV* were already 4,000 (45: 68; qtd. *L* 2: 62n4); sales eventually ran to 10,000 (*BPW* 2: 316). The advance on *Childe Harold IV* (at 12 shillings) would yield £2,400, nearly a tenth of Murray's last sale. My thanks to Peter Manning and Jerry McGann for helping me sort out the math of Keats's report.

21. Woodhouse dates the sonnet "To Lord Byron" December 1814; it was first published in Milnes's *Life, Letters, and Literary Remains* (1848), with a remark that the "the proud and successful" poet's "harsh judgment and late remorse" about Keats were uttered in ignorance "of this imperfect utterance of boyish sympathy and respect" (1: 13).

22. The first edition (1809) sold out its run of 1,000; a second augmented edition, the same year, also sold out. By 1811, there was a 4th edition and there would have been a 5th, had not Byron suppressed it (*BLJ* 4: 318). Even so, his disappointed publisher issued spurious editions across the decade, and there were several piracies (McGann, *BPW* 1: 397).

23. In the early lyrics, argues Anthony Paul Vital, Byron's sentimental regard of women, as creatures passive and vulnerable, yet still able to wield power over men, is something of an embarrassment to male self-possession (277). For *English Bards* in relation to this sentimentalism, see Marlon Ross, *Contours* 28–34; and Jerome McGann, "My Brain is Feminine" (esp. 54–57).

24. Keats celebrated Hunt's principles and patronage in *Poems,* heading it with a dedicatory sonnet, *To Leigh Hunt, Esq.* (v), and opening the volume proper with an untitled poem (*I stood tip-toe*), the title-line occupied by a quotation from Hunt, with the controversial source advertised: STORY OF RIMINI (1).

25. Reviewing Hunt's *Literary Pocket-Book; or, Companion for the Lover of Nature and Art* (December 1819), which included Keats's sonnets *The Human Seasons* and *To Ailsa Rock* (225); *Blackwood's* reprinted these "two feats of Johnny Keates" (with a reminder of its signature discourse of "the Muses' Son of Promise"), linked to a satire of Keats in the fashions of Cockaigne (a faux Cockney suburb) apostrophizing the ocean pyramid. That this was not Z's sketch but John Wilson's (unsigned; *RR* C 125) reflects not only an assumed consensus, but the ease with which "Johnny Keates" had been assimilated to its pattern Cockney.

26. See Gillen Wood's report, including Swift's alarm in 1728 about the "*Italian Effeminacy*" infecting English culture through opera ("Crying Game" 975).

27. Nov. 1820; *BLJ* 7: 217. The *Blackwood's* connection was understood: in September 1818, Murray told Byron he had recently "purchased half the copyright" (Smiles 1: 398). Marjorie Levinson notes the use of *stretch* in *London Magazine,* and gives a sharp reading to how Byron's comment and his anecdotal simile of a pathetic sexual sport convey disgust; Byron's underlined *outstretched* concentrates his disdain of "the ambitiousness, elaboration and sexual tension of Keats's poetry" (*Keats's Life* 22–23).

28. That is, the premature ending of his career in *Blackwood's,* that burgh's chief magazine. While Keats's spelling is not rigorous, the only other time he spells the city

this way is in a report of "a flaming attack on Hunt in the Endinburgh Magazine," Z's first Cockney School paper (*L* 1: 179–80). Keats is a notorious punster, especially in rueful moments, and apparent misspellings have the look of "Joycean or Carrollean acts of imagination, their portmanteaux hastily packed," proposes Christopher Ricks (58–59), citing "rediculous" (like a blush) and "irrisistable" (unable to resist resibility); for one instance, see *L* 1: 187–88. *Endinburgh* belongs on this list, and as Jack Cragwall commented to me, the attack-mode punning also involves *Magazine*.

29. "Was ever a more unsatisfactory statement of intention put into words? Keats [. . .] has so little idea of how this is to be done that all he can think of is to conjure up a fairy-tale of a charioteer whirling over a world of mysterious visions, the most concrete of which is 'a wreath of girls'" (1: 223). This collapse is shadowed by Milton's contempt for a poetry of no higher desire than "To sport with *Amaryllis* in the shade, / Or with the tangles of *Neara's* hair" (*Lycidas* 68–69).

30. See "Some Observations upon an Article in *Blackwood's Edinburgh Magazine.*" It was a censure of *Don Juan* (Aug. 1819, 512–18), not by John Wilson (as Byron thought; *BLJ* 7: 83) but by John Gibson Lockhart (Nicholson, *CMP* 360). Byron wrote "Observations" in March 1820, intending publication, but it didn't appear until 1833, in *Works* (15: 55–98; for the remarks on Keats see 92–95).

31. The other I-rhyme is also in a syntax of dubious though devoted capacity: "how shall I / Revive the dying tones of minstrelsy" (*Specimen of an Induction to a Poem* 30–31).

32. Wells and Keats "quarrelled about some trifle or other; the quarrel being ended by Wells' present of roses," Thomas Wade informed R. M. Milnes (27 Jan. 1845; *KC* 2: 115). Keats broke with Wells for good after a transvestite practical joke on Tom, in which he sent him letters from "Amena Bellefila"; Tom fell for the ruse, and Keats was furious over his humiliation.

33. The Leander Gem is one of Tassie's ten reproductions of gems engraved with scenes from classical stories. Keats thought to buy some of Tassie's popular set of letter seals for his sister, the "heads of great Men such as Shakspeare, Milton &—or fancy pieces of art: such as Fame, Adonis & c" (*KL* 2: 45–46). He owned and used a Tassie Shakespeare for his letters (*L* 1: 167, 178, 209; 2: 153). Fulfilling this commodity formation, the poem itself was first published by Thomas Hood in the 1829 volume of the annual he edited, *The Gem* (128; there titled *On a Picture of Leander*).

34. On Tom Keats's ms. of *Calidore* (one of two extant), Hunt underscored *portcullis* and *kiss;* and approvingly marked the metapoetic *feet/sweet* rhyme (Stillinger, ed., *Poems* 549).

35. Mathew's tart review elaborates: "in after times we presume he is to become the hero of some marvelous achievements," though the guess is somewhat attenuated by the present "fragment [. . .] as pretty and as innocent as childishness can make it" ("Keats's Poems" 435–36).

36. The new sentence at 445, "His heart leapt up as to its rightful throne," gives the rhyme for "Endymion," but it is weakened both by the syntactic break at 444 and by the atonality that lets "Endymion" chime more audibly with *run / sun* (442–43) than

with *throne;* in *I stood tip-toe,* Keats rhymes "Endymion" with *won* (203–4); see my *Questioning Presence* 230n4. As if he wanted to set this triple rhyme, Keats discarded "Because in sunshine treacherous wax would melt, / Even at the fatal melting thereof, felt . . ."); see Stillinger *Poems* 205.

37. The conception of Apollo is Keats's (23 Jan. 1818; *L* 1: 207). Reprising a nineteenth-century consensus, Léonie Villard indicts "the weakness and effeminacy" of Keatsian lovers, including even Porphyro, "who 'grows faint' and 'sinks upon his knees,' 'pale as smooth-sculptured stone'" (87). Stillinger ("Hoodwinking") was the first to expose Porphyro's genealogy of ravishers: Satan, Peeping Tom, Tereus, Iachimo, and Lovelace. Daniel Watkins finds Porphyro a "political and patriarchal" ravisher as well: Madeline "is woman as the Other, as the silent and passive object of masculine power" (78–79*ff*). I think Keats gives Madeline (a feminized dreaming poet) more complicity in the lovemaking (her expectations, desires, and dreams are very hot, and when Porphyro "melt[s] into" her dream, it is unclear who has conquered whom); but it matters that Keats's poetry can produce readers such as Stillinger and Watkins.

38. Marjorie Levinson comments on the way the conditional mode involves the strong central claim of the informing passion (232–33). J. Burke Severs suggests a hyper-alienation from socially potent manhood, arguing that the lament is not about the lack of manly form, but of any human form at all through which to court a woman (110).

39. See Byron's Medora and Gulnare in *The Corsair* 2.402; 433–34, 489–90; 3.95, 298, 550. A hyper-feminizing version of this epithet, "fairy form," is applied to Zuleika in *The Bride of Abydos* (1813) 1.285–86; and the Maid of Saragoza in *Childe Harold* (1812) 1.54–55.

40. Keats's revisions hone the staginess of this posture. The first draft was "He who has lingerd in a . . ." (Stillinger, *Poems* 79n). Levinson comments on the social meanings: "what class [. . .] stands tip-toe? children, short grown-ups, and people struggling to penetrate a defended view or to seize a remote one. Keats, from a political standpoint, was in 1817 all those things"—"visually disenfranchised," curious, and greedy (*Keats's Life* 239). His repetition of this phrase in 1819 to depict Lamia's rising "tiptoe" (1.286–87) to flirt with Lycius underscores the longing. Jeffrey Cox notes the echo of Wordsworth (*Poetry and Politics* 105).

41. Ricks nicely notes the passage's "verbal germination" from the initial verb *shrunk* (35).

42. Pre-Raphaelite images of Keatsian women tend to the androgynous, swelled with passion to masculine proportions. D. G. Rossetti paints a large-framed impassive Mnemosyne of tragic grandeur (1881). Holman Hunt's *Isabella and Pot of Basil* (1868) features a big-boned gal, and his *The Flight of Madelaine and Porphyro* (1848) gives Madeline a robust physique.

43. Stillinger, *Poems* 356n. Keats's only other use of *luscious* is in a feminine figure, Arethusa's "luscious lips" (*Endymion* 2.942).

44. Ricks, *Keats and Embarrassment* 12–13; Swann, "*Endymion*'s Beautiful Dreamers" 22–23. Swann suggests the embarrassment of the scene is not what Ricks argues, Adonis's

vulnerability to Endymion's (and our) gaze; it is the disconcerting over-solicitation of the image.

45. I am grateful to Peter Manning for putting the question to me in this form.

46. *Several Questions Answer'd* 11–14. As for the unequal schemes: Susan Fox sees Blake's arguments for equality between sexes embarrassed by stereotypes and a tendency to use "female" as a negative term (518, 516); Anne Mellor finds the "liberated vision" contradicted by recurrent sexism, especially women's status as "emanation" of masculine selfhood, and by recourse to an "gender-identified metaphors inherent in the literary and religious culture" ("Blake's Portrayal" 148, 154); Blake's "richly developed anti-patriarchal and proto-feminist sensibility," notes Alicia Ostriker, coexists with "homocentric gynophobia" (158, 164).

47. This important essay tracks Keats's defensiveness in his "feminine" self-identifications and the counter-assertions of masculinity (*SiR* 29: 344–45). Grant Scott gives a sharp reading to Keats's fears of feminine influence in competition with a "half anxious" interest in postures prone to regard and ridicule as feminine (*Sculpted Word* 112–13).

48. Homans notes this sentence only in a parenthetical coda, as if a troubling afterthought, while Trilling endows Indolent Keats with power and agency, asserting "the virtue of a specifically 'masculine' energy" by affirming "the active principle" in his "conscious [. . .] surrender to the passive, unconscious life"; indolence is about "the *power* of passivity" (28–29).

49. For the anti-indolent poetics (the "fitful rhythm of refusal"), see Helen Vendler's attention to vacillation and recurrence (21–25, 38), and my *Questioning Presence* 328–29. A month or so later, 15 April 1819, Keats tells George and Georgiana, "I am affraid more from indolence of mind than anything else" (*L* 2: 83).

50. To both Anne Mellor and Grant Scott, this unmeek maiden is a negative image of Keats's favorite poetic subjects, Love and Poesy (Mellor, *Romanticism & Gender* 182), or of their popularity in feminized literary taste (Scott, *Sculpted Word* 105). I think both the possessive *my* and the sense of *daemon* in *demon* complicate the purely negative vector.

51. Grant Scott sees the odist's vacillation between indolence and inspiration aggravated by the implicit emasculation of paralysis in marble, and always by a consciousness "that his own poetic is closely allied with femininity" (97).

52. In anticipation of *Poems*, Hunt advertised Keats in *The Examiner*, 1 December 1816, in a trio of rising "Young Poets" (with Reynolds and Shelley); in the 16 March 1817 issue, he granted Keats a "true claim" to the title "young poet": "the youngest he/That sits in the shadow of Apollo's tree" (quoting Ben Jonson). On the eve of the debut of *Poems*, Reynolds recited to Keats a sonnet assuring him that his "genius" shall win a "coronal for thy young head"; even the publisher Charles Ollier managed a rare sonnet, beholding a laurel crown gracing Keats's "eager grasp at immortality" (Amy Lowell 1: 270), and helping out with a lavish compliment of gratis copies.

53. For Keats's letters and poetic practices in relation to a feminized marketplace, see Sonia Hofkosh ("The Writer's Ravishment") and Margaret Homans ("Keats Reading").

54. Hofkosh provides a sharp discussion of these sonnets as staging Keats's defensive "desire for the recognition that both constitutes and subverts his authorship, both empowers him to write and undermines the singularity of his writing" (97).

55. *L* 2: 94. *The Pet-Lamb: A Pastoral* (*Lyrical Ballads* 1800) was classed in the 1815 *Poems* with *Poems of Childhood*. Barbara Esthwaite, treating this pet as her baby, foresees gentle Samson-lite thraldom: "I'll yoke thee to my cart . . . / My playmate thou shalt be" (46–47). As for *Woman!* according to Woodhouse, "when Keats had written these lines he burst into tears overpowered by the tenderness of his own imagination" (Sperry's *Woodhouse* 145). Alexander Smith was perhaps more documentary than partisan when he wrote of the "Cockney" taint of "effeminacy and puerile sentimentalism" in the way that Keats "weeps for the mere delight he has in weeping" (*Encyclopædia Britannica* 56)—or the license that a tenderness for "woman" gives to a man's tears.

Chapter Eight

1. In *Victorian Keats*, especially the chapter on "Keats's 'Posthumous Life'" (11–51), James Najarian gives a fresh review, from the angle of homoerotic reception (9), to much of the material in the essay from which my present chapter develops ("Feminizing Keats" 1990).

2. 17 March 1832; *TT* 2: 158. Eve Sedgwick observes the double misogyny in *effeminate:* defined against both "feminine" and normative "masculine" (*Between Men* 20).

3. "Cockney School, No. IV" (*Blackwood's* 3: 524, 519, 521). The socio-political invective, remarks John Barnard, was aimed at Keats's class aspirations (5). It wasn't just the praises of Hunt in *Poems*, and the cry against monarchs in *Endymion* 3; it was also, argues Nicholas Roe, Keats's aesthetics, read as "the stylistic signature of the 'natural freedom' that defined [. . .] political opposition" (37–38, 40). Cockney poets, proposes Linda Dowling, looked like "agents of a dangerous and unappeasable social modernity" that was served by, or even fronted by, gender transgression (60; see 59–64).

4. *Blackwood's* 2: 38, 194; 3: 519, 521, 522, 524. See also *Blackwood's* May 1818 (3: 197) and reprises of "Johnny" across 1819: January (4: 482), April (5: 97), September (5: 640), and repeatedly in the lead article of December (6: 236–39), followed in July 1822 (11: 60); then June (13: 689–90), July (14: 60), and August (14: 85) 1823; then January (14: 85), May (5: 559) and June 1824 (5: 712). The diminutive took hold, even in affection. Decades on, George Gilfillan, who admired Keats's "elegant effeminacy" of mind, spoke of "the hapless apothecary's boy [. . .] the Cockney boy!" (*Gallery* 379, 380). For the census of "Johnny Keats," see MacGillivray xxii, and his compendium, xxv. Twinned to ridicule of Keats as "The Muses' son of promise," notes Rollins, the epithet was applied "by very many later writers" (*L* 1: 180 n3).

5. "Shabby genteel" appears in an 1820 essay on the Pope/Bowles controversy that was not published until 1830 (*Some Observations; Prose* 116). Ridiculing the anti-establishment poet of *Sleep and Poetry* (181–206) as "a Mr. John Ketch," Byron named the "grand distinction of the Under forms of the New School of poets" as the "*Vulgarity*" of "shabby-genteel." He claimed to despise affectation only, not class origin: "Burns

is often coarse—but never vulgar —— —— —— Chatterton is never vulgar;—nor Wordsworth." Also protesting Hazlitt's polemic on class bias, he insists that style, not station, is the issue: "there is Nobility of thought and of Style—open to all Stations— and derived partly from talent—& partly from education," but never from display: "It is in their finery that the New-under School are most vulgar;—and they may be known by this at once—as what we called at Harrow—'a Sunday Blood' might be easily distinguished from a Gentleman." Yet as the cozy "we at Harrow" suggests, the distinction is not disinterested: "Your vulgar writer is always most vulgar the higher his subject" (*Prose* 157–60).

6. This last comment, from 1824 (*BLJ* 1: 124), is not directly about Keats. The others are from letters written in 1820–1821 (8: 102; 7: 200, 202, 217, 229); for Byron's contempt of Keatsian erotics, see Marjorie Levinson, *Keats's Life* 22–23.

7. George Ford notes that by the 1840s the name was more often misspelled in the reviews than not (94)—usually "Keates" with "Johnny" or "Jack." See the template of *Blackwood's* alone: January 1818 (2: 415), December 1819 (6: 236*ff.*); March 1822 (11: 346); May 1824 (15: 559); September 1825 (19: 378); and in 1834, answering the legend that "we killed Keates" (36: 525).

8. *Blackwood's* 3: 524. Byron to Murray, November 1820 (*BLJ* 7: 229), probably referring to an unsigned two-part review in *Scots Edinburgh* (Aug./Oct. 1820), on *Endymion* and the *Lamia* volume, which opened, "MR KEATS is a poet of high and undoubted powers" (7: 107).

9. By 1820 *Blackwood's* boasted a monthly circulation of 17,000 (19,500, counting private subscribers). For the (admittedly exuberant) accounting, see *An Hour's Tete-a-Tete with the Public* (Oct. 1820, 8: 88; cf. 81). For a survey of *Blackwood's* Cockney rants, ranging from ridicule to demonization, see Emily Lorraine de Montluzin.

10. "On the Qualifications Necessary to Success in Life" (*W* 12: 208), a piece Hazlitt wrote fresh from being dubbed the "Cockney Aristotle" by Z ("Cockney School V," April 1819). Snarking that "Mr Hazlitt cannot look round him at the Surrey [Institute, the site of Hazlitt's lectures] without resting his smart eye on the idiot admiring grin of several dozens of aspiring apprentices and critical clerks" (*Blackwood's* 5: 97), Z made him compere to faux Petrarch Hunt, and the vulgar poets of Byron's *English Bards*.

11. "The Modern Gradus ad Parnassum," in *London Weekly Review,* 17 May 1828 (*W* 20: 159).

12. "On Effeminacy of Character," *W* 8: 248–49 (quoting Pope's *Essay on Man* 1.200), and 254–55. Pope's line is set in verse exhorting contentment and cautioning against higher refinements, but the image was too irresistible not to be appropriated for satire. In a Wollstonecraft-era ridicule of sensibility, *Monthly Magazine*'s Enquirer exclaimed, "Who can endure, with patience, the weakness or the affectation which shrieks at the sight of a spider; faints at a drop of blood produced by the puncture of a needle; and 'Dies of a rose in aromatic pain?'" (2 [1796]: 707).

13. *Blackwood's* 3: 197. Z is quoting two passages from Hunt's *The Nymphs,* the first an image of startled stag (1.30); the second, a nymph-nurtured gazelle (1.139).

14. When Wilde submitted his erotic elegy, *The Grave of Keats*, to the *Irish Monthly*, Father Russell, ably reading the "boy" code, asked him to substitute "youth"; Wilde refused (Ellman 74n). The primary denotation of "effeminacy" as culpable luxury and civic irresponsibility always carried a whiff of a sexual deviance.

15. For contemporary comments on androgynous Shelley, see William Veeder (40–41, 239n16) and Timothy Webb (8–17), who insists Shelley is not "effeminate" (17). Queer theorist *avant le lettre* Edward Carpenter collates Shelley's contrarian idealism with his "peculiarities" of gender: a strong "feminine" element, serial and thus ambivalent heterosexual involvements, and a "warm and faithful attachment" to "men friends" (7–8, 25). Shelley's "intermediate (or double) in character—*intermediate* as between the masculine and feminine, or *double* as having the twofold outlook," Carpenter proposes, is not yet at that "*higher* level of evolution" of androgynous character (46).

16. Medwin's *Memoir* was serialized in *Athenæum* in 1832, then collected as *The Shelley Papers* in 1833. Even David Masson, while calling Shelley "etherial, and feminine," uncovers the fearless rebel: "At Eton the sensitive boy, almost girlish in his look and demeanour, had nerved himself, with meek obstinacy [. . .] against every part of the established system—not only against the tyranny of his fellows, but also against the teaching of the masters" (339–40). For pointing me to Greg, Rossetti, and Dowden, I'm indebted to Eric Clarke.

17. This female sympathy could even gain credit as a kind of Wollstonecrafted "masculinity." Thinking of *The Revolt of Islam* and *The Cenci*, G. H. Lewes dubs Shelley "*par excellence*, the 'poet of women'"—able to comprehend a woman's "delicacies of mind and heart," "undisguised fervour of passion," "the graces of mind, the beauty of person, and the confiding innocence of nature." Though the anatomy is by the book, Lewes means to praise a progress "learnt in a measure from Mary Wolstencraft": Shelley "clearly perceived the true relations of the sexes, and with him women are neither slaves nor angels"; Shelley offers "the true ideal of woman" as "a *partner* of your life" (*Westminster Review* 1841; 35: 330–31).

18. In a late-century brief for Keats as a "manly Englishman," Saintsbury used Shelley as an ethical foil: atheist, infidel, adulterer, absconder, debt-evader, cultural outcast Shelley was "hardly a man, and still less an Englishman" (88).

19. While *Blackwood's* was harsher, the *Quarterly's* influence and circulation (12,000 by January 1818, with nearly 500,000 readers) made it the icon for Keats's champions. Croker, the unsigned *Quarterly* reviewer of *Endymion*, identifies Keats as a Cockney (19: 204), not in politics (he advances "no dogmas" [205]), but in aesthetics.

20. *Chambers'* 363–64. For Brown, see *KC* 2: 51–53. For the force of *Adonais* in Keats's nineteenth-century reception, see my "Keats Enters History."

21. *On the Aristocracy of Letters* (*W* 8: 211). His quotations, in order, are from *Winter's Tale* (4.4.81–85), *Hamlet* (4.5.173–78), and *Paradise Lost* (7.37–8).

22. Hazlitt quotes 1.1.157; Romeo himself later voices the judgment: "O sweet Juliet, / Thy beauty hath made me effeminate / And in my temper soften'd valour's steel" (3.1.115–17). Hazlitt cites the same lines to gloss Keats's fate in Gifford's political bias

("Mr. Keats's ostensible crime was that he had been praised in the *Examiner Newspaper*"; "Mr. Gifford," 261).

23. See *Blackwood's* 75: 346; *Cornhill* 34: 558. The persistent refutations confirm the adhesiveness. Alluding to Shelley's Preface, Masson works to dispel the legend of Keats's death from "the savage article in the *Quarterly*" (*Macmillan's*, 1860, 7). "'Snuffed out by an article,' indeed!" said Cowden Clarke (*Atlantic* [1861]; *Recollections* [1878] 147).

24. Ford 68. MacGillivray remarks that the story of Keats was made to order for "the popular Victorian and feminine ideal of the unhappy and beautiful youth of genius" (xiii).

25. "Poor Keats," born on his deathbed, became as frequent as "Johnny Keats," and abetted the effeminizing diminution: "the closing scene of poor Keats's life [. . .] the poor fellow," said Shelley in his Preface (5); "poor Keats was of too gentle a disposition for severity," echoed *Literary Chronicle,* in a preface to a reprinting of *Adonais* late in 1821 (133: 751). At the close of his *Keats*, Milnes prints Severn's letters, the historically prior, and now canonical, record of the deathbed genesis of "Poor Keats" (2: 218–25). Clarke's *Recollection* is only one of many to sound the refrain "Poor Keats!" (141).

26. For the nineteenth-century feminizing of the disease, see Paul Fry's remark that Severn's narrative of Keats's death "and the deaths of far too many sensitive heroines both in literature and life inspired a group of French poetasters to call themselves *les jeunes tubercules*" (184).

27. *Edinburgh* 90: 428. Allingham 205; my spell-checker keeps proposing "Bighorn" for Byron.

28. Though, as the title suggests, the annual was marketed for female purchase and gifting, the company within was gender-mixed, and the *Gem*s in which poems by "The Late John Keats" appeared (still in the aura of *Adonais*) also featured many men, including Hood himself, Sir Walter Scott, Hartley Coleridge, Barry Cornwall, John Clare, James Hogg, William Howitt. Hood was tied in to the Keats circle through his marriage to John Hamilton Reynolds's sister Jane.

29. *Guardian,* in Schwartz 228, 230. *Woman's Will* is a play. The most popular feature of *The Ladies Diary,* reports Marilyn Gaull, was the "enigma, often in verse, to which readers replied by mail, five hundred of them, including men, some of them using women's names, competing for a free subscription" (126); she refers to Teri Perl's essay for further information.

30. For this bit of Keatsiana, see Ford 105. OED reports several she-inflected contemporary senses of *dainty: fine, valuable, choice, excellent, delicate, of delicate or tender beauty or grace, delicately pretty.* Keats knew Spenser's *Shepearde's Calendar* (June 6): "daintye Daysies." For both sexes, OED defines *dainty* as "possessing or displaying delicate taste, perception, sensibility; nice, fastidious, particular; sometimes overnice," citing a text Keats also knew: "The hand of little Imployment hath the daintier sense" (*Hamlet* 5.1.78). Keats's uses tend to name quaint delights—"most dainty Tales from many bards of yore" (*I stood tip-toe* 122/123 draft); or food: Porphyro's banquet of "cates and dainties" (*Eve of St. Agnes* 173; cf. "spiced dainties" [269]); or (with grotesque

freezing) Isabella's bosom, "Those dainties made to still an infant's cries" (*Isabella* 374). The word is most frequent in *Endymion*, mostly in scenes of erotic longing: Alpheus yearns for Arethusa's "dainty fairness" (2.939); Glaucus yearning for Scylla's "dainty hue" (3.408) is mocked by Circe's naming him "Sir Dainty" (3.570). Endymion's sense of "life so dainty real" as he listens to the Indian Maid (4.104–5, draft) bodes his enthrallment and forecasts the comedy, a little later, of his reluctant "Adieu" to the "daintiest Dream" that has beckoned him from such life (4.556).

31. For *The Girl's Second Help*, see *KCH* 10. Woodhouse was pleased to have launched the circulation of *Endymion* among his cousin "Miss Frogley," "the Misses Porter (of romance Celebrity)" and their friend "Miss Fitzgerald" (*KL* 2: 9–10); for Keats's regret of this admiration, see Homans (*Keats Reading Women* 347–48). For the popularity of *Endymion* with Victorian women, see Ford 105, and for the lavish editions, see Helen Haworth.

32. "To interest the feelings is to [woman] much easier than to convince the judgment; the heart is far more accessible to her influence than the head," writes Mrs. Sandford (16). This was among the passages Jewsbury despised in her review for *Athenæum* (282). Like Courthope's essay (quoted in the epigraph to this section), Patmore's was first published as a review of Colvin's *Keats*.

33. *Fraser's* 48: 571, 465, 466. For Victorian attitudes about the feminization of literature, see Thomas Meade Harwell, *Keats and the Critics* 13.

34. See Altick 7; David Newsome, *Godliness and Good Learning* 196–97; and J. R. de S. Honey: however erratic and imperfectly developed, the code was "anti-effeminacy, stiff-upper-lippery, and physical hardness" (*Tom Brown's Universe* 209).

35. Carol Christ reads this charge even in Patmore's "angel in the house," a figure endowing Victorian man with "an ideal freedom from those very qualities he finds most difficult to accept in himself" (147).

36. See Sonia Hofkosh's resourceful discussion (66–69, 77–78).

37. Swinburne, *W* 16: 373; *Blackwood's* 3: 524; *Endymion* 2.194; Swinburne 14: 296–97.

38. Patmore, *Keats* 62; Hopkins, 20 Oct. 1887 (*Further Letters* 233; he had just read Patmore's review) and 6 May 1888 (237). Hopkins's homosexual orientation, argues James Najarian, informs a "tortured relationship to sensual perception and through it his ambivalence about Keats" (101). Thus he labors to link masculine to sensual poetry, writing to Canon Dixon about the "male gift" of "masterly execution" that "marks off men from women," and in which Keats participates (Najarian 103, without a source citation).

39. Recall the self-indictment of Milton's Samson (p. 346n21), which collapses enamoration with effeminate lapse and catastrophic cultural consequence. For the Miltonic coordination of male sensuality and effeminacy, see Jean H. Hagstrum 34–41.

40. Étienne equates "le paganisme" with "sensualité" (292), both in recoil from the demands of modern life: "Son paganisme [. . .] c'est une de ces fleurs étranges [. . .]

elles naissent d'un accident de la nature.[. . .] Keats se fit un monde idéal qui n'était ni l'antique ni le moderne, ni sur la terre ni dans le ciel, un monde qui résidait dans sa pensée" (294–95). Courthope saw Keats retreating from "social influences" and spiritual "severity" alike, opting for "the mythological spirit of pagan times" (*History* 6: 323). This is different from the anti-establishment paganism of Cockney aesthetics. Hearing Keats recite the "Ode to Pan" in *Endymion*, Wordsworth (recollected Haydon) "drily said 'a Very pretty piece of Paganism—,'" a term Haydon understood to reflect an offense to his "puling Christian feelings" (*KC* 2: 143–44), but which may also have disciplined his own half yearning for the sensibility of a "pagan suckled in a creed outworn" ("The world is too much with us").

41. From Wilde's first lecture in New York, 1882, reported in *New York World* (quoted by Walter Hamilton 115–16). Such praise was "vital to the complete acceptance of Keats's poetry" by D. G. Rossetti and his circle (Ford 115). *Victoria* observed that a "dainty pre-raphaelitism marks [his] glorious word-pictures" (65).

42. Anticipating Buchanan by a year, *Edinburgh Review* arraigned Swinburne's "cloying" feminine muse as a corruption of the male body social: "incontinent, not only in the details of licentious indulgence, but [. . .] naked and not ashamed, destitute of any natural sense," and inspiring an "hysterical admiration for things essentially contemptible and base" (134: 75). The issue, as always, was bigger than Swinburne: the "principles of the school which Mr. Swinburne represents would, indeed, if successful, not only overturn all existing order, but in the end prove fatal to art, literature, and civilisation itself" (99). Buchanan was reviving *Blackwood's* stock of slanders, and giving the scandals fresh social anxiety, but his strictures on sensuousness were resisted by social liberals and even developing middle-class sanctions (see Linda Dowling, *Hellenism* 60–66).

43. *The Tomb of Keats* 304–5. "Adonais to most English ears sounds strange in its loving and highly imaginative glorification of a *Man*," comments Carpenter (14; cf. 10), but it was continuous with the resort to Keats as site and medium of otherwise inhibited homosocial love. "Keats must get himself well, again, Severn, if but for us," said Haslam; " I, for one, cannot afford to lose him. If I know what it is to love, I truly love John Keats" (Sharp 72; in *KC* 1: lxxxviii). After reading *Life of Keats,* Bailey wrote to Milnes: "Socially, he was the most <u>loveable</u> creature, in the proper sense of that word as distinguished from <u>amiable</u>, that I ever knew as a man" (*KC* 2: 261).

44. See also *Autobiography* 2: 212–13.

45. Bailey, *KC* 2: 274; "Her voice was ever soft, / Gentle and low, an excellent thing in woman" (*King Lear* 5.3.274–75).

46. Nicholas Roe describes Masson's hulking Keats as Sweeney-Keats (52).

47. See Chorley on Hemans: "her hair long, curling, and golden:—in the latter years of her life its hue deepened into brown, but it remained silken, and profuse, and wavy" (*CMH* 1: 12; cf. *Personal Recollections, Athenæum* 398: 452).

48. *KC* 2: 268; Milnes quotes Mrs. Procter (1: 103–4). Owen echoes Bailey's use of

Coleridge's term, placing it in the main clause of a sentence that begins, "Although his face was strong and manly" (8), and including Coleridge's remark.

49. From 1854–1908, copies, or versions of it by Severn and others appear in forty editions: see MacGillivray's appendices B–F, 8–52; Allott uses this portrait as a frontispiece.

50. Bailey, *KC* 2: 269; Severn is quoted by Sharp 540. For Severn's quasi-spousal devotion to a homoerotically attractive Keats as a romance for male Victorian poets, see Najarian 45–51.

51. A detail of an engraving of this portrait, tilted slightly counterclockwise to give Keats's face a more upward look, is on the dust-cover of *Keats: The Critical Heritage*—an ironic icon given that Hilton's *Keats*, gracing few more than a dozen editions in the nineteenth century, is less a heritage than Severn's.

52. Hilton's *Keats* was controversial. For credits to Severn's *Keats* (inflected by gratitude for his devotion to Keats and awareness of his rivalry with Hilton), see Sharp, who judged Hilton's "in almost no respect faithful to recognized detail" ("Portraits" 545), and Fanny Keats, who found it "not at all favorable"; "the only real likeness" was Severn's (537). Cowden Clarke agreed, calling Severn's *Keats* "absolutely perfect, both in feature, manner, and expression," while Severn himself complained of Hilton's "singular error" in failing to show Keats's "strikingly large" eyes (*KC* 2: 152, 98). Hilton's chief reference, Haydon's life mask, was also found wanting. The mouth, said Fanny Keats, "renders the expression more severe than the sweet and mild original" (Sharp 537).

53. Hunt, *Mr Keats* 1: 410, 419. Galignani, in *KCH* 262. This *Memoir of Keats,* by Cyrus Redding, Whig editor of *New Monthly Magazine,* relies on Hunt (Matthews, *KCH* 261).

54. Hunt, *Mr Keats* 409; Saintsbury 91. Milnes also suppressed Keats's romance with Fanny Brawne, his skeptical views on religion, and his comments about Wordsworth, by then Poet Laureate (see Marquess 37–57).

55. Milnes, *Keats* 1: 4; Colvin 4; J. R. Lowell 219. These narratives also retuned Keats's patrilineage. His father, "employed in the establishment of Mr. Jennings, the proprietor of large livery-stables on the Pavement in Moorfields, nearly opposite the entrance into Finsbury Circus," insisted Milnes, was "a man of excellent natural sense" and "entire freedom from any vulgarity or assumption on account of his prosperous alliance" (1: 4–5). By the time Masson has the account, the alliance had indeed prospered: Keats's father was now "a livery-stable keeper of some wealth" (1). W. M. Rossetti saw the silliness: "I hardly know why the biographer of the poet should call Keats's origins 'the upper rank of the middle class,' save as a concession to that deadly spirit of flunkeyism in the British people which, after doing its pitiful best to embitter Keats's life on the score of his unexalted origin, and after the nation had accepted him warmly at a later date as a poet of splendid and exquisite gifts, is still capable of wishing to suppose that he was more like a member of 'the upper rank of the middle class' than what he really was—a member of a middling rank in the middle class" ("Sketch" vii). Satirizing the contempt spun in the word *vulgar,* Lowell guesses that Keats may have "resented

with becoming pride the vulgar Blackwood and quarterly standard, which measured genius by genealogies" (220); "it is not pleasant to be ridiculous, even if you are a lord; but to be ridiculous and an apothecary at the same time is almost as bad as it was formerly to excommunicated. *A priori*, there was something absurd in poetry written by the son of an assistant in the livery-stables of Mr. Jennings, even though they were an establishment, and a large establishment, and nearly opposite Finsbury Circus" (226).

56. Carlyle thought his own temperament rather feminine; Ruskin himself, for all his conduct-booking, knew that his aesthetic and ethical values might convey "effeminate sentimentality" (Ruskin, *W* 36: xcvi–vii and 28: 81). See Dinah Birch, who discusses Ruskin's identification of his intellectual interests with "feminine" tendencies. In 1851 F. J. Furnivall described Ruskin's charms as "partly feminine" in character (Ruskin, *W* 8: xxxiv); when in the 1870s the adjective morphed into *effeminate*, Ruskin challenged the judgment.

57. *Edinburgh Review* (1871) 134: 74, 91, riffing on Keats's call for "sunburnt mirth! . . . a beaker full of the warm South" (*Ode to a Nightingale*). Browning called Swinburne "effeminate" (*Dearest Isa* 333), and Austin ranted in *Temple Bar* (1869), "What have men [. . .] brave, muscular, bold, upright, chivalrous [. . .] men daring, enduring, short of speech, terrible in action—what have these to do with Mr. Swinburne's Venuses and Chastelards, his Anactorias and Faustines, his Dolores, his Sapphos, or his Hermaphroditus?" (86); he is less "masculine even than Mr. Tennyson" (88). Shocked that Chastelard's "intrinsically feminine" poetry issues from "a man—a man!" Austin declared, "I scarcely like to own sex with him" (107). Courthope's 1872 review for the *Quarterly*, noting Keatsian influence (59), cautiously congratulates Swinburne for some recent poems of "more manly tone" and "manly self-restraint" (68–69). I thank Thaïs Morgan for these references; George Ford remarks that the frequency of *manly* in Swinburne's invectives against Keats reflects not just aristocratic disdain but also his own insecurities (169).

58. It was Patmore who provoked Leslie Stephen to refresh Coleridge: "Every man ought to be feminine, *i.e.,* to have quick and delicate feelings; but no man ought to be effeminate, *i.e.,* to let his feelings get the better of his intellect and produce a cowardly view of life and the world" (quoted by Maitland 314).

59. 29 Sept. 1848; *L* 93. Arnold and Clough liked to address each other as "my love," in no campy affectation but in passionate affection. Back in 1832, notes Najarian (81), editor Howard Foster Lowry felt compelled to rationalize "this curious expression" as a private language; the letter prompting his intervention (late 1844/1845) ends in a gush of "my love, lovers of one another," "Oh my love," "Oh my love, goodnight" (*L* 1: 63)

60. Defining "masculine power of intellect" as that "tenacity of spirit which cleaves to and assimilates the truth when it is found, and which steadfastly refuses to be blown about by every wind of doctrine and feeling," Patmore thinks that "the impressionable and feminine element, which is manifest in all genius, but which in truly effective genius is always subordinate to power of intellect, had in Clough's mind the preponderance" ("Clough" 88).

61. 1848 or ?1849; *Letters to Clough* 97; *Note-Books* 510.

62. The discussion in *Romantic Movement* (298–315) first appeared in *Monthly Review*, 1901.

63. Buchanan 70; Milnes in Reid 1: 201; Patmore, *Keats* 62; Rossetti, quoted by Ford 118; Hunt, "Mr. Keats" 441 and *Autobiography* 211; Colvin 210; van Dyke 911–12.

64. Among the witnesses called are G. F. Mathew, who indirectly reveals Keats's "virility" (56–57); and B. W. Procter, who testifies to "manly" (113).

65. Anticipating Bate and Ward, Parson, noting that Severn did not enjoy a reputation for good draftsmanship (49), proposes that he subordinated realism to "poetical interpretations of the form, face, and expression of his adored friend" (94.).

66. *Table Talk* 2: 190–91; Woolf, *Room* 102, 107.

67. Trilling, *Opposing Self* x, 24, 28–29. When Carpenter writes, "No one can contemplate Shelley's portrait, or read the descriptions of his personality left by his contemporaries without feeling that therein a double nature (at once both masculine and feminine) is implied and portrayed" (46), it is to enlist Shelley among "the great leaders of mankind" who "have so often shown this fusion," including Byron, Jesus, and St. Francis (44). There is no need to deny weakness, effeminacy, disease, or degeneracy in this canon of visionary power.

68. Homans 240n25, 251n15; Rich 115, referring to Chodorow, *Family Structure and Feminine Personality* 44, 58–60. Gelpi summons "negative capability" to gloss D. G. Rossetti's identification of the artist with the prostitute ("Feminization" 105): both depend "on the whims and fancies" of the market (*L* 3: 1175; see also 2: 849–50). Yet she elides Keats's description of hack writing as "trafficking," a commercial prostitution that may be an extension of mobility, but with no strength of negative capability, and (moreover) tinged with misogyny and anti-semitism.

69. "Visionary Anger" 171–72. Two years later, Jong published her own love-letter to Keats, incorporating Keats's voice (from letters and poems) into her poetic measures. Reading the interview, Anne Mellor describes an "anti-masculine conception of identity" (*Romanticism and Gender* 174).

70. "The exchanges upon which patriarchal societies are based take place exclusively among men. Women, signs, commodities, and currency always pass from one man to another" (Luce Irigaray, "Commodities" 192). Homans, *Keats Reading* 343.

71. 20 Oct. 1887; *Further Letters* 234. Claude Colleer Abbott (234n2) suggests that this paper was "Why Women Are Dissatisfied" (*St. James Gazette*, 29 Sept. 1887).

72. For anti-patriarchy, see Rich 114; Jong 172. For Keats's irritation at women of learning (e.g., *KL* 1: 163), see Grant Scott, *Sculpted Word* 106–7.

73. Ross, "Patrilineal" 110, 122. Among the features: a "will to power, the desire to overcome his foes and win their allegiance [. . .] schematizing compromise; performance, purposiveness, and spectatorship; and, perhaps most important, the establishment of territorial claims for the sake of engendering a lasting line of powerful discourse within culture" (122). On Moneta, Homans is in accord. The goddess may greet the poet as his "most severe reader-critic," but it is with the entailment of her severe suffer-

ing, and her function as a text for the "extraordinary egotism" of a dreaming poet, for whom she is a store of history and the screen on to which to project the text of *Hyperion* (*Keats Reading* 356–58).

74. *Romanticism & Gender* 171; Mellor follows the Rich-feminist equations of negative capability and "camelion" poetics as "anti-masculine" (174–75), and adds Keats's metaphors of creation as pregnancy and birth, as female weaving and tale-telling. She means to modify Homans's defensive-misogynist Keats into a Keats beset by "discomfort," "anxiety," and "ambivalence" about his sensibility, about his attraction to genres and subjects associated with female writing, and his inability to succeed at "masculine" epic and tragedy (179–84).

Chapter Nine

1. Woolf is reading a report in Godwin's *Memoirs* (46).

2. *VRM* 113; Burke's gendered aesthetics, based on a view of female "duty and happiness in this life" that "must clash with any preparation for a more exalted state," made her "tremble for the souls of women" (114–15).

3. The title she gives Chapter 5 is "Animadversions on Some of the Writers Who Have Rendered Women Objects of Pity, Bordering on Contempt" (198); *anima* is *soul*.

4. In *Serious Proposal to the Ladies, for the Advancement of their true and greatest Interest* (London, 1694), Astell protests, "since GOD has given Women as well as Men intelligent Souls, why should they be forbidden to improve them?" Although, as her vision of female retirement suggests, she was not arguing for social revolution ("We pretend not that women shou'd [. . .] usurp Authority where it is not allow'd them; permit us only to understand our *own* duty"; 80–81), her analysis of social habits and expectations might imply it.

5. The title-page credits "Rowe." In Nicholas Rowe's popular tragedy, *The Fair Penitent* (1703), it is a female protest, voiced by Calista: "How hard is the condition of our sex, / Thro' ev'ry state of life the slaves of man! / In all the dear delightful days of youth / A rigid father dictates to our wills, / And deals out pleasure with a scanty hand. / To his, the tyrant husband's reign succeeds; / Proud with opinion of superior reason, / He holds domestick bus'ness and devotion, / All we are capable to know, and shuts us, / Like cloyster'd ideots, from the world's acquaintance, / And all the joys of freedom. Wherefore are we / Born with high souls, but to assert our selves, / Shake off this vile obedience they exact, / And claim an equal empire o'er the world?" (3.1.40–53).

6. I owe my interest in Colls' poem to a quotation in Caroline Franklin's *Mary Wollstonecraft* (83). I supply line numbers, along with page-number references.

7. To recall that Victorian gender-sorter Coventry Patmore, prompted by the puzzle of Meynell to that "theory, not unknown to philosophy and theology, that sex in the soul lies in aspect rather than in substance" ("Meynell" 118): he almost says (without knowing it, without meaning to) that not just spiritual identity, but existential character is no guarantee of anatomy. Aspect/substance corresponds to the gender-critic's binary, construction/essence.

8. This effect is more apparent on the next page: "Not satisfied with masculine ideas, and masculine habits, Mary Wolstonecraft wished, as the consummation of female independence, to introduce the sex into the Camp, the Rostrum and the Cabinet; and although she does not recommend a total dereliction of *the household good,* still she would not cramp the female energies" (24). Editor Ben Harris McClary reports that Silliman's *Letters*—notwithstanding the anti-Republican flag (with the imprimatur of Federalist publishers John Russell and James Cutler)—"sparked a new interest" in Wollstonecraft and her *Vindication,* with a spate of letters in the Boston magazines in the months following publication (xii).

9. *Ignorant* puns a negation of the title-word *noscere* (to know). Bate and Engell (*BL* 2: 7) note that Coleridge takes the verse from an imperfect transcription: see *Notebooks* 3: 4112 (f14v–f15), Oct.–Nov. 1811. His edition was Robert Anderson's *Works of the British Poets* (13 vols.; Edinburgh and London, 1792–95; 2: 689), reports R. A. Foakes (*Lectures* 1: 246n23). My supplementary quotations draw on the first seven stanzas of the text in *The Renaissance in England,* ed. Rollins and Baker (476).

10. Writing in 1925 about such soul-sympathy, Edward Carpenter is explicit about the queer, non- (or anti-) hetero-normative liberty: "Love between two persons of like sex is nowadays widely accepted, as being an attachment resting on a sympathy and soul-union very deep and sincere—even though it may elude the physical ties or take little account of them" (27).

11. I refer to Margaret Homans's view of women's poetry under masculine tradition as troubled by a sensation of "alien centers" and "sources of poetic power [. . .] not felt to be within the self" (*Women Writers* 104). I'm proposing that men may be, if not similarly, then analogously beset, especially in events of creative crisis.

12. Quotations follow Reed's A-B Stage Reading Text, a collation of 1805 mss., cited as *1805.*

13. Such lines of diagnosis impel Wordsworth to revise a passage in *The Excursion* about social discontent. The 1814 text speaks of "a soul perplexed, / And finding in itself no steady power" able to distinguish divine chastisement from human injustice (2.73–74; p. 54); by 1850, this would be gender-marked incapacity, "in herself" (2.70–71).

14. See Marlon Ross, "Romantic Quest and Conquest," and Anne Mellor, for whom such moments epitomize the poem's politics of gender, showing a "surpassing confidence [in] the construction of an autonomous poetic self that can stand alone" (*Romanticism & Gender* 148), precisely because it has mastered the feminine (18, 144–53).

15. Quotations of the 1850 *Prelude* follow Ms. D (in Owen) rather than the 1850 publication, which was corrupted by the poet's executors.

16. For the self-constituting rhetoric, see Jonathan Culler, "Apostrophe."

17. *Poems of Wordsworth,* Preface xxiv (cf. xxii). "Is a pen a metaphorical penis?" ask Gilbert and Gubar in the now famous opening of *Madwoman in the Attic* (3). If so, Arnold's report is a scandal, and he was reading not just Wordsworth but the spirit of the age (he summons the trope again to describe Byron's style; "Byron"; *W* 9: 234).

18. This death (around his eighth birthday) is not named in this memory but it is deducible from the frame of biography and traceable in the psychology of the poetry.

19. For the ambiguous place of the feminine in homosocial dynamics, see Eve Sedgwick, *Between Men,* especially the chapter on Shakespeare's sonnets.

20. The epigraph first appears in *Poems* of 1815, the year Shelley was composing *Alastor.* For its attenuated language and the consequences for the *Ode,* see Frances Ferguson, *Language as Counter-Spirit* 98–101. For the involvement of *Alastor* with the *Ode,* especially its least stable configurations, see William Keach.

21. In a fragment of *Athanase* (b.12–14), Shelley proposes that if there be none "near to love," one "Loves then the shade of his own soul, half seen / In any mirror"—in the dynamics of self-regard, a distinction nearly without a difference (*Poems,* ed. Everest and Matthews, 326). Mary Shelley's note in her edition describes *Athanase* (the name means "immortality") as "a good deal modelled on *Alastor*" (156).

22. For the root, prefix, and suffix of *Epi-psych-idion,* see Earl Wasserman 418–19. Irene Tayler and Gina Luria note how often figures of inspiration in Romantic poetry appear "as sister image or mirror image of the poet" (115), his "counterpart," or "feminized alter-ego" (120); and they examine the implications for the idea of "the Poet."

23. This iconography would reverse after 1815, when the fallen eagle signified, in Byron's poetry and elsewhere, defeated Napoleon.

24. For this dyad, see Tilottama Rajan (76; although she is not discussing gender).

25. Noting Marlon Ross's claim that "in his 'mature' poetry [Keats] is forced to contain or crystallize the feminine as a sign of his manhood, as evidence of his self-control" (*Contours* 173), I'd emphasize the urgency of "forced to" rather than any accomplished shape. The late poems to Fanny Brawne were published posthumously, with severe damage to Keats's reputation, especially for manly self-possession. For the gender crises of these lyrics and the consequences for the poet's mastery of his forms, see my *Formal Charges,* ch. 6.

26. *Enthusiast* 43. John Wilson was professor of philosophy at Edinburgh University.

27. *On Shakespeare and Milton,* in *Lectures on the English Poets* (1818; *W* 5: 50).

28. The end of *A Defence of Poetry* sets "Poets" as heroic servants to "the power which is seated on the throne of their own soul," and destined to speak as "hierophants" and "legislators" (535); the *Defence* had not been published by 1830, but Jewsbury would know its themes from her immersion in Shelley's poetry, much of it, like *Adonais,* a virtual defense of poetry.

29. *Letters to Mitford* 2: 88. Barrett alludes to "The Psalter" 105 (18), in *The Book of Common Prayer.* Wollstonecraft sarcastically quotes same line in *Rights of Woman* (188) to describe the souls of women so degraded by subservience that they would feel no particular change in chaining.

30. Barrett would have had fresh in mind the late religious poetry that seeks consolation in the soul's release from the dying body: *The Angels' Call, A Thought of the Sea, Distant Sound of the Sea, The Return to Poetry, Intellectual Powers,* and *Sickness Like Night.*

31. Although Eva Hope was sure that "Miss Jewsbury" had written these remarks (*Queens of Literature* 270), the essay, by *Dublin*'s editor William Archer Butler, appeared four years after her death. Hope probably confused its title ("The Poetesses of Our Day.—No. I. Felicia Hemans") with Jewsbury's "Literary Sketches No. I.—Felicia Hemans."

32. In the "exhortatory melancholy," combining "resiliance and weariness, heroism and victimisation, importance and hopelessness," abides the appeal to female readers, proposes Angela Leighton (*Writing Against* 12). Thus Chorley could see in *Evening Prayer* Hemans's signature theme, "the peculiar trails appointed to her sex" (*Athenæum* 395: 392).

33. First published in *Literary Souvenir* for 1825 as *Arria; an Historical Sketch*; I quote the version in *Phantasmagoria* (1: 122–24).

34. 1: 114–15. See also, for instance, *The Lonely Grave* and *The Emir's Daughter*, in *Phantasmagoria*.

35. Although Aikin's introduction "disclaim[s] entirely the absurd idea that the two sexes ever can be, or ever ought to be, placed in all respects on a footing of equality" (v), the respects it does consider were quite broad: "let the daily observation of mankind bear witness, that no talent, no virtue, is masculine alone; no fault or folly exclusively feminine" (vi).

36. *CMH* 1: 304n. Chorley quotes more fully the passage that this sentence concludes: "De toutes mes facultés la plus puissante est la faculté de souffrir. Je suis née pour le bonheur, mon caractère est confiant, mon imagination est animée; mais la peine excite en moi je ne sais quelle impétuosité qui peut trouble ma raison, ou me donner de la mort. Je vous le répète encore, ménagez-moi; la gaieté, la mobilité ne me servent qu'en apparence: mais il ya a dans mon âme des abîmes de tristesse dont je ne pouvais me défendre qu'en me préservant de l'amour" (bk. 4, ch. 6; p. 304: Of all my endowments, the most powerful is the capacity for suffering. I was born for happiness, my character is confident, my imagination is soulful; but pain excites in me a strange impetuosity that can trouble my sanity or drive me to death. I repeat to you again, be caring of me; gaiety, mobilité help me only in appearance: but there are in my soul abysses of sadness from which I cannot defend myself except by saving myself from love). For Romantic alignments of gender and genius, see Battersby 13, 35–38, 46–47, ch. 8 and ch. 10.

37. The canny observation about "MWS" is Anne Mellor's (*Mary Shelley* 54).

38. 28 Sept. 1833, p. 646; the review closed: "We shall not again dip our pen in this mire of blood and dirt, over which, by a strange perversity of feeling, the talent of the writer, and that writer a woman! has contrived to throw a lurid, fearful and unhallowed light" (347). Angela Leighton (*Writing Against* 81) alerted me to this review.

39. Quoted from *Littell's Living Age,* 609–10. The by-line is "From the London Review."

40. *Brownings' Correspondence* 1: 361; the editors date the composition of this untitled essay in the early 1840s, and discern Elizabeth Barrett in the portrait of Beth.

Works Cited

attr.   attributed by (author identification)
&c   other works / other publishing partners
/e   edition
rev.   revised
tr.   translated by

Adams, James Eli. *Dandies and Desert Saints: Styles of Victorian Manhood.* Ithaca: Cornell UP, 1995.
Aikin, Lucy. *Epistles on Women, Exemplifying Their Character and Condition in Various Ages and Nations. With Miscellaneous Poems.* London: J. Johnson, 1810.
Alfieri, Vittorio. *Mirra.* Trans. as *Myrrha,* in *The Tragedies of Vittorio Alfieri.* Ed. Edgar Alfred Bowring. 2 vols. London: George Bell and Sons, 1876. 2: 311–64.
Allingham, William. *William Allingham: A Diary, 1824–1889.* Ed. H. Allingham and D. Radford. 1907; Middlesex, UK: Penguin, 1967.
Allott, Miriam, ed. *The Poems of John Keats.* New York: Norton, 1970.
Altick, Richard D. *Victorian People and Ideas.* New York: Norton, 1973.
The Amulet, or Christian and Literary Remembrancer. Ed. S. C. Hall. London: Frederick Westley and A. H. Davis, and Wightman, 1829.
Analytical Review, or history of literature, domestic and foreign, on an enlarged plan 8 (1790): 416–19; on Wollstonecraft, *A Vindication of the Rights of Men.*
Anti-Jacobin; or, Weekly Examiner 1 (20 Nov. 1798): 7–8. "Introduction to the Poetry of the *Anti-Jacobin.*"
Anti-Jacobin Review and Magazine, or, Monthly Political and Literary Censor 9 (April-Aug. 1801): 515–20. *The Vision of Liberty,* by C. K. (C. Kirkpatrick Sharpe).
Approaches to Teaching British Women Poets of the Romantic Period. Ed. Stephen C. Behrendt and Harriet Kramer Linkin. New York: MLA, 1997.
Armstrong, Isobel. "The Gush of the Feminine: How Can We Read Women's Poetry

of the Romantic Period?" *Romantic Women: Voices and Counter-Voices.* Ed. Paula Feldman and Theresa M. Kelley. Hanover, NH: UP of New England, 1995. 13–32.

Arnold, Matthew. "Byron." Preface to *Poetry of Byron* (1881); *Essays in Criticism, Second Series* (1895). *Prose* 9: 217–37.

———. *The Complete Prose Works of Matthew Arnold.* Ed. R. H. Super. 11 vols. Ann Arbor: U Michigan P, 1960–77.

———. "John Keats." Ward's *English Poets*, vol. 4 (1880): 428–37; *Essays and Criticism, Second Series*, 1888. *Prose* 9: 205–16.

———. *Letters of Matthew Arnold, 1848–1888.* Ed. George W. E. Russell. 2 vols. New York: Macmillan, 1896.

———. *The Letters of Matthew Arnold to Arthur Hugh Clough.* Ed. Howard Foster Lowry, 1932; London: Oxford UP, 1968.

———. *The Note-Books of Matthew Arnold.* Ed. Howard Foster Lowry, Karl Young, and Waldo Hilary Dunn. London: Oxford UP, 1952.

———. Preface, *Poems of Wordsworth.* London: Macmillan, 1879. v–xxvi.

"Shelley." *Nineteenth Century,* January 1888; *Prose* 2: 305–27.

Astell, Mary. *Reflections Upon Marriage. The Third Edition. To which is Added A Preface, in Answer to some Objections.* London: Richard Wilkin, 1706.

———. *A Serious Proposal to the Ladies, for the Advancement of their true and greatest Interest.* London: Richard Wilkin, 1694; ed. Patricia Springborg. Peterborough, ON.: Broadview P, 2002.

The Athenæum: Weekly Review of English and Foreign Literature, Fine Arts, and Works of Embellishment 131 (1 May 1830): 258–60; on Jewsbury, *The Three Histories.*

The Athenæum, Journal of English and Foreign Literature, Science, and the Fine Arts 228 (10 March 1832): 162. [B.], "Original Papers: An Elegy on the Death of the Poet Keats."

——— 263 (10 Nov. 1832): 730. "'On *Frankenstein.*' By the Late Percy Bysshe Shelley."

——— 275 (2 Feb. 1833): 74. "Paris Correspondence."

——— 309 (28 Sept. 1833): 346–47. "*Lelia*: a Novel. By George Sand."

——— 347 (21 June 1834): 473. "Original Papers: Mrs. Fletcher."

[Austen, Henry]. "Biographical Notice of the Author." *Northanger Abbey AND Persuasion.* 4 vols. London: John Murray, 1818. 1: 3–8.

———. "Memoir of Miss Austen." *Sense and Sensibility.* London: Richard Bentley, 1833. Rpt. *J. E. Austen-Leigh, "A Memoir of Jane Austen" and Other Family Recollections.* Ed. Kathryn Sutherland. Oxford: Oxford UP, 2002. 145–54.

Austen, Jane. *Northanger Abbey.* London: John Murray, 1818.

———. *Persuasion.* 1818; ed. Linda Bree. Peterborough, ON: Broadview P, 1998.

———. *Pride and Prejudice.* 1813; ed. Claudia L. Johnson and Susan J. Wolfson. New York: Longman, 2003.

———. *Sense and Sensibility.* 1811; ed. Claudia L. Johnson. New York: Norton, 2002.

Austin, Alfred. "Mr. Swinburne." *Temple Bar* 24 (July 1869); *The Poetry of the Period.* London: Richard Bentley, 1870. 77–117.

Baillie, Joanna. *The Collected Letters of Joanna Baillie*. Ed. Judith Bayley Slagle. 2 vols. London: Associated UPs, 1999.

———. *Plays on the Passions* (1798); ed. Peter Duthie. Peterborough, ON.: Broadview P, 2001.

———. *A Series of Plays: In Which It Is Attempted to Delineate the Stronger Passions of the Mind* (1798; 1802; 1812). *The Dramatic and Poetic Works of Joanna Baillie*. 2/e; London: Longman & c., 1853.

Barker-Benfield, G. J. *The Culture of Sensibility: Sex and Society in Eighteenth-Century Britain*. Chicago: U Chicago P, 1992.

Barnard, John. *John Keats*. Cambridge: Cambridge UP, 1987.

Barnefield, George. "The Psychology of the Poet Shelley." Edward Carpenter and George Barnefield. *The Psychology of the Poet Shelley*. London: George Allen & Unwin, 1925. 53–125.

Barrett, Elizabeth. *The Brownings' Correspondence*. Ed. Philip Kelley and Ronald Hudson. 10 vols. Winfield, KS: Wedgestone P, 1984–92.

———. *The Complete Poetical Works of Elizabeth Barrett Browning*. Ed. Harriet Waters Preston. Boston: Houghton Mifflin, 1900.

———. *The Letters of Elizabeth Barrett Browning to Mary Russell Mitford, 1836–1854*. Ed. Meredith B. Raymond and Mary Rose Sullivan. 3 vols. Winfield, KS: Wedgestone P, 1983.

———. "Stanzas Addressed to Miss Landon, and Suggested by Her 'Stanzas on the Death of Mrs Hemans.'" *New Monthly Magazine* 45 (1835): 82.

Bate, Walter Jackson. *John Keats*. Cambridge: Harvard UP, 1963.

Battersby, Christine. *Gender and Genius: Towards a Feminist Aesthetics*. Bloomington: Indiana UP, 1989.

Baudelaire, Charles. *The Painter of Modern Life and Other Essays*. Tr. and ed. Jonathan Mayne. New York: Da Capo, 1985.

Behrendt, Stephen C. "'Certainly not a Female Pen': Felicia Hemans's Early Public Reception." Sweet and Melnyk, eds. 95–114.

———, and Harriet Kramer Linkin, eds. See *Approaches*.

Belsey, Catherine. "Disrupting Sexual Difference: Meaning and Gender in the Comedies." *Alternative Shakespeares*. Ed. John Drakakis. London: Methuen, 1985. 166–90.

Benét, Stephen Vincent. *John Brown's Body*. 1927. New York: Farrar & Rhinehart, 1928.

Benson, Arthur C. *Rossetti*. London: Macmillan, 1904.

Bierce, Ambrose. *The Devil's Dictionary*. 1881–1906; 1911; *Collected Works of Ambrose Bierce*, vol. 7; rpt. Mineola, NY: Dover, 1993.

Biographium Fæmineum. The Female Worthies: or, Memoirs of the Most Illustrious Ladies of all Ages and Nations . . . who have shone with a particular Lustre, and given the noblest Proofs of the most exalted Genius. 2 vols. London: S. Crowder &c, 1766.

Birch, Dinah. "Ruskin's 'Womanly Mind.'" *Essays in Criticism* 38 (1988): 308–24.

Blackstone, Bernard. *Byron: A Survey*. London: Longman, 1975.

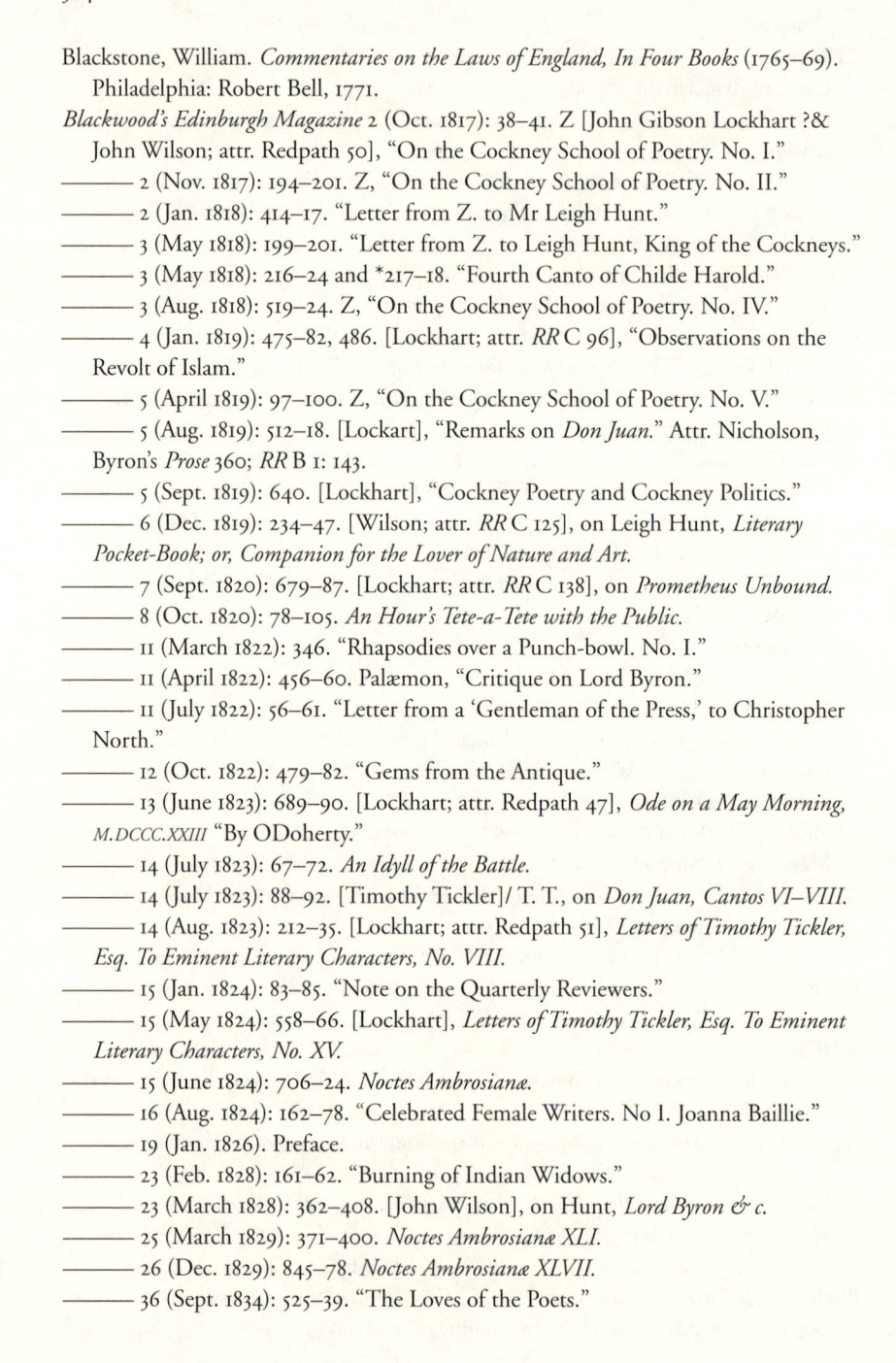

Blackstone, William. *Commentaries on the Laws of England, In Four Books* (1765–69). Philadelphia: Robert Bell, 1771.

Blackwood's Edinburgh Magazine 2 (Oct. 1817): 38–41. Z [John Gibson Lockhart ?& John Wilson; attr. Redpath 50], "On the Cockney School of Poetry. No. I."

——— 2 (Nov. 1817): 194–201. Z, "On the Cockney School of Poetry. No. II."

——— 2 (Jan. 1818): 414–17. "Letter from Z. to Mr Leigh Hunt."

——— 3 (May 1818): 199–201. "Letter from Z. to Leigh Hunt, King of the Cockneys."

——— 3 (May 1818): 216–24 and *217–18. "Fourth Canto of Childe Harold."

——— 3 (Aug. 1818): 519–24. Z, "On the Cockney School of Poetry. No. IV."

——— 4 (Jan. 1819): 475–82, 486. [Lockhart; attr. *RR* C 96], "Observations on the Revolt of Islam."

——— 5 (April 1819): 97–100. Z, "On the Cockney School of Poetry. No. V."

——— 5 (Aug. 1819): 512–18. [Lockart], "Remarks on *Don Juan*." Attr. Nicholson, Byron's *Prose* 360; *RR* B 1: 143.

——— 5 (Sept. 1819): 640. [Lockhart], "Cockney Poetry and Cockney Politics."

——— 6 (Dec. 1819): 234–47. [Wilson; attr. *RR* C 125], on Leigh Hunt, *Literary Pocket-Book; or, Companion for the Lover of Nature and Art*.

——— 7 (Sept. 1820): 679–87. [Lockhart; attr. *RR* C 138], on *Prometheus Unbound*.

——— 8 (Oct. 1820): 78–105. *An Hour's Tete-a-Tete with the Public*.

——— 11 (March 1822): 346. "Rhapsodies over a Punch-bowl. No. I."

——— 11 (April 1822): 456–60. Palæmon, "Critique on Lord Byron."

——— 11 (July 1822): 56–61. "Letter from a 'Gentleman of the Press,' to Christopher North."

——— 12 (Oct. 1822): 479–82. "Gems from the Antique."

——— 13 (June 1823): 689–90. [Lockhart; attr. Redpath 47], *Ode on a May Morning, M.DCCC.XXIII* "By ODoherty."

——— 14 (July 1823): 67–72. *An Idyll of the Battle*.

——— 14 (July 1823): 88–92. [Timothy Tickler]/ T. T., on *Don Juan, Cantos VI–VIII*.

——— 14 (Aug. 1823): 212–35. [Lockhart; attr. Redpath 51], *Letters of Timothy Tickler, Esq. To Eminent Literary Characters, No. VIII*.

——— 15 (Jan. 1824): 83–85. "Note on the Quarterly Reviewers."

——— 15 (May 1824): 558–66. [Lockhart], *Letters of Timothy Tickler, Esq. To Eminent Literary Characters, No. XV*.

——— 15 (June 1824): 706–24. *Noctes Ambrosianæ*.

——— 16 (Aug. 1824): 162–78. "Celebrated Female Writers. No I. Joanna Baillie."

——— 19 (Jan. 1826). Preface.

——— 23 (Feb. 1828): 161–62. "Burning of Indian Widows."

——— 23 (March 1828): 362–408. [John Wilson], on Hunt, *Lord Byron &c*.

——— 25 (March 1829): 371–400. *Noctes Ambrosianæ XLI*.

——— 26 (Dec. 1829): 845–78. *Noctes Ambrosianæ XLVII*.

——— 36 (Sept. 1834): 525–39. "The Loves of the Poets."

———— 38 (July 1835): 96–97. Δ/ "Delta" / [David Macbeth Moir], obituary essay on Hemans.
———— 39 (1836). Preface.
———— 39 (Feb. 1836): 265–80. Review of Baillie's *Dramas*.
———— 56 (Sept. 1844): 331–42. [James Ferrier; attr. *KCH* 21n2], "Poems by Coventry Patmore."
———— 75 (March 1854): 345–51. "Alexander Smith's Poems."
———— 86 (July 1859): 99–113. [G. H. Lewes], "The Novels of Jane Austen."
Blake, William. *The Complete Poetry and Prose of William Blake*. Ed. David V. Erdman. 1965; rev. New York: Anchor, 1982.
Blakemore, Steven. *Crisis in Representation*. Cranbury NJ: Associated UPs, 1993.
———— *Intertextual War*. Madison, NJ: Fairleigh Dickinson UP, 1997.
Blanchard, Laman. *Life and Literary Remains of L.E.L.* 2 vols. London: Henry Colburn, 1841.
Blessington, Marguerite, Lady. *Conversations of Lord Byron*. 1834; ed. Ernest J. Lovell, Jr. Princeton: Princeton UP, 1969.
————. "Le Bas Bleu." *Heath's Book of Beauty for 1845*. Ed. Countess of Blessington. London: Longman, Brown, Green, and Longman's, 1845. 232–49.
Bloom, Harold. "*Frankenstein, or, The Modern Prometheus*." *Partisan Review*, 1965; Afterword, *Frankenstein* (Signet Classic; New York: NAL, 1965); *The Ringers in the Tower: Studies in Romantic Tradition*. Chicago: U Chicago P, 1971.
Blyth, Henry. *Caro: The Fatal Passion: The Life of Lady Caroline Lamb*. 1972; New York: Coward, McCann & Goeghegan, 1973.
Boswell, James. *Life of Johnson*. 1791–95; abridged and ed. Charles G. Osgood. New York: Charles Scribner's Sons, 1917.
Bowles, William Lisle. *To Miss Stephens, on first hearing her sing "Auld Robin Gray." Literary Souvenir* (1825): 83–84.
Boyle, Andrew. *An Index to the Annuals*. Vol. 1, *The Authors (1820–1850)*. Worcester: Andrew Boyle, 1967.
Breen, Jennifer, ed. *Women Romantic Poets, 1785–1832, an Anthology*. London: J. M. Dent; Vermont: Charles E. Tuttle, 1992.
British Critic 7 (June 1796): 602–10; on Wollstonecraft, *Letters Written during a Short Residence in Sweden, Norway, Denmark*.
———— ns 20 (July 1823): 50–61; on Hemans, *The Siege of Valencia &c.*
British Lady's Magazine 25 (May 1817): 262.
British Review 11 (May 1818): 327–33. [William Roberts; attr. B 1: 455] on Byron, *Beppo*.
———— 15 (June 1820): 299–310. "Mrs. Hemans's Poems."
———— 19 (March 1822): 72–102. [William Roberts; attr. *RR* B1: 495], on Byron, *Sardanapalus*.
Bromwich, David. *Hazlitt: The Mind of a Critic*. New York: Oxford UP, 1983.
[Brown, John]. *An Estimate of the Manners and Principles of the Times*. 2/e; London: L. Davis and C. Reymers, 1757.

Brown, Laura. *Alexander Pope*. Oxford: Basil Blackwell, 1985.
Browning, Robert. *Dearest Isa: Robert Browning's Letters to Isabella Blagden*. Ed. Edward C. McAleer. Austin: U of Texas P, 1951.
Buchanan, Robert. *The Fleshly School of Poetry and Other Phenomena of the Day*. London: Strahan, 1872.
Burke, Edmund. *A Letter From the Right Hon. Edmund Burke, to a Noble Lord, on the Attacks Made Upon Him and His Pension, in the House of Lords, by the Duke of Bedford and the Earl of Lauderdale, Early in the Present Sessions of Parliament*. 1796; *Works* 4: 281–328.
———. *Letter I: On the Overtures of Peace. Three Letters Addressed to a Member of the Present Parliament, on the Proposals for Peace with the Regicide Directory of France*. 1796; *Works* 4: 331–417.
———. *Reflections on the Revolution in France*. 1790; Garden City, NY: Anchor/Doubleday, 1973.
———. *The Works of Edmund Burke*. 9 vols. Boston: Charles C. Little and James Brown, 1839.
[Burton, Robert] / Democritus Junior. *The Anatomy of Melancholy, What it is, With all the Kinds, Causes, Symptoms, Prognostics, and Several Cures of it*. A New Edition, corrected and enriched by Democritus Minor. London: William Tegg, n.d.
Bush, Douglas. *Mythology and the Romantic Tradition*. 1937; New York: Norton, 1963.
Butler, Judith. *Gender Trouble: Feminism and the Subversion of Identity*. New York: Routledge, 1990.
Butler, Marilyn. "John Bull's Other Kingdom: Byron's Intellectual Comedy." *Studies in Romanticism* 31 (1992): 281–95.
———. *Romantics, Rebels, and Reactionaries: English Literature and Its Backgrounds, 1760–1830*. New York: Oxford UP, 1982.
[Butler, William Archer] / W. A. B. "Poetry, and Decline of the Poetical Genius." *Dublin University Magazine* (Aug. 1834): 174–83.
Byron, George Gordon, Lord. *Byron's Letters and Journals*. Ed. Leslie A. Marchand. 12 vols. Cambridge: Harvard UP, 1973–82.
———. *Childe Harold's Pilgrimage, Canto the Third*. London: John Murray, 1816.
———. *Childe Harold's Pilgrimage, Canto the Fourth*. London: John Murray, 1818.
———. *Complete Miscellaneous Prose*. Ed. Andrew Nicholson. Oxford: Clarendon P, 1991.
———. *The Complete Poetical Works*. Ed. Jerome J. McGann. 7 vols. Oxford: Clarendon P, 1980–93. Vol. 6, co-ed. Barry Weller.
———. *Conversations*. See Blessington, Lovell, Medwin.
———. *English Bards and Scotch Reviewers. A Satire*. 4/e; London: James Cawthorn, 1811.
———. *Letter to John Murray, Esqre. Prose* 121–60.
———. *Sardanapalus, A Tragedy. The Two Foscari, A Tragedy. Cain, A Mystery*. London: John Murray, 1821.

---. *The Works of Lord Byron: With His Letters and Journals, and His Life.* By Thomas Moore, Esq. 17 vols. London: John Murray, 1832–34. *Sardanapalus*, vol. 13 (1834).

---. *The Works of Lord Byron: Poetry.* Ed. Ernest Hartley Coleridge. 7 vols. London: John Murray, 1898–1904. *Sardanapalus*, vol. 5.

Callender, Michelle. "'The Grand Theatre of Political Changes': Marie Antoinette, the Republic, and the Politics of Spectacle in Mary Wollstonecraft's *An Historical and Moral View of the French Revolution.*" *European Romantic Review* 11 (2000): 375–92.

Cambridge University Magazine 1/2 (May 1839): 81–101. "The Poets of England Who Have Died Young: No. II: Percy Bysshe Shelley."

Carlyle, Thomas. "Burns." *Edinburgh Review* 48 (1828). 1: 258–319.

[---]. "Characteristics." Art. IV, *Edinburgh Review* 54 (Dec. 1831): 351–86.

---. *Critical and Miscellaneous Essays.* London: Chapman and Hall, 1899. 5 vols. New York: AMS, 1969.

---. "Goethe." *Foreign Review* 3 (1828); *Critical and Miscellaneous Essays* 1: 198–257.

---. *On Heroes, Hero-Worship, and the Heroic in History.* 1840–41; ed. Carl Niemeyer. Lincoln: U Nebraska P, 1966.

---. *Sartor Resartus.* 1833–38; *The Carlyle Reader.* Ed. G. B. Tennyson. New York: Modern Library, 1969.

Carpenter, Edward. "The Psychology of the Poet Shelley." Edward Carpenter and George Barnefield, *The Psychology of the Poet Shelley.* London: George Allen & Unwin, 1925. 7–51.

Castle, Terry. "The Carnivalization of Eighteenth-Century English Narrative." *PMLA* 99 (1984): 903–16.

---. "Eros and Liberty at the English Masquerade, 1710–90." *Eighteenth-Century Studies* 17 (1983–84): 156–76.

Certain Homilies Appointed to be Read in the Churches in the Time of Queen Elizabeth. London: Society for Promoting Christian Knowledge, 1908.

Chambers's Cyclopedia of English Literature. Ed. Robert Chambers. 2 vols. London and Edinburgh: William and Robert Chambers, 1858. "John Keats," 2: 363–68. See also 1866 (Boston: Gould and Lincoln), 2: 402–7; 1870, 2: 402–6.

Champion (11 Feb. 1816): 45–46. Review of Byron, *Siege of Corinth* and *Parisina*.

Chandler, James K. *Wordsworth's Second Nature: A Study of the Poetry and Politics.* Chicago: U of Chicago P, 1984.

Chew, Samuel. *Byron in England: His Fame and After-Fame.* London: John Murray, 1924.

---. *The Dramas of Lord Byron: A Critical Study.* 1915; New York: Russell & Russell, 1964.

Chilcott, Tim. *A Publisher and his Circle: The Life and Work of John Taylor, Keats's Publisher.* London: Routledge and Kegan Paul, 1972.

Chodorow, Nancy. *The Reproduction of Mothering: Psychoanalysis and the Sociology of Gender.* Stanford: Stanford UP, 1978.

Chorley, Henry F[othergill]. *Memorials of Mrs. Hemans, with Illustrations of her Literary Character from her Private Correspondence.* 2 vols. London: Saunders and Otley, 1836.

[———]. "Mrs. Hemans." *Athenæum* 395 (May 1835): 391–92.

[———] / H. F. C., "Personal Recollections of the Late Mrs. Hemans." *Athenæum* 398 (13 June 1835): 452–54; 400 (27 June 1835): 493–95; 402 (11 July 1835): 527–30.

Christ, Carol. "Victorian Masculinity and the Angel in the House." *A Widening Sphere: Changing Roles of Victorian Women.* Ed. Martha Vicinus. Bloomington: Indiana UP, 1977. 146–62.

Christensen, Jerome. *Lord Byron's Strength: Romantic Writing and Commercial Society.* Baltimore: Johns Hopkins UP, 1993.

———. *Romanticism at the End of History.* Baltimore: Johns Hopkins UP, 2000.

Clark, Anna. "Queen Caroline and the Sexual Politics of Popular Culture in London, 1820." *Representations* 31 (Summer 1990): 47–68.

Clarke, Charles Cowden. "Recollections of Keats." *Atlantic Monthly* 7 (Jan. 1861); rev. *Gentleman's Magazine* ns 12 (Feb. 1874); rpt. "Recollections of John Keats," *Recollections of Writers* (with Mary Cowden Clarke), 1878; Sussex, UK: Centaur P, 1969. 120–57.

Clarke, Eric O. "Shelley's Heart." *Virtuous Vice: Homoeroticism and the Public Sphere.* Durham: Duke UP, 2000.

Clarke, Norma. *Ambitious Heights: Writing, Friendship, Love—The Jewsbury Sisters, Felicia Hemans, and Jane Welsh Carlyle.* London: Routledge, 1990.

Cline, C. L. "Unpublished Notes on the Romantic Poets by Isaac D'Israeli." *Studies in English* 21 (1941): 138–46.

Cobbe, Frances Power. *Life of Frances Power Cobbe.* 2 vols. Boston: Riverside, 1894.

Coleridge, Hartley. *Complete Poetical Works.* Ed. Ramsay Colles. London: George Routledge & Sons, 1908.

Coleridge, Samuel Taylor. *Aids to Reflection.* 1825; ed. John Beer. Princeton: Princeton UP, 1993.

———. *Biographia Literaria; or, Biographical Sketches of My Literary Life and Opinions.* 1817; ed. James Engell and W. Jackson Bate. 2 vols. Princeton: Princeton UP, 1983.

———. *Collected Letters of Samuel Taylor Coleridge.* Ed. Earl Leslie Griggs. 6 vols. Oxford: Clarendon P, 1956–71.

———. *Fears in Solitude, Written, April 1798, during the Alarms of an Invasion, To which are added, France, an Ode; and Frost at Midnight.* London: J. Johnson, 1798.

———. *Lectures 1808–1819, On Literature.* Ed. R. A. Foakes. 2 vols. Princeton: Princeton UP, 1987.

———. *The Notebooks of Samuel Taylor Coleridge.* Ed. Kathleen Coburn. 4 vols. Princeton: Princeton UP, 1957–90.

———. *On the Constitution of the Church and State.* 1829; ed. John Colmer. Princeton: Princeton UP, 1976.

———. *Samuel Taylor Coleridge: The Complete Poems.* Ed. William Keach. London: Penguin, 1997.

---. *Satyrane's Letters: Letter II (To a Lady), The Friend* 16 (7 Dec. 1809). *The Friend.* Ed. Barbara E. Rooke. 2 vols. Princeton: Princeton UP, 1969. 2: 209–21.

---. *Table Talk* (Recorded by Henry Nelson Coleridge and John Taylor Coleridge). 1835; rev. and ed. Carl Woodring. 2 vols. Princeton: Princeton UP, 1990.

---. *The Watchman.* 1796; ed. Lewis Patton. Princeton: Princeton UP, 1970.

---. *Zapolya.* 1817; *The Complete Poetic & Dramatic Works of Samuel Taylor Coleridge.* Ed. James Dykes Campbell. London: Macmillan, 1893.

Colley, Linda. *Britons: Forging the Nation, 1707–1837.* New Haven: Yale UP 1992.

Colls, John Henry. *A Poetic Epistle Addressed to Miss Wollstonecraft, Occasioned by Reading Her Celebrated* Essay on the Rights of Woman, *and her* Historical and Moral View of the French Revolution. London: Vernor and Hood, G. and T. Wilkie, 1795.

Colvin, Sidney. *John Keats.* New York: Harper, 1887.

Corbett, Martyn. *Byron and Tragedy.* London: Macmillan; New York: St. Martin's P, 1988.

Cornhill Magazine 34 (1876): 556–69. "Thoughts on Criticism, by a Critic."

Cornwall, Barry / [Bryan Waller Procter]. *An Autobiographical Fragment and Biographical Notes, with Personal Sketches of Contemporaries, Unpublished Lyrics, and Letters of Literary Friends.* London: George Bell and Sons, 1877.

[Courthope, William John]. On Swinburne, *Song Before Sunrise;* Rossetti, *Poems;* and Morris, *The Earthly Paradise. Quarterly Review* 132 (Jan. 1872): 59–84. Attr. *KCH* 33.

Courthope, William John. "Keats' Place In English Poetry." *National Review* 10 (Sept. 1887): 11–24.

---. "Poetry, Music, and Painting: Coleridge and Keats." *The Liberal Movement in English Literature.* London: John Murray, 1885. 159–94.

---. "Romanticism in English Poetry: Poetry and Painting: John Keats." *A History of English Poetry.* 6 vols. London: Macmillan, 1910. 6: 320–56.

Cox, Jeffrey N. *Poetry and Politics in the Cockney School: Keats, Shelley, Hunt, and Their Circle.* Cambridge: Cambridge UP, 1998.

Critical Review; or, Annals of literature; extended and improved by a society of gentlemen 70 (1790): 694–96; on Wollstonecraft, *Rights of Men.*

--- 2d ser. 4 (1792): 389–98; and 5 (1792): 132–41; on Wollstonecraft, *Rights of Woman.*

[Croker, John Wilson]. On Barbauld, *Eighteen Hundred and Eleven. Quarterly Review* 7 (June 1812): 309–13. Attr. *The Quarterly Review Under Gifford, 1809–24,* ed. Hill Chadwick and Here Shins. Chapel Hill: U North Carolina P, 1949. 31.

[---]. On *Frankenstein. Quarterly Review* 18 (Jan. 1818): 379–85. Attr. *RR* C 764.

[---]. On Keats, *Endymion. Quarterly Review* 19 (April 1818; pub. Sept.): 204–8. Attr. *RR* C 767.

Crompton, Louis. *Byron and Greek Love: Homophobia in 19th-Century England.* Berkeley: U of California P, 1985.

Culler, Jonathan. "Apostrophe." 1977; *The Pursuit of Signs: Semiotics, Literature, Deconstruction.* Ithaca: Cornell UP, 1981. 135–54.

Curran, Stuart. "Romantic Poetry: The 'I' Altered." Mellor, ed. 185–207.

———. "Women Readers, Women Writers." *The Cambridge Companion to British Romanticism.* Ed. Stuart Curran. Cambridge: Cambridge UP, 1993. 177–95.

Dallas, E[neas]. S[weetland]. *The Gay Science.* 2 vols. London: Chapman and Hall, 1866.

Darlington, Beth, ed. *The Love Letters of William and Mary Wordsworth.* Ithaca: Cornell UP, 1981.

David, Deirdre. *Intellectual Women and Victorian Patriarchy: Harriet Martineau, Elizabeth Barrett Browning, George Eliot.* Ithaca: Cornell UP, 1987.

Davies, Sir John. *Nosce Teipsum: This Oracle Expounded in Two Elegies.* 2, *Of the Soul of Man and the Immortality Thereof.* Hyder E. Rollins and Herschel Baker, eds., *The Renaissance in England: Non-Dramatic Prose and Verse of the Sixteenth Century.* Lexington, MA.: D. C. Heath, 1954. 476–79.

Davis, Natalie Zemon. "Women on Top." *Society and Culture in Early Modern France.* Stanford: Stanford UP, 1975. 124–51.

De Montluzin, Emily Lorraine. "Killing the Cockneys: *Blackwood's* Weapons of Choice Against Hunt, Hazlitt, Keats." *Keats-Shelley Journal* 47 (1998): 33–62.

Dennis, John. *The Critical Works of John Dennis.* Ed. Edward Niles Hooker. 2 vols. Baltimore: Johns Hopkins UP, 1939–43.

[De Quincey, Thomas]. *Confessions of an English Opium-Eater. London Magazine* 4 (1821): 293–312. Ed. Grevel Lindop. New York: Oxford UP, 1985.

———. "John Keats." "Notes on George Gilfillan's *Gallery of Literary Portraits* (1845)." *Tait's Edinburgh Magazine* ns 13 (April 1846): 249–54.

Derrida, Jacques. "La Loi du Genre." Tr. Avital Ronell, "The Law of Genre." 1980. Rpt. with some editorial modification, *Jacques Derrida: Acts of Literature.* Ed. Derek Attridge. New York: Routledge, 1992. 223–52.

Dickstein, Morris. *Keats and His Poetry: A Study in Development.* Chicago: U Chicago P, 1971.

Diodorus Siculus. Trans. C. H. Oldfather. 10 vols. London: William Heinemann, 1946. "Sardanapallus" (Book 2, ¶s 23–28) 1: 425–45.

Disher, M. Wilson. *Clowns and Pantomimes.* New York: Benjamin Blom, 1968.

Donaldson, Ian. *The World Upside-Down: Comedy from Jonson to Fielding.* Oxford: Clarendon P, 1970.

Dowden, Edward. *Life of Percy Bysshe Shelley.* 1886; New York: Barnes and Noble, 1966.

Dowling, Linda. *Hellenism and Homosexuality in Victorian Oxford.* Ithaca: Cornell UP, 1994.

Dublin Review 2 (Dec. 1836): 245–75. "Life and Writing of Mrs. Hemans."

Dublin University Magazine 10.56 (Aug. 1837): 123–41. [William Archer Butler], "The Poetesses of Our Day—No. I. Felicia Hemans."

DuPlessis, Rachel Blau. *Writing Beyond the Ending: Narrative Strategies of Twentieth-Century Women Writers.* Bloomington: Indiana UP, 1985.

Dusinberre, Juliet. *Shakespeare and the Nature of Women.* New York: Macmillan, 1975.

Eagleton, Terry. "Ideology and Literary Form." *Criticism and Ideology: A Study in Marxist Literary Theory.* 1976; London: Verso, 1978. 102–61.

The Eclectic Review 2d ser. 2 (Oct. 1814): 393–400. [Josiah Conder; attr. *RR* B 2: 727], on Byron's *Lara.*

——— 2d ser. 8 (Sept. 1817): 67–75. [Josiah Conder; attr. *RR* C 329], "Keats's *Poems.*"

Edgcumbe, Fred, ed. *Letters of Fanny Brawne to Fanny Keats.* London: Oxford UP, 1936.

Edinburgh Journal; or, Weekly Register of Criticism and Belles Lettres (8 May 1830): 270; on Jewsbury, *The Three Histories.*

Edinburgh Magazine, and Literary Miscellany 2 (1818): 249–53; on [M. Shelley], *Frankenstein.*

Edinburgh Monthly Review 3 (1820): 373–83; on Hemans, *The Sceptic.*

Edinburgh Review, or Critical Journal 90 (October 1849): 388–433. [Aubrey Thomas de Vere; attr. *KCH* 341] on Tennyson, *The Princess* (5/e, 1848), P. B. Shelley, *Poetical Works* (1847), and Milnes, *John Keats: Life, Letters, and Literary Remains* (1848).

Edinburgh Review 134 (July 1871): 71–99. [T. S. Baynes], and on Swinburne. Attr. *The Wellesley Index to Victorian Periodicals 1824–1900*, ed. Walter E. Houghton (U Toronto P, 1966), 1: 52.

Elfenbein, Andrew. *Byron and the Victorians.* Cambridge: Cambridge UP, 1995.

———. *Romantic Genius: The Prehistory of a Homosexual Role.* New York: Columbia UP, 1999.

Elledge, W. Paul. *Byron and the Dynamics of Metaphor.* Nashville: Vanderbilt UP, 1968.

[Ellis, George; attr. *BCH* 43]. On *Childe Harold's Pilgrimage I–II. Quarterly Review* 7 (1812): 180–200.

Ellis, Mrs. [Sarah Stickney]. *The Daughters of England: Their Position in Society, Characters, and Responsibilities.* New York: D. Appleton, 1842.

———. "Mrs. Fletcher, Late Miss Jewsbury." *The Christian Keepsake, and Missionary Annual.* Ed. William Ellis. London, Paris, and New York: Fisher, 1838. 30–42.

Ellman, Richard. *Oscar Wilde.* 1987; New York: Vintage, 1988.

Elwood, Mrs. [Anne Katharine Curteis]. "Mrs. Mary Wollstonecroft [*sic*] Godwin." *Memoirs of the Literary Ladies of England from the Commencement of the Last Century.* 2 vols. London: Henry Colburn, 1843. 2: 125–54.

English Review 17 (1791): 59–61; on Wollstonecraft, *Rights of Men.*

Erdman, David V. "Byron's Stage Fright: The History of His Ambition and Fear of Writing for the Stage." *ELH* 6 (1939): 219–43.

Erskine, Mrs. Steuart, ed. *Anna Jameson: Letters and Friendships.* London: Fletcher Unwin, 1915.

Espinasse, Francis. *Lancashire Worthies.* 2d ser.; London: Simpkin, Marshall, 1877. "Felicia Hemans," 286–95; "Maria Jane Jewsbury," 323–39.

Étienne, Louis. "La Poésie Paienne en Angleterre"/"Le Paganisme Poétique en Angleterre: John Keats et Algernon Charles Swinburne." *Revue des Deux Mondes* 69, part 1 (15 May 1867): 291–317.

European Magazine, and London Review 4 (Nov. 1783): 330–34. "Account of the Life and Writings of Mrs. Catherine Macaulay Graham."

Evert, Walter H., and Jack W. Rhodes, eds. *Approaches to Teaching Keats's Poetry.* New York: MLA, 1991.

Examiner. 23 Dec. 1821: 808–10. Q. on Byron, *Sardanapalus.*

———. 8 Jan. 1848: 21–22; on Ellis Bell, *Wuthering Heights.*

Fairchild, Hoxie Neale. *Religious Trends in English Poetry.* 3 vols. New York: Columbia UP, 1949.

Farrell, John P. *Revolution as Tragedy: The Dilemma of the Moderate from Scott to Arnold.* Ithaca: Cornell UP, 1980.

Feldman, Paula R. "The Poet and Her Profits: Felicia Hemans and the Literary Marketplace." *Keats-Shelley Journal* 46 (1997): 148–76.

———, ed. *British Women Poets of the Romantic Era, An Anthology.* Baltimore: Johns Hopkins UP, 1997.

Felman, Shoshana. "Rereading Femininity." *Yale French Studies* 62 (Spring 1981): 19–44.

———. "Woman and Madness: The Critical Phallacy." *Diacritics* 5.4 (1975): 2–10.

Fenichel, Otto. "The Psychology of Transvestitism." 1930; *The Collected Papers of Otto Fenichel, First Series.* New York: Norton, 1953. 1.167–80.

Ferguson, Frances. *Solitude and the Sublime: Romanticism and the Aesthetics of Individuation.* New York: Routledge, 1992.

———. *Wordsworth: Language as Counter-Spirit.* New Haven: Yale UP, 1977.

Fields, Mrs. James T. / [Annie Adams]. *A Shelf of Old Books.* New York: Charles Scribner's Sons, 1894.

Ford, George H. *Keats and the Victorians: A Study of His Influence and Rise to Fame 1821–1895.* New Haven: Yale UP, 1944.

Fordyce, James. *Sermons to Young Women, in Two Volumes.* 1765; 6/e; London: T. Cadell &c., 1769.

Forman, Harry Buxton. *Letters of John Keats to Fanny Brawne.* New York: Charles Scribner's Sons,, 1878.

Forsyth, P. T. *Religion in Recent Art: Expository Lectures on Rossetti, Burne Jones, James Watts, Holman Hunt and Wagner.* 1889; 3/e; London: Hodder and Stroughton, 1905.

Foucault, Michel. *The History of Sexuality.* Vol. 1, *An Introduction.* Trans. Robert Hurley. New York: Vintage, 1990.

Fox, Susan. "The Female as Metaphor in William Blake's Poetry." *Critical Inquiry* 3 (1977): 507–19.

Franklin, Caroline. *Byron's Heroines.* Oxford: Clarendon P, 1992.

———. "Juan's Sea Changes." *Don Juan, Theory and Practice.* Ed. Nigel Wood. Buckingham and Philadelphia: Open UP, 1993. 56–89.

———. *Mary Wollstonecraft: A Literary Life*. New York: Palgrave Macmillan, 2004.

Fraser's Magazine for Town and Country 7 (May 1833): 591–601. "The Female Character."

——— 48 (Nov. 1853): 568–76. Charles Kingsley, "Thoughts on Shelley and Byron."

Freud, Sigmund. "Negation." *The Standard Edition of the Complete Works of Sigmund Freud*. Trans. James Strachey. London: Hogarth P, 1953–74. 19: 235–39.

Fry, Paul H. *A Defense of Poetry: Reflections on the Occasion of Writing*. Stanford: Stanford UP, 1995.

Fryckstedt, Monica C. "The Hidden Rill: The Life and Career of Maria Jane Jewsbury." *Bulletin of the John Rylands University Library, University of Manchester* 66–67 (1984): 177–203, 450–73.

Furniss, Tom. "Nasty Tricks and Tropes: Sexuality and Language in Mary Wollstonecraft's *Rights of Woman*." *Studies in Romanticism* 32 (1993): 177–209.

Galignani, A. and William. *The Poetical Works of Coleridge, Shelley, and Keats*. Paris, 1829.

Galperin, William H. *The Historical Austen*. Philadelphia: U Pennsylvania P, 2003.

Garber, Marjorie. *Vested Interests: Cross-Dressing & Cultural Anxiety*. New York: Routledge, 1992.

Gaskell, Elizabeth. *Life of Charlotte Brontë*. London: J. M. Dent, 1908.

Gaull, Marilyn. "Romantic Numeracy: The 'Tuneless Numbers' and 'Shadows Numberless." *The Wordsworth Circle* 22 (1991): 124–30.

Gelpi, Barbara Charlesworth. "The Feminization of D. G. Rossetti." *The Victorian Experience: The Poets*. Ed. Richard A. Levine. Athens: Ohio UP, 1982. 94–114.

General Magazine and Impartial Review (Dec. 1790); 541–43; on H. M. Williams, *Letters written in France in the summer of 1790*.

———. 543–45; on Catharine Macaulay, *Observations on the Reflections of the Right Honourable Edmund Burke, on the Revolution in France*.

Gentleman's Magazine 61.1 (1791): 151–154; on Wollstonecraft, *A Vindication of the Rights of Men*.

Gilbert, Sandra M., and Susan Gubar. *The Madwoman in the Attic: The Woman Writer and the Nineteenth-Century Literary Imagination*. New Haven: Yale UP, 1979.

———. *No Man's Land: The Place of the Woman Writer in the Twentieth Century*. Vol. 2, *Sexchanges*. New Haven: Yale UP, 1989.

Gilfillan, George. "Female Authors. No. I—Mrs. Hemans." *Tait's Edinburgh Magazine* ns 14 (1847): 359–63.

———. "Female Authors. No. II—Mrs. Elizabeth Barrett Browning." *Tait's Edinburgh Magazine* ns 14 (1847): 620–25.

———. "John Keats." *A Gallery of Literary Portraits*. London: Simpkin, Marshall / Edinburgh: William Tait, 1845. 372–85.

Gilmartin, Sophie. "The Sati, the Bride, and the Widow: Sacrificial Woman in the Nineteenth Century." *Victorian Literature and Culture* 25.1 (1997): 141–58.

Gillett, Eric. *Maria Jane Jewsbury: Occasional Papers, Selected with a Memoir*. London: Oxford UP, 1932.
The Girl's Second Help to Reading. 1854. Matthews, *KCH* 10.
Gisborne, Thomas. *An Inquiry into the Duties of the Female Sex*. 1796; 7/e; London: T. Cadell and W. Davies, 1806.
Gitter, Elisabeth G. "The Power of Women's Hair in the Victorian Imagination." *PMLA* 99 (October 1984): 936–54.
Godwin, William. *Memoirs of the Author of* A Vindication of the Rights of Woman. London: J. Johnson, 1798; ed. Pamela Clemit and Gina Luria. Peterborough, ON: Broadview P, 2001.
Gorton, John. *A General Biographical Dictionary*. 3 vols. London: Whitaker, 1828.
Gouges, Olympe de. *Déclaration des Droits de la Femme et de la Citoyenne*. 1791; ed. Levy & c., 87–96.
Graham, Peter W. *Don Juan and Regency England*. Charlottesville: UP Virginia, 1990.
Green, Peter. *Juvenal: The Sixteen Satires*. London: Penguin, 1998.
Greenblatt, Stephen. "Culture." *Critical Terms for Literary Study*. Ed. Frank Lentricchia and Thomas McLaughlin. Chicago: U of Chicago P, 1990, 1995. 225–32.
———. *Renaissance Self-Fashioning: From More to Shakespeare*. Chicago: U of Chicago P, 1980.
Greer, Germaine. *Slip-Shod Sibyls: Recognition, Rejection, and the Woman Poet*. London: Viking, 1995.
Greg, W. R. "Kingsley and Carlyle." *Literary and Social Judgements*. Boston: James Osgood, 1873. 115–45.
Gregory, John. *A Father's Legacy to his Daughters*. London: Strahan and Cadell, 1774.
Grenby, M. O. *The Anti-Jacobin Novel: British Conservatism and the French Revolution*. Cambridge: Cambridge UP, 2001.
Guardian, or Historical and Literary Review. On Keats, *Lamia & c* (1820); Schwartz, 228–32.
"Gulnare." *Heath's Book of Beauty for 1847*. Ed. Countess of Blessington. London: Longman &c 1847. 158–63. Signed "E.A.H.O."
Gutwirth, Madelyn. "Forging a Vocation: Germaine de Staël on Fiction, Power, and Passion." *Bulletin of Research in the Humanities* 86.3 (1983–85): 242–54.
Hagstrum, Jean H. *Sex and Sensibility: Ideal and Erotic Love from Milton to Mozart*. Chicago: U Chicago P, 1980.
Hamilton, Walter. *The Aesthetic Movement in England*. 3/e; London: Reeves & Turner, 1882.
Harrison, William. *The Description of England*, ed. Georges Edelen, *1587*. Ithaca: Cornell UP, 1968.
Harwell, Thomas Meade. *Keats and the Critics, 1848–1900*. Salzburg: Institut für Englische Sprache und Literatur, U Salzburg, 1972.
Hawkins, Laetitia Matilda. *Letters on the Female Mind, Its Powers and Pursuits*.

Addressed to Miss H. M. Williams, with Particular Reference to Her Letters from France. 2 vols. London: Hookham & Carpenter, 1793.
Haworth, Helen. E. "'A Thing of Beauty Is a Joy Forever'? Early Illustrated Editions of Keats's Poetry." *Harvard Library Bulletin* 21 (1973): 88–103.
Haydon, Benjamin Robert. *Autobiography and Memoirs*. Ed. Tom Taylor and Aldous Huxley. 2 vols. New York: Harcourt Brace, 1926.
———. *The Diary of Benjamin Robert Haydon*. Ed. Willard Bissell Pope. 5 vols. Cambridge: Harvard UP, 1960.
[Hays, Mary]. *Appeal to the Men of Great Britain in Behalf of Woman*. London: J. Johnson and J. Bell, 1798.
[———]. "Improvements Suggested in Female Education." *Monthly Magazine* 3 (March 1797): 193–95. Signed H. M.
[———]. "Mary Wollstonecraft." *The Annual Necrology for 1797–8*. London: Richard Phillips, 1800. 411–60.
———. *The Memoirs of Emma Courtney*. London: G. G. and J. Robinson, 1796; ed. Marilyn R. Brooks. Peterborough, ON: Broadview P, 2000.
[———]. Obit. Wollstonecraft. *Monthly Magazine* 4 (Sept. 1797): 232–33. Hays identifies herself as the author in a letter to *Monthly Magazine* 4 (Oct. 1797): 245.
Hazlitt, William. *Characters of Shakespear's Plays*. 1817; London: Taylor and Hessey, 1818.
———. *The Complete Works of William Hazlitt*. Ed. P. P. Howe. 21 vols. 1930–34; New York: AMS P, 1967.
———. *Lectures on the English Poets, Delivered at the Surrey Institution*. London: Taylor and Hessey, 1818.
[———]. "Lord Byron." *Spirit of the Age*, 149–68.
Remarks (1824). *Works* 9: 233–45.
———. "The Merchant of Venice." *Characters* 269–77.
———. "The Modern Gradus ad Parnassum." *London Weekly Review*, 17 May 1828. *Works* 20: 157–62.
[———]. "Mr. Gifford." *Spirit of the Age* 251–74.
[———]. "Mr. Wordsworth." *Spirit of the Age* 187–206.
———. "On Effeminacy of Character." *Table-Talk*, 1822; *Works* 8: 248–55.
———. "On Great and Little Things." *Table-Talk*, 1821; *Works* 8: 226–42.
———. "On Living to One's-Self." *Table-Talk*, 1821–1822; *Works* 8: 90–100.
———. "On Shakespeare and Milton." *Lectures on the English Poets*. 86–134.
———. "On the Aristocracy of Letters." *Table-Talk; or, Original Essays*. 1821–22; *Works* 8: 205–14.
———. "On the Living Poets." *Lectures on the English Poets*. 283–331.
———. "On the Qualifications Necessary to Success in Life." *Baldwin's London Magazine,* June 1820. *Works* 12: 195–209.
———. Preface ("A Critical List of Authors Contained in this Volume"), *Select*

British Poets, or New Elegant Extracts from Chaucer to the Present Time, with Critical Remarks. 1824; *Works* 9: 233–45.

———. "Richard II." *Characters* 178–87.

[———] / W. H., "The Round Table." No. 7. *Examiner,* 12 Feb. 1815: 107–8.

[———.] *The Spirit of the Age; or, Contemporary Portraits.* 2/e; London: Henry Colburn, 1825.

[Heber, Reginald]. "Lord Byron's Dramas." *Quarterly Review* 27 (1822): 476–524. Attr. *BCH* 236.

Hemans, Felicia. *Felicia Hemans, Selected Poems, Letters, and Reception Materials.* Ed. Susan J. Wolfson. Princeton: Princeton UP, 2000.

———. *Poems of Felicia Hemans.* Edinburgh and London: William Blackwood and Sons, 1873.

———. *The Poetical Works of Mrs. Felicia Hemans.* London and Edinburgh: Gall and Inglis, 1876.

———. *The Poetical Works of Mrs. Hemans.* London: Frederick Warne, 1874.

———. *The Poetical Works of Mrs. Hemans.* Albion Edition. London: Frederick Warne, 1900.

———. *The Works of Mrs Hemans; with a Memoir by Her Sister.* 7 vols. Edinburgh: William Blackwood and Sons; London: Thomas Cadell, 1839.

Hewlett, Dorothy. *Adonais: A Life of John Keats.* London: Hurst and Blackett, 1937.

Hill, Alan G., ed. *Letters of Dorothy Wordsworth: A Selection.* Oxford: Clarendon P, 1985.

Hoeveler, Diane Long. *Romantic Androgyny: The Women Within.* University Park: Pennsylvania State UP, 1990.

Hofkosh, Sonia. *Sexual Politics and the Romantic Author.* Cambridge: Cambridge UP, 1998.

Hollander, John. *Melodious Guile: Fictive Pattern in Poetic Language.* New Haven: Yale UP, 1988.

Homans, Margaret. "Keats Reading Women, Women Reading Keats." *Studies in Romanticism* 29 (1990): 341–70.

———. *Women Writers and Poetic Identity: Dorothy Wordsworth, Emily Brontë, and Emily Dickinson.* Princeton: Princeton UP, 1980.

Honey, J. R. de S. *Tom Brown's Universe: The Development of the Victorian Public School.* London: Millington, 1977.

Hopkins, Gerard Manley. *Further Letters of Gerard Manley Hopkins.* Ed. Claude Colleer Abbott. London: Oxford UP, 1938.

Howard, Jean E. "Crossdressing, the Theatre, and Gender Struggle in Early Modern England." *Shakespeare Quarterly* 39 (1998): 418–40.

Howell, Margaret J. *Byron Tonight: A Poet's Plays on the Nineteenth-Century Stage.* Surrey, UK: Springwood, 1982.

Howitt, William. "Keats." *Homes and Haunts of the Most Eminent British Poets.* 2 vols. London: Richard Bentley, 1847. 1: 423–36.

[Hughes, Harriett Mary]. *Memoir of Mrs. Hemans.* Hemans, *Works* (1839) 1: 1–315.
Hunt, Leigh. *The Autobiography of Leigh Hunt with Reminiscences of Friends and Contemporaries.* 3 vols. London: Smith, Elder, 1850.
[———]. "Keats." *Gorton's Biographical Dictionary* 2: 241–2. Attr. *KC* 1: xcv.
———. "Keats." *Imagination and Fancy; or, Selections from the English Poets. Illustrative of those first requisites of their art; with markings of the best passages, critical notices of the writers, and an essay in answer to the question "What is Poetry?"* 1844; London: Smith, Elder, 1891. 283–315.
———. *Lord Byron and Some of His Contemporaries; With Recollections of the Author's Life, and of His Visit to Italy.* 2/e; 2 vols. London: Henry Colburn, 1828.
———. "Mr. Keats, with a Criticism on His Writings." *Lord Byron* 1: 407–50.
[———]. On Byron, *Don Juan, Cantos 1–2. Examiner* 618 (31 Oct. 1819): 700–701.
———. On Keats, *Lamia & c. Indicator* 44 (9 Aug. 1820): 345–52.
[———]. On Keats, *Poems. Examiner* 492 (1 June 1817): 345; 497–98 (6/13 July 1817): 428–29; 443–44.
———. *The Poetical Works of Leigh Hunt.* London: Edward Moxon, 1832.
———. *The Poetical Works of Leigh Hunt.* London: Ward, Lock, 1884.
———. "The Political Examiner. No. 258: Sentence Against the Examiner." *Examiner* 267 (7 Feb. 1813): 81–83.
[———]. "Porcupine Renewing His Old Quills; or, Remarks on Mr. Cobbett's Strange and Sudden Bristling Up Against Sir Francis Burdett." *Examiner* 510 (5 Aug. 1817): 625–27.
[———]. "Young Poets." *Examiner* 466 (1 Dec. 1816): 761–62.
Hunt, Lynn. *Politics, Culture, and Class in the French Revolution.* Berkeley: U California P, 1984.
[? Iley, Matthew]. *The Life, Writings, Opinions, and Times of the Right Hon. George Gordon Noel Byron, Lord Byron.* "By an English Gentleman, in the Greek Military Service, and Comrade of His Lordship." 3 vols. London: Matthew Iley, 1825. Attr. Chew, Lovell.
Irigaray, Luce. "Des Marchandises Entre Elles." 1975; tr. Catherine Porter and Carolyn Burke, "Commodities Among Themselves." *This Sex Which is Not One.* Ithaca: Cornell UP, 1985. 192–97.
———. "Le Marché des Femmes." 1978; trans. Porter and Burke, "Woman on the Market." *This Sex,* 170–91.
———. "Questions." *This Sex,* 119–69.
Jackson, H. J. "Coleridge's Women, or Girls, Girls, Girls Are Made to Love." *Studies in Romanticism* 32 (1993): 577–600.
Jacobus, Mary. *Reading Woman.* New York: Columbia UP, 1986.
Jameson, Mrs. [Anna]. *Characteristics of Women, Moral, Poetical, and Historical.* London: Saunders and Otley, 1832; 2/e, 1833. Revised as *Shakspeare's Heroines: Characteristics of Women, Moral, Poetical, and Historical.* London: George Bell and Sons, 1913.

———. *Memoirs of Celebrated Female Sovereigns.* 2 vols. London: Henry Colburn and Richard Bentley, 1831.

[Jeffrey, Francis]. *Edinburgh Review* 2 (July 1803): 269–86; on Baillie, *Plays* [. . .] *to delineate the Stronger Passions*, vol. 2 (1802).

[———] 5 (Jan. 1805): 405–21; on Baillie, *Miscellaneous Plays.*

[———] 12 (April 1808): 131–51; on Crabbe, 1807 *Poems.*

[———] 19 (Feb. 1812): 261–90; on Baillie, *Plays on the Passions,* vol. 3 (1812).

[———] 20 (Nov. 1812): 434–51; on Smith and Smith, *Rejected Addresses.*

[———] 23 (April 1814): 198–229; on Byron, *The Corsair* and *The Bride of Abydos.*

[———] 34 (Aug. 1820): 203–13; on Keats's *Lamia & c.*; attr., *KCH.*

[——— and William Hazlitt]. 36 (1822): 413–52. "Lord Byron's Tragedies."

[———] 40 (March 1824): 67–92; on Landor, *Imaginary Conversations.*

[———] 50 (Oct. 1829): 32–47; on Hemans, *Records of Woman* (2/e), *The Forest Sanctuary* (2/e).

[———]. 63 (April 1836): 73–101. "Dramas."

———. *Life of Lord Jeffrey with a Selection from his Correspondence.* By Lord Cockburn. 2 vols. Edinburgh: Adam and Charles Black, 1852.

Jewsbury, Maria Jane. *Lays of Leisure Hours.* London: J. Hatchard & Son, 1829.

———. Letters to Dora Wordsworth. Dove Cottage Archives, Grasmere, England.

———. *Letters to the Young.* London: J. Hatchard & Son, 1828.

———. *The Three Histories. The History of an Enthusiast. The History of a Nonchalant. The History of a Realist.* 1830. Boston: Perkins & Marvin, 1831.

———. "To My Own Heart." *Lays of Leisure Hours.*

[———]/M. J. J. "Arria; an Historical Sketch." *Literary Souvenir.* Ed. Alaric A. Watts. London: Longman &c, 1825. 330–33. Rpt. "Historical Sketches," *Phantasmagoria* 1: 122–24.

[———]/M. J. J. "A Farewell to the Muse." *Literary Souvenir; or, Cabinet of Poetry and Romance.* Ed. Alaric A. Watts. London: Hurst & Robinson, 1826. 379–80.

[———]/M. J. J. "First Efforts in Criticism." *Phantasmagoria* 1: 233–48.

[———]/M. J. J. *Phantasmagoria; or, Sketches of Life and Literature.* 2 vols. London: Hurst & Robinson; Edinburgh: Archibald Constable, 1825.

[———]/M. J. J. "Religious Novels." *Phantasmagoria* 1: 41–49.

[———]/M. J. J. "The Military Spectacle." *Literary Souvenir.* Ed. Alaric A. Watts. London: Longman &c, 1825. 243–48; rev. *Phantasmagoria.* 2: 103–9.

[———]/M. J. J. "The Young Author." *Phantasmagoria* 1: 189–98. First pub. *Literary Souvenir* (1825), 85–93.

[———]/M. J. J. "To a Poet's Infant Child." *Literary Souvenir.* London: Hurst & Robinson, 1826. 78–80.

[———]. Contributions to *The Athenæum* 1830–31 are identified in a file, reported by Fryckstedt 470–73, 65–70; reviews of 1831 are identified by City University Contributor Record (http://www.soi.city.ac.uk). For 1832, I concur with Norma Clarke's guesses [?] "on the basis of subject matter and style" (229–30n40).

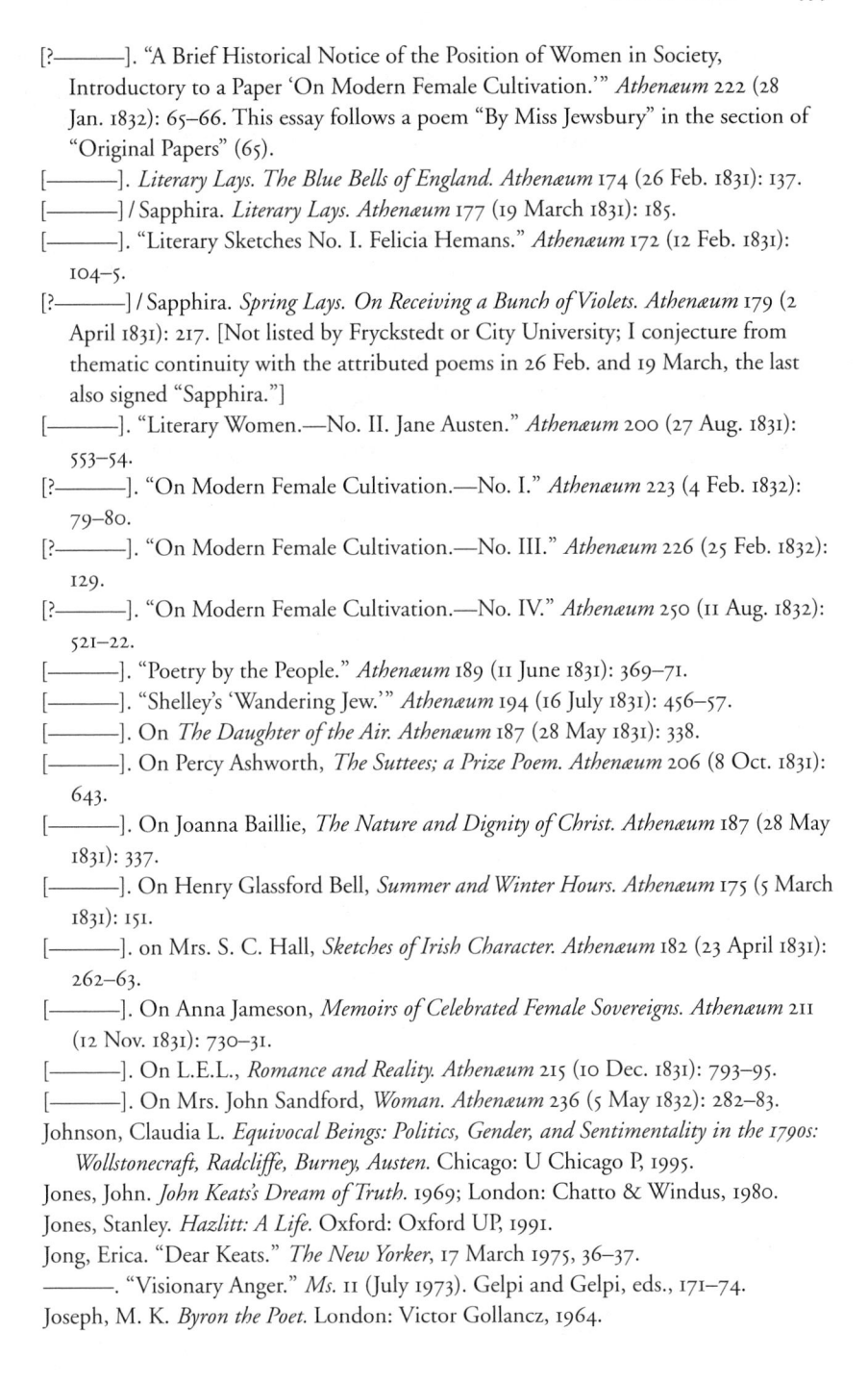

[?———]. "A Brief Historical Notice of the Position of Women in Society, Introductory to a Paper 'On Modern Female Cultivation.'" *Athenæum* 222 (28 Jan. 1832): 65–66. This essay follows a poem "By Miss Jewsbury" in the section of "Original Papers" (65).

[———]. *Literary Lays. The Blue Bells of England. Athenæum* 174 (26 Feb. 1831): 137.

[———] / Sapphira. *Literary Lays. Athenæum* 177 (19 March 1831): 185.

[———]. "Literary Sketches No. I. Felicia Hemans." *Athenæum* 172 (12 Feb. 1831): 104–5.

[?———] / Sapphira. *Spring Lays. On Receiving a Bunch of Violets. Athenæum* 179 (2 April 1831): 217. [Not listed by Fryckstedt or City University; I conjecture from thematic continuity with the attributed poems in 26 Feb. and 19 March, the last also signed "Sapphira."]

[———]. "Literary Women.—No. II. Jane Austen." *Athenæum* 200 (27 Aug. 1831): 553–54.

[?———]. "On Modern Female Cultivation.—No. I." *Athenæum* 223 (4 Feb. 1832): 79–80.

[?———]. "On Modern Female Cultivation.—No. III." *Athenæum* 226 (25 Feb. 1832): 129.

[?———]. "On Modern Female Cultivation.—No. IV." *Athenæum* 250 (11 Aug. 1832): 521–22.

[———]. "Poetry by the People." *Athenæum* 189 (11 June 1831): 369–71.

[———]. "Shelley's 'Wandering Jew.'" *Athenæum* 194 (16 July 1831): 456–57.

[———]. On *The Daughter of the Air. Athenæum* 187 (28 May 1831): 338.

[———]. On Percy Ashworth, *The Suttees; a Prize Poem. Athenæum* 206 (8 Oct. 1831): 643.

[———]. On Joanna Baillie, *The Nature and Dignity of Christ. Athenæum* 187 (28 May 1831): 337.

[———]. On Henry Glassford Bell, *Summer and Winter Hours. Athenæum* 175 (5 March 1831): 151.

[———]. on Mrs. S. C. Hall, *Sketches of Irish Character. Athenæum* 182 (23 April 1831): 262–63.

[———]. On Anna Jameson, *Memoirs of Celebrated Female Sovereigns. Athenæum* 211 (12 Nov. 1831): 730–31.

[———]. On L.E.L., *Romance and Reality. Athenæum* 215 (10 Dec. 1831): 793–95.

[———]. On Mrs. John Sandford, *Woman. Athenæum* 236 (5 May 1832): 282–83.

Johnson, Claudia L. *Equivocal Beings: Politics, Gender, and Sentimentality in the 1790s: Wollstonecraft, Radcliffe, Burney, Austen.* Chicago: U Chicago P, 1995.

Jones, John. *John Keats's Dream of Truth.* 1969; London: Chatto & Windus, 1980.

Jones, Stanley. *Hazlitt: A Life.* Oxford: Oxford UP, 1991.

Jong, Erica. "Dear Keats." *The New Yorker,* 17 March 1975, 36–37.

———. "Visionary Anger." *Ms.* 11 (July 1973). Gelpi and Gelpi, eds., 171–74.

Joseph, M. K. *Byron the Poet.* London: Victor Gollancz, 1964.

Kadish, Doris Y. *Politicizing Gender: Narrative Strategies in the Aftermath of the French Revolution.* New Brunswick: Rutgers UP, 1991.

Kaplan, Cora. "Pandora's Box: Subjectivity, Class, and Sexuality in Socialist Feminist Criticism." *Making a Difference: Feminist Literary Criticism.* Ed. Gayle Greene and Coppélia Kahn. London: Methuen, 1985. 146–76.

———. *Salt and Bitter and Good: Three Centuries of English and American Women Poets.* New York and London: Paddington, 1973.

Keach, William. *Arbitrary Power: Romanticism, Language, Politics.* Princeton: Princeton UP, 2004.

———. "Obstinate Questionings: The Immortality Ode and *Alastor*." *The Wordsworth Circle* 12 (1981): 36–44.

———. "A Regency Prophecy and the End of Anna Barbauld's Career." *Studies in Romanticism* 33 (1994): 569–77.

———. "Romanticism and Language." *The Cambridge Companion to British Romanticism.* Ed. Stuart Curran. Cambridge: Cambridge UP, 1993. 95–119.

Keats, John. *John Keats.* Ed. Elizabeth Cook. New York: Oxford UP, 1990.

———. / The Late John Keats. "On a Picture of Leander." *The Gem: A Literary Annual.* Ed. Thomas Hood. London: W. Marshall, 1829. 108.

———. "Stanzas" ("In drear-nighted December"). *The Gem: A Literary Annual.* [Ed. Thomas Hood.] London: W. Marshall, 1830. 80.

———. *The Letters of John Keats.* Ed. Hyder E. Rollins, 2 vols. Cambridge: Harvard UP, 1958.

———. *The Poems of John Keats.* Ed. Jack Stillinger. Cambridge: Harvard UP, 1978.

The Keats Circle. Ed. Hyder E. Rollins. 2 vols. Cambridge: Harvard UP, 1948.

Keats: The Critical Heritage. See Matthews.

The Keepsake for MDCCCXXIX. Ed. Frederic Mansel Reynolds. London: Hurst, Chance, 1829.

Kelsall, Malcolm. "Byron and the Women of the Harem." Levine and Keane, eds., 165–73.

———. "The Slave-Woman in the Harem." *Studies in Romanticism* 31 (1992): 315–31.

Kern, Robert. "Keats and the Problem of Romance." *Philological Quarterly* 58 (1979): 171–91.

Kernberger, Katherine. "Power and Sex: The Implication of Role Reversal in Catherine's Russia." *Byron Journal* 8 (1980): 42–49.

Kingsley, Charles. "Alexander Smith and Alexander Pope." *Fraser's Magazine* 48 (Oct. 1853): 452–66.

———. "Thoughts on Shelley and Byron." *Fraser's Magazine* 48 (Nov. 1853): 568–76.

Knight, G. Wilson. *Lord Byron's Marriage: The Evidence of the Asterisks.* London: Routledge and Kegan Paul, 1957.

———. "The Two Eternities: An Essay on Byron." *The Burning Oracle: Studies in the Poetry of Action.* London: Oxford UP, 1939. 199–288.

Knoepflmacher, U. C. "Genre and the Integration of Gender: From Wordsworth to

George Eliot to Virginia Woolf." *Victorian Literature and Society: Essays Presented to Richard D. Altick.* Ed. James R. Kincaid and Albert J. Kuhn. Columbus: Ohio State UP, 1984. 94–118.

Kucich, Greg. "Cockney Chivalry: Hunt, Keats, and the Aesthetics of Excess." *Leigh Hunt: Life, Poetics, Politics.* Ed. Nicholas Roe. Routledge, 2003. 118–34.

———. "Gendering the Canons of Romanticism: Past and Present." *The Wordsworth Circle* 27 (1995): 95–102.

———. "Mary Shelley's *Lives* and the Reengendering of History." *Mary Shelley in Her Times.* Ed. Betty T. Bennett and Stuart Curran. Baltimore: Johns Hopkins UP, 2000. 198–213.

The Ladies' Companion. August 1837. 186–87.

[Lamb, Caroline]. *A New Canto.* London: William Wright, 1819.

Landon, Laetitia Elizabeth. "On the Character of Mrs. Hemans's Writings." *New Monthly Magazine* 44 (Aug. 1835): 425–33.

———. "Stanzas on the Death of Mrs. Hemans." *New Monthly Magazine* 44, Part 2 (1835): 286–88.

Lang, Cecil. "Narcissus Jilted: Byron, *Don Juan*, and the Biographical Imperative." *Historical Studies and Literary Criticism.* Ed. Jerome J. McGann. Madison: U Wisconsin P, 1985. 143–79.

Lansdown, Richard. *Byron's Historical Dramas.* Oxford: Clarendon P, 1992.

Lawrence, Mrs. [Rose D'Aguilar]. *Recollections of Mrs. Hemans. The Last Autumn at a Favourite Residence, with other Poems.* Liverpool: G. and J. Robinson &c.; London: John Murray, 1836. 287–419.

Leighton, Angela. *Victorian Women Poets: Writing Against the Heart.* New York: Wheatsheaf / Harvester, 1992.

——— and Margaret Reynolds, eds. *Victorian Women Poets: An Anthology.* Oxford: Basil Blackwell, 1995.

Lemprière, J. *A Classical Dictionary.* 1788; 8/e; London: T. Cadell and W. Davies, 1812. Fifth American Edition, Corrected and Improved by Charles Anthon. New York: Evert Duyckinck &c, 1825.

Levine, Alice and Robert N. Keane, eds. *Rereading Byron: Essays Selected from Hofstra University's Byron Bicentennial Conference.* New York: Garland, 1993.

Levine, Laura. "Men in Women's Clothing: Anti-Theatricality and Effeminization from 1579 to 1642." *Criticism* 28 (1986): 121–44.

Levinson, Marjorie. *Keats's Life of Allegory: The Origins of a Style.* London: Basil Blackwell, 1988.

Levy, Darline Gay, Harriet Branson Applewhite, and Mary Durham Johnson, eds. *Women in Revolutionary Paris, 1789–95.* Urbana: U Illinois P, 1979.

Lewes, George Henry. "Charles Kean and Sardanapalus." *The Leader*, 25 July 1853. *Dramatic Essays by John Forster and George Henry Lewes.* Ed. William Archer and Robert W. Lowe. London: Walter Scott, 1896. 250–52.

[———]. "The Novels of Jane Austen." *Blackwood's Edinburgh Magazine* 86 (July 1859): 99–113.

[———] / G.H.L. On P. Shelley, *Poetical Works* (1839); *Letters and Essays from Abroad* (1840); *Die Cenci* (Germany; 1838); *Adone* (Italy; 1830). *Westminster Review* 35 (1841): 303–44.

Lindsay, Jack. "The Metrics of William Blake." POETICAL SKETCHES *by William Blake*. London: Scholartis P, 1927. 1–20.

Linkin, Harriet Kramer. "The Current Canon in British Romantics Studies." *College English* 53 (1991): 548–70.

Literary Chronicle and Weekly Review 133 (1 Dec. 1821): 751–54; on Shelley, *Adonais*.

——— 336 (22 Oct. 1825): 673–76; on Jewsbury, *Phantasmagoria*.

Literary Gazette (8 Dec. 1821): 772–73. "Adonais."

——— (22 and 29 Oct. 1825): 673 and 692; on M. J. J., *Phantasmagoria*.

——— (24 April 1830): 271; on Jewsbury, *The Three Histories*.

Literary Magnet of Belles Lettres, Science, and the Fine Arts 4. London: Wrightman & Cramp, 1826.

Literary Souvenir; or, Cabinet of Poetry and Romance. Ed. Alaric A. Watts. London: Hurst, Robinson, 1825, 1826; London: Longman &c , 1827, 1829.

London Chronicle, 4–6 May, 1775, 429. "Remarks *on the* Pictures *in the* Exhibition *of the* Royal Academy . . . *Despair of Achilles on being informed by Antilochus of the Death of Patroclus. Iliad, Book* 18*th:* By Angelica Kauffman, R.A."

London Magazine and Monthly Critical and Dramatic Review (Gold's) 2 (Aug. 1820). On Keats, *Lamia& c. KCH* 181–201.

London Magazine 2d ser. 10 (Dec. 1827): 541–52. "Hindoo Widows."

London Review 8 (1864): 329. "Literary Women." Rpt. *Littell's Living Age* 81 (1864): 609–10.

London Weekly Review: A Miscellany of English and Foreign Literature, Science, and the Fine Arts 1.7 (27 Nov. 1839): 107–8; on P. Shelley's *Poetical Works* (1839).

Longman Anthology of British Literature. Gen. ed., David Damrosch. Vol. 2a *The Romantics and Their Contemporaries,* ed. Susan J. Wolfson and Peter J. Manning. New York: Longman, 1998, 2003, 2006.

Lootens, Tricia. "Hemans and Home: Victorianism, "Feminine 'Internal Enemies,' and the Domestication of National Identity." *PMLA* 109 (1994): 238–53.

Lovell, Ernest J. Jr., ed. *Byron: The Record of a Quest*. 1949; Hamden, CT: Archon, 1966.

———. *His Very Self and Voice: Collected Conversations of Lord Byron*. New York: Macmillan, 1954.

Low, Dennis. "Maria Jane Jewsbury." *Four Literary Protégées of the Lake Poets: Caroline Bowles, Maria Gowen Brooks, Sara Coleridge, and Maria Jane Jewsbury*. University of Hull, 2003.

Lowell, Amy. *John Keats*. 2 vols. Cambridge: Riverside P, 1925.

Lowell, James Russell. "Keats." 1854; *The Writings of James Russell Lowell.* 11 vols. Boston: Houghton Mifflin, 1897. 1: 218–47.

Lydgate, John. *Fall of Princes.* Ed. Henry Bergen. 4 vols. Early English Text Society, 1924; London: Oxford UP, 1967.

Mabie, Hamilton Wright. "John Keats: Poet and Man." *Essays in Literary Interpretation.* New York: Dodd, Mead, 1892. 138–74.

Macaulay, Catharine (Graham). *Letters on Education, With Observations on Religious and Metaphysical Subjects.* London: C. Dilly, 1790.

MacGillivray, J. R. *Keats: A Bibliography and Reference Guide with an Essay on Keats' Reputation.* Toronto: U of Toronto P, 1949.

Mackenzie, Henry. *The Man of Feeling.* 1771; ed. Brian Vickers. London: Oxford UP, 1967.

Maitland, Frederick William. *The Life and Letters of Leslie Stephen.* New York: G. P. Putnam's Sons, 1906.

Manning, Peter J. *Byron and His Fictions.* Detroit: Wayne State UP, 1978.

———. "The Hone-ing of Byron's *Corsair.*" 1985; *Reading* 216–37.

———. "The Nameless Broken Dandy and the Structure of Authorship." *Reading* 145–62.

———. *Reading Romantics: Texts and Contexts.* New York: Oxford UP, 1990.

———. "Reading and Ravishing: The 'Ode on a Grecian Urn.'" Evert and Rhodes, 131–36.

———. "Tales and Politics: *The Corsair, Lara,* and *The White Doe of Rylstone.*" 1980; *Reading* 195–215.

Marchand, Leslie A. *The Athenaeum: A Mirror of Victorian Culture.* 1941; New York: Octagon, 1971.

———. *Byron: A Biography.* 3 vols. New York: Knopf, 1957.

———. *Byron's Poetry: A Critical Introduction.* Cambridge: Harvard UP, 1968.

———, ed. *Don Juan by Lord Byron.* Boston: Houghton Mifflin, 1958.

Marquess, William Henry. *Lives of the Poet: The First Century of Keats Biography.* University Park: Pennsylvania State UP, 1985.

Masson, David. "The Life and Poetry of Keats." *Macmillan's Magazine* 3 (Nov. 1860): 1–16.

———. "The Life and Poetry of Shelley." *Macmillan's Magazine* 2 (Sept. 1860): 338–50.

[Mathew, George Felton] / G. F. M. On Keats, *Poems* (1817). *European Magazine and London Review* 71 (May 1817): 434–37.

Matthews, G. M., ed. *Keats: The Critical Heritage.* New York: Barnes and Noble, 1971.

McClary, Ben Harris. "Introduction." Silliman, *Letters.* v–xxii.

McCluskie, Kathleen. *Renaissance Dramatists.* Atlantic Highlands, NJ: Humanities P, 1989.

McGann, Jerome J. "The Book of Byron and the Book of a World." 1982–83; *The*

Beauty of Inflections: Literary Investigations in Historical Method & Theory. Oxford: Clarendon P, 1988. 255–93.

———. *Byron and Romanticism.* Ed. James Soderholm. Cambridge: Cambridge UP, 2002.

———. "Byron, Mobility, and the Poetics of Historical Ventriloquism." 1985; *Byron and Romanticism* 36–52.

———. *Fiery Dust: Byron's Poetic Development.* Chicago: U Chicago P, 1968.

———. "Hero with a Thousand Faces: The Rhetoric of Byronism." 1992; *Byron and Romanticism* 141–59.

———. *The Romantic Ideology: A Critical Investigation.* Chicago: U Chicago P, 1983.

[———]. Anne Mack, J. J. Rome, and Georg Mannejc. "Literary History, Romanticism, and Felicia Hemans." *Modern Language Quarterly* 54.2 (June 1993): 215–35.

Medwin, Thomas. *Conversations of Lord Byron: Noted During a Residence with His Lordship at Pisa, in the Years 1821 and 1822.* London: Henry Colburn, 1824.

———. *Medwin's Conversations of Lord Byron.* Rev. 3/e, annotated by contemporaries, ed. Ernest J. Lovell, Jr. Princeton: Princeton UP, 1966. Cited as *MCB.*

[———]. *Memoir of Shelley. Athenæum* 246 (21 July 1832): 472–4.

Meiners, Christoph. *History of the Female Sex.* 4 vols. London, 1808.

Mellor, Anne K. "Blake's Portrayal of Women." *Blake: An Illustrated Quarterly* 16 (1982–83): 148–55.

———. "A Criticism of Their Own: Romantic Women Literary Critics." *Questioning Romanticism.* Ed. John Beer. Baltimore: Johns Hopkins UP, 1995. 29–48.

———. *English Romantic Irony.* Cambridge: Harvard UP, 1980.

———. "The Female Poet and the Poetess: Two Traditions of British Women's Poetry, 1780–1830." *Studies in Romanticism* 36 (1997): 261–76.

———. *Mary Shelley: Her Life, Her Fiction, Her Monsters.* New York: Methuen, 1988.

———. *Mothers of the Nation: Women's Political Writing in England, 1780–1830.* Bloomington: Indiana UP, 2000.

———. "On Romanticism and Feminism." *Romanticism and Feminism* 3–9.

———. *Romanticism & Gender.* New York: Routledge, 1992.

———, ed. *Romanticism and Feminism.* Bloomington: Indiana UP, 1988.

——— and Richard Matlak, eds. *British Literature, 1780–1830.* Fort Worth: Harcourt Brace, 1996.

Milnes, Richard Monckton (Lord Houghton). *Life, Letters, and Literary Remains, of John Keats.* 2 vols. London: Edward Moxon, 1848.

Milton, John. *Complete Poems and Major Prose.* Ed. Merritt Y. Hughes. New York: Odyssey, 1957.

Moers, Ellen. *The Dandy: Brummell to Beerbohm.* London: Secker & Warburg, 1960.

———. *Literary Women: The Great Writers.* 1963; Garden City, NY: Anchor/Doubleday, 1977.

Moi, Toril. *Sexual/Textual Politics: Feminist Literary Theory.* London: Methuen, 1985.

Montagu, Lady Mary Wortley. *The Complete Letters of Lady Mary Wortley Montagu*. Ed. Robert Halsband. 3 vols. Oxford: Clarendon P, 1965–67.

Monthly Magazine 43 (April 1817): 248. Notice of Keats, *Poems*.

Monthly Magazine, and British Register 1 (April 1796): 181–84. "The Enquirer No. III. Question: 'Are Literary and Scientific Pursuits Suited to the Female Character?'"

———— 2 (Oct. 1796): 706–9; "The Enquirer No. IX. Question: 'Ought Sensibility to Be Cherished, or Repressed?'"

Monthly Review ns 8 (1792): 198–209; on Wollstonecraft, *Rights of Woman*.

Monthly Review 108 (1825): 134–35; on M.J. J., *Phantasmagoria*.

Moore, Doris Langley. "Byronic Dress." *Costume* 5 (1971): 1–13.

Moore, Thomas. *Letters and Journals of Lord Byron: With Notices of His Life*. 2 vols. London: John Murray, 1830. 2/e; *The Works of Lord Byron: With His Letters and Journals, and His Life*. 17 vols. London: John Murray, 1832–34.

More, Hannah. *The Bas Bleu; or, Conversation*. 1786; *Works* (1835) 5: 314–27.

————. *Essays on Various Subjects Principally Designed for Young Ladies*. 1777; *Works* (1835) 6: 257–358.

————. "On Dissipation." *Essays* 267–75.

————. "On the Importance of Religion to the Female Character." *Essays* 333–41.

————. *Strictures on the Modern System of Female Education*. 1799; *The Works of Hannah More*. 11 vols. London: T. Cadell, 1830. Vol. 5.

————. "Thoughts on the Cultivation of the Heart and Temper in the Education of Daughters." *Essays* 317–31.

————. *The Works of Hannah More*. 6 vols. London: H. Fisher, R. Fisher, and P. Jackson, 1835.

Morely, Edith J., ed. *Henry Crabb Robinson on Books and Their Writers*. 3 vols. London: J. M. Dent, 1938.

Morgan, Thaïs E. "Mixed Metaphor and Mixed Genre: Swinburne and the Victorian Critics." Paper delivered at the MLA Convention, 1986, session 694.

Mulvey, Laura. "Visual Pleasure and Narrative Cinema." *Screen* 16 (1975). *Feminisms: An Anthology of Literary Theory and Criticism*. Ed. Robyn R. Warhol and Diane Price Herndl. New Brunswick: Rutgers UP, 1991. 432–42.

Myers, Sylvia Harcstark. *The Bluestocking Circle: Women, Friendship, and the Life of the Mind in Eighteenth-Century England*. Oxford: Clarendon P, 1990.

Najarian, James. *Victorian Keats: Manliness, Sexuality, and Desire*. New York: Palgrave, 2002.

National Review 9 (Oct. 1859): 370–90. [?Bagehot], "Tennyson's Idylls." Attri. *KCH* 355.

New Monthly Magazine 14 (Sept. 1820): 306. "Modern Periodical Literature."

———— 15 (Oct. 1820): 547; on M. J. J., *Phantasmagoria*.

———— 30 (May 1830): 233; on Jewsbury, *The Three Histories*.

———— 81: 23 (1847): 288–94. "A Graybeard's Gossip About His Literary Acquaintance. No. IX."

Nemoianu, Virgil. "Literary Canons and Social Value Options." *The Hospitable*

Canon: Essays on Literary Play, Scholarly Choice, and Popular Pressures. Ed. Virgil Nemoianu and Robert Royal. Philadelphia: John Benjamins, 1991. 215–47.

Newsome, David. *Godliness and Good Learning: Four Studies in a Victorian Ideal.* London: John Murray, 1961.

Nicholson, Andrew, ed. *The Manuscripts of the Younger Romantics. Lord Byron, vol. IX: Don Juan, Cantos X, XI, XII and XVII.* New York: Garland, 1993.

———. *The Manuscripts of the Younger Romantics. Lord Byron, vol. XII: Poems 1807–1824 and Beppo.* New York: Garland, 1998.

Nicholson, Francis. "Correspondence Between Mrs. Hemans and Matthew Nicholson." *Memoirs and Proceedings of the Manchester Literary and Philosophical Society* 54.9 (1910): 1–40.

Norton Anthology of English Literature. "The Romantic Period." Ed. M. H. Abrams and Jack Stillinger. Vol. 2. 6/e; New York: Norton, 1993; 7/e, 2000; 8/e (ed. Jack Stillinger and Deirdre Shauna Lynch) 2006.

Nurmi, Martin K. "The Prompt Copy of Charles Kean's 1838 Production of Byron's *Sardanapalus*." *The Serif* (June 1968): 3–13.

Odell, George Clinton Densmore. *Annals of the New York Stage.* 15 vols. New York: Columbia UP, 1927–49.

Oliphant, Mrs. [Margaret]. "John Keats." *The Literary History of England in the End of the Eighteenth and Beginning of the Nineteenth Century.* 3 vols. London: Macmillan, 1882. 3: 133–55.

Osgood, Charles G., ed. *Boswell's LIFE OF JOHNSON.* New York: Charles Scribner's Sons, 1917.

Ostriker, Alicia. "Desire Gratified and Ungratified: William Blake and Sexuality." *Blake: An Illustrated Quarterly* 16 (1982–83): 156–65.

Ovid. *Metamorphoses.* Tr. Frank Justus Miller. 2 vols. 1916; Cambridge: Harvard UP, 1976.

Owen, F[rances]. M[ary]. *John Keats: A Study.* London: C. Kegan Paul, 1880.

Oxford Book of English Verse. Ed. Arthur Quiller-Couch. Oxford: Clarendon P, 1906.

Oxford English Dictionary. London: Oxford UP, 1971.

Paine, Thomas. *The Rights of Man* (1791–93). *Two Classics of the French Revolution.* New York: Anchor, 1973. 267–515.

Paley, Morton D. *The Apocalyptic Sublime.* New Haven: Yale UP, 1986.

Parson, Donald. *Portraits of Keats.* Cleveland: World, 1954.

Patmore, Coventry. "Arthur Hugh Clough." *Principle* 86–90.

———. "Keats." (on Colvin's *Keats*). *St. James Gazette* 2 July 1887. *Principle* 60–65.

———. "Mrs. Meynell." *Principle* 118–28.

———. *Principle in Art, Religio Poetæ, and Other Essays.* London: Duckworth, 1889.

———. "What Shelley Was." *Principle* 66–73.

Perkins, David, ed. *English Romantic Writers.* 2/e; Fort Worth: Harcourt Brace, 1995.

Perl, Teri. "The Ladies Diary of *Woman's Almanack*, 1704–1841." *Historia Mathematica* 6 (1979): 36–53.

Perry, Ruth. *The Celebrated Mary Astell: An Early English Feminist.* Chicago: U Chicago P, 1986.
Pocket Magazine of Classic and Polite Literature 1 (4 April 1821): 333–38. J. W. Dalby, "Remarks on Keats."
Pollak, Ellen. *The Poetics of Sexual Myth: Gender and Ideology in the Verse of Swift and Pope.* Chicago: U of Chicago P, 1985.
[Polwhele, Richard]. *The Unsex'd Females, A Poem. Addressed to the Author of* THE PURSUITS OF LITERATURE. London: T. Cadell and W. Davies, 1798.
Poovey, Mary. *The Proper Lady and the Woman Writer: Ideology as Style in the Works of Mary Wollstonecraft, Mary Shelley, and Jane Austen.* Chicago: U Chicago P, 1984.
Pope, Alexander. *Epistle from Mr. Pope to Dr. Arbuthnot.* 1735; *Poems* 2 (ed. John Butt): 91–127.
———. *Poems of Alexander Pope.* Ed. John Butt. 6 vols. New Haven: Yale UP, 1961.
———. *To a Lady, Of the Characters of Women.* 1735; *Poems* 3 (2/e, ed. F. W. Bateson): 39–74.
Poston, Carol H., ed. *Mary Wollstonecraft, A Vindication of the Rights of Woman.* 2/e; New York: Norton, 1988.
Pratt, Willis W. "Notes on the Variorum Edition." Steffan and Pratt. Vol. 4.
Priestly, J. B. *The Prince of Pleasure and His Regency, 1811–20.* New York: Harper and Row, 1969.
Priestley, Joseph. *Letters to the Right Honourable Edmund Burke, Occasioned by his Reflections on the Revolution in France, &c.* Birmingham: Thomas Pearson, 1791.
Quarterly Review 7 (June 1812): 309–13. [John Wilson Croker], on A. L. Barbauld's *Eighteen Hundred and Eleven: A Poem.*
——— 18 (1817–18): 379–85. [Croker], on [M. Shelley], *Frankenstein.*
——— 19 (April 1818; pub. Sept.). [Croker], on Keats, *Endymion.*
——— 24 (Oct. 1820): 130–39. [William Gifford], on Hemans.
——— 27 (July 1822): 476–524. [Reginald Heber], "Lord Byron's Dramas." Pub. Oct. (*RR* B 5: 2057).
——— 67 (1841): 437–52; on Joanna Baillie, *Fugitive Verses.*
Queens of Literature of the Victorian Era. [Eva Hope]. London: Walter Scott, 1886. "Felicia Hemans: The Poet of Womanhood." 261–301.
Rackin, Phyllis. "Androgyny, Mimesis, and the Marriage of the Boy Heroine on the English Renaissance Stage." *PMLA* 102 (1987): 29–41.
Radcliffe, Mary Anne. *The Female Advocate; or, An Attempt to Recover the Rights of Women from Male Usurpation.* London: Vernor and Hood, 1799.
Rajan, Tilottama. *Dark Interpreter: The Discourse of Romanticism.* Ithaca: Cornell UP, 1980.
Redpath, Theodore. *The Young Romantics and Critical Opinion, 1807–1824: Poetry of Byron, Shelley, and Keats as Seen by Their Contemporary Critics.* New York: St. Martin's P, 1973.
R[eeve], C[lara]. *The Progress of Romance, Through Times, Countries, and Manners;*

with Remarks on the Good and Bad Effects of It, on Them Respectively; in a Course of Evening Conversations. 2 vols. Colchester: W. Keymer; London: J. & J. Robinson, 1785.

Reid, T. Wemyss. *The Life, Letters, and Friendships of Richard Monckton Milnes, First Lord Houghton*. 3/e; 2 vols. London: Cassell, 1891.

Reiman, Donald H., ed. *The Romantics Reviewed: Contemporary Reviews of British Romantic Writers*. New York: Garland, 1972. Part B: *Byron and Regency Society Poets*. Part C: *Shelley, Keats, and London Radical Writers*.

Reynolds, John Hamilton. *The Letters of John Hamilton Reynolds*. Ed. Leonidas M. Jones Lincoln: U of Nebraska P, 1973.

[―――]. On Keats, *Poems. Champion* 9 (March 1817): 78. Attr. *KCH* 45.

[―――]. On Keats, *Endymion. The Alfred, West of England Journal and General Advertiser* 6 Oct. 1818. Rpt. *Examiner* 12 Oct. 1818: 648–49. Attr. Keats; *KL* 1: 393.

Reynolds, Margaret. "Maria Jane Jewsbury." Leighton and Reynolds, eds. 25–29.

Rich, Adrienne. "Three Conversations." *Adrienne Rich's Poetry: Texts of the Poems, the Poet on Her Work, Reviews, and Criticism*. Ed. Barbara Charlesworth Gelpi and Albert Gelpi. New York: Norton, 1975. 105–22.

Richardson, Alan. "Escape from the Seraglio: Cultural Transvestism in *Don Juan*." Levine and Keane, eds. 175–85.

―――. "Romanticism and the Colonization of the Feminine." Mellor, ed. 13–25.

Ricks, Christopher. *Keats and Embarrassment*. London: Oxford UP, 1976.

Ridenour, George M. *The Style of Don Juan*. New Haven: Yale UP, 1960.

Riviere, Joan. "Womanliness as a Masquerade." *International Journal of Psychoanalysis* 10 (1929). *Formations of Fantasy*. Ed. Victor Burgin, James Donald, Cora Kaplan. London: Methuen, 1986. 35–44.

[Roberts, William]. See *British Review*.

Robinson, A[gnes] Mary F. "Felicia Hemans." Ward 4: 334–35.

Robinson, Henry Crabb. See Morley, Edith J.

[Robinson, Mary] / Anne Frances Randall. *A Letter to the Women of England, on the Injustice of Mental Subordination*. London: Longman and Reese, 1799.

Roe, Nicholas. "Keats's Lisping Sedition." *Essays in Criticism* 42 (1992): 36–55.

Roland, Citizenness [de la Platière, Jeanne Manon (Philipon)]. *An appeal to impartial posterity, by Citizenness Roland* (London: J. Johnson, 1795). Translation of *Appel a L'impartiale Postérité, Par La Citoyenne Roland* (Paris: Chez Louvet, 26 germinal, an 3e de la République [9 April, 1795]).

Romantic Women Writers: Voices and Counter-Voices. Ed. Paula Feldman and Theresa M. Kelley. Hanover, NH: UP of New England, 1995.

Ross, Marlon B. "Beyond the Fragmented Word: Keats and the Limits of Patrilineal Language." *Out of Bounds: Male Writers and Gender(ed) Criticism*. Ed. Laura Claridge and Elizabeth Langland. Amherst: U Massachusetts P, 1990. 110–31.

―――. *The Contours of Masculine Desire: Romanticism and the Rise of Women's Poetry*. New York: Oxford UP, 1989.

———. "Romantic Quest and Conquest: Troping Masculine Power in the Crisis of Poetic Identity." Mellor, ed. 26–51.

Rossetti, Dante Gabriel. *The Letters of Dante Gabriel Rossetti*. Ed. Oswald Doughty and John Robert Wahl. 4 vols. Oxford: Clarendon, 1965–67.

Rossetti, William Michael. "Biographical Sketch." *Poems of John Keats*. New York: Cooperative Publication Society, 1872. vii–xix.

———. "Critical Memoir." 1873; rpt. "Prefatory Notice," *The Poetical Works of Mrs. Hemans*. New York: Thomas Y. Crowell / Philadelphia: J. B. Lippincott, 1881. 11–24.

———. *Life of John Keats*. London: Walter Scott, 1887.

———. "Memoir of Shelley." *The Poetical Works of Percy Bysshe Shelley*. 2 vols. London: E. Moxon, 1870. 1: xxvix–clxxix.

———, ed. *Shelley / Adonais*. Oxford: Clarendon P, 1891.

Rousseau, Jean Jacques. *Émile ou de l'Education*. Trans. Barbara Foxley. London: J. M. Dent; New York: E. P. Dutton, 1911.

Rowton, Frederic. *The Female Poets of Great Britain, Chronologically Arranged: With Copious Selections and Critical Remarks*. London: Longman &c., 1848.

Runge, Laura L. *Gender and Language in British Literary Criticism, 1660–1790*. Cambridge: Cambridge UP, 1997.

Ruskin, John. *The Complete Works of John Ruskin*. Ed. E. T. Cook and Alexander Wedderburn. 39 vols. London: George Allen, 1904.

———. "Of Queens' Gardens." *Sesame and Lilies: Two Lectures Delivered at Manchester in 1864*. 1865; rev. 1871; London: Oxford UP, 1936. 84–123.

———. "Pre-Raphaelitism." 1851; *Works* 12: 338–93.

Rutherford, Andrew. *Byron: A Critical Study*. Stanford: Stanford UP, 1961.

———, ed. *Byron: The Critical Heritage*. New York: Barnes and Noble, 1970.

Saintsbury, George. *A History of Nineteenth-Century Literature (1780–1895)*. London: Macmillan, 1896.

Sales, Roger. *English Literature in History, 1780–1830: Pastoral and Politics*. New York: St. Martin's P, 1983.

Sandford [Elizabeth], Mrs. John. *Woman, In Her Social and Domestic Character*. 1831; 2/e London: Longman, 1832.

The Satirist, or Monthly Meteor 14 (April 1814): 327–31. Review of Leigh Hunt, *The Feast of the Poets*.

Savage, Anne. "Kaled." *Heath's Book of Beauty for 1847*. Ed. Countess of Blessington. London: Longman, Brown, Green, and Longman's, 1847. 203–8.

Schama, Simon. *Citizens: A Chronicle of the French Revolution*. New York: Knopf, 1989.

Schwartz, Lewis M. *Keats Reviewed by His Contemporaries: A Collection of Notices for the Years 1816–1821*. Metuchen, NJ: Scarecrow P, 1973.

Scots Edinburgh Magazine, and Literary Miscellany 2d ser. 1 (Oct. 1817): 255–57; on Keats's *Poems*.

——— 7 (Aug. 1820): 107–10. "Remarks on Keats's Poems."

——— 7 (Oct. 1820): 313–16. "Continuation of Remarks on the Poetry of Keats."

——— 10 (Jan. 1822) 102–14; on Byron's *Sardanapalus*.
Scott, Grant. "The Fragile Image: Felicia Hemans and Romantic Ekphrasis." *Felicia Hemans: Reimagining Poetry in the Nineteenth Century.* Ed. Julie Melnyk and Nanora Sweet. Houndsmill, UK: Palgrave, 2001. 36–54.
———. *The Sculpted Word: Keats, Ekphrasis, and the Visual Arts.* Hanover: UP New Hampshire, 1994.
Scott, Joan Wallach. "'A Woman Who Has Only Paradoxes to Offer': Olympe de Gouges Claims Rights for Women." *Rebel Daughters: Women and the French Revolution.* Ed. Sara E. Melzer and Leslie W. Rabine. New York: Oxford UP, 1992. 102–20.
Scott, Walter. *The Heart of Midlothian.* 1818; New York: Holt, Rinehart, and Winston, 1963.
[———]. "Remarks on *Frankenstein, or the Modern Prometheus*: A Novel." *Blackwood's Edinburgh Magazine* 12 (March 1818): 613–20.
Sedgwick, Eve Kosofsky. *Between Men: English Literature and Male Homosocial Desire.* New York: Columbia UP, 1985.
Severs, J. Burke. "Keats's Fairy Sonnet." *Keats-Shelley Journal* 6 (1957): 109–13.
Shairp, J. C. *On Poetic Interpretation of Nature.* Boston: Houghton Mifflin, 1898.
Shakespeare, William. *Antony and Cleopatra.* Ed. M. R. Ridley. 1954; London: NAL, 1981.
———. *Coriolanus.* Ed. Philip Brockbank. London: Methuen, 1976.
———. *Hamlet.* Ed. Harold Jenkins. New York: Methuen, 1982.
———. *Henry V.* Ed. Gary Taylor. Oxford: Oxford UP, 1984.
———. *Macbeth.* Ed. G. K. Hunter. Middlesex, UK: Penguin, 1967.
———. *Richard III.* Ed. Antony Hammond. London: Methuen, 1981.
———. *Romeo and Juliet.* Ed. Brian Gibbons. 1980; London: Routledge, 1983.
———. *Troilus and Cressida.* Ed. Kenneth Palmer. 1982; London: Routledge, 1990.
———. *The Winter's Tale.* Ed. J. H. P. Pafford. 1963; New York: Routledge, 1988.
Sharp, W[illiam]. *The Life and Letters of Joseph Severn.* New York: Charles Scribner's Sons, 1892.
———. "The Portraits of Keats, with Special Reference to Those By Severn." *Century Magazine* 49 (Feb. 1906): 535–51.
[Shelley, Mary Wollstonecraft]. *Frankenstein; or, The Modern Prometheus.* 1818. Ed. Susan J. Wolfson. New York: Longman, 2003.
[———]. "Giovanni Villani." *The Liberal* 4 (1823): 281–97. Ext. *The Mary Shelley Reader.* Ed. Betty T. Bennett and Charles E. Robinson. New York: Oxford UP, 1990. 329–33
———. *The Journals of Mary Shelley, 1814–1844.* Ed. Paula R. Feldman and Diana Scott-Kilvert. 2 vols. Baltimore: Johns Hopkins UP, 1987.
———. *The Letters of Mary Wollstonecraft Shelley.* Ed. Betty T. Bennett. 3 vols. Baltimore: Johns Hopkins UP, 1980–88.

———. *Lodore*. London: Richard Bentley, 1835; ed. Lisa Vargo; Peterborough, ON: Broadview P, 1997.

———, ed. *Essays, Letters from Abroad, Translations and Fragments by Percy Bysshe Shelley.* 2 vols. London: Edward Moxon, 1840 [1839]; Philadelphia: Lea and Blanchard, 1840.

———, ed. *The Poetical Works of Percy Bysshe Shelley.* London: Moxon, 1840; notes rpt. in *The Complete Works of Percy Bysshe Shelley.* Ed. Thomas Hutchinson. London: Oxford UP, 1917.

Shelley, Percy Bysshe. *Adonais / An Elegy on the Death of John Keats, / Author of Endymion, Hyperion, etc. / By Percy B. Shelley.* Pisa, 1821; fac. rpt. New York: Payson & Clarke, 1927. .

———. *A Defence of Poetry.* 1840; *Poetry and Prose* 480–508.

———. *The Letters of Percy Bysshe Shelley.* Ed. Frederick L. Jones. 2 vols. Oxford: Clarendon P, 1964.

———. *On Love. The Keepsake for MDCCCXXIX.* Ed. Frederic Mansel Reynolds. London: Hurst, Chance, 1828. 47–49.

———. *The Poems of Shelley.* Vol. 2. Ed. Kelvin Everest and Geoffrey Matthews. Harlow: Pearson, 2000.

———. *Shelley's Poetry and Prose.* 2/e; ed. Donald H. Reiman and Neil Fraistat. New York: Norton, 2002.

Shevelow, Kathryn. *Women and Print Culture: The Construction of Femininity in the Early Periodical.* New York: Routledge, 1989.

Showalter, Elaine. "Critical Cross-Dressing: Male Feminists and the Woman of the Year." *Raritan* 3.2 (Fall 1983): 130–49.

———. *A Literature of Their Own: British Women Novelists from Brontë to Lessing.* Princeton: Princeton UP, 1977.

Sigourney, Mrs. [Lydia Huntley]. "Essay on the Genius of Mrs. Hemans." *Memoir of the Life and Writings of Felicia Hemans: By Her Sister; with an Essay on Her Genius: By Mrs. Sigourney.* New York: C. S. Francis; Boston: J. H. Francis, 1845. vii–xxiii.

Silliman, Benjamin. *The Letters of Shahcoolen, A Hindu Philosopher, Residing in Philadelphia, to His Friend El Hassan, An inhabitant of Delhi.* Boston: Russel and Cutler, 1802. Rpt. with introduction by Ben Harris McClary. Gainesville, FL: Scholars' Facsimiles & Reprints, 1962.

Sinfield, Alan. *The Wilde Century.* New York: Columbia UP, 1994.

Smiles, Samuel. *A Publisher and His Friends: Memoir and Correspondence of the Late John Murray with an Account of the Origin and Progress of the House, 1768–1843.* 2 vols. London: John Murray, 1891.

S[mith], A[lexander]. "John Keats." *The Encyclopædia Britannica.* 8/e. Edinburgh: Adam and Charles Black, 1887. 13: 55–57.

Smith, Charlotte. *Desmond, A Novel, in Three Volumes.* London: G. G. J. & J. Robinson, 1792. Ed. Antje Blank and Janet Todd. Peterborough, ON: Broadview P, 2001.

Soderholm, James. *Fantasy, Forgery, and the Byron Legend.* Lexington: U Kentucky P, 1996.

———. "Lady Caroline Lamb: Byron's Miniature Writ Large." *Keats-Shelley Journal* 40 (1991): 24–46.

Spectator 39 (1866): 1229. "Mr. Swinburne on His Critics."

Spence, Gordon. "Moral and Sexual Ambivalence in *Sardanapalus.*" *Byron Journal* 12 (1984): 59–69.

Spenser, Edmund. *The Faerie Queene.* Ed. Thomas P. Roche, Jr., with C. Patrick O'Donnell, Jr. New Haven: Yale UP, 1981.

Sperry, Stuart M. *Keats the Poet.* Princeton: Princeton UP, 1973.

———. "Richard Woodhouse's Interleaved and Annotated Edition of Keats's 1817 *Poems.*" *Literary Monographs*, vol. 1. Ed. Eric Rothstein and Thomas Dunseath. Madison: U Wisconsin P, 1967. 101–64; 308–11.

Stabler, Jane. *Byron: Poetics and History.* Cambridge UP, 2002.

Staël, Germaine de. *Corinne, ou l'Italie.* 1807; ed. Simone Balayé. France: Gallimard, 1985.

———. *De l'Influence des Passions sur le bonheur des Individus et des Nations.* Vol. 3, *Ouvres Completes.* Paris: Treuttel et Würtz, 1820.

Stedman, Jane W. "From Dame to Woman: W. S. Gilbert and Theatrical Transvestism." *Suffer and Be Still: Women in the Victorian Age.* Ed. Martha Vicinus. Bloomington: Indiana UP, 1972. 20–37.

Steffan, Truman Guy. *Lord Byron's Cain: Twelve Essays and a Text with Variants and Annotations.* Austin: U of Texas P, 1968.

——— and Willis W. Pratt, eds. *Byron's Don Juan: A Variorum Edition.* 4 vols. Austin: U of Texas P, 1957.

Stillinger, Jack. "The Hoodwinking of Madeline: Skepticism in *The Eve of St. Agnes.*" 1961; *"The Hoodwinking of Madeline" and Other Essays on Keats's Poems.* Urbana: U Illinois P, 1971. 67–93.

———. "The Order of Poems in Keats's First Volume." 1969; *Hoodwinking* 1–13.

———. *Reading* The Eve of St. Agnes: *The Multiples of Complex Literary Transaction.* New York: Oxford UP, 1999.

———, ed. See Keats, John.

Stodart, M[ary] A[nn]. *Female Writers: Thoughts on Their Proper Sphere, and on Their Powers of Usefulness.* London: R. B. Seeley and W. Burnside, 1842.

Stoller, Robert J. *Sex and Gender: On the Development of Masculinity and Femininity.* New York: Science House, 1968.

Straub, Kristina. *Sexual Suspects: Eighteenth-Century Players and Sexual Ideology.* Princeton: Princeton UP, 1992.

Stubbes, Phillip. *Anatomie of the Abuses in England in Shakespeare's Youth, A.D. 1583.* Part I. Ed. Frederick J. Furnivall. London: N. Trüber, 1877–79.

The Sultana: or, A Trip to Turkey: A Melo-drama, in Three Acts, founded on Lord Byron's Don Juan. Anon.; attributed to Jonathan S. Bailey. New York: N. B. Holmes, 1822.

Surrey, Henry Howard, Earl. *Poems*. Annotated by Emrys Jones. Oxford: Clarendon P, 1964.
Swann, Karen. "*Endymion*'s Beautiful Dreamers." *The Cambridge Companion to Keats.* Ed. Susan J. Wolfson. Cambridge: Cambridge UP, 2001. 20–36.
———. "Harassing the Muse." Mellor, ed. 81–92.
Sweet, Nanora. "Felicia Hemans." *Cambridge Bibliography of English Literature: The Nineteenth Century.* Ed. Joanne Shattock. Cambridge: Cambridge UP, 1999.
———. "'The Inseparables': Hemans, the Brownes and the Milan Commission." *Modern Language Studies* 39.2 (2003): 165–77.
———, and Julie Melnyk, eds. *Felicia Hemans: Reimagining Poetry in the Nineteenth Century.* New York: Palgrave, 2001.
Swinburne, Algernon Charles. *The Complete Works of Algernon Charles Swinburne.* Ed. Edmund Gosse and Thomas James Wise. 20 vols. London: William Heinemann, 1925–27.
———. "Keats." *Works* 14: 295–302.
———. *Notes on Poems and Reviews*. 1866; *Works* 16: 351–73.
Symons, Arthur. "John Keats." *Monthly Review* 13 (Oct. 1901): 139–55.
———. *The Romantic Movement in English Poetry.* New York: E. P. Dutton, 1909.
The Tatler 172 (Tuesday, 16 May 1710). *The Tatler; or, Lucubrations of Isaac Bickerstaff, Esq.* 4 vols. London: J. and R. Tonson, &c, 1764. 3: 246–50.
Tayler, Irene and Gina Luria. "Women in British Romantic Literature." *What Manner of Woman.* Ed. Marlene Springer. New York: New York UP, 1977. 98–123.
Taylor, W[illiam]. C[ooke]. "Miss Jewsbury." *The National Portrait Gallery of Illustrious and Eminent Personages, Chiefly of the Nineteenth Century.* London: P. Jackson, 1846–48. 3: 36–38.
Tennyson, Alfred Lord. *The Poems of Tennyson.* Ed. Christopher Ricks. London: Longmans, Green, 1969.
Tennyson, Hallam Lord. *Alfred Lord Tennyson: A Memoir.* 2 vols. London: Macmillan, 1897.
The Times [London] (19 Sept. 1848): 3. [Samuel Phillips; attr. *KCH* 320], on Milnes, "Life of John Keats."
Tomalin, Claire. *The Life and Death of Mary Wollstonecraft.* New York: Harcourt Brace Jovanovich, 1974.
Trelawny, E[dward] J[ohn]. *Recollections of the Last Days of Shelley and Keats.* Boston: Tricknor and Fields, 1858.
Trilling, Lionel. Introduction, *The Selected Letters of John Keats.* (1951); rpt. "The Poet as Hero: Keats in His Letters." *The Opposing Self.* New York: Viking, 1955. 3–49.
Trinder, Peter W. *Mrs Hemans*. Wales: U Wales P, 1984.
Trott, Nicola. "Sexing the Critic: Mary Wollstonecraft at the Turn of the Century." *1798: The Year of the LYRICAL BALLADS*. Ed. Richard Cronin. London: Macmillan, 1998. 32–67.
Union Magazine of Literature and Art 2 (June 1848): 287; on *Wuthering Heights*.
Van Dyke, Henry. "The Influence of Keats." *Century Magazine* 50 (Oct. 1895): 910–14.

Vance, Norman. *The Sinews of the Spirit: The Ideal of Christian Manliness in Victorian Literature and Religious Thought.* Cambridge: Cambridge UP, 1985.

Veeder, William. *Mary Shelley, Frankenstein, and Androgyny.* Chicago: U Chicago P, 1986.

Vendler, Helen. *The Odes of John Keats.* Cambridge: Harvard UP, 1983.

Victoria Magazine 15 (May 1870): 1–11. "Our Censors and Satirists."

——— 15 (May 1870): 55–67. "The Daintiest of Poets—Keats."

Villard, Léonie. *The Influence of Keats on Tennyson and Rossetti.* 1914; Folcroft P, 1970.

Vincent, Howard P., ed. *Letters of Dora Wordsworth.* Chicago: Packard, 1944.

Vincent, Leon. "A Reading of the Letters of John Keats." *Atlantic Monthly* 74 (Sept. 1894): 399–408.

Vital, Anthony Paul. "Lord Byron's Embarrassment: Poesy and the Feminine." *Bulletin of Research in the Humanities* 86 (1983–85): 269–90.

Voltaire. *Sémiramis.* 1748. Tr. William F. Fleming. *The Works of Voltaire.* 42 vols. Paris: E. R. Dumont. 17: 147–225.

Wadsworth, Frank W. "Hamlet and Iago: Nineteenth-Century Breeches Parts." *Shakespeare Quarterly* 17 (Spring 1966): 130–39.

Wakefield, Priscilla. *Reflections on the Present Condition of the Female Sex; With Suggestions for its Improvement.* London: J. Johnson, Darton, and Harvey, 1798.

Ward, Aileen. *John Keats: The Making of a Poet.* New York: Viking, 1963.

Ward, Thomas Humphry, ed. *The English Poets: Selections with Critical Introductions.* 5 vols. London: Macmillan, 1880.

Wasserman, Earl R. *Shelley: A Critical Reading.* Baltimore: Johns Hopkins UP, 1981.

Watkins, Daniel P. *Keats's Poetry and the Politics of the Imagination.* Rutherford, NJ: Associated UPs, 1989.

———. "Violence, Class Consciousness, and Ideology in Byron's History Plays." *ELH* 48 (1981): 799–816.

Watson, Jean. "Coleridge's Androgynous Ideal." *Prose Studies* 6 (1983): 37–56.

Watson, Sir William. "Keats and Mr. Colvin." *Excursions in Criticism: Being Some Prose Recreations of a Rhymer.* London: Elkins, Matthews, & John Lane, 1893. 37–45.

Watts, Alaric Alfred. *Alaric Watts: A Narrative of His Life.* 2 vols. London: Richard Bentley & Son, 1884.

———. "A Remonstrance / To the Authoress of the Forgoing 'Farewell to the Muse'." *Literary Souvenir* for 1826, pp. 382–84.

Webb, Timothy. *Shelley: A Voice Not Understood.* Atlantic Highlands, NJ: Humanities, 1977.

West, Kenyon. "Keats in Hampstead." *Century Magazine* 50 (Oct. 1895): 898–910.

[Whately, Richard]. "*Northanger Abbey and Persuasion.*" *Quarterly Review* 24 (1821): 352–76.

Whitmore, Allen Perry. *The Major Characters of Lord Byron's Dramas.* Salzburg: Institut für Englische Sprache und Literatur, Salzburg, 1974.

Wilde, Oscar. *Glykypikros Eros. The Writings of Oscar Wilde.* 12 vols. New York: Doubleday, Page, 1923. 1: 243–46.

———. *The Portrait of Mr. W. H. Selected Critical Prose.* Ed. Linda Dowling. New York: Penguin, 2001. 31–101.

———. *The Tomb of Keats. Irish Monthly* 5 (July 1887): 476–78; *Writings* 12: 301–5.

Wilkes, Joanne. "'Only the Broken Music'? The Critical Writings of Maria Jane Jewsbury." *Women's Writing* 7 (2000): 105–18.

Williams, Jane. *The Literary Women of England, Including a Biographical Epitome of All the Most Eminent to the Year 1700; and Sketches of the Poetesses to the Year 1850; With Extracts from their Works, and Critical Remarks.* London: Saunders, Otley, 1861.

Wilson, Carol Shiner and Joel Haefner, eds. *Re-Visioning Romanticism: British Women Writers, 1776–1837.* Philadelphia: U Pennsylvania P, 1994.

[Wilson, John.] On Byron, *Childe Harold's Pilgrimage, Canto the Fourth. Blackwood's Edinburgh Magazine* 3 (May 1818): 216–24 and *217–*18. Attr. John Murray, letter to Byron 22 Sept. 1818 (Smiles 1: 397).

Winslow, Hubbard. *Woman As She Should Be.* Philadelphia: Henry Perkins, 1838.

Wolfson, Susan J. "Editorial Privilege: Mary Shelley and Percy Shelley's Works." *The Other Mary Shelley.* Ed. Anne K. Mellor, Esther Schor, and Audrey Fisch. New York: Oxford UP, 1993. 39–72.

———. "Felicia Hemans and the Revolving Doors of Reception." *Romanticism and Women Poets: Opening the Doors of Reception.* Ed. Harriet Kramer Linkin and Stephen C. Behrendt. Lexington: U Kentucky P, 1999. 214–41.

———. *Formal Charges: The Shaping of Poetry in British Romanticism.* Stanford: Stanford UP, 1997.

———. "Keats Enters History: Autopsy, *Adonais*, and the Fame of Keats." *Keats and History.* Ed. Nicholas Roe. Cambridge : Cambridge UP, 1994. 17–45.

———. *The Questioning Presence: Wordsworth, Keats, and the Interrogative Mode in Romantic Poetry.* Ithaca: Cornell UP, 1986.

———. "Shakespeare and the Romantic Girl Reader." *Nineteenth-Century Contexts* 21 (1999): 191–234.

———. "Wollstonecraft and the Poets." *The Cambridge Companion to Mary Wollstonecraft.* Ed. Claudia Johnson. Cambridge UP, 2002.

———. "Wordsworth and the Language of (Men) Feeling." *Men Writing the Feminine.* Ed. Thaïs Morgan. New York: State U New York P, 1994. 29–57.

——— and Peter J. Manning, eds. *The Romantics and Their Contemporaries.* Vol. 2a of *Longman Anthology of British Literature.* Gen. ed., David Damrosch. New York: Longman, 1998, 2002, 2006.

Wollstonecraft, Mary. *An Historical and Moral View of the Origin and Progress of the French Revolution; and the Effect It Has Produced in Europe.* London: J. Johnson, 1794.

———. *Letter on the Present Character of the French Nation.* 1793. *Posthumous Works of the Author of a Vindication of the Rights of Woman.* Ed. William Godwin (1798). *Works* 6: 439–46.

———. *Letters Written During a Short Residence in Sweden, Norway, and Denmark.* London: J. Johnson, 1796; *Works* 6: 237–348.

[———] / M., on Catharine Macaulay Graham, *Letters on Education. Analytical Review* 8 (Nov. 1790): 241–54. *Works* 7: 309–22.

———. *A Vindication of the Rights of Men, in a Letter to the Right Honourable Edmund Burke; Occasioned by His "Reflections on the Revolution in France."* 2/e; London: J. Johnson, 1790; Gainesville, FL: Scholars' Facsimiles and Reprints, 1960.

———. *A Vindication of the Rights of Woman.* 1792; ed. Lorne Macdonald and Kathleen Scherf. Peterborough, ON: Broadview P, 1997.

———. *The Works of Mary Wollstonecraft.* Ed. Janet Todd and Marilyn Butler. 7 vols. New York: New York UP, 1989.

Woman: As She Is and As She Should Be. London: James Cochrane, 1835.

Wood, Gillen D'Arcy. "Crying Game: Operatic Strains in Wordsworth's *Lyrical Ballads.*" *ELH* 71 (2004): 969–1000.

Woodring, Carl. *Politics in English Romantic Poetry.* Cambridge: Harvard UP, 1970.

Woolf, Virginia. "Mary Wollstonecraft." *The Second Common Reader.* New York: Harcourt Brace Jovanovich, 1932. 168–76.

———. *Orlando, A Biography.* New York: Harcourt Brace Jovanovich, 1928.

———. *A Room of One's Own.* 1929; New York: Harcourt, Brace, 1957.

———. *A Writer's Diary.* Ed. Leonard Woolf. New York: Harcourt Brace Jovanovich, 1954.

Wordsworth, Dorothy. *The Grasmere Journals.* Ed. Pamela Woof. Oxford: Oxford UP, 1991.

Wordsworth, William. "Essay, Supplementary to the Preface" [of 1815]. *The Prose Works of William Wordsworth.* Ed. W. J. B. Owen and Jane Worthington Smyser. 3 vols. Oxford: Clarendon P, 1974. 3: 62–84.

———. *The Excursion, Being a Portion of The Recluse, A Poem.* London: Longman &c, 1814.

———. *Ode: Intimations of Immortality from Recollections of Early Childhood.* 1815. *Wordsworth's Selected Poems and Prefaces.* Ed. Jack Stillinger. Boston: Houghton Mifflin, 1969.

———. *The Poems.* Ed. John O. Hayden. 2 vols. 1977; New Haven: Yale UP, 1981.

———. POEMS, IN TWO VOLUMES, *and Other Poems, 1800–1807.* Ed. Jared Curtis. Ithaca: Cornell UP, 1983.

———. *The Poetical Works of William Wordsworth.* Ed. Ernest de Selincourt. 2/e rev. Helen Darbishire. 5 vols. Oxford: Clarendon P, 1952–59.

———. Preface to *Lyrical Ballads.* 1800–1802. LYRICAL BALLADS *and Other Poems, 1797–1800, by William Wordsworth.* Ed. James Butler and Karen Green. Ithaca: Cornell UP, 1992.

———. *The Thirteen-Book PRELUDE*. Ed. Mark L. Reed. 2 vols. Ithaca: Cornell UP, 1991.
———. *The Fourteen-Book PRELUDE*. Ed. W. J. B. Owen. Ithaca: Cornell UP, 1985.
——— and Dorothy Wordsworth. *The Letters of William and Dorothy Wordsworth*. Ed. Ernest de Selincourt. *The Early Years, 1787– 1805*, 2/e rev. Chester L. Shaver; Oxford: Clarendon P, 1967. *The Middle Years, 1806–1820: Part 1, 1806–1811*, 2/e rev. Mary Moorman; Oxford: Clarendon P, 1969; *Part 2, 1812–1820*, 2/e rev. Mary Moorman and Alan G. Hill. Oxford: Clarendon P, 1970. *The Later Years, 1821–1853*, 2/e rev. Alan G. Hill. 4 Parts. Oxford: Oxford UP, 1978–88.
Wu, Duncan. "Appropriating Byron: Lady Caroline Lamb's *A New Canto*." *The Wordsworth Circle* 26 (1995): 140–46.
———. "Talking Pimples: Hazlitt and Byron in Love." *Romanticism* 10.2 (2004): 158–72.
———, ed. *Romantic Woman Poets: An Anthology*. Oxford: Basil Blackwell, 1997.
———, ed. *Romanticism: An Anthology.* Oxford: Basil Blackwell, 1994.
Yeats, William Butler. *The Variorum Edition of the Poems*. Ed. Peter Allt and Russell K. Alspach. 1940; New York: Macmillan, 1973.
The Young Lady's Book of Elegant Poetry. Philadelphia: Key and Biddle, 1835. Keats, *To Autumn*, 314–15.

Index

f: a separate reference on the next page
ff: separate references on the next two pages
Italics: page-runs of chapters or subsections on the subject, with the relevant footnotes
n: note; nn: notes
For full information on short titles, see Works Cited
Not indexed: Works Cited, Acknowledgments, illustration credits, incidental mentions

Adams, James Eli, 258, 344n7.
Adonis, 232–33, 258, 366–67n44.
Aikin, Lucy, *Epistles on Women*, 93, 310, 380n35.
Alexander the Great, 141–42, 211.
Alfieri, Vittorio (*Mirra*), 351–52n59.
Altick, Richard, 372n34.
Amazon, 16, 69, 80, 84, 86, 88–89, 198, 329n24, 350n47.
Ambition. See *Fame, Indolence* (antonym).
Androgyny, 30, 88–90, 244, 278–79, 293; and Byron 351n53, 376n67; and Keats 335n21; and Caroline Lamb 354n16; Coventry Patmore on 87–88, 278, 375n60; and Pre-Raphaelite art 278, 366n42; and Shakespeare 335n20; and P. Shelley 335n17, 370n15, 376n67; Tennyson on 325n40; Woolf on 335nn20–21. See also *Carpenter, Coleridge, Genius (male)*.
Annuals, 96, 98, 102–3, 371n28; and Hemans 73, 306; and Jewsbury 96, 98, 102–03, 113–14, 337n10, 341n37; and Keats 255f, 365n33, 371n28; and Wordsworth 338n15. See also *Heath's Book of Beauty, Literary Souvenir*.
Anti-Jacobin Review, 184.
Antony, Mark, 68, 144–45, 160, 179, 191, 346n21, 357n42.
Apollo, 232, 366n37.
Armstrong, Isobel, 58.

Arnold, Matthew, on Keats 209–10, 256, 261, 273, 275–75f, 362n11; and male intimacy 277, 375n59; on Shelley 32, 325n42; on Wordsworth 294, 378n17. See also *Clough*.
Arria (wife of Paetus), 63, 309, 380n33.
Astell, Mary, 12, 187, 359n54; *Reflections Upon Marriage* 4; *Serious Proposal* 289, 292, 377n4.
Athenæum, 334n1; on P. Shelley 340n32, 370n16. See also *Jewsbury, Sand*.
Austen, Jane, xvi, 45, 114, 320n3, 322n22, 334n5, 336n5, 356n28; and Byron 181; and Jewsbury 94–96f, 114, 127, 131, 336nn4–5, 343nn58–59; *Northanger Abbey* 95, 323n31, 336–38nn6, 12; *Persuasion* 358n46; Woolf on 288.
Austin, Alfred, 31–32, 181, 325n43, 363n13, 375n57.

Baillie, Joanna, 327n8, 334n9; and *Blackwood's* 22–23, 44; and Byron 22, 25, 152, 194, 356n32; *Count Basil* 194; *Countess Albini*, 80; *Plays on the Passions*, 22; and Hazlitt 41; and Hemans 40, 47–48; and Jewsbury 96–97, 337n9.
Barbauld, Anna, 17, 41, 45–46, 327n8; *Eighteen Hundred and Eleven* 17, 22, 323n28; *Song V* 183.
Barker-Benfield, G. J., 322n18, 343–44n2, 361n74, 362n2.
Barnard, John, 368n3.
Barrett, Elizabeth [later Browning], 19, 72, 79, 314, 333n60, 335–36nn18, 25, 380n40; Lady Dacre, 87; Hemans 72, 304, 379nn29–30; Jewsbury 87; Wollstonecraft, 314, 336n25.
Bate, W. J., 280–81.
Battersby, Christine, 380n36.
Baudelaire, Charles, 217.
Behrendt, Stephen, 326n51, 327n7.

419

Bell, H. G., *The Favourite Actress*, 113.
Belsey, Catherine, 355n19.
Benét, Stephen Vincent, 280.
Bible and gender: Deuteronomy, 18, 169; Galatians (Paul to), 28, 324n37.
Bierce, Ambrose, 172–73.
Biographium Fæmineum, 285, 302.
Birch, Dinah, 375n56.
Blackstone, Bernard, 358n48.
Blackwood's Edinburgh Magazine, 214; Austen 131; Baillie 22–23, 25; Byron 25, 139, 162, 182, 184, 200, 218, 299; Hazlitt 246, 369n10; Hemans 43f, 85; Hunt 85, 139, 216–18, 246, 369nn10, 13; Keats 85, 206–7, 212, 216, 218, 221f, *245–48*, 252, 259, 283, 364–65nn25, 27, 28, *368–69nn3–10, 13*, 371n23; Jewsbury 85, 337n10; Patmore, 277; P. Shelley 246, 248; Alexander Smith 276; suttee 332n52; Wordsworth 206, 218. See also *Cockney School*.
Blake, William, xv, 235, 367n46.
Blakemore, Steven, 321n13, 322n19.
Blessington, Lady Marguerite, 165, 178, 355–56n26, 357n37; *Le Bas Bleu* 21, 173–74.
Bluestocking women, 18–22, 32–33, 42, 97–99, 173–74, 191–92, 209, 211, 288, 290–91, 323–24nn29–32, 337n11, 360nn62–63.
Bowles, Caroline, 44, 98, 337n9.
Bowles, William Lisle, 100, 206, 215.
Breen, Jennifer, 328n17.
British Critic, on Hemans 20; on Wollstonecraft 86.
British Review, on Hemans 77; on Byron 137, 139.
Bromwich, David, 345n9.
Brontë, Charlotte, 279, 324–25nn36, 45.
Brontë, Emily, 32, 325n44.
Brown, Charles (friend of Keats), 237, 242, 251, 262–63, 266.
Brown, Ford Madox, 185–86.
Brown, John "Estimate," 3, 136, 138, 146, 245, 344n3.
Brown, Laura, 334n10.
Browning, Robert, 32, 262
Buchanan, Robert ("The Fleshly School"), 262, 276, 278, 373n42.
Burke, Edmund, 5, 8–11, 13, 32, 288, 322–23nn16, 29, 332n50, 377n2.
Burton, Robert, *The Anatomy of Melancholy*, 212f, 363nn16–17.
Bush, Douglas, 280.
Butler, Judith, 189, 224, 320n2, 354n8, 359n58.
Butler, Marilyn, 344–45nn, 4, 12–13, 349n37.

Byron, George Gordon, Lord, xv, xvii, 1, 34, 61, *135–204*, 112, 115; Albanian costume 163, 170, 194–96; Annabella Byron (wife) 153, 166, 177, 182, 191, 348n34; Austen 181; Catherine Byron (mother) 197–98, 355n25, 360n68; Byronism 139, 151, 162, 197, 201, 243f, 359n52; Carbonari 140–43, 345n15; Cavalier Servente 188–91; character of 28–29, 31, 177, 179 357n40, 360n62; John Edleston 170, 177, 354n6, 357n35; effeminacy *135–63*, 191–92, 215–16, 344nn6, 8, 360nn62–63; female readers 173, 176, 182, 188, 191–92, 242, 314, 360nn62–63; Gynocrasy 176–77, 201, 360n63; homosexuality 16, 147, 154, 165–67, 170–71, 175, 177, 185, 194, 293, 252n4, 349–50nn44–45, 353–54nn4, 6–7, 357n35, 360n66; Hemans 20, 123; Lord and Lady Holland, 164–65, 353n3; Keats 133, 217, 222, 246, 252–53, 364nn21, 27, 368–69nn5, 6, 8; mobility 177–80, 187, 357n38; portraits 163, 196–97; on rape 200, 361n72; Shakespeare's characters 137, 140–45, 154, 158, 179 192, 194, 350–51n 52 (see also *Shakespeare*); sentiment 176, 364n23; Wordsworth 215, 369. See also *Arnold, Baillie, Class, Dandy, Guiccioli, Harem, Hazlitt, Hemans, Hunt, Same-sex passion, Staël*.
Works & characters: *Beppo* 137, 360n62; *Bride of Abydos* 153, 359n52, 360n60, 366n39; *Childe Harold* 181 (Maid of Saragoza, 350n47, 366n39; Thyrza 165–66, 354n6; Canto III 309; IV 214, 299–300, 364n20); *Corsair* 192, 331–32nn42, 49, 356n32, 359n52, 366n39 (Hemans 61, 64, 66; Jewsbury 119); *Deformed Transformed* 341n35; *English Bards and Scotch Reviewers* 215–19, 236, 345n9, 353n3, 362n4, 364nn22–23, 369n10; *Giaour* 154, 174, 189, 356n30; *Hints from Horace* 142, 345–46n17; *Hours of Idleness* 215, 356–57n34; *Lara* 356n33, 360n60 (Kaled, 174–75, 356n30); *Marino Faliero* 146, 161, 351n54; *Prometheus* 304–5; *The Vision of Judgment* 201.
Don Juan xvii, 18, 34, 140, *164–84*, 212, 239; Lady Adeline 176–78, 180; Castlereagh, 171–72; Empress Catherine 33, 158, 168f, 172, 185–86, 191, 198, 200, 350n51, 360n61; Queen Elizabeth 172; Duchess Fitz-Fulke 168, 172, 184, 187, 201–3, 359n52; Sultana Gulbeyaz 172, 175–76, 190–93, 198, 200, 359n52; Haidée 166, 168, 172, 175f, 180, 185–87, 191, 194, 359nn52–53; Lord Henry 166; Donna Inez 173, 182, 184, 197; Donna Julia 168, 171–72, 177, 180–82, 185, 187,

191, 256, 358–60nn45–46, 48, 52–53, 65; Southey 172. See also *Bluestockings, Harem, Slavery.*
Sardanapalus 34, *135–63;* Diodorus Siculus 141, 146–47, 159–60, 352n62; Hemans 56, 64–66; Jewsbury 56; Myrrha 56, 66–67, 144, 146, 148f, 155–60, 347n33, 350–53nn49, 58–60, 66, 359n52; Nimrod 144, 146, 152–53, 157–58f; Semiramis 145f, 148, 152–58, 350n49; Zarina 144, 149f. See also *Effeminacy, George IV, Semiramis, Slavery.*

Callender, Michelle, 322n15.
Calvert, Charles Alexander, 163.
Camp and gender, 20; Byron xviii, 154, 165, 172, 176, 193–94, 353n67; Hemans 53; Keats 207, 223–24, 236. See also *Drag.*
Caprice(s), 5, 111, 158, 179f, 198, 360n62. See also *Byron, mobility.*
Carlyle, Thomas, on Byron 243, 248; dandyism 138, 344n8; as feminine 375n56; heroes, 257–58, 281; Dr. Johnson 252, 258; Keats 254–55, 258.
Carnival, 198–200. See also *Masquerade.*
Caroline, Queen of England, 150, 348nn36–37.
Carpenter, Edward, 232, 281, 335n17, 370n15, 373n43, 376n67, 378n10.
Castle, Terry, 202, 361n75.
Castrato. See *Eunuch.*
Catherine, Empress of Russia, 9, 33, 152, 340n28, 355n23. See also *Byron, Don Juan.*
Certain Homilies . . . in the Time of Queen Elizabeth, 356n27.
Champion, 179–80.
Chandler, James, 321n9.
Chew, Samuel, 360n65; on Byron 345n14.
Chivalry, 375n57; Hemans 43–6, 48, 329n20; Burke 8–9, 11–13, Keats 226–29.
Chodorow, Nancy, xvi, 282, 376n68.
Cixous, Hélène, xvi.
Chorley, Henry, on female genius 17–18, 72, 105, 117–18, 333n60; Hemans 17, 39, 43–44, 47, 49–51, 113, 326n2, 327nn10–11, 328n15, 328–29n19, 329n22, 332n55, 333n57, 373n47, 380nn32, 36; Jewsbury 85, 87, 93, 105, 338n21.
Christ, Carol, 372n35.
Christensen, Jerome, 126, 352n60, 355n22, 357n43.
Clark, Anna, 348n36.
Clarke, Charles Cowden (friend of Keats), 264, 371nn23, 25, 374n52.
Clarke, Eric O., 248, 370n16.

Clarke, Norma, 77, 323n30, 328n18, 329n25, 330–31nn38, 336n24; Jewsbury 113, 131, 399, 334n6, 336n3, 338n17, 340–43nn32, 36, 41–42, 55–57.
Class and gender, 138, 165, 216–17, 248, 277, 331n43, 357n35, 369nn10–11; Byron vii, 115, 137–38, 177, 192, 215–16, 246f, 368–69n5; Jewsbury 337n8; Keats 206–7, 231, 245f, 258–59, 275–76, 280, 282, 368nn3, 5, 374–75nn55, 57; Wollstonecraft on 6, 11, 13, 322n16. See also *Cockney, Dandy.*
Cleopatra, 350n45, 354n5; Byron 144–55, 154, 160f, 179, 346n21; Hemans 68; in Jewsbury 111. See also *Antony.*
Clough, Arthur Hugh, feminine/effeminate 87, 277, 335n16, 375n60; male intimacy 277, 375n59. See also *Arnold.*
Cobbe, Frances Power, 181.
Cockney School 85, 206, 216–19, 224, 227 234, *245–48,* 276, 363n15, 364–65nn25, 28, 368n55, 368–69nn3–5, 9–10, 370n19. See also *Blackwood's Edinburgh Magazine, Hunt, Keats.*
Coleridge, Hartley, *Prometheus* 117; *To Somebody* 120–21, 342n46.
Coleridge, S. T., xv, 33, 50, 324n34, 325n39, 335n23; *Aids to Reflection* 29; androgyny 89–90, 281, 325n47, 335–36nn19–22, 373–74n48; Bowles 206; *Christabel* 195; effeminacy 29, 136, 145, 152, 244, 265, 346n23, 375n58; *Kubla Khan* 155; *Remorse* 111; sensibility and delicacy 100, 206; *Zapolya* 341n33. See also *Soul.*
Colley, Linda, 356n27, 361n75.
Colvin, Sidney, on Keats, 254, 260, 263–65, 274, 276, 278, 372n32.
Conduct books and gender, 322–23nn22, 32. See also *Ellis, Fordyce, Gisborne, More, Sandford, Stodart.*
Corbett, Martyn, 346n28.
Corinna (Greek poet), 75. See also *Staël, Corinne.*
Cornhill Magazine, on Keats 249, 253.
Cornwall, Barry / [Bryan Waller Procter], on Keats, 243.
Courthope, W. J., Keats, 232, 254, 257f, 260, 261, 275, 373n40; Swinburne, 375n57.
Coverture, 174, 356n28.
Cox, Jeffrey, 366n40.
Cross-dressing and gender, 80, *164–204,* 354nn8, 10, 12; female 6–7, 11–12, 18–19, 34, 61, 69, 163, 314, 321n12, 333n56, 340n28, 353n68, 354n7, 16, 356nn30–31, 361n75 (see

also *Joan of Arc, Lamb, Sand*); male 146–47, 163, 165, 247–48, 354n5, 360nn64–65, 356n32. See also *Byron, Drag*.
Croker, J. W. (*Quarterly* reviewer), Barbauld 17, 323n28; *Frankenstein* 325n24; Keats 370n19. See also *Quarterly Review*.
Crompton, Louis, 147, 162, 349n44, 353–54nn4–7.
Culler, Jonathan, 378n16.
Curran, Stuart, 48, 62, 320n5, 324n38, 330n28.

Dallas, E. S., 32.
Dandy, dandyism, 151, 217, 277, 344nn7–8; Byron 34, 137–38, 143, 169, 195, 197, 360n66; Keats 228.
Dante, 216, 258, 260, 331n39.
David, Deirdre, 334n2.
Davies, Sir John, *Nosce Teipsum*, 292.
Davis, Natalie, 167, 198.
Delicacy, 371–72n30; female, 13, 17, 22, 42f, 45f, 68, 76, 81, 84, 86ff, 94f, 303, 370n17, 375n58; male, vii, 11, 84, 100, 138, 147, 244, 247, 249f, 252, 255, 263, 273, 275. See also *Effeminacy, Sensibility*.
Della Cruscan poets, 362n4.
de Montluzin, Emily Lorraine, 369n9.
Dennis, John, on feminine rhyme, 355n22.
De Quincey, Thomas, 24–25, 324n34.
Derrida, Jacques, 171.
Dickens, Charles, 257.
Dickstein, Morris, 298.
Donaldson, Ian, 173.
Dowden, Edward, 249.
Dowling, Linda, 343–44n2, 368n3, 373n42.
Drag, 189, 345n8; female 187, 359n58; male 80, 154, 160, 169, 193–95.
Dublin University Magazine, 42, 305, 328nn15, 19.
DuPlessis, Rachel Blau, 342–43nn48, 51.
Dusinberre, Juliet, 361n75.

Eagleton, Terry, 1, 282, 320n2, 339n24.
Eclectic Review, Byron, 175; Keats, 223.
Écriture féminine, xvi.
Edgeworth, Maria, 213.
Edinburgh Review, 20; Byron 153, 156, 162, 182, 215, 345n13, 354n6; the canon 326n50; Hemans 20, 29–30, 43, 303, 327n9; Keats 254, 277, 375n57; Swinburne 373n42, 375n57; Wordsworth and Coleridge 324n29, 332n48. See also *Jeffrey*.
Effeminacy, xviii, 3, 214, *135–63, 243–84*, 331n43, 343–44nn2–8, 355n22, 360n67,

364n26, 368n2, 370n14; Bowles 215; Carlyle 344n7, 375n56; Coleridge 29, 31, 215, 244, 265; Hunt 216–17, 344n6, 364n25; Kingsley 257; Milton 346n21; Otho 154, 349–50nn44–45; and D. G. Rossetti 262; Ruskin 375n56; Wollstonecraft on 13. See also *John Brown, Byron, Camp, Cockney, Dandy, Hercules, Hunt, Keats, Sardanapalus, Shakespeare (Antony, Macbeth, Romeo, Richard II); P. B. Shelley, Swinburne*.
Elfenbein, Andrew, 343–44nn2, 8, 360n63.
Elledge, Paul, 351nn53, 55.
Ellis, Sarah Stickney, *Daughters of England* 340n29; Jewsbury 126, 128, 303; Gilfillan 323–24n32.
Elwood, Mrs. [Anne Katharine Curteis], 105, 339n22.
Epicene, 168–69, 171, 195, 277.
Erdman, David, 352n61.
Espinasse, Francis, on Hemans 42; Jewsbury, 126, 128, 130, 338–39n21.
Étienne, Louis, 260f, 276–77, 372–73n40.
Eunuch, 335n21; 346n21; Byron 154, 171–72, 191; Keats 210, 212, 247.
Eve / Milton's Eve, 14–15; 25, 81, 208–9, 290, 332n50.
Examiner, 20, 334–35n11; Byron 160, 162, 182; Hunt 216f; Keats, 222, 239, 248, 250, 367n52, 369–70n22; *Wuthering Heights*, 32.

Fairchild, H. N., 280.
Fame and gender, 30; female 24, 39, 49–51, 92, 120, 123, 128, 130, 176, 303, 305, 311, 333nn59, 60, 62–64 (Hemans *68–77*, 333nn59, 60–61; Jewsbury *108–15*, 304); male 55, 115, 191, 238, 305, 332n54 (Byron 141–2, 180, 191–92, 239; Keats 216, 226, 230, *237–42*). See also *Genius*.
Farrell, John, 346–47n28.
Feldman, Paula, 326n51, 328–29nn18–19, 355n21.
Felman, Shoshana, 279, 284, 354n8.
Female friendship, 77, 292.
Ferguson, Frances, 220, 379n20.
Ford, George, 253, 276, 280, 369n7, 371–73nn30, 31, 41, 375n57.
Fordyce, Revd. James, *Sermons to Young Women* 13, 80–84, 244, 322n22, 346n24.
Forman, H. B., 251.
Foucault, Michel, 293.
Fox, Susan, 367n46.
Franklin, Caroline, 322–23nn19, 21, 25, 350nn49, 51, 358n49, 377n6.

INDEX 423

Fraser's Magazine, "Female Character" 54, 310, 356n31; male poets, 31, 257. See also *Kingsley.*
French Revolution, xviii, *3–11;* Mme Roland 109, 120, 340nn29–30; women 6–8, 109, 120, 198, 321–22nn8–14.
Freud, Sigmund, 106.
Fry, Paul, 371n26.
Fryckstedt, Monica, 130–31, 399, 343n56.
Furniss, Tom, 322n19.

Galperin, William, 320n3.
Garber, Marjorie, 333n56, 354–55nn10, 18, 357n35, 359n58, 361n73.
Gaull, Marilyn, 371n29.
Gelpi, Barbara, 282, 376n68.
General Magazine, 15; on C. Macaulay, 80.
Genius and gender, 18, 178–79, 201, 285, 311, 327n8, 371n24, 380n36; women 16, 17ff, 22, 24, 32, 33, 42, 45–46, 47, 67, 74–75, 77, 85, 87–88, 91, 96, *105–28,* 201, 289, 312, 333n65, 339n25, 343n53, 359n50; men 29, 49, 55, 88f, 90, 208, 216, 230, 239, 244, 248, 250, 278–81, 300, 303, 329n26, 333n63, 335n21, 340–41n32, 374–75nn55, 60. See also *Androgyny, Fame.*
Genre and gender, xv, 15, 17, 21–25, 41–42, 45–46, 88, 171, 247, 324n33, 335n18, 338n13; and Byron 25, 171, 184, 189, 193–95, 360n64; and Hemans 21–22, 42–43, 39, 71–72, 92; and Keats 211–14, 222, 260–61, 275, 298, 377n74. See also *Poetess.*
Gentleman's Magazine 11–12, 18.
George IV, King of England (Prince Regent), 150–51, 348–49nn35–37. See also *Caroline, Queen of England.*
Gifford, William, 349n44; Della Cruscans 207, 362n4; Keats 251, 370–71n22. See also *Quarterly Review.*
Gilbert, Sandra, and Susan Gubar, 336n4, 341n36, 356n28, 361n69, 378n17.
Gillett, Eric, 338n21, 343n56.
Gilfillan, George, 323–24n32; E. B. Browning 79; Hemans 21–22, 30, 41, 43, 49, 327n11, 330n30; Keats 254f, 368n4; "lady authors" 22, 323–24n32; P. Shelley 30.
Gilligan, Carol, xvi.
Gilmartin, Sophie, 332n52
Gisborne, Thomas, 201, 205–6, 254, 259, 262.
Gitter, Elisabeth, 332n50.
Godwin, William, 184–85; Wollstonecraft 15, 86–87, 325n48, 377n1.
Graham, Peter, 354n15.

Greenblatt, Stephen, on "Culture" 2, 33, 320n4.
Greer, Germaine, 328n17.
Greg, W. R., 249.
Grenby, M. O., 344n4.
Guardian, 255.
Guiccioli, Teresa Gamba (Byron's mistress), 20, 74, 140, 142, 179, 181, 188–90, 354n13, 359n55.
Gutwirth, Madelyn, 333n63.

Hagstrum, Jean, 372n39.
Harem, 247, 290, 359–60nn59, 60; Byron 66, 140, 144–48, 152–53, 166, 168, 174f, 189–90, *192–95,* 356n32, 360n60; Macaulay on 190; Wollstonecraft 190. See also *Slavery.*
Harrison, William, 169.
Harwell, Thomas Meade, 372n33.
Hawkins, Laetitia, 14.
Haworth, Helen, 372n21.
Haydon, B. R., 217f, 222, 230, 263, 265, 271–73, 374n52.
Hays, Mary, 282, 359n59; Pope 183, 358–59n50; soul 289; Wollstonecraft 11, 86, 335n14; *Appeal to the Men* 5, 83–84, 168, 183, 282, 335n13, 358–59nn50, 362n10; *Emma Courtney* 83.
Hazlitt, William, 41; *Blackwood's* 246, 369n10; women 20, 41, 288, 327n6, 363n15; Byron 138, 153, 156, 158, 162, 168, 174, 184, 231, 246, 345n9, 350–53n52; class prejudice 246, 369n5; effeminacy 135–38, 246–47, 260, 276; *Elegant Extracts* 247; fame 241; Keats 138, 246–47, 251–52f, 260, 277; Milton, 324n35; Samuel Rogers 239; Shakespeare 301, Shakespeare's characters and gender 301 (Antony 179; the Macbeths 25, 32; Ophelia 251; Perdita 251; Portia and Nerissa 174, 356n29; Richard II 154; Romeo 252, 370–71n22).
Heath's Book of Beauty, 21, 175, 356n32.
Heber, Reginald. See *Quarterly Review,* on Byron.
Helen of Troy, 166.
Hemans, Felicia (Browne), xvii, 29–30, 34, *39–77,* 79, 85, 88, 102, 113, 117, *303–9,* 323–24nn32–33, 353n65; Baillie 47–48; and Byron 49, 60–61, 64–66, 74–75, 304–5, 307–9; girlhood 48; celebrity 39–41, 71–76 (see also *Fame*); death of 71; genre 20; history and historiography 60–62, 331nn43, 45; infanticide 59–61, 331nn40–41; Jewsbury 76–77, 95, 108, 128 ("Egeria" 44, 95–96, 128,

327n11); marriage 48–49, 329n22; portraits 40, 51; reception 20, 30, *39–50*, 303–5, 330nn28, 30; and P. Shelley 312, 332n51; Staël 73–74, 311, 357n39, 380n36; Tighe 71–72, 333nn58–59; Wordsworth 49, 52–53, 312, 329–30nn26, 29, 33, 338n14. See also *Fame, Genius, Melancholy, Soul.*
Works: *Arabella Stuart* 64; *Bride of the Greek Isle* 64–67, 70, 159, 304–5; *Casabianca* 46, 50, 327–28nn14, 17; *Corinne at the Capitol* 73–75, 77; *Design and Performance* 312; *The Domestic Affections* 47, 54–56f, 305–6f; *England's Dead* 50; *Evening Prayer, at a Girls' School* 306–7, 380n32; *Forest Sanctuary* 46f, 108, 330n35; *Gertrude* 63; *Grave of a Poetess* 71–72; *Imelda* 64; *Indian City* 70, 307–9; *Indian Woman's Death-Song* 60, 70, 306; *Joan of Arc* 69–70; *Lady of the Castle* 54; *Last Banquet of Antony and Cleopatra* 68; *Last Song of Sappho* 71; *Madeline* 53; *Maremma* 57; *Our Daily Paths* 56–57; *Pauline* 53–54; *Properzia Rossi* 72–73, 120, 311, 333n61; *Records of Woman* 47f, *53–67*, 331nn46, 47; *Sicilian Captive* 310–11; *Siege of Valencia* 47, 64, 332n54; *Songs of the Affections* 47, 75; *Suliote Mother* 59–60; *Switzer's Wife* 63f; *Tales, and Historic Scenes, in Verse* 47, 61–62; *To My Own Portrait* 39–41; *Widow of Crescentius* (Stephania) 61–62, 70, 93; *Wife of Asdrubal* 58–59, 64, 70; *Woman and Fame* 69, 72–76; *Woman on the Field of Battle* 306.
Hercules and Omphale, 18, 146, 346n25.
Hermaphrodites and hermaphrodism, 171, 278, 293, 375n57.
Hic Mulier / Haec Vir, 171.
Hilton, William (portrait-artist), 265, 269–70, 273, 281, 374nn51–52.
Hoeveler, Diane Long, 336n22, 351n53.
Hofkosh, Sonia, 360n62, 367–68nn53–54, 372n36.
Hollander, John, 235.
Homans, Margaret, xvi, 235f, 282–83, 320n5, 359n52, 363n18, 367nn47–48, 53, 372n31, 376–77nn73–74, 378n11.
Honey, J. R. de S., 372n34.
Hopkins, Gerard Manley, 282; gender confusion, 277, 372n38; on Keats, 259, 261.
Horace, 355n23.
Howard, Jean, 355–56nn18–19, 29.
Howell, Margaret, 345n13, 352–53nn65–66, 68.
Howitt, William, 261.
Hughes, Harriett (Hemans's sister), 40, 79.
Hunt, Leigh, 261; *Blackwood's* 100–1, 139, 216–18, 247, 363n15, 364–65nn25, 28; Byron 138f, 182, 344n6; *Blue-Stocking Revels* 337n11; *Feast of the Poets* 263; *Nymphs* 138–39, 182, 369n13; and Keats 211, 216–18, 222, 227, 232, 250, 255–56, 263, 276, 278, 364nn24–25, 367n52; on M. W. Shelley 334–45n11. See also *Cockney School, Effeminacy, Examiner.*
Hunt, Lynn, 321n8.

Indolence and gender, 82, 136; Byron 148, 345n13; Keats, 207, *234–42*, 367nn48–51; Wordsworth 234. See also *Effeminacy.*
Irigaray, Luce. xvi, 188f, 376n70.
Irving, Washington, 79.

Jackson, H. J., 336n22.
Jacobus, Mary, 354n8.
Jameson, Anna, 44, 99, 337n9; Hemans 44; Shakespeare's women 25, 63; *Characteristics of Women* 86; *Diary of an Ennuyée* 98, 103, 121; *Memoirs of Celebrated Female Sovereigns* 86.
Jeffrey, Francis, 29–30, 101; Bluestockings 20; public esteem 35; on Byron 45, 182, 326n50; Dickens 257; "Female Poetry" 45–46; Hemans 29–30, 42ff, 45–47, 86, 303, 327n13; Keats 45, 326n50; Wordsworth, 63, 324–25n39, 332n48, 363n13. See also *Edinburgh Review, Poetess.*
Jewsbury, M. J., xvii, *92–131*; 78, 25–26, 28, 90–91; and *The Athenæum* 19, 76, 78, 80, 90, 93, 95–97, 103, 125, 129, 131, 336n2, 343nn53, 58 ; Austen 94–96f, 131, 336n4, 343nn58, 59; Baillie 96–97; *Blackwood's* 85; Byron 56, 99, 112, 119; death of 76, 104, 128, 334n67; female "accomplishment" 96; on female fame 92, *108–17*; Mrs. S. C. Hall 90–91; Hemans 33–34, 44, 53, 63, 76–77, 95–97, 102, 108, 120f, 304, 330n33, 342n44; historiography 106, 120, 126; Anna Jameson 86; on L.E.L. 124; Geraldine Jewsbury (sister) 106, 336n3, 339n25; marriage to W. K. Fletcher 104–5 127–28; Mrs. Sandford 19, 372n32; Sappho 71; P. Shelley 101, 108–12, 119–25, 301–3, 340–41nn32, 34, 379n28; suttee 67, 332n53; Wollstonecraft 90, 96, 105, 108, 110ff, 121, 325n48; women in society 93–95; Wm. Wordsworth xvii, 79, 96, *99–105*, 107f, 111, 116, 119, 131, 338–39nn14–21, 341nn36, 43. See also *Soul.*
Works: *Arria* 63, 309; *The Blue Bells of England* 97–99; *Farewell after a Visit* 123–24; *A Farewell to the Muse*, 113–14, 341–42nn36,

INDEX 425

45; *First Efforts at Criticism* 100–1; *Gold & Silver Fish to their Poet* 102–3; *History of an Enthusiast* 19–20, 90, 92–94, 105, *125–31*, 300–3, 343n53; *History of a Nonchalant*, 44, 95–96; *Letters to the Young* 102, 130f; *On Modern Female Cultivation* 93, 290, 334n6, 340n30; *On Receiving a Bunch of Violets* 98–99; *Phantasmagoria* 79, 99, 85, 101, 113–14, 124, 128; *Reply to a Letter of Advice*, 122–23; *Religious Novels* 119, 130; *Song, of the Hindoo Women*, 67; *To a Poet's Infant Child*, 113–14; *To My Own Heart* 340n27, 342n45; *Woman's Love* 56, 309–10; *Writing a Love Tale* 100f; *The Young Author* 99–100.
Joan of Arc, 69–70; 333n56.
Johnson, Claudia L., 321–22nn7, 9, 16.
Johnson, Samuel, 252, 258, 328n16.
Jones, John, 280.
Jong, Erica, 282, 376n69.
Joseph, M. K., 346n28.
Juvenal (Roman poet), on homosexuality, 154, 349–50nn44–45.

Kaplan, Cora, 50, 330n27.
Kauffman, Angelica (painter), 334n11.
Keach, William, 320n6, 323n28, 379n20.
Kean, Charles, 163, 353n66.
Keats, John. xv, xvii, 28, 34f, 87, 113, *205–84*; Fanny Brawne 209, 227–28, 230–31, 240, 242, 251f, 275, 277, 299, 362n11, 374n54, 379n25; bluestockings 20, 209, 376n72; Byron 212, 242; "camelion" poet 207, 357n40, 377n74; effeminacy 138, 221, 232, 236, *243–84*, 366n37, 368n55, 371n25; female readers and writers 207–9, 212, 213–14, 219, 242, 253–56, 282, 367–68nn50, 53, 372n31 (see also Gelpi, Homans, Jong, Amy Lowell, Rich); height 133, 205, 207, 211, 230–31, 262–64; indolence *234–41*; manliness 261, *262–74*, 370n18, 376n64; Negative Capability 208–9, 282, 376n68; poetics 221–23, 230, 246, 365nn31, 34, 36, 368n3; "Romance" 21, 259–601; portraits 265–73; women 207–8, 210–11, 275, 287–88, 363n15; Wordsworth 230, 374n54. See also Blackwood's, Byron, Cockney, Dandy, Fame, Genre, Hunt, Effeminacy, Same-sex passion (male), Shelley (Adonais), Soul.
Works: *Addressed to Haydon* 218, 230; *Another on Fame* 241; *Calidore* 226, 228–29f; *Endymion* 211, 216, 227f, 230, 232–33, 239–40, 250, 256, 258–59 275, 277, 281–82, 298, 366–67n 36, 44, 368n3, 371–73nn30–31,

40 (Preface 233, 273–74, 280, 283); *Eve of St. Agnes* 184, 211–12, 214, 227, 229, 255, 260, 275, 363n14, 366nn37, 42, 371n30; *Fall of Hyperion* 116, 231–32, 283, 376–77n73; "Fill for me a brimming Bowl" 210; "Had I a man's fair form" 229–30; *Hyperion* 211–12, 214, 232, 280, 283; "I cry your mercy" 299; "I stood tip-toe" 230, 255, 280, 298, 364n24, 366nn36, 40, 371n30; *Isabella* 212, 214, 258–59, 363n13, 366n42, 371–72n30; *Lamia* 212–13, 230, 255, 298–99, 363n17, 366n40; *Ode on Indolence* 236–38; *Ode on Melancholy* 275, 299; *Ode to a Nightingale* 277, 375n57; *Ode to Psyche* 293, 298–99; *Ode on a Grecian Urn* 75–76, 259; *On a Leander* 225, 365n33; *On Fame* 240; *On first looking into Chapman's Homer* 230, 273f, 280–81; *Poems* (1817) 206, *218–30*, 238, 255–56, 273, 362n3, 367n52, 368n3; *Sleep and Poetry* 214, 218–24, 239, 247, 280, 298, 365n29, 369n5; *Specimen of an Induction* 225; *To a Friend who sent me some Roses* 224, 365n32; *To Fanny* 299; *To Lord Byron* 364n21; "What can I do?" 299; "Woman! when I behold thee" 225, 237, 241, 256, 368n55.
Kelley, Theresa, 326n51.
Kelsall, Malcolm, 347n30.
Kern, Robert, 363n12.
Kernberger, Katherine, 359n57.
Kingsley, Charles, 249, 257, 276, 325n41; Byron 31–32; P. Shelley 31, 248.
Knight, G. Wilson, 152, 165, 346n28, 351n53, 354n6.
Knoepflmacher, U. C., 33.
Kristeva, Julia, xviff.
Kucich, Greg, 227, 331nn43, 45.

L.E.L. See *Landon*.
Ladies' Companion, 253, 255.
Ladies of Llangollen, 357n35.
Lamb, Caroline , 169, 184, 188, 201, 354n16, 356n30; portrait 170. *A New Canto* 171, 355n21.
Landon, Laetitia Elizabeth / L.E.L., 28, 44, 100, 98; Jewsbury 110, 122. 340n31; *Romance and Reality* 124; *Stanzas on the Death of Mrs. Hemans* 71–72.
Lang, Cecil, 355n24, 360nn61, 66.
Lansdown, Richard, 345n15.
Lawrence, Rose, 47, 77.
Leighton, Angela, 314, 323–24n32, 333n64, 380nn32, 38; and Margaret Reynolds (eds.), 328n18, 342n45.

Levine, Laura, 355n20.
Levinson, Marjorie, 298, 364n27, 366nn38, 40, 369n6.
Lewes, G. H., on Austen 131, 343n59; Byron's *Sardanapalus*, 163; P. Shelley, 30, 370n17.
Lindsay, Jack, 261.
Linkin, Harriet Kramer, xvi, 326n51.
Literary Chronicle and Weekly, M.J.J.'s *Phantasmagoria* 79; Keats 371n25.
Literary Gazette, Jewsbury 127, 343n53; Shelley's *Adonais*.
Literary Souvenir, 75; Jewsbury 100, 113–14, 332n53.
Lockhart, J. G. (aka Z). See *Blackwood's Edinburgh Magazine, Cockney*.
London Magazine, Keats 217, 364n27; suttee 332n52.
Longman Anthology of British Literature, xvi, 326n51, 328n18.
Lootens, Tricia, 48, 61, 328n17, 330–31n27, 45.
Low, Dennis, 341n38, 343nn56–57.
Lowell, Amy, 221, 224, 253–54, 276, 365n29.
Lowell, James Russell, 264, 276, 374–75n55.
Lydgate, John, *Fall of Princes*, 147, 160.

Mabie, H. W., on Keats, 263, 274, 278–79.
Macaulay, Catharine, xix, 2, 11, 78–82f, 88–89, 340n28, 362n10; Pope 81, 183, 358–59n50; Rousseau 189–90.
MacGillivray, J. R., on Keats 280, 368n4, 371n24, 374n49.
Macready, Charles, 162–63, 352–53n65.
Manning, Peter, xvi, 152, 173, 326n51, 349nn39–40, 351n56, 355n25, 359–60nn51, 53, 60, 62, 68, 366n45.
Marchand, Leslie, 148, 334n1, 345nn15–16, 353–54nn4, 16–17.
Marie Antoinette, Queen of France, 8–9.
Marquess, William Henry, 374n54.
Marriage & marriage plots, 81, 182, 188, 288, 359n55; female critique 4, 19–20, 174, 181, 342n48, 355–56n26; Byron 149, 152, 166, 190f; Hemans 48–49, 53, 65, 67, 305, 329n22; Jewsbury 105, 110–11, 128, 303, 339–40n26. See also *Coverture*.
Martin, John, 163, 352–53n65.
Masculine woman, xviii, 1, 7, 13, 20, 22, 25, 32–33, *78–91*, 291, 293, 310, 322n24, 340n28, 351n55. See also *Phallic woman*.
Masson, David, on Keats 264, 274, 371n23, 373–74nn46, 55; Shelley 370n16.
Masquerade, 97, 177, 179, 189, 198, 354n8, 361nn73–76; women 82, 169, 171, 197, 201–2; 356n30; men, 152, 154f, 189, 195–97, 201–2, 354n16. See also *Camp*.
Mathew, George Felton, 365n35, 376n64.
Mathias, T. J., 32
Matthews, G. M., 248.
McClary, Ben Harris, 378n8.
McGann, Jerome, on Byron 179, 345nn11–13, 347–48nn28–29, 34, 35, 350–51nn49, 56, 353n3, 358n46, 361nn72, 77, 364n23; Hemans 50, 330n27; *Romantic Ideology* 320n2.
Medusa, 158, 187, 332n50.
Medwin, Thomas, on P. Shelley 249, 370n16..
Meiners, Christoph, 13–14, 323n25, 358n49.
Melancholy, 346n22, Coleridge 206; Corinne (Staël) 380n36; Hemans 47, 50, 51, 56–57, 72–73, 113, 306, 330n27, 380n32; Jewsbury 126–27, 180; Keats 247, 275, 299. See also *Burton*.
Mellor, Anne, xvi, 50, 202, 283, 320n5, 325–26nn44, 51, 327–28nn8, 18, 330n27, 334n7, 367nn46, 50, 376–77nn69, 74, 378n14, 380n37; and Richard Matlak 326n51, 328n17.
Meynell, Alice, 87–88, 335n18, 377n7.
Milnes, R. M. (Lord Houghton), on Keats, 254–55, 263–65, 268, 273–78, 281, 326n52, 371n25, 374–75nn54, 55.
Milton, John, 30, 250; *Comus* 210–11; Eve 4–5, 25, 70, 81, 147, 187, 332n50; *Lycidas* 238, 242, 365n29; *Paradise Lost* 10, 13, 21, 112, 208, 224f, 322n17, 332n49; Samson 145, 260, 346n21, 372n39.
Mitford, Mary Russell. 44, 53, 71, 87, 98, 337n9.
Moers, Ellen, 137, 151, 333n65.
Moi, Toril, xvii-xviii, 335n21.
Montagu, Lady Mary W., 24–25, 89; Byron 194; female learning, 21, 41, 323n31; portrait 199; Mary Shelley 15; Turkish habit 194, 196, 199, 201–2.
Moore, Doris Langley, 197, 360n66.
Moore, Thomas, 99, 215, 218; Byron, 28.
More, Hannah, 41, 69, 80, 89, 324nn32, 37, 327n8; women's poetry, 22, 24, 28, 214; Macaulay 88; Wollstonecraft 26–27f, 359n50. Works: *The Bas Bleu* 97, 290–91, 323n29; *On Dissipation* 18; *Essays for Young Ladies* 16ff, 22, 26–27, 220, 290, 323n27; *Strictures on Female Education* 13, 15–17, 26–28, 68, 147, 259–60, 324n37, 340n29, 359n50; *Thoughts on the Education of Daughters* 27.
Morgan, Lady (Sidney Owenson), 85, 103, 250.

Morgan, Thaïs, 375n57.
Mulvey, Laura, 228.
Murray, John (publisher), 17, 20, 323n28, 338n15, 345n9, 358n46.
Myers, Sylvia Harcstark, 323n29.

Najarian, James, 277, 362n11, 368n1, 372n38, 374n50, 375n59.
"Nature" and "Natural Law" of gender, xviii, 2, 4, 5, 7–8, 11, 12, 14–17, 20, 22–31, 45, 47, 54, 57, 70, 81–87, 95, 105, 117, 126, 128, 149–50, 152–54, 156, 168–69, 175–76, 184, 198, 200–01, 204, 291, 314, 321–22n14, 19, 333n63, 335n12, 339n23, 344nn2, 4, 349n41, 355–56nn24, 29, 32, 359n57.
Needlework 17, 39, 41–42, 52, 314, 330n31, 326–27n4.
Nemoianu, Virgil, 35, 328n17.
New Monthly Magazine on Jewsbury, 118, 126, 343n53; Keats, 250.
Newsome, David, 372n34.
Norton Anthology of English Literature, xvi, 326n51, 328nn17, 18
Nurmi, Martin, 353n66.

Oliphant, Margaret, 253, 256.
Ostriker, Alicia, 367n46.
Owen, F. M., 253, 256, 373–74n48.

Paley, Morton, 352–53n65.
Parson, Donald, 265, 376n65.
Patmore, Coventry, 282, 372n35, 377n7; E. B. Browning 335n18; Clough 87, 375n60; effeminate 277, 375n58; Keats 87, 249, 256–57, 259f, 278, 375n58; Meynell 87–88, 377n7; P. Shelley 87, 249, 335n16. See also *Androgyny*.
Perkins, David, 326n51, 328n18.
Perl, Teri, 371n29.
Phallic woman, 193, 195, 197–98, 360–61nn67, 69.
Pocket Magazine on Keats, 255, 260.
Poetess, xviii, 22–23, 29, 33–34, 39, 41–42, 46–50, 71–72, 79, 96, 114, 247, 304, 326n2, 327n8, 330n28, 380n31.
Pollak, Ellen, 362n8.
Polwhele, Richard, 16–17, 23–24, 32, 214, 290, 323n27.
Poovey, Mary, 320n2, 322n14, 22, 323n30, 334n2.
Pope, Alexander, 222, 247, 253, 369n12; *Eloisa to Abelard* 62, 93, 203; *To a Lady, Of the Characters of Women* 13, 81–82, 89, 183, 208, 334–35nn10, 12, 358–59n50; *Sappho to Phaon* 333n57; Sporus 146, 345n10.
Pre-Raphaelite Brotherhood, 261–62; and Keats 366n42, 373n41.
Priestley, Joseph, 8–9.

Quarterly Review, Baillie 334n9; Barbauld 17, 20, 25, 42, 323n28; Byron 144, 149, 155, 182, 345n13, 352n64; Hemans 43; Keats 228, 239–41, 250, 253, 370–71nn19, 23.
Queens of Literature of the Victorian Era, 39, 42.

Rackin, Phyllis, 355n19.
Radcliffe, Ann, 96, 100, 208, 213–14, 327n6.
Radcliffe, M. A., *The Female Advocate*, 84, 168.
Rajan, Tilottama, 379n24.
Reeve, Clara, *The Progress of Romance* 136.
Reynolds, Margaret, 339–40, n26, 341n36. See also *Leighton*.
Rich, Adrienne, 282, 376–77nn72, 74.
Richardson, Alan, 320n5, 324n38, 359n59.
Ricks, Christopher, 233, 281–82, 363n13, 365–67nn28, 41, 44.
Ridenour, George, 179, 357nn37, 41.
Riviere, Joan, 189.
Roberts, William. See *British Review*.
Robinson, A. Mary F., 46–47, 58.
Robinson, Mary, 333n57; [Anne Frances Randall], *Letter to the Women of England* 84, 289.
Roe, Nicholas, 368n3, 373n46.
Rogers, Samuel, 30, 35, 41, 239.
Romantic canon, xvi, 326nn51–52, 328n17, 342n45; feminist critique of xv, 2–3, 320n5; male canon xv-xvii, 2–3, 34–35; "masculinist" values xv, 2–3, 320n5, 331n43.
Ross, Marlon, xvi, 283, 320n5, 329–30nn18, 22, 33, 364n23, 376n73, 378–79nn14, 25.
Rossetti, D. G., 261–62, 278, 366n42, 373n42, 376n68. See also *Buchanan, Courthope, Pre-Raphaelite, Villard*.
Rossetti, W. M., on Hemans 46, 49, 62, 327n11, 329–30nn22, 34; Keats 258, 260, 261, 264f, 275, 374n55; P. Shelley 249.
Rousseau, J.- J., 4, 321nn9–10; *Émile* and Sophy 4–6, 152, 189–90, 322n24, 349n41, 359n59. See also *Macaulay, Wollstonecraft*.
Rowe, Nicholas, *The Fair Penitent* 377n5.
Rowton, Frederic, *Female Poets of Great Britain* 23; Hemans 43, 303–4.
Runge, Laura, 323n24.
Ruskin, John, 375n56; *Of Queens' Gardens*, 260.
Rutherford, Andrew, 361n72.

428   INDEX

Saintsbury, George, 276, 279, 370n18.
Same-sex passion, 354n8, 378n10; female: 181, 340n28, 357n35; male: 162, 165, 262, 354nn5, 7, 357–58nn35, 44 (Arnold 277; Hopkins 372n38; Keats 224, 232, 247–48, 277, 293, 368n1, 370n14, 372n8, 373–74nn43, 50; Shelley, 357–58n44, 370n15). See also *Barnefield, Byron, Carpenter, Crompton, Cross-dressing, Najarian, Sedgwick, Wilde.*
Sand, George, 201, 313–14, 324n36, 380n38.
Sandford, Mrs. John, *Woman* 18–19, 30, 49, 211, 254ff, 282, 329n24, 372n32.
Sappho, 71, 223, 333n57, 340n28, 375n57.
Satirist, on Hunt 217.
Scots Edinburgh Magazine, on Byron 139, 160; on Keats 206–7, 369n8.
Scott, Grant, 283, 333n61, 367nn47, 50–51, 376n72.
Scott, Walter, 50; Shelley's *Frankenstein* 325n44; *The Heart of Midlothian* 198, 361n70.
Sedgwick, Eve Kosofsky, 368n2, 379n19.
Semiramis, Empress of Assyria, 349n42, 350nn45, 50. See also Byron, *Sardanapalus* 145f, 148, 152–58, 350n49.
Sensibility and sentiment, 247, 253, 322n18, 324n38, 369n12, 371n30; female 63, 102, 205–6, 255, 291, 303, 335n14; in men 11, 13, 84, 118, 135, 243–44, 247, 249, 252–54, 257, 262, 278–79, 356–57n34, 360n63, 362–63nn2, 13, 368n55, 375n56. See also *Delicacy, Effeminacy.*
Seraglio. See *Harem.*
Severn, Joseph, on Keats 265, 268, 270, 272–73, 281, 371nn25–26, 374nn49–52, 376n65.
Severs, J. Burke, 366n38.
Shairp, J. C., 279.
Shakespeare, William, 20, 30, 63, 103, 107, 208, 211, 216, 256, 300f, 303–4n32, 324n39, 335n20, 342n49, 354n5, 365n33, 379n19; *Antony and Cleopatra* 137, 144f; *Coriolanus* 192; *Hamlet* 19–20, 31, 112, 140, 251, 275, 341n34, 345n14, 346n28, 353n68, 371n30; *Henry IV* 300; *Henry V* 140, 158, 345n14; *King Lear* 211, 373n45; *Macbeth* 25, 142 (Lady Macbeth 16, 25, 32, 107); *Merchant of Venice* (Portia) 142, 174, 354n5, 356n29; *Othello* 143, 176; *Richard II* 154; *Richard III* 346n27; *Romeo and Juliet* 107, 252, 370–71n22; *Troilus and Cressida* 144, 194–95; *Twelfth Night* 61; *Winter's Tale* (Perdita) 251. See also *Cross-dressing, Effeminacy, Same-sex passion.*

Shaw-Hamblin, Mrs. (actress), 163, 353n68.
Shelley, Mary W., xvi, 331n45, 334–45n11, 352n59; Byron 138, 180, 200, 354n9, 358–59nn45, 56; *Frankenstein* xvff, 32, 325n44, 326n51 (Victor 346n22; Walton 313; Safie 290); *Lodore* 138; M. W. Montagu 15; Wollstonecraft 15, 312–13.
Shelley, P. B., xv, 66, 246, 248, 264, 276f, 301–3, 325–26nn42–43, 52; Byron 167, 180, 188, 192, 195, 354n9, 357n40; gender of 28, 30–32, 87, 244, 248–49, 281, 335nn16–17, 357–58n44, 370nn15–18, 376n67.
Works: *Adonais* 249–53, 275, 302–3, 370–71nn21, 23, 25, 373n43; *Alastor* 108, 295–98, 302–3, 332n51, 379n20; *Athanase* 379n21; *Epipsychidion* 296, 312, 379n22; *Hymn to Intellectual Beauty* 110; *Ode to Liberty* 312; *Ode to the West Wind* 125, 303; *On Love* 296; *Prometheus Unbound* 119, 302; *To a Sky-lark* 121, 341n34; *The Triumph of Life* 112, 341n34. See also *Androgyny, Arnold, Carpenter, Hemans, Jewsbury, Kingsley.*
Shevelow, Kathryn, 323n24.
Showalter, Elaine, 193, 282, 324n36, 335n21, 336n3, 342n48, 361n69.
Siddons, Sarah, 361n75.
Sigourney, Lydia Huntley, 329nn23, 25.
Silliman, Benjamin, 291, 378n8.
Sinfield, Alan, 345n11, 362n2.
Slavery and thraldom, 150–51; 164, 347n32; male 145, 164–65, 173–74, 184, 190–92, 254, 260, 275, 346–48n21, 33, 360n60, 372nn30, 39; female 65, 93, 149–50, 164, 183, 189–90, 198, 290, 301, 347n30, 359n59, 377n5 (Hemans 59–60, 64–67, 379n30; Wollstonecraft 13, 14–15, 111, 149, 189–90, 301, 347n32, 379n29). See also *Byron (Cavalier Servente, Juan in the harem, Sardanapalus); Harem, Hays, Hercules.*
Smith, Alexander, as unmanly 253; on Keats 224, 245, 258, 274, 276, 368n55.
Smith, Charlotte, 82.
Soderholm, James, 355n21, 357n36.
Soul, sex and gender, 28, 34, 122, *287–314;* Aikin 310; Coleridge 285, 291–92, 296; Hazlitt 288; Hemans 303–12; Keats 287–88, 293, 298–99; Patmore, 377n7; M. W. Shelley 312–13; P. Shelley, 295–98, 312, 379nn21–22, 28; Wollstonecraft 28, 285, 288–90; Wordsworth 287f, 292–95, 378n13.
Southey, Robert, on women writers 325n45. See also *Byron.*
Spence, Gordon, 145, 148.

INDEX 429

Spenser, Edmund, 216, 371n30; *Faerie Queene* 70, 225–27; *Visions of the World's Vanities* 106–7, 111.
Sperry, Stuart, 363n12.
Stabler, Jane, 361n71.
Staël, Germaine de, 12, 47, 322n21; Byron 25, 32, 74, 178–81, 358n46; Hemans 47, 73–75, 311, 333n65; Jewsbury, 302, 333n65. Works: *Corinne* 67, 73–75, 120f, 188, 311, 333nn64, 65, 357n39, 380n36; *De l'Influence des Passions* 74, 333n63.
Stedman, Jane, 360n64.
Steinem, Gloria, 189.
Stephen, Leslie, 375n58.
Stillinger, Jack, 224, 363n14, 366n37.
Stodart, M. A., 65, 146, 300, 324n37, 355n24; *Female Writers* 12, 29, 88–89, 105; Eve, 14–15.
Stoller, Robert. See *Phallic woman*.
Straub, Kristina, 360n64.
Stubbes, Phillip (*Anatomie of Abuses*), 169ff.
The Sultana: or, A Trip to Turkey, 166, 185.
Surrey, Henry Howard, Earl, sonnet on Sardanapalus, 155, 160, 348n35.
Suttee, 67, 159, 332n52.
Swann, Karen, 233, 366–67n44.
Sweet, Nanora, 348n36.
Swift, Jonathan, 142–43, 345–46n17, 364n26.
Swinburne, Algernon Charles, on Keats 252, 259, 275; as unmanly 32, 252, 261f, 276–77, 325n43, 373n42, 375n57.
Symons, Arthur, on Byron 133, 248; Hemans 41–42, 327n14; Keats 279.

Talleyrand, report on education 12, 320n7, 321n11.
The Tatler, 285, 287.
Taylor, Jane, 80, 213; and Ann Taylor, 364n19.
Taylor and Hessey (publishers), 212f, 240f.
Tayler, Irene and Gina Luria, 379n22.
Taylor, William Cooke, *National Portrait Gallery*, 128.
The Ten Plagues of England, 136.
Tennyson, Alfred Lord, 258f; androgyny 325n40; effeminacy 30; gender 32, 259, 325n43, 363n13, 375n57; on Keats, 254–55; *The Lady of Shalott*, 73.
Terence (Roman poet), *Eunuch* 210.
Tighe, Mary, 71–72, 208, 333n59. See also Hemans.
The Times (London) on Keats, 274.
Tiresias, 166–67.
Trelawny, E. J., on Byron 138; P. B. Shelley 248–49, 325n42.

Trilling, Lionel, 280–81, 367n48.
Trott, Nicola, 80, 334n8.

Van Dyke, Henry, 278.
Vance, Norman, 325n41.
Veeder, William, 370n15.
Vendler, Helen, 367n49.
Victoria Magazine on Keats 253, 255–56, 373n41; women 255.
Villard, Léonie, 260, 366n37.
Vincent, Leon, 279–80.
Vital, Anthony Paul, 356–57n34, 360n63, 364n23.
Voltaire, 25; *Sémiramis* 350n50.

Wadsworth, Frank, 361n75.
Wakefield, Priscilla, 167–68.
Ward, Aileen, 281.
Wasserman, Earl, 379n22.
Watkins, Daniel, 349n38, 366n37.
Watson, Jean, 325n46, 336n22.
Watson, Sir William, 279.
Watts, Alaric A., and Hemans 40; Jewsbury 79, 101, 113–14.
Webb, Timothy, 370n15.
West, Kenyon, 280.
Whately, Richard, on Austen, 131, 343nn58–59.
Whitmore, Allen Perry, 349nn39–40.
Wilde, Oscar, on effeminacy 261; on Keats 262, 370n14; on Pre-Raphaelite aesthetics 261, 373n41; on Shakespeare's boy actors 248, 354n5. See also *Same-sex passion*.
Wilkes, Joanne, 336n25, 343nn56, 59.
Williams, Helen Maria, 323n26.
Williams, Jane, *Literary Women of England* 76, 334n3; Hemans 327n11; Jewsbury 127–28, 338n21, 340n31.
Wilson, Carol Shiner, 326n51, 330n31.
Wilson, John, 379n26; Byron 299–300; "Christopher North" on female writers 85; *An Evening in Furness Abbey* 300–1; Keats, 364n25.
Winslow, Hubbard, *Woman As She Should Be* 31.
Wollstonecraft, Mary, xvi–xix, *1–18*, 24, 27, 42, 65, 78ff, 86–8, 108f, 116, 339n22, 370n17, 378n8; *Analytical Review* 11, 81–82, 359n59; *Anti-Jacobin* 80; Burke, 10–13, 288, 322nn16, 19–20, 22, 377n2; J. H. Colls 289–90; *Critical Review* 23, 80; on effeminacy 136–37; *English Review* 11; Macaulay 81–82, 340n28, 360n59; Milton 4–5, 13; *Monthly Review* 22; Pope, 13, 81–82, 89, 183, 358–

59n50; Rousseau 4–6, 13, 189–90. See also *Slavery, Soul.*
Works: *French Revolution* 9, 11; *Letters During a Short Residence* 15, 86; *Rights of Men* 10–12; *Rights of Woman* xviii, 4–5, 12–13, 15–16, 23, 26, 62f, 80–83, 90, 110, 149, 174, 314, 320–21n7, 339–40nn23, 28, 362n10, 379n29.
Wood, Gillen, 364n26.
Woodring, Carl, 348–49n37.
Woolf, Virginia, 230–31, 324n36; androgyny 89–90, 166–67, 281, 335nn20–21; Byron 28, 164–65; *Orlando* 166–67, 354n8; Wollstonecraft 288.
Wordsworth, Dorothy, xvi, 330n31; Jewsbury, 79, 92–93.
Wordsworth, William, xv–xvi, 5, 22, 30, 35, 41, 49, 119, 206, 215, 326n52, 330–31n38, 338n14, 369n5; *Blackwood's* on 218; Byronic portrait 272; Hemans xvii, 39, 41, 49, 50, 52–53, 329–30nn26, 30, 33; indolence 234; Jeffrey 324–25n39, 363n13; Keats 338n14, 373n40. See also *Arnold, Jewsbury, Soul.*
Works: Advertisement of 1798 (*Lyrical Ballads*); Composed on Westminster Bridge 312; *The Excursion* 96, 107, 116, 205, 230, 292–93, 378n13; *Extempore Effusion* 50; *Gold and Silver Fishes in a Vase* 102; "It is a beauteous evening" 49; *Laodamia* 53, 63, 332n48; *Liberty* 104–5; *Lyrical Ballads*, 324n38; *Morning Exercise*, 341n43; *Ode: Intimations of Immortality* 99–100, 116, 287–88, 295–96, 298, 330n37, 379n20; *The Pet-Lamb* 241, 368n55; Preface to *Lyrical Ballads* xvii, 41, 126, 205, 324–25n39, 341n34; *The Prelude* 293–95; "She dwelt among th'untrodden ways" 95; "The world is too much with us" 373n40; "Three years she grew" 111; *Tintern Abbey* 107; *To a Skylark* 119; *To the Cuckoo* 119.
Wu, Duncan, 326nn51, 52, 326n51, 328n18, 331n47, 342n45, 349n43.

Yeats, William Butler, on Keats, 259, 276.

Z. (signature of J. G. Lockhart & c.). See *Blackwood's Edinburgh Magazine, Cockney School.*